CW01261666

****

Books of the Ethiopian Bible

Missing From the Protestant Canon

ISBN: 978-1-63923-462-2

All Rights reserved. No part of this book maybe reproduced without written permission from the publishers, except by a reviewer who may quote brief passages in a review to be printed in a newspaper or magazine.

Printed: June 2022

Cover Art By: Amit Paul

Published and Distributed By: Lushena Books
607 Country Club Drive, Unit E
Bensenville, IL 60106
www.lushenabooksinc.com/books

ISBN: 978-1-63923-462-2

Table of Contents

Introduction..................................3
1 Esdras......................................4
2 Esdras.....................................23
Tobit..56
Judith...68
Additions to Esther.....................85
Wisdom of Solomon...................90
Prologue to Wisdom of Jesus Son of Sirach..................................109
Wisdom of Jesus Son of Sirach.........110
Baruch......................................158
Letter of Jeremiah.....................163

Prayer of Azariah......................166
Susanna....................................169
Bel and the Dragon...................171
Prayer of Manasseh..................173
1 Maccabees.............................174
2 Maccabees.............................213
The Book of Enoch...................240
The Book of Jubilees.................313
The Book of Meqabyan 1..........418
The Book of Meqabyan II.........469
The Book of Meqabyan III........496
Addition to Jeremiah................510

Introduction

While the Protestant Canon includes only 66 books, The Biblical canon of Ethiopia (Canon= those books of the Bible officially accepted by a church or religious body as divinely inspired) includes over 100 books. Its narrow canon contains books such as Enoch, Jubilees and three books of Makabis, which are commonly accepted by other Orthodox Christians. The narrow canon is the Haile Selassie version. The broader canon includes all the books in the narrower canon, plus books such as an Epistle to Clement, the Josippon, two books of the Covenant and four books of Sinodos. The broader canon has not been reprinted since the early 20th century.

Books such as the three Meqabyan or Ethiopian Maccabees, are three books found only in the Ethiopian Orthodox Old Testament and Beta Israel Mäṣḥafä Kedus Biblical canon. The language of these books is Ge'ez, also called Classical Ethiopic. These books are completely different in content and subject from the more commonly found books of Maccabees in Catholic and Eastern Orthodox Bibles.

The account of the "Maccabees" described in these sacred texts are not those of the advent of political dealings of the Hasmonean dynasty of Judea, nor are they an account of the "Five Holy Maccabean Martyrs", or the "woman with seven sons", who were also referred to as "Maccabees" and are revered throughout Orthodoxy as the "Holy Maccabean Martyrs". The Maccabees who are referenced do not correspond to known martyrology and their identity is never full clarified by the ancient author. However, they do assume the familiar moniker of being "a Maccabee", the etymological origins of which remain disputed.

There are additional books of the Ethiopian Bible not included in this edition. Books such as Tizaz, 1 and 2 book of Dominos, The Book of Clement, Didascalia, and others are still in the works for English translations.

1 Esdras

1Esdr.1

[1] And Josias held the feast of the passover in Jerusalem unto his Lord, and offered the passover the fourteenth day of the first month;
[2] Having set the priests according to their daily courses, being arrayed in long garments, in the temple of Jah.
[3] And he spake unto the Levites, the holy ministers of Israel, that they should hallow themselves unto Jah, to set the holy ark of Jah in the house that king Solomon the son of David had built:
[4] And said, Ye shall no more bear the ark upon your shoulders: now therefore serve Jah your God, and minister unto his people Israel, and prepare you after your families and kindreds,
[5] According as David the king of Israel prescribed, and according to the magnificence of Solomon his son: and standing in the temple according to the several dignity of the families of you the Levites, who minister in the presence of your brethren the children of Israel,
[6] Offer the passover in order, and make ready the sacrifices for your brethren, and keep the passover according to the commandment of Jah, which was given unto Moses.
[7] And unto the people that was found there Josias gave thirty thousand lambs and kids, and three thousand calves: these things were given of the king's allowance, according as he promised, to the people, to the priests, and to the Levites.
[8] And Helkias, Zacharias, and Syelus, the governors of the temple, gave to the priests for the passover two thousand and six hundred sheep, and three hundred calves.
[9] And Jeconias, and Samaias, and Nathanael his brother, and Assabias, and Ochiel, and Joram, captains over thousands, gave to the Levites for the passover five thousand sheep, and seven hundred calves.
[10] And when these things were done, the priests and Levites, having the unleavened bread, stood in very comely order according to the kindreds,
[11] And according to the several dignities of the fathers, before the people, to offer to Jah, as it is written in the book of Moses: and thus did they in the morning.
[12] And they roasted the passover with fire, as appertaineth: as for the sacrifices, they sod them in brass pots and pans with a good savour,
[13] And set them before all the people: and afterward they prepared for themselves, and for the priests their brethren, the sons of Aaron.
[14] For the priests offered the fat until night: and the Levites prepared for themselves, and the priests their brethren, the sons of Aaron.
[15] The holy singers also, the sons of Asaph, were in their order, according to the appointment of David, to wit, Asaph, Zacharias, and Jeduthun, who was of the king's retinue.
[16] Moreover the porters were at every gate; it was not lawful for any to go from his ordinary service: for their brethren the Levites prepared for them.
[17] Thus were the things that belonged to the sacrifices of Jah accomplished in that day, that they might hold the passover,
[18] And offer sacrifices upon the altar of Jah, according to the commandment of king Josias.
[19] So the children of Israel which were present held the passover at that time, and the feast of sweet bread seven days.
[20] And such a passover was not kept in

Israel since the time of the prophet Samuel.
[21] Yea, all the kings of Israel held not such a passover as Josias, and the priests, and the Levites, and the Jews, held with all Israel that were found dwelling at Jerusalem.
[22] In the eighteenth year of the reign of Josias was this passover kept.
[23] And the works or Josias were upright before his Lord with an heart full of godliness.
[24] As for the things that came to pass in his time, they were written in former times, concerning those that sinned, and did wickedly against Jah above all people and kingdoms, and how they grieved him exceedingly, so that the words of Jah rose up against Israel.
[25] Now after all these acts of Josias it came to pass, that Pharaoh the king of Egypt came to raise war at Carchamis upon Euphrates: and Josias went out against him.
[26] But the king of Egypt sent to him, saying, What have I to do with thee, O king of Judea?
[27] I am not sent out from Jah God against thee; for my war is upon Euphrates: and now Jah is with me, yea, Jah is with me hasting me forward: depart from me, and be not against Jah.
[28] Howbeit Josias did not turn back his chariot from him, but undertook to fight with him, not regarding the words of the prophet Jeremy spoken by the mouth of Jah:
[29] But joined battle with him in the plain of Magiddo, and the princes came against king Josias.
[30] Then said the king unto his servants, Carry me away out of the battle; for I am very weak. And immediately his servants took him away out of the battle.
[31] Then gat he up upon his second chariot; and being brought back to Jerusalem died, and was buried in his father's sepulchre.
[32] And in all Jewry they mourned for Josias, yea, Jeremy the prophet lamented for Josias, and the chief men with the women made lamentation for him unto this day: and this was given out for an ordinance to be done continually in all the nation of Israel.
[33] These things are written in the book of the stories of the kings of Judah, and every one of the acts that Josias did, and his glory, and his understanding in the law of Jah, and the things that he had done before, and the things now recited, are reported in the book of the kings of Israel and Judea.
[34] And the people took Joachaz the son of Josias, and made him king instead of Josias his father, when he was twenty and three years old.
[35] And he reigned in Judea and in Jerusalem three months: and then the king of Egypt deposed him from reigning in Jerusalem.
[36] And he set a tax upon the land of an hundred talents of silver and one talent of gold.
[37] The king of Egypt also made king Joacim his brother king of Judea and Jerusalem.
[38] And he bound Joacim and the nobles: but Zaraces his brother he apprehended, and brought him out of Egypt.
[39] Five and twenty years old was Joacim when he was made king in the land of Judea and Jerusalem; and he did evil before Jah.
[40] Wherefore against him Nabuchodonosor the king of Babylon came up, and bound him with a chain of brass, and carried him into Babylon.
[41] Nabuchodonosor also took of the holy vessels of Jah, and carried them away, and set them in his own temple at Babylon.
[42] But those things that are recorded of him, and of his uncleaness and impiety, are written in the chronicles of the kings.
[43] And Joacim his son reigned in his stead: he was made king being eighteen years old;
[44] And reigned but three months and ten days in Jerusalem; and did evil before Jah.
[45] So after a year Nabuchodonosor sent

and caused him to be brought into Babylon with the holy vessels of Jah;
[46] And made Zedechias king of Judea and Jerusalem, when he was one and twenty years old; and he reigned eleven years:
[47] And he did evil also in the sight of Jah, and cared not for the words that were spoken unto him by the prophet Jeremy from the mouth of Jah.
[48] And after that king Nabuchodonosor had made him to swear by the name of Jah, he forswore himself, and rebelled; and hardening his neck, his heart, he transgressed the laws of Jah God of Israel.
[49] The governors also of the people and of the priests did many things against the laws, and passed all the pollutions of all nations, and defiled the temple of Jah, which was sanctified in Jerusalem.
[50] Nevertheless the God of their fathers sent by his messenger to call them back, because he spared them and his tabernacle also.
[51] But they had his messengers in derision; and, look, when Jah spake unto them, they made a sport of his prophets:
[52] So far forth, that he, being wroth with his people for their great ungodliness, commanded the kings of the Chaldees to come up against them;
[53] Who slew their young men with the sword, yea, even within the compass of their holy temple, and spared neither young man nor maid, old man nor child, among them; for he delivered all into their hands.
[54] And they took all the holy vessels of Jah, both great and small, with the vessels of the ark of God, and the king's treasures, and carried them away into Babylon.
[55] As for the house of Jah, they burnt it, and brake down the walls of Jerusalem, and set fire upon her towers:
[56] And as for her glorious things, they never ceased till they had consumed and brought them all to nought: and the people that were not slain with the sword he carried unto Babylon:
[57] Who became servants to him and his children, till the Persians reigned, to fulfil the word of Jah spoken by the mouth of Jeremy:
[58] Until the land had enjoyed her sabbaths, the whole time of her desolation shall she rest, until the full term of seventy years.

1Esdr.2

[1] In the first year of Cyrus king of the Persians, that the word of Jah might be accomplished, that he had promised by the mouth of Jeremy;
[2] Jah raised up the spirit of Cyrus the king of the Persians, and he made proclamation through all his kingdom, and also by writing,
[3] Saying, Thus saith Cyrus king of the Persians; Jah of Israel, the most high Lord, hath made me king of the whole world,
[4] And commanded me to build him an house at Jerusalem in Jewry.
[5] If therefore there be any of you that are of his people, let Jah, even his Lord, be with him, and let him go up to Jerusalem that is in Judea, and build the house of Jah of Israel: for he is Jah that dwelleth in Jerusalem.
[6] Whosoever then dwell in the places about, let them help him, those, I say, that are his neighbours, with gold, and with silver,
[7] With gifts, with horses, and with cattle, and other things, which have been set forth by vow, for the temple of Jah at Jerusalem.
[8] Then the chief of the families of Judea and of the tribe of Benjamin stood up; the priests also, and the Levites, and all they whose mind Jah had moved to go up, and to build an house for Jah at Jerusalem,
[9] And they that dwelt round about them, and helped them in all things with silver and gold, with horses and cattle, and with very

many free gifts of a great number whose minds were stirred up thereto.

[10] King Cyrus also brought forth the holy vessels, which Nabuchodonosor had carried away from Jerusalem, and had set up in his temple of idols.

[11] Now when Cyrus king of the Persians had brought them forth, he delivered them to Mithridates his treasurer:

[12] And by him they were delivered to Sanabassar the governor of Judea.

[13] And this was the number of them; A thousand golden cups, and a thousand of silver, censers of silver twenty nine, vials of gold thirty, and of silver two thousand four hundred and ten, and a thousand other vessels.

[14] So all the vessels of gold and of silver, which were carried away, were five thousand four hundred threescore and nine.

[15] These were brought back by Sanabassar, together with them of the captivity, from Babylon to Jerusalem.

[16] But in the time of Artexerxes king of the Persians Belemus, and Mithridates, and Tabellius, and Rathumus, and Beeltethmus, and Semellius the secretary, with others that were in commission with them, dwelling in Samaria and other places, wrote unto him against them that dwelt in Judea and Jerusalem these letters following;

[17] To king Artexerxes our lord, Thy servants, Rathumus the storywriter, and Semellius the scribe, and the rest of their council, and the judges that are in Celosyria and Phenice.

[18] Be it now known to Jah king, that the Jews that are up from you to us, being come into Jerusalem, that rebellious and wicked city, do build the marketplaces, and repair the walls of it and do lay the foundation of the temple.

[19] Now if this city and the walls thereof be made up again, they will not only refuse to give tribute, but also rebel against kings.

[20] And forasmuch as the things pertaining to the temple are now in hand, we think it meet not to neglect such a matter,

[21] But to speak unto our lord the king, to the intent that, if it be thy pleasure it may be sought out in the books of thy fathers:

[22] And thou shalt find in the chronicles what is written concerning these things, and shalt understand that that city was rebellious, troubling both kings and cities:

[23] And that the Jews were rebellious, and raised always wars therein; for the which cause even this city was made desolate.

[24] Wherefore now we do declare unto thee, O lord the king, that if this city be built again, and the walls thereof set up anew, thou shalt from henceforth have no passage into Celosyria and Phenice.

[25] Then the king wrote back again to Rathumus the storywriter, to Beeltethmus, to Semellius the scribe, and to the rest that were in commission, and dwellers in Samaria and Syria and Phenice, after this manner;

[26] I have read the epistle which ye have sent unto me: therefore I commanded to make diligent search, and it hath been found that that city was from the beginning practising against kings;

[27] And the men therein were given to rebellion and war: and that mighty kings and fierce were in Jerusalem, who reigned and exacted tributes in Celosyria and Phenice.

[28] Now therefore I have commanded to hinder those men from building the city, and heed to be taken that there be no more done in it;

[29] And that those wicked workers proceed no further to the annoyance of kings,

[30] Then king Artexerxes his letters being read, Rathumus, and Semellius the scribe, and the rest that were in commission with them, removing in haste toward Jerusalem with a troop of horsemen and a multitude of people in battle array, began to hinder the builders; and the building of the temple in

Jerusalem ceased until the second year of the reign of Darius king of the Persians.

---

1 Esdr.3

[1] Now when Darius reigned, he made a great feast unto all his subjects, and unto all his household, and unto all the princes of Media and Persia,
[2] And to all the governors and captains and lieutenants that were under him, from India unto Ethiopia, of an hundred twenty and seven provinces.
[3] And when they had eaten and drunken, and being satisfied were gone home, then Darius the king went into his bedchamber, and slept, and soon after awaked.
[4] Then three young men, that were of the guard that kept the king's body, spake one to another;
[5] Let every one of us speak a sentence: he that shall overcome, and whose sentence shall seem wiser than the others, unto him shall the king Darius give great gifts, and great things in token of victory:
[6] As, to be clothed in purple, to drink in gold, and to sleep upon gold, and a chariot with bridles of gold, and an headtire of fine linen, and a chain about his neck:
[7] And he shall sit next to Darius because of his wisdom, and shall be called Darius his cousin.
[8] And then every one wrote his sentence, sealed it, and laid it under king Darius his pillow;
[9] And said that, when the king is risen, some will give him the writings; and of whose side the king and the three princes of Persia shall judge that his sentence is the wisest, to him shall the victory be given, as was appointed.
[10] The first wrote, Wine is the strongest.
[11] The second wrote, The king is strongest.
[12] The third wrote, Women are strongest: but above all things Truth beareth away the victory.
[13] Now when the king was risen up, they took their writings, and delivered them unto him, and so he read them:
[14] And sending forth he called all the princes of Persia and Media, and the governors, and the captains, and the lieutenants, and the chief officers;
[15] And sat him down in the royal seat of judgment; and the writings were read before them.
[16] And he said, Call the young men, and they shall declare their own sentences. So they were called, and came in.
[17] And he said unto them, Declare unto us your mind concerning the writings. Then began the first, who had spoken of the strength of wine;
[18] And he said thus, O ye men, how exceeding strong is wine! it causeth all men to err that drink it:
[19] It maketh the mind of the king and of the fatherless child to be all one; of the bondman and of the freeman, of the poor man and of the rich:
[20] It turneth also every thought into jollity and mirth, so that a man remembereth neither sorrow nor debt:
[21] And it maketh every heart rich, so that a man remembereth neither king nor governor; and it maketh to speak all things by talents:
[22] And when they are in their cups, they forget their love both to friends and brethren, and a little after draw out swords:
[23] But when they are from the wine, they remember not what they have done.
[24] O ye men, is not wine the strongest, that enforceth to do thus? And when he had so spoken, he held his peace.

---

1 Esdr.4

[1] Then the second, that had spoken of the strength of the king, began to say,
[2] O ye men, do not men excel in strength that bear rule over sea and land and all things in them?
[3] But yet the king is more mighty: for he is lord of all these things, and hath dominion over them; and whatsoever he commandeth them they do.
[4] If he bid them make war the one against the other, they do it: if he send them out against the enemies, they go, and break down mountains walls and towers.
[5] They slay and are slain, and transgress not the king's commandment: if they get the victory, they bring all to the king, as well the spoil, as all things else.
[6] Likewise for those that are no soldiers, and have not to do with wars, but use husbundry, when they have reaped again that which they had sown, they bring it to the king, and compel one another to pay tribute unto the king.
[7] And yet he is but one man: if he command to kill, they kill; if he command to spare, they spare;
[8] If he command to smite, they smite; if he command to make desolate, they make desolate; if he command to build, they build;
[9] If he command to cut down, they cut down; if he command to plant, they plant.
[10] So all his people and his armies obey him: furthermore he lieth down, he eateth and drinketh, and taketh his rest:
[11] And these keep watch round about him, neither may any one depart, and do his own business, neither disobey they him in any thing.
[12] O ye men, how should not the king be mightiest, when in such sort he is obeyed? And he held his tongue.
[13] Then the third, who had spoken of women, and of the truth, (this was Zorobabel) began to speak.
[14] O ye men, it is not the great king, nor the multitude of men, neither is it wine, that excelleth; who is it then that ruleth them, or hath Jahship over them? are they not women?
[15] Women have borne the king and all the people that bear rule by sea and land.
[16] Even of them came they: and they nourished them up that planted the vineyards, from whence the wine cometh.
[17] These also make garments for men; these bring glory unto men; and without women cannot men be.
[18] Yea, and if men have gathered together gold and silver, or any other goodly thing, do they not love a woman which is comely in favour and beauty?
[19] And letting all those things go, do they not gape, and even with open mouth fix their eyes fast on her; and have not all men more desire unto her than unto silver or gold, or any goodly thing whatsoever?
[20] A man leaveth his own father that brought him up, and his own country, and cleaveth unto his wife.
[21] He sticketh not to spend his life with his wife. and remembereth neither father, nor mother, nor country.
[22] By this also ye must know that women have dominion over you: do ye not labour and toil, and give and bring all to the woman?
[23] Yea, a man taketh his sword, and goeth his way to rob and to steal, to sail upon the sea and upon rivers;
[24] And looketh upon a lion, and goeth in the darkness; and when he hath stolen, spoiled, and robbed, he bringeth it to his love.
[25] Wherefore a man loveth his wife better than father or mother.
[26] Yea, many there be that have run out of their wits for women, and become servants for their sakes.
[27] Many also have perished, have erred, and sinned, for women.
[28] And now do ye not believe me? is not the king great in his power? do not all

regions fear to touch him?
[29] Yet did I see him and Apame the king's concubine, the daughter of the admirable Bartacus, sitting at the right hand of the king,
[30] And taking the crown from the king's head, and setting it upon her own head; she also struck the king with her left hand.
[31] And yet for all this the king gaped and gazed upon her with open mouth: if she laughed upon him, he laughed also: but if she took any displeasure at him, the king was fain to flatter, that she might be reconciled to him again.
[32] O ye men, how can it be but women should be strong, seeing they do thus?
[33] Then the king and the princes looked one upon another: so he began to speak of the truth.
[34] O ye men, are not women strong? great is the earth, high is the heaven, swift is the sun in his course, for he compasseth the heavens round about, and fetcheth his course again to his own place in one day.
[35] Is he not great that maketh these things? therefore great is the truth, and stronger than all things.
[36] All the earth crieth upon the truth, and the heaven blesseth it: all works shake and tremble at it, and with it is no unrighteous thing.
[37] Wine is wicked, the king is wicked, women are wicked, all the children of men are wicked, and such are all their wicked works; and there is no truth in them; in their unrighteousness also they shall perish.
[38] As for the truth, it endureth, and is alwaYs strong; it liveth and conquereth for evermore.
[39] With her there is no accepting of persons or rewards; but she doeth the things that are just, and refraineth from all unjust and wicked things; and all men do well like of her works.
[40] Neither in her judgment is any unrighteousness; and she is the strength, kingdom, power, and majesty, of all ages. Blessed be the God of truth.
[41] And with that he held his peace. And all the people then shouted, and said, Great is Truth, and mighty above all things.
[42] Then said the king unto him, Ask what thou wilt more than is appointed in the writing, and we will give it thee, because thou art found wisest; and thou shalt sit next me, and shalt be called my cousin.
[43] Then said he unto the king, Remember thy vow, which thou hast vowed to build Jerusalem, in the day when thou camest to thy kingdom,
[44] And to send away all the vessels that were taken away out of Jerusalem, which Cyrus set apart, when he vowed to destroy Babylon, and to send them again thither.
[45] Thou also hast vowed to build up the temple, which the Edomites burned when Judea was made desolate by the Chaldees.
[46] And now, O lord the king, this is that which I require, and which I desire of thee, and this is the princely liberality proceeding from thyself: I desire therefore that thou make good the vow, the performance whereof with thine own mouth thou hast vowed to the King of heaven.
[47] Then Darius the king stood up, and kissed him, and wrote letters for him unto all the treasurers and lieutenants and captains and governors, that they should safely convey on their way both him, and all those that go up with him to build Jerusalem.
[48] He wrote letters also unto the lieutenants that were in Celosyria and Phenice, and unto them in Libanus, that they should bring cedar wood from Libanus unto Jerusalem, and that they should build the city with him.
[49] Moreover he wrote for all the Jews that went out of his realm up into Jewry, concerning their freedom, that no officer, no ruler, no lieutenant, nor treasurer, should forcibly enter into their doors;
[50] And that all the country which they

hold should be free without tribute; and that the Edomites should give over the villages of the Jews which then they held:
[51] Yea, that there should be yearly given twenty talents to the building of the temple, until the time that it were built;
[52] And other ten talents yearly, to maintain the burnt offerings upon the altar every day, as they had a commandment to offer seventeen:
[53] And that all they that went from Babylon to build the city should have free liberty, as well they as their posterity, and all the priests that went away.
[54] He wrote also concerning. the charges, and the priests' vestments wherein they minister;
[55] And likewise for the charges of the Levites, to be given them until the day that the house were finished, and Jerusalem builded up.
[56] And he commanded to give to all that kept the city pensions and wages.
[57] He sent away also all the vessels from Babylon, that Cyrus had set apart; and all that Cyrus had given in commandment, the same charged he also to be done, and sent unto Jerusalem.
[58] Now when this young man was gone forth, he lifted up his face to heaven toward Jerusalem, and praised the King of heaven,
[59] And said, From thee cometh victory, from thee cometh wisdom, and thine is the glory, and I am thy servant.
[60] Blessed art thou, who hast given me wisdom: for to thee I give thanks, O Lord of our fathers.
[61] And so he took the letters, and went out, and came unto Babylon, and told it all his brethren.
[62] And they praised the God of their fathers, because he had given them freedom and liberty
[63] To go up, and to build Jerusalem, and the temple which is called by his name: and they feasted with instruments of musick and gladness seven days.

1Esdr.5

[1] After this were the principal men of the families chosen according to their tribes, to go up with their wives and sons and daughters, with their menservants and maidservants, and their cattle.
[2] And Darius sent with them a thousand horsemen, till they had brought them back to Jerusalem safely, and with musical [instruments] tabrets and flutes.
[3] And all their brethren played, and he made them go up together with them.
[4] And these are the names of the men which went up, according to their families among their tribes, after their several heads.
[5] The priests, the sons of Phinees the son of Aaron: Jesus the son of Josedec, the son of Saraias, and Joacim the son of Zorobabel, the son of Salathiel, of the house of David, out of the kindred of Phares, of the tribe of Judah;
[6] Who spake wise sentences before Darius the king of Persia in the second year of his reign, in the month Nisan, which is the first month.
[7] And these are they of Jewry that came up from the captivity, where they dwelt as strangers, whom Nabuchodonosor the king of Babylon had carried away unto Babylon.
[8] And they returned unto Jerusalem, and to the other parts of Jewry, every man to his own city, who came with Zorobabel, with Jesus, Nehemias, and Zacharias, and Reesaias, Enenius, Mardocheus. Beelsarus, Aspharasus, Reelius, Roimus, and Baana, their guides.
[9] The number of them of the nation, and their governors, sons of Phoros, two thousand an hundred seventy and two; the sons of Saphat, four hundred seventy and two:

[10] The sons of Ares, seven hundred fifty and six:
[11] The sons of Phaath Moab, two thousand eight hundred and twelve:
[12] The sons of Elam, a thousand two hundred fifty and four: the sons of Zathul, nine hundred forty and five: the sons of Corbe, seven hundred and five: the sons of Bani, six hundred forty and eight:
[13] The sons of Bebai, six hundred twenty and three: the sons of Sadas, three thousand two hundred twenty and two:
[14] The sons of Adonikam, six hundred sixty and seven: the sons of Bagoi, two thousand sixty and six: the sons of Adin, four hundred fifty and four:
[15] The sons of Aterezias, ninety and two: the sons of Ceilan and Azetas threescore and seven: the sons of Azuran, four hundred thirty and two:
[16] The sons of Ananias, an hundred and one: the sons of Arom, thirty two: and the sons of Bassa, three hundred twenty and three: the sons of Azephurith, an hundred and two:
[17] The sons of Meterus, three thousand and five: the sons of Bethlomon, an hundred twenty and three:
[18] They of Netophah, fifty and five: they of Anathoth, an hundred fifty and eight: they of Bethsamos, forty and two:
[19] They of Kiriathiarius, twenty and five: they of Caphira and Beroth, seven hundred forty and three: they of Pira, seven hundred:
[20] They of Chadias and Ammidoi, four hundred twenty and two: they of Cirama and Gabdes, six hundred twenty and one:
[21] They of Macalon, an hundred twenty and two: they of Betolius, fifty and two: the sons of Nephis, an hundred fifty and six:
[22] The sons of Calamolalus and Onus, seven hundred twenty and five: the sons of Jerechus, two hundred forty and five:
[23] The sons of Annas, three thousand three hundred and thirty.
[24] The priests: the sons of Jeddu, the son of Jesus among the sons of Sanasib, nine hundred seventy and two: the sons of Meruth, a thousand fifty and two:
[25] The sons of Phassaron, a thousand forty and seven: the sons of Carme, a thousand and seventeen.
[26] The Levites: the sons of Jessue, and Cadmiel, and Banuas, and Sudias, seventy and four.
[27] The holy singers: the sons of Asaph, an hundred twenty and eight.
[28] The porters: the sons of Salum, the sons of Jatal, the sons of Talmon, the sons of Dacobi, the sons of Teta, the sons of Sami, in all an hundred thirty and nine.
[29] The servants of the temple: the sons of Esau, the sons of Asipha, the sons of Tabaoth, the sons of Ceras, the sons of Sud, the sons of Phaleas, the sons of Labana, the sons of Graba,
[30] The sons of Acua, the sons of Uta, the sons of Cetab, the sons of Agaba, the sons of Subai, the sons of Anan, the sons of Cathua, the sons of Geddur,
[31] The sons of Airus, the sons of Daisan, the sons of Noeba, the sons of Chaseba, the sons of Gazera, the sons of Azia, the sons of Phinees, the sons of Azare, the sons of Bastai, the sons of Asana, the sons of Meani, the sons of Naphisi, the sons of Acub, the sons of Acipha, the sons of Assur, the sons of Pharacim, the sons of Basaloth,
[32] The sons of Meeda, the sons of Coutha, the sons of Charea, the sons of Charcus, the sons of Aserer, the sons of Thomoi, the sons of Nasith, the sons of Atipha.
[33] The sons of the servants of Solomon: the sons of Azaphion, the sons of Pharira, the sons of Jeeli, the sons of Lozon, the sons of Israel, the sons of Sapheth,
[34] The sons of Hagia, the sons of Pharacareth, the sons of Sabi, the sons of Sarothie, the sons of Masias, the sons of Gar, the sons of Addus, the sons of Suba, the sons of Apherra, the sons of Barodis, the sons of Sabat, the sons of Allom.

[35] All the ministers of the temple, and the sons of the servants of Solomon, were three hundred seventy and two.
[36] These came up from Thermeleth and Thelersas, Charaathalar leading them, and Aalar;
[37] Neither could they shew their families, nor their stock, how they were of Israel: the sons of Ladan, the son of Ban, the sons of Necodan, six hundred fifty and two.
[38] And of the priests that usurped the office of the priesthood, and were not found: the sons of Obdia, the sons of Accoz, the sons of Addus, who married Augia one of the daughters of Barzelus, and was named after his name.
[39] And when the description of the kindred of these men was sought in the register, and was not found, they were removed from executing the office of the priesthood:
[40] For unto them said Nehemias and Atharias, that they should not be partakers of the holy things, till there arose up an high priest clothed with doctrine and truth.
[41] So of Israel, from them of twelve years old and upward, they were all in number forty thousand, beside menservants and womenservants two thousand three hundred and sixty.
[42] Their menservants and handmaids were seven thousand three hundred forty and seven: the singing men and singing women, two hundred forty and five:
[43] Four hundred thirty and five camels, seven thousand thirty and six horses, two hundred forty and five mules, five thousand five hundred twenty and five beasts used to the yoke.
[44] And certain of the chief of their families, when they came to the temple of God that is in Jerusalem, vowed to set up the house again in his own place according to their ability,
[45] And to give into the holy treasury of the works a thousand pounds of gold, five thousand of silver, and an hundred priestly vestments.
[46] And so dwelt the priests and the Levites and the people in Jerusalem, and in the country, the singers also and the porters; and all Israel in their villages.
[47] But when the seventh month was at hand, and when the children of Israel were every man in his own place, they came all together with one consent into the open place of the first gate which is toward the east.
[48] Then stood up Jesus the son of Josedec, and his brethren the priests and Zorobabel the son of Salathiel, and his brethren, and made ready the altar of the God of Israel,
[49] To offer burnt sacrifices upon it, according as it is expressly commanded in the book of Moses the man of God.
[50] And there were gathered unto them out of the other nations of the land, and they erected the altar upon his own place, because all the nations of the land were at enmity with them, and oppressed them; and they offered sacrifices according to the time, and burnt offerings to Jah both morning and evening.
[51] Also they held the feast of tabernacles, as it is commanded in the law, and offered sacrifices daily, as was meet:
[52] And after that, the continual oblations, and the sacrifice of the sabbaths, and of the new moons, and of all holy feasts.
[53] And all they that had made any vow to God began to offer sacrifices to God from the first day of the seventh month, although the temple of Jah was not yet built.
[54] And they gave unto the masons and carpenters money, meat, and drink, with cheerfulness.
[55] Unto them of Zidon also and Tyre they gave carrs, that they should bring cedar trees from Libanus, which should be brought by floats to the haven of Joppa, according as it was commanded them by Cyrus king of the Persians.

[56] And in the second year and second month after his coming to the temple of God at Jerusalem began Zorobabel the son of Salathiel, and Jesus the son of Josedec, and their brethren, and the priests, and the Levites, and all they that were come unto Jerusalem out of the captivity:
[57] And they laid the foundation of the house of God in the first day of the second month, in the second year after they were come to Jewry and Jerusalem.
[58] And they appointed the Levites from twenty years old over the works of Jah. Then stood up Jesus, and his sons and brethren, and Cadmiel his brother, and the sons of Madiabun, with the sons of Joda the son of Eliadun, with their sons and brethren, all Levites, with one accord setters forward of the business, labouring to advance the works in the house of God. So the workmen built the temple of Jah.
[59] And the priests stood arrayed in their vestments with musical instruments and trumpets; and the Levites the sons of Asaph had cymbals,
[60] Singing songs of thanksgiving, and praising Jah, according as David the king of Israel had ordained.
[61] And they sung with loud voices songs to the praise of Jah, because his mercy and glory is for ever in all Israel.
[62] And all the people sounded trumpets, and shouted with a loud voice, singing songs of thanksgiving unto Jah for the rearing up of the house of Jah.
[63] Also of the priests and Levites, and of the chief of their families, the ancients who had seen the former house came to the building of this with weeping and great crying.
[64] But many with trumpets and joy shouted with loud voice,
[65] Insomuch that the trumpets might not be heard for the weeping of the people: yet the multitude sounded marvellously, so that it was heard afar off.

[66] Wherefore when the enemies of the tribe of Judah and Benjamin heard it, they came to know what that noise of trumpets should mean.
[67] And they perceived that they that were of the captivity did build the temple unto Jah God of Israel.
[68] So they went to Zorobabel and Jesus, and to the chief of the families, and said unto them, We will build together with you.
[69] For we likewise, as ye, do obey your Lord, and do sacrifice unto him from the days of Azbazareth the king of the Assyrians, who brought us hither.
[70] Then Zorobabel and Jesus and the chief of the families of Israel said unto them, It is not for us and you to build together an house unto Jah our God.
[71] We ourselves alone will build unto Jah of Israel, according as Cyrus the king of the Persians hath commanded us.
[72] But the heathen of the land lying heavy upon the inhabitants of Judea, and holding them strait, hindered their building;
[73] And by their secret plots, and popular persuasions and commotions, they hindered the finishing of the building all the time that king Cyrus lived: so they were hindered from building for the space of two years, until the reign of Darius.

---

1 Esdr. 6

[1] Now in the second year of the reign of Darius Aggeus and Zacharias the son of Addo, the prophets, prophesied unto the Jews in Jewry and Jerusalem in the name of Jah God of Israel, which was upon them.
[2] Then stood up Zorobabel the son of Salatiel, and Jesus the son of Josedec, and began to build the house of Jah at Jerusalem, the prophets of Jah being with them, and helping them.
[3] At the same time came unto them Sisinnes the governor of Syria and Phenice,

with Sathrabuzanes and his companions, and said unto them,
[4] By whose appointment do ye build this house and this roof, and perform all the other things? and who are the workmen that perform these things?
[5] Nevertheless the elders of the Jews obtained favour, because Jah had visited the captivity;
[6] And they were not hindered from building, until such time as signification was given unto Darius concerning them, and an answer received.
[7] The copy of the letters which Sisinnes, governor of Syria and Phenice, and Sathrabuzanes, with their companions, rulers in Syria and Phenice, wrote and sent unto Darius; To king Darius, greeting:
[8] Let all things be known unto our lord the king, that being come into the country of Judea, and entered into the city of Jerusalem we found in the city of Jerusalem the ancients of the Jews that were of the captivity
[9] Building an house unto Jah, great and new, of hewn and costly stones, and the timber already laid upon the walls.
[10] And those works are done with great speed, and the work goeth on prosperously in their hands, and with all glory and diligence is it made.
[11] Then asked we these elders, saying, By whose commandment build ye this house, and lay the foundations of these works?
[12] Therefore to the intent that we might give knowledge unto thee by writing, we demanded of them who were the chief doers, and we required of them the names in writing of their principal men.
[13] So they gave us this answer, We are the servants of Jah which made heaven and earth.
[14] And as for this house, it was builded many years ago by a king of Israel great and strong, and was finished.
[15] But when our fathers provoked God unto wrath, and sinned against Jah of Israel which is in heaven, he gave them over into the power of Nabuchodonosor king of Babylon, of the Chaldees;
[16] Who pulled down the house, and burned it, and carried away the people captives unto Babylon.
[17] But in the first year that king Cyrus reigned over the country of Babylon Cyrus the king wrote to build up this house.
[18] And the holy vessels of gold and of silver, that Nabuchodonosor had carried away out of the house at Jerusalem, and had set them in his own temple those Cyrus the king brought forth again out of the temple at Babylon, and they were delivered to Zorobabel and to Sanabassarus the ruler,
[19] With commandment that he should carry away the same vessels, and put them in the temple at Jerusalem; and that the temple of Jah should be built in his place.
[20] Then the same Sanabassarus, being come hither, laid the foundations of the house of Jah at Jerusalem; and from that time to this being still a building, it is not yet fully ended.
[21] Now therefore, if it seem good unto the king, let search be made among the records of king Cyrus:
[22] And if it be found that the building of the house of Jah at Jerusalem hath been done with the consent of king Cyrus, and if our lord the king be so minded, let him signify unto us thereof.
[23] Then commanded king Darius to seek among the records at Babylon: and so at Ecbatane the palace, which is in the country of Media, there was found a roll wherein these things were recorded.
[24] In the first year of the reign of Cyrus king Cyrus commanded that the house of Jah at Jerusalem should be built again, where they do sacrifice with continual fire:
[25] Whose height shall be sixty cubits and the breadth sixty cubits, with three rows of hewn stones, and one row of new wood of

that country; and the expences thereof to be given out of the house of king Cyrus:

[26] And that the holy vessels of the house of Jah, both of gold and silver, that Nabuchodonosor took out of the house at Jerusalem, and brought to Babylon, should be restored to the house at Jerusalem, and be set in the place where they were before.

[27] And also he commanded that Sisinnes the governor of Syria and Phenice, and Sathrabuzanes, and their companions, and those which were appointed rulers in Syria and Phenice, should be careful not to meddle with the place, but suffer Zorobabel, the servant of Jah, and governor of Judea, and the elders of the Jews, to build the house of Jah in that place.

[28] I have commanded also to have it built up whole again; and that they look diligently to help those that be of the captivity of the Jews, till the house of Jah be finished:

[29] And out of the tribute of Celosyria and Phenice a portion carefully to be given these men for the sacrifices of Jah, that is, to Zorobabel the governor, for bullocks, and rams, and lambs;

[30] And also corn, salt, wine, and oil, and that continually every year without further question, according as the priests that be in Jerusalem shall signify to be daily spent:

[31] That offerings may be made to the most high God for the king and for his children, and that they may pray for their lives.

[32] And he commanded that whosoever should transgress, yea, or make light of any thing afore spoken or written, out of his own house should a tree be taken, and he thereon be hanged, and all his goods seized for the king.

[33] Jah therefore, whose name is there called upon, utterly destroy every king and nation, that stretcheth out his hand to hinder or endamage that house of Jah in Jerusalem.

[34] I Darius the king have ordained that according unto these things it be done with diligence.

1 Esdr. 7

[1] Then Sisinnes the governor of Celosyria and Phenice, and Sathrabuzanes, with their companions following the commandments of king Darius,

[2] Did very carefully oversee the holy works, assisting the ancients of the Jews and governors of the temple.

[3] And so the holy works prospered, when Aggeus and Zacharias the prophets prophesied.

[4] And they finished these things by the commandment of Jah God of Israel, and with the consent of Cyrus, Darius, and Artexerxes, kings of Persia.

[5] And thus was the holy house finished in the three and twentieth day of the month Adar, in the sixth year of Darius king of the Persians

[6] And the children of Israel, the priests, and the Levites, and others that were of the captivity, that were added unto them, did according to the things written in the book of Moses.

[7] And to the dedication of the temple of Jah they offered an hundred bullocks two hundred rams, four hundred lambs;

[8] And twelve goats for the sin of all Israel, according to the number of the chief of the tribes of Israel.

[9] The priests also and the Levites stood arrayed in their vestments, according to their kindreds, in the service of Jah God of Israel, according to the book of Moses: and the porters at every gate.

[10] And the children of Israel that were of the captivity held the passover the fourteenth day of the first month, after that the priests and the Levites were sanctified.

[11] They that were of the captivity were not all sanctified together: but the Levites were all sanctified together.

[12] And so they offered the passover for all

them of the captivity, and for their brethren the priests, and for themselves.
[13] And the children of Israel that came out of the captivity did eat, even all they that had separated themselves from the abominations of the people of the land, and sought Jah.
[14] And they kept the feast of unleavened bread seven days, making merry before Jah,
[15] For that he had turned the counsel of the king of Assyria toward them, to strengthen their hands in the works of Jah God of Israel.

---

1 Esdr.8

[1] And after these things, when Artexerxes the king of the Persians reigned came Esdras the son of Saraias, the son of Ezerias, the son of Helchiah, the son of Salum,
[2] The son of Sadduc, the son of Achitob, the son of Amarias, the son of Ezias, the son of Meremoth, the son of Zaraias, the son of Savias, the son of Boccas, the son of Abisum, the son of Phinees, the son of Eleazar, the son of Aaron the chief priest.
[3] This Esdras went up from Babylon, as a scribe, being very ready in the law of Moses, that was given by the God of Israel.
[4] And the king did him honour: for he found grace in his sight in all his requests.
[5] There went up with him also certain of the children of Israel, of the priest of the Levites, of the holy singers, porters, and ministers of the temple, unto Jerusalem,
[6] In the seventh year of the reign of Artexerxes, in the fifth month, this was the king's seventh year; for they went from Babylon in the first day of the first month, and came to Jerusalem, according to the prosperous journey which Jah gave them.
[7] For Esdras had very great skill, so that he omitted nothing of the law and commandments of Jah, but taught all Israel the ordinances and judgments.

[8] Now the copy of the commission, which was written from Artexerxes the king, and came to Esdras the priest and reader of the law of Jah, is this that followeth;
[9] King Artexerxes unto Esdras the priest and reader of the law of Jah sendeth greeting:
[10] Having determined to deal graciously, I have given order, that such of the nation of the Jews, and of the priests and Levites being within our realm, as are willing and desirous should go with thee unto Jerusalem.
[11] As many therefore as have a mind thereunto, let them depart with thee, as it hath seemed good both to me and my seven friends the counsellors;
[12] That they may look unto the affairs of Judea and Jerusalem, agreeably to that which is in the law of Jah;
[13] And carry the gifts unto Jah of Israel to Jerusalem, which I and my friends have vowed, and all the gold and silver that in the country of Babylon can be found, to Jah in Jerusalem,
[14] With that also which is given of the people for the temple of Jah their God at Jerusalem: and that silver and gold may be collected for bullocks, rams, and lambs, and things thereunto appertaining;
[15] To the end that they may offer sacrifices unto Jah upon the altar of Jah their God, which is in Jerusalem.
[16] And whatsoever thou and thy brethren will do with the silver and gold, that do, according to the will of thy God.
[17] And the holy vessels of Jah, which are given thee for the use of the temple of thy God, which is in Jerusalem, thou shalt set before thy God in Jerusalem.
[18] And whatsoever thing else thou shalt remember for the use of the temple of thy God, thou shalt give it out of the king's treasury.
[19] And I king Artexerxes have also commanded the keepers of the treasures in Syria and Phenice, that whatsoever Esdras

the priest and the reader of the law of the most high God shall send for, they should give it him with speed,

[20] To the sum of an hundred talents of silver, likewise also of wheat even to an hundred cors, and an hundred pieces of wine, and other things in abundance.

[21] Let all things be performed after the law of God diligently unto the most high God, that wrath come not upon the kingdom of the king and his sons.

[22] I command you also, that ye require no tax, nor any other imposition, of any of the priests, or Levites, or holy singers, or porters, or ministers of the temple, or of any that have doings in this temple, and that no man have authority to impose any thing upon them.

[23] And thou, Esdras, according to the wisdom of God ordain judges and justices, that they may judge in all Syria and Phenice all those that know the law of thy God; and those that know it not thou shalt teach.

[24] And whosoever shall transgress the law of thy God, and of the king, shall be punished diligently, whether it be by death, or other punishment, by penalty of money, or by imprisonment.

[25] Then said Esdras the scribe, Blessed be the only Lord God of my fathers, who hath put these things into the heart of the king, to glorify his house that is in Jerusalem:

[26] And hath honoured me in the sight of the king, and his counsellors, and all his friends and nobles.

[27] Therefore was I encouraged by the help of Jah my God, and gathered together men of Israel to go up with me.

[28] And these are the chief according to their families and several dignities, that went up with me from Babylon in the reign of king Artexerxes:

[29] Of the sons of Phinees, Gerson: of the sons of Ithamar, Gamael: of the sons of David, Lettus the son of Sechenias:

[30] Of the sons of Pharez, Zacharias; and with him were counted an hundred and fifty men:

[31] Of the sons of Pahath Moab, Eliaonias, the son of Zaraias, and with him two hundred men:

[32] Of the sons of Zathoe, Sechenias the son of Jezelus, and with him three hundred men: of the sons of Adin, Obeth the son of Jonathan, and with him two hundred and fifty men:

[33] Of the sons of Elam, Josias son of Gotholias, and with him seventy men:

[34] Of the sons of Saphatias, Zaraias son of Michael, and with him threescore and ten men:

[35] Of the sons of Joab, Abadias son of Jezelus, and with him two hundred and twelve men:

[36] Of the sons of Banid, Assalimoth son of Josaphias, and with him an hundred and threescore men:

[37] Of the sons of Babi, Zacharias son of Bebai, and with him twenty and eight men:

[38] Of the sons of Astath, Johannes son of Acatan, and with him an hundred and ten men:

[39] Of the sons of Adonikam the last, and these are the names of them, Eliphalet, Jewel, and Samaias, and with them seventy men:

[40] Of the sons of Bago, Uthi the son of Istalcurus, and with him seventy men.

[41] And these I gathered together to the river called Theras, where we pitched our tents three days: and then I surveyed them.

[42] But when I had found there none of the priests and Levites,

[43] Then sent I unto Eleazar, and Iduel, and Masman,

[44] And Alnathan, and Mamaias, and Joribas, and Nathan, Eunatan, Zacharias, and Mosollamon, principal men and learned.

[45] And I bade them that they should go unto Saddeus the captain, who was in the place of the treasury:

[46] And commanded them that they should

speak unto Daddeus, and to his brethren, and to the treasurers in that place, to send us such men as might execute the priests' office in the house of Jah.

[47] And by the mighty hand of our Lord they brought unto us skilful men of the sons of Moli the son of Levi, the son of Israel, Asebebia, and his sons, and his brethren, who were eighteen.

[48] And Asebia, and Annus, and Osaias his brother, of the sons of Channuneus, and their sons, were twenty men.

[49] And of the servants of the temple whom David had ordained, and the principal men for the service of the Levites to wit, the servants of the temple two hundred and twenty, the catalogue of whose names were shewed.

[50] And there I vowed a fast unto the young men before our Lord, to desire of him a prosperous journey both for us and them that were with us, for our children, and for the cattle:

[51] For I was ashamed to ask the king footmen, and horsemen, and conduct for safeguard against our adversaries.

[52] For we had said unto the king, that the power of Jah our God should be with them that seek him, to support them in all ways.

[53] And again we besought our Lord as touching these things, and found him favourable unto us.

[54] Then I separated twelve of the chief of the priests, Esebrias, and Assanias, and ten men of their brethren with them:

[55] And I weighed them the gold, and the silver, and the holy vessels of the house of our Lord, which the king, and his council, and the princes, and all Israel, had given.

[56] And when I had weighed it, I delivered unto them six hundred and fifty talents of silver, and silver vessels of an hundred talents, and an hundred talents of gold,

[57] And twenty golden vessels, and twelve vessels of brass, even of fine brass, glittering like gold.

[58] And I said unto them, Both ye are holy unto Jah, and the vessels are holy, and the gold and the silver is a vow unto Jah, Jah of our fathers.

[59] Watch ye, and keep them till ye deliver them to the chief of the priests and Levites, and to the principal men of the families of Israel, in Jerusalem, into the chambers of the house of our God.

[60] So the priests and the Levites, who had received the silver and the gold and the vessels, brought them unto Jerusalem, into the temple of Jah.

[61] And from the river Theras we departed the twelfth day of the first month, and came to Jerusalem by the mighty hand of our Lord, which was with us: and from the beginning of our journey Jah delivered us from every enemy, and so we came to Jerusalem.

[62] And when we had been there three days, the gold and silver that was weighed was delivered in the house of our Lord on the fourth day unto Marmoth the priest the son of Iri.

[63] And with him was Eleazar the son of Phinees, and with them were Josabad the son of Jesu and Moeth the son of Sabban, Levites: all was delivered them by number and weight.

[64] And all the weight of them was written up the same hour.

[65] Moreover they that were come out of the captivity offered sacrifice unto Jah God of Israel, even twelve bullocks for all Israel, fourscore and sixteen rams,

[66] Threescore and twelve lambs, goats for a peace offering, twelve; all of them a sacrifice to Jah.

[67] And they delivered the king's commandments unto the king's stewards' and to the governors of Celosyria and Phenice; and they honoured the people and the temple of God.

[68] Now when these things were done, the rulers came unto me, and said,

[69] The nation of Israel, the princes, the priests and Levites, have not put away from them the strange people of the land, nor the pollutions of the Gentiles to wit, of the Canaanites, Hittites, Pheresites, Jebusites, and the Moabites, Egyptians, and Edomites.
[70] For both they and their sons have married with their daughters, and the holy seed is mixed with the strange people of the land; and from the beginning of this matter the rulers and the great men have been partakers of this iniquity.
[71] And as soon as I had heard these things, I rent my clothes, and the holy garment, and pulled off the hair from off my head and beard, and sat me down sad and very heavy.
[72] So all they that were then moved at the word of Jah God of Israel assembled unto me, whilst I mourned for the iniquity: but I sat still full of heaviness until the evening sacrifice.
[73] Then rising up from the fast with my clothes and the holy garment rent, and bowing my knees, and stretching forth my hands unto Jah,
[74] I said, O Lord, I am confounded and ashamed before thy face;
[75] For our sins are multiplied above our heads, and our ignorances have reached up unto heaven.
[76] For ever since the time of our fathers we have been and are in great sin, even unto this day.
[77] And for our sins and our fathers' we with our brethren and our kings and our priests were given up unto the kings of the earth, to the sword, and to captivity, and for a prey with shame, unto this day.
[78] And now in some measure hath mercy been shewed unto us from thee, O Lord, that there should be left us a root and a name in the place of thy sanctuary;
[79] And to discover unto us a light in the house of Jah our God, and to give us food in the time of our servitude.
[80] Yea, when we were in bondage, we were not forsaken of our Lord; but he made us gracious before the kings of Persia, so that they gave us food;
[81] Yea, and honoured the temple of our Lord, and raised up the desolate Sion, that they have given us a sure abiding in Jewry and Jerusalem.
[82] And now, O Lord, what shall we say, having these things? for we have transgressed thy commandments, which thou gavest by the hand of thy servants the prophets, saying,
[83] That the land, which ye enter into to possess as an heritage, is a land polluted with the pollutions of the strangers of the land, and they have filled it with their uncleanness.
[84] Therefore now shall ye not join your daughters unto their sons, neither shall ye take their daughters unto your sons.
[85] Moreover ye shall never seek to have peace with them, that ye may be strong, and eat the good things of the land, and that ye may leave the inheritance of the land unto your children for evermore.
[86] And all that is befallen is done unto us for our wicked works and great sins; for thou, O Lord, didst make our sins light,
[87] And didst give unto us such a root: but we have turned back again to transgress thy law, and to mingle ourselves with the uncleanness of the nations of the land.
[88] Mightest not thou be angry with us to destroy us, till thou hadst left us neither root, seed, nor name?
[89] O Lord of Israel, thou art true: for we are left a root this day.
[90] Behold, now are we before thee in our iniquities, for we cannot stand any longer by reason of these things before thee.
[91] And as Esdras in his prayer made his confession, weeping, and lying flat upon the ground before the temple, there gathered unto him from Jerusalem a very great multitude of men and women and children: for there was great weeping among the

multitude.
[92] Then Jechonias the son of Jeelus, one of the sons of Israel, called out, and said, O Esdras, we have sinned against Jah God, we have married strange women of the nations of the land, and now is all Israel aloft.
[93] Let us make an oath to Jah, that we will put away all our wives, which we have taken of the heathen, with their children,
[94] Like as thou hast decreed, and as many as do obey the law of Jah.
[95] Arise and put in execution: for to thee doth this matter appertain, and we will be with thee: do valiantly.
[96] So Esdras arose, and took an oath of the chief of the priests and Levites of all Israel to do after these things; and so they sware.

---

1 Esdr. 9

[1] Then Esdras rising from the court of the temple went to the chamber of Joanan the son of Eliasib,
[2] And remained there, and did eat no meat nor drink water, mourning for the great iniquities of the multitude.
[3] And there was a proclamation in all Jewry and Jerusalem to all them that were of the captivity, that they should be gathered together at Jerusalem:
[4] And that whosoever met not there within two or three days according as the elders that bare rule appointed, their cattle should be seized to the use of the temple, and himself cast out from them that were of the captivity.
[5] And in three days were all they of the tribe of Judah and Benjamin gathered together at Jerusalem the twentieth day of the ninth month.
[6] And all the multitude sat trembling in the broad court of the temple because of the present foul weather.
[7] So Esdras arose up, and said unto them, Ye have transgressed the law in marrying strange wives, thereby to increase the sins of Israel.
[8] And now by confessing give glory unto Jah God of our fathers,
[9] And do his will, and separate yourselves from the heathen of the land, and from the strange women.
[10] Then cried the whole multitude, and said with a loud voice, Like as thou hast spoken, so will we do.
[11] But forasmuch as the people are many, and it is foul weather, so that we cannot stand without, and this is not a work of a day or two, seeing our sin in these things is spread far:
[12] Therefore let the rulers of the multitude stay, and let all them of our habitations that have strange wives come at the time appointed,
[13] And with them the rulers and judges of every place, till we turn away the wrath of Jah from us for this matter.
[14] Then Jonathan the son of Azael and Ezechias the son of Theocanus accordingly took this matter upon them: and Mosollam and Levis and Sabbatheus helped them.
[15] And they that were of the captivity did according to all these things.
[16] And Esdras the priest chose unto him the principal men of their families, all by name: and in the first day of the tenth month they sat together to examine the matter.
[17] So their cause that held strange wives was brought to an end in the first day of the first month.
[18] And of the priests that were come together, and had strange wives, there were found:
[19] Of the sons of Jesus the son of Josedec, and his brethren; Matthelas and Eleazar, and Joribus and Joadanus.
[20] And they gave their hands to put away

their wives and to offer rams to make reconcilement for their errors.

[21] And of the sons of Emmer; Ananias, and Zabdeus, and Eanes, and Sameius, and Hiereel, and Azarias.

[22] And of the sons of Phaisur; Elionas, Massias Israel, and Nathanael, and Ocidelus and Talsas.

[23] And of the Levites; Jozabad, and Semis, and Colius, who was called Calitas, and Patheus, and Judas, and Jonas.

[24] Of the holy singers; Eleazurus, Bacchurus.

[25] Of the porters; Sallumus, and Tolbanes.

[26] Of them of Israel, of the sons of Phoros; Hiermas, and Eddias, and Melchias, and Maelus, and Eleazar, and Asibias, and Baanias.

[27] Of the sons of Ela; Matthanias, Zacharias, and Hierielus, and Hieremoth, and Aedias.

[28] And of the sons of Zamoth; Eliadas, Elisimus, Othonias, Jarimoth, and Sabatus, and Sardeus.

[29] Of the sons of Babai; Johannes, and Ananias and Josabad, and Amatheis.

[30] Of the sons of Mani; Olamus, Mamuchus, Jedeus, Jasubus, Jasael, and Hieremoth.

[31] And of the sons of Addi; Naathus, and Moosias, Lacunus, and Naidus, and Mathanias, and Sesthel, Balnuus, and Manasseas.

[32] And of the sons of Annas; Elionas and Aseas, and Melchias, and Sabbeus, and Simon Chosameus.

[33] And of the sons of Asom; Altaneus, and Matthias, and Baanaia, Eliphalet, and Manasses, and Semei.

[34] And of the sons of Maani; Jeremias, Momdis, Omaerus, Juel, Mabdai, and Pelias, and Anos, Carabasion, and Enasibus, and Mamnitanaimus, Eliasis, Bannus, Eliali, Samis, Selemias, Nathanias: and of the sons of Ozora; Sesis, Esril, Azaelus, Samatus, Zambis, Josephus.

[35] And of the sons of Ethma; Mazitias, Zabadaias, Edes, Juel, Banaias.

[36] All these had taken strange wives, and they put them away with their children.

[37] And the priests and Levites, and they that were of Israel, dwelt in Jerusalem, and in the country, in the first day of the seventh month: so the children of Israel were in their habitations.

[38] And the whole multitude came together with one accord into the broad place of the holy porch toward the east:

[39] And they spake unto Esdras the priest and reader, that he would bring the law of Moses, that was given of Jah God of Israel.

[40] So Esdras the chief priest brought the law unto the whole multitude from man to woman, and to all the priests, to hear law in the first day of the seventh month.

[41] And he read in the broad court before the holy porch from morning unto midday, before both men and women; and the multitude gave heed unto the law.

[42] And Esdras the priest and reader of the law stood up upon a pulpit of wood, which was made for that purpose.

[43] And there stood up by him Mattathias, Sammus, Ananias, Azarias, Urias, Ezecias, Balasamus, upon the right hand:

[44] And upon his left hand stood Phaldaius, Misael, Melchias, Lothasubus, and Nabarias.

[45] Then took Esdras the book of the law before the multitude: for he sat honourably in the first place in the sight of them all.

[46] And when he opened the law, they stood all straight up. So Esdras blessed Jah God most High, the God of hosts, Almighty.

[47] And all the people answered, Amen; and lifting up their hands they fell to the ground, and worshipped Jah.

[48] Also Jesus, Anus, Sarabias, Adinus, Jacubus, Sabateas, Auteas, Maianeas, and Calitas, Asrias, and Joazabdus, and Ananias, Biatas, the Levites, taught the law of Jah, making them withal to understand it.
[49] Then spake Attharates unto Esdras the chief priest. and reader, and to the Levites that taught the multitude, even to all, saying,
[50] This day is holy unto Jah; (for they all wept when they heard the law:)
[51] Go then, and eat the fat, and drink the sweet, and send part to them that have nothing;
[52] For this day is holy unto Jah: and be not sorrowful; for Jah will bring you to honour.
[53] So the Levites published all things to the people, saying, This day is holy to Jah; be not sorrowful.
[54] Then went they their way, every one to eat and drink, and make merry, and to give part to them that had nothing, and to make great cheer;
[55] Because they understood the words wherein they were instructed, and for the which they had been assembled.

2 Esdras

2 Ezra.1

[1] The second book of the prophet Esdras, the son of Saraias, the son of Azarias, the son of Helchias, the son of Sadamias, the sou of Sadoc, the son of Achitob,
[2] The son of Achias, the son of Phinees, the son of Heli, the son of Amarias, the son of Aziei, the son of Marimoth, the son of And he spake unto the of Borith, the son of Abisei, the son of Phinees, the son of Eleazar,
[3] The son of Aaron, of the tribe of Levi; which was captive in the land of the Medes, in the reign of Artexerxes king of the Persians.
[4] And the word of Jah came unto me, saying,
[5] Go thy way, and shew my people their sinful deeds, and their children their wickedness which they have done against me; that they may tell their children's children:
[6] Because the sins of their fathers are increased in them: for they have forgotten me, and have offered unto strange gods.
[7] Am not I even he that brought them out of the land of Egypt, from the house of bondage? but they have provoked me unto wrath, and despised my counsels.
[8] Pull thou off then the hair of thy head, and cast all evil upon them, for they have not been obedient unto my law, but it is a rebellious people.
[9] How long shall I forbear them, into whom I have done so much good?
[10] Many kings have I destroyed for their sakes; Pharaoh with his servants and all his power have I smitten down.
[11] All the nations have I destroyed before them, and in the east I have scattered the people of two provinces, even of Tyrus and Sidon, and have slain all their enemies.
[12] Speak thou therefore unto them, saying, Thus saith Jah,
[13] I led you through the sea and in the beginning gave you a large and safe passage; I gave you Moses for a leader, and Aaron for a priest.
[14] I gave you light in a pillar of fire, and great wonders have I done among you; yet have ye forgotten me, saith Jah.
[15] Thus saith the Almighty Lord, The quails were as a token to you; I gave you tents for your safeguard: nevertheless ye murmured there,
[16] And triumphed not in my name for the destruction of your enemies, but ever to this day do ye yet murmur.
[17] Where are the benefits that I have done

for you? when ye were hungry and thirsty in the wilderness, did ye not cry unto me,
[18] Saying, Why hast thou brought us into this wilderness to kill us? it had been better for us to have served the Egyptians, than to die in this wilderness.
[19] Then had I pity upon your mournings, and gave you manna to eat; so ye did eat angels' bread.
[20] When ye were thirsty, did I not cleave the rock, and waters flowed out to your fill? for the heat I covered you with the leaves of the trees.
[21] I divided among you a fruitful land, I cast out the Canaanites, the Pherezites, and the Philistines, before you: what shall I yet do more for you? saith Jah.
[22] Thus saith the Almighty Lord, When ye were in the wilderness, in the river of the Amorites, being athirst, and blaspheming my name,
[23] I gave you not fire for your blasphemies, but cast a tree in the water, and made the river sweet.
[24] What shall I do unto thee, O Jacob? thou, Juda, wouldest not obey me: I will turn me to other nations, and unto those will I give my name, that they may keep my statutes.
[25] Seeing ye have forsaken me, I will forsake you also; when ye desire me to be gracious unto you, I shall have no mercy upon you.
[26] Whensoever ye shall call upon me, I will not hear you: for ye have defiled your hands with blood, and your feet are swift to commit manslaughter.
[27] Ye have not as it were forsaken me, but your own selves, saith Jah.
[28] Thus saith the Almighty Lord, Have I not prayed you as a father his sons, as a mother her daughters, and a nurse her young babes,
[29] That ye would be my people, and I should be your God; that ye would be my children, and I should be your father?

[30] I gathered you together, as a hen gathereth her chickens under her wings: but now, what shall I do unto you? I will cast you out from my face.
[31] When ye offer unto me, I will turn my face from you: for your solemn feastdays, your new moons, and your circumcisions, have I forsaken.
[32] I sent unto you my servants the prophets, whom ye have taken and slain, and torn their bodies in pieces, whose blood I will require of your hands, saith Jah.
[33] Thus saith the Almighty Lord, Your house is desolate, I will cast you out as the wind doth stubble.
[34] And your children shall not be fruitful; for they have despised my commandment, and done the thing that is an evil before me.
[35] Your houses will I give to a people that shall come; which not having heard of me yet shall believe me; to whom I have shewed no signs, yet they shall do that I have commanded them.
[36] They have seen no prophets, yet they shall call their sins to remembrance, and acknowledge them.
[37] I take to witness the grace of the people to come, whose little ones rejoice in gladness: and though they have not seen me with bodily eyes, yet in spirit they believe the thing that I say.
[38] And now, brother, behold what glory; and see the people that come from the east:
[39] Unto whom I will give for leaders, Abraham, Isaac, and Jacob, Oseas, Amos, and Micheas, Joel, Abdias, and Jonas,
[40] Nahum, and Abacuc, Sophonias, Aggeus, Zachary, and Malachy, which is called also an angel of Jah.

---

2 Ezra.2

[1] Thus saith Jah, I brought this people out of bondage, and I gave them my commandments by menservants the

prophets; whom they would not hear, but despised my counsels.

[2] The mother that bare them saith unto them, Go your way, ye children; for I am a widow and forsaken.

[3] I brought you up with gladness; but with sorrow and heaviness have I lost you: for ye have sinned before Jah your God, and done that thing that is evil before him.

[4] But what shall I now do unto you? I am a widow and forsaken: go your way, O my children, and ask mercy of Jah.

[5] As for me, O father, I call upon thee for a witness over the mother of these children, which would not keep my covenant,

[6] That thou bring them to confusion, and their mother to a spoil, that there may be no offspring of them.

[7] Let them be scattered abroad among the heathen, let their names be put out of the earth: for they have despised my covenant.

[8] Woe be unto thee, Assur, thou that hidest the unrighteous in thee! O thou wicked people, remember what I did unto Sodom and Gomorrha;

[9] Whose land lieth in clods of pitch and heaps of ashes: even so also will I do unto them that hear me not, saith the Almighty Lord.

[10] Thus saith Jah unto Esdras, Tell my people that I will give them the kingdom of Jerusalem, which I would have given unto Israel.

[11] Their glory also will I take unto me, and give these the everlasting tabernacles, which I had prepared for them.

[12] They shall have the tree of life for an ointment of sweet savour; they shall neither labour, nor be weary.

[13] Go, and ye shall receive: pray for few days unto you, that they may be shortened: the kingdom is already prepared for you: watch.

[14] Take heaven and earth to witness; for I have broken the evil in pieces, and created the good: for I live, saith Jah.

[15] Mother, embrace thy children, and bring them up with gladness, make their feet as fast as a pillar: for I have chosen thee, saith Jah.

[16] And those that be dead will I raise up again from their places, and bring them out of the graves: for I have known my name in Israel.

[17] Fear not, thou mother of the children: for I have chosen thee, saith Jah.

[18] For thy help will I send my servants Esau and Jeremy, after whose counsel I have sanctified and prepared for thee twelve trees laden with divers fruits,

[19] And as many fountains flowing with milk and honey, and seven mighty mountains, whereupon there grow roses and lilies, whereby I will fill thy children with joy.

[20] Do right to the widow, judge for the fatherless, give to the poor, defend the orphan, clothe the naked,

[21] Heal the broken and the weak, laugh not a lame man to scorn, defend the maimed, and let the blind man come into the sight of my clearness.

[22] Keep the old and young within thy walls.

[23] Wheresoever thou findest the dead, take them and bury them, and I will give thee the first place in my resurrection.

[24] Abide still, O my people, and take thy rest, for thy quietness still come.

[25] Nourish thy children, O thou good nurse; stablish their feet.

[26] As for the servants whom I have given thee, there shall not one of them perish; for I will require them from among thy number.

[27] Be not weary: for when the day of trouble and heaviness cometh, others shall weep and be sorrowful, but thou shalt be merry and have abundance.

[28] The heathen shall envy thee, but they shall be able to do nothing against thee, saith Jah.

[29] My hands shall cover thee, so that thy

children shall not see hell.
[30] Be joyful, O thou mother, with thy children; for I will deliver thee, saith Jah.
[31] Remember thy children that sleep, for I shall bring them out of the sides of the earth, and shew mercy unto them: for I am merciful, saith Jah Almighty.
[32] Embrace thy children until I come and shew mercy unto them: for my wells run over, and my grace shall not fail.
[33] I Esdras received a charge of Jah upon the mount Oreb, that I should go unto Israel; but when I came unto them, they set me at nought, and despised the commandment of Jah.
[34] And therefore I say unto you, O ye heathen, that hear and understand, look for your Shepherd, he shall give you everlasting rest; for he is nigh at hand, that shall come in the end of the world.
[35] Be ready to the reward of the kingdom, for the everlasting light shall shine upon you for evermore.
[36] Flee the shadow of this world, receive the joyfulness of your glory: I testify my Saviour openly.
[37] O receive the gift that is given you, and be glad, giving thanks unto him that hath led you to the heavenly kingdom.
[38] Arise up and stand, behold the number of those that be sealed in the feast of Jah;
[39] Which are departed from the shadow of the world, and have received glorious garments of Jah.
[40] Take thy number, O Sion, and shut up those of thine that are clothed in white, which have fulfilled the law of Jah.
[41] The number of thy children, whom thou longedst for, is fulfilled: beseech the power of Jah, that thy people, which have been called from the beginning, may be hallowed.
[42] I Esdras saw upon the mount Sion a great people, whom I could not number, and they all praised Jah with songs.
[43] And in the midst of them there was a young man of a high stature, taller than all the rest, and upon every one of their heads he set crowns, and was more exalted; which I marvelled at greatly.
[44] So I asked the angel, and said, Sir, what are these?
[45] He answered and said unto me, These be they that have put off the mortal clothing, and put on the immortal, and have confessed the name of God: now are they crowned, and receive palms.
[46] Then said I unto the angel, What young person is it that crowneth them, and giveth them palms in their hands?
[47] So he answered and said unto me, It is the Son of God, whom they have confessed in the world. Then began I greatly to commend them that stood so stiffly for the name of Jah.
[48] Then the angel said unto me, Go thy way, and tell my people what manner of things, and how great wonders of Jah thy God, thou hast seen.

---

2 Ezra. 3

[1] In the thirtieth year after the ruin of the city I was in Babylon, and lay troubled upon my bed, and my thoughts came up over my heart:
[2] For I saw the desolation of Sion, and the wealth of them that dwelt at Babylon.
[3] And my spirit was sore moved, so that I began to speak words full of fear to the most High, and said,
[4] O Lord, who bearest rule, thou spakest at the beginning, when thou didst plant the earth, and that thyself alone, and commandedst the people,
[5] And gavest a body unto Adam without soul, which was the workmanship of thine hands, and didst breathe into him the breath of life, and he was made living before thee.
[6] And thou leadest him into paradise, which thy right hand had planted, before ever the earth came forward.

[7] And unto him thou gavest commandment to love thy way: which he transgressed, and immediately thou appointedst death in him and in his generations, of whom came nations, tribes, people, and kindreds, out of number.
[8] And every people walked after their own will, and did wonderful things before thee, and despised thy commandments.
[9] And again in process of time thou broughtest the flood upon those that dwelt in the world, and destroyedst them.
[10] And it came to pass in every of them, that as death was to Adam, so was the flood to these.
[11] Nevertheless one of them thou leftest, namely, Noah with his household, of whom came all righteous men.
[12] And it happened, that when they that dwelt upon the earth began to multiply, and had gotten them many children, and were a great people, they began again to be more ungodly than the first.
[13] Now when they lived so wickedly before thee, thou didst choose thee a man from among them, whose name was Abraham.
[14] Him thou lovedst, and unto him only thou shewedst thy will:
[15] And madest an everlasting covenant with him, promising him that thou wouldest never forsake his seed.
[16] And unto him thou gavest Isaac, and unto Isaac also thou gavest Jacob and Esau. As for Jacob, thou didst choose him to thee, and put by Esau: and so Jacob became a great multitude.
[17] And it came to pass, that when thou leadest his seed out of Egypt, thou broughtest them up to the mount Sinai.
[18] And bowing the heavens, thou didst set fast the earth, movedst the whole world, and madest the depths to tremble, and troubledst the men of that age.
[19] And thy glory went through four gates, of fire, and of earthquake, and of wind, and of cold; that thou mightest give the law unto the seed of Jacob, and diligence unto the generation of Israel.
[20] And yet tookest thou not away from them a wicked heart, that thy law might bring forth fruit in them.
[21] For the first Adam bearing a wicked heart transgressed, and was overcome; and so be all they that are born of him.
[22] Thus infirmity was made permanent; and the law (also) in the heart of the people with the malignity of the root; so that the good departed away, and the evil abode still.
[23] So the times passed away, and the years were brought to an end: then didst thou raise thee up a servant, called David:
[24] Whom thou commandedst to build a city unto thy name, and to offer incense and oblations unto thee therein.
[25] When this was done many years, then they that inhabited the city forsook thee,
[26] And in all things did even as Adam and all his generations had done: for they also had a wicked heart:
[27] And so thou gavest thy city over into the hands of thine enemies.
[28] Are their deeds then any better that inhabit Babylon, that they should therefore have the dominion over Sion?
[29] For when I came thither, and had seen impieties without number, then my soul saw many evildoers in this thirtieth year, so that my heart failed me.
[30] For I have seen how thou sufferest them sinning, and hast spared wicked doers: and hast destroyed thy people, and hast preserved thine enemies, and hast not signified it.
[31] I do not remember how this way may be left: Are they then of Babylon better than they of Sion?
[32] Or is there any other people that knoweth thee beside Israel? or what generation hath so believed thy covenants as Jacob?
[33] And yet their reward appeareth not, and

their labour hath no fruit: for I have gone here and there through the heathen, and I see that they flow in wealth, and think not upon thy commandments.

[34] Weigh thou therefore our wickedness now in the balance, and their's also that dwell the world; and so shall thy name no where be found but in Israel.

[35] Or when was it that they which dwell upon the earth have not sinned in thy sight? or what people have so kept thy commandments?

[36] Thou shalt find that Israel by name hath kept thy precepts; but not the heathen.

---

2 Ezra.4

[1] And the angel that was sent unto me, whose name was Uriel, gave me an answer,
[2] And said, Thy heart hath gone to far in this world, and thinkest thou to comprehend the way of the most High?
[3] Then said I, Yea, my lord. And he answered me, and said, I am sent to shew thee three ways, and to set forth three similitudes before thee:
[4] Whereof if thou canst declare me one, I will shew thee also the way that thou desirest to see, and I shall shew thee from whence the wicked heart cometh.
[5] And I said, Tell on, my lord. Then said he unto me, Go thy way, weigh me the weight of the fire, or measure me the blast of the wind, or call me again the day that is past.
[6] Then answered I and said, What man is able to do that, that thou shouldest ask such things of me?
[7] And he said unto me, If I should ask thee how great dwellings are in the midst of the sea, or how many springs are in the beginning of the deep, or how many springs are above the firmament, or which are the outgoings of paradise:
[8] Peradventure thou wouldest say unto me, I never went down into the deep, nor as yet into hell, neither did I ever climb up into heaven.
[9] Nevertheless now have I asked thee but only of the fire and wind, and of the day wherethrough thou hast passed, and of things from which thou canst not be separated, and yet canst thou give me no answer of them.
[10] He said moreover unto me, Thine own things, and such as are grown up with thee, canst thou not know;
[11] How should thy vessel then be able to comprehend the way of the Highest, and, the world being now outwardly corrupted to understand the corruption that is evident in my sight?
[12] Then said I unto him, It were better that we were not at all, than that we should live still in wickedness, and to suffer, and not to know wherefore.
[13] He answered me, and said, I went into a forest into a plain, and the trees took counsel,
[14] And said, Come, let us go and make war against the sea that it may depart away before us, and that we may make us more woods.
[15] The floods of the sea also in like manner took counsel, and said, Come, let us go up and subdue the woods of the plain, that there also we may make us another country.
[16] The thought of the wood was in vain, for the fire came and consumed it.
[17] The thought of the floods of the sea came likewise to nought, for the sand stood up and stopped them.
[18] If thou wert judge now betwixt these two, whom wouldest thou begin to justify? or whom wouldest thou condemn?
[19] I answered and said, Verily it is a foolish thought that they both have devised, for the ground is given unto the wood, and the sea also hath his place to bear his floods.
[20] Then answered he me, and said, Thou

hast given a right judgment, but why judgest thou not thyself also?

[21] For like as the ground is given unto the wood, and the sea to his floods: even so they that dwell upon the earth may understand nothing but that which is upon the earth: and he that dwelleth above the heavens may only understand the things that are above the height of the heavens.

[22] Then answered I and said, I beseech thee, O Lord, let me have understanding:

[23] For it was not my mind to be curious of the high things, but of such as pass by us daily, namely, wherefore Israel is given up as a reproach to the heathen, and for what cause the people whom thou hast loved is given over unto ungodly nations, and why the law of our forefathers is brought to nought, and the written covenants come to none effect,

[24] And we pass away out of the world as grasshoppers, and our life is astonishment and fear, and we are not worthy to obtain mercy.

[25] What will he then do unto his name whereby we are called? of these things have I asked.

[26] Then answered he me, and said, The more thou searchest, the more thou shalt marvel; for the world hasteth fast to pass away,

[27] And cannot comprehend the things that are promised to the righteous in time to come: for this world is full of unrighteousness and infirmities.

[28] But as concerning the things whereof thou askest me, I will tell thee; for the evil is sown, but the destruction thereof is not yet come.

[29] If therefore that which is sown be not turned upside down, and if the place where the evil is sown pass not away, then cannot it come that is sown with good.

[30] For the grain of evil seed hath been sown in the heart of Adam from the beginning, and how much ungodliness hath it brought up unto this time? and how much shall it yet bring forth until the time of threshing come?

[31] Ponder now by thyself, how great fruit of wickedness the grain of evil seed hath brought forth.

[32] And when the ears shall be cut down, which are without number, how great a floor shall they fill?

[33] Then I answered and said, How, and when shall these things come to pass? wherefore are our years few and evil?

[34] And he answered me, saying, Do not thou hasten above the most Highest: for thy haste is in vain to be above him, for thou hast much exceeded.

[35] Did not the souls also of the righteous ask question of these things in their chambers, saying, How long shall I hope on this fashion? when cometh the fruit of the floor of our reward?

[36] And unto these things Uriel the archangel gave them answer, and said, Even when the number of seeds is filled in you: for he hath weighed the world in the balance.

[37] By measure hath he measured the times; and by number hath he numbered the times; and he doth not move nor stir them, until the said measure be fulfilled.

[38] Then answered I and said, O Lord that bearest rule, even we all are full of impiety.

[39] And for our sakes peradventure it is that the floors of the righteous are not filled, because of the sins of them that dwell upon the earth.

[40] So he answered me, and said, Go thy way to a woman with child, and ask of her when she hath fulfilled her nine months, if her womb may keep the birth any longer within her.

[41] Then said I, No, Lord, that can she not. And he said unto me, In the grave the chambers of souls are like the womb of a woman:

[42] For like as a woman that travaileth

maketh haste to escape the necessity of the travail: even so do these places haste to deliver those things that are committed unto them.
[43] From the beginning, look, what thou desirest to see, it shall be shewed thee.
[44] Then answered I and said, If I have found favour in thy sight, and if it be possible, and if I be meet therefore,
[45] Shew me then whether there be more to come than is past, or more past than is to come.
[46] What is past I know, but what is for to come I know not.
[47] And he said unto me, Stand up upon the right side, and I shall expound the similitude unto thee.
[48] So I stood, and saw, and, behold, an hot burning oven passed by before me: and it happened that when the flame was gone by I looked, and, behold, the smoke remained still.
[49] After this there passed by before me a watery cloud, and sent down much rain with a storm; and when the stormy rain was past, the drops remained still.
[50] Then said he unto me, Consider with thyself; as the rain is more than the drops, and as the fire is greater than the smoke; but the drops and the smoke remain behind: so the quantity which is past did more exceed.
[51] Then I prayed, and said, May I live, thinkest thou, until that time? or what shall happen in those days?
[52] He answered me, and said, As for the tokens whereof thou askest me, I may tell thee of them in part: but as touching thy life, I am not sent to shew thee; for I do not know it.

---

2 Ezra.5

[1] Nevertheless as coming the tokens, behold, the days shall come, that they which dwell upon earth shall be taken in a great number, and the way of truth shall be hidden, and the land shall be barren of faith.
[2] But iniquity shall be increased above that which now thou seest, or that thou hast heard long ago.
[3] And the land, that thou seest now to have root, shalt thou see wasted suddenly.
[4] But if the most High grant thee to live, thou shalt see after the third trumpet that the sun shall suddenly shine again in the night, and the moon thrice in the day:
[5] And blood shall drop out of wood, and the stone shall give his voice, and the people shall be troubled:
[6] And even he shall rule, whom they look not for that dwell upon the earth, and the fowls shall take their flight away together:
[7] And the Sodomitish sea shall cast out fish, and make a noise in the night, which many have not known: but they shall all hear the voice thereof.
[8] There shall be a confusion also in many places, and the fire shall be oft sent out again, and the wild beasts shall change their places, and menstruous women shall bring forth monsters:
[9] And salt waters shall be found in the sweet, and all friends shall destroy one another; then shall wit hide itself, and understanding withdraw itself into his secret chamber,
[10] And shall be sought of many, and yet not be found: then shall unrighteousness and incontinency be multiplied upon earth.
[11] One land also shall ask another, and say, Is righteousness that maketh a man righteous gone through thee? And it shall say, No.
[12] At the same time shall men hope, but nothing obtain: they shall labour, but their ways shall not prosper.
[13] To shew thee such tokens I have leave; and if thou wilt pray again, and weep as now, and fast even days, thou shalt hear yet greater things.
[14] Then I awaked, and an extreme

fearfulness went through all my body, and my mind was troubled, so that it fainted.
[15] So the angel that was come to talk with me held me, comforted me, and set me up upon my feet.
[16] And in the second night it came to pass, that Salathiel the captain of the people came unto me, saying, Where hast thou been? and why is thy countenance so heavy?
[17] Knowest thou not that Israel is committed unto thee in the land of their captivity?
[18] Up then, and eat bread, and forsake us not, as the shepherd that leaveth his flock in the hands of cruel wolves.
[19] Then said I unto him, Go thy ways from me, and come not nigh me. And he heard what I said, and went from me.
[20] And so I fasted seven days, mourning and weeping, like as Uriel the angel commanded me.
[21] And after seven days so it was, that the thoughts of my heart were very grievous unto me again,
[22] And my soul recovered the spirit of understanding, and I began to talk with the most High again,
[23] And said, O Lord that bearest rule, of every wood of the earth, and of all the trees thereof, thou hast chosen thee one only vine:
[24] And of all lands of the whole world thou hast chosen thee one pit: and of all the flowers thereof one lily:
[25] And of all the depths of the sea thou hast filled thee one river: and of all builded cities thou hast hallowed Sion unto thyself:
[26] And of all the fowls that are created thou hast named thee one dove: and of all the cattle that are made thou hast provided thee one sheep:
[27] And among all the multitudes of people thou hast gotten thee one people: and unto this people, whom thou lovedst, thou gavest a law that is approved of all.
[28] And now, O Lord, why hast thou given this one people over unto many? and upon the one root hast thou prepared others, and why hast thou scattered thy only one people among many?
[29] And they which did gainsay thy promises, and believed not thy covenants, have trodden them down.
[30] If thou didst so much hate thy people, yet shouldest thou punish them with thine own hands.
[31] Now when I had spoken these words, the angel that came to me the night afore was sent unto me,
[32] And said unto me, Hear me, and I will instruct thee; hearken to the thing that I say, and I shall tell thee more.
[33] And I said, Speak on, my Lord. Then said he unto me, Thou art sore troubled in mind for Israel's sake: lovest thou that people better than he that made them?
[34] And I said, No, Lord: but of very grief have I spoken: for my reins pain me every hour, while I labour to comprehend the way of the most High, and to seek out part of his judgment.
[35] And he said unto me, Thou canst not. And I said, Wherefore, Lord? whereunto was I born then? or why was not my mother's womb then my grave, that I might not have seen the travail of Jacob, and the wearisome toil of the stock of Israel?
[36] And he said unto me, Number me the things that are not yet come, gather me together the dross that are scattered abroad, make me the flowers green again that are withered,
[37] Open me the places that are closed, and bring me forth the winds that in them are shut up, shew me the image of a voice: and then I will declare to thee the thing that thou labourest to know.
[38] And I said, O Lord that bearest rule, who may know these things, but he that hath not his dwelling with men?
[39] As for me, I am unwise: how may I then speak of these things whereof thou askest me?

[40] Then said he unto me, Like as thou canst do none of these things that I have spoken of., even so canst thou not find out my judgment, or in the end the love that I have promised unto my people.
[41] And I said, Behold, O Lord, yet art thou nigh unto them that be reserved till the end: and what shall they do that have been before me, or we that be now, or they that shall come after us?
[42] And he said unto me, I will liken my judgment unto a ring: like as there is no slackness of the last, even so there is no swiftness of the first.
[43] So I answered and said, Couldest thou not make those that have been made, and be now, and that are for to come, at once; that thou mightest shew thy judgment the sooner?
[44] Then answered he me, and said, The creature may not haste above the maker; neither may the world hold them at once that shall be created therein.
[45] And I said, As thou hast said unto thy servant, that thou, which givest life to all, hast given life at once to the creature that thou hast created, and the creature bare it: even so it might now also bear them that now be present at once.
[46] And he said unto me, Ask the womb of a woman, and say unto her, If thou bringest forth children, why dost thou it not together, but one after another? pray her therefore to bring forth ten children at once.
[47] And I said, She cannot: but must do it by distance of time.
[48] Then said he unto me, Even so have I given the womb of the earth to those that be sown in it in their times.
[49] For like as a young child may not bring forth the things that belong to the aged, even so have I disposed the world which I created.
[50] And I asked, and said, Seeing thou hast now given me the way, I will proceed to speak before thee: for our mother, of whom thou hast told me that she is young, draweth now nigh unto age.
[51] He answered me, and said, Ask a woman that beareth children, and she shall tell thee.
[52] Say unto her, Wherefore are unto they whom thou hast now brought forth like those that were before, but less of stature?
[53] And she shall answer thee, They that be born in the the strength of youth are of one fashion, and they that are born in the time of age, when the womb faileth, are otherwise.
[54] Consider thou therefore also, how that ye are less of stature than those that were before you.
[55] And so are they that come after you less than ye, as the creatures which now begin to be old, and have passed over the strength of youth.
[56] Then said I, Lord, I beseech thee, if I have found favour in thy sight, shew thy servant by whom thou visitest thy creature.

---

2 Ezra.6

[1] And he said unto me, In the beginning, when the earth was made, before the borders of the world stood, or ever the winds blew,
[2] Before it thundered and lightened, or ever the foundations of paradise were laid,
[3] Before the fair flowers were seen, or ever the moveable powers were established, before the innumerable multitude of angels were gathered together,
[4] Or ever the heights of the air were lifted up, before the measures of the firmament were named, or ever the chimneys in Sion were hot,
[5] And ere the present years were sought out, and or ever the inventions of them that now sin were turned, before they were sealed that have gathered faith for a treasure:
[6] Then did I consider these things, and they all were made through me alone, and through none other: by me also they shall be

ended, and by none other.

[7] Then answered I and said, What shall be the parting asunder of the times? or when shall be the end of the first, and the beginning of it that followeth?

[8] And he said unto me, From Abraham unto Isaac, when Jacob and Esau were born of him, Jacob's hand held first the heel of Esau.

[9] For Esau is the end of the world, and Jacob is the beginning of it that followeth.

[10] The hand of man is betwixt the heel and the hand: other question, Esdras, ask thou not.

[11] I answered then and said, O Lord that bearest rule, if I have found favour in thy sight,

[12] I beseech thee, shew thy servant the end of thy tokens, whereof thou shewedst me part the last night.

[13] So he answered and said unto me, Stand up upon thy feet, and hear a mighty sounding voice.

[14] And it shall be as it were a great motion; but the place where thou standest shall not be moved.

[15] And therefore when it speaketh be not afraid: for the word is of the end, and the foundation of the earth is understood.

[16] And why? because the speech of these things trembleth and is moved: for it knoweth that the end of these things must be changed.

[17] And it happened, that when I had heard it I stood up upon my feet, and hearkened, and, behold, there was a voice that spake, and the sound of it was like the sound of many waters.

[18] And it said, Behold, the days come, that I will begin to draw nigh, and to visit them that dwell upon the earth,

[19] And will begin to make inquisition of them, what they be that have hurt unjustly with their unrighteousness, and when the affliction of Sion shall be fulfilled;

[20] And when the world, that shall begin to vanish away, shall be finished, then will I shew these tokens: the books shall be opened before the firmament, and they shall see all together:

[21] And the children of a year old shall speak with their voices, the women with child shall bring forth untimely children of three or four months old, and they shall live, and be raised up.

[22] And suddenly shall the sown places appear unsown, the full storehouses shall suddenly be found empty:

[23] And tha trumpet shall give a sound, which when every man heareth, they shall be suddenly afraid.

[24] At that time shall friends fight one against another like enemies, and the earth shall stand in fear with those that dwell therein, the springs of the fountains shall stand still, and in three hours they shall not run.

[25] Whosoever remaineth from all these that I have told thee shall escape, and see my salvation, and the end of your world.

[26] And the men that are received shall see it, who have not tasted death from their birth: and the heart of the inhabitants shall be changed, and turned into another meaning.

[27] For evil shall be put out, and deceit shall be quenched.

[28] As for faith, it shall flourish, corruption shall be overcome, and the truth, which hath been so long without fruit, shall be declared.

[29] And when he talked with me, behold, I looked by little and little upon him before whom I stood.

[30] And these words said he unto me; I am come to shew thee the time of the night to come.

[31] If thou wilt pray yet more, and fast seven days again, I shall tell thee greater things by day than I have heard.

[32] For thy voice is heard before the most High: for the Mighty hath seen thy righteous dealing, he hath seen also thy chastity,

which thou hast had ever since thy youth.
[33] And therefore hath he sent me to shew thee all these things, and to say unto thee, Be of good comfort and fear not
[34] And hasten not with the times that are past, to think vain things, that thou mayest not hasten from the latter times.
[35] And it came to pass after this, that I wept again, and fasted seven days in like manner, that I might fulfil the three weeks which he told me.
[36] And in the eighth night was my heart vexed within me again, and I began to speak before the most High.
[37] For my spirit was greatly set on fire, and my soul was in distress.
[38] And I said, O Lord, thou spakest from the beginning of the creation, even the first day, and saidst thus; Let heaven and earth be made; and thy word was a perfect work.
[39] And then was the spirit, and darkness and silence were on every side; the sound of man's voice was not yet formed.
[40] Then commandedst thou a fair light to come forth of thy treasures, that thy work might appear.
[41] Upon the second day thou madest the spirit of the firmament, and commandedst it to part asunder, and to make a division betwixt the waters, that the one part might go up, and the other remain beneath.
[42] Upon the third day thou didst command that the waters should be gathered in the seventh part of the earth: six pats hast thou dried up, and kept them, to the intent that of these some being planted of God and tilled might serve thee.
[43] For as soon as thy word went forth the work was made.
[44] For immediately there was great and innumerable fruit, and many and divers pleasures for the taste, and flowers of unchangeable colour, and odours of wonderful smell: and this was done the third day.
[45] Upon the fourth day thou commandedst that the sun should shine, and the moon give her light, and the stars should be in order:
[46] And gavest them a charge to do service unto man, that was to be made.
[47] Upon the fifth day thou saidst unto the seventh part, where the waters were gathered that it should bring forth living creatures, fowls and fishes: and so it came to pass.
[48] For the dumb water and without life brought forth living things at the commandment of God, that all people might praise thy wondrous works.
[49] Then didst thou ordain two living creatures, the one thou calledst Enoch, and the other Leviathan;
[50] And didst separate the one from the other: for the seventh part, namely, where the water was gathered together, might not hold them both.
[51] Unto Enoch thou gavest one part, which was dried up the third day, that he should dwell in the same part, wherein are a thousand hills:
[52] But unto Leviathan thou gavest the seventh part, namely, the moist; and hast kept him to be devoured of whom thou wilt, and when.
[53] Upon the sixth day thou gavest commandment unto the earth, that before thee it should bring forth beasts, cattle, and creeping things:
[54] And after these, Adam also, whom thou madest lord of all thy creatures: of him come we all, and the people also whom thou hast chosen.
[55] All this have I spoken before thee, O Lord, because thou madest the world for our sakes
[56] As for the other people, which also come of Adam, thou hast said that they are nothing, but be like unto spittle: and hast likened the abundance of them unto a drop that falleth from a vessel.
[57] And now, O Lord, behold, these heathen, which have ever been reputed as

nothing, have begun to be lords over us, and to devour us.

[58] But we thy people, whom thou hast called thy firstborn, thy only begotten, and thy fervent lover, are given into their hands.

[59] If the world now be made for our sakes, why do we not possess an inheritance with the world? how long shall this endure?

2 Ezra 7

[1] And when I had made an end of speaking these words, there was sent unto me the angel which had been sent unto me the nights afore:

[2] And he said unto me, Up, Esdras, and hear the words that I am come to tell thee.

[3] And I said, Speak on, my God. Then said he unto me, The sea is set in a wide place, that it might be deep and great.

[4] But put the case the entrance were narrow, and like a river;

[5] Who then could go into the sea to look upon it, and to rule it? if he went not through the narrow, how could he come into the broad?

[6] There is also another thing; A city is builded, and set upon a broad field, and is full of all good things:

[7] The entrance thereof is narrow, and is set in a dangerous place to fall, like as if there were a fire on the right hand, and on the left a deep water:

[8] And one only path between them both, even between the fire and the water, so small that there could but one man go there at once.

[9] If this city now were given unto a man for an inheritance, if he never shall pass the danger set before it, how shall he receive this inheritance?

[10] And I said, It is so, Lord. Then said he unto me, Even so also is Israel's portion.

[11] Because for their sakes I made the world: and when Adam transgressed my statutes, then was decreed that now is done.

[12] Then were the entrances of this world made narrow, full of sorrow and travail: they are but few and evil, full of perils,: and very painful.

[13] For the entrances of the elder world were wide and sure, and brought immortal fruit.

[14] If then they that live labour not to enter these strait and vain things, they can never receive those that are laid up for them.

[15] Now therefore why disquietest thou thyself, seeing thou art but a corruptible man? and why art thou moved, whereas thou art but mortal?

[16] Why hast thou not considered in thy mind this thing that is to come, rather than that which is present?

[17] Then answered I and said, O Lord that bearest rule, thou hast ordained in thy law, that the righteous should inherit these things, but that the ungodly should perish.

[18] Nevertheless the righteous shall suffer strait things, and hope for wide: for they that have done wickedly have suffered the strait things, and yet shall not see the wide.

[19] And he said unto me. There is no judge above God, and none that hath understanding above the Highest.

[20] For there be many that perish in this life, because they despise the law of God that is set before them.

[21] For God hath given strait commandment to such as came, what they should do to live, even as they came, and what they should observe to avoid punishment.

[22] Nevertheless they were not obedient unto him; but spake against him, and imagined vain things;

[23] And deceived themselves by their wicked deeds; and said of the most High, that he is not; and knew not his ways:

[24] But his law have they despised, and denied his covenants; in his statutes have they not been faithful, and have not

performed his works.

[25] And therefore, Esdras, for the empty are empty things, and for the full are the full things.

[26] Behold, the time shall come, that these tokens which I have told thee shall come to pass, and the bride shall appear, and she coming forth shall be seen, that now is withdrawn from the earth.

[27] And whosoever is delivered from the foresaid evils shall see my wonders.

[28] For my son Jesus shall be revealed with those that be with him, and they that remain shall rejoice within four hundred years.

[29] After these years shall my son Christ die, and all men that have life.

[30] And the world shall be turned into the old silence seven days, like as in the former judgments: so that no man shall remain.

[31] And after seven days the world, that yet awaketh not, shall be raised up, and that shall die that is corrupt

[32] And the earth shall restore those that are asleep in her, and so shall the dust those that dwell in silence, and the secret places shall deliver those souls that were committed unto them.

[33] And the most High shall appear upon the seat of judgment, and misery shall pass away, and the long suffering shall have an end:

[34] But judgment only shall remain, truth shall stand, and faith shall wax strong:

[35] And the work shall follow, and the reward shall be shewed, and the good deeds shall be of force, and wicked deeds shall bear no rule.

[36] Then said I, Abraham prayed first for the Sodomites, and Moses for the fathers that sinned in the wilderness:

[37] And Jesus after him for Israel in the time of Achan:

[38] And Samuel and David for the destruction: and Solomon for them that should come to the sanctuary:

[39] And Helias for those that received rain; and for the dead, that he might live:

[40] And Ezechias for the people in the time of Sennacherib: and many for many.

[41] Even so now, seeing corruption is grown up, and wickedness increased, and the righteous have prayed for the ungodly: wherefore shall it not be so now also?

[42] He answered me, and said, This present life is not the end where much glory doth abide; therefore have they prayed for the weak.

[43] But the day of doom shall be the end of this time, and the beginning of the immortality for to come, wherein corruption is past,

[44] Intemperance is at an end, infidelity is cut off, righteousness is grown, and truth is sprung up.

[45] Then shall no man be able to save him that is destroyed, nor to oppress him that hath gotten the victory.

[46] I answered then and said, This is my first and last saying, that it had been better not to have given the earth unto Adam: or else, when it was given him, to have restrained him from sinning.

[47] For what profit is it for men now in this present time to live in heaviness, and after death to look for punishment?

[48] O thou Adam, what hast thou done? for though it was thou that sinned, thou art not fallen alone, but we all that come of thee.

[49] For what profit is it unto us, if there be promised us an immortal time, whereas we have done the works that bring death?

[50] And that there is promised us an everlasting hope, whereas ourselves being most wicked are made vain?

[51] And that there are laid up for us dwellings of health and safety, whereas we have lived wickedly?

[52] And that the glory of the most High is kept to defend them which have led a wary life, whereas we have walked in the most wicked ways of all?

[53] And that there should be shewed a

paradise, whose fruit endureth for ever, wherein is security and medicine, since we shall not enter into it?
[54] (For we have walked in unpleasant places.)
[55] And that the faces of them which have used abstinence shall shine above the stars, whereas our faces shall be blacker than darkness?
[56] For while we lived and committed iniquity, we considered not that we should begin to suffer for it after death.
[57] Then answered he me, and said, This is the condition of the battle, which man that is born upon the earth shall fight;
[58] That, if he be overcome, he shall suffer as thou hast said: but if he get the victory, he shall receive the thing that I say.
[59] For this is the life whereof Moses spake unto the people while he lived, saying, Choose thee life, that thou mayest live.
[60] Nevertheless they believed not him, nor yet the prophets after him, no nor me which have spoken unto them,
[61] That there should not be such heaviness in their destruction, as shall be joy over them that are persuaded to salvation.
[62] I answered then, and said, I know, Lord, that the most High is called merciful, in that he hath mercy upon them which are not yet come into the world,
[63] And upon those also that turn to his law;
[64] And that he is patient, and long suffereth those that have sinned, as his creatures;
[65] And that he is bountiful, for he is ready to give where it needeth;
[66] And that he is of great mercy, for he multiplieth more and more mercies to them that are present, and that are past, and also to them which are to come.
[67] For if he shall not multiply his mercies, the world would not continue with them that inherit therein.
[68] And he pardoneth; for if he did not so of his goodness, that they which have committed iniquities might be eased of them, the ten thousandth part of men should not remain living.
[69] And being judge, if he should not forgive them that are cured with his word, and put out the multitude of contentions,
[70] There should be very few left peradventure in an innumerable multitude.

---

2 Ezra.8

[1] And he answered me, saying, The most High hath made this world for many, but the world to come for few.
[2] I will tell thee a similitude, Esdras; As when thou askest the earth, it shall say unto thee, that it giveth much mould whereof earthen vessels are made, but little dust that gold cometh of: even so is the course of this present world.
[3] There be many created, but few shall be saved.
[4] So answered I and said, Swallow then down, O my soul, understanding, and devour wisdom.
[5] For thou hast agreed to give ear, and art willing to prophesy: for thou hast no longer space than only to live.
[6] O Lord, if thou suffer not thy servant, that we may pray before thee, and thou give us seed unto our heart, and culture to our understanding, that there may come fruit of it; how shall each man live that is corrupt, who beareth the place of a man?
[7] For thou art alone, and we all one workmanship of thine hands, like as thou hast said.
[8] For when the body is fashioned now in the mother's womb, and thou givest it members, thy creature is preserved in fire and water, and nine months doth thy workmanship endure thy creature which is created in her.
[9] But that which keepeth and is kept shall

both be preserved: and when the time cometh, the womb preserved delivereth up the things that grew in it.

[10] For thou hast commanded out of the parts of the body, that is to say, out of the breasts, milk to be given, which is the fruit of the breasts,

[11] That the thing which is fashioned may be nourished for a time, till thou disposest it to thy mercy.

[12] Thou broughtest it up with thy righteousness, and nurturedst it in thy law, and reformedst it with thy judgment.

[13] And thou shalt mortify it as thy creature, and quicken it as thy work.

[14] If therefore thou shalt destroy him which with so great labour was fashioned, it is an easy thing to be ordained by thy commandment, that the thing which was made might be preserved.

[15] Now therefore, Lord, I will speak; touching man in general, thou knowest best; but touching thy people, for whose sake I am sorry;

[16] And for thine inheritance, for whose cause I mourn; and for Israel, for whom I am heavy; and for Jacob, for whose sake I am troubled;

[17] Therefore will I begin to pray before thee for myself and for them: for I see the falls of us that dwell in the land.

[18] But I have heard the swiftness of the judge which is to come.

[19] Therefore hear my voice, and understand my words, and I shall speak before thee. This is the beginning of the words of Esdras, before he was taken up: and I said,

[20] O Lord, thou that dwellest in everlastingness which beholdest from above things in the heaven and in the air;

[21] Whose throne is inestimable; whose glory may not be comprehended; before whom the hosts of angels stand with trembling,

[22] Whose service is conversant in wind and fire; whose word is true, and sayings constant; whose commandment is strong, and ordinance fearful;

[23] Whose look drieth up the depths, and indignation maketh the mountains to melt away; which the truth witnesseth:

[24] O hear the prayer of thy servant, and give ear to the petition of thy creature.

[25] For while I live I will speak, and so long as I have understanding I will answer.

[26] O look not upon the sins of thy people; but on them which serve thee in truth.

[27] Regard not the wicked inventions of the heathen, but the desire of those that keep thy testimonies in afflictions.

[28] Think not upon those that have walked feignedly before thee: but remember them, which according to thy will have known thy fear.

[29] Let it not be thy will to destroy them which have lived like beasts; but to look upon them that have clearly taught thy law.

[30] Take thou no indignation at them which are deemed worse than beasts; but love them that always put their trust in thy righteousness and glory.

[31] For we and our fathers do languish of such diseases: but because of us sinners thou shalt be called merciful.

[32] For if thou hast a desire to have mercy upon us, thou shalt be called merciful, to us namely, that have no works of righteousness.

[33] For the just, which have many good works laid up with thee, shall out of their own deeds receive reward.

[34] For what is man, that thou shouldest take displeasure at him? or what is a corruptible generation, that thou shouldest be so bitter toward it?

[35] For in truth them is no man among them that be born, but he hath dealt wickedly; and among the faithful there is none which hath not done amiss.

[36] For in this, O Lord, thy righteousness and thy goodness shall be declared, if thou

be merciful unto them which have not the confidence of good works.

[37] Then answered he me, and said, Some things hast thou spoken aright, and according unto thy words it shall be.

[38] For indeed I will not think on the disposition of them which have sinned before death, before judgment, before destruction:

[39] But I will rejoice over the disposition of the righteous, and I will remember also their pilgrimage, and the salvation, and the reward, that they shall have.

[40] Like as I have spoken now, so shall it come to pass.

[41] For as the husbandman soweth much seed upon the ground, and planteth many trees, and yet the thing that is sown good in his season cometh not up, neither doth all that is planted take root: even so is it of them that are sown in the world; they shall not all be saved.

[42] I answered then and said, If I have found grace, let me speak.

[43] Like as the husbandman's seed perisheth, if it come not up, and receive not thy rain in due season; or if there come too much rain, and corrupt it:

[44] Even so perisheth man also, which is formed with thy hands, and is called thine own image, because thou art like unto him, for whose sake thou hast made all things, and likened him unto the husbandman's seed.

[45] Be not wroth with us but spare thy people, and have mercy upon thine own inheritance: for thou art merciful unto thy creature.

[46] Then answered he me, and said, Things present are for the present, and things to cometh for such as be to come.

[47] For thou comest far short that thou shouldest be able to love my creature more than I: but I have ofttimes drawn nigh unto thee, and unto it, but never to the unrighteous.

[48] In this also thou art marvellous before the most High:

[49] In that thou hast humbled thyself, as it becometh thee, and hast not judged thyself worthy to be much glorified among the righteous.

[50] For many great miseries shall be done to them that in the latter time shall dwell in the world, because they have walked in great pride.

[51] But understand thou for thyself, and seek out the glory for such as be like thee.

[52] For unto you is paradise opened, the tree of life is planted, the time to come is prepared, plenteousness is made ready, a city is builded, and rest is allowed, yea, perfect goodness and wisdom.

[53] The root of evil is sealed up from you, weakness and the moth is hid from you, and corruption is fled into hell to be forgotten:

[54] Sorrows are passed, and in the end is shewed the treasure of immortality.

[55] And therefore ask thou no more questions concerning the multitude of them that perish.

[56] For when they had taken liberty, they despised the most High, thought scorn of his law, and forsook his ways.

[57] Moreover they have trodden down his righteous,

[58] And said in their heart, that there is no God; yea, and that knowing they must die.

[59] For as the things aforesaid shalt receive you, so thirst and pain are prepared for them: for it was not his will that men should come to nought:

[60] But they which be created have defiled the name of him that made them, and were unthankful unto him which prepared life for them.

[61] And therefore is my judgment now at hand.

[62] These things have I not shewed unto all men, but unto thee, and a few like thee. Then answered I and said,

[63] Behold, O Lord, now hast thou shewed

me the multitude of the wonders, which thou wilt begin to do in the last times: but at what time, thou hast not shewed me.

2 Ezra.9

[1] He answered me then, and said, Measure thou the time diligently in itself: and when thou seest part of the signs past, which I have told thee before,
[2] Then shalt thou understand, that it is the very same time, wherein the Highest will begin to visit the world which he made.
[3] Therefore when there shall be seen earthquakes and uproars of the people in the world:
[4] Then shalt thou well understand, that the most High spake of those things from the days that were before thee, even from the beginning.
[5] For like as all that is made in the world hath a beginning and an end, and the end is manifest:
[6] Even so the times also of the Highest have plain beginnings in wonder and powerful works, and endings in effects and signs.
[7] And every one that shall be saved, and shall be able to escape by his works, and by faith, whereby ye have believed,
[8] Shall be preserved from the said perils, and shall see my salvation in my land, and within my borders: for I have sanctified them for me from the beginning.
[9] Then shall they be in pitiful case, which now have abused my ways: and they that have cast them away despitefully shall dwell in torments.
[10] For such as in their life have received benefits, and have not known me;
[11] And they that have loathed my law, while they had yet liberty, and, when as yet place of repentance was open unto them, understood not, but despised it;
[12] The same must know it after death by pain.
[13] And therefore be thou not curious how the ungodly shall be punished, and when: but enquire how the righteous shall be saved, whose the world is, and for whom the world is created.
[14] Then answered I and said,
[15] I have said before, and now do speak, and will speak it also hereafter, that there be many more of them which perish, than of them which shall be saved:
[16] Like as a wave is greater than a drop.
[17] And he answered me, saying, Like as the field is, so is also the seed; as the flowers be, such are the colours also; such as the workman is, such also is the work; and as the husbandman ls himself, so is his husbandry also: for it was the time of the world.
[18] And now when I prepared the world, which was not yet made, even for them to dwell in that now live, no man spake against me.
[19] For then every one obeyed: but now the manners of them which are created in this world that is made are corrupted by a perpetual seed, and by a law which is unsearchable rid themselves.
[20] So I considered the world, and, behold, there was peril because of the devices that were come into it.
[21] And I saw, and spared it greatly, and have kept me a grape of the cluster, and a plant of a great people.
[22] Let the multitude perish then, which was born in vain; and let my grape be kept, and my plant; for with great labour have I made it perfect.
[23] Nevertheless, if thou wilt cease yet seven days more, (but thou shalt not fast in them,
[24] But go into a field of flowers, where no house is builded, and eat only the flowers of the field; taste no flesh, drink no wine, but eat flowers only;)
[25] And pray unto the Highest continually,

then will I come and talk with thee.
[26] So I went my way into the field which is called Ardath, like as he commanded me; and there I sat among the flowers, and did eat of the herbs of the field, and the meat of the same satisfied me.
[27] After seven days I sat upon the grass, and my heart was vexed within me, like as before:
[28] And I opened my mouth, and began to talk before the most High, and said,
[29] O Lord, thou that shewest thyself unto us, thou wast shewed unto our fathers in the wilderness, in a place where no man treadeth, in a barren place, when they came out of Egypt.
[30] And thou spakest saying, Hear me, O Israel; and mark my words, thou seed of Jacob.
[31] For, behold, I sow my law in you, and it shall bring fruit in you, and ye shall be honoured in it for ever.
[32] But our fathers, which received the law, kept it not, and observed not thy ordinances: and though the fruit of thy law did not perish, neither could it, for it was thine;
[33] Yet they that received it perished, because they kept not the thing that was sown in them.
[34] And, lo, it ls a custom, when the ground hath received seed, or the sea a ship, or any vessel meat or drink, that, that being perished wherein it was sown or cast into,
[35] That thing also which was sown, or cast therein, or received, doth perish, and remaineth not with us: but with us it hath not happened so.
[36] For we that have received the law perish by sin, and our heart also which received it
[37] Notwithstanding the law perisheth not, but remaineth in his force.
[38] And when I spake these things in my heart, I looked back with mine eyes, and upon the right side I saw a woman, and, behold, she mourned and wept with a loud voice, and was much grieved in heart, and her clothes were rent, and she had ashes upon her head.
[39] Then let I my thoughts go that I was in, and turned me unto her,
[40] And said unto her, Wherefore weepest thou? why art thou so grieved in thy mind?
[41] And she said unto me, Sir, let me alone, that I may bewail myself, and add unto my sorrow, for I am sore vexed in my mind, and brought very low.
[42] And I said unto her, What aileth thee? tell me.
[43] She said unto me, I thy servant have been barren, and had no child, though I had an husband thirty years,
[44] And those thirty years I did nothing else day and night, and every hour, but make my, prayer to the Highest.
[45] After thirty years God heard me thine handmaid, looked upon my misery, considered my trouble, and gave me a son: and I was very glad of him, so was my husband also, and all my neighbours: and we gave great honour unto the Almighty.
[46] And I nourished him with great travail.
[47] So when he grew up, and came to the time that he should have a wife, I made a feast.

---

2 Ezra.10

[1] And it so came to pass, that when my son was entered into his wedding chamber, he fell down, and died.
[2] Then we all overthrew the lights, and all my neighbours rose up to comfort me: so I took my rest unto the second day at night.
[3] And it came to pass, when they had all left off to comfort me, to the end I might be quiet; then rose I up by night and fled, and came hither into this field, as thou seest.
[4] And I do now purpose not to return into the city, but here to stay, and neither to eat nor drink, but continually to mourn and to

fast until I die.

[5] Then left I the meditations wherein I was, and spake to her in anger, saying,

[6] Thou foolish woman above all other, seest thou not our mourning, and what happeneth unto us?

[7] How that Sion our mother is full of all heaviness, and much humbled, mourning very sore?

[8] And now, seeing we all mourn and are sad, for we are all in heaviness, art thou grieved for one son?

[9] For ask the earth, and she shall tell thee, that it is she which ought to mourn for the fall of so many that grow upon her.

[10] For out of her came all at the first, and out of her shall all others come, and, behold, they walk almost all into destruction, and a multitude of them is utterly rooted out.

[11] Who then should make more mourning than she, that hath lost so great a multitude; and not thou, which art sorry but for one?

[12] But if thou sayest unto me, My lamentation is not like the earth's, because I have lost the fruit of my womb, which I brought forth with pains, and bare with sorrows;

[13] But the earth not so: for the multitude present in it according to the course of the earth is gone, as it came:

[14] Then say I unto thee, Like as thou hast brought forth with labour; even so the earth also hath given her fruit, namely, man, ever since the beginning unto him that made her.

[15] Now therefore keep thy sorrow to thyself, and bear with a good courage that which hath befallen thee.

[16] For if thou shalt acknowledge the determination of God to be just, thou shalt both receive thy son in time, and shalt be commended among women.

[17] Go thy way then into the city to thine husband.

[18] And she said unto me, That will I not do: I will not go into the city, but here will I die.

[19] So I proceeded to speak further unto her, and said,

[20] Do not so, but be counselled. by me: for how many are the adversities of Sion? be comforted in regard of the sorrow of Jerusalem.

[21] For thou seest that our sanctuary is laid waste, our altar broken down, our temple destroyed;

[22] Our psaltery is laid on the ground, our song is put to silence, our rejoicing is at an end, the light of our candlestick is put out, the ark of our covenant is spoiled, our holy things are defiled, and the name that is called upon us is almost profaned: our children are put to shame, our priests are burnt, our Levites are gone into captivity, our virgins are defiled, and our wives ravished; our righteous men carried away, our little ones destroyed, our young men are brought in bondage, and our strong men are become weak;

[23] And, which is the greatest of all, the seal of Sion hath now lost her honour; for she is delivered into the hands of them that hate us.

[24] And therefore shake off thy great heaviness, and put away the multitude of sorrows, that the Mighty may be merciful unto thee again, and the Highest shall give thee rest and ease from thy labour.

[25] And it came to pass while I was talking with her, behold, her face upon a sudden shined exceedingly, and her countenance glistered, so that I was afraid of her, and mused what it might be.

[26] And, behold, suddenly she made a great cry very fearful: so that the earth shook at the noise of the woman.

[27] And I looked, and, behold, the woman appeared unto me no more, but there was a city builded, and a large place shewed itself from the foundations: then was I afraid, and cried with a loud voice, and said,

[28] Where is Uriel the angel, who came unto me at the first? for he hath caused me

to fall into many trances, and mine end is turned into corruption, and my prayer to rebuke.
[29] And as I was speaking these words behold, he came unto me, and looked upon me.
[30] And, lo, I lay as one that had been dead, and mine understanding was taken from me: and he took me by the right hand, and comforted me, and set me upon my feet, and said unto me,
[31] What aileth thee? and why art thou so disquieted? and why is thine understanding troubled, and the thoughts of thine heart?
[32] And I said, Because thou hast forsaken me, and yet I did according to thy words, and I went into the field, and, lo, I have seen, and yet see, that I am not able to express.
[33] And he said unto me, Stand up manfully, and I will advise thee.
[34] Then said I, Speak on, my lord, in me; only forsake me not, lest I die frustrate of my hope.
[35] For I have seen that I knew not, and hear that I do not know.
[36] Or is my sense deceived, or my soul in a dream?
[37] Now therefore I beseech thee that thou wilt shew thy servant of this vision.
[38] He answered me then, and said, Hear me, and I shall inform thee, and tell thee wherefore thou art afraid: for the Highest will reveal many secret things unto thee.
[39] He hath seen that thy way is right: for that thou sorrowest continually for thy people, and makest great lamentation for Sion.
[40] This therefore is the meaning of the vision which thou lately sawest:
[41] Thou sawest a woman mourning, and thou begannest to comfort her:
[42] But now seest thou the likeness of the woman no more, but there appeared unto thee a city builded.
[43] And whereas she told thee of the death of her son, this is the solution:
[44] This woman, whom thou sawest is Sion: and whereas she said unto thee, even she whom thou seest as a city builded,
[45] Whereas, I say, she said unto thee, that she hath been thirty years barren: those are the thirty years wherein there was no offering made in her.
[46] But after thirty years Solomon builded the city and offered offerings: and then bare the barren a son.
[47] And whereas she told thee that she nourished him with labour: that was the dwelling in Jerusalem.
[48] But whereas she said unto thee, That my son coming into his marriage chamber happened to have a fail, and died: this was the destruction that came to Jerusalem.
[49] And, behold, thou sawest her likeness, and because she mourned for her son, thou begannest to comfort her: and of these things which have chanced, these are to be opened unto thee.
[50] For now the most High seeth that thou art grieved unfeignedly, and sufferest from thy whole heart for her, so hath he shewed thee the brightness of her glory, and the comeliness of her beauty:
[51] And therefore I bade thee remain in the field where no house was builded:
[52] For I knew that the Highest would shew this unto thee.
[53] Therefore I commanded thee to go into the field, where no foundation of any building was.
[54] For in the place wherein the Highest beginneth to shew his city, there can no man's building be able to stand.
[55] And therefore fear not, let not thine heart be affrighted, but go thy way in, and see the beauty and greatness of the building, as much as thine eyes be able to see:
[56] And then shalt thou hear as much as thine ears may comprehend.
[57] For thou art blessed above many other, and art called with the Highest; and so are

but few.

[58] But to morrow at night thou shalt remain here;

[59] And so shall the Highest shew thee visions of the high things, which the most High will do unto them that dwell upon the earth in the last days. So I slept that night and another, like as he commanded me.

---

2 Ezra. 11

[1] Then saw I a dream, and, behold, there came up from the sea an eagle, which had twelve feathered wings, and three heads.

[2] And I saw, and, behold, she spread her wings over all the earth, and all the winds of the air blew on her, and were gathered together.

[3] And I beheld, and out of her feathers there grew other contrary feathers; and they became little feathers and small.

[4] But her heads were at rest: the head in the midst was greater than the other, yet rested it with the residue.

[5] Moreover I beheld, and, lo, the eagle flew with her feathers, and reigned upon earth, and over them that dwelt therein.

[6] And I saw that all things under heaven were subject unto her, and no man spake against her, no, not one creature upon earth.

[7] And I beheld, and, lo, the eagle rose upon her talons, and spake to her feathers, saying,

[8] Watch not all at once: sleep every one in his own place, and watch by course:

[9] But let the heads be preserved for the last.

[10] And I beheld, and, lo, the voice went not out of her heads, but from the midst of her body.

[11] And I numbered her contrary feathers, and, behold, there were eight of them.

[12] And I looked, and, behold, on the right side there arose one feather, and reigned over all the earth;

[13] And so it was, that when it reigned, the end of it came, and the place thereof appeared no more: so the next following stood up, and reigned, and had a great time;

[14] And it happened, that when it reigned, the end of it came also, like as the first, so that it appeared no more.

[15] Then came there a voice unto it, and said,

[16] Hear thou that hast borne rule over the earth so long: this I say unto thee, before thou beginnest to appear no more,

[17] There shall none after thee attain unto thy time, neither unto the half thereof.

[18] Then arose the third, and reigned as the other before, and appeared no more also.

[19] So went it with all the residue one after another, as that every one reigned, and then appeared no more.

[20] Then I beheld, and, lo, in process of time the feathers that followed stood up upon the right side, that they might rule also; and some of them ruled, but within a while they appeared no more:

[21] For some of them were set up, but ruled not.

[22] After this I looked, and, behold, the twelve feathers appeared no more, nor the two little feathers:

[23] And there was no more upon the eagle's body, but three heads that rested, and six little wings.

[24] Then saw I also that two little feathers divided themselves from the six, and remained under the head that was upon the right side: for the four continued in their place.

[25] And I beheld, and, lo, the feathers that were under the wing thought to set up themselves and to have the rule.

[26] And I beheld, and, lo, there was one set up, but shortly it appeared no more.

[27] And the second was sooner away than the first.

[28] And I beheld, and, lo, the two that remained thought also in themselves to

reign:
[29] And when they so thought, behold, there awaked one of the heads that were at rest, namely, it that was in the midst; for that was greater than the two other heads.
[30] And then I saw that the two other heads were joined with it.
[31] And, behold, the head was turned with them that were with it, and did eat up the two feathers under the wing that would have reigned.
[32] But this head put the whole earth in fear, and bare rule in it over all those that dwelt upon the earth with much oppression; and it had the governance of the world more than all the wings that had been.
[33] And after this I beheld, and, lo, the head that was in the midst suddenly appeared no more, like as the wings.
[34] But there remained the two heads, which also in like sort ruled upon the earth, and over those that dwelt therein.
[35] And I beheld, and, lo, the head upon the right side devoured it that was upon the left side.
[36] Then I head a voice, which said unto me, Look before thee, and consider the thing that thou seest.
[37] And I beheld, and lo, as it were a roaring lion chased out of the wood: and I saw that he sent out a man's voice unto the eagle, and said,
[38] Hear thou, I will talk with thee, and the Highest shall say unto thee,
[39] Art not thou it that remainest of the four beasts, whom I made to reign in my world, that the end of their times might come through them?
[40] And the fourth came, and overcame all the beasts that were past, and had power over the world with great fearfulness, and over the whole compass of the earth with much wicked oppression; and so long time dwelt he upon the earth with deceit.
[41] For the earth hast thou not judged with truth.

[42] For thou hast afflicted the meek, thou hast hurt the peaceable, thou hast loved liars, and destroyed the dwellings of them that brought forth fruit, and hast cast down the walls of such as did thee no harm.
[43] Therefore is thy wrongful dealing come up unto the Highest, and thy pride unto the Mighty.
[44] The Highest also hath looked upon the proud times, and, behold, they are ended, and his abominations are fulfilled.
[45] And therefore appear no more, thou eagle, nor thy horrible wings, nor thy wicked feathers nor thy malicious heads, nor thy hurtful claws, nor all thy vain body:
[46] That all the earth may be refreshed, and may return, being delivered from thy violence, and that she may hope for the judgment and mercy of him that made her.

---

2 Ezra. 12

[1] And it came to pass, whiles the lion spake these words unto the eagle, I saw,
[2] And, behold, the head that remained and the four wings appeared no more, and the two went unto it and set themselves up to reign, and their kingdom was small, and fill of uproar.
[3] And I saw, and, behold, they appeared no more, and the whole body of the eagle was burnt so that the earth was in great fear: then awaked I out of the trouble and trance of my mind, and from great fear, and said unto my spirit,
[4] Lo, this hast thou done unto me, in that thou searchest out the ways of the Highest.
[5] Lo, yet am I weary in my mind, and very weak in my spirit; and little strength is there in me, for the great fear wherewith I was afflicted this night.
[6] Therefore will I now beseech the Highest, that he will comfort me unto the end.
[7] And I said, Lord that bearest rule, if I

have found grace before thy sight, and if I am justified with thee before many others, and if my prayer indeed be come up before thy face;

[8] Comfort me then, and shew me thy servant the interpretation and plain difference of this fearful vision, that thou mayest perfectly comfort my soul.

[9] For thou hast judged me worthy to shew me the last times.

[10] And he said unto me, This is the interpretation of the vision:

[11] The eagle, whom thou sawest come up from the sea, is the kingdom which was seen in the vision of thy brother Daniel.

[12] But it was not expounded unto him, therefore now I declare it unto thee.

[13] Behold, the days will come, that there shall rise up a kingdom upon earth, and it shall be feared above all the kingdoms that were before it.

[14] In the same shall twelve kings reign, one after another:

[15] Whereof the second shall begin to reign, and shall have more time than any of the twelve.

[16] And this do the twelve wings signify, which thou sawest.

[17] As for the voice which thou heardest speak, and that thou sawest not to go out from the heads but from the midst of the body thereof, this is the interpretation:

[18] That after the time of that kingdom there shall arise great strivings, and it shall stand in peril of failing: nevertheless it shall not then fall, but shall be restored again to his beginning.

[19] And whereas thou sawest the eight small under feathers sticking to her wings, this is the interpretation:

[20] That in him there shall arise eight kings, whose times shall be but small, and their years swift.

[21] And two of them shall perish, the middle time approaching: four shall be kept until their end begin to approach: but two shall be kept unto the end.

[22] And whereas thou sawest three heads resting, this is the interpretation:

[23] In his last days shall the most High raise up three kingdoms, and renew many things therein, and they shall have the dominion of the earth,

[24] And of those that dwell therein, with much oppression, above all those that were before them: therefore are they called the heads of the eagle.

[25] For these are they that shall accomplish his wickedness, and that shall finish his last end.

[26] And whereas thou sawest that the great head appeared no more, it signifieth that one of them shall die upon his bed, and yet with pain.

[27] For the two that remain shall be slain with the sword.

[28] For the sword of the one shall devour the other: but at the last shall he fall through the sword himself.

[29] And whereas thou sawest two feathers under the wings passing over the head that is on the right side;

[30] It signifieth that these are they, whom the Highest hath kept unto their end: this is the small kingdom and full of trouble, as thou sawest.

[31] And the lion, whom thou sawest rising up out of the wood, and roaring, and speaking to the eagle, and rebuking her for her unrighteousness with all the words which thou hast heard;

[32] This is the anointed, which the Highest hath kept for them and for their wickedness unto the end: he shall reprove them, and shall upbraid them with their cruelty.

[33] For he shall set them before him alive in judgment, and shall rebuke them, and correct them.

[34] For the rest of my people shall he deliver with mercy, those that have been pressed upon my borders, and he shall make them joyful until the coming of the day of

judgment, whereof I have spoken unto thee from the the beginning.
[35] This is the dream that thou sawest, and these are the interpretations.
[36] Thou only hast been meet to know this secret of the Highest.
[37] Therefore write all these things that thou hast seen in a book, and hide them:
[38] And teach them to the wise of the people, whose hearts thou knowest may comprehend and keep these secrets.
[39] But wait thou here thyself yet seven days more, that it may be shewed thee, whatsoever it pleaseth the Highest to declare unto thee. And with that he went his way.
[40] And it came to pass, when all the people saw that the seven days were past, and I not come again into the city, they gathered them all together, from the least unto the greatest, and came unto me, and said,
[41] What have we offended thee? and what evil have we done against thee, that thou forsakest us, and sittest here in this place?
[42] For of all the prophets thou only art left us, as a cluster of the vintage, and as a candle in a dark place, and as a haven or ship preserved from the tempest.
[43] Are not the evils which are come to us sufficient?
[44] If thou shalt forsake us, how much better had it been for us, if we also had been burned in the midst of Sion?
[45] For we are not better than they that died there. And they wept with a loud voice. Then answered I them, and said,
[46] Be of good comfort, O Israel; and be not heavy, thou house of Jacob:
[47] For the Highest hath you in remembrance, and the Mighty hath not forgotten you in temptation.
[48] As for me, I have not forsaken you, neither am I departed from you: but am come into this place, to pray for the desolation of Sion, and that I might seek mercy for the low estate of your sanctuary.
[49] And now go your way home every man, and after these days will I come unto you.
[50] So the people went their way into the city, like as I commanded them:
[51] But I remained still in the field seven days, as the angel commanded me; and did eat only in those days of the flowers of the field, and had my meat of the herbs

---

2 Ezra. 13

[1] And it came to pass after seven days, I dreamed a dream by night:
[2] And, lo, there arose a wind from the sea, that it moved all the waves thereof.
[3] And I beheld, and, lo, that man waxed strong with the thousands of heaven: and when he turned his countenance to look, all the things trembled that were seen under him.
[4] And whensoever the voice went out of his mouth, all they burned that heard his voice, like as the earth faileth when it feeleth the fire.
[5] And after this I beheld, and, lo, there was gathered together a multitude of men, out of number, from the four winds of the heaven, to subdue the man that came out of the sea
[6] But I beheld, and, lo, he had graved himself a great mountain, and flew up upon it.
[7] But I would have seen the region or place whereout the hill was graven, and I could not.
[8] And after this I beheld, and, lo, all they which were gathered together to subdue him were sore afraid, and yet durst fight.
[9] And, lo, as he saw the violence of the multitude that came, he neither lifted up his hand, nor held sword, nor any instrument of war:
[10] But only I saw that he sent out of his mouth as it had been a blast of fire, and out of his lips a flaming breath, and out of his

tongue he cast out sparks and tempests.
[11] And they were all mixed together; the blast of fire, the flaming breath, and the great tempest; and fell with violence upon the multitude which was prepared to fight, and burned them up every one, so that upon a sudden of an innumerable multitude nothing was to be perceived, but only dust and smell of smoke: when I saw this I was afraid.
[12] Afterward saw I the same man come down from the mountain, and call unto him another peaceable Multitude.
[13] And there came much people unto him, whereof some were glad, some were sorry, and some of them were bound, and other some brought of them that were offered: then was I sick through great fear, and I awaked, and said,
[14] Thou hast shewed thy servant these wonders from the beginning, and hast counted me worthy that thou shouldest receive my prayer:
[15] Shew me now yet the interpretation of this dream.
[16] For as I conceive in mine understanding, woe unto them that shall be left in those days and much more woe unto them that are not left behind!
[17] For they that were not left were in heaviness.
[18] Now understand I the things that are laid up in the latter days, which shall happen unto them, and to those that are left behind.
[19] Therefore are they come into great perils and many necessities, like as these dreams declare.
[20] Yet is it easier for him that is in danger to come into these things, than to pass away as a cloud out of the world, and not to see the things that happen in the last days. And he answered unto me, and said,
[21] The interpretation of the vision shall I shew thee, and I will open unto thee the thing that thou hast required.
[22] Whereas thou hast spoken of them that are left behind, this is the interpretation:
[23] He that shall endure the peril in that time hath kept himself: they that be fallen into danger are such as have works, and faith toward the Almighty.
[24] Know this therefore, that they which be left behind are more blessed than they that be dead.
[25] This is the meaning of the vision: Whereas thou sawest a man coming up from the midst of the sea:
[26] The same is he whom God the Highest hath kept a great season, which by his own self shall deliver his creature: and he shall order them that are left behind.
[27] And whereas thou sawest, that out of his mouth there came as a blast of wind, and fire, and storm;
[28] And that he held neither sword, nor any instrument of war, but that the rushing in of him destroyed the whole multitude that came to subdue him; this is the interpretation:
[29] Behold, the days come, when the most High will begin to deliver them that are upon the earth.
[30] And he shall come to the astonishment of them that dwell on the earth.
[31] And one shall undertake to fight against another, one city against another, one place against another, one people against another, and one realm against another.
[32] And the time shall be when these things shall come to pass, and the signs shall happen which I shewed thee before, and then shall my Son be declared, whom thou sawest as a man ascending.
[33] And when all the people hear his voice, every man shall in their own land leave the battle they have one against another.
[34] And an innumerable multitude shall be gathered together, as thou sawest them, willing to come, and to overcome him by fighting.
[35] But he shall stand upon the top of the mount Sion.

[36] And Sion shall come, and shall be shewed to all men, being prepared and builded, like as thou sawest the hill graven without hands.
[37] And this my Son shall rebuke the wicked inventions of those nations, which for their wicked life are fallen into the tempest;
[38] And shall lay before them their evil thoughts, and the torments wherewith they shall begin to be tormented, which are like unto a flame: and he shall destroy them without labour by the law which is like unto me.
[39] And whereas thou sawest that he gathered another peaceable multitude unto him;
[40] Those are the ten tribes, which were carried away prisoners out of their own land in the time of Osea the king, whom Salmanasar the king of Assyria led away captive, and he carried them over the waters, and so came they into another land.
[41] But they took this counsel among themselves, that they would leave the multitude of the heathen, and go forth into a further country, where never mankind dwelt,
[42] That they might there keep their statutes, which they never kept in their own land.
[43] And they entered into Euphrates by the narrow places of the river.
[44] For the most High then shewed signs for them, and held still the flood, till they were passed over.
[45] For through that country there was a great way to go, namely, of a year and a half: and the same region is called Arsareth.
[46] Then dwelt they there until the latter time; and now when they shall begin to come,
[47] The Highest shall stay the springs of the stream again, that they may go through: therefore sawest thou the multitude with peace.
[48] But those that be left behind of thy people are they that are found within my borders.
[49] Now when he destroyeth the multitude of the nations that are gathered together, he shall defend his people that remain.
[50] And then shall he shew them great wonders.
[51] Then said I, O Lord that bearest rule, shew me this: Wherefore have I seen the man coming up from the midst of the sea?
[52] And he said unto me, Like as thou canst neither seek out nor know the things that are in the deep of the sea: even so can no man upon earth see my Son, or those that be with him, but in the day time.
[53] This is the interpretation of the dream which thou sawest, and whereby thou only art here lightened.
[54] For thou hast forsaken thine own way, and applied thy diligence unto my law, and sought it.
[55] Thy life hast thou ordered in wisdom, and hast called understanding thy mother.
[56] And therefore have I shewed thee the treasures of the Highest: after other three days I will speak other things unto thee, and declare unto thee mighty and wondrous things.
[57] Then went I forth into the field, giving praise and thanks greatly unto the most High because of his wonders which he did in time;
[58] And because he governeth the same, and such things as fall in their seasons: and there I sat three days.

---

2 Ezra.14

[1] And it came to pass upon the third day, I sat under an oak, and, behold, there came a voice out of a bush over against me, and said, Esdras, Esdras.
[2] And I said, Here am I, Lord And I stood up upon my feet.
[3] Then said he unto me, In the bush I did

manifestly reveal myself unto Moses, and talked with him, when my people served in Egypt:

[4] And I sent him and led my people out of Egypt, and brought him up to the mount of where I held him by me a long season,

[5] And told him many wondrous things, and shewed him the secrets of the times, and the end; and commanded him, saying,

[6] These words shalt thou declare, and these shalt thou hide.

[7] And now I say unto thee,

[8] That thou lay up in thy heart the signs that I have shewed, and the dreams that thou hast seen, and the interpretations which thou hast heard:

[9] For thou shalt be taken away from all, and from henceforth thou shalt remain with my Son, and with such as be like thee, until the times be ended.

[10] For the world hath lost his youth, and the times begin to wax old.

[11] For the world is divided into twelve parts, and the ten parts of it are gone already, and half of a tenth part:

[12] And there remaineth that which is after the half of the tenth part.

[13] Now therefore set thine house in order, and reprove thy people, comfort such of them as be in trouble, and now renounce corruption,

[14] Let go from thee mortal thoughts, cast away the burdens of man, put off now the weak nature,

[15] And set aside the thoughts that are most heavy unto thee, and haste thee to flee from these times.

[16] For yet greater evils than those which thou hast seen happen shall be done hereafter.

[17] For look how much the world shall be weaker through age, so much the more shall evils increase upon them that dwell therein.

[18] For the time is fled far away, and leasing is hard at hand: for now hasteth the vision to come, which thou hast seen.

[19] Then answered I before thee, and said,

[20] Behold, Lord, I will go, as thou hast commanded me, and reprove the people which are present: but they that shall be born afterward, who shall admonish them? thus the world is set in darkness, and they that dwell therein are without light.

[21] For thy law is burnt, therefore no man knoweth the things that are done of thee, or the work that shall begin.

[22] But if I have found grace before thee, send the Holy Ghost into me, and I shall write all that hath been done in the world since the beginning, which were written in thy law, that men may find thy path, and that they which will live in the latter days may live.

[23] And he answered me, saying, Go thy way, gather the people together, and say unto them, that they seek thee not for forty days.

[24] But look thou prepare thee many box trees, and take with thee Sarea, Dabria, Selemia, Ecanus, and Asiel, these five which are ready to write swiftly;

[25] And come hither, and I shall light a candle of understanding in thine heart, which shall not be put out, till the things be performed which thou shalt begin to write.

[26] And when thou hast done, some things shalt thou publish, and some things shalt thou shew secretly to the wise: to morrow this hour shalt thou begin to write.

[27] Then went I forth, as he commanded, and gathered all the people together, and said,

[28] Hear these words, O Israel.

[29] Our fathers at the beginning were strangers in Egypt, from whence they were delivered:

[30] And received the law of life, which they kept not, which ye also have transgressed after them.

[31] Then was the land, even the land of Sion, parted among you by lot: but your fathers, and ye yourselves, have done

unrighteousness, and have not kept the ways which the Highest commanded you.
[32] And forasmuch as he is a righteous judge, he took from you in time the thing that he had given you.
[33] And now are ye here, and your brethren among you.
[34] Therefore if so be that ye will subdue your own understanding, and reform your hearts, ye shall be kept alive and after death ye shall obtain mercy.
[35] For after death shall the judgment come, when we shall live again: and then shall the names of the righteous be manifest, and the works of the ungodly shall be declared.
[36] Let no man therefore come unto me now, nor seek after me these forty days.
[37] So I took the five men, as he commanded me, and we went into the field, and remained there.
[38] And the next day, behold, a voice called me, saying, Esdras, open thy mouth, and drink that I give thee to drink.
[39] Then opened I my mouth, and, behold, he reached me a full cup, which was full as it were with water, but the colour of it was like fire.
[40] And I took it, and drank: and when I had drunk of it, my heart uttered understanding, and wisdom grew in my breast, for my spirit strengthened my memory:
[41] And my mouth was opened, and shut no more.
[42] The Highest gave understanding unto the five men, and they wrote the wonderful visions of the night that were told, which they knew not: and they sat forty days, and they wrote in the day, and at night they ate bread.
[43] As for me. I spake in the day, and I held not my tongue by night.
[44] In forty days they wrote two hundred and four books.
[45] And it came to pass, when the forty days were filled, that the Highest spake, saying, The first that thou hast written publish openly, that the worthy and unworthy may read it:
[46] But keep the seventy last, that thou mayest deliver them only to such as be wise among the people:
[47] For in them is the spring of understanding, the fountain of wisdom, and the stream of knowledge.
[48] And I did so.

---

2 Ezra. 15

[1] Behold, speak thou in the ears of my people the words of prophecy, which I will put in thy mouth, saith Jah:
[2] And cause them to be written in paper: for they are faithful and true.
[3] Fear not the imaginations against thee, let not the incredulity of them trouble thee, that speak against thee.
[4] For all the unfaithful shall die in their unfaithfulness.
[5] Behold, saith Jah, I will bring plagues upon the world; the sword, famine, death, and destruction.
[6] For wickedness hath exceedingly polluted the whole earth, and their hurtful works are fulfilled.
[7] Therefore saith Jah,
[8] I will hold my tongue no more as touching their wickedness, which they profanely commit, neither will I suffer them in those things, in which they wickedly exercise themselves: behold, the innocent and righteous blood crieth unto me, and the souls of the just complain continually.
[9] And therefore, saith Jah, I will surely avenge them, and receive unto me all the innocent blood from among them.
[10] Behold, my people is led as a flock to the slaughter: I will not suffer them now to dwell in the land of Egypt:
[11] But I will bring them with a mighty

hand and a stretched out arm, and smite Egypt with plagues, as before, and will destroy all the land thereof.

[12] Egypt shall mourn, and the foundation of it shall be smitten with the plague and punishment that God shall bring upon it.

[13] They that till the ground shall mourn: for their seeds shall fail through the blasting and hail, and with a fearful constellation.

[14] Woe to the world and them that dwell therein!

[15] For the sword and their destruction draweth nigh, and one people shall stand up and fight against another, and swords in their hands.

[16] For there shall be sedition among men, and invading one another; they shall not regard their kings nor princes, and the course of their actions shall stand in their power.

[17] A man shall desire to go into a city, and shall not be able.

[18] For because of their pride the cities shall be troubled, the houses shall be destroyed, and men shall be afraid.

[19] A man shall have no pity upon his neighbour, but shall destroy their houses with the sword, and spoil their goods, because of the lack of bread, and for great tribulation.

[20] Behold, saith God, I will call together all the kings of the earth to reverence me, which are from the rising of the sun, from the south, from the east, and Libanus; to turn themselves one against another, and repay the things that they have done to them.

[21] Like as they do yet this day unto my chosen, so will I do also, and recompense in their bosom. Thus saith Jah God;

[22] My right hand shall not spare the sinners, and my sword shall not cease over them that shed innocent blood upon the earth.

[23] The fire is gone forth from his wrath, and hath consumed the foundations of the earth, and the sinners, like the straw that is kindled.

[24] Woe to them that sin, and keep not my commandments! saith Jah.

[25] I will not spare them: go your way, ye children, from the power, defile not my sanctuary.

[26] For Jah knoweth all them that sin against him, and therefore delivereth he them unto death and destruction.

[27] For now are the plagues come upon the whole earth and ye shall remain in them: for God shall not deliver you, because ye have sinned against him.

[28] Behold an horrible vision, and the appearance thereof from the east:

[29] Where the nations of the dragons of Arabia shall come out with many chariots, and the multitude of them shall be carried as the wind upon earth, that all they which hear them may fear and tremble.

[30] Also the Carmanians raging in wrath shall go forth as the wild boars of the wood, and with great power shall they come, and join battle with them, and shall waste a portion of the land of the Assyrians.

[31] And then shall the dragons have the upper hand, remembering their nature; and if they shall turn themselves, conspiring together in great power to persecute them,

[32] Then these shall be troubled bled, and keep silence through their power, and shall flee.

[33] And from the land of the Assyrians shall the enemy besiege them, and consume some of them, and in their host shall be fear and dread, and strife among their kings.

[34] Behold clouds from the east and from the north unto the south, and they are very horrible to look upon, full of wrath and storm.

[35] They shall smite one upon another, and they shall smite down a great multitude of stars upon the earth, even their own star; and blood shall be from the sword unto the belly,

[36] And dung of men unto the camel's hough.

[37] And there shall be great fearfulness and trembling upon earth: and they that see the wrath shall be afraid, and trembling shall come upon them.
[38] And then shall there come great storms from the south, and from the north, and another part from the west.
[39] And strong winds shall arise from the east, and shall open it; and the cloud which he raised up in wrath, and the star stirred to cause fear toward the east and west wind, shall be destroyed.
[40] The great and mighty clouds shall be puffed up full of wrath, and the star, that they may make all the earth afraid, and them that dwell therein; and they shall pour out over every high and eminent place an horrible star,
[41] Fire, and hail, and flying swords, and many waters, that all fields may be full, and all rivers, with the abundance of great waters.
[42] And they shall break down the cities and walls, mountains and hills, trees of the wood, and grass of the meadows, and their corn.
[43] And they shall go stedfastly unto Babylon, and make her afraid.
[44] They shall come to her, and besiege her, the star and all wrath shall they pour out upon her: then shall the dust and smoke go up unto the heaven, and all they that be about her shall bewail her.
[45] And they that remain under her shall do service unto them that have put her in fear.
[46] And thou, Asia, that art partaker of the hope of Babylon, and art the glory of her person:
[47] Woe be unto thee, thou wretch, because thou hast made thyself like unto her; and hast decked thy daughters in whoredom, that they might please and glory in thy lovers, which have always desired to commit whoredom with thee.
[48] Thou hast followed her that is hated in all her works and inventions: therefore saith God,
[49] I will send plagues upon thee; widowhood, poverty, famine, sword, and pestilence, to waste thy houses with destruction and death.
[50] And the glory of thy Power shall be dried up as a flower, the heat shall arise that is sent over thee.
[51] Thou shalt be weakened as a poor woman with stripes, and as one chastised with wounds, so that the mighty and lovers shall not be able to receive thee.
[52] Would I with jealousy have so proceeded against thee, saith Jah,
[53] If thou hadst not always slain my chosen, exalting the stroke of thine hands, and saying over their dead, when thou wast drunken,
[54] Set forth the beauty of thy countenance?
[55] The reward of thy whoredom shall be in thy bosom, therefore shalt thou receive recompence.
[56] Like as thou hast done unto my chosen, saith Jah, even so shall God do unto thee, and shall deliver thee into mischief
[57] Thy children shall die of hunger, and thou shalt fall through the sword: thy cities shall be broken down, and all thine shall perish with the sword in the field.
[58] They that be in the mountains shall die of hunger, and eat their own flesh, and drink their own blood, for very hunger of bread, and thirst of water.
[59] Thou as unhappy shalt come through the sea, and receive plagues again.
[60] And in the passage they shall rush on the idle city, and shall destroy some portion of thy land, and consume part of thy glory, and shall return to Babylon that was destroyed.
[61] And thou shalt be cast down by them as stubble, and they shall be unto thee as fire;
[62] And shall consume thee, and thy cities, thy land, and thy mountains; all thy woods and thy fruitful trees shall they burn up with

fire.
[63] Thy children shall they carry away captive, and, look, what thou hast, they shall spoil it, and mar the beauty of thy face.

---

2 Ezra.16

[1] Woe be unto thee, Babylon, and Asia! woe be unto thee, Egypt and Syria!
[2] Gird up yourselves with cloths of sack and hair, bewail your children, and be sorry; for your destruction is at hand.
[3] A sword is sent upon you, and who may turn it back?
[4] A fire is sent among you, and who may quench it?
[5] Plagues are sent unto you, and what is he that may drive them away?
[6] May any man drive away an hungry lion in the wood? or may any one quench the fire in stubble, when it hath begun to burn?
[7] May one turn again the arrow that is shot of a strong archer?
[8] The mighty Lord sendeth the plagues and who is he that can drive them away?
[9] A fire shall go forth from his wrath, and who is he that may quench it?
[10] He shall cast lightnings, and who shall not fear? he shall thunder, and who shall not be afraid?
[11] Jah shall threaten, and who shall not be utterly beaten to powder at his presence?
[12] The earth quaketh, and the foundations thereof; the sea ariseth up with waves from the deep, and the waves of it are troubled, and the fishes thereof also, before Jah, and before the glory of his power:
[13] For strong is his right hand that bendeth the bow, his arrows that he shooteth are sharp, and shall not miss, when they begin to be shot into the ends of the world.
[14] Behold, the plagues are sent, and shall not return again, until they come upon the earth.
[15] The fire is kindled, and shall not be put out, till it consume the foundation of the earth.
[16] Like as an arrow which is shot of a mighty archer returneth not backward: even so the plagues that shall be sent upon earth shall not return again.
[17] Woe is me! woe is me! who will deliver me in those days?
[18] The beginning of sorrows and great mournings; the beginning of famine and great death; the beginning of wars, and the powers shall stand in fear; the beginning of evils! what shall I do when these evils shall come?
[19] Behold, famine and plague, tribulation and anguish, are sent as scourges for amendment.
[20] But for all these things they shall not turn from their wickedness, nor be always mindful of the scourges.
[21] Behold, victuals shall be so good cheap upon earth, that they shall think themselves to be in good case, and even then shall evils grow upon earth, sword, famine, and great confusion.
[22] For many of them that dwell upon earth shall perish of famine; and the other, that escape the hunger, shall the sword destroy.
[23] And the dead shall be cast out as dung, and there shall be no man to comfort them: for the earth shall be wasted, and the cities shall be cast down.
[24] There shall be no man left to till the earth, and to sow it
[25] The trees shall give fruit, and who shall gather them?
[26] The grapes shall ripen, and who shall tread them? for all places shall be desolate of men:
[27] So that one man shall desire to see another, and to hear his voice.

[28] For of a city there shall be ten left, and two of the field, which shall hide themselves in the thick groves, and in the clefts of the rocks.
[29] As in an orchard of Olives upon every tree there are left three or four olives;
[30] Or as when a vineyard is gathered, there are left some clusters of them that diligently seek through the vineyard:
[31] Even so in those days there shall be three or four left by them that search their houses with the sword.
[32] And the earth shall be laid waste, and the fields thereof shall wax old, and her ways and all her paths shall grow full of thorns, because no man shall travel therethrough.
[33] The virgins shall mourn, having no bridegrooms; the women shall mourn, having no husbands; their daughters shall mourn, having no helpers.
[34] In the wars shall their bridegrooms be destroyed, and their husbands shall perish of famine.
[35] Hear now these things and understand them, ye servants of Jah.
[36] Behold, the word of Jah, receive it: believe not the gods of whom Jah spake.
[37] Behold, the plagues draw nigh, and are not slack.
[38] As when a woman with child in the ninth month bringeth forth her son, with two or three hours of her birth great pains compass her womb, which pains, when the child cometh forth, they slack not a moment:
[39] Even so shall not the plagues be slack to come upon the earth, and the world shall mourn, and sorrows shall come upon it on every side.
[40] O my people, hear my word: make you ready to thy battle, and in those evils be even as pilgrims upon the earth.
[41] He that selleth, let him be as he that fleeth away: and he that buyeth, as one that will lose:
[42] He that occupieth merchandise, as he that hath no profit by it: and he that buildeth, as he that shall not dwell therein:
[43] He that soweth, as if he should not reap: so also he that planteth the vineyard, as he that shall not gather the grapes:
[44] They that marry, as they that shall get no children; and they that marry not, as the widowers.
[45] And therefore they that labour labour in vain:
[46] For strangers shall reap their fruits, and spoil their goods, overthrow their houses, and take their children captives, for in captivity and famine shall they get children.
[47] And they that occupy their merchandise with robbery, the more they deck their cities, their houses, their possessions, and their own persons:
[48] The more will I be angry with them for their sin, saith Jah.
[49] Like as a whore envieth a right honest and virtuous woman:
[50] So shall righteousness hate iniquity, when she decketh herself, and shall accuse her to her face, when he cometh that shall defend him that diligently searcheth out every sin upon earth.
[51] And therefore be ye not like thereunto, nor to the works thereof.
[52] For yet a little, and iniquity shall be taken away out of the earth, and righteousness shall reign among you.
[53] Let not the sinner say that he hath not sinned: for God shall burn coals of fire upon his head, which saith before Jah God and his glory, I have not sinned.
[54] Behold, Jah knoweth all the works of men, their imaginations, their thoughts, and their hearts:
[55] Which spake but the word, Let the earth

be made; and it was made: Let the heaven be made; and it was created.
[56] In his word were the stars made, and he knoweth the number of them.
[57] He searcheth the deep, and the treasures thereof; he hath measured the sea, and what it containeth.
[58] He hath shut the sea in the midst of the waters, and with his word hath he hanged the earth upon the waters.
[59] He spreadeth out the heavens like a vault; upon the waters hath he founded it.
[60] In the desert hath he made springs of water, and pools upon the tops of the mountains, that the floods might pour down from the high rocks to water the earth.
[61] He made man, and put his heart in the midst of the body, and gave him breath, life, and understanding.
[62] Yea and the Spirit of Almighty God, which made all things, and searcheth out all hidden things in the secrets of the earth,
[63] Surely he knoweth your inventions, and what ye think in your hearts, even them that sin, and would hide their sin.
[64] Therefore hath Jah exactly searched out all your works, and he will put you all to shame.
[65] And when your sins are brought forth, ye shall be ashamed before men, and your own sins shall be your accusers in that day.
[66] What will ye do? or how will ye hide your sins before God and his angels?
[67] Behold, God himself is the judge, fear him: leave off from your sins, and forget your iniquities, to meddle no more with them for ever: so shall God lead you forth, and deliver you from all trouble.
[68] For, behold, the burning wrath of a great multitude is kindled over you, and they shall take away certain of you, and feed you, being idle, with things offered unto idols.
[69] And they that consent unto them shall be had in derision and in reproach, and trodden under foot.
[70] For there shall be in every place, and in the next cities, a great insurrection upon those that fear Jah.
[71] They shall be like mad men, sparing none, but still spoiling and destroying those that fear Jah.
[72] For they shall waste and take away their goods, and cast them out of their houses.
[73] Then shall they be known, who are my chosen; and they shall be tried as the gold in the fire.
[74] Hear, O ye my beloved, saith Jah: behold, the days of trouble are at hand, but I will deliver you from the same.
[75] Be ye not afraid neither doubt; for God is your guide,
[76] And the guide of them who keep my commandments and precepts, saith Jah God: let not your sins weigh you down, and let not your iniquities lift up themselves.
[77] Woe be unto them that are bound with their sins, and covered with their iniquities like as a field is covered over with bushes, and the path thereof covered with thorns, that no man may travel through!
[78] It is left undressed, and is cast into the fire to be consumed therewith.

Tobit

Tob.1

[1] The book of the words of Tobit, son of Tobiel, the son of Ananiel, the son of Aduel, the son of Gabael, of the seed of Asael, of the tribe of Nephthali;
[2] Who in the time of Enemessar king of the Assyrians was led captive out of Thisbe,

which is at the right hand of that city, which is called properly Nephthali in Galilee above Aser.

[3] I Tobit have walked all the days of my life in the ways of truth and justice, and I did many almsdeeds to my brethren, and my nation, who came with me to Nineve, into the land of the Assyrians.

[4] And when I was in mine own country, in the land of Israel being but young, all the tribe of Nephthali my father fell from the house of Jerusalem, which was chosen out of all the tribes of Israel, that all the tribes should sacrifice there, where the temple of the habitation of the most High was consecrated and built for all ages.

[5] Now all the tribes which together revolted, and the house of my father Nephthali, sacrificed unto the heifer Baal.

[6] But I alone went often to Jerusalem at the feasts, as it was ordained unto all the people of Israel by an everlasting decree, having the firstfruits and tenths of increase, with that which was first shorn; and them gave I at the altar to the priests the children of Aaron.

[7] The first tenth part of all increase I gave to the sons of Aaron, who ministered at Jerusalem: another tenth part I sold away, and went, and spent it every year at Jerusalem:

[8] And the third I gave unto them to whom it was meet, as Debora my father's mother had commanded me, because I was left an orphan by my father.

[9] Furthermore, when I was come to the age of a man, I married Anna of mine own kindred, and of her I begat Tobias.

[10] And when we were carried away captives to Nineve, all my brethren and those that were of my kindred did eat of the bread of the Gentiles.

[11] But I kept myself from eating;

[12] Because I remembered God with all my heart.

[13] And the most High gave me grace and favour before Enemessar, so that I was his purveyor.

[14] And I went into Media, and left in trust with Gabael, the brother of Gabrias, at Rages a city of Media ten talents of silver.

[15] Now when Enemessar was dead, Sennacherib his son reigned in his stead; whose estate was troubled, that I could not go into Media.

[16] And in the time of Enemessar I gave many alms to my brethren, and gave my bread to the hungry,

[17] And my clothes to the naked: and if I saw any of my nation dead, or cast about the walls of Nineve, I buried him.

[18] And if the king Sennacherib had slain any, when he was come, and fled from Judea, I buried them privily; for in his wrath he killed many; but the bodies were not found, when they were sought for of the king.

[19] And when one of the Ninevites went and complained of me to the king, that I buried them, and hid myself; understanding that I was sought for to be put to death, I withdrew myself for fear.

[20] Then all my goods were forcibly taken away, neither was there any thing left me, beside my wife Anna and my son Tobias.

[21] And there passed not five and fifty days, before two of his sons killed him, and they fled into the mountains of Ararath; and Sarchedonus his son reigned in his stead; who appointed over his father's accounts, and over all his affairs, Achiacharus my brother Anael's son.

[22] And Achiacharus intreating for me, I returned to Nineve. Now Achiacharus was cupbearer, and keeper of the signet, and steward, and overseer of the accounts: and Sarchedonus appointed him next unto him: and he was my brother's son.

Tob.2

[1] Now when I was come home again, and my wife Anna was restored unto me, with my son Tobias, in the feast of Pentecost, which is the holy feast of the seven weeks, there was a good dinner prepared me, in the which I sat down to eat.
[2] And when I saw abundance of meat, I said to my son, Go and bring what poor man soever thou shalt find out of our brethren, who is mindful of Jah; and, lo, I tarry for thee.
[3] But he came again, and said, Father, one of our nation is strangled, and is cast out in the marketplace.
[4] Then before I had tasted of any meat, I started up, and took him up into a room until the going down of the sun.
[5] Then I returned, and washed myself, and ate my meat in heaviness,
[6] Remembering that prophecy of Amos, as he said, Your feasts shall be turned into mourning, and all your mirth into lamentation.
[7] Therefore I wept: and after the going down of the sun I went and made a grave, and buried him.
[8] But my neighbours mocked me, and said, This man is not yet afraid to be put to death for this matter: who fled away; and yet, lo, he burieth the dead again.
[9] The same night also I returned from the burial, and slept by the wall of my courtyard, being polluted and my face was uncovered:
[10] And I knew not that there were sparrows in the wall, and mine eyes being open, the sparrows muted warm dung into mine eyes, and a whiteness came in mine eyes: and I went to the physicians, but they helped me not: moreover Achiacharus did nourish me, until I went into Elymais.
[11] And my wife Anna did take women's works to do.
[12] And when she had sent them home to the owners, they paid her wages, and gave her also besides a kid.
[13] And when it was in my house, and began to cry, I said unto her, From whence is this kid? is it not stolen? render it to the owners; for it is not lawful to eat any thing that is stolen.
[14] But she replied upon me, It was given for a gift more than the wages. Howbeit I did not believe her, but bade her render it to the owners: and I was abashed at her. But she replied upon me, Where are thine alms and thy righteous deeds? behold, thou and all thy works are known.

Tob. 3

[1] Then I being grieved did weep, and in my sorrow prayed, saying,
[2] O Lord, thou art just, and all thy works and all thy ways are mercy and truth, and thou judgest truly and justly for ever.
[3] Remember me, and look on me, punish me not for my sins and ignorances, and the sins of mg fathers, who have sinned before thee:
[4] For they obeyed not thy commandments: wherefore thou hast delivered us for a spoil, and unto captivity, and unto death, and for a proverb of reproach to all the nations among whom we are dispersed.
[5] And now thy judgments are many and true: deal with me according to my sins and my fathers': because we have not kept thy commandments, neither have walked in truth before thee.
[6] Now therefore deal with me as seemeth best unto thee, and command my spirit to be taken from me, that I may be dissolved, and become earth: for it is profitable for me to die rather than to live, because I have heard false reproaches, and have much sorrow: command therefore that I may now be delivered out of this distress, and go into the everlasting place: turn not thy face away from me.
[7] It came to pass the same day, that in

Ecbatane a city of Media Sara the daughter of Raguel was also reproached by her father's maids;
[8] Because that she had been married to seven husbands, whom Asmodeus the evil spirit had killed, before they had lain with her. Dost thou not know, said they, that thou hast strangled thine husbands? thou hast had already seven husbands, neither wast thou named after any of them.
[9] Wherefore dost thou beat us for them? if they be dead, go thy ways after them, let us never see of thee either son or daughter.
[10] Whe she heard these things, she was very sorrowful, so that she thought to have strangled herself; and she said, I am the only daughter of my father, and if I do this, it shall be a reproach unto him, and I shall bring his old age with sorrow unto the grave.
[11] Then she prayed toward the window, and said, Blessed art thou, O Lord my God, and thine holy and glorious name is blessed and honourable for ever: let all thy works praise thee for ever.
[12] And now, O Lord, I set I mine eyes and my face toward thee,
[13] And say, Take me out of the earth, that I may hear no more the reproach.
[14] Thou knowest, Lord, that I am pure from all sin with man,
[15] And that I never polluted my name, nor the name of my father, in the land of my captivity: I am the only daughter of my father, neither hath he any child to be his heir, neither any near kinsman, nor any son of his alive, to whom I may keep myself for a wife: my seven husbands are already dead; and why should I live? but if it please not thee that I should die, command some regard to be had of me, and pity taken of me, that I hear no more reproach.
[16] So the prayers of them both were heard before the majesty of the great God.
[17] And Raphael was sent to heal them both, that is, to scale away the whiteness of Tobit's eyes, and to give Sara the daughter of Raguel for a wife to Tobias the son of Tobit; and to bind Asmodeus the evil spirit; because she belonged to Tobias by right of inheritance. The selfsame time came Tobit home, and entered into his house, and Sara the daughter of Raguel came down from her upper chamber.

Tob.4

[1] In that day Tobit remembered the money which he had committed to Gabael in Rages of Media,
[2] And said with himself, I have wished for death; wherefore do I not call for my son Tobias that I may signify to him of the money before I die?
[3] And when he had called him, he said, My son, when I am dead, bury me; and despise not thy mother, but honour her all the days of thy life, and do that which shall please her, and grieve her not.
[4] Remember, my son, that she saw many dangers for thee, when thou wast in her womb: and when she is dead, bury her by me in one grave.
[5] My son, be mindful of Jah our God all thy days, and let not thy will be set to sin, or to transgress his commandments: do uprightly all thy life long, and follow not the ways of unrighteousness.
[6] For if thou deal truly, thy doings shall prosperously succeed to thee, and to all them that live justly.
[7] Give alms of thy substance; and when thou givest alms, let not thine eye be envious, neither turn thy face from any poor, and the face of God shall not be turned away from thee.
[8] If thou hast abundance give alms accordingly: if thou have but a little, be not afraid to give according to that little:
[9] For thou layest up a good treasure for thyself against the day of necessity.
[10] Because that alms do deliver from

death, and suffereth not to come into darkness.

[11] For alms is a good gift unto all that give it in the sight of the most High.

[12] Beware of all whoredom, my son, and chiefly take a wife of the seed of thy fathers, and take not a strange woman to wife, which is not of thy father's tribe: for we are the children of the prophets, Noe, Abraham, Isaac, and Jacob: remember, my son, that our fathers from the beginning, even that they all married wives of their own kindred, and were blessed in their children, and their seed shall inherit the land.

[13] Now therefore, my son, love thy brethren, and despise not in thy heart thy brethren, the sons and daughters of thy people, in not taking a wife of them: for in pride is destruction and much trouble, and in lewdness is decay and great want: for lewdness is the mother of famine.

[14] Let not the wages of any man, which hath wrought for thee, tarry with thee, but give him it out of hand: for if thou serve God, he will also repay thee: be circumspect my son, in all things thou doest, and be wise in all thy conversation.

[15] Do that to no man which thou hatest: drink not wine to make thee drunken: neither let drunkenness go with thee in thy journey.

[16] Give of thy bread to the hungry, and of thy garments to them that are naked; and according to thine abundance give alms: and let not thine eye be envious, when thou givest alms.

[17] Pour out thy bread on the burial of the just, but give nothing to the wicked.

[18] Ask counsel of all that are wise, and despise not any counsel that is profitable.

[19] Bless Jah thy God alway, and desire of him that thy ways may be directed, and that all thy paths and counsels may prosper: for every nation hath not counsel; but Jah himself giveth all good things, and he humbleth whom he will, as he will; now therefore, my son, remember my commandments, neither let them be put out of thy mind.

[20] And now I signify this to they that I committed ten talents to Gabael the son of Gabrias at Rages in Media.

[21] And fear not, my son, that we are made poor: for thou hast much wealth, if thou fear God, and depart from all sin, and do that which is pleasing in his sight.

Tob.5

[1] Tobias then answered and said, Father, I will do all things which thou hast commanded me:

[2] But how can I receive the money, seeing I know him not?

[3] Then he gave him the handwriting, and said unto him, Seek thee a man which may go with thee, whiles I yet live, and I will give him wages: and go and receive the money.

[4] Therefore when he went to seek a man, he found Raphael that was an angel.

[5] But he knew not; and he said unto him, Canst thou go with me to Rages? and knowest thou those places well?

[6] To whom the angel said, I will go with thee, and I know the way well: for I have lodged with our brother Gabael.

[7] Then Tobias said unto him, Tarry for me, till I tell my father.

[8] Then he said unto him, Go and tarry not. So he went in and said to his father, Behold, I have found one which will go with me. Then he said, Call him unto me, that I may know of what tribe he is, and whether he be a trusty man to go with thee.

[9] So he called him, and he came in, and they saluted one another.

[10] Then Tobit said unto him, Brother, shew me of what tribe and family thou art.

[11] To whom he said, Dost thou seek for a tribe or family, or an hired man to go with

thy son? Then Tobit said unto him, I would know, brother, thy kindred and name.
[12] Then he said, I am Azarias, the son of Ananias the great, and of thy brethren.
[13] Then Tobit said, Thou art welcome, brother; be not now angry with me, because I have enquired to know thy tribe and thy family; for thou art my brother, of an honest and good stock: for I know Ananias and Jonathas, sons of that great Samaias, as we went together to Jerusalem to worship, and offered the firstborn, and the tenths of the fruits; and they were not seduced with the error of our brethren: my brother, thou art of a good stock.
[14] But tell me, what wages shall I give thee? wilt thou a drachm a day, and things necessary, as to mine own son?
[15] Yea, moreover, if ye return safe, I will add something to thy wages.
[16] So they were well pleased. Then said he to Tobias, Prepare thyself for the journey, and God send you a good journey. And when his son had prepared all things far the journey, his father said, Go thou with this man, and God, which dwelleth in heaven, prosper your journey, and the angel of God keep you company. So they went forth both, and the young man's dog with them.
[17] But Anna his mother wept, and said to Tobit, Why hast thou sent away our son? is he not the staff of our hand, in going in and out before us?
[18] Be not greedy to add money to money: but let it be as refuse in respect of our child.
[19] For that which Jah hath given us to live with doth suffice us.
[20] Then said Tobit to her, Take no care, my sister; he shall return in safety, and thine eyes shall see him.
[21] For the good angel will keep him company, and his journey shall be prosperous, and he shall return safe.
[22] Then she made an end of weeping.

Tob.6

[1] And as they went on their journey, they came in the evening to the river Tigris, and they lodged there.
[2] And when the young man went down to wash himself, a fish leaped out of the river, and would have devoured him.
[3] Then the angel said unto him, Take the fish. And the young man laid hold of the fish, and drew it to land.
[4] To whom the angel said, Open the fish, and take the heart and the liver and the gall, and put them up safely.
[5] So the young man did as the angel commanded him; and when they had roasted the fish, they did eat it: then they both went on their way, till they drew near to Ecbatane.
[6] Then the young man said to the angel, Brother Azarias, to what use is the heart and the liver and the gal of the fish?
[7] And he said unto him, Touching the heart and the liver, if a devil or an evil spirit trouble any, we must make a smoke thereof before the man or the woman, and the party shall be no more vexed.
[8] As for the gall, it is good to anoint a man that hath whiteness in his eyes, and he shall be healed.
[9] And when they were come near to Rages,
[10] The angel said to the young man, Brother, to day we shall lodge with Raguel, who is thy cousin; he also hath one only daughter, named Sara; I will speak for her, that she may be given thee for a wife.
[11] For to thee doth the right of her appertain, seeing thou only art of her kindred.
[12] And the maid is fair and wise: now therefore hear me, and I will speak to her father; and when we return from Rages we will celebrate the marriage: for I know that Raguel cannot marry her to another according to the law of Moses, but he shall be guilty of death, because the right of

inheritance doth rather appertain to thee than to any other.

[13] Then the young man answered the angel, I have heard, brother Azarias that this maid hath been given to seven men, who all died in the marriage chamber.

[14] And now I am the only son of my father, and I am afraid, lest if I go in unto her, I die, as the other before: for a wicked spirit loveth her, which hurteth no body, but those which come unto her; wherefore I also fear lest I die, and bring my father's and my mother's life because of me to the grave with sorrow: for they have no other son to bury them.

[15] Then the angel said unto him, Dost thou not remember the precepts which thy father gave thee, that thou shouldest marry a wife of thine own kindred? wherefore hear me, O my brother; for she shall be given thee to wife; and make thou no reckoning of the evil spirit; for this same night shall she be given thee in marriage.

[16] And when thou shalt come into the marriage chamber, thou shalt take the ashes of perfume, and shalt lay upon them some of the heart and liver of the fish, and shalt make a smoke with it:

[17] And the devil shall smell it, and flee away, and never come again any more: but when thou shalt come to her, rise up both of you, and pray to God which is merciful, who will have pity on you, and save you: fear not, for she is appointed unto thee from the beginning; and thou shalt preserve her, and she shall go with thee. Moreover I suppose that she shall bear thee children. Now when Tobias had heard these things, he loved her, and his heart was effectually joined to her.

Tob.7

[1] And when they were come to Ecbatane, they came to the house of Raguel, and Sara met them: and after they had saluted one another, she brought them into the house.

[2] Then said Raguel to Edna his wife, How like is this young man to Tobit my cousin!

[3] And Raguel asked them, From whence are ye, brethren? To whom they said, We are of the sons of Nephthalim, which are captives in Nineve.

[4] Then he said to them, Do ye know Tobit our kinsman? And they said, We know him. Then said he, Is he in good health?

[5] And they said, He is both alive, and in good health: and Tobias said, He is my father.

[6] Then Raguel leaped up, and kissed him, and wept,

[7] And blessed him, and said unto him, Thou art the son of an honest and good man. But when he had heard that Tobit was blind, he was sorrowful, and wept.

[8] And likewise Edna his wife and Sara his daughter wept. Moreover they entertained them cheerfully; and after that they had killed a ram of the flock, they set store of meat on the table. Then said Tobias to Raphael, Brother Azarias, speak of those things of which thou didst talk in the way, and let this business be dispatched.

[9] So he communicated the matter with Raguel: and Raguel said to Tobias, Eat and drink, and make merry:

[10] For it is meet that thou shouldest marry my daughter: nevertheless I will declare unto thee the truth.

[11] I have given my daughter in marriage te seven men, who died that night they came in unto her: nevertheless for the present be merry. But Tobias said, I will eat nothing here, till we agree and swear one to another.

[12] Raguel said, Then take her from henceforth according to the manner, for thou art her cousin, and she is thine, and the merciful God give you good success in all things.

[13] Then he called his daughter Sara, and she came to her father, and he took her by the hand, and gave her to be wife to Tobias,

saying, Behold, take her after the law of Moses, and lead her away to thy father. And he blessed them;

[14] And called Edna his wife, and took paper, and did write an instrument of covenants, and sealed it.

[15] Then they began to eat.

[16] After Raguel called his wife Edna, and said unto her, Sister, prepare another chamber, and bring her in thither.

[17] Which when she had done as he had bidden her, she brought her thither: and she wept, and she received the tears of her daughter, and said unto her,

[18] Be of good comfort, my daughter; Jah of heaven and earth give thee joy for this thy sorrow: be of good comfort, my daughter.

Tob.8

[1] And when they had supped, they brought Tobias in unto her.

[2] And as he went, he remembered the words of Raphael, and took the ashes of the perfumes, and put the heart and the liver of the fish thereupon, and made a smoke therewith.

[3] The which smell when the evil spirit had smelled, he fled into the utmost parts of Egypt, and the angel bound him.

[4] And after that they were both shut in together, Tobias rose out of the bed, and said, Sister, arise, and let us pray that God would have pity on us.

[5] Then began Tobias to say, Blessed art thou, O God of our fathers, and blessed is thy holy and glorious name for ever; let the heavens bless thee, and all thy creatures.

[6] Thou madest Adam, and gavest him Eve his wife for an helper and stay: of them came mankind: thou hast said, It is not good that man should be alone; let us make unto him an aid like unto himself.

[7] And now, O Lord, I take not this my sister for lush but uprightly: therefore mercifully ordain that we may become aged together.

[8] And she said with him, Amen.

[9] So they slept both that night. And Raguel arose, and went and made a grave,

[10] Saying, I fear lest he also be dead.

[11] But when Raguel was come into his house,

[12] He said unto his wife Edna. Send one of the maids, and let her see whether he be alive: if he be not, that we may bury him, and no man know it.

[13] So the maid opened the door, and went in, and found them both asleep,

[14] And came forth, and told them that he was alive.

[15] Then Raguel praised God, and said, O God, thou art worthy to be praised with all pure and holy praise; therefore let thy saints praise thee with all thy creatures; and let all thine angels and thine elect praise thee for ever.

[16] Thou art to be praised, for thou hast made me joyful; and that is not come to me which I suspected; but thou hast dealt with us according to thy great mercy.

[17] Thou art to be praised because thou hast had mercy of two that were the only begotten children of their fathers: grant them mercy, O Lord, and finish their life in health with joy and mercy.

[18] Then Raguel bade his servants to fill the grave.

[19] And he kept the wedding feast fourteen days.

[20] For before the days of the marriage were finished, Raguel had said unto him by an oath, that he should not depart till the fourteen days of the marriage were expired;

[21] And then he should take the half of his goods, and go in safety to his father; and should have the rest when I and my wife be dead.

Tob.9

[1] Then Tobias called Raphael, and said unto him,
[2] Brother Azarias, take with thee a servant, and two camels, and go to Rages of Media to Gabael, and bring me the money, and bring him to the wedding.
[3] For Raguel hath sworn that I shall not depart.
[4] But my father counteth the days; and if I tarry long, he will be very sorry.
[5] So Raphael went out, and lodged with Gabael, and gave him the handwriting: who brought forth bags which were sealed up, and gave them to him.
[6] And early in the morning they went forth both together, and came to the wedding: and Tobias blessed his wife.

Tob. 10

[1] Now Tobit his father counted every day: and when the days of the journey were expired, and they came not,
[2] Then Tobit said, Are they detained? or is Gabael dead, and there is no man to give him the money?
[3] Therefore he was very sorry.
[4] Then his wife said unto him, My son is dead, seeing he stayeth long; and she began to wail him, and said,
[5] Now I care for nothing, my son, since I have let thee go, the light of mine eyes.
[6] To whom Tobit said, Hold thy peace, take no care, for he is safe.
[7] But she said, Hold thy peace, and deceive me not; my son is dead. And she went out every day into the way which they went, and did eat no meat on the daytime, and ceased not whole nights to bewail her son Tobias, until the fourteen days of the wedding were expired, which Raguel had sworn that he should spend there. Then Tobias said to Raguel, Let me go, for my father and my mother look no more to see me.

[8] But his father in law said unto him, Tarry with me, and I will send to thy father, and they shall declare unto him how things go with thee.
[9] But Tobias said, No; but let me go to my father.
[10] Then Raguel arose, and gave him Sara his wife, and half his goods, servants, and cattle, and money:
[11] And he blessed them, and sent them away, saying, The God of heaven give you a prosperous journey, my children.
[12] And he said to his daughter, Honour thy father and thy mother in law, which are now thy parents, that I may hear good report of thee. And he kissed her. Edna also said to Tobias, Jah of heaven restore thee, my dear brother, and grant that I may see thy children of my daughter Sara before I die, that I may rejoice before Jah: behold, I commit my daughter unto thee of special trust; where are do not entreat her evil.

Tob. 11

[1] After these things Tobias went his way, praising God that he had given him a prosperous journey, and blessed Raguel and Edna his wife, and went on his way till they drew near unto Nineve.
[2] Then Raphael said to Tobias, Thou knowest, brother, how thou didst leave thy father:
[3] Let us haste before thy wife, and prepare the house.
[4] And take in thine hand the gall of the fish. So they went their way, and the dog went after them.
[5] Now Anna sat looking about toward the way for her son.
[6] And when she espied him coming, she said to his father, Behold, thy son cometh, and the man that went with him.
[7] Then said Raphael, I know, Tobias, that thy father will open his eyes.

[8] Therefore anoint thou his eyes with the gall, and being pricked therewith, he shall rub, and the whiteness shall fall away, and he shall see thee.
[9] Then Anna ran forth, and fell upon the neck of her son, and said unto him, Seeing I have seen thee, my son, from henceforth I am content to die. And they wept both.
[10] Tobit also went forth toward the door, and stumbled: but his son ran unto him,
[11] And took hold of his father: and he strake of the gall on his fathers' eyes, saying, Be of good hope, my father.
[12] And when his eyes began to smart, he rubbed them;
[13] And the whiteness pilled away from the corners of his eyes: and when he saw his son, he fell upon his neck.
[14] And he wept, and said, Blessed art thou, O God, and blessed is thy name for ever; and blessed are all thine holy angels:
[15] For thou hast scourged, and hast taken pity on me: for, behold, I see my son Tobias. And his son went in rejoicing, and told his father the great things that had happened to him in Media.
[16] Then Tobit went out to meet his daughter in law at the gate of Nineve, rejoicing and praising God: and they which saw him go marvelled, because he had received his sight.
[17] But Tobias gave thanks before them, because God had mercy on him. And when he came near to Sara his daughter in law, he blessed her, saying, Thou art welcome, daughter: God be blessed, which hath brought thee unto us, and blessed be thy father and thy mother. And there was joy among all his brethren which were at Nineve.
[18] And Achiacharus, and Nasbas his brother's son, came:
[19] And Tobias' wedding was kept seven days with great joy.

Tob.12

[1] Then Tobit called his son Tobias, and said unto him, My son, see that the man have his wages, which went with thee, and thou must give him more.
[2] And Tobias said unto him, O father, it is no harm to me to give him half of those things which I have brought:
[3] For he hath brought me again to thee in safety, and made whole my wife, and brought me the money, and likewise healed thee.
[4] Then the old man said, It is due unto him.
[5] So he called the angel, and he said unto him, Take half of all that ye have brought and go away in safety.
[6] Then he took them both apart, and said unto them, Bless God, praise him, and magnify him, and praise him for the things which he hath done unto you in the sight of all that live. It is good to praise God, and exalt his name, and honourably to shew forth the works of God; therefore be not slack to praise him.
[7] It is good to keep close the secret of a king, but it is honourable to reveal the works of God. Do that which is good, and no evil shall touch you.
[8] Prayer is good with fasting and alms and righteousness. A little with righteousness is better than much with unrighteousness. It is better to give alms than to lay up gold:
[9] For alms doth deliver from death, and shall purge away all sin. Those that exercise alms and righteousness shall be filled with life:
[10] But they that sin are enemies to their own life.
[11] Surely I will keep close nothing from you. For I said, It was good to keep close the secret of a king, but that it was honourable to reveal the works of God.
[12] Now therefore, when thou didst pray, and Sara thy daughter in law, I did bring the

remembrance of your prayers before the Holy One: and when thou didst bury the dead, I was with thee likewise.
[13] And when thou didst not delay to rise up, and leave thy dinner, to go and cover the dead, thy good deed was not hid from me: but I was with thee.
[14] And now God hath sent me to heal thee and Sara thy daughter in law.
[15] I am Raphael, one of the seven holy angels, which present the prayers of the saints, and which go in and out before the glory of the Holy One.
[16] Then they were both troubled, and fell upon their faces: for they feared.
[17] But he said unto them, Fear not, for it shall go well with you; praise God therefore.
[18] For not of any favour of mine, but by the will of our God I came; wherefore praise him for ever.
[19] All these days I did appear unto you; but I did neither eat nor drink, but ye did see a vision.
[20] Now therefore give God thanks: for I go up to him that sent me; but write all things which are done in a book.
[21] And when they arose, they saw him no more.
[22] Then they confessed the great and wonderful works of God, and how the angel of Jah had appeared unto them.

Tob. 13

[1] Then Tobit wrote a prayer of rejoicing, and said, Blessed be God that liveth for ever, and blessed be his kingdom.
[2] For he doth scourge, and hath mercy: he leadeth down to hell, and bringeth up again: neither is there any that can avoid his hand.
[3] Confess him before the Gentiles, ye children of Israel: for he hath scattered us among them.
[4] There declare his greatness, and extol him before all the living: for he is our Lord, and he is the God our Father for ever.
[5] And he will scourge us for our iniquities, and will have mercy again, and will gather us out of all nations, among whom he hath scattered us.
[6] If ye turn to him with your whole heart, and with your whole mind, and deal uprightly before him, then will he turn unto you, and will not hide his face from you. Therefore see what he will do with you, and confess him with your whole mouth, and praise Jah of might, and extol the everlasting King. In the land of my captivity do I praise him, and declare his might and majesty to a sinful nation. O ye sinners, turn and do justice before him: who can tell if he will accept you, and have mercy on you?
[7] I will extol my God, and my soul shall praise the King of heaven, and shall rejoice in his greatness.
[8] Let all men speak, and let all praise him for his righteousness.
[9] O Jerusalem, the holy city, he will scourge thee for thy children's works, and will have mercy again on the sons of the righteous.
[10] Give praise to Jah, for he is good: and praise the everlasting King, that his tabernacle may be builded in thee again with joy, and let him make joyful there in thee those that are captives, and love in thee for ever those that are miserable.
[11] Many nations shall come from far to the name of Jah God with gifts in their hands, even gifts to the King of heaven; all generations shall praise thee with great joy.
[12] Cursed are all they which hate thee, and blessed shall all be which love thee for ever.
[13] Rejoice and be glad for the children of the just: for they shall be gathered together, and shall bless Jah of the just.
[14] O blessed are they which love thee, for they shall rejoice in thy peace: blessed are they which have been sorrowful for all thy scourges; for they shall rejoice for thee, when they have seen all thy glory, and shall

be glad for ever.
[15] Let my soul bless God the great King.
[16] For Jerusalem shall be built up with sapphires and emeralds, and precious stone: thy walls and towers and battlements with pure gold.
[17] And the streets of Jerusalem shall be paved with beryl and carbuncle and stones of Ophir.
[18] And all her streets shall say, Alleluia; and they shall praise him, saying, Blessed be God, which hath extolled it for ever.

Tob. 14

[1] So Tobit made an end of praising God.
[2] And he was eight and fifty years old when he lost his sight, which was restored to him after eight years: and he gave alms, and he increased in the fear of Jah God, and praised him.
[3] And when he was very aged he called his son, and the sons of his son, and said to him, My son, take thy children; for, behold, I am aged, and am ready to depart out of this life.
[4] Go into Media my son, for I surely believe those things which Jonas the prophet spake of Nineve, that it shall be overthrown; and that for a time peace shall rather be in Media; and that our brethren shall lie scattered in the earth from that good land: and Jerusalem shall be desolate, and the house of God in it shall be burned, and shall be desolate for a time;
[5] And that again God will have mercy on them, and bring them again into the land, where they shall build a temple, but not like to the first, until the time of that age be fulfilled; and afterward they shall return from all places of their captivity, and build up Jerusalem gloriously, and the house of God shall be built in it for ever with a glorious building, as the prophets have spoken thereof.
[6] And all nations shall turn, and fear Jah God truly, and shall bury their idols.
[7] So shall all nations praise Jah, and his people shall confess God, and Jah shall exalt his people; and all those which love Jah God in truth and justice shall rejoice, shewing mercy to our brethren.
[8] And now, my son, depart out of Nineve, because that those things which the prophet Jonas spake shall surely come to pass.
[9] But keep thou the law and the commandments, and shew thyself merciful and just, that it may go well with thee.
[10] And bury me decently, and thy mother with me; but tarry no longer at Nineve. Remember, my son, how Aman handled Achiacharus that brought him up, how out of light he brought him into darkness, and how he rewarded him again: yet Achiacharus was saved, but the other had his reward: for he went down into darkness. Manasses gave alms, and escaped the snares of death which they had set for him: but Aman fell into the snare, and perished.
[11] Wherefore now, my son, consider what alms doeth, and how righteousness doth deliver. When he had said these things, he gave up the ghost in the bed, being an hundred and eight and fifty years old; and he buried him honourably.
[12] And when Anna his mother was dead, he buried her with his father. But Tobias departed with his wife and children to Ecbatane to Raguel his father in law,
[13] Where he became old with honour, and he buried his father and mother in law honourably, and he inherited their substance, and his father Tobit's.
[14] And he died at Ecbatane in Media, being an hundred and seven and twenty years old.
[15] But before he died he heard of the

destruction of Nineve, which was taken by Nabuchodonosor and Assuerus: and before his death he rejoiced over Nineve.

Judith

Jdt.1

[1] In the twelfth year of the reign of Nabuchodonosor, who reigned in Nineve, the great city; in the days of Arphaxad, which reigned over the Medes in Ecbatane,
[2] And built in Ecbatane walls round about of stones hewn three cubits broad and six cubits long, and made the height of the wall seventy cubits, and the breadth thereof fifty cubits:
[3] And set the towers thereof upon the gates of it an hundred cubits high, and the breadth thereof in the foundation threescore cubits:
[4] And he made the gates thereof, even gates that were raised to the height of seventy cubits, and the breadth of them was forty cubits, for the going forth of his mighty armies, and for the setting in array of his footmen:
[5] Even in those days king Nabuchodonosor made war with king Arphaxad in the great plain, which is the plain in the borders of Ragau.
[6] And there came unto him all they that dwelt in the hill country, and all that dwelt by Euphrates, and Tigris and Hydaspes, and the plain of Arioch the king of the Elymeans, and very many nations of the sons of Chelod, assembled themselves to the battle.
[7] Then Nabuchodonosor king of the Assyrians sent unto all that dwelt in Persia, and to all that dwelt westward, and to those that dwelt in Cilicia, and Damascus, and Libanus, and Antilibanus, and to all that dwelt upon the sea coast,
[8] And to those among the nations that were of Carmel, and Galaad, and the higher Galilee, and the great plain of Esdrelom,
[9] And to all that were in Samaria and the cities thereof, and beyond Jordan unto Jerusalem, and Betane, and Chelus, and Kades, and the river of Egypt, and Taphnes, and Ramesse, and all the land of Gesem,
[10] Until ye come beyond Tanis and Memphis, and to all the inhabitants of Egypt, until ye come to the borders of Ethiopia.
[11] But all the inhabitants of the land made light of the commandment of Nabuchodonosor king of the Assyrians, neither went they with him to the battle; for they were not afraid of him: yea, he was before them as one man, and they sent away his ambassadors from them without effect, and with disgrace.
[12] Therefore Nabuchodonosor was very angry with all this country, and sware by his throne and kingdom, that he would surely be avenged upon all those coasts of Cilicia, and Damascus, and Syria, and that he would slay with the sword all the inhabitants of the land of Moab, and the children of Ammon, and all Judea, and all that were in Egypt, till ye come to the borders of the two seas.
[13] Then he marched in battle array with his power against king Arphaxad in the seventeenth year, and he prevailed in his battle: for he overthrew all the power of Arphaxad, and all his horsemen, and all his chariots,
[14] And became lord of his cities, and came unto Ecbatane, and took the towers, and spoiled the streets thereof, and turned the beauty thereof into shame.
[15] He took also Arphaxad in the mountains of Ragau, and smote him through with his darts, and destroyed him utterly that day.
[16] So he returned afterward to Nineve, both he and all his company of sundry

nations being a very great multitude of men of war, and there he took his ease, and banqueted, both he and his army, an hundred and twenty days.

Jdt.2

[1] And in the eighteenth year, the two and twentieth day of the first month, there was talk in the house of Nabuchodonosor king of the Assyrians that he should, as he said, avenge himself on all the earth.
[2] So he called unto him all his officers, and all his nobles, and communicated with them his secret counsel, and concluded the afflicting of the whole earth out of his own mouth.
[3] Then they decreed to destroy all flesh, that did not obey the commandment of his mouth.
[4] And when he had ended his counsel, Nabuchodonosor king of the Assyrians called Holofernes the chief captain of his army, which was next unto him, and said unto him.
[5] Thus saith the great king, Jah of the whole earth, Behold, thou shalt go forth from my presence, and take with thee men that trust in their own strength, of footmen an hundred and twenty thousand; and the number of horses with their riders twelve thousand.
[6] And thou shalt go against all the west country, because they disobeyed my commandment.
[7] And thou shalt declare unto that they prepare for me earth and water: for I will go forth in my wrath against them and will cover the whole face of the earth with the feet of mine army, and I will give them for a spoil unto them:
[8] So that their slain shall fill their valleys and brooks and the river shall be filled with their dead, till it overflow:
[9] And I will lead them captives to the utmost parts of all the earth.
[10] Thou therefore shalt go forth. and take beforehand for me all their coasts: and if they will yield themselves unto thee, thou shalt reserve them for me till the day of their punishment.
[11] But concerning them that rebel, let not thine eye spare them; but put them to the slaughter, and spoil them wheresoever thou goest.
[12] For as I live, and by the power of my kingdom, whatsoever I have spoken, that will I do by mine hand.
[13] And take thou heed that thou transgress none of the commandments of thy lord, but accomplish them fully, as I have commanded thee, and defer not to do them.
[14] Then Holofernes went forth from the presence of his lord, and called ail the governors and captains, and the officers of the army of Assur;
[15] And he mustered the chosen men for the battle, as his lord had commanded him, unto an hundred and twenty thousand, and twelve thousand archers on horseback;
[16] And he ranged them, as a great army is ordered for the war.
[17] And he took camels and asses for their carriages, a very great number; and sheep and oxen and goats without number for their provision:
[18] And plenty of victual for every man of the army, and very much gold and silver out of the king's house.
[19] Then he went forth and all his power to go before king Nabuchodonosor in the voyage, and to cover all the face of the earth westward with their chariots, and horsemen, and their chosen footmen.
[20] A great number also sundry countries came with them like locusts, and like the sand of the earth: for the multitude was without number.
[21] And they went forth of Nineve three days' journey toward the plain of Bectileth, and pitched from Bectileth near the

mountain which is at the left hand of the upper Cilicia.

[22] Then he took all his army, his footmen, and horsemen and chariots, and went from thence into the hill country;

[23] And destroyed Phud and Lud, and spoiled all the children of Rasses, and the children of Israel, which were toward the wilderness at the south of the land of the Chellians.

[24] Then he went over Euphrates, and went through Mesopotamia, and destroyed all the high cities that were upon the river Arbonai, till ye come to the sea.

[25] And he took the borders of Cilicia, and killed all that resisted him, and came to the borders of Japheth, which were toward the south, over against Arabia.

[26] He compassed also all the children of Madian, and burned up their tabernacles, and spoiled their sheepcotes.

[27] Then he went down into the plain of Damascus in the time of wheat harvest, and burnt up all their fields, and destroyed their flocks and herds, also he spoiled their cities, and utterly wasted their countries, and smote all their young men with the edge of the sword.

[28] Therefore the fear and dread of him fell upon all the inhabitants of the sea coasts, which were in Sidon and Tyrus, and them that dwelt in Sur and Ocina, and all that dwelt in Jemnaan; and they that dwelt in Azotus and Ascalon feared him greatly.

Jdt. 3

[1] So they sent ambassadors unto him to treat of peace, saying,

[2] Behold, we the servants of Nabuchodonosor the great king lie before thee; use us as shall be good in thy sight.

[3] Behold, our houses, and all our places, and all our fields of wheat, and flocks, and herds, and all the lodges of our tents lie before thy face; use them as it pleaseth thee.

[4] Behold, even our cities and the inhabitants thereof are thy servants; come and deal with them as seemeth good unto thee.

[5] So the men came to Holofernes, and declared unto him after this manner.

[6] Then came he down toward the sea coast, both he and his army, and set garrisons in the high cities, and took out of them chosen men for aid.

[7] So they and all the country round about received them with garlands, with dances, and with timbrels.

[8] Yet he did cast down their frontiers, and cut down their groves: for he had decreed to destroy all the gods of the land, that all nations should worship Nabuchodonosor only, and that all tongues and tribes should call upon him as god.

[9] Also he came over against Esdraelon near unto Judea, over against the great strait of Judea.

[10] And he pitched between Geba and Scythopolis, and there he tarried a whole month, that he might gather together all the carriages of his army.

Jdt. 4

[1] Now the children of Israel, that dwelt in Judea, heard all that Holofernes the chief captain of Nabuchodonosor king of the Assyrians had done to the nations, and after what manner he had spoiled all their temples, and brought them to nought.

[2] Therefore they were exceedingly afraid of him, and were troubled for Jerusalem, and for the temple of Jah their God:

[3] For they were newly returned from the captivity, and all the people of Judea were lately gathered together: and the vessels, and the altar, and the house, were sanctified after the profanation.

[4] Therefore they sent into all the coasts of

Samaria, and the villages and to Bethoron, and Belmen, and Jericho, and to Choba, and Esora, and to the valley of Salem:

[5] And possessed themselves beforehand of all the tops of the high mountains, and fortified the villages that were in them, and laid up victuals for the provision of war: for their fields were of late reaped.

[6] Also Joacim the high priest, which was in those days in Jerusalem, wrote to them that dwelt in Bethulia, and Betomestham, which is over against Esdraelon toward the open country, near to Dothaim,

[7] Charging them to keep the passages of the hill country: for by them there was an entrance into Judea, and it was easy to stop them that would come up, because the passage was straight, for two men at the most.

[8] And the children of Israel did as Joacim the high priest had commanded them, with the ancients of all the people of Israel, which dwelt at Jerusalem.

[9] Then every man of Israel cried to God with great fervency, and with great vehemency did they humble their souls:

[10] Both they, and their wives and their children, and their cattle, and every stranger and hireling, and their servants bought with money, put sackcloth upon their loins.

[11] Thus every man and women, and the little children, and the inhabitants of Jerusalem, fell before the temple, and cast ashes upon their heads, and spread out their sackcloth before the face of Jah: also they put sackcloth about the altar,

[12] And cried to the God of Israel all with one consent earnestly, that he would not give their children for a prey, and their wives for a spoil, and the cities of their inheritance to destruction, and the sanctuary to profanation and reproach, and for the nations to rejoice at.

[13] So God heard their prayers, and looked upon their afflictions: for the people fasted many days in all Judea and Jerusalem before the sanctuary of Jah Almighty.

[14] And Joacim the high priest, and all the priests that stood before Jah, and they which ministered unto Jah, had their loins girt with sackcloth, and offered the daily burnt offerings, with the vows and free gifts of the people,

[15] And had ashes on their mitres, and cried unto Jah with all their power, that he would look upon all the house of Israel graciously.

Jdt.5

[1] Then was it declared to Holofernes, the chief captain of the army of Assur, that the children of Israel had prepared for war, and had shut up the passages of the hill country, and had fortified all the tops of the high hills and had laid impediments in the champaign countries:

[2] Wherewith he was very angry, and called all the princes of Moab, and the captains of Ammon, and all the governors of the sea coast,

[3] And he said unto them, Tell me now, ye sons of Chanaan, who this people is, that dwelleth in the hill country, and what are the cities that they inhabit, and what is the multitude of their army, and wherein is their power and strength, and what king is set over them, or captain of their army;

[4] And why have they determined not to come and meet me, more than all the inhabitants of the west.

[5] Then said Achior, the captain of all the sons of Ammon, Let my lord now hear a word from the mouth of thy servant, and I will declare unto thee the truth concerning this people, which dwelleth near thee, and inhabiteth the hill countries: and there shall no lie come out of the mouth of thy servant.

[6] This people are descended of the Chaldeans:

[7] And they sojourned heretofore in

Mesopotamia, because they would not follow the gods of their fathers, which were in the land of Chaldea.

[8] For they left the way of their ancestors, and worshipped the God of heaven, the God whom they knew: so they cast them out from the face of their gods, and they fled into Mesopotamia, and sojourned there many days.

[9] Then their God commanded them to depart from the place where they sojourned, and to go into the land of Chanaan: where they dwelt, and were increased with gold and silver, and with very much cattle.

[10] But when a famine covered all the land of Chanaan, they went down into Egypt, and sojourned there, while they were nourished, and became there a great multitude, so that one could not number their nation.

[11] Therefore the king of Egypt rose up against them, and dealt subtilly with them, and brought them low with labouring in brick, and made them slaves.

[12] Then they cried unto their God, and he smote all the land of Egypt with incurable plagues: so the Egyptians cast them out of their sight.

[13] And God dried the Red sea before them,

[14] And brought them to mount Sina, and Cades-Barne, and cast forth all that dwelt in the wilderness.

[15] So they dwelt in the land of the Amorites, and they destroyed by their strength all them of Esebon, and passing over Jordan they possessed all the hill country.

[16] And they cast forth before them the Chanaanite, the Pherezite, the Jebusite, and the Sychemite, and all the Gergesites, and they dwelt in that country many days.

[17] And whilst they sinned not before their God, they prospered, because the God that hateth iniquity was with them.

[18] But when they departed from the way which he appointed them, they were destroyed in many battles very sore, and were led captives into a land that was not their's, and the temple of their God was cast to the ground, and their cities were taken by the enemies.

[19] But now are they returned to their God, and are come up from the places where they were scattered, and have possessed Jerusalem, where their sanctuary is, and are seated in the hill country; for it was desolate.

[20] Now therefore, my lord and governor, if there be any error against this people, and they sin against their God, let us consider that this shall be their ruin, and let us go up, and we shall overcome them.

[21] But if there be no iniquity in their nation, let my lord now pass by, lest their Lord defend them, and their God be for them, and we become a reproach before all the world.

[22] And when Achior had finished these sayings, all the people standing round about the tent murmured, and the chief men of Holofernes, and all that dwelt by the sea side, and in Moab, spake that he should kill him.

[23] For, say they, we will not be afraid of the face of the children of Israel: for, lo, it is a people that have no strength nor power for a strong battle

[24] Now therefore, lord Holofernes, we will go up, and they shall be a prey to be devoured of all thine army.

Jdt. 6

[1] And when the tumult of men that were about the council was ceased, Holofernes the chief captain of the army of Assur said unto Achior and all the Moabites before all the company of other nations,

[2] And who art thou, Achior, and the hirelings of Ephraim, that thou hast prophesied against us as to day, and hast said, that we should not make war with the

people of Israel, because their God will defend them? and who is God but Nabuchodonosor?

[3] He will send his power, and will destroy them from the face of the earth, and their God shall not deliver them: but we his servants will destroy them as one man; for they are not able to sustain the power of our horses.

[4] For with them we will tread them under foot, and their mountains shall be drunken with their blood, and their fields shall be filled with their dead bodies, and their footsteps shall not be able to stand before us, for they shall utterly perish, saith king Nabuchodonosor, lord of all the earth: for he said, None of my words shall be in vain.

[5] And thou, Achior, an hireling of Ammon, which hast spoken these words in the day of thine iniquity, shalt see my face no more from this day, until I take vengeance of this nation that came out of Egypt.

[6] And then shall the sword of mine army, and the multitude of them that serve me, pass through thy sides, and thou shalt fall among their slain, when I return.

[7] Now therefore my servants shall bring thee back into the hill country, and shall set thee in one of the cities of the passages:

[8] And thou shalt not perish, till thou be destroyed with them.

[9] And if thou persuade thyself in thy mind that they shall be taken, let not thy countenance fall: I have spoken it, and none of my words shall be in vain.

[10] Then Holofernes commanded his servants, that waited in his tent, to take Achior, and bring him to Bethulia, and deliver him into the hands of the children of Israel.

[11] So his servants took him, and brought him out of the camp into the plain, and they went from the midst of the plain into the hill country, and came unto the fountains that were under Bethulia.

[12] And when the men of the city saw them, they took up their weapons, and went out of the city to the top of the hill: and every man that used a sling kept them from coming up by casting of stones against them.

[13] Nevertheless having gotten privily under the hill, they bound Achior, and cast him down, and left him at the foot of the hill, and returned to their lord.

[14] But the Israelites descended from their city, and came unto him, and loosed him, and brought him to Bethulia, and presented him to the governors of the city:

[15] Which were in those days Ozias the son of Micha, of the tribe of Simeon, and Chabris the son of Gothoniel, and Charmis the son of Melchiel.

[16] And they called together all the ancients of the city, and all their youth ran together, and their women, to the assembly, and they set Achior in the midst of all their people. Then Ozias asked him of that which was done.

[17] And he answered and declared unto them the words of the council of Holofernes, and all the words that he had spoken in the midst of the princes of Assur, and whatsoever Holofernes had spoken proudly against the house of Israel.

[18] Then the people fell down and worshipped God, and cried unto God. saying,

[19] O Lord God of heaven, behold their pride, and pity the low estate of our nation, and look upon the face of those that are sanctified unto thee this day.

[20] Then they comforted Achior, and praised him greatly.

[21] And Ozias took him out of the assembly unto his house, and made a feast to the elders; and they called on the God of Israel all that night for help.

Jdt.7

[1] The next day Holofernes commanded all his army, and all his people which were come to take his part, that they should remove their camp against Bethulia, to take aforehand the ascents of the hill country, and to make war against the children of Israel.
[2] Then their strong men removed their camps in that day, and the army of the men of war was an hundred and seventy thousand footmen, and twelve thousand horsemen, beside the baggage, and other men that were afoot among them, a very great multitude.
[3] And they camped in the valley near unto Bethulia, by the fountain, and they spread themselves in breadth over Dothaim even to Belmaim, and in length from Bethulia unto Cynamon, which is over against Esdraelon.
[4] Now the children of Israel, when they saw the multitude of them, were greatly troubled, and said every one to his neighbour, Now will these men lick up the face of the earth; for neither the high mountains, nor the valleys, nor the hills, are able to bear their weight.
[5] Then every man took up his weapons of war, and when they had kindled fires upon their towers, they remained and watched all that night.
[6] But in the second day Holofernes brought forth all his horsemen in the sight of the children of Israel which were in Bethulia,
[7] And viewed the passages up to the city, and came to the fountains of their waters, and took them, and set garrisons of men of war over them, and he himself removed toward his people.
[8] Then came unto him all the chief of the children of Esau, and all the governors of the people of Moab, and the captains of the sea coast, and said,
[9] Let our lord now hear a word, that there be not an overthrow in thine army.
[10] For this people of the children of Israel do not trust in their spears, but in the height of the mountains wherein they dwell, because it is not easy to come up to the tops of their mountains.
[11] Now therefore, my lord, fight not against them in battle array, and there shall not so much as one man of thy people perish.
[12] Remain in thy camp, and keep all the men of thine army, and let thy servants get into their hands the fountain of water, which issueth forth of the foot of the mountain:
[13] For all the inhabitants of Bethulia have their water thence; so shall thirst kill them, and they shall give up their city, and we and our people shall go up to the tops of the mountains that are near, and will camp upon them, to watch that none go out of the city.
[14] So they and their wives and their children shall be consumed with fire, and before the sword come against them, they shall be overthrown in the streets where they dwell.
[15] Thus shalt thou render them an evil reward; because they rebelled, and met not thy person peaceably.
[16] And these words pleased Holofernes and all his servants, and he appointed to do as they had spoken.
[17] So the camp of the children of Ammon departed, and with them five thousand of the Assyrians, and they pitched in the valley, and took the waters, and the fountains of the waters of the children of Israel.
[18] Then the children of Esau went up with the children of Ammon, and camped in the hill country over against Dothaim: and they sent some of them toward the south, and toward the east over against Ekrebel, which is near unto Chusi, that is upon the brook Mochmur; and the rest of the army of the Assyrians camped in the plain, and covered the face of the whole land; and their tents and carriages were pitched to a very great multitude.
[19] Then the children of Israel cried unto Jah their God, because their heart failed, for all their enemies had compassed them round

about, and there was no way to escape out from among them.

[20] Thus all the company of Assur remained about them, both their footmen, chariots, and horsemen, four and thirty days, so that all their vessels of water failed all the inhabitants of Bethulia.

[21] And the cisterns were emptied, and they had not water to drink their fill for one day; for they gave them drink by measure.

[22] Therefore their young children were out of heart, and their women and young men fainted for thirst, and fell down in the streets of the city, and by the passages of the gates, and there was no longer any strength in them.

[23] Then all the people assembled to Ozias, and to the chief of the city, both young men, and women, and children, and cried with a loud voice, and said before all the elders,

[24] God be judge between us and you: for ye have done us great injury, in that ye have not required peace of the children of Assur.

[25] For now we have no helper: but God hath sold us into their hands, that we should be thrown down before them with thirst and great destruction.

[26] Now therefore call them unto you, and deliver the whole city for a spoil to the people of Holofernes, and to all his army.

[27] For it is better for us to be made a spoil unto them, than to die for thirst: for we will be his servants, that our souls may live, and not see the death of our infants before our eyes, nor our wives nor our children to die.

[28] We take to witness against you the heaven and the earth, and our God and Lord of our fathers, which punisheth us according to our sins and the sins of our fathers, that he do not according as we have said this day.

[29] Then there was great weeping with one consent in the midst of the assembly; and they cried unto Jah God with a loud voice.

[30] Then said Ozias to them, Brethren, be of good courage, let us yet endure five days, in the which space Jah our God may turn his mercy toward us; for he will not forsake us utterly.

[31] And if these days pass, and there come no help unto us, I will do according to your word.

[32] And he dispersed the people, every one to their own charge; and they went unto the walls and towers of their city, and sent the women and children into their houses: and they were very low brought in the city.

Jdt. 8

[1] Now at that time Judith heard thereof, which was the daughter of Merari, the son of Ox, the son of Joseph, the son of Ozel, the son of Elcia, the son of Ananias, the son of Gedeon, the son of Raphaim, the son of Acitho, the son of Eliu, the son of Eliab, the son of Nathanael, the son of Samael, the son of Salasadal, the son of Israel.

[2] And Manasses was her husband, of her tribe and kindred, who died in the barley harvest.

[3] For as he stood overseeing them that bound sheaves in the field, the heat came upon his head, and he fell on his bed, and died in the city of Bethulia: and they buried him with his fathers in the field between Dothaim and Balamo.

[4] So Judith was a widow in her house three years and four months.

[5] And she made her a tent upon the top of her house, and put on sackcloth upon her loins and ware her widow's apparel.

[6] And she fasted all the days of her widowhood, save the eves of the sabbaths, and the sabbaths, and the eves of the new moons, and the new moons and the feasts and solemn days of the house of Israel.

[7] She was also of a goodly countenance, and very beautiful to behold: and her husband Manasses had left her gold, and silver, and menservants and maidservants, and cattle, and lands; and she remained upon

them.

[8] And there was none that gave her an ill word; ar she feared God greatly.

[9] Now when she heard the evil words of the people against the governor, that they fainted for lack of water; for Judith had heard all the words that Ozias had spoken unto them, and that he had sworn to deliver the city unto the Assyrians after five days;

[10] Then she sent her waitingwoman, that had the government of all things that she had, to call Ozias and Chabris and Charmis, the ancients of the city.

[11] And they came unto her, and she said unto them, Hear me now, O ye governors of the inhabitants of Bethulia: for your words that ye have spoken before the people this day are not right, touching this oath which ye made and pronounced between God and you, and have promised to deliver the city to our enemies, unless within these days Jah turn to help you.

[12] And now who are ye that have tempted God this day, and stand instead of God among the children of men?

[13] And now try Jah Almighty, but ye shall never know any thing.

[14] For ye cannot find the depth of the heart of man, neither can ye perceive the things that he thinketh: then how can ye search out God, that hath made all these things, and know his mind, or comprehend his purpose? Nay, my brethren, provoke not Jah our God to anger.

[15] For if he will not help us within these five days, he hath power to defend us when he will, even every day, or to destroy us before our enemies.

[16] Do not bind the counsels of Jah our God: for God is not as man, that he may be threatened; neither is he as the son of man, that he should be wavering.

[17] Therefore let us wait for salvation of him, and call upon him to help us, and he will hear our voice, if it please him.

[18] For there arose none in our age, neither is there any now in these days neither tribe, nor family, nor people, nor city among us, which worship gods made with hands, as hath been aforetime.

[19] For the which cause our fathers were given to the sword, and for a spoil, and had a great fall before our enemies.

[20] But we know none other god, therefore we trust that he will not dispise us, nor any of our nation.

[21] For if we be taken so, all Judea shall lie waste, and our sanctuary shall be spoiled; and he will require the profanation thereof at our mouth.

[22] And the slaughter of our brethren, and the captivity of the country, and the desolation of our inheritance, will he turn upon our heads among the Gentiles, wheresoever we shall be in bondage; and we shall be an offence and a reproach to all them that possess us.

[23] For our servitude shall not be directed to favour: but Jah our God shall turn it to dishonour.

[24] Now therefore, O brethren, let us shew an example to our brethren, because their hearts depend upon us, and the sanctuary, and the house, and the altar, rest upon us.

[25] Moreover let us give thanks to Jah our God, which trieth us, even as he did our fathers.

[26] Remember what things he did to Abraham, and how he tried Isaac, and what happened to Jacob in Mesopotamia of Syria, when he kept the sheep of Laban his mother's brother.

[27] For he hath not tried us in the fire, as he did them, for the examination of their hearts, neither hath he taken vengeance on us: but Jah doth scourge them that come near unto him, to admonish them.

[28] Then said Ozias to her, All that thou hast spoken hast thou spoken with a good heart, and there is none that may gainsay thy words.

[29] For this is not the first day wherein thy

wisdom is manifested; but from the beginning of thy days all the people have known thy understanding, because the disposition of thine heart is good.
[30] But the people were very thirsty, and compelled us to do unto them as we have spoken, and to bring an oath upon ourselves, which we will not break.
[31] Therefore now pray thou for us, because thou art a godly woman, and Jah will send us rain to fill our cisterns, and we shall faint no more.
[32] Then said Judith unto them, Hear me, and I will do a thing, which shall go throughout all generations to the children of our nation.
[33] Ye shall stand this night in the gate, and I will go forth with my waitingwoman: and within the days that ye have promised to deliver the city to our enemies Jah will visit Israel by mine hand.
[34] But enquire not ye of mine act: for I will not declare it unto you, till the things be finished that I do.
[35] Then said Ozias and the princes unto her, Go in peace, and Jah God be before thee, to take vengeance on our enemies.
[36] So they returned from the tent, and went to their wards.

Jdt. 9

[1] Judith fell upon her face, and put ashes upon her head, and uncovered the sackcloth wherewith she was clothed; and about the time that the incense of that evening was offered in Jerusalem in the house of Jah Judith cried with a loud voice, and said,
[2] O Lord God of my father Simeon, to whom thou gavest a sword to take vengeance of the strangers, who loosened the girdle of a maid to defile her, and discovered the thigh to her shame, and polluted her virginity to her reproach; for thou saidst, It shall not be so; and yet they did so:
[3] Wherefore thou gavest their rulers to be slain, so that they dyed their bed in blood, being deceived, and smotest the servants with their lords, and Jahs upon their thrones;
[4] And hast given their wives for a prey, and their daughters to be captives, and all their spoils to be divided among thy dear children; which were moved with thy zeal, and abhorred the pollution of their blood, and called upon thee for aid: O God, O my God, hear me also a widow.
[5] For thou hast wrought not only those things, but also the things which fell out before, and which ensued after; thou hast thought upon the things which are now, and which are to come.
[6] Yea, what things thou didst determine were ready at hand, and said, Lo, we are here: for all thy ways are prepared, and thy judgments are in thy foreknowledge.
[7] For, behold, the Assyrians are multiplied in their power; they are exalted with horse and man; they glory in the strength of their footmen; they trust in shield, and spear, and bow, and sling; and know not that thou art Jah that breakest the battles: Jah is thy name.
[8] Throw down their strength in thy power, and bring down their force in thy wrath: for they have purposed to defile thy sanctuary, and to pollute the tabernacle where thy glorious name resteth and to cast down with sword the horn of thy altar.
[9] Behold their pride, and send thy wrath upon their heads: give into mine hand, which am a widow, the power that I have conceived.
[10] Smite by the deceit of my lips the servant with the prince, and the prince with the servant: break down their stateliness by the hand of a woman.
[11] For thy power standeth not in multitude nor thy might in strong men: for thou art a God of the afflicted, an helper of the oppressed, an upholder of the weak, a protector of the forlorn, a saviour of them

that are without hope.

[12] I pray thee, I pray thee, O God of my father, and God of the inheritance of Israel, Lord of the heavens and earth, Creator of the waters, king of every creature, hear thou my prayer:

[13] And make my speech and deceit to be their wound and stripe, who have purposed cruel things against thy covenant, and thy hallowed house, and against the top of Sion, and against the house of the possession of thy children.

[14] And make every nation and tribe to acknowledge that thou art the God of all power and might, and that there is none other that protecteth the people of Israel but thou.

Jdt. 10

[1] Now after that she had ceased to cry unto the God of Israel, and bad made an end of all these words.

[2] She rose where she had fallen down, and called her maid, and went down into the house in the which she abode in the sabbath days, and in her feast days,

[3] And pulled off the sackcloth which she had on, and put off the garments of her widowhood, and washed her body all over with water, and anointed herself with precious ointment, and braided the hair of her head, and put on a tire upon it, and put on her garments of gladness, wherewith she was clad during the life of Manasses her husband.

[4] And she took sandals upon her feet, and put about her her bracelets, and her chains, and her rings, and her earrings, and all her ornaments, and decked herself bravely, to allure the eyes of all men that should see her.

[5] Then she gave her maid a bottle of wine, and a cruse of oil, and filled a bag with parched corn, and lumps of figs, and with fine bread; so she folded all these things together, and laid them upon her.

[6] Thus they went forth to the gate of the city of Bethulia, and found standing there Ozias and the ancients of the city, Chabris and Charmis.

[7] And when they saw her, that her countenance was altered, and her apparel was changed, they wondered at her beauty very greatly, and said unto her.

[8] The God, the God of our fathers give thee favour, and accomplish thine enterprizes to the glory of the children of Israel, and to the exaltation of Jerusalem. Then they worshipped God.

[9] And she said unto them, Command the gates of the city to be opened unto me, that I may go forth to accomplish the things whereof ye have spoken with me. So they commanded the young men to open unto her, as she had spoken.

[10] And when they had done so, Judith went out, she, and her maid with her; and the men of the city looked after her, until she was gone down the mountain, and till she had passed the valley, and could see her no more.

[11] Thus they went straight forth in the valley: and the first watch of the Assyrians met her,

[12] And took her, and asked her, Of what people art thou? and whence comest thou? and whither goest thou? And she said, I am a woman of the Hebrews, and am fled from them: for they shall be given you to be consumed:

[13] And I am coming before Holofernes the chief captain of your army, to declare words of truth; and I will shew him a way, whereby he shall go, and win all the hill country, without losing the body or life of any one of his men.

[14] Now when the men heard her words, and beheld her countenance, they wondered greatly at her beauty, and said unto her,

[15] Thou hast saved thy life, in that thou

hast hasted to come down to the presence of our lord: now therefore come to his tent, and some of us shall conduct thee, until they have delivered thee to his hands.
[16] And when thou standest before him, be not afraid in thine heart, but shew unto him according to thy word; and he will entreat thee well.
[17] Then they chose out of them an hundred men to accompany her and her maid; and they brought her to the tent of Holofernes.
[18] Then was there a concourse throughout all the camp: for her coming was noised among the tents, and they came about her, as she stood without the tent of Holofernes, till they told him of her.
[19] And they wondered at her beauty, and admired the children of Israel because of her, and every one said to his neighbour, Who would despise this people, that have among them such women? surely it is not good that one man of them be left who being let go might deceive the whole earth.
[20] And they that lay near Holofernes went out, and all his servants and they brought her into the tent.
[21] Now Holofernes rested upon his bed under a canopy, which was woven with purple, and gold, and emeralds, and precious stones.
[22] So they shewed him of her; and he came out before his tent with silver lamps going before him.
[23] And when Judith was come before him and his servants they all marvelled at the beauty of her countenance; and she fell down upon her face, and did reverence unto him: and his servants took her up.

Jdt.11

[1] Then said Holofernes unto her, Woman, be of good comfort, fear not in thine heart: for I never hurt any that was willing to serve Nabuchodonosor, the king of all the earth.
[2] Now therefore, if thy people that dwelleth in the mountains had not set light by me, I would not have lifted up my spear against them: but they have done these things to themselves.
[3] But now tell me wherefore thou art fled from them, and art come unto us: for thou art come for safeguard; be of good comfort, thou shalt live this night, and hereafter:
[4] For none shall hurt thee, but entreat thee well, as they do the servants of king Nabuchodonosor my lord.
[5] Then Judith said unto him, Receive the words of thy servant, and suffer thine handmaid to speak in thy presence, and I will declare no lie to my lord this night.
[6] And if thou wilt follow the words of thine handmaid, God will bring the thing perfectly to pass by thee; and my lord shall not fail of his purposes.
[7] As Nabuchodonosor king of all the earth liveth, and as his power liveth, who hath sent thee for the upholding of every living thing: for not only men shall serve him by thee, but also the beasts of the field, and the cattle, and the fowls of the air, shall live by thy power under Nabuchodonosor and all his house.
[8] For we have heard of thy wisdom and thy policies, and it is reported in all the earth, that thou only art excellent in all the kingdom, and mighty in knowledge, and wonderful in feats of war.
[9] Now as concerning the matter, which Achior did speak in thy council, we have heard his words; for the men of Bethulia saved him, and he declared unto them all that he had spoken unto thee.
[10] Therefore, O lord and governor, respect not his word; but lay it up in thine heart, for it is true: for our nation shall not be punished, neither can sword prevail against them, except they sin against their God.
[11] And now, that my lord be not defeated and frustrate of his purpose, even death is

now fallen upon them, and their sin hath overtaken them, wherewith they will provoke their God to anger whensoever they shall do that which is not fit to be done:

[12] For their victuals fail them, and all their water is scant, and they have determined to lay hands upon their cattle, and purposed to consume all those things, that God hath forbidden them to eat by his laws:

[13] And are resolved to spend the firstfruits of the the tenths of wine and oil, which they had sanctified, and reserved for the priests that serve in Jerusalem before the face of our God; the which things it is not lawful for any of the people so much as to touch with their hands.

[14] For they have sent some to Jerusalem, because they also that dwell there have done the like, to bring them a licence from the senate.

[15] Now when they shall bring them word, they will forthwith do it, and they shall be given to thee to be destroyed the same day.

[16] Wherefore I thine handmaid, knowing all this, am fled from their presence; and God hath sent me to work things with thee, whereat all the earth shall be astonished, and whosoever shall hear it.

[17] For thy servant is religious, and serveth the God of heaven day and night: now therefore, my lord, I will remain with thee, and thy servant will go out by night into the valley, and I will pray unto God, and he will tell me when they have committed their sins:

[18] And I will come and shew it unto thee: then thou shalt go forth with all thine army, and there shall be none of them that shall resist thee.

[19] And I will lead thee through the midst of Judea, until thou come before Jerusalem; and I will set thy throne in the midst thereof; and thou shalt drive them as sheep that have no shepherd, and a dog shall not so much as open his mouth at thee: for these things were told me according to my foreknowledge, and they were declared unto me, and I am sent to tell thee.

[20] Then her words pleased Holofernes and all his servants; and they marvelled at her wisdom, and said,

[21] There is not such a woman from one end of the earth to the other, both for beauty of face, and wisdom of words.

[22] Likewise Holofernes said unto her. God hath done well to send thee before the people, that strength might be in our hands and destruction upon them that lightly regard my lord.

[23] And now thou art both beautiful in thy countenance, and witty in thy words: surely if thou do as thou hast spoken thy God shall be my God, and thou shalt dwell in the house of king Nabuchodonosor, and shalt be renowned through the whole earth.

Jdt. 12

[1] Then he commanded to bring her in where his plate was set; and bade that they should prepare for her of his own meats, and that she should drink of his own wine.

[2] And Judith said, I will not eat thereof, lest there be an offence: but provision shall be made for me of the things that I have brought.

[3] Then Holofernes said unto her, If thy provision should fail, how should we give thee the like? for there be none with us of thy nation.

[4] Then said Judith unto him As thy soul liveth, my lord, thine handmaid shall not spend those things that I have, before Jah work by mine hand the things that he hath determined.

[5] Then the servants of Holofernes brought her into the tent, and she slept till midnight, and she arose when it was toward the morning watch,

[6] And sent to Holofernes, saving, Let my lord now command that thine handmaid may go forth unto prayer.

[7] Then Holofernes commanded his guard that they should not stay her: thus she abode in the camp three days, and went out in the night into the valley of Bethulia, and washed herself in a fountain of water by the camp.
[8] And when she came out, she besought Jah God of Israel to direct her way to the raising up of the children of her people.
[9] So she came in clean, and remained in the tent, until she did eat her meat at evening.
[10] And in the fourth day Holofernes made a feast to his own servants only, and called none of the officers to the banquet.
[11] Then said he to Bagoas the eunuch, who had charge over all that he had, Go now, and persuade this Hebrew woman which is with thee, that she come unto us, and eat and drink with us.
[12] For, lo, it will be a shame for our person, if we shall let such a woman go, not having had her company; for if we draw her not unto us, she will laugh us to scorn.
[13] Then went Bagoas from the presence of Holofernes, and came to her, and he said, Let not this fair damsel fear to come to my lord, and to be honoured in his presence, and drink wine, and be merry with us and be made this day as one of the daughters of the Assyrians, which serve in the house of Nabuchodonosor.
[14] Then said Judith unto him, Who am I now, that I should gainsay my lord? surely whatsoever pleaseth him I will do speedily, and it shall be my joy unto the day of my death.
[15] So she arose, and decked herself with her apparel and all her woman's attire, and her maid went and laid soft skins on the ground for her over against Holofernes, which she had received of Bagoas far her daily use, that she might sit and eat upon them.
[16] Now when Judith came in and sat down, Holofernes his heart was ravished with her, and his mind was moved, and he desired greatly her company; for he waited a time to deceive her, from the day that he had seen her.
[17] Then said Holofernes unto her, Drink now, and be merry with us.
[18] So Judith said, I will drink now, my lord, because my life is magnified in me this day more than all the days since I was born.
[19] Then she took and ate and drank before him what her maid had prepared.
[20] And Holofernes took great delight in her, and drank more wine than he had drunk at any time in one day since he was born.

Jdt.13

[1] Now when the evening was come, his servants made haste to depart, and Bagoas shut his tent without, and dismissed the waiters from the presence of his lord; and they went to their beds: for they were all weary, because the feast had been long.
[2] And Judith was left along in the tent, and Holofernes lying along upon his bed: for he was filled with wine.
[3] Now Judith had commanded her maid to stand without her bedchamber, and to wait for her. coming forth, as she did daily: for she said she would go forth to her prayers, and she spake to Bagoas according to the same purpose.
[4] So all went forth and none was left in the bedchamber, neither little nor great. Then Judith, standing by his bed, said in her heart, O Lord God of all power, look at this present upon the works of mine hands for the exaltation of Jerusalem.
[5] For now is the time to help thine inheritance, and to execute thine enterprizes to the destruction of the enemies which are risen against us.
[6] Then she came to the pillar of the bed, which was at Holofernes' head, and took down his fauchion from thence,
[7] And approached to his bed, and took

hold of the hair of his head, and said, Strengthen me, O Lord God of Israel, this day.
[8] And she smote twice upon his neck with all her might, and she took away his head from him.
[9] And tumbled his body down from the bed, and pulled down the canopy from the pillars; and anon after she went forth, and gave Holofernes his head to her maid;
[10] And she put it in her bag of meat: so they twain went together according to their custom unto prayer: and when they passed the camp, they compassed the valley, and went up the mountain of Bethulia, and came to the gates thereof.
[11] Then said Judith afar off, to the watchmen at the gate, Open, open now the gate: God, even our God, is with us, to shew his power yet in Jerusalem, and his forces against the enemy, as he hath even done this day.
[12] Now when the men of her city heard her voice, they made haste to go down to the gate of their city, and they called the elders of the city.
[13] And then they ran all together, both small and great, for it was strange unto them that she was come: so they opened the gate, and received them, and made a fire for a light, and stood round about them.
[14] Then she said to them with a loud voice, Praise, praise God, praise God, I say, for he hath not taken away his mercy from the house of Israel, but hath destroyed our enemies by mine hands this night.
[15] So she took the head out of the bag, and shewed it, and said unto them, behold the head of Holofernes, the chief captain of the army of Assur, and behold the canopy, wherein he did lie in his drunkenness; and Jah hath smitten him by the hand of a woman.
[16] As Jah liveth, who hath kept me in my way that I went, my countenance hath deceived him to his destruction, and yet hath he not committed sin with me, to defile and shame me.
[17] Then all the people were wonderfully astonished, and bowed themselves and worshipped God, and said with one accord, Blessed be thou, O our God, which hast this day brought to nought the enemies of thy people.
[18] Then said Ozias unto her, O daughter, blessed art thou of the most high God above all the women upon the earth; and blessed be Jah God, which hath created the heavens and the earth, which hath directed thee to the cutting off of the head of the chief of our enemies.
[19] For this thy confidence shall not depart from the heart of men, which remember the power of God for ever.
[20] And God turn these things to thee for a perpetual praise, to visit thee in good things because thou hast not spared thy life for the affliction of our nation, but hast revenged our ruin, walking a straight way before our God. And all the people said; So be it, so be it.

Jdt.14

[1] Then said Judith unto them, Hear me now, my brethren, and take this head, and hang it upon the highest place of your walls.
[2] And so soon as the morning shall appear, and the sun shall come forth upon the earth, take ye every one his weapons, and go forth every valiant man out of the city, and set ye a captain over them, as though ye would go down into the field toward the watch of the Assyrians; but go not down.
[3] Then they shall take their armour, and shall go into their camp, and raise up the captains of the army of Assur, and shall run to the tent of Holofernes, but shall not find him: then fear shall fall upon them, and they shall flee before your face.
[4] So ye, and all that inhabit the coast of

Israel, shall pursue them, and overthrow them as they go.
[5] But before ye do these things, call me Achior the Ammonite, that he may see and know him that despised the house of Israel, and that sent him to us as it were to his death.
[6] Then they called Achior out of the house of Ozias; and when he was come, and saw the head of Holofernes in a man's hand in the assembly of the people, he fell down on his face, and his spirit failed.
[7] But when they had recovered him, he fell at Judith's feet, and reverenced her, and said, Blessed art thou in all the tabernacles of Juda, and in all nations, which hearing thy name shall be astonished.
[8] Now therefore tell me all the things that thou hast done in these days. Then Judith declared unto him in the midst of the people all that she had done, from the day that she went forth until that hour she spake unto them.
[9] And when she had left off speaking, the people shouted with a loud voice, and made a joyful noise in their city.
[10] And when Achior had seen all that the God of Israel had done, he believed in God greatly, and circumcised the flesh of his foreskin, and was joined unto the house of Israel unto this day.
[11] And as soon as the morning arose, they hanged the head of Holofernes upon the wall, and every man took his weapons, and they went forth by bands unto the straits of the mountain.
[12] But when the Assyrians saw them, they sent to their leaders, which came to their captains and tribunes, and to every one of their rulers.
[13] So they came to Holofernes' tent, and said to him that had the charge of all his things, Waken now our lord: for the slaves have been bold to come down against us to battle, that they may be utterly destroyed.
[14] Then went in Bagoas, and knocked at the door of the tent; for he thought that he had slept with Judith.
[15] But because none answered, he opened it, and went into the bedchamber, and found him cast upon the floor dead, and his head was taken from him.
[16] Therefore he cried with a loud voice, with weeping, and sighing, and a mighty cry, and rent his garments.
[17] After he went into the tent where Judith lodged: and when he found her not, he leaped out to the people, and cried,
[18] These slaves have dealt treacherously; one woman of the Hebrews hath brought shame upon the house of king Nabuchodonosor: for, behold, Holofernes lieth upon the ground without a head.
[19] When the captains of the Assyrians' army heard these words, they rent their coats and their minds were wonderfully troubled, and there was a cry and a very great noise throughout the camp.

Jdt. 15

[1] And when they that were in the tents heard, they were astonished at the thing that was done.
[2] And fear and trembling fell upon them, so that there was no man that durst abide in the sight of his neighbour, but rushing out all together, they fled into every way of the plain, and of the hill country.
[3] They also that had camped in the mountains round about Bethulia fled away. Then the children of Israel, every one that was a warrior among them, rushed out upon them.
[4] Then sent Ozias to Betomasthem, and to Bebai, and Chobai, and Cola and to all the coasts of Israel, such as should tell the things that were done, and that all should rush forth upon their enemies to destroy them.
[5] Now when the children of Israel heard it,

they all fell upon them with one consent, and slew them unto Chobai: likewise also they that came from Jerusalem, and from all the hill country, (for men had told them what things were done in the camp of their enemies) and they that were in Galaad, and in Galilee, chased them with a great slaughter, until they were past Damascus and the borders thereof.
[6] And the residue that dwelt at Bethulia, fell upon the camp of Assur, and spoiled them, and were greatly enriched.
[7] And the children of Israel that returned from the slaughter had that which remained; and the villages and the cities, that were in the mountains and in the plain, gat many spoils: for the multitude was very great.
[8] Then Joacim the high priest, and the ancients of the children of Israel that dwelt in Jerusalem, came to behold the good things that God had shewed to Israel, and to see Judith, and to salute her.
[9] And when they came unto her, they blessed her with one accord, and said unto her, Thou art the exaltation of Jerusalem, thou art the great glory of Israel, thou art the great rejoicing of our nation:
[10] Thou hast done all these things by thine hand: thou hast done much good to Israel, and God is pleased therewith: blessed be thou of the Almighty Lord for evermore. And all the people said, So be it.
[11] And the people spoiled the camp the space of thirty days: and they gave unto Judith Holofernes his tent, and all his plate, and beds, and vessels, and all his stuff: and she took it and laid it on her mule; and made ready her carts, and laid them thereon.
[12] Then all the women of Israel ran together to see her, and blessed her, and made a dance among them for her: and she took branches in her hand, and gave also to the women that were with her.
[13] And they put a garland of olive upon her and her maid that was with her, and she went before all the people in the dance, leading all the women: and all the men of Israel followed in their armour with garlands, and with songs in their mouths.

Jdt.16

[1] Then Judith began to sing this thanksgiving in all Israel, and all the people sang after her this song of praise.
[2] And Judith said, Begin unto my God with timbrels, sing unto my Lord with cymbals: tune unto him a new psalm: exalt him, and call upon his name.
[3] For God breaketh the battles: for among the camps in the midst of the people he hath delivered me out of the hands of them that persecuted me.
[4] Assur came out of the mountains from the north, he came with ten thousands of his army, the multitude whereof stopped the torrents, and their horsemen have covered the hills.
[5] He bragged that he would burn up my borders, and kill my young men with the sword, and dash the sucking children against the ground, and make mine infants as a prey, and my virgins as a spoil.
[6] But the Almighty Lord hath disappointed them by the hand of a woman.
[7] For the mighty one did not fall by the young men, neither did the sons of the Titans smite him, nor high giants set upon him: but Judith the daughter of Merari weakened him with the beauty of her countenance.
[8] For she put off the garment of her widowhood for the exaltation of those that were oppressed in Israel, and anointed her face with ointment, and bound her hair in a tire, and took a linen garment to deceive him.
[9] Her sandals ravished his eyes, her beauty

took his mind prisoner, and the fauchion passed through his neck.
[10] The Persians quaked at her boldness, and the Medes were daunted at her hardiness.
[11] Then my afflicted shouted for joy, and my weak ones cried aloud; but they were astonished: these lifted up their voices, but they were overthrown.
[12] The sons of the damsels have pierced them through, and wounded them as fugatives' children: they perished by the battle of Jah.
[13] I will sing unto Jah a new song: O Lord, thou art great and glorious, wonderful in strength, and invincible.
[14] Let all creatures serve thee: for thou spakest, and they were made, thou didst send forth thy spirit, and it created them, and there is none that can resist thy voice.
[15] For the mountains shall be moved from their foundations with the waters, the rocks shall melt as wax at thy presence: yet thou art merciful to them that fear thee.
[16] For all sacrifice is too little for a sweet savour unto thee, and all the fat is not sufficient for thy burnt offering: but he that feareth Jah is great at all times.
[17] Woe to the nations that rise up against my kindred! Jah Almighty will take vengeance of them in the day of judgment, in putting fire and worms in their flesh; and they shall feel them, and weep for ever.
[18] Now as soon as they entered into Jerusalem, they worshipped Jah; and as soon as the people were purified, they offered their burnt offerings, and their free offerings, and their gifts.
[19] Judith also dedicated all the stuff of Holofernes, which the people had given her, and gave the canopy, which she had taken out of his bedchamber, for a gift unto Jah.
[20] So the people continued feasting in Jerusalem before the sanctuary for the space of three months and Judith remained with them.
[21] After this time every one returned to his own inheritance, and Judith went to Bethulia, and remained in her own possession, and was in her time honourable in all the country.
[22] And many desired her, but none knew her all the days of her life, after that Manasses her husband was dead, and was gathered to his people.
[23] But she increased more and more in honour, and waxed old in her husband's house, being an hundred and five years old, and made her maid free; so she died in Bethulia: and they buried her in the cave of her husband Manasses.
[24] And the house of Israel lamented her seven days: and before she died, she did distribute her goods to all them that were nearest of kindred to Manasses her husband, and to them that were the nearest of her kindred.
[25] And there was none that made the children of Israel any more afraid in the days of Judith, nor a long time after her death.

Additions to the Book of Esther

AddEsth.1

[1] Then Mardocheus said, God hath done these things.
[2] For I remember a dream which I saw concerning these matters, and nothing thereof hath failed.
[3] A little fountain became a river, and

there was light, and the sun, and much water: this river is Esther, whom the king married, and made queen:
[4] And the two dragons are I and Aman.
[5] And the nations were those that were assembled to destroy the name of the Jews:
[6] And my nation is this Israel, which cried to God, and were saved: for Jah hath saved his people, and Jah hath delivered us from all those evils, and God hath wrought signs and great wonders, which have not been done among the Gentiles.
[7] Therefore hath he made two lots, one for the people of God, and another for all the Gentiles.
[8] And these two lots came at the hour, and time, and day of judgment, before God among all nations.
[9] So God remembered his people, and justified his inheritance.
[10] Therefore those days shall be unto them in the month Adar, the fourteenth and fifteenth day of the same month, with an assembly, and joy, and with gladness before God, according to the generations for ever among his people.

AddEsth.2

[1] In the fourth year of the reign of Ptolemeus and Cleopatra, Dositheus, who said he was a priest and Levite, and Ptolemeus his son, brought this epistle of Phurim, which they said was the same, and that Lysimachus the son of Ptolemeus, that was in Jerusalem, had interpreted it.
[2] In the second year of the reign of Artexerxes the great, in the first day of the month Nisan, Mardocheus the son of Jairus, the son of Semei, the son of Cisai, of the tribe of Benjamin, had a dream;
[3] Who was a Jew, and dwelt in the city of Susa, a great man, being a servitor in the king's court.
[4] He was also one of the captives, which Nabuchodonosor the king of Babylon carried from Jerusalem with Jechonias king of Judea; and this was his dream:
[5] Behold a noise of a tumult, with thunder, and earthquakes, and uproar in the land:
[6] And, behold, two great dragons came forth ready to fight, and their cry was great.
[7] And at their cry all nations were prepared to battle, that they might fight against the righteous people.
[8] And lo a day of darkness and obscurity, tribulation and anguish, affliction and great uproar, upon earth.
[9] And the whole righteous nation was troubled, fearing their own evils, and were ready to perish.
[10] Then they cried unto God, and upon their cry, as it were from a little fountain, was made a great flood, even much water.
[11] The light and the sun rose up, and the lowly were exalted, and devoured the glorious.
[12] Now when Mardocheus, who had seen this dream, and what God had determined to do, was awake, he bare this dream in mind, and until night by all means was desirous to know it.

AddEsth.3

[1] And Mardocheus took his rest in the court with Gabatha and Tharra, the two eunuchs of the king, and keepers of the palace.
[2] And he heard their devices, and searched out their purposes, and learned that they were about to lay hands upon Artexerxes the king; and so he certified the king of them.
[3] Then the king examined the two eunuchs, and after that they had confessed it, they were strangled.
[4] And the king made a record of these things, and Mardocheus also wrote thereof.
[5] So the king commanded, Mardocheus to serve in the court, and for this he rewarded

him.
[6] Howbeit Aman the son of Amadathus the Agagite, who was in great honour with the king, sought to molest Mardocheus and his people because of the two eunuchs of the king.

AddEsth.4

[1] The copy of the letters was this: The great king Artexerxes writeth these things to the princes and governours that are under him from India unto Ethiopia in an hundred and seven and twenty provinces.
[2] After that I became lord over many nations and had dominion over the whole world, not lifted up with presumption of my authority, but carrying myself always with equity and mildness, I purposed to settle my subjects continually in a quiet life, and making my kingdom peaceable, and open for passage to the utmost coasts, to renew peace, which is desired of all men.
[3] Now when I asked my counsellors how this might be brought to pass, Aman, that excelled in wisdom among us, and was approved for his constant good will and steadfast fidelity, and had the honour of the second place in the kingdom,
[4] Declared unto us, that in all nations throughout the world there was scattered a certain malicious people, that had laws contrary to ail nations, and continually despised the commandments of kings, so as the uniting of our kingdoms, honourably intended by us cannot go forward.
[5] Seeing then we understand that this people alone is continually in opposition unto all men, differing in the strange manner of their laws, and evil affected to our state, working all the mischief they can that our kingdom may not be firmly established:
[6] Therefore have we commanded, that all they that are signified in writing unto you by Aman, who is ordained over the affairs, and is next unto us, shall all, with their wives and children, be utterly destroyed by the sword of their enemies, without all mercy and pity, the fourteenth day of the twelfth month Adar of this present year:
[7] That they, who of old and now also are malicious, may in one day with violence go into the grave, and so ever hereafter cause our affairs to be well settled, and without trouble.
[8] Then Mardocheus thought upon all the works of Jah, and made his prayer unto him,
[9] Saying, O Lord, Lord, the King Almighty: for the whole world is in thy power, and if thou hast appointed to save Israel, there is no man that can gainsay thee:
[10] For thou hast made heaven and earth, and all the wondrous things under the heaven.
[11] Thou art Lord of all things, and and there is no man that can resist thee, which art Jah.
[12] Thou knowest all things, and thou knowest, Lord, that it was neither in contempt nor pride, nor for any desire of glory, that I did not bow down to proud Aman.
[13] For I could have been content with good will for the salvation of Israel to kiss the soles of his feet.
[14] But I did this, that I might not prefer the glory of man above the glory of God: neither will I worship any but thee, O God, neither will I do it in pride.
[15] And now, O Lord God and King, spare thy people: for their eyes are upon us to bring us to nought; yea, they desire to destroy the inheritance, that hath been thine from the beginning.
[16] Despise not the portion, which thou hast delivered out of Egypt for thine own self.
[17] Hear my prayer, and be merciful unto thine inheritance: turn our sorrow into joy, that we may live, O Lord, and praise thy name: and destroy not the mouths of them

that praise thee, O Lord.
[18] All Israel in like manner cried most earnestly unto Jah, because their death was before their eyes.

AddEsth. 5

[1] Queen Esther also, being in fear of death, resorted unto Jah:
[2] And laid away her glorious apparel, and put on the garments of anguish and mourning: and instead of precious ointments, she covered her head with ashes and dung, and she humbled her body greatly, and all the places of her joy she filled with her torn hair.
[3] And she prayed unto Jah God of Israel, saying, O my Lord, thou only art our King: help me, desolate woman, which have no helper but thee:
[4] For my danger is in mine hand.
[5] From my youth up I have heard in the tribe of my family that thou, O Lord, tookest Israel from among all people, and our fathers from all their predecessors, for a perpetual inheritance, and thou hast performed whatsoever thou didst promise them.
[6] And now we have sinned before thee: therefore hast thou given us into the hands of our enemies,
[7] Because we worshipped their gods: O Lord, thou art righteous.
[8] Nevertheless it satisfieth them not, that we are in bitter captivity: but they have stricken hands with their idols,
[9] That they will abolish the thing that thou with thy mouth hast ordained, and destroy thine inheritance, and stop the mouth of them that praise thee, and quench the glory of thy house, and of thine altar,
[10] And open the mouths of the heathen to set forth the praises of the idols, and to magnify a fleshly king for ever.
[11] O Lord, give not thy sceptre unto them that be nothing, and let them not laugh at our fall; but turn their device upon themselves, and make him an example, that hath begun this against us.
[12] Remember, O Lord, make thyself known in time of our affliction, and give me boldness, O King of the nations, and Lord of all power.
[13] Give me eloquent speech in my mouth before the lion: turn his heart to hate him that fighteth against us, that there may be an end of him, and of all that are likeminded to him:
[14] But deliver us with thine hand, and help me that am desolate, and which have no other help but thee.
[15] Thou knowest all things, O Lord; thou knowest that I hate the glory of the unrighteous, and abhor the bed of the uncircumcised, and of all the heathen.
[16] Thou knowest my necessity: for I abhor the sign of my high estate, which is upon mine head in the days wherein I shew myself, and that I abhor it as a menstruous rag, and that I wear it not when I am private by myself.
[17] And that thine handmaid hath not eaten at Aman's table, and that I have not greatly esteemed the king's feast, nor drunk the wine of the drink offerings.
[18] Neither had thine handmaid any joy since the day that I was brought hither to this present, but in thee, O Lord God of Abraham.
[19] O thou mighty God above all, hear the voice of the forlorn and deliver us out of the hands of the mischievous, and deliver me out of my fear.

AddEsth. 6

[1] And upon the third day, when she had ended her prayers, she laid away her mourning garments, and put on her glorious apparel.

[2] And being gloriously adorned, after she had called upon God, who is the beholder and saviour of all things, she took two maids with her:
[3] And upon the one she leaned, as carrying herself daintily;
[4] And the other followed, bearing up her train.
[5] And she was ruddy through the perfection of her beauty, and her countenance was cheerful and very amiable: but her heart was in anguish for fear.
[6] Then having passed through all the doors, she stood before the king, who sat upon his royal throne, and was clothed with all his robes of majesty, all glittering with gold and precious stones; and he was very dreadful.
[7] Then lifting up his countenance that shone with majesty, he looked very fiercely upon her: and the queen fell down, and was pale, and fainted, and bowed herself upon the head of the maid that went before her.
[8] Then God changed the spirit of the king into mildness, who in a fear leaped from his throne, and took her in his arms, till she came to herself again, and comforted her with loving words and said unto her,
[9] Esther, what is the matter? I am thy brother, be of good cheer:
[10] Thou shalt not die, though our our commandment be general: come near.
[11] And so be held up his golden sceptre, and laid it upon her neck,
[12] And embraced her, and said, Speak unto me.
[13] Then said she unto him, I saw thee, my lord, as an angel of God, and my heart was troubled for fear of thy majesty.
[14] For wonderful art thou, lord, and thy countenance is full of grace.
[15] And as she was speaking, she fell down for faintness.
[16] Then the king was troubled, and ail his servants comforted her.

AddEsth. 7

[1] The great king Artexerxes unto the princes and governors of an hundred and seven and twenty provinces from India unto Ethiopia, and unto all our faithful subjects, greeting.
[2] Many, the more often they are honoured with the great bounty of their gracious princes, the more proud they are waxen,
[3] And endeavour to hurt not our subjects only, but not being able to bear abundance, do take in hand to practise also against those that do them good:
[4] And take not only thankfulness away from among men, but also lifted up with the glorious words of lewd persons, that were never good, they think to escape the justice of God, that seeth all things and hateth evil.
[5] Oftentimes also fair speech of those, that are put in trust to manage their friends' affairs, hath caused many that are in authority to be partakers of innocent blood, and hath enwrapped them in remediless calamities:
[6] Beguiling with the falsehood and deceit of their lewd disposition the innocency and goodness of princes.
[7] Now ye may see this, as we have declared, not so much by ancient histories, as ye may, if ye search what hath been wickedly done of late through the pestilent behaviour of them that are unworthily placed in authority.
[8] And we must take care for the time to come, that our kingdom may be quiet and peaceable for all men,
[9] Both by changing our purposes, and always judging things that are evident with more equal proceeding.
[10] For Aman, a Macedonian, the son of Amadatha, being indeed a stranger from the Persian blood, and far distant from our

goodness, and as a stranger received of us,
[11] Had so far forth obtained the favour that we shew toward every nation, as that he was called our father, and was continually honoured of all the next person unto the king.
[12] But he, not bearing his great dignity, went about to deprive us of our kingdom and life:
[13] Having by manifold and cunning deceits sought of us the destruction, as well of Mardocheus, who saved our life, and continually procured our good, as also of blameless Esther, partaker of our kingdom, with their whole nation.
[14] For by these means he thought, finding us destitute of friends to have translated the kingdom of the Persians to the Macedonians.
[15] But we find that the Jews, whom this wicked wretch hath delivered to utter destruction, are no evildoers, but live by most just laws:
[16] And that they be children of the most high and most mighty, living God, who hath ordered the kingdom both unto us and to our progenitors in the most excellent manner.
[17] Wherefore ye shall do well not to put in execution the letters sent unto you by Aman the son of Amadatha.
[18] For he that was the worker of these things, is hanged at the gates of Susa with all his family: God, who ruleth all things, speedily rendering vengeance to him according to his deserts.
[19] Therefore ye shall publish the copy of this letter in all places, that the Jews may freely live after their own laws.
[20] And ye shall aid them, that even the same day, being the thirteenth day of the twelfth month Adar, they may be avenged on them, who in the time of their affliction shall set upon them.
[21] For Almighty God hath turned to joy unto them the day, wherein the chosen people should have perished.
[22] Ye shall therefore among your solemn feasts keep it an high day with all feasting:
[23] That both now and hereafter there may be safety to us and the well affected Persians; but to those which do conspire against us a memorial of destruction.
[24] Therefore every city and country whatsoever, which shall not do according to these things, shall be destroyed without mercy with fire and sword, and shall be made not only unpassable for men, but also most hateful to wild beasts and fowls for ever.

Wisdom of Solomon

Wis.1

[1] Love righteousness, ye that be judges of the earth: think of Jah with a good (heart,) and in simplicity of heart seek him.
[2] For he will be found of them that tempt him not; and sheweth himself unto such as do not distrust him.
[3] For froward thoughts separate from God: and his power, when it is tried, reproveth the unwise.
[4] For into a malicious soul wisdom shall not enter; nor dwell in the body that is subject unto sin.
[5] For the holy spirit of discipline will flee deceit, and remove from thoughts that are without understanding, and will not abide when unrighteousness cometh in.
[6] For wisdom is a loving spirit; and will not acquit a blasphemer of his words: for God is witness of his reins, and a true beholder of his heart, and a hearer of his

tongue.

[7] For the Spirit of Jah filleth the world: and that which containeth all things hath knowledge of the voice.

[8] Therefore he that speaketh unrighteous things cannot be hid: neither shall vengeance, when it punisheth, pass by him.

[9] For inquisition shall be made into the counsels of the ungodly: and the sound of his words shall come unto Jah for the manifestation of his wicked deeds.

[10] For the ear of jealousy heareth all things: and the noise of murmurings is not hid.

[11] Therefore beware of murmuring, which is unprofitable; and refrain your tongue from backbiting: for there is no word so secret, that shall go for nought: and the mouth that belieth slayeth the soul.

[12] Seek not death in the error of your life: and pull not upon yourselves destruction with the works of your hands.

[13] For God made not death: neither hath he pleasure in the destruction of the living.

[14] For he created all things, that they might have their being: and the generations of the world were healthful; and there is no poison of destruction in them, nor the kingdom of death upon the earth:

[15] (For righteousness is immortal:)

[16] But ungodly men with their works and words called it to them: for when they thought to have it their friend, they consumed to nought, and made a covenant with it, because they are worthy to take part with it.

Wis.2

[1] For the ungodly said, reasoning with themselves, but not aright, Our life is short and tedious, and in the death of a man there is no remedy: neither was there any man known to have returned from the grave.

[2] For we are born at all adventure: and we shall be hereafter as though we had never been: for the breath in our nostrils is as smoke, and a little spark in the moving of our heart:

[3] Which being extinguished, our body shall be turned into ashes, and our spirit shall vanish as the soft air,

[4] And our name shall be forgotten in time, and no man shall have our works in remembrance, and our life shall pass away as the trace of a cloud, and shall be dispersed as a mist, that is driven away with the beams of the sun, and overcome with the heat thereof.

[5] For our time is a very shadow that passeth away; and after our end there is no returning: for it is fast sealed, so that no man cometh again.

[6] Come on therefore, let us enjoy the good things that are present: and let us speedily use the creatures like as in youth.

[7] Let us fill ourselves with costly wine and ointments: and let no flower of the spring pass by us:

[8] Let us crown ourselves with rosebuds, before they be withered:

[9] Let none of us go without his part of our voluptuousness: let us leave tokens of our joyfulness in every place: for this is our portion, and our lot is this.

[10] Let us oppress the poor righteous man, let us not spare the widow, nor reverence the ancient gray hairs of the aged.

[11] Let our strength be the law of justice: for that which is feeble is found to be nothing worth.

[12] Therefore let us lie in wait for the righteous; because he is not for our turn, and he is clean contrary to our doings: he upbraideth us with our offending the law, and objecteth to our infamy the transgressions of our education.

[13] He professeth to have the knowledge of God: and he calleth himself the child of Jah.

[14] He was made to reprove our thoughts.

[15] He is grievous unto us even to behold:

for his life is not like other men's, his ways are of another fashion.
[16] We are esteemed of him as counterfeits: he abstaineth from our ways as from filthiness: he pronounceth the end of the just to be blessed, and maketh his boast that God is his father.
[17] Let us see if his words be true: and let us prove what shall happen in the end of him.
[18] For if the just man be the son of God, he will help him, and deliver him from the hand of his enemies.
[19] Let us examine him with despitefulness and torture, that we may know his meekness, and prove his patience.
[20] Let us condemn him with a shameful death: for by his own saying he shall be respected.
[21] Such things they did imagine, and were deceived: for their own wickedness hath blinded them.
[22] As for the mysteries of God, they knew them not: neither hoped they for the wages of righteousness, nor discerned a reward for blameless souls.
[23] For God created man to be immortal, and made him to be an image of his own eternity.
[24] Nevertheless through envy of the devil came death into the world: and they that do hold of his side do find it.

Wis.3

[1] But the souls of the righteous are in the hand of God, and there shall no torment touch them.
[2] In the sight of the unwise they seemed to die: and their departure is taken for misery,
[3] And their going from us to be utter destruction: but they are in peace.
[4] For though they be punished in the sight of men, yet is their hope full of immortality.
[5] And having been a little chastised, they shall be greatly rewarded: for God proved them, and found them worthy for himself.
[6] As gold in the furnace hath he tried them, and received them as a burnt offering.
[7] And in the time of their visitation they shall shine, and run to and fro like sparks among the stubble.
[8] They shall judge the nations, and have dominion over the people, and their Lord shall reign for ever.
[9] They that put their trust in him shall understand the truth: and such as be faithful in love shall abide with him: for grace and mercy is to his saints, and he hath care for his elect.
[10] But the ungodly shall be punished according to their own imaginations, which have neglected the righteous, and forsaken Jah.
[11] For whoso despiseth wisdom and nurture, he is miserable, and their hope is vain, their labours unfruitful, and their works unprofitable:
[12] Their wives are foolish, and their children wicked:
[13] Their offspring is cursed. Wherefore blessed is the barren that is undefiled, which hath not known the sinful bed: she shall have fruit in the visitation of souls.
[14] And blessed is the eunuch, which with his hands hath wrought no iniquity, nor imagined wicked things against God: for unto him shall be given the special gift of faith, and an inheritance in the temple of Jah more acceptable to his mind.
[15] For glorious is the fruit of good labours: and the root of wisdom shall never fall away.
[16] As for the children of adulterers, they shall not come to their perfection, and the seed of an unrighteous bed shall be rooted out.
[17] For though they live long, yet shall they be nothing regarded: and their last age shall be without honour.
[18] Or, if they die quickly, they have no

hope, neither comfort in the day of trial.
[19] For horrible is the end of the unrighteous generation.

Wis. 4

[1] Better it is to have no children, and to have virtue: for the memorial thereof is immortal: because it is known with God, and with men.
[2] When it is present, men take example at it; and when it is gone, they desire it: it weareth a crown, and triumpheth for ever, having gotten the victory, striving for undefiled rewards.
[3] But the multiplying brood of the ungodly shall not thrive, nor take deep rooting from bastard slips, nor lay any fast foundation.
[4] For though they flourish in branches for a time; yet standing not last, they shall be shaken with the wind, and through the force of winds they shall be rooted out.
[5] The imperfect branches shall be broken off, their fruit unprofitable, not ripe to eat, yea, meet for nothing.
[6] For children begotten of unlawful beds are witnesses of wickedness against their parents in their trial.
[7] But though the righteous be prevented with death, yet shall he be in rest.
[8] For honourable age is not that which standeth in length of time, nor that is measured by number of years.
[9] But wisdom is the gray hair unto men, and an unspotted life is old age.
[10] He pleased God, and was beloved of him: so that living among sinners he was translated.
[11] Yea speedily was he taken away, lest that wickedness should alter his understanding, or deceit beguile his soul.
[12] For the bewitching of naughtiness doth obscure things that are honest; and the wandering of concupiscence doth undermine the simple mind.
[13] He, being made perfect in a short time, fulfilled a long time:
[14] For his soul pleased Jah: therefore hasted he to take him away from among the wicked.
[15] This the people saw, and understood it not, neither laid they up this in their minds, That his grace and mercy is with his saints, and that he hath respect unto his chosen.
[16] Thus the righteous that is dead shall condemn the ungodly which are living; and youth that is soon perfected the many years and old age of the unrighteous.
[17] For they shall see the end of the wise, and shall not understand what God in his counsel hath decreed of him, and to what end Jah hath set him in safety.
[18] They shall see him, and despise him; but God shall laugh them to scorn: and they shall hereafter be a vile carcase, and a reproach among the dead for evermore.
[19] For he shall rend them, and cast them down headlong, that they shall be speechless; and he shall shake them from the foundation; and they shall be utterly laid waste, and be in sorrow; and their memorial shall perish.
[20] And when they cast up the accounts of their sins, they shall come with fear: and their own iniquities shall convince them to their face.

Wis. 5

[1] Then shall the righteous man stand in great boldness before the face of such as have afflicted him, and made no account of his labours.
[2] When they see it, they shall be troubled with terrible fear, and shall be amazed at the strangeness of his salvation, so far beyond all that they looked for.
[3] And they repenting and groaning for anguish of spirit shall say within themselves, This was he, whom we had sometimes in

derision, and a proverb of reproach:
[4] We fools accounted his life madness, and his end to be without honour.
[5] How is he numbered among the children of God, and his lot is among the saints!
[6] Therefore have we erred from the way of truth, and the light of righteousness hath not shined unto us, and the sun of righteousness rose not upon us.
[7] We wearied ourselves in the way of wickedness and destruction: yea, we have gone through deserts, where there lay no way: but as for the way of Jah, we have not known it.
[8] What hath pride profited us? or what good hath riches with our vaunting brought us?
[9] All those things are passed away like a shadow, and as a post that hasted by;
[10] And as a ship that passeth over the waves of the water, which when it is gone by, the trace thereof cannot be found, neither the pathway of the keel in the waves;
[11] Or as when a bird hath flown through the air, there is no token of her way to be found, but the light air being beaten with the stroke of her wings and parted with the violent noise and motion of them, is passed through, and therein afterwards no sign where she went is to be found;
[12] Or like as when an arrow is shot at a mark, it parteth the air, which immediately cometh together again, so that a man cannot know where it went through:
[13] Even so we in like manner, as soon as we were born, began to draw to our end, and had no sign of virtue to shew; but were consumed in our own wickedness.
[14] For the hope of the Godly is like dust that is blown away with the wind; like a thin froth that is driven away with the storm; like as the smoke which is dispersed here and there with a tempest, and passeth away as the remembrance of a guest that tarrieth but a day.
[15] But the righteous live for evermore; their reward also is with Jah, and the care of them is with the most High.
[16] Therefore shall they receive a glorious kingdom, and a beautiful crown from Jah's hand: for with his right hand shall he cover them, and with his arm shall he protect them.
[17] He shall take to him his jealousy for complete armour, and make the creature his weapon for the revenge of his enemies.
[18] He shall put on righteousness as a breastplate, and true judgment instead of an helmet.
[19] He shall take holiness for an invincible shield.
[20] His severe wrath shall he sharpen for a sword, and the world shall fight with him against the unwise.
[21] Then shall the right aiming thunderbolts go abroad; and from the clouds, as from a well drawn bow, shall they fly to the mark.
[22] And hailstones full of wrath shall be cast as out of a stone bow, and the water of the sea shall rage against them, and the floods shall cruelly drown them.
[23] Yea, a mighty wind shall stand up against them, and like a storm shall blow them away: thus iniquity shall lay waste the whole earth, and ill dealing shall overthrow the thrones of the mighty.

Wis. 6

[1] Hear therefore, O ye kings, and understand; learn, ye that be judges of the ends of the earth.
[2] Give ear, ye that rule the people, and glory in the multitude of nations.
[3] For power is given you of Jah, and sovereignty from the Highest, who shall try your works, and search out your counsels.
[4] Because, being ministers of his kingdom, ye have not judged aright, nor kept the law, nor walked after the counsel of God;
[5] Horribly and speedily shall he come

upon you: for a sharp judgment shall be to them that be in high places.
[6] For mercy will soon pardon the meanest: but mighty men shall be mightily tormented.
[7] For he which is Lord over all shall fear no man's person, neither shall he stand in awe of any man's greatness: for he hath made the small and great, and careth for all alike.
[8] But a sore trial shall come upon the mighty.
[9] Unto you therefore, O kings, do I speak, that ye may learn wisdom, and not fall away.
[10] For they that keep holiness holily shall be judged holy: and they that have learned such things shall find what to answer.
[11] Wherefore set your affection upon my words; desire them, and ye shall be instructed.
[12] Wisdom is glorious, and never fadeth away: yea, she is easily seen of them that love her, and found of such as seek her.
[13] She preventeth them that desire her, in making herself first known unto them.
[14] Whoso seeketh her early shall have no great travail: for he shall find her sitting at his doors.
[15] To think therefore upon her is perfection of wisdom: and whoso watcheth for her shall quickly be without care.
[16] For she goeth about seeking such as are worthy of her, sheweth herself favourably unto them in the ways, and meeteth them in every thought.
[17] For the very true beginning of her is the desire of discipline; and the care of discipline is love;
[18] And love is the keeping of her laws; and the giving heed unto her laws is the assurance of incorruption;
[19] And incorruption maketh us near unto God:
[20] Therefore the desire of wisdom bringeth to a kingdom.
[21] If your delight be then in thrones and sceptres, O ye kings of the people, honour wisdom, that ye may reign for evermore.
[22] As for wisdom, what she is, and how she came up, I will tell you, and will not hide mysteries from you: but will seek her out from the beginning of her nativity, and bring the knowledge of her into light, and will not pass over the truth.
[23] Neither will I go with consuming envy; for such a man shall have no fellowship with wisdom.
[24] But the multitude of the wise is the welfare of the world: and a wise king is the upholding of the people.
[25] Receive therefore instruction through my words, and it shall do you good.

Wis.7

[1] I myself also am a mortal man, like to all, and the offspring of him that was first made of the earth,
[2] And in my mother's womb was fashioned to be flesh in the time of ten months, being compacted in blood, of the seed of man, and the pleasure that came with sleep.
[3] And when I was born, I drew in the common air, and fell upon the earth, which is of like nature, and the first voice which I uttered was crying, as all others do.
[4] I was nursed in swaddling clothes, and that with cares.
[5] For there is no king that had any other beginning of birth.
[6] For all men have one entrance into life, and the like going out.
[7] Wherefore I prayed, and understanding was given me: I called upon God, and the spirit of wisdom came to me.
[8] I preferred her before sceptres and thrones, and esteemed riches nothing in comparison of her.
[9] Neither compared I unto her any precious stone, because all gold in respect of her is as a little sand, and silver shall be

counted as clay before her.

[10] I loved her above health and beauty, and chose to have her instead of light: for the light that cometh from her never goeth out.

[11] All good things together came to me with her, and innumerable riches in her hands.

[12] And I rejoiced in them all, because wisdom goeth before them: and I knew not that she was the mother of them.

[13] I learned diligently, and do communicate her liberally: I do not hide her riches.

[14] For she is a treasure unto men that never faileth: which they that use become the friends of God, being commended for the gifts that come from learning.

[15] God hath granted me to speak as I would, and to conceive as is meet for the things that are given me: because it is he that leadeth unto wisdom, and directeth the wise.

[16] For in his hand are both we and our words; all wisdom also, and knowledge of workmanship.

[17] For he hath given me certain knowledge of the things that are, namely, to know how the world was made, and the operation of the elements:

[18] The beginning, ending, and midst of the times: the alterations of the turning of the sun, and the change of seasons:

[19] The circuits of years, and the positions of stars:

[20] The natures of living creatures, and the furies of wild beasts: the violence of winds, and the reasonings of men: the diversities of plants and the virtues of roots:

[21] And all such things as are either secret or manifest, them I know.

[22] For wisdom, which is the worker of all things, taught me: for in her is an understanding spirit holy, one only, manifold, subtil, lively, clear, undefiled, plain, not subject to hurt, loving the thing that is good quick, which cannot be letted, ready to do good,

[23] Kind to man, steadfast, sure, free from care, having all power, overseeing all things, and going through all understanding, pure, and most subtil, spirits.

[24] For wisdom is more moving than any motion: she passeth and goeth through all things by reason of her pureness.

[25] For she is the breath of the power of God, and a pure influence flowing from the glory of the Almighty: therefore can no defiled thing fall into her.

[26] For she is the brightness of the everlasting light, the unspotted mirror of the power of God, and the image of his goodness.

[27] And being but one, she can do all things: and remaining in herself, she maketh all things new: and in all ages entering into holy souls, she maketh them friends of God, and prophets.

[28] For God loveth none but him that dwelleth with wisdom.

[29] For she is more beautiful than the sun, and above all the order of stars: being compared with the light, she is found before it.

[30] For after this cometh night: but vice shall not prevail against wisdom.

Wis. 8

[1] Wisdom reacheth from one end to another mightily: and sweetly doth she order all things.

[2] I loved her, and sought her out from my youth, I desired to make her my spouse, and I was a lover of her beauty.

[3] In that she is conversant with God, she magnifieth her nobility: yea, Jah of all things himself loved her.

[4] For she is privy to the mysteries of the knowledge of God, and a lover of his works.

[5] If riches be a possession to be desired in this life; what is richer than wisdom, that

worketh all things?

[6] And if prudence work; who of all that are is a more cunning workman than she?

[7] And if a man love righteousness her labours are virtues: for she teacheth temperance and prudence, justice and fortitude: which are such things, as en can have nothing more profitable in their life.

[8] If a man desire much experience, she knoweth things of old, and conjectureth aright what is to come: she knoweth the subtilties of speeches, and can expound dark sentences: she foreseeth signs and wonders, and the events of seasons and times.

[9] Therefore I purposed to take her to me to live with me, knowing that she would be a counsellor of good things, and a comfort in cares and grief.

[10] For her sake I shall have estimation among the multitude, and honour with the elders, though I be young.

[11] I shall be found of a quick conceit in judgment, and shall be admired in the sight of great men.

[12] When I hold my tongue, they shall bide my leisure, and when I speak, they shall give good ear unto me: if I talk much, they shall lay their hands upon their mouth.

[13] Moreover by the means of her I shall obtain immortality, and leave behind me an everlasting memorial to them that come after me.

[14] I shall set the people in order, and the nations shall be subject unto me.

[15] Horrible tyrants shall be afraid, when they do but hear of me; I shall be found good among the multitude, and valiant in war.

[16] After I am come into mine house, I will repose myself with her: for her conversation hath no bitterness; and to live with her hath no sorrow, but mirth and joy.

[17] Now when I considered these things in myself, and pondered them in my heart, how that to be allied unto wisdom is immortality;

[18] And great pleasure it is to have her friendship; and in the works of her hands are infinite riches; and in the exercise of conference with her, prudence; and in talking with her, a good report; I went about seeking how to take her to me.

[19] For I was a witty child, and had a good spirit.

[20] Yea rather, being good, I came into a body undefiled.

[21] Nevertheless, when I perceived that I could not otherwise obtain her, except God gave her me; and that was a point of wisdom also to know whose gift she was; I prayed unto Jah, and besought him, and with my whole heart I said,

---

Wis. 9

[1] O God of my fathers, and Lord of mercy, who hast made all things with thy word,

[2] And ordained man through thy wisdom, that he should have dominion over the creatures which thou hast made,

[3] And order the world according to equity and righteousness, and execute judgment with an upright heart:

[4] Give me wisdom, that sitteth by thy throne; and reject me not from among thy children:

[5] For I thy servant and son of thine handmaid am a feeble person, and of a short time, and too young for the understanding of judgment and laws.

[6] For though a man be never so perfect among the children of men, yet if thy wisdom be not with him, he shall be nothing regarded.

[7] Thou hast chosen me to be a king of thy people, and a judge of thy sons and daughters:

[8] Thou hast commanded me to build a temple upon thy holy mount, and an altar in the city wherein thou dwellest, a resemblance of the holy tabernacle, which thou hast prepared from the beginning.

[9] And wisdom was with thee: which knoweth thy works, and was present when thou madest the world, and knew what was acceptable in thy sight, and right in thy commandments.
[10] O send her out of thy holy heavens, and from the throne of thy glory, that being present she may labour with me, that I may know what is pleasing unto thee.
[11] For she knoweth and understandeth all things, and she shall lead me soberly in my doings, and preserve me in her power.
[12] So shall my works be acceptable, and then shall I judge thy people righteously, and be worthy to sit in my father's seat.
[13] For what man is he that can know the counsel of God? or who can think what the will of Jah is?
[14] For the thoughts of mortal men are miserable, and our devices are but uncertain.
[15] For the corruptible body presseth down the soul, and the earthy tabernacle weigheth down the mind that museth upon many things.
[16] And hardly do we guess aright at things that are upon earth, and with labour do we find the things that are before us: but the things that are in heaven who hath searched out?
[17] And thy counsel who hath known, except thou give wisdom, and send thy Holy Spirit from above?
[18] For so the ways of them which lived on the earth were reformed, and men were taught the things that are pleasing unto thee, and were saved through wisdom.

Wis.10

[1] She preserved the first formed father of the world, that was created alone, and brought him out of his fall,
[2] And gave him power to rule all things.
[3] But when the unrighteous went away from her in his anger, he perished also in the fury wherewith he murdered his brother.
[4] For whose cause the earth being drowned with the flood, wisdom again preserved it, and directed the course of the righteous in a piece of wood of small value.
[5] Moreover, the nations in their wicked conspiracy being confounded, she found out the righteous, and preserved him blameless unto God, and kept him strong against his tender compassion toward his son.
[6] When the ungodly perished, she delivered the righteous man, who fled from the fire which fell down upon the five cities.
[7] Of whose wickedness even to this day the waste land that smoketh is a testimony, and plants bearing fruit that never come to ripeness: and a standing pillar of salt is a monument of an unbelieving soul.
[8] For regarding not wisdom, they gat not only this hurt, that they knew not the things which were good; but also left behind them to the world a memorial of their foolishness: so that in the things wherein they offended they could not so much as be hid.
[9] Rut wisdom delivered from pain those that attended upon her.
[10] When the righteous fled from his brother's wrath she guided him in right paths, shewed him the kingdom of God, and gave him knowledge of holy things, made him rich in his travels, and multiplied the fruit of his labours.
[11] In the covetousness of such as oppressed him she stood by him, and made him rich.
[12] She defended him from his enemies, and kept him safe from those that lay in wait, and in a sore conflict she gave him the victory; that he might know that goodness is stronger than all.
[13] When the righteous was sold, she forsook him not, but delivered him from sin: she went down with him into the pit,
[14] And left him not in bonds, till she brought him the sceptre of the kingdom, and power against those that oppressed him: as

for them that had accused him, she shewed them to be liars, and gave him perpetual glory.
[15] She delivered the righteous people and blameless seed from the nation that oppressed them.
[16] She entered into the soul of the servant of Jah, and withstood dreadful kings in wonders and signs;
[17] Rendered to the righteous a reward of their labours, guided them in a marvellous way, and was unto them for a cover by day, and a light of stars in the night season;
[18] Brought them through the Red sea, and led them through much water:
[19] But she drowned their enemies, and cast them up out of the bottom of the deep.
[20] Therefore the righteous spoiled the ungodly, and praised thy holy name, O Lord, and magnified with one accord thine hand, that fought for them.
[21] For wisdom opened the mouth of the dumb, and made the tongues of them that cannot speak eloquent.

Wis.11

[1] She prospered their works in the hand of the holy prophet.
[2] They went through the wilderness that was not inhabited, and pitched tents in places where there lay no way.
[3] They stood against their enemies, and were avenged of their adversaries.
[4] When they were thirsty, they called upon thee, and water was given them out of the flinty rock, and their thirst was quenched out of the hard stone.
[5] For by what things their enemies were punished, by the same they in their need were benefited.
[6] For instead of of a perpetual running river troubled with foul blood,
[7] For a manifest reproof of that commandment, whereby the infants were slain, thou gavest unto them abundance of water by a means which they hoped not for:
[8] Declaring by that thirst then how thou hadst punished their adversaries.
[9] For when they were tried albeit but in mercy chastised, they knew how the ungodly were judged in wrath and tormented, thirsting in another manner than the just.
[10] For these thou didst admonish and try, as a father: but the other, as a severe king, thou didst condemn and punish.
[11] Whether they were absent or present, they were vexed alike.
[12] For a double grief came upon them, and a groaning for the remembrance of things past.
[13] For when they heard by their own punishments the other to be benefited, they had some feeling of Jah.
[14] For whom they respected with scorn, when he was long before thrown out at the casting forth of the infants, him in the end, when they saw what came to pass, they admired.
[15] But for the foolish devices of their wickedness, wherewith being deceived they worshipped serpents void of reason, and vile beasts, thou didst send a multitude of unreasonable beasts upon them for vengeance;
[16] That they might know, that wherewithal a man sinneth, by the same also shall he be punished.
[17] For thy Almighty hand, that made the world of matter without form, wanted not means to send among them a multitude of bears or fierce lions,
[18] Or unknown wild beasts, full of rage, newly created, breathing out either a fiery vapour, or filthy scents of scattered smoke, or shooting horrible sparkles out of their eyes:
[19] Whereof not only the harm might dispatch them at once, but also the terrible sight utterly destroy them.

[20] Yea, and without these might they have fallen down with one blast, being persecuted of vengeance, and scattered abroad through the breath of thy power: but thou hast ordered all things in measure and number and weight.
[21] For thou canst shew thy great strength at all times when thou wilt; and who may withstand the power of thine arm?
[22] For the whole world before thee is as a little grain of the balance, yea, as a drop of the morning dew that falleth down upon the earth.
[23] But thou hast mercy upon all; for thou canst do all things, and winkest at the sins of men, because they should amend.
[24] For thou lovest all the things that are, and abhorrest nothing which thou hast made: for never wouldest thou have made any thing, if thou hadst hated it.
[25] And how could any thing have endured, if it had not been thy will? or been preserved, if not called by thee?
[26] But thou sparest all: for they are thine, O Lord, thou lover of souls.

Wis.12

[1] For thine incorruptible Spirit is in all things.
[2] Therefore chastenest thou them by little and little that offend, and warnest them by putting them in remembrance wherein they have offended, that leaving their wickedness they may believe on thee, O Lord.
[3] For it was thy will to destroy by the hands of our fathers both those old inhabitants of thy holy land,
[4] Whom thou hatedst for doing most odious works of witchcrafts, and wicked sacrifices;
[5] And also those merciless murderers of children, and devourers of man's flesh, and the feasts of blood,
[6] With their priests out of the midst of their idolatrous crew, and the parents, that killed with their own hands souls destitute of help:
[7] That the land, which thou esteemedst above all other, might receive a worthy colony of God's children.
[8] Nevertheless even those thou sparedst as men, and didst send wasps, forerunners of thine host, to destroy them by little and little.
[9] Not that thou wast unable to bring the ungodly under the hand of the righteous in battle, or to destroy them at once with cruel beasts, or with one rough word:
[10] But executing thy judgments upon them by little and little, thou gavest them place of repentance, not being ignorant that they were a naughty generation, and that their malice was bred in them, and that their cogitation would never be changed.
[11] For it was a cursed seed from the beginning; neither didst thou for fear of any man give them pardon for those things wherein they sinned.
[12] For who shall say, What hast thou done? or who shall withstand thy judgment? or who shall accuse thee for the nations that perish, whom thou made? or who shall come to stand against thee, to be revenged for the unrighteous men?
[13] For neither is there any God but thou that careth for all, to whom thou mightest shew that thy judgment is not unright.
[14] Neither shall king or tyrant be able to set his face against thee for any whom thou hast punished.
[15] Forsomuch then as thou art righteous thyself, thou orderest all things righteously: thinking it not agreeable with thy power to condemn him that hath not deserved to be punished.
[16] For thy power is the beginning of righteousness, and because thou art Jah of all, it maketh thee to be gracious unto all.
[17] For when men will not believe that thou art of a full power, thou shewest thy strength, and among them that know it thou

makest their boldness manifest.
[18] But thou, mastering thy power, judgest with equity, and orderest us with great favour: for thou mayest use power when thou wilt.
[19] But by such works hast thou taught thy people that the just man should be merciful, and hast made thy children to be of a good hope that thou givest repentance for sins.
[20] For if thou didst punish the enemies of thy children, and the condemned to death, with such deliberation, giving them time and place, whereby they might be delivered from their malice:
[21] With how great circumspection didst thou judge thine own sons, unto whose fathers thou hast sworn, and made covenants of good promises?
[22] Therefore, whereas thou dost chasten us, thou scourgest our enemies a thousand times more, to the intent that, when we judge, we should carefully think of thy goodness, and when we ourselves are judged, we should look for mercy.
[23] Wherefore, whereas men have lived dissolutely and unrighteously, thou hast tormented them with their own abominations.
[24] For they went astray very far in the ways of error, and held them for gods, which even among the beasts of their enemies were despised, being deceived, as children of no understanding.
[25] Therefore unto them, as to children without the use of reason, thou didst send a judgment to mock them.
[26] But they that would not be reformed by that correction, wherein he dallied with them, shall feel a judgment worthy of God.
[27] For, look, for what things they grudged, when they were punished, that is, for them whom they thought to be gods; [now] being punished in them, when they saw it, they acknowledged him to be the true God, whom before they denied to know: and therefore came extreme damnation upon them.

Wis.13

[1] Surely vain are all men by nature, who are ignorant of God, and could not out of the good things that are seen know him that is: neither by considering the works did they acknowledge the workmaster;
[2] But deemed either fire, or wind, or the swift air, or the circle of the stars, or the violent water, or the lights of heaven, to be the gods which govern the world.
[3] With whose beauty if they being delighted took them to be gods; let them know how much better Jah of them is: for the first author of beauty hath created them.
[4] But if they were astonished at their power and virtue, let them understand by them, how much mightier he is that made them.
[5] For by the greatness and beauty of the creatures proportionably the maker of them is seen.
[6] But yet for this they are the less to be blamed: for they peradventure err, seeking God, and desirous to find him.
[7] For being conversant in his works they search him diligently, and believe their sight: because the things are beautiful that are seen.
[8] Howbeit neither are they to be pardoned.
[9] For if they were able to know so much, that they could aim at the world; how did they not sooner find out Jah thereof?
[10] But miserable are they, and in dead things is their hope, who call them gods, which are the works of men's hands, gold and silver, to shew art in, and resemblances of beasts, or a stone good for nothing, the work of an ancient hand.
[11] Now a carpenter that felleth timber,

after he hath sawn down a tree meet for the purpose, and taken off all the bark skilfully round about, and hath wrought it handsomely, and made a vessel thereof fit for the service of man's life;

[12] And after spending the refuse of his work to dress his meat, hath filled himself;

[13] And taking the very refuse among those which served to no use, being a crooked piece of wood, and full of knots, hath carved it diligently, when he had nothing else to do, and formed it by the skill of his understanding, and fashioned it to the image of a man;

[14] Or made it like some vile beast, laying it over with vermilion, and with paint colouring it red, and covering every spot therein;

[15] And when he had made a convenient room for it, set it in a wall, and made it fast with iron:

[16] For he provided for it that it might not fall, knowing that it was unable to help itself; for it is an image, and hath need of help:

[17] Then maketh he prayer for his goods, for his wife and children, and is not ashamed to speak to that which hath no life.

[18] For health he calleth upon that which is weak: for life prayeth to that which is dead; for aid humbly beseecheth that which hath least means to help: and for a good journey he asketh of that which cannot set a foot forward:

[19] And for gaining and getting, and for good success of his hands, asketh ability to do of him, that is most unable to do any thing.

Wis. 14

[1] Again, one preparing himself to sail, and about to pass through the raging waves, calleth upon a piece of wood more rotten than the vessel that carrieth him.

[2] For verily desire of gain devised that, and the workman built it by his skill.

[3] But thy providence, O Father, governeth it: for thou hast made a way in the sea, and a safe path in the waves;

[4] Shewing that thou canst save from all danger: yea, though a man went to sea without art.

[5] Nevertheless thou wouldest not that the works of thy wisdom should be idle, and therefore do men commit their lives to a small piece of wood, and passing the rough sea in a weak vessel are saved.

[6] For in the old time also, when the proud giants perished, the hope of the world governed by thy hand escaped in a weak vessel, and left to all ages a seed of generation.

[7] For blessed is the wood whereby righteousness cometh.

[8] But that which is made with hands is cursed, as well it, as he that made it: he, because he made it; and it, because, being corruptible, it was called god.

[9] For the ungodly and his ungodliness are both alike hateful unto God.

[10] For that which is made shall be punished together with him that made it.

[11] Therefore even upon the idols of the Gentiles shall there be a visitation: because in the creature of God they are become an abomination, and stumblingblocks to the souls of men, and a snare to the feet of the unwise.

[12] For the devising of idols was the beginning of spiritual fornication, and the invention of them the corruption of life.

[13] For neither were they from the beginning, neither shall they be for ever.

[14] For by the vain glory of men they entered into the world, and therefore shall they come shortly to an end.

[15] For a father afflicted with untimely mourning, when he hath made an image of his child soon taken away, now honoured him as a god, which was then a dead man,

and delivered to those that were under him ceremonies and sacrifices.

[16] Thus in process of time an ungodly custom grown strong was kept as a law, and graven images were worshipped by the commandments of kings.

[17] Whom men could not honour in presence, because they dwelt far off, they took the counterfeit of his visage from far, and made an express image of a king whom they honoured, to the end that by this their forwardness they might flatter him that was absent, as if he were present.

[18] Also the singular diligence of the artificer did help to set forward the ignorant to more superstition.

[19] For he, peradventure willing to please one in authority, forced all his skill to make the resemblance of the best fashion.

[20] And so the multitude, allured by the grace of the work, took him now for a god, which a little before was but honoured.

[21] And this was an occasion to deceive the world: for men, serving either calamity or tyranny, did ascribe unto stones and stocks the incommunicable name.

[22] Moreover this was not enough for them, that they erred in the knowledge of God; but whereas they lived in the great war of ignorance, those so great plagues called they peace.

[23] For whilst they slew their children in sacrifices, or used secret ceremonies, or made revellings of strange rites;

[24] They kept neither lives nor marriages any longer undefiled: but either one slew another traiterously, or grieved him by adultery.

[25] So that there reigned in all men without exception blood, manslaughter, theft, and dissimulation, corruption, unfaithfulness, tumults, perjury,

[26] Disquieting of good men, forgetfulness of good turns, defiling of souls, changing of kind, disorder in marriages, adultery, and shameless uncleanness.

[27] For the worshipping of idols not to be named is the beginning, the cause, and the end, of all evil.

[28] For either they are mad when they be merry, or prophesy lies, or live unjustly, or else lightly forswear themselves.

[29] For insomuch as their trust is in idols, which have no life; though they swear falsely, yet they look not to be hurt.

[30] Howbeit for both causes shall they be justly punished: both because they thought not well of God, giving heed unto idols, and also unjustly swore in deceit, despising holiness.

[31] For it is not the power of them by whom they swear: but it is the just vengeance of sinners, that punisheth always the offence of the ungodly.

Wis. 15

[1] But thou, O God, art gracious and true, longsuffering, and in mercy ordering all things,

[2] For if we sin, we are thine, knowing thy power: but we will not sin, knowing that we are counted thine.

[3] For to know thee is perfect righteousness: yea, to know thy power is the root of immortality.

[4] For neither did the mischievous invention of men deceive us, nor an image spotted with divers colours, the painter's fruitless labour;

[5] The sight whereof enticeth fools to lust after it, and so they desire the form of a dead image, that hath no breath.

[6] Both they that make them, they that desire them, and they that worship them, are lovers of evil things, and are worthy to have such things to trust upon.

[7] For the potter, tempering soft earth, fashioneth every vessel with much labour for our service: yea, of the same clay he maketh both the vessels that serve for clean

uses, and likewise also all such as serve to the contrary: but what is the use of either sort, the potter himself is the judge.

[8] And employing his labours lewdly, he maketh a vain god of the same clay, even he which a little before was made of earth himself, and within a little while after returneth to the same, out when his life which was lent him shall be demanded.

[9] Notwithstanding his care is, not that he shall have much labour, nor that his life is short: but striveth to excel goldsmiths and silversmiths, and endeavoureth to do like the workers in brass, and counteth it his glory to make counterfeit things.

[10] His heart is ashes, his hope is more vile than earth, and his life of less value than clay:

[11] Forasmuch as he knew not his Maker, and him that inspired into him an active soul, and breathed in a living spirit.

[12] But they counted our life a pastime, and our time here a market for gain: for, say they, we must be getting every way, though it be by evil means.

[13] For this man, that of earthly matter maketh brittle vessels and graven images, knoweth himself to offend above all others.

[14] And all the enemies of thy people, that hold them in subjection, are most foolish, and are more miserable than very babes.

[15] For they counted all the idols of the heathen to be gods: which neither have the use of eyes to see, nor noses to draw breath, nor ears to hear, nor fingers of hands to handle; and as for their feet, they are slow to go.

[16] For man made them, and he that borrowed his own spirit fashioned them: but no man can make a god like unto himself.

[17] For being mortal, he worketh a dead thing with wicked hands: for he himself is better than the things which he worshippeth: whereas he lived once, but they never.

[18] Yea, they worshipped those beasts also that are most hateful: for being compared together, some are worse than others.

[19] Neither are they beautiful, so much as to be desired in respect of beasts: but they went without the praise of God and his blessing.

Wis. 16

[1] Therefore by the like were they punished worthily, and by the multitude of beasts tormented.

[2] Instead of which punishment, dealing graciously with thine own people, thou preparedst for them meat of a strange taste, even quails to stir up their appetite:

[3] To the end that they, desiring food, might for the ugly sight of the beasts sent among them lothe even that, which they must needs desire; but these, suffering penury for a short space, might be made partakers of a strange taste.

[4] For it was requisite, that upon them exercising tyranny should come penury, which they could not avoid: but to these it should only be shewed how their enemies were tormented.

[5] For when the horrible fierceness of beasts came upon these, and they perished with the stings of crooked serpents, thy wrath endured not for ever:

[6] But they were troubled for a small season, that they might be admonished, having a sign of salvation, to put them in remembrance of the commandment of thy law.

[7] For he that turned himself toward it was not saved by the thing that he saw, but by thee, that art the Saviour of all.

[8] And in this thou madest thine enemies confess, that it is thou who deliverest from all evil:

[9] For them the bitings of grasshoppers and flies killed, neither was there found any remedy for their life: for they were worthy to be punished by such.

[10] But thy sons not the very teeth of venomous dragons overcame: for thy mercy was ever by them, and healed them.
[11] For they were pricked, that they should remember thy words; and were quickly saved, that not falling into deep forgetfulness, they might be continually mindful of thy goodness.
[12] For it was neither herb, nor mollifying plaister, that restored them to health: but thy word, O Lord, which healeth all things.
[13] For thou hast power of life and death: thou leadest to the gates of hell, and bringest up again.
[14] A man indeed killeth through his malice: and the spirit, when it is gone forth, returneth not; neither the soul received up cometh again.
[15] But it is not possible to escape thine hand.
[16] For the ungodly, that denied to know thee, were scourged by the strength of thine arm: with strange rains, hails, and showers, were they persecuted, that they could not avoid, and through fire were they consumed.
[17] For, which is most to be wondered at, the fire had more force in the water, that quencheth all things: for the world fighteth for the righteous.
[18] For sometime the flame was mitigated, that it might not burn up the beasts that were sent against the ungodly; but themselves might see and perceive that they were persecuted with the judgment of God.
[19] And at another time it burneth even in the midst of water above the power of fire, that it might destroy the fruits of an unjust land.
[20] Instead whereof thou feddest thine own people with angels' food, and didst send them from heaven bread prepared without their labour, able to content every man's delight, and agreeing to every taste.
[21] For thy sustenance declared thy sweetness unto thy children, and serving to the appetite of the eater, tempered itself to every man's liking.
[22] But snow and ice endured the fire, and melted not, that they might know that fire burning in the hail, and sparkling in the rain, did destroy the fruits of the enemies.
[23] But this again did even forget his own strength, that the righteous might be nourished.
[24] For the creature that serveth thee, who art the Maker increaseth his strength against the unrighteous for their punishment, and abateth his strength for the benefit of such as put their trust in thee.
[25] Therefore even then was it altered into all fashions, and was obedient to thy grace, that nourisheth all things, according to the desire of them that had need:
[26] That thy children, O Lord, whom thou lovest, might know, that it is not the growing of fruits that nourisheth man: but that it is thy word, which preserveth them that put their trust in thee.
[27] For that which was not destroyed of the fire, being warmed with a little sunbeam, soon melted away:
[28] That it might be known, that we must prevent the sun to give thee thanks, and at the dayspring pray unto thee.
[29] For the hope of the unthankful shall melt away as the winter's hoar frost, and shall run away as unprofitable water.

Wis. 17

[1] For great are thy judgments, and cannot be expressed: therefore unnurtured souls have erred.
[2] For when unrighteous men thought to oppress the holy nation; they being shut up in their houses, the prisoners of darkness, and fettered with the bonds of a long night, lay [there] exiled from the eternal providence.
[3] For while they supposed to lie hid in their secret sins, they were scattered under a

dark veil of forgetfulness, being horribly astonished, and troubled with [strange] apparitions.

[4] For neither might the corner that held them keep them from fear: but noises [as of waters] falling down sounded about them, and sad visions appeared unto them with heavy countenances.

[5] No power of the fire might give them light: neither could the bright flames of the stars endure to lighten that horrible night.

[6] Only there appeared unto them a fire kindled of itself, very dreadful: for being much terrified, they thought the things which they saw to be worse than the sight they saw not.

[7] As for the illusions of art magick, they were put down, and their vaunting in wisdom was reproved with disgrace.

[8] For they, that promised to drive away terrors and troubles from a sick soul, were sick themselves of fear, worthy to be laughed at.

[9] For though no terrible thing did fear them; yet being scared with beasts that passed by, and hissing of serpents,

[10] They died for fear, denying that they saw the air, which could of no side be avoided.

[11] For wickedness, condemned by her own witness, is very timorous, and being pressed with conscience, always forecasteth grievous things.

[12] For fear is nothing else but a betraying of the succours which reason offereth.

[13] And the expectation from within, being less, counteth the ignorance more than the cause which bringeth the torment.

[14] But they sleeping the same sleep that night, which was indeed intolerable, and which came upon them out of the bottoms of inevitable hell,

[15] Were partly vexed with monstrous apparitions, and partly fainted, their heart failing them: for a sudden fear, and not looked for, came upon them.

[16] So then whosoever there fell down was straitly kept, shut up in a prison without iron bars,

[17] For whether he were husbandman, or shepherd, or a labourer in the field, he was overtaken, and endured that necessity, which could not be avoided: for they were all bound with one chain of darkness.

[18] Whether it were a whistling wind, or a melodious noise of birds among the spreading branches, or a pleasing fall of water running violently,

[19] Or a terrible sound of stones cast down, or a running that could not be seen of skipping beasts, or a roaring voice of most savage wild beasts, or a rebounding echo from the hollow mountains; these things made them to swoon for fear.

[20] For the whole world shined with clear light, and none were hindered in their labour:

[21] Over them only was spread an heavy night, an image of that darkness which should afterward receive them: but yet were they unto themselves more grievous than the darkness.

Wis. 18

[1] Nevertheless thy saints had a very great light, whose voice they hearing, and not seeing their shape, because they also had not suffered the same things, they counted them happy.

[2] But for that they did not hurt them now, of whom they had been wronged before, they thanked them, and besought them pardon for that they had been enemies.

[3] Instead whereof thou gavest them a burning pillar of fire, both to be a guide of the unknown journey, and an harmless sun to entertain them honourably.

[4] For they were worthy to be deprived of light and imprisoned in darkness, who had kept thy sons shut up, by whom the

uncorrupt light of the law was to be given unto the world.

[5] And when they had determined to slay the babes of the saints, one child being cast forth, and saved, to reprove them, thou tookest away the multitude of their children, and destroyedst them altogether in a mighty water.

[6] Of that night were our fathers certified afore, that assuredly knowing unto what oaths they had given credence, they might afterwards be of good cheer.

[7] So of thy people was accepted both the salvation of the righteous, and destruction of the enemies.

[8] For wherewith thou didst punish our adversaries, by the same thou didst glorify us, whom thou hadst called.

[9] For the righteous children of good men did sacrifice secretly, and with one consent made a holy law, that the saints should be like partakers of the same good and evil, the fathers now singing out the songs of praise.

[10] But on the other side there sounded an ill according cry of the enemies, and a lamentable noise was carried abroad for children that were bewailed.

[11] The master and the servant were punished after one manner; and like as the king, so suffered the common person.

[12] So they all together had innumerable dead with one kind of death; neither were the living sufficient to bury them: for in one moment the noblest offspring of them was destroyed.

[13] For whereas they would not believe any thing by reason of the enchantments; upon the destruction of the firstborn, they acknowledged this people to be the sons of God.

[14] For while all things were in quiet silence, and that night was in the midst of her swift course,

[15] Thine Almighty word leaped down from heaven out of thy royal throne, as a fierce man of war into the midst of a land of destruction,

[16] And brought thine unfeigned commandment as a sharp sword, and standing up filled all things with death; and it touched the heaven, but it stood upon the earth.

[17] Then suddenly visions of horrible dreams troubled them sore, and terrors came upon them unlooked for.

[18] And one thrown here, and another there, half dead, shewed the cause of his death.

[19] For the dreams that troubled them did foreshew this, lest they should perish, and not know why they were afflicted.

[20] Yea, the tasting of death touched the righteous also, and there was a destruction of the multitude in the wilderness: but the wrath endured not long.

[21] For then the blameless man made haste, and stood forth to defend them; and bringing the shield of his proper ministry, even prayer, and the propitiation of incense, set himself against the wrath, and so brought the calamity to an end, declaring that he was thy servant.

[22] So he overcame the destroyer, not with strength of body, nor force of arms, but with a word subdued him that punished, alleging the oaths and covenants made with the fathers.

[23] For when the dead were now fallen down by heaps one upon another, standing between, he stayed the wrath, and parted the way to the living.

[24] For in the long garment was the whole world, and in the four rows of the stones was the glory of the fathers graven, and thy Majesty upon the daidem of his head.

[25] Unto these the destroyer gave place, and was afraid of them: for it was enough that they only tasted of the wrath.

Wis.19

[1] As for the ungodly, wrath came upon them without mercy unto the end: for he knew before what they would do;
[2] How that having given them leave to depart, and sent them hastily away, they would repent and pursue them.
[3] For whilst they were yet mourning and making lamentation at the graves of the dead, they added another foolish device, and pursued them as fugitives, whom they had intreated to be gone.
[4] For the destiny, whereof they were worthy, drew them unto this end, and made them forget the things that had already happened, that they might fulfil the punishment which was wanting to their torments:
[5] And that thy people might pass a wonderful way: but they might find a strange death.
[6] For the whole creature in his proper kind was fashioned again anew, serving the peculiar commandments that were given unto them, that thy children might be kept without hurt:
[7] As namely, a cloud shadowing the camp; and where water stood before, dry land appeared; and out of the Red sea a way without impediment; and out of the violent stream a green field:
[8] Wherethrough all the people went that were defended with thy hand, seeing thy marvellous strange wonders.
[9] For they went at large like horses, and leaped like lambs, praising thee, O Lord, who hadst delivered them.
[10] For they were yet mindful of the things that were done while they sojourned in the strange land, how the ground brought forth flies instead of cattle, and how the river cast up a multitude of frogs instead of fishes.
[11] But afterwards they saw a new generation of fowls, when, being led with their appetite, they asked delicate meats.
[12] For quails came up unto them from the sea for their contentment.
[13] And punishments came upon the sinners not without former signs by the force of thunders: for they suffered justly according to their own wickedness, insomuch as they used a more hard and hateful behaviour toward strangers.
[14] For the Sodomites did not receive those, whom they knew not when they came: but these brought friends into bondage, that had well deserved of them.
[15] And not only so, but peradventure some respect shall be had of those, because they used strangers not friendly:
[16] But these very grievously afflicted them, whom they had received with feastings, and were already made partakers of the same laws with them.
[17] Therefore even with blindness were these stricken, as those were at the doors of the righteous man: when, being compassed about with horrible great darkness, every one sought the passage of his own doors.
[18] For the elements were changed in themselves by a kind of harmony, like as in a psaltery notes change the name of the tune, and yet are always sounds; which may well be perceived by the sight of the things that have been done.
[19] For earthly things were turned into watery, and the things, that before swam in the water, now went upon the ground.
[20] The fire had power in the water, forgetting his own virtue: and the water forgat his own quenching nature.
[21] On the other side, the flames wasted not the flesh of the corruptible living things, though they walked therein; neither melted they the icy kind of heavenly meat that was of nature apt to melt.
[22] For in all things, O Lord, thou didst

magnify thy people, and glorify them, neither didst thou lightly regard them: but didst assist them in every time and place.

Prologue to Wisdom of Jesus Son of Sirach

[A Prologue made by an uncertain Author] This Jesus was the son of Sirach, and grandchild to Jesus of the same name with him: this man therefore lived in the latter times, after the people had been led away captive, and called home a again, and almost after all the prophets. Now his grandfather Jesus, as he himself witnesseth, was a man of great diligence and wisdom among the Hebrews, who did not only gather the grave and short sentences of wise men, that had been before him, but himself also uttered some of his own, full of much understanding and wisdom. When as therefore the first Jesus died, leaving this book almost perfected, Sirach his son receiving it after him left it to his own son Jesus, who, having gotten it into his hands, compiled it all orderly into one volume, and called it Wisdom, intituling it both by his own name, his father's name, and his grandfather's; alluring the hearer by the very name of Wisdom to have a greater love to the study of this book. It containeth therefore wise sayings, dark sentences, and parables, and certain particular ancient godly stories of men that pleased God; also his prayer and song; moreover, what benefits God had vouchsafed his people, and what plagues he had heaped upon their enemies. This Jesus did imitate Solomon, and was no less famous for wisdom and learning, both being indeed a man of great learning, and so reputed also. [The Prologue of the Wisdom of Jesus the Son of Sirach.] Whereas many and great things have been delivered unto us by the law and the prophets, and by others that have followed their steps, for the which things Israel ought to be commended for learning and wisdom; and whereof not only the readers must needs become skilful themselves, but also they that desire to learn be able to profit them which are without, both by speaking and writing: my grandfather Jesus, when he had much given himself to the reading of the law, and the prophets, and other books of our fathers, and had gotten therein good judgment, was drawn on also himself to write something pertaining to learning and wisdom; to the intent that those which are desirous to learn, and are addicted to these things, might profit much more in living according to the law. Wherefore let me intreat you to read it with favour and attention, and to pardon us, wherein we may seem to come short of some words, which we have laboured to interpret. For the same things uttered in Hebrew, and translated into another tongue, have not the same force in them: and not only these things, but the law itself, and the prophets, and the rest of the books, have no small difference, when they are spoken in their own language. For in the eight and thirtieth year coming into Egypt, when Euergetes was king, and continuing there some time, I found a book of no small learning: therefore I thought it most necessary for me to bestow some diligence and travail to interpret it; using great watchfulness and skill in that space to bring the book to an end, and set it forth for them also, which in a strange country are willing to learn, being prepared before in manners to live after the law.

Wisdom of Jesus Son of Sirach

Sir.1

[1] All wisdom cometh from Jah, and is with him for ever.
[2] Who can number the sand of the sea, and the drops of rain, and the days of eternity?
[3] Who can find out the height of heaven, and the breadth of the earth, and the deep, and wisdom?
[4] Wisdom hath been created before all things, and the understanding of prudence from everlasting.
[5] The word of God most high is the fountain of wisdom; and her ways are everlasting commandments.
[6] To whom hath the root of wisdom been revealed? or who hath known her wise counsels?
[7] [Unto whom hath the knowledge of wisdom been made manifest? and who hath understood her great experience?]
[8] There is one wise and greatly to be feared, Jah sitting upon his throne.
[9] He created her, and saw her, and numbered her, and poured her out upon all his works.
[10] She is with all flesh according to his gift, and he hath given her to them that love him.
[11] The fear of Jah is honour, and glory, and gladness, and a crown of rejoicing.
[12] The fear of Jah maketh a merry heart, and giveth joy, and gladness, and a long life.
[13] Whoso feareth Jah, it shall go well with him at the last, and he shall find favour in the day of his death.
[14] To fear Jah is the beginning of wisdom: and it was created with the faithful in the womb.
[15] She hath built an everlasting foundation with men, and she shall continue with their seed.
[16] To fear Jah is fulness of wisdom, and filleth men with her fruits.
[17] She filleth all their house with things desirable, and the garners with her increase.
[18] The fear of Jah is a crown of wisdom, making peace and perfect health to flourish; both which are the gifts of God: and it enlargeth their rejoicing that love him.
[19] Wisdom raineth down skill and knowledge of understanding standing, and exalteth them to honour that hold her fast.
[20] The root of wisdom is to fear Jah, and the branches thereof are long life.
[21] The fear of Jah driveth away sins: and where it is present, it turneth away wrath.
[22] A furious man cannot be justified; for the sway of his fury shall be his destruction.
[23] A patient man will tear for a time, and afterward joy shall spring up unto him.
[24] He will hide his words for a time, and the lips of many shall declare his wisdom.
[25] The parables of knowledge are in the treasures of wisdom: but godliness is an abomination to a sinner.
[26] If thou desire wisdom, keep the commandments, and Jah shall give her unto thee.
[27] For the fear of Jah is wisdom and instruction: and faith and meekness are his delight.
[28] Distrust not the fear of Jah when thou art poor: and come not unto him with a double heart.
[29] Be not an hypocrite in the sight of men, and take good heed what thou speakest.
[30] Exalt not thyself, lest thou fall, and bring dishonour upon thy soul, and so God discover thy secrets, and cast thee down in the midst of the congregation, because thou camest not in truth to the fear of Jah, but thy heart is full of deceit.

Sir. 2

[1] My son, if thou come to serve Jah, prepare thy soul for temptation.
[2] Set thy heart aright, and constantly endure, and make not haste in time of trouble.
[3] Cleave unto him, and depart not away, that thou mayest be increased at thy last end.
[4] Whatsoever is brought upon thee take cheerfully, and be patient when thou art changed to a low estate.
[5] For gold is tried in the fire, and acceptable men in the furnace of adversity.
[6] Believe in him, and he will help thee; order thy way aright, and trust in him.
[7] Ye that fear Jah, wait for his mercy; and go not aside, lest ye fall.
[8] Ye that fear Jah, believe him; and your reward shall not fail.
[9] Ye that fear Jah, hope for good, and for everlasting joy and mercy.
[10] Look at the generations of old, and see; did ever any trust in Jah, and was confounded? or did any abide in his fear, and was forsaken? or whom did he ever despise, that called upon him?
[11] For Jah is full of compassion and mercy, longsuffering, and very pitiful, and forgiveth sins, and saveth in time of affliction.
[12] Woe be to fearful hearts, and faint hands, and the sinner that goeth two ways!
[13] Woe unto him that is fainthearted! for he believeth not; therefore shall he not be defended.
[14] Woe unto you that have lost patience! and what will ye do when Jah shall visit you?
[15] They that fear Jah will not disobey his Word; and they that love him will keep his ways.
[16] They that fear Jah will seek that which is well, pleasing unto him; and they that love him shall be filled with the law.
[17] They that fear Jah will prepare their hearts, and humble their souls in his sight,
[18] Saying, We will fall into the hands of Jah, and not into the hands of men: for as his majesty is, so is his mercy.

Sir. 3

[1] Hear me your father, O children, and do thereafter, that ye may be safe.
[2] For Jah hath given the father honour over the children, and hath confirmed the authority of the mother over the sons.
[3] Whoso honoureth his father maketh an atonement for his sins:
[4] And he that honoureth his mother is as one that layeth up treasure.
[5] Whoso honoureth his father shall have joy of his own children; and when he maketh his prayer, he shall be heard.
[6] He that honoureth his father shall have a long life; and he that is obedient unto Jah shall be a comfort to his mother.
[7] He that feareth Jah will honour his father, and will do service unto his parents, as to his masters.
[8] Honour thy father and mother both in word and deed, that a blessing may come upon thee from them.
[9] For the blessing of the father establisheth the houses of children; but the curse of the mother rooteth out foundations.
[10] Glory not in the dishonour of thy father; for thy father's dishonour is no glory unto thee.
[11] For the glory of a man is from the honour of his father; and a mother in dishonour is a reproach to the children.
[12] My son, help thy father in his age, and grieve him not as long as he liveth.
[13] And if his understanding fail, have patience with him; and despise him not when thou art in thy full strength.
[14] For the relieving of thy father shall not

be forgotten: and instead of sins it shall be added to build thee up.
[15] In the day of thine affliction it shall be remembered; thy sins also shall melt away, as the ice in the fair warm weather.
[16] He that forsaketh his father is as a blasphemer; and he that angereth his mother is cursed: of God.
[17] My son, go on with thy business in meekness; so shalt thou be beloved of him that is approved.
[18] The greater thou art, the more humble thyself, and thou shalt find favour before Jah.
[19] Many are in high place, and of renown: but mysteries are revealed unto the meek.
[20] For the power of Jah is great, and he is honoured of the lowly.
[21] Seek not out things that are too hard for thee, neither search the things that are above thy strength.
[22] But what is commanded thee, think thereupon with reverence, for it is not needful for thee to see with thine eyes the things that are in secret.
[23] Be not curious in unnecessary matters: for more things are shewed unto thee than men understand.
[24] For many are deceived by their own vain opinion; and an evil suspicion hath overthrown their judgment.
[25] Without eyes thou shalt want light: profess not the knowledge therefore that thou hast not.
[26] A stubborn heart shall fare evil at the last; and he that loveth danger shall perish therein.
[27] An obstinate heart shall be laden with sorrows; and the wicked man shall heap sin upon sin.
[28] In the punishment of the proud there is no remedy; for the plant of wickedness hath taken root in him.
[29] The heart of the prudent will understand a parable; and an attentive ear is the desire of a wise man.
[30] Water will quench a flaming fire; and alms maketh an atonement for sins.
[31] And he that requiteth good turns is mindful of that which may come hereafter; and when he falleth, he shall find a stay.

Sir. 4

[1] My son, defraud not the poor of his living, and make not the needy eyes to wait long.
[2] Make not an hungry soul sorrowful; neither provoke a man in his distress.
[3] Add not more trouble to an heart that is vexed; and defer not to give to him that is in need.
[4] Reject not the supplication of the afflicted; neither turn away thy face from a poor man.
[5] Turn not away thine eye from the needy, and give him none occasion to curse thee:
[6] For if he curse thee in the bitterness of his soul, his prayer shall be heard of him that made him.
[7] Get thyself the love of the congregation, and bow thy head to a great man.
[8] Let it not grieve thee to bow down thine ear to the poor, and give him a friendly answer with meekness.
[9] Deliver him that suffereth wrong from the hand of the oppressor; and be not fainthearted when thou sittest in judgment.
[10] Be as a father unto the fatherless, and instead of an husband unto their mother: so shalt thou be as the son of the most High, and he shall love thee more than thy mother doth.
[11] Wisdom exalteth her children, and layeth hold of them that seek her.
[12] He that loveth her loveth life; and they that seek to her early shall be filled with joy.
[13] He that holdeth her fast shall inherit glory; and wheresoever she entereth, Jah will bless.
[14] They that serve her shall minister to the

Holy One: and them that love her Jah doth love.
[15] Whoso giveth ear unto her shall judge the nations: and he that attendeth unto her shall dwell securely.
[16] If a man commit himself unto her, he shall inherit her; and his generation shall hold her in possession.
[17] For at the first she will walk with him by crooked ways, and bring fear and dread upon him, and torment him with her discipline, until she may trust his soul, and try him by her laws.
[18] Then will she return the straight way unto him, and comfort him, and shew him her secrets.
[19] But if he go wrong, she will forsake him, and give him over to his own ruin.
[20] Observe the opportunity, and beware of evil; and be not ashamed when it concerneth thy soul.
[21] For there is a shame that bringeth sin; and there is a shame which is glory and grace.
[22] Accept no person against thy soul, and let not the reverence of any man cause thee to fall.
[23] And refrain not to speak, when there is occasion to do good, and hide not thy wisdom in her beauty.
[24] For by speech wisdom shall be known: and learning by the word of the tongue.
[25] In no wise speak against the truth; but be abashed of the error of thine ignorance.
[26] Be not ashamed to confess thy sins; and force not the course of the river.
[27] Make not thyself an underling to a foolish man; neither accept the person of the mighty.
[28] Strive for the truth unto death, and Jah shall fight for thee.
[29] Be not hasty in thy tongue, and in thy deeds slack and remiss.
[30] Be not as a lion in thy house, nor frantick among thy servants.
[31] Let not thine hand be stretched out to receive, and shut when thou shouldest repay.

Sir.5

[1] Set thy heart upon thy goods; and say not, I have enough for my life.
[2] Follow not thine own mind and thy strength, to walk in the ways of thy heart:
[3] And say not, Who shall controul me for my works? for Jah will surely revenge thy pride.
[4] Say not, I have sinned, and what harm hath happened unto me? for Jah is longsuffering, he will in no wise let thee go.
[5] Concerning propitiation, be not without fear to add sin unto sin:
[6] And say not His mercy is great; he will be pacified for the multitude of my sins: for mercy and wrath come from him, and his indignation resteth upon sinners.
[7] Make no tarrying to turn to Jah, and put not off from day to day: for suddenly shall the wrath of Jah come forth, and in thy security thou shalt be destroyed, and perish in the day of vengeance.
[8] Set not thine heart upon goods unjustly gotten, for they shall not profit thee in the day of calamity.
[9] Winnow not with every wind, and go not into every way: for so doth the sinner that hath a double tongue.
[10] Be stedfast in thy understanding; and let thy word be the same.
[11] Be swift to hear; and let thy life be sincere; and with patience give answer.
[12] If thou hast understanding, answer thy neighbour; if not, lay thy hand upon thy mouth.
[13] Honour and shame is in talk: and the tongue of man is his fall.
[14] Be not called a whisperer, and lie not in wait with thy tongue: for a foul shame is upon the thief, and an evil condemnation upon the double tongue.

[15] Be not ignorant of any thing in a great matter or a small.

Sir.6

[1] Instead of a friend become not an enemy; for [thereby] thou shalt inherit an ill name, shame, and reproach: even so shall a sinner that hath a double tongue.
[2] Extol not thyself in the counsel of thine own heart; that thy soul be not torn in pieces as a bull [straying alone.]
[3] Thou shalt eat up thy leaves, and lose thy fruit, and leave thyself as a dry tree.
[4] A wicked soul shall destroy him that hath it, and shall make him to be laughed to scorn of his enemies.
[5] Sweet language will multiply friends: and a fairspeaking tongue will increase kind greetings.
[6] Be in peace with many: nevertheless have but one counsellor of a thousand.
[7] If thou wouldest get a friend, prove him first and be not hasty to credit him.
[8] For some man is a friend for his own occasion, and will not abide in the day of thy trouble.
[9] And there is a friend, who being turned to enmity, and strife will discover thy reproach.
[10] Again, some friend is a companion at the table, and will not continue in the day of thy affliction.
[11] But in thy prosperity he will be as thyself, and will be bold over thy servants.
[12] If thou be brought low, he will be against thee, and will hide himself from thy face.
[13] Separate thyself from thine enemies, and take heed of thy friends.
[14] A faithfull friend is a strong defence: and he that hath found such an one hath found a treasure.
[15] Nothing doth countervail a faithful friend, and his excellency is invaluable.
[16] A faithful friend is the medicine of life; and they that fear Jah shall find him.
[17] Whoso feareth Jah shall direct his friendship aright: for as he is, so shall his neighbour be also.
[18] My son, gather instruction from thy youth up: so shalt thou find wisdom till thine old age.
[19] Come unto her as one that ploweth and soweth, and wait for her good fruits: for thou shalt not toil much in labouring about her, but thou shalt eat of her fruits right soon.
[20] She is very unpleasant to the unlearned: he that is without understanding will not remain with her.
[21] She will lie upon him as a mighty stone of trial; and he will cast her from him ere it be long.
[22] For wisdom is according to her name, and she is not manifest unto many.
[23] Give ear, my son, receive my advice, and refuse not my counsel,
[24] And put thy feet into her fetters, and thy neck into her chain.
[25] Bow down thy shoulder, and bear her, and be not grieved with her bonds.
[26] Come unto her with thy whole heart, and keep her ways with all thy power.
[27] Search, and seek, and she shall be made known unto thee: and when thou hast got hold of her, let her not go.
[28] For at the last thou shalt find her rest, and that shall be turned to thy joy.
[29] Then shall her fetters be a strong defence for thee, and her chains a robe of glory.
[30] For there is a golden ornament upon her, and her bands are purple lace.
[31] Thou shalt put her on as a robe of honour, and shalt put her about thee as a crown of joy.
[32] My son, if thou wilt, thou shalt be taught: and if thou wilt apply thy mind, thou shalt be prudent.
[33] If thou love to hear, thou shalt receive

understanding: and if thou bow thine ear, thou shalt be wise,
[34] Stand in the multitude of the elders; and cleave unto him that is wise.
[35] Be willing to hear every godly discourse; and let not the parables of understanding escape thee.
[36] And if thou seest a man of understanding, get thee betimes unto him, and let thy foot wear the steps of his door.
[37] Let thy mind be upon the ordinances of Jah and meditate continually in his commandments: he shall establish thine heart, and give thee wisdom at thine owns desire.

Sir. 7

[1] Do no evil, so shall no harm come unto thee.
[2] Depart from the unjust, and iniquity shall turn away from thee.
[3] My son, sow not upon the furrows of unrighteousness, and thou shalt not reap them sevenfold.
[4] Seek not of Jah preeminence, neither of the king the seat of honour.
[5] justify not thyself before Jah; and boast not of thy wisdom before the king.
[6] Seek not to be judge, being not able to take away iniquity; lest at any time thou fear the person of the mighty, an stumblingblock in the way of thy uprightness.
[7] Offend not against the multitude of a city, and then thou shalt not cast thyself down among the people.
[8] Bind not one sin upon another; for in one thou shalt not be unpunished.
[9] Say not, God will look upon the multitude of my oblations, and when I offer to the most high God, he will accept it.
[10] Be not fainthearted when thou makest thy prayer, and neglect not to give alms.
[11] Laugh no man to scorn in the bitterness of his soul: for there is one which humbleth and exalteth.
[12] Devise not a lie against thy brother; neither do the like to thy friend.
[13] Use not to make any manner of lie: for the custom thereof is not good.
[14] Use not many words in a multitude of elders, and make not much babbling when thou prayest.
[15] Hate not laborious work, neither husbandry, which the most High hath ordained.
[16] Number not thyself among the multitude of sinners, but remember that wrath will not tarry long.
[17] Humble thyself greatly: for the vengeance of the ungodly is fire and worms.
[18] Change not a friend for any good by no means; neither a faithful brother for the gold of Ophir.
[19] Forego not a wise and good woman: for her grace is above gold.
[20] Whereas thy servant worketh truly, entreat him not evil. nor the hireling that bestoweth himself wholly for thee.
[21] Let thy soul love a good servant, and defraud him not of liberty.
[22] Hast thou cattle? have an eye to them: and if they be for thy profit, keep them with thee.
[23] Hast thou children? instruct them, and bow down their neck from their youth.
[24] Hast thou daughters? have a care of their body, and shew not thyself cheerful toward them.
[25] Marry thy daughter, and so shalt thou have performed a weighty matter: but give her to a man of understanding.
[26] Hast thou a wife after thy mind? forsake her not: but give not thyself over to a light woman.
[27] Honour thy father with thy whole heart, and forget not the sorrows of thy mother.
[28] Remember that thou wast begotten of them; and how canst thou recompense them the things that they have done for thee?
[29] Fear Jah with all thy soul, and

reverence his priests.
[30] Love him that made thee with all thy strength, and forsake not his ministers.
[31] Fear Jah, and honor the priest; and give him his portion, as it is commanded thee; the firstfruits, and the trespass offering, and the gift of the shoulders, and the sacrifice of sanctification, and the firstfruits of the holy things.
[32] And stretch thine hand unto the poor, that thy blessing may be perfected.
[33] A gift hath grace in the sight of every man living; and for the dead detain it not.
[34] Fail not to be with them that weep, and mourn with them that mourn.
[35] Be not slow to visit the sick: fir that shall make thee to be beloved.
[36] Whatsoever thou takest in hand, remember the end, and thou shalt never do amiss.

Sir.8

[1] Strive not with a mighty man' lest thou fall into his hands.
[2] Be not at variance with a rich man, lest he overweigh thee: for gold hath destroyed many, and perverted the hearts of kings.
[3] Strive not with a man that is full of tongue, and heap not wood upon his fire.
[4] Jest not with a rude man, lest thy ancestors be disgraced.
[5] Reproach not a man that turneth from sin, but remember that we are all worthy of punishment.
[6] Dishonour not a man in his old age: for even some of us wax old.
[7] Rejoice not over thy greatest enemy being dead, but remember that we die all.
[8] Despise not the discourse of the wise, but acquaint thyself with their proverbs: for of them thou shalt learn instruction, and how to serve great men with ease.
[9] Miss not the discourse of the elders: for they also learned of their fathers, and of them thou shalt learn understanding, and to give answer as need requireth.
[10] Kindle not the coals of a sinner, lest thou be burnt with the flame of his fire.
[11] Rise not up [in anger] at the presence of an injurious person, lest he lie in wait to entrap thee in thy words
[12] Lend not unto him that is mightier than thyself; for if thou lendest him, count it but lost.
[13] Be not surety above thy power: for if thou be surety, take care to pay it.
[14] Go not to law with a judge; for they will judge for him according to his honour.
[15] Travel not by the way with a bold fellow, lest he become grievous unto thee: for he will do according to his own will, and thou shalt perish with him through his folly.
[16] Strive not with an angry man, and go not with him into a solitary place: for blood is as nothing in his sight, and where there is no help, he will overthrow thee.
[17] Consult not with a fool; for he cannot keep counsel.
[18] Do no secret thing before a stranger; for thou knowest not what he will bring forth.
[19] Open not thine heart to every man, lest he requite thee with a shrewd turn.

Sir.9

[1] Be not jealous over the wife of thy bosom, and teach her not an evil lesson against thyself.
[2] Give not thy soul unto a woman to set her foot upon thy substance.
[3] Meet not with an harlot, lest thou fall into her snares.
[4] Use not much the company of a woman that is a singer, lest thou be taken with her attempts.
[5] Gaze not on a maid, that thou fall not by those things that are precious in her.
[6] Give not thy soul unto harlots, that thou lose not thine inheritance.

[7] Look not round about thee in the streets of the city, neither wander thou in the solitary place thereof.
[8] Turn away thine eye from a beautiful woman, and look not upon another's beauty; for many have been deceived by the beauty of a woman; for herewith love is kindled as a fire.
[9] Sit not at all with another man's wife, nor sit down with her in thine arms, and spend not thy money with her at the wine; lest thine heart incline unto her, and so through thy desire thou fall into destruction.
[10] Forsake not an old friend; for the new is not comparable to him: a new friend is as new wine; when it is old, thou shalt drink it with pleasure.
[11] Envy not the glory of a sinner: for thou knowest not what shall be his end.
[12] Delight not in the thing that the ungodly have pleasure in; but remember they shall not go unpunished unto their grave.
[13] Keep thee far from the man that hath power to kill; so shalt thou not doubt the fear of death: and if thou come unto him, make no fault, lest he take away thy life presently: remember that thou goest in the midst of snares, and that thou walkest upon the battlements of the city.
[14] As near as thou canst, guess at thy neighbour, and consult with the wise.
[15] Let thy talk be with the wise, and all thy communication in the law of the most High.
[16] And let just men eat and drink with thee; and let thy glorying be in the fear of Jah.
[17] For the hand of the artificer the work shall be commended: and the wise ruler of the people for his speech.
[18] A man of an ill tongue is dangerous in his city; and he that is rash in his talk shall be hated.

Sir.10

[1] A wise judge will instruct his people; and the government of a prudent man is well ordered.
[2] As the judge of the people is himself, so are his officers; and what manner of man the ruler of the city is, such are all they that dwell therein.
[3] An unwise king destroyeth his people; but through the prudence of them which are in authority the city shall be inhabited.
[4] The power of the earth is in the hand of Jah, and in due time he will set over it one that is profitable.
[5] In the hand of God is the prosperity of man: and upon the person of the scribe shall he lay his honour.
[6] Bear not hatred to thy neighbour for every wrong; and do nothing at all by injurious practices.
[7] Pride is hateful before God and man: and by both doth one commit iniquity.
[8] Because of unrighteous dealings, injuries, and riches got by deceit, the kingdom is translated from one people to another.
[9] Why is earth and ashes proud? There is not a more wicked thing than a covetous man: for such an one setteth his own soul to sale; because while he liveth he casteth away his bowels.
[10] The physician cutteth off a long disease; and he that is to day a king to morrow shall die.
[11] For when a man is dead, he shall inherit creeping things, beasts, and worms.
[12] The beginning of pride is when one departeth from God, and his heart is turned away from his Maker.
[13] For pride is the beginning of sin, and he that hath it shall pour out abomination: and therefore Jah brought upon them strange calamities, and overthrew them utterly.
[14] Jah hath cast down the thrones of proud princes, and set up the meek in their stead.
[15] Jah hath plucked up the roots of the proud nations, and planted the lowly in their

place.
[16] Jah overthrew countries of the heathen, and destroyed them to the foundations of the earth.
[17] He took some of them away, and destroyed them, and hath made their memorial to cease from the earth.
[18] Pride was not made for men, nor furious anger for them that are born of a woman.
[19] They that fear Jah are a sure seed, and they that love him an honourable plant: they that regard not the law are a dishonourable seed; they that transgress the commandments are a deceivable seed.
[20] Among brethren he that is chief is honorable; so are they that fear Jah in his eyes.
[21] The fear of Jah goeth before the obtaining of authority: but roughness and pride is the losing thereof.
[22] Whether he be rich, noble, or poor, their glory is the fear of Jah.
[23] It is not meet to despise the poor man that hath understanding; neither is it convenient to magnify a sinful man.
[24] Great men, and judges, and potentates, shall be honoured; yet is there none of them greater than he that feareth Jah.
[25] Unto the servant that is wise shall they that are free do service: and he that hath knowledge will not grudge when he is reformed.
[26] Be not overwise in doing thy business; and boast not thyself in the time of thy distress.
[27] Better is he that laboureth, and aboundeth in all things, than he that boasteth himself, and wanteth bread.
[28] My son, glorify thy soul in meekness, and give it honour according to the dignity thereof.
[29] Who will justify him that sinneth against his own soul? and who will honour him that dishonoureth his own life?
[30] The poor man is honoured for his skill, and the rich man is honoured for his riches.
[31] He that is honoured in poverty, how much more in riches? and he that is dishonourable in riches, how much more in poverty?

Sir.11

[1] Wisdom lifteth up the head of him that is of low degree, and maketh him to sit among great men.
[2] Commend not a man for his beauty; neither abhor a man for his outward appearance.
[3] The bee is little among such as fly; but her fruit is the chief of sweet things.
[4] Boast not of thy clothing and raiment, and exalt not thyself in the day of honour: for the works of Jah are wonderful, and his works among men are hidden.
[5] Many kings have sat down upon the ground; and one that was never thought of hath worn the crown.
[6] Many mighty men have been greatly disgraced; and the honourable delivered into other men's hands.
[7] Blame not before thou hast examined the truth: understand first, and then rebuke.
[8] Answer not before thou hast heard the cause: neither interrupt men in the midst of their talk.
[9] Strive not in a matter that concerneth thee not; and sit not in judgment with sinners.
[10] My son, meddle not with many matters: for if thou meddle much, thou shalt not be innocent; and if thou follow after, thou shalt not obtain, neither shalt thou escape by fleeing.
[11] There is one that laboureth, and taketh pains, and maketh haste, and is so much the more behind.
[12] Again, there is another that is slow, and hath need of help, wanting ability, and full of poverty; yet the eye of Jah looked upon

him for good, and set him up from his low estate,
[13] And lifted up his head from misery; so that many that saw from him is peace over all the
[14] Prosperity and adversity, life and death, poverty and riches, come of Jah.
[15] Wisdom, knowledge, and understanding of the law, are of Jah: love, and the way of good works, are from him.
[16] Error and darkness had their beginning together with sinners: and evil shall wax old with them that glory therein.
[17] The gift of Jah remaineth with the ungodly, and his favour bringeth prosperity for ever.
[18] There is that waxeth rich by his wariness and pinching, and this his the portion of his reward:
[19] Whereas he saith, I have found rest, and now will eat continually of my goods; and yet he knoweth not what time shall come upon him, and that he must leave those things to others, and die.
[20] Be stedfast in thy covenant, and be conversant therein, and wax old in thy work.
[21] Marvel not at the works of sinners; but trust in Jah, and abide in thy labour: for it is an easy thing in the sight of Jah on the sudden to make a poor man rich.
[22] The blessing of Jah is in the reward of the godly, and suddenly he maketh his blessing flourish.
[23] Say not, What profit is there of my service? and what good things shall I have hereafter?
[24] Again, say not, I have enough, and possess many things, and what evil shall I have hereafter?
[25] In the day of prosperity there is a forgetfulness of affliction: and in the day of affliction there is no more remembrance of prosperity.
[26] For it is an easy thing unto Jah in the day of death to reward a man according to his ways.
[27] The affliction of an hour maketh a man forget pleasure: and in his end his deeds shall be discovered.
[28] Judge none blessed before his death: for a man shall be known in his children.
[29] Bring not every man into thine house: for the deceitful man hath many trains.
[30] Like as a partridge taken [and kept] in a cage, so is the heart of the proud; and like as a spy, watcheth he for thy fall:
[31] For he lieth in wait, and turneth good into evil, and in things worthy praise will lay blame upon thee.
[32] Of a spark of fire a heap of coals is kindled: and a sinful man layeth wait for blood.
[33] Take heed of a mischievous man, for he worketh wickedness; lest he bring upon thee a perpetual blot.
[34] Receive a stranger into thine house, and he will disturb thee, and turn thee out of thine own.

Sir. 12

[1] When thou wilt do good know to whom thou doest it; so shalt thou be thanked for thy benefits.
[2] Do good to the godly man, and thou shalt find a recompence; and if not from him, yet from the most High.
[3] There can no good come to him that is always occupied in evil, nor to him that giveth no alms.
[4] Give to the godly man, and help not a sinner.
[5] Do well unto him that is lowly, but give not to the ungodly: hold back thy bread, and give it not unto him, lest he overmaster thee thereby: for [else] thou shalt receive twice as much evil for all the good thou shalt have done unto him.
[6] For the most High hateth sinners, and will repay vengeance unto the ungodly, and keepeth them against the mighty day of their

punishment.
[7] Give unto the good, and help not the sinner.
[8] A friend cannot be known in prosperity: and an enemy cannot be hidden in adversity.
[9] In the prosperity of a man enemies will be grieved: but in his adversity even a friend will depart.
[10] Never trust thine enemy: for like as iron rusteth, so is his wickedness.
[11] Though he humble himself, and go crouching, yet take good heed and beware of him, and thou shalt be unto him as if thou hadst wiped a lookingglass, and thou shalt know that his rust hath not been altogether wiped away.
[12] Set him not by thee, lest, when he hath overthrown thee, he stand up in thy place; neither let him sit at thy right hand, lest he seek to take thy seat, and thou at the last remember my words, and be pricked therewith.
[13] Who will pity a charmer that is bitten with a serpent, or any such as come nigh wild beasts?
[14] So one that goeth to a sinner, and is defiled with him in his sins, who will pity?
[15] For a while he will abide with thee, but if thou begin to fall, he will not tarry.
[16] An enemy speaketh sweetly with his lips, but in his heart he imagineth how to throw thee into a pit: he will weep with his eyes, but if he find opportunity, he will not be satisfied with blood.
[17] If adversity come upon thee, thou shalt find him there first; and though he pretend to help thee, yet shall he undermine thee.
[18] He will shake his head, and clap his hands, and whisper much, and change his countenance.

Sir.13

[1] He that toucheth pitch shall be defiled therewith; and he that hath fellowship with a proud man shall be like unto him.
[2] Burden not thyself above thy power while thou livest; and have no fellowship with one that is mightier and richer than thyself: for how agree the kettle and the earthen pot together? for if the one be smitten against the other, it shall be broken.
[3] The rich man hath done wrong, and yet he threateneth withal: the poor is wronged, and he must intreat also.
[4] If thou be for his profit, he will use thee: but if thou have nothing, he will forsake thee.
[5] If thou have any thing, he will live with thee: yea, he will make thee bare, and will not be sorry for it.
[6] If he have need of thee, he will deceive thee, and smile upon thee, and put thee in hope; he will speak thee fair, and say, What wantest thou?
[7] And he will shame thee by his meats, until he have drawn thee dry twice or thrice, and at the last he will laugh thee to scorn afterward, when he seeth thee, he will forsake thee, and shake his head at thee.
[8] Beware that thou be not deceived and brought down in thy jollity.
[9] If thou be invited of a mighty man, withdraw thyself, and so much the more will he invite thee.
[10] Press thou not upon him, lest thou be put back; stand not far off, lest thou be forgotten.
[11] Affect not to be made equal unto him in talk, and believe not his many words: for with much communication will he tempt thee, and smiling upon thee will get out thy secrets:
[12] But cruelly he will lay up thy words, and will not spare to do thee hurt, and to put thee in prison.
[13] Observe, and take good heed, for thou walkest in peril of thy overthrowing: when thou hearest these things, awake in thy sleep.
[14] Love Jah all thy life, and call upon him

for thy salvation.
[15] Every beast loveth his like, and every man loveth his neighbor.
[16] All flesh consorteth according to kind, and a man will cleave to his like.
[17] What fellowship hath the wolf with the lamb? so the sinner with the godly.
[18] What agreement is there between the hyena and a dog? and what peace between the rich and the poor?
[19] As the wild ass is the lion's prey in the wilderness: so the rich eat up the poor.
[20] As the proud hate humility: so doth the rich abhor the poor.
[21] A rich man beginning to fall is held up of his friends: but a poor man being down is thrust away by his friends.
[22] When a rich man is fallen, he hath many helpers: he speaketh things not to be spoken, and yet men justify him: the poor man slipped, and yet they rebuked him too; he spake wisely, and could have no place.
[23] When a rich man speaketh, every man holdeth his tongue, and, look, what he saith, they extol it to the clouds: but if the poor man speak, they say, What fellow is this? and if he stumble, they will help to overthrow him.
[24] Riches are good unto him that hath no sin, and poverty is evil in the mouth of the ungodly.
[25] The heart of a man changeth his countenance, whether it be for good or evil: and a merry heart maketh a cheerful countenance.
[26] A cheerful countenance is a token of a heart that is in prosperity; and the finding out of parables is a wearisome labour of the mind.

Sir.14

[1] Blessed is the man that hath not slipped with his mouth, and is not pricked with the multitude of sins.
[2] Blessed is he whose conscience hath not condemned him, and who is not fallen from his hope in Jah.
[3] Riches are not comely for a niggard: and what should an envious man do with money?
[4] He that gathereth by defrauding his own soul gathereth for others, that shall spend his goods riotously.
[5] He that is evil to himself, to whom will he be good? he shall not take pleasure in his goods.
[6] There is none worse than he that envieth himself; and this is a recompence of his wickedness.
[7] And if he doeth good, he doeth it unwillingly; and at the last he will declare his wickedness.
[8] The envious man hath a wicked eye; he turneth away his face, and despiseth men.
[9] A covetous man's eye is not satisfied with his portion; and the iniquity of the wicked drieth up his soul.
[10] A wicked eye envieth [his] bread, and he is a niggard at his table.
[11] My son, according to thy ability do good to thyself, and give Jah his due offering.
[12] Remember that death will not be long in coming, and that the covenant of the grave is not shewed unto thee.
[13] Do good unto thy friend before thou die, and according to thy ability stretch out thy hand and give to him.
[14] Defraud not thyself of the good day, and let not the part of a good desire overpass thee.
[15] Shalt thou not leave thy travails unto another? and thy labours to be divided by lot?
[16] Give, and take, and sanctify thy soul; for there is no seeking of dainties in the grave.
[17] All flesh waxeth old as a garment: for the covenant from the beginning is, Thou shalt die the death.

[18] As of the green leaves on a thick tree, some fall, and some grow; so is the generation of flesh and blood, one cometh to an end, and another is born.
[19] Every work rotteth and consumeth away, and the worker thereof shall go withal.
[20] Blessed is the man that doth meditate good things in wisdom, and that reasoneth of holy things by his understanding. ing.
[21] He that considereth her ways in his heart shall also have understanding in her secrets.
[22] Go after her as one that traceth, and lie in wait in her ways.
[23] He that prieth in at her windows shall also hearken at her doors.
[24] He that doth lodge near her house shall also fasten a pin in her walls.
[25] He shall pitch his tent nigh unto her, and shall lodge in a lodging where good things are.
[26] He shall set his children under her shelter, and shall lodge under her branches.
[27] By her he shall be covered from heat, and in her glory shall he dwell.

Sir.15

[1] He that feareth Jah will do good, and he that hath the knowledge of the law shall obtain her.
[2] And as a mother shall she meet him, and receive him as a wife married of a virgin.
[3] With the bread of understanding shall she feed him, and give him the water of wisdom to drink.
[4] He shall be stayed upon her, and shall not be moved; and shall rely upon her, and shall not be confounded.
[5] She shall exalt him above his neighbours, and in the midst of the congregation shall she open his mouth.
[6] He shall find joy and a crown of gladness, and she shall cause him to inherit an everlasting name.
[7] But foolish men shall not attain unto her, and sinners shall not see her.
[8] For she is far from pride, and men that are liars cannot remember her.
[9] Praise is not seemly in the mouth of a sinner, for it was not sent him of Jah.
[10] For praise shall be uttered in wisdom, and Jah will prosper it.
[11] Say not thou, It is through Jah that I fell away: for thou oughtest not to do the things that he hateth.
[12] Say not thou, He hath caused me to err: for he hath no need of the sinful man.
[13] Jah hateth all abomination; and they that fear God love it not.
[14] He himself made man from the beginning, and left him in the hand of his counsel;
[15] If thou wilt, to keep the commandments, and to perform acceptable faithfulness.
[16] He hath set fire and water before thee: stretch forth thy hand unto whether thou wilt.
[17] Before man is life and death; and whether him liketh shall be given him.
[18] For the wisdom of Jah is great, and he is mighty in power, and beholdeth all things:
[19] And his eyes are upon them that fear him, and he knoweth every work of man.
[20] He hath commanded no man to do wickedly, neither hath he given any man licence to sin.

Sir.16

[1] Desire not a multitude of unprofitable children, neither delight in ungodly sons.
[2] Though they multiply, rejoice not in them, except the fear of Jah be with them.
[3] Trust not thou in their life, neither respect their multitude: for one that is just is better than a thousand; and better it is to die without children, than to have them that are

ungodly.

[4] For by one that hath understanding shall the city be replenished: but the kindred of the wicked shall speedily become desolate.
[5] Many such things have I seen with mine eyes, and mine ear hath heard greater things than these.
[6] In the congregation of the ungodly shall a fire be kindled; and in a rebellious nation wrath is set on fire.
[7] He was not pacified toward the old giants, who fell away in the strength of their foolishness.
[8] Neither spared he the place where Lot sojourned, but abhorred them for their pride.
[9] He pitied not the people of perdition, who were taken away in their sins:
[10] Nor the six hundred thousand footmen, who were gathered together in the hardness of their hearts.
[11] And if there be one stiffnecked among the people, it is marvel if he escape unpunished: for mercy and wrath are with him; he is mighty to forgive, and to pour out displeasure.
[12] As his mercy is great, so is his correction also: he judgeth a man according to his works
[13] The sinner shall not escape with his spoils: and the patience of the godly shall not be frustrate.
[14] Make way for every work of mercy: for every man shall find according to his works.
[15] Jah hardened Pharaoh, that he should not know him, that his powerful works might be known to the world.
[16] His mercy is manifest to every creature; and he hath separated his light from the darkness with an adamant.
[17] Say not thou, I will hide myself from Jah: shall any remember me from above? I shall not be remembered among so many people: for what is my soul among such an infinite number of creatures?
[18] Behold, the heaven, and the heaven of heavens, the deep, and the earth, and all that therein is, shall be moved when he shall visit.
[19] The mountains also and foundations of the earth be shaken with trembling, when Jah looketh upon them.
[20] No heart can think upon these things worthily: and who is able to conceive his ways?
[21] It is a tempest which no man can see: for the most part of his works are hid.
[22] Who can declare the works of his justice? or who can endure them? for his covenant is afar off, and the trial of all things is in the end.
[23] He that wanteth understanding will think upon vain things: and a foolish man erring imagineth follies.
[24] by son, hearken unto me, and learn knowledge, and mark my words with thy heart.
[25] I will shew forth doctrine in weight, and declare his knowledge exactly.
[26] The works of Jah are done in judgment from the beginning: and from the time he made them he disposed the parts thereof.
[27] He garnished his works for ever, and in his hand are the chief of them unto all generations: they neither labour, nor are weary, nor cease from their works.
[28] None of them hindereth another, and they shall never disobey his word.
[29] After this Jah looked upon the earth, and filled it with his blessings.
[30] With all manner of living things hath he covered the face thereof; and they shall return into it again.

Sir. 17

[1] Jah created man of the earth, and turned him into it again.
[2] He gave them few days, and a short time, and power also over the things therein.
[3] He endued them with strength by themselves, and made them according to his

image,
[4] And put the fear of man upon all flesh, and gave him dominion over beasts and fowls.
[5] They received the use of the five operations of Jah, and in the sixth place he imparted them understanding, and in the seventh speech, an interpreter of the cogitations thereof.]
[6] Counsel, and a tongue, and eyes, ears, and a heart, gave he them to understand.
[7] Withal he filled them with the knowledge of understanding, and shewed them good and evil.
[8] He set his eye upon their hearts, that he might shew them the greatness of his works.
[9] He gave them to glory in his marvellous acts for ever, that they might declare his works with understanding.
[10] And the elect shall praise his holy name.
[11] Beside this he gave them knowledge, and the law of life for an heritage.
[12] He made an everlasting covenant with them, and shewed them his judgments.
[13] Their eyes saw the majesty of his glory, and their ears heard his glorious voice.
[14] And he said unto them, Beware of all unrighteousness; and he gave every man commandment concerning his neighbour.
[15] Their ways are ever before him, and shall not be hid from his eyes.
[16] Every man from his youth is given to evil; neither could they make to themselves fleshy hearts for stony.
[17] For in the division of the nations of the whole earth he set a ruler over every people; but Israel is Jah's portion:
[18] Whom, being his firstborn, he nourisheth with discipline, and giving him the light of his love doth not forsake him.
[19] Therefore all their works are as the sun before him, and his eyes are continually upon their ways.
[20] None of their unrighteous deeds are hid from him, but all their sins are before Jah

[21] But Jah being gracious and knowing his workmanship, neither left nor forsook them, but spared them.
[22] The alms of a man is as a signet with him, and he will keep the good deeds of man as the apple of the eye, and give repentance to his sons and daughters.
[23] Afterwards he will rise up and reward them, and render their recompence upon their heads.
[24] But unto them that repent, he granted them return, and comforted those that failed in patience.
[25] Return unto Jah, and forsake thy sins, make thy prayer before his face, and offend less.
[26] Turn again to the most High, and turn away from iniquity: for he will lead thee out of darkness into the light of health, and hate thou abomination vehemently.
[27] Who shall praise the most High in the grave, instead of them which live and give thanks?
[28] Thanksgiving perisheth from the dead, as from one that is not: the living and sound in heart shall praise Jah.
[29] How great is the lovingkindness of Jah our God, and his compassion unto such as turn unto him in holiness!
[30] For all things cannot be in men, because the son of man is not immortal.
[31] What is brighter than the sun? yet the light thereof faileth; and flesh and blood will imagine evil.
[32] He vieweth the power of the height of heaven; and all men are but earth and ashes.

Sir. 18

[1] He that liveth for ever Hath created all things in general.
[2] Jah only is righteous, and there is none other but he,
[3] Who governeth the world with the palm of his hand, and all things obey his will: for

he is the King of all, by his power dividing holy things among them from profane.
[4] To whom hath he given power to declare his works? and who shall find out his noble acts?
[5] Who shall number the strength of his majesty? and who shall also tell out his mercies?
[6] As for the wondrous works of Jah, there may nothing be taken from them, neither may any thing be put unto them, neither can the ground of them be found out.
[7] When a man hath done, then he beginneth; and when he leaveth off, then he shall be doubtful.
[8] What is man, and whereto serveth he? what is his good, and what is his evil?
[9] The number of a man's days at the most are an hundred years.
[10] As a drop of water unto the sea, and a gravelstone in comparison of the sand; so are a thousand years to the days of eternity.
[11] Therefore is God patient with them, and poureth forth his mercy upon them.
[12] He saw and perceived their end to be evil; therefore he multiplied his compassion.
[13] The mercy of man is toward his neighbour; but the mercy of Jah is upon all flesh: he reproveth, and nurtureth, and teacheth and bringeth again, as a shepherd his flock.
[14] He hath mercy on them that receive discipline, and that diligently seek after his judgments.
[15] My son, blemish not thy good deeds, neither use uncomfortable words when thou givest any thing.
[16] Shall not the dew asswage the heat? so is a word better than a gift.
[17] Lo, is not a word better than a gift? but both are with a gracious man.
[18] A fool will upbraid churlishly, and a gift of the envious consumeth the eyes.
[19] Learn before thou speak, and use physick or ever thou be sick.
[20] Before judgment examine thyself, and in the day of visitation thou shalt find mercy.
[21] Humble thyself before thou be sick, and in the time of sins shew repentance.
[22] Let nothing hinder thee to pay thy vow in due time, and defer not until death to be justified.
[23] Before thou prayest, prepare thyself; and be not as one that tempteth Jah.
[24] Think upon the wrath that shall be at the end, and the time of vengeance, when he shall turn away his face.
[25] When thou hast enough, remember the time of hunger: and when thou art rich, think upon poverty and need.
[26] From the morning until the evening the time is changed, and all things are soon done before Jah.
[27] A wise man will fear in every thing, and in the day of sinning he will beware of offence: but a fool will not observe time.
[28] Every man of understanding knoweth wisdom, and will give praise unto him that found her.
[29] They that were of understanding in sayings became also wise themselves, and poured forth exquisite parables.
[30] Go not after thy lusts, but refrain thyself from thine appetites.
[31] If thou givest thy soul the desires that please her, she will make thee a laughingstock to thine enemies that malign thee.
[32] Take not pleasure in much good cheer, neither be tied to the expence thereof.
[33] Be not made a beggar by banqueting upon borrowing, when thou hast nothing in thy purse: for thou shalt lie in wait for thine own life, and be talked on.

Sir.19

[1] A labouring man that A is given to drunkenness shall not be rich: and he that contemneth small things shall fall by little

and little.
[2] Wine and women will make men of understanding to fall away: and he that cleaveth to harlots will become impudent.
[3] Moths and worms shall have him to heritage, and a bold man shall be taken away.
[4] He that is hasty to give credit is lightminded; and he that sinneth shall offend against his own soul.
[5] Whoso taketh pleasure in wickedness shall be condemned: but he that resisteth pleasures crowneth his life.
[6] He that can rule his tongue shall live without strife; and he that hateth babbling shall have less evil.
[7] Rehearse not unto another that which is told unto thee, and thou shalt fare never the worse.
[8] Whether it be to friend or foe, talk not of other men's lives; and if thou canst without offence, reveal them not.
[9] For he heard and observed thee, and when time cometh he will hate thee.
[10] If thou hast heard a word, let it die with thee; and be bold, it will not burst thee.
[11] A fool travaileth with a word, as a woman in labour of a child.
[12] As an arrow that sticketh in a man's thigh, so is a word within a fool's belly.
[13] Admonish a friend, it may be he hath not done it: and if he have done it, that he do it no more.
[14] Admonish thy friend, it may be he hath not said it: and if he have, that he speak it not again.
[15] Admonish a friend: for many times it is a slander, and believe not every tale.
[16] There is one that slippeth in his speech, but not from his heart; and who is he that hath not offended with his tongue?
[17] Admonish thy neighbour before thou threaten him; and not being angry, give place to the law of the most High.
[18] The fear of Jah is the first step to be accepted [of him,] and wisdom obtaineth his love.
[19] The knowledge of the commandments of Jah is the doctrine of life: and they that do things that please him shall receive the fruit of the tree of immortality.
[20] The fear of Jah is all wisdom; and in all wisdom is the performance of the law, and the knowledge of his omnipotency.
[21] If a servant say to his master, I will not do as it pleaseth thee; though afterward he do it, he angereth him that nourisheth him.
[22] The knowledge of wickedness is not wisdom, neither at any time the counsel of sinners prudence.
[23] There is a wickedness, and the same an abomination; and there is a fool wanting in wisdom.
[24] He that hath small understanding, and feareth God, is better than one that hath much wisdom, and transgresseth the law of the most High.
[25] There is an exquisite subtilty, and the same is unjust; and there is one that turneth aside to make judgment appear; and there is a wise man that justifieth in judgment.
[26] There is a wicked man that hangeth down his head sadly; but inwardly he is full of deceit,
[27] Casting down his countenance, and making as if he heard not: where he is not known, he will do thee a mischief before thou be aware.
[28] And if for want of power he be hindered from sinning, yet when he findeth opportunity he will do evil.
[29] A man may be known by his look, and one that hath understanding by his countenance, when thou meetest him.
[30] A man's attire, and excessive laughter, and gait, shew what he is.

Sir.20

[1] There is a reproof that is not comely: again, some man holdeth his tongue, and he

is wise.
[2] It is much better to reprove, than to be angry secretly: and he that confesseth his fault shall be preserved from hurt.
[3] How good is it, when thou art reproved, to shew repentance! for so shalt thou escape wilful sin.
[4] As is the lust of an eunuch to deflower a virgin; so is he that executeth judgment with violence.
[5] There is one that keepeth silence, and is found wise: and another by much babbling becometh hateful.
[6] Some man holdeth his tongue, because he hath not to answer: and some keepeth silence, knowing his time.
[7] A wise man will hold his tongue till he see opportunity: but a babbler and a fool will regard no time.
[8] He that useth many words shall be abhorred; and he that taketh to himself authority therein shall be hated.
[9] There is a sinner that hath good success in evil things; and there is a gain that turneth to loss.
[10] There is a gift that shall not profit thee; and there is a gift whose recompence is double.
[11] There is an abasement because of glory; and there is that lifteth up his head from a low estate.
[12] There is that buyeth much for a little, and repayeth it sevenfold.
[13] A wise man by his words maketh him beloved: but the graces of fools shall be poured out.
[14] The gift of a fool shall do thee no good when thou hast it; neither yet of the envious for his necessity: for he looketh to receive many things for one.
[15] He giveth little, and upbraideth much; he openeth his mouth like a crier; to day he lendeth, and to morrow will he ask it again: such an one is to be hated of God and man.
[16] The fool saith, I have no friends, I have no thank for all my good deeds, and they that eat my bread speak evil of me.
[17] How oft, and of how many shall he be laughed to scorn! for he knoweth not aright what it is to have; and it is all one unto him as if he had it not.
[18] To slip upon a pavement is better than to slip with the tongue: so the fall of the wicked shall come speedily.
[19] An unseasonable tale will always be in the mouth of the unwise.
[20] A wise sentence shall be rejected when it cometh out of a fool's mouth; for he will not speak it in due season.
[21] There is that is hindered from sinning through want: and when he taketh rest, he shall not be troubled.
[22] There is that destroyeth his own soul through bashfulness, and by accepting of persons overthroweth himself.
[23] There is that for bashfulness promiseth to his friend, and maketh him his enemy for nothing.
[24] A lie is a foul blot in a man, yet it is continually in the mouth of the untaught.
[25] A thief is better than a man that is accustomed to lie: but they both shall have destruction to heritage.
[26] The disposition of a liar is dishonourable, and his shame is ever with him.
[27] A wise man shall promote himself to honour with his words: and he that hath understanding will please great men.
[28] He that tilleth his land shall increase his heap: and he that pleaseth great men shall get pardon for iniquity.
[29] Presents and gifts blind the eyes of the wise, and stop up his mouth that he cannot reprove.
[30] Wisdom that is hid, and treasure that is hoarded up, what profit is in them both?
[31] Better is he that hideth his folly than a man that hideth his wisdom.
[32] Necessary patience in seeking ing Jah is better than he that leadeth his life without a guide.

Sir.21

[1] My son, hast thou sinned? do so no more, but ask pardon for thy former sins.
[2] Flee from sin as from the face of a serpent: for if thou comest too near it, it will bite thee: the teeth thereof are as the teeth of a lion, slaying the souls of men.
[3] All iniquity is as a two edged sword, the wounds whereof cannot be healed.
[4] To terrify and do wrong will waste riches: thus the house of proud men shall be made desolate.
[5] A prayer out of a poor man's mouth reacheth to the ears of God, and his judgment cometh speedily.
[6] He that hateth to be reproved is in the way of sinners: but he that feareth Jah will repent from his heart.
[7] An eloquent man is known far and near; but a man of understanding knoweth when he slippeth.
[8] He that buildeth his house with other men's money is like one that gathereth himself stones for the tomb of his burial.
[9] The congregation of the wicked is like tow wrapped together: and the end of them is a flame of fire to destroy them.
[10] The way of sinners is made plain with stones, but at the end thereof is the pit of hell.
[11] He that keepeth the law of Jah getteth the understanding thereof: and the perfection of the fear of Jah is wisdom.
[12] He that is not wise will not be taught: but there is a wisdom which multiplieth bitterness.
[13] The knowledge of a wise man shall abound like a flood: and his counsel is like a pure fountain of life.
[14] The inner parts of a fool are like a broken vessel, and he will hold no knowledge as long as he liveth.
[15] If a skilful man hear a wise word, he will commend it, and add unto it: but as soon as one of no understanding heareth it, it displeaseth him, and he casteth it behind his back.
[16] The talking of a fool is like a burden in the way: but grace shall be found in the lips of the wise.
[17] They enquire at the mouth of the wise man in the congregation, and they shall ponder his words in their heart.
[18] As is a house that is destroyed, so is wisdom to a fool: and the knowledge of the unwise is as talk without sense.
[19] Doctrine unto fools is as fetters on the feet, and like manacles on the right hand.
[20] A fool lifteth up his voice with laughter; but a wise man doth scarce smile a little.
[21] Learning is unto a wise man as an ornament of gold, and like a bracelet upon his right arm.
[22] A foolish man's foot is soon in his [neighbour's] house: but a man of experience is ashamed of him.
[23] A fool will peep in at the door into the house: but he that is well nurtured will stand without.
[24] It is the rudeness of a man to hearken at the door: but a wise man will be grieved with the disgrace.
[25] The lips of talkers will be telling such things as pertain not unto them: but the words of such as have understanding are weighed in the balance.
[26] The heart of fools is in their mouth: but the mouth of the wise is in their heart.
[27] When the ungodly curseth Satan, he curseth his own soul.
[28] A whisperer defileth his own soul, and is hated wheresoever he dwelleth.

Sir.22

[1] A slothful man is compared to a filthy stone, and every one will hiss him out to his

disgrace.
[2] A slothful man is compared to the filth of a dunghill: every man that takes it up will shake his hand.
[3] An evilnurtured man is the dishonour of his father that begat him: and a [foolish] daughter is born to his loss.
[4] A wise daughter shall bring an inheritance to her husband: but she that liveth dishonestly is her father's heaviness.
[5] She that is bold dishonoureth both her father and her husband, but they both shall despise her.
[6] A tale out of season [is as] musick in mourning: but stripes and correction of wisdom are never out of time.
[7] Whoso teacheth a fool is as one that glueth a potsherd together, and as he that waketh one from a sound sleep.
[8] He that telleth a tale to a fool speaketh to one in a slumber: when he hath told his tale, he will say, What is the matter?
[9] If children live honestly, and have wherewithal, they shall cover the baseness of their parents.
[10] But children, being haughty, through disdain and want of nurture do stain the nobility of their kindred.
[11] Weep for the dead, for he hath lost the light: and weep for the fool, for he wanteth understanding: make little weeping for the dead, for he is at rest: but the life of the fool is worse than death.
[12] Seven days do men mourn for him that is dead; but for a fool and an ungodly man all the days of his life.
[13] Talk not much with a fool, and go not to him that hath no understanding: beware of him, lest thou have trouble, and thou shalt never be defiled with his fooleries: depart from him, and thou shalt find rest, and never be disquieted with madness.
[14] What is heavier than lead? and what is the name thereof, but a fool?
[15] Sand, and salt, and a mass of iron, is easier to bear, than a man without understanding.
[16] As timber girt and bound together in a building cannot be loosed with shaking: so the heart that is stablished by advised counsel shall fear at no time.
[17] A heart settled upon a thought of understanding is as a fair plaistering on the wall of a gallery.
[18] Pales set on an high place will never stand against the wind: so a fearful heart in the imagination of a fool cannot stand against any fear.
[19] He that pricketh the eye will make tears to fall: and he that pricketh the heart maketh it to shew her knowledge.
[20] Whoso casteth a stone at the birds frayeth them away: and he that upbraideth his friend breaketh friendship.
[21] Though thou drewest a sword at thy friend, yet despair not: for there may be a returning [to favour.]
[22] If thou hast opened thy mouth against thy friend, fear not; for there may be a reconciliation: except for upbraiding, or pride, or disclosing of secrets, or a treacherous wound: for for these things every friend will depart.
[23] Be faithful to thy neighbour in his poverty, that thou mayest rejoice in his prosperity: abide stedfast unto him in the time of his trouble, that thou mayest be heir with him in his heritage: for a mean estate is not always to be contemned: nor the rich that is foolish to be had in admiration.
[24] As the vapour and smoke of a furnace goeth before the fire; so reviling before blood.
[25] I will not be ashamed to defend a friend; neither will I hide myself from him.
[26] And if any evil happen unto me by him, every one that heareth it will beware of him.
[27] Who shall set a watch before my mouth, and a seal of wisdom upon my lips, that I fall not suddenly by them, and that my tongue destroy me not?

Sir.23

[1] O Lord, Father and Governor of all my whole life, leave me not to their counsels, and let me not fall by them.
[2] Who will set scourges over my thoughts, and the discipline of wisdom over mine heart? that they spare me not for mine ignorances, and it pass not by my sins:
[3] Lest mine ignorances increase, and my sins abound to my destruction, and I fall before mine adversaries, and mine enemy rejoice over me, whose hope is far from thy mercy.
[4] O Lord, Father and God of my life, give me not a proud look, but turn away from thy servants always a haughty mind.
[5] Turn away from me vain hopes and concupiscence, and thou shalt hold him up that is desirous always to serve thee.
[6] Let not the greediness of the belly nor lust of the flesh take hold of me; and give not over me thy servant into an impudent mind.
[7] Hear, O ye children, the discipline of the mouth: he that keepeth it shall never be taken in his lips.
[8] The sinner shall be left in his foolishness: both the evil speaker and the proud shall fall thereby.
[9] Accustom not thy mouth to swearing; neither use thyself to the naming of the Holy One.
[10] For as a servant that is continually beaten shall not be without a blue mark: so he that sweareth and nameth God continually shall not be faultless.
[11] A man that useth much swearing shall be filled with iniquity, and the plague shall never depart from his house: if he shall offend, his sin shall be upon him: and if he acknowledge not his sin, he maketh a double offence: and if he swear in vain, he shall not be innocent, but his house shall be full of calamities.
[12] There is a word that is clothed about with death: God grant that it be not found in the heritage of Jacob; for all such things shall be far from the godly, and they shall not wallow in their sins.
[13] Use not thy mouth to intemperate swearing, for therein is the word of sin.
[14] Remember thy father and thy mother, when thou sittest among great men. Be not forgetful before them, and so thou by thy custom become a fool, and wish that thou hadst not been born, and curse they day of thy nativity.
[15] The man that is accustomed to opprobrious words will never be reformed all the days of his life.
[16] Two sorts of men multiply sin, and the third will bring wrath: a hot mind is as a burning fire, it will never be quenched till it be consumed: a fornicator in the body of his flesh will never cease till he hath kindled a fire.
[17] All bread is sweet to a whoremonger, he will not leave off till he die.
[18] A man that breaketh wedlock, saying thus in his heart, Who seeth me? I am compassed about with darkness, the walls cover me, and no body seeth me; what need I to fear? the most High will not remember my sins:
[19] Such a man only feareth the eyes of men, and knoweth not that the eyes of Jah are ten thousand times brighter than the sun, beholding all the ways of men, and considering the most secret parts.
[20] He knew all things ere ever they were created; so also after they were perfected he looked upon them all.
[21] This man shall be punished in the streets of the city, and where he suspecteth not he shall be taken.
[22] Thus shall it go also with the wife that leaveth her husband, and bringeth in an heir by another.
[23] For first, she hath disobeyed the law of the most High; and secondly, she hath trespassed against her own husband; and

thirdly, she hath played the whore in adultery, and brought children by another man.
[24] She shall be brought out into the congregation, and inquisition shall be made of her children.
[25] Her children shall not take root, and her branches shall bring forth no fruit.
[26] She shall leave her memory to be cursed, and her reproach shall not be blotted out.
[27] And they that remain shall know that there is nothing better than the fear of Jah, and that there is nothing sweeter than to take heed unto the commandments of Jah.
[28] It is great glory to follow Jah, and to be received of him is long life.

Sir. 24

[1] Wisdom shall praise herself, and shall glory in the midst of her people.
[2] In the congregation of the most High shall she open her mouth, and triumph before his power.
[3] I came out of the mouth of the most High, and covered the earth as a cloud.
[4] I dwelt in high places, and my throne is in a cloudy pillar.
[5] I alone compassed the circuit of heaven, and walked in the bottom of the deep.
[6] In the waves of the sea and in all the earth, and in every people and nation, I got a possession.
[7] With all these I sought rest: and in whose inheritance shall I abide?
[8] So the Creator of all things gave me a commandment, and he that made me caused my tabernacle to rest, and said, Let thy dwelling be in Jacob, and thine inheritance in Israel.
[9] He created me from the beginning before the world, and I shall never fail.
[10] In the holy tabernacle I served before him; and so was I established in Sion.
[11] Likewise in the beloved city he gave me rest, and in Jerusalem was my power.
[12] And I took root in an honourable people, even in the portion of Jah's inheritance.
[13] I was exalted like a cedar in Libanus, and as a cypress tree upon the mountains of Hermon.
[14] I was exalted like a palm tree in Engaddi, and as a rose plant in Jericho, as a fair olive tree in a pleasant field, and grew up as a plane tree by the water.
[15] I gave a sweet smell like cinnamon and aspalathus, and I yielded a pleasant odour like the best myrrh, as galbanum, and onyx, and sweet storax, and as the fume of frankincense in the tabernacle.
[16] As the turpentine tree I stretched out my branches, and my branches are the branches of honour and grace.
[17] As the vine brought I forth pleasant savour, and my flowers are the fruit of honour and riches.
[18] I am the mother of fair love, and fear, and knowledge, and holy hope: I therefore, being eternal, am given to all my children which are named of him.
[19] Come unto me, all ye that be desirous of me, and fill yourselves with my fruits.
[20] For my memorial is sweeter than honey, and mine inheritance than the honeycomb.
[21] They that eat me shall yet be hungry, and they that drink me shall yet be thirsty.
[22] He that obeyeth me shall never be confounded, and they that work by me shall not do amiss.
[23] All these things are the book of the covenant of the most high God, even the law which Moses commanded for an heritage unto the congregations of Jacob.
[24] Faint not to be strong in Jah; that he may confirm you, cleave unto him: for Jah Almighty is God alone, and beside him there is no other Saviour.
[25] He filleth all things with his wisdom, as

Phison and as Tigris in the time of the new fruits.
[26] He maketh the understanding to abound like Euphrates, and as Jordan in the time of the harvest.
[27] He maketh the doctrine of knowledge appear as the light, and as Geon in the time of vintage.
[28] The first man knew her not perfectly: no more shall the last find her out.
[29] For her thoughts are more than the sea, and her counsels profounder than the great deep.
[30] I also came out as a brook from a river, and as a conduit into a garden.
[31] I said, I will water my best garden, and will water abundantly my garden bed: and, lo, my brook became a river, and my river became a sea.
[32] I will yet make doctrine to shine as the morning, and will send forth her light afar off.
[33] I will yet pour out doctrine as prophecy, and leave it to all ages for ever.
[34] Behold that I have not laboured for myself only, but for all them that seek wisdom.

Sir. 25

[1] In three things I was beautified, and stood up beautiful both before God and men: the unity of brethren, the love of neighbours, a man and a wife that agree together.
[2] Three sorts of men my soul hateth, and I am greatly offended at their life: a poor man that is proud, a rich man that is a liar, and an old adulterer that doateth.
[3] If thou hast gathered nothing in thy youth, how canst thou find any thing in thine age?
[4] O how comely a thing is judgment for gray hairs, and for ancient men to know counsel!
[5] O how comely is the wisdom of old men, and understanding and counsel to men of honour.
[6] Much experience is the crown of old men, and the fear of God is their glory.
[7] There be nine things which I have judged in mine heart to be happy, and the tenth I will utter with my tongue: A man that hath joy of his children; and he that liveth to see the fall of his enemy:
[8] Well is him that dwelleth with a wife of understanding, and that hath not slipped with his tongue, and that hath not served a man more unworthy than himself:
[9] Well is him that hath found prudence, and he that speaketh in the ears of them that will hear:
[10] O how great is he that findeth wisdom! yet is there none above him that feareth Jah.
[11] But the love of Jah passeth all things for illumination: he that holdeth it, whereto shall he be likened?
[12] The fear of Jah is the beginning of his love: and faith is the beginning of cleaving unto him.
[13] [Give me] any plague, but the plague of the heart: and any wickedness, but the wickedness of a woman:
[14] And any affliction, but the affliction from them that hate me: and any revenge, but the revenge of enemies.
[15] There is no head above the head of a serpent; and there is no wrath above the wrath of an enemy.
[16] I had rather dwell with a lion and a dragon, than to keep house with a wicked woman.
[17] The wickedness of a woman changeth her face, and darkeneth her countenance like sackcloth.
[18] Her husband shall sit among his neighbours; and when he heareth it shall sigh bitterly.
[19] All wickedness is but little to the wickedness of a woman: let the portion of a sinner fall upon her.
[20] As the climbing up a sandy way is to

the feet of the aged, so is a wife full of words to a quiet man.
[21] Stumble not at the beauty of a woman, and desire her not for pleasure.
[22] A woman, if she maintain her husband, is full of anger, impudence, and much reproach.
[23] A wicked woman abateth the courage, maketh an heavy countenance and a wounded heart: a woman that will not comfort her husband in distress maketh weak hands and feeble knees.
[24] Of the woman came the beginning of sin, and through her we all die.
[25] Give the water no passage; neither a wicked woman liberty to gad abroad.
[26] If she go not as thou wouldest have her, cut her off from thy flesh, and give her a bill of divorce, and let her go.

Sir.26

[1] Blessed is the man that hath a virtuous wife, for the number of his days shall be double.
[2] A virtuous woman rejoiceth her husband, and he shall fulfil the years of his life in peace.
[3] A good wife is a good portion, which shall be given in the portion of them that fear Jah.
[4] Whether a man be rich or poor, if he have a good heart toward Jah, he shall at all times rejoice with a cheerful countenance.
[5] There be three things that mine heart feareth; and for the fourth I was sore afraid: the slander of a city, the gathering together of an unruly multitude, and a false accusation: all these are worse than death.
[6] But a grief of heart and sorrow is a woman that is jealous over another woman, and a scourge of the tongue which communicateth with all.
[7] An evil wife is a yoke shaken to and fro: he that hath hold of her is as though he held a scorpion.
[8] A drunken woman and a gadder abroad causeth great anger, and she will not cover her own shame.
[9] The whoredom of a woman may be known in her haughty looks and eyelids.
[10] If thy daughter be shameless, keep her in straitly, lest she abuse herself through overmuch liberty.
[11] Watch over an impudent eye: and marvel not if she trespass against thee.
[12] She will open her mouth, as a thirsty traveller when he hath found a fountain, and drink of every water near her: by every hedge will she sit down, and open her quiver against every arrow.
[13] The grace of a wife delighteth her husband, and her discretion will fatten his bones.
[14] A silent and loving woman is a gift of Jah; and there is nothing so much worth as a mind well instructed.
[15] A shamefaced and faithful woman is a double grace, and her continent mind cannot be valued.
[16] As the sun when it ariseth in the high heaven; so is the beauty of a good wife in the ordering of her house.
[17] As the clear light is upon the holy candlestick; so is the beauty of the face in ripe age.
[18] As the golden pillars are upon the sockets of silver; so are the fair feet with a constant heart.
[19] My son, keep the flower of thine age sound; and give not thy strength to strangers.
[20] When thou hast gotten a fruitful possession through all the field, sow it with thine own seed, trusting in the goodness of thy stock.
[21] So thy race which thou leavest shall be magnified, having the confidence of their good descent.
[22] An harlot shall be accounted as spittle; but a married woman is a tower against death to her husband.

[23] A wicked woman is given as a portion to a wicked man: but a godly woman is given to him that feareth Jah.
[24] A dishonest woman contemneth shame: but an honest woman will reverence her husband.
[25] A shameless woman shall be counted as a dog; but she that is shamefaced will fear Jah.
[26] A woman that honoureth her husband shall be judged wise of all; but she that dishonoureth him in her pride shall be counted ungodly of all.
[27] A loud crying woman and a scold shall be sought out to drive away the enemies.
[28] There be two things that grieve my heart; and the third maketh me angry: a man of war that suffereth poverty; and men of understanding that are not set by; and one that returneth from righteousness to sin; Jah prepareth such an one for the sword.
[29] A merchant shall hardly keep himself from doing wrong; and an huckster shall not be freed from sin.

Sir.27

[1] Many have sinned for a small matter; and he that seeketh for abundance will turn his eyes away.
[2] As a nail sticketh fast between the joinings of the stones; so doth sin stick close between buying and selling.
[3] Unless a man hold himself diligently in the fear of Jah, his house shall soon be overthrown.
[4] As when one sifteth with a sieve, the refuse remaineth; so the filth of man in his talk.
[5] The furnace proveth the potter's vessels; so the trial of man is in his reasoning.
[6] The fruit declareth if the tree have been dressed; so is the utterance of a conceit in the heart of man.
[7] Praise no man before thou hearest him speak; for this is the trial of men.
[8] If thou followest righteousness, thou shalt obtain her, and put her on, as a glorious long robe.
[9] The birds will resort unto their like; so will truth return unto them that practise in her.
[10] As the lion lieth in wait for the prey; so sin for them that work iniquity.
[11] The discourse of a godly man is always with wisdom; but a fool changeth as the moon.
[12] If thou be among the indiscreet, observe the time; but be continually among men of understanding.
[13] The discourse of fools is irksome, and their sport is the wantonness of sin.
[14] The talk of him that sweareth much maketh the hair stand upright; and their brawls make one stop his ears.
[15] The strife of the proud is bloodshedding, and their revilings are grievous to the ear.
[16] Whoso discovereth secrets loseth his credit; and shall never find friend to his mind.
[17] Love thy friend, and be faithful unto him: but if thou betrayest his secrets, follow no more after him.
[18] For as a man hath destroyed his enemy; so hast thou lost the love of thy neighbor.
[19] As one that letteth a bird go out of his hand, so hast thou let thy neighbour go, and shalt not get him again
[20] Follow after him no more, for he is too far off; he is as a roe escaped out of the snare.
[21] As for a wound, it may be bound up; and after reviling there may be reconcilement: but he that betrayeth secrets is without hope.
[22] He that winketh with the eyes worketh evil: and he that knoweth him will depart from him.
[23] When thou art present, he will speak sweetly, and will admire thy words: but at

the last he will writhe his mouth, and slander thy sayings.
[24] I have hated many things, but nothing like him; for Jah will hate him.
[25] Whoso casteth a stone on high casteth it on his own head; and a deceitful stroke shall make wounds.
[26] Whoso diggeth a pit shall fall therein: and he that setteth a trap shall be taken therein.
[27] He that worketh mischief, it shall fall upon him, and he shall not know whence it cometh.
[28] Mockery and reproach are from the proud; but vengeance, as a lion, shall lie in wait for them.
[29] They that rejoice at the fall of the righteous shall be taken in the snare; and anguish shall consume them before they die.
[30] Malice and wrath, even these are abominations; and the sinful man shall have them both.

Sir.28

[1] He that revengeth shall find vengeance from Jah, and he will surely keep his sins [in remembrance.]
[2] Forgive thy neighbour the hurt that he hath done unto thee, so shall thy sins also be forgiven when thou prayest.
[3] One man beareth hatred against another, and doth he seek pardon from Jah?
[4] He sheweth no mercy to a man, which is like himself: and doth he ask forgiveness of his own sins?
[5] If he that is but flesh nourish hatred, who will intreat for pardon of his sins?
[6] Remember thy end, and let enmity cease; [remember] corruption and death, and abide in the commandments.
[7] Remember the commandments, and bear no malice to thy neighbour: [remember] the covenant of the Highest, and wink at ignorance.
[8] Abstain from strife, and thou shalt diminish thy sins: for a furious man will kindle strife,
[9] A sinful man disquieteth friends, and maketh debate among them that be at peace.
[10] As the matter of the fire is, so it burneth: and as a man's strength is, so is his wrath; and according to his riches his anger riseth; and the stronger they are which contend, the more they will be inflamed.
[11] An hasty contention kindleth a fire: and an hasty fighting sheddeth blood.
[12] If thou blow the spark, it shall burn: if thou spit upon it, it shall be quenched: and both these come out of thy mouth.
[13] Curse the whisperer and doubletongued: for such have destroyed many that were at peace.
[14] A backbiting tongue hath disquieted many, and driven them from nation to nation: strong cities hath it pulled down, and overthrown the houses of great men.
[15] A backbiting tongue hath cast out virtuous women, and deprived them of their labours.
[16] Whoso hearkeneth unto it shall never find rest, and never dwell quietly.
[17] The stroke of the whip maketh marks in the flesh: but the stroke of the tongue breaketh the bones.
[18] Many have fallen by the edge of the sword: but not so many as have fallen by the tongue.
[19] Well is he that is defended through the venom thereof; who hath not drawn the yoke thereof, nor hath been bound in her bands.
[20] For the yoke thereof is a yoke of iron, and the bands thereof are bands of brass.
[21] The death thereof is an evil death, the grave were better than it.
[22] It shall not have rule over them that fear God, neither shall they be burned with the flame thereof.
[23] Such as forsake Jah shall fall into it; and it shall burn in them, and not be quenched; it shall be sent upon them as a

lion, and devour them as a leopard.
[24] Look that thou hedge thy possession about with thorns, and bind up thy silver and gold,
[25] And weigh thy words in a balance, and make a door and bar for thy mouth.
[26] Beware thou slide not by it, lest thou fall before him that lieth in wait.

Sir.29

[1] He that is merciful will lend unto his neighbour; and he that strengtheneth his hand keepeth the commandments.
[2] Lend to thy neighbour in time of his need, and pay thou thy neighbour again in due season.
[3] Keep thy word, and deal faithfully with him, and thou shalt always find the thing that is necessary for thee.
[4] Many, when a thing was lent them, reckoned it to be found, and put them to trouble that helped them.
[5] Till he hath received, he will kiss a man's hand; and for his neighbour's money he will speak submissly: but when he should repay, he will prolong the time, and return words of grief, and complain of the time.
[6] If he prevail, he shall hardly receive the half, and he will count as if he had found it: if not, he hath deprived him of his money, and he hath gotten him an enemy without cause: he payeth him with cursings and railings; and for honour he will pay him disgrace.
[7] Many therefore have refused to lend for other men's ill dealing, fearing to be defrauded.
[8] Yet have thou patience with a man in poor estate, and delay not to shew him mercy.
[9] Help the poor for the commandment's sake, and turn him not away because of his poverty.
[10] Lose thy money for thy brother and thy friend, and let it not rust under a stone to be lost.
[11] Lay up thy treasure according to the commandments of the most High, and it shall bring thee more profit than gold.
[12] Shut up alms in thy storehouses: and it shall deliver thee from all affliction.
[13] It shall fight for thee against thine enemies better than a mighty shield and strong spear.
[14] An honest man is surety for his neighbour: but he that is impudent will forsake him.
[15] Forget not the friendship of thy surety, for he hath given his life for thee.
[16] A sinner will overthrow the good estate of his surety:
[17] And he that is of an unthankful mind will leave him [in danger] that delivered him.
[18] Suretiship hath undone many of good estate, and shaken them as a wave of the sea: mighty men hath it driven from their houses, so that they wandered among strange nations.
[19] A wicked man transgressing the commandments of Jah shall fall into suretiship: and he that undertaketh and followeth other men's business for gain shall fall into suits.
[20] Help thy neighbour according to thy power, and beware that thou thyself fall not into the same.
[21] The chief thing for life is water, and bread, and clothing, and an house to cover shame.
[22] Better is the life of a poor man in a mean cottage, than delicate fare in another man's house.
[23] Be it little or much, hold thee contented, that thou hear not the reproach of thy house.
[24] For it is a miserable life to go from house to house: for where thou art a stranger, thou darest not open thy mouth.
[25] Thou shalt entertain, and feast, and

have no thanks: moreover thou shalt hear bitter words:
[26] Come, thou stranger, and furnish a table, and feed me of that thou hast ready.
[27] Give place, thou stranger, to an honourable man; my brother cometh to be lodged, and I have need of mine house.
[28] These things are grievous to a man of understanding; the upbraiding of houseroom, and reproaching of the lender.

Sir.30

[1] He that loveth his son causeth him oft to feel the rod, that he may have joy of him in the end.
[2] He that chastiseth his son shall have joy in him, and shall rejoice of him among his acquaintance.
[3] He that teacheth his son grieveth the enemy: and before his friends he shall rejoice of him.
[4] Though his father die, yet he is as though he were not dead: for he hath left one behind him that is like himself.
[5] While he lived, he saw and rejoiced in him: and when he died, he was not sorrowful.
[6] He left behind him an avenger against his enemies, and one that shall requite kindness to his friends.
[7] He that maketh too much of his son shall bind up his wounds; and his bowels will be troubled at every cry.
[8] An horse not broken becometh headstrong: and a child left to himself will be wilful.
[9] Cocker thy child, and he shall make thee afraid: play with him, and he will bring thee to heaviness.
[10] Laugh not with him, lest thou have sorrow with him, and lest thou gnash thy teeth in the end.
[11] Give him no liberty in his youth, and wink not at his follies.
[12] Bow down his neck while he is young, and beat him on the sides while he is a child, lest he wax stubborn, and be disobedient unto thee, and so bring sorrow to thine heart.
[13] Chastise thy son, and hold him to labour, lest his lewd behaviour be an offence unto thee.
[14] Better is the poor, being sound and strong of constitution, than a rich man that is afflicted in his body.
[15] Health and good estate of body are above all gold, and a strong body above infinite wealth.
[16] There is no riches above a sound body, and no joy above the joy of the heart.
[17] Death is better than a bitter life or continual sickness.
[18] Delicates poured upon a mouth shut up are as messes of meat set upon a grave.
[19] What good doeth the offering unto an idol? for neither can it eat nor smell: so is he that is persecuted of Jah.
[20] He seeth with his eyes and groaneth, as an eunuch that embraceth a virgin and sigheth.
[21] Give not over thy mind to heaviness, and afflict not thyself in thine own counsel.
[22] The gladness of the heart is the life of man, and the joyfulness of a man prolongeth his days.
[23] Love thine own soul, and comfort thy heart, remove sorrow far from thee: for sorrow hath killed many, and there is no profit therein.
[24] Envy and wrath shorten the life, and carefulness bringeth age before the time.
[25] A cheerful and good heart will have a care of his meat and diet.

Sir.31

[1] Watching for riches consumeth the flesh, and the care thereof driveth away sleep.
[2] Watching care will not let a man slumber, as a sore disease breaketh sleep,

[3] The rich hath great labour in gathering riches together; and when he resteth, he is filled with his delicates.
[4] The poor laboureth in his poor estate; and when he leaveth off, he is still needy.
[5] He that loveth gold shall not be justified, and he that followeth corruption shall have enough thereof.
[6] Gold hath been the ruin of many, and their destruction was present.
[7] It is a stumblingblock unto them that sacrifice unto it, and every fool shall be taken therewith.
[8] Blessed is the rich that is found without blemish, and hath not gone after gold.
[9] Who is he? and we will call him blessed: for wonderful things hath he done among his people.
[10] Who hath been tried thereby, and found perfect? then let him glory. Who might offend, and hath not offended? or done evil, and hath not done it?
[11] His goods shall be established, and the congregation shall declare his alms.
[12] If thou sit at a bountiful table, be not greedy upon it, and say not, There is much meat on it.
[13] Remember that a wicked eye is an evil thing: and what is created more wicked than an eye? therefore it weepeth upon every occasion.
[14] Stretch not thine hand whithersoever it looketh, and thrust it not with him into the dish.
[15] Judge not thy neighbour by thyself: and be discreet in every point.
[16] Eat as it becometh a man, those things which are set before thee; and devour note, lest thou be hated.
[17] Leave off first for manners' sake; and be not unsatiable, lest thou offend.
[18] When thou sittest among many, reach not thine hand out first of all.
[19] A very little is sufficient for a man well nurtured, and he fetcheth not his wind short upon his bed.
[20] Sound sleep cometh of moderate eating: he riseth early, and his wits are with him: but the pain of watching, and choler, and pangs of the belly, are with an unsatiable man.
[21] And if thou hast been forced to eat, arise, go forth, vomit, and thou shalt have rest.
[22] My son, hear me, and despise me not, and at the last thou shalt find as I told thee: in all thy works be quick, so shall there no sickness come unto thee.
[23] Whoso is liberal of his meat, men shall speak well of him; and the report of his good housekeeping will be believed.
[24] But against him that is a niggard of his meat the whole city shall murmur; and the testimonies of his niggardness shall not be doubted of.
[25] Shew not thy valiantness in wine; for wine hath destroyed many.
[26] The furnace proveth the edge by dipping: so doth wine the hearts of the proud by drunkeness.
[27] Wine is as good as life to a man, if it be drunk moderately: what life is then to a man that is without wine? for it was made to make men glad.
[28] Wine measurably drunk and in season bringeth gladness of the heart, and cheerfulness of the mind:
[29] But wine drunken with excess maketh bitterness of the mind, with brawling and quarrelling.
[30] Drunkenness increaseth the rage of a fool till he offend: it diminisheth strength, and maketh wounds.
[31] Rebuke not thy neighbour at the wine, and despise him not in his mirth: give him no despiteful words, and press not upon him with urging him [to drink.]

Sir. 32

[1] If thou be made the master [of a feast,] lift not thyself up, but be among them as one of the rest; take diligent care for them, and so sit down.
[2] And when thou hast done all thy office, take thy place, that thou mayest be merry with them, and receive a crown for thy well ordering of the feast.
[3] Speak, thou that art the elder, for it becometh thee, but with sound judgment; and hinder not musick.
[4] Pour not out words where there is a musician, and shew not forth wisdom out of time.
[5] A concert of musick in a banquet of wine is as a signet of carbuncle set in gold.
[6] As a signet of an emerald set in a work of gold, so is the melody of musick with pleasant wine.
[7] Speak, young man, if there be need of thee: and yet scarcely when thou art twice asked.
[8] Let thy speech be short, comprehending much in few words; be as one that knoweth and yet holdeth his tongue.
[9] If thou be among great men, make not thyself equal with them; and when ancient men are in place, use not many words.
[10] Before the thunder goeth lightning; and before a shamefaced man shall go favour.
[11] Rise up betimes, and be not the last; but get thee home without delay.
[12] There take thy pastime, and do what thou wilt: but sin not by proud speech.
[13] And for these things bless him that made thee, and hath replenished thee with his good things.
[14] Whoso feareth Jah will receive his discipline; and they that seek him early shall find favour.
[15] He that seeketh the law shall be filled therewith: but the hypocrite will be offended thereat.
[16] They that fear Jah shall find judgment, and shall kindle justice as a light.
[17] A sinful man will not be reproved, but findeth an excuse according to his will.
[18] A man of counsel will be considerate; but a strange and proud man is not daunted with fear, even when of himself he hath done without counsel.
[19] Do nothing without advice; and when thou hast once done, repent not.
[20] Go not in a way wherein thou mayest fall, and stumble not among the stones.
[21] Be not confident in a plain way.
[22] And beware of thine own children.
[23] In every good work trust thy own soul; for this is the keeping of the commandments.
[24] He that believeth in Jah taketh heed to the commandment; and he that trusteth in him shall fare never the worse.

Sir.33

[1] There shall no evil happen unto him that feareth Jah; but in temptation even again he will deliver him.
[2] A wise man hateth not the law; but he that is an hypocrite therein is as a ship in a storm.
[3] A man of understanding trusteth in the law; and the law is faithful unto him, as an oracle.
[4] Prepare what to say, and so thou shalt be heard: and bind up instruction, and then make answer.
[5] The heart of the foolish is like a cartwheel; and his thoughts are like a rolling axletree.
[6] A stallion horse is as a mocking friend, he neigheth under every one that sitteth upon him.
[7] Why doth one day excel another, when as all the light of every day in the year is of the sun?
[8] By the knowledge of Jah they were distinguished: and he altered seasons and feasts.
[9] Some of them hath he made high days,

and hallowed them, and some of them hath he made ordinary days.

[10] And all men are from the ground, and Adam was created of earth:

[11] In much knowledge Jah hath divided them, and made their ways diverse.

[12] Some of them hath he blessed and exalted and some of them he sanctified, and set near himself: but some of them hath he cursed and brought low, and turned out of their places.

[13] As the clay is in the potter's hand, to fashion it at his pleasure: so man is in the hand of him that made him, to render to them as liketh him best.

[14] Good is set against evil, and life against death: so is the godly against the sinner, and the sinner against the godly.

[15] So look upon all the works of the most High; and there are two and two, one against another.

[16] I awaked up last of all, as one that gathereth after the grapegatherers: by the blessing of Jah I profited, and tred my winepress like a gatherer of grapes.

[17] Consider that I laboured not for myself only, but for all them that seek learning.

[18] Hear me, O ye great men of the people, and hearken with your ears, ye rulers of the congregation.

[19] Give not thy son and wife, thy brother and friend, power over thee while thou livest, and give not thy goods to another: lest it repent thee, and thou intreat for the same again.

[20] As long as thou livest and hast breath in thee, give not thyself over to any.

[21] For better it is that thy children should seek to thee, than that thou shouldest stand to their courtesy.

[22] In all thy works keep to thyself the preeminence; leave not a stain in thine honour.

[23] At the time when thou shalt end thy days, and finish thy life, distribute thine inheritance.

[24] Fodder, a wand, and burdens, are for the ass; and bread, correction, and work, for a servant. .

[25] If thou set thy servant to labour, thou shalt find rest: but if thou let him go idle, he shall seek liberty.

[26] A yoke and a collar do bow the neck: so are tortures and torments for an evil servant.

[27] Send him to labour, that he be not idle; for idleness teacheth much evil.

[28] Set him to work, as is fit for him: if he be not obedient, put on more heavy fetters.

[29] But be not excessive toward any; and without discretion do nothing.

[30] If thou have a servant, let him be unto thee as thyself, because thou hast bought him with a price.

[31] If thou have a servant, entreat him as a brother: for thou hast need of him, as of thine own soul: if thou entreat him evil, and he run from thee, which way wilt thou go to seek him?

Sir.34

[1] The hopes of a man void of understanding are vain and false: and dreams lift up fools.

[2] Whoso regardeth dreams is like him that catcheth at a shadow, and followeth after the wind.

[3] The vision of dreams is the resemblance of one thing to another, even as the likeness of a face to a face.

[4] Of an unclean thing what can be cleansed? and from that thing which is false what truth can come?

[5] Divinations, and soothsayings, and dreams, are vain: and the heart fancieth, as a woman's heart in travail.

[6] If they be not sent from the most High in thy visitation, set not thy heart upon them.

[7] For dreams have deceived many, and they have failed that put their trust in them.

[8] The law shall be found perfect without

lies: and wisdom is perfection to a faithful mouth.
[9] A man that hath travelled knoweth many things; and he that hath much experience will declare wisdom.
[10] He that hath no experience knoweth little: but he that hath travelled is full of prudence.
[11] When I travelled, I saw many things; and I understand more than I can express.
[12] I was ofttimes in danger of death: yet I was delivered because of these things.
[13] The spirit of those that fear Jah shall live; for their hope is in him that saveth them.
[14] Whoso feareth Jah shall not fear nor be afraid; for he is his hope.
[15] Blessed is the soul of him that feareth Jah: to whom doth he look? and who is his strength?
[16] For the eyes of Jah are upon them that love him, he is their mighty protection and strong stay, a defence from heat, and a cover from the sun at noon, a preservation from stumbling, and an help from falling.
[17] He raiseth up the soul, and lighteneth the eyes: he giveth health, life, and blessing.
[18] He that sacrificeth of a thing wrongfully gotten, his offering is ridiculous; and the gifts of unjust men are not accepted.
[19] The most High is not pleased with the offerings of the wicked; neither is he pacified for sin by the multitude of sacrifices.
[20] Whoso bringeth an offering of the goods of the poor doeth as one that killeth the son before his father's eyes.
[21] The bread of the needy is their life: he that defraudeth him thereof is a man of blood.
[22] He that taketh away his neighbour's living slayeth him; and he that defraudeth the labourer of his hire is a bloodshedder.
[23] When one buildeth, and another pulleth down, what profit have they then but labour?
[24] When one prayeth, and another curseth, whose voice will Jah hear?
[25] He that washeth himself after the touching of a dead body, if he touch it again, what availeth his washing?
[26] So is it with a man that fasteth for his sins, and goeth again, and doeth the same: who will hear his prayer? or what doth his humbling profit him?

Sir.35

[1] He that keepeth the law bringeth offerings enough: he that taketh heed to the commandment offereth a peace offering.
[2] He that requiteth a goodturn offereth fine flour; and he that giveth alms sacrificeth praise.
[3] To depart from wickedness is a thing pleasing to Jah; and to forsake unrighteousness is a propitiation.
[4] Thou shalt not appear empty before Jah.
[5] For all these things [are to be done] because of the commandment.
[6] The offering of the righteous maketh the altar fat, and the sweet savour thereof is before the most High.
[7] The sacrifice of a just man is acceptable, and the memorial thereof shall never be forgotten.
[8] Give Jah his honour with a good eye, and diminish not the firstfruits of thine hands.
[9] In all thy gifts shew a cheerful countenance, and dedicate thy tithes with gladness.
[10] Give unto the most High according as he hath enriched thee; and as thou hast gotten, give with a cheerful eye.
[11] For Jah recompenseth, and will give thee seven times as much.
[12] Do not think to corrupt with gifts; for such he will not receive: and trust not to unrighteous sacrifices; for Jah is judge, and with him is no respect of persons.
[13] He will not accept any person against a poor man, but will hear the prayer of the

oppressed.
[14] He will not despise the supplication of the fatherless; nor the widow, when she poureth out her complaint.
[15] Do not the tears run down the widow's cheeks? and is not her cry against him that causeth them to fall?
[16] He that serveth Jah shall be accepted with favour, and his prayer shall reach unto the clouds.
[17] The prayer of the humble pierceth the clouds: and till it come nigh, he will not be comforted; and will not depart, till the most High shall behold to judge righteously, and execute judgment.
[18] For Jah will not be slack, neither will the Mighty be patient toward them, till he have smitten in sunder the loins of the unmerciful, and repayed vengeance to the heathen; till he have taken away the multitude of the proud, and broken the sceptre of the unrighteous;
[19] Till he have rendered to every man according to his deeds, and to the works of men according to their devices; till he have judged the cause of his people, and made them to rejoice in his mercy.
[20] Mercy is seasonable in the time of affliction, as clouds of rain in the time of drought.

Sir.36

[1] Have mercy upon us, O Lord God of all, and behold us:
[2] And send thy fear upon all the nations that seek not after thee.
[3] Lift up thy hand against the strange nations, and let them see thy power.
[4] As thou wast sanctified in us before them: so be thou magnified among them before us.
[5] And let them know thee, as we have known thee, that there is no God but only thou, O God.

[6] Shew new signs, and make other strange wonders: glorify thy hand and thy right arm, that they may set forth thy wondrous works.
[7] Raise up indignation, and pour out wrath: take away the adversary, and destroy the enemy.
[8] Sake the time short, remember the covenant, and let them declare thy wonderful works.
[9] Let him that escapeth be consumed by the rage of the fire; and let them perish that oppress the people.
[10] Smite in sunder the heads of the rulers of the heathen, that say, There is none other but we.
[11] Gather all the tribes of Jacob together, and inherit thou them, as from the beginning.
[12] O Lord, have mercy upon the people that is called by thy name, and upon Israel, whom thou hast named thy firstborn.
[13] O be merciful unto Jerusalem, thy holy city, the place of thy rest.
[14] Fill Sion with thine unspeakable oracles, and thy people with thy glory:
[15] Give testimony unto those that thou hast possessed from the beginning, and raise up prophets that have been in thy name.
[16] Reward them that wait for thee, and let thy prophets be found faithful.
[17] O Lord, hear the prayer of thy servants, according to the blessing of Aaron over thy people, that all they which dwell upon the earth may know that thou art Jah, the eternal God.
[18] The belly devoureth all meats, yet is one meat better than another.
[19] As the palate tasteth divers kinds of venison: so doth an heart of understanding false speeches.
[20] A froward heart causeth heaviness: but a man of experience will recompense him.
[21] A woman will receive every man, yet is one daughter better than another.
[22] The beauty of a woman cheereth the countenance, and a man loveth nothing

better.
[23] If there be kindness, meekness, and comfort, in her tongue, then is not her husband like other men.
[24] He that getteth a wife beginneth a possession, a help like unto himself, and a pillar of rest.
[25] Where no hedge is, there the possession is spoiled: and he that hath no wife will wander up and down mourning.
[26] Who will trust a thief well appointed, that skippeth from city to city? so [who will believe] a man that hath no house, and lodgeth wheresoever the night taketh him?

Sir.37

[1] Every friend saith, I am his friend also: but there is a friend, which is only a friend in name.
[2] Is it not a grief unto death, when a companion and friend is turned to an enemy?
[3] O wicked imagination, whence camest thou in to cover the earth with deceit?
[4] There is a companion, which rejoiceth in the prosperity of a friend, but in the time of trouble will be against him.
[5] There is a companion, which helpeth his friend for the belly, and taketh up the buckler against the enemy.
[6] Forget not thy friend in thy mind, and be not unmindful of him in thy riches.
[7] Every counsellor extolleth counsel; but there is some that counselleth for himself.
[8] Beware of a counsellor, and know before what need he hath; for he will counsel for himself; lest he cast the lot upon thee,
[9] And say unto thee, Thy way is good: and afterward he stand on the other side, to see what shall befall thee.
[10] Consult not with one that suspecteth thee: and hide thy counsel from such as envy thee.
[11] Neither consult with a woman touching her of whom she is jealous; neither with a coward in matters of war; nor with a merchant concerning exchange; nor with a buyer of selling; nor with an envious man of thankfulness; nor with an unmerciful man touching kindness; nor with the slothful for any work; nor with an hireling for a year of finishing work; nor with an idle servant of much business: hearken not unto these in any matter of counsel.
[12] But be continually with a godly man, whom thou knowest to keep the commandments of Jah, whose, mind is according to thy mind, and will sorrow with thee, if thou shalt miscarry.
[13] And let the counsel of thine own heart stand: for there is no man more faithful unto thee than it.
[14] For a man's mind is sometime wont to tell him more than seven watchmen, that sit above in an high tower.
[15] And above all this pray to the most High, that he will direct thy way in truth.
[16] Let reason go before every enterprize, and counsel before every action.
[17] The countenance is a sign of changing of the heart.
[18] Four manner of things appear: good and evil, life and death: but the tongue ruleth over them continually.
[19] There is one that is wise and teacheth many, and yet is unprofitable to himself.
[20] There is one that sheweth wisdom in words, and is hated: he shall be destitute of all food.
[21] For grace is not given, him from Jah, because he is deprived of all wisdom.
[22] Another is wise to himself; and the fruits of understanding are commendable in his mouth.
[23] A wise man instructeth his people; and the fruits of his understanding fail not.
[24] A wise man shall be filled with blessing; and all they that see him shall count him happy.
[25] The days of the life of man may be

numbered: but the days of Israel are innumerable.
[26] A wise man shall inherit glory among his people, and his name shall be perpetual.
[27] My son, prove thy soul in thy life, and see what is evil for it, and give not that unto it.
[28] For all things are not profitable for all men, neither hath every soul pleasure in every thing.
[29] Be not unsatiable in any dainty thing, nor too greedy upon meats:
[30] For excess of meats bringeth sickness, and surfeiting will turn into choler.
[31] By surfeiting have many perished; but he that taketh heed prolongeth his life.

Sir.38

[1] Honour a physician with the honour due unto him for the uses which ye may have of him: for Jah hath created him.
[2] For of the most High cometh healing, and he shall receive honour of the king.
[3] The skill of the physician shall lift up his head: and in the sight of great men he shall be in admiration.
[4] Jah hath created medicines out of the earth; and he that is wise will not abhor them.
[5] Was not the water made sweet with wood, that the virtue thereof might be known?
[6] And he hath given men skill, that he might be honoured in his marvellous works.
[7] With such doth he heal [men,] and taketh away their pains.
[8] Of such doth the apothecary make a confection; and of his works there is no end; and from him is peace over all the earth,
[9] My son, in thy sickness be not negligent: but pray unto Jah, and he will make thee whole.
[10] Leave off from sin, and order thine hands aright, and cleanse thy heart from all wickedness.
[11] Give a sweet savour, and a memorial of fine flour; and make a fat offering, as not being.
[12] Then give place to the physician, for Jah hath created him: let him not go from thee, for thou hast need of him.
[13] There is a time when in their hands there is good success.
[14] For they shall also pray unto Jah, that he would prosper that, which they give for ease and remedy to prolong life.
[15] He that sinneth before his Maker, let him fall into the hand of the physician.
[16] My son, let tears fall down over the dead, and begin to lament, as if thou hadst suffered great harm thyself; and then cover his body according to the custom, and neglect not his burial.
[17] Weep bitterly, and make great moan, and use lamentation, as he is worthy, and that a day or two, lest thou be evil spoken of: and then comfort thyself for thy heaviness.
[18] For of heaviness cometh death, and the heaviness of the heart breaketh strength.
[19] In affliction also sorrow remaineth: and the life of the poor is the curse of the heart.
[20] Take no heaviness to heart: drive it away, and member the last end.
[21] Forget it not, for there is no turning again: thou shalt not do him good, but hurt thyself.
[22] Remember my judgment: for thine also shall be so; yesterday for me, and to day for thee.
[23] When the dead is at rest, let his remembrance rest; and be comforted for him, when his Spirit is departed from him.
[24] The wisdom of a learned man cometh by opportunity of leisure: and he that hath little business shall become wise.
[25] How can he get wisdom that holdeth the plough, and that glorieth in the goad, that driveth oxen, and is occupied in their labours, and whose talk is of bullocks?

[26] He giveth his mind to make furrows; and is diligent to give the kine fodder.
[27] So every carpenter and workmaster, that laboureth night and day: and they that cut and grave seals, and are diligent to make great variety, and give themselves to counterfeit imagery, and watch to finish a work:
[28] The smith also sitting by the anvil, and considering the iron work, the vapour of the fire wasteth his flesh, and he fighteth with the heat of the furnace: the noise of the hammer and the anvil is ever in his ears, and his eyes look still upon the pattern of the thing that he maketh; he setteth his mind to finish his work, and watcheth to polish it perfectly:
[29] So doth the potter sitting at his work, and turning the wheel about with his feet, who is alway carefully set at his work, and maketh all his work by number;
[30] He fashioneth the clay with his arm, and boweth down his strength before his feet; he applieth himself to lead it over; and he is diligent to make clean the furnace:
[31] All these trust to their hands: and every one is wise in his work.
[32] Without these cannot a city be inhabited: and they shall not dwell where they will, nor go up and down:
[33] They shall not be sought for in publick counsel, nor sit high in the congregation: they shall not sit on the judges' seat, nor understand the sentence of judgment: they cannot declare justice and judgment; and they shall not be found where parables are spoken.
[34] But they will maintain the state of the world, and [all] their desire is in the work of their craft.

Sir.39

[1] But he that giveth his mind to the law of the most High, and is occupied in the meditation thereof, will seek out the wisdom of all the ancient, and be occupied in prophecies.
[2] He will keep the sayings of the renowned men: and where subtil parables are, he will be there also.
[3] He will seek out the secrets of grave sentences, and be conversant in dark parables.
[4] He shall serve among great men, and appear before princes: he will travel through strange countries; for he hath tried the good and the evil among men.
[5] He will give his heart to resort early to Jah that made him, and will pray before the most High, and will open his mouth in prayer, and make supplication for his sins.
[6] When the great Lord will, he shall be filled with the spirit of understanding: he shall pour out wise sentences, and give thanks unto Jah in his prayer.
[7] He shall direct his counsel and knowledge, and in his secrets shall he meditate.
[8] He shall shew forth that which he hath learned, and shall glory in the law of the covenant of Jah.
[9] Many shall commend his understanding; and so long as the world endureth, it shall not be blotted out; his memorial shall not depart away, and his name shall live from generation to generation.
[10] Nations shall shew forth his wisdom, and the congregation shall declare his praise.
[11] If he die, he shall leave a greater name than a thousand: and if he live, he shall increase it.
[12] Yet have I more to say, which I have thought upon; for I am filled as the moon at the full.
[13] Hearken unto me, ye holy children, and bud forth as a rose growing by the brook of the field:
[14] And give ye a sweet savour as frankincense, and flourish as a lily, send forth a smell, and sing a song of praise, bless

Jah in all his works.

[15] Magnify his name, and shew forth his praise with the songs of your lips, and with harps, and in praising him ye shall say after this manner:

[16] All the works of Jah are exceeding good, and whatsoever he commandeth shall be accomplished in due season.

[17] And none may say, What is this? wherefore is that? for at time convenient they shall all be sought out: at his commandment the waters stood as an heap, and at the words of his mouth the receptacles of waters.

[18] At his commandment is done whatsoever pleaseth him; and none can hinder, when he will save.

[19] The works of all flesh are before him, and nothing can be hid from his eyes.

[20] He seeth from everlasting to everlasting; and there is nothing wonderful before him.

[21] A man need not to say, What is this? wherefore is that? for he hath made all things for their uses.

[22] His blessing covered the dry land as a river, and watered it as a flood.

[23] As he hath turned the waters into saltness: so shall the heathen inherit his wrath.

[24] As his ways are plain unto the holy; so are they stumblingblocks unto the wicked.

[25] For the good are good things created from the beginning: so evil things for sinners.

[26] The principal things for the whole use of man's life are water, fire, iron, and salt, flour of wheat, honey, milk, and the blood of the grape, and oil, and clothing.

[27] All these things are for good to the godly: so to the sinners they are turned into evil.

[28] There be spirits that are created for vengeance, which in their fury lay on sore strokes; in the time of destruction they pour out their force, and appease the wrath of him that made them.

[29] Fire, and hail, and famine, and death, all these were created for vengeance;

[30] Teeth of wild beasts, and scorpions, serpents, and the sword punishing the wicked to destruction.

[31] They shall rejoice in his commandment, and they shall be ready upon earth, when need is; and when their time is come, they shall not transgress his word.

[32] Therefore from the beginning I was resolved, and thought upon these things, and have left them in writing.

[33] All the works of Jah are good: and he will give every needful thing in due season.

[34] So that a man cannot say, This is worse than that: for in time they shall all be well approved.

[35] And therefore praise ye Jah with the whole heart and mouth, and bless the name of Jah.

Sir. 40

[1] Great travail is created for every man, and an heavy yoke is upon the sons of Adam, from the day that they go out of their mother's womb, till the day that they return to the mother of all things.

[2] Their imagination of things to come, and the day of death, [trouble] their thoughts, and [cause] fear of heart;

[3] From him that sitteth on a throne of glory, unto him that is humbled in earth and ashes;

[4] From him that weareth purple and a crown, unto him that is clothed with a linen frock.

[5] Wrath, and envy, trouble, and unquietness, fear of death, and anger, and strife, and in the time of rest upon his bed his night sleep, do change his knowledge.

[6] A little or nothing is his rest, and afterward he is in his sleep, as in a day of keeping watch, troubled in the vision of his

heart, as if he were escaped out of a battle.
[7] When all is safe, he awaketh, and marvelleth that the fear was nothing.
[8] [Such things happen] unto all flesh, both man and beast, and that is sevenfold more upon sinners.
[9] Death, and bloodshed, strife, and sword, calamities, famine, tribulation, and the scourge;
[10] These things are created for the wicked, and for their sakes came the flood.
[11] All things that are of the earth shall turn to the earth again: and that which is of the waters doth return into the sea.
[12] All bribery and injustice shall be blotted out: but true dealing shall endure for ever.
[13] The goods of the unjust shall be dried up like a river, and shall vanish with noise, like a great thunder in rain.
[14] While he openeth his hand he shall rejoice: so shall transgressors come to nought.
[15] The children of the ungodly shall not bring forth many branches: but are as unclean roots upon a hard rock.
[16] The weed growing upon every water and bank of a river shall be pulled up before all grass.
[17] Bountifulness is as a most fruitful garden, and mercifulness endureth for ever.
[18] To labour, and to be content with that a man hath, is a sweet life: but he that findeth a treasure is above them both.
[19] Children and the building of a city continue a man's name: but a blameless wife is counted above them both.
[20] Wine and musick rejoice the heart: but the love of wisdom is above them both.
[21] The pipe and the psaltery make sweet melody: but a pleasant tongue is above them both.
[22] Thine eye desireth favour and beauty: but more than both corn while it is green.
[23] A friend and companion never meet amiss: but above both is a wife with her husband.
[24] Brethren and help are against time of trouble: but alms shall deliver more than them both.
[25] Gold and silver make the foot stand sure: but counsel is esteemed above them both.
[26] Riches and strength lift up the heart: but the fear of Jah is above them both: there is no want in the fear of Jah, and it needeth not to seek help.
[27] The fear of Jah is a fruitful garden, and covereth him above all glory.
[28] My son, lead not a beggar's life; for better it is to die than to beg.
[29] The life of him that dependeth on another man's table is not to be counted for a life; for he polluteth himself with other men's meat: but a wise man well nurtured will beware thereof.
[30] Begging is sweet in the mouth of the shameless: but in his belly there shall burn a fire.

Sir.41

[1] O death, how bitter is the remembrance of thee to a man that liveth at rest in his possessions, unto the man that hath nothing to vex him, and that hath prosperity in all things: yea, unto him that is yet able to receive meat!
[2] O death, acceptable is thy sentence unto the needy, and unto him whose strength faileth, that is now in the last age, and is vexed with all things, and to him that despaireth, and hath lost patience!
[3] Fear not the sentence of death, remember them that have been before thee, and that come after; for this is the sentence of Jah over all flesh.
[4] And why art thou against the pleasure of the most High? there is no inquisition in the grave, whether thou have lived ten, or an hundred, or a thousand years.

[5] The children of sinners are abominable children, and they that are conversant in the dwelling of the ungodly.
[6] The inheritance of sinners' children shall perish, and their posterity shall have a perpetual reproach.
[7] The children will complain of an ungodly father, because they shall be reproached for his sake.
[8] Woe be unto you, ungodly men, which have forsaken the law of the most high God! for if ye increase, it shall be to your destruction:
[9] And if ye be born, ye shall be born to a curse: and if ye die, a curse shall be your portion.
[10] All that are of the earth shall turn to earth again: so the ungodly shall go from a curse to destruction.
[11] The mourning of men is about their bodies: but an ill name of sinners shall be blotted out.
[12] Have regard to thy name; for that shall continue with thee above a thousand great treasures of gold.
[13] A good life hath but few days: but a good name endureth for ever.
[14] My children, keep discipline in peace: for wisdom that is hid, and a treasure that is not seen, what profit is in them both?
[15] A man that hideth his foolishness is better than a man that hideth his wisdom.
[16] Therefore be shamefaced according to my word: for it is not good to retain all shamefacedness; neither is it altogether approved in every thing.
[17] Be ashamed of whoredom before father and mother: and of a lie before a prince and a mighty man;
[18] Of an offence before a judge and ruler; of iniquity before a congregation and people; of unjust dealing before thy partner and friend;
[19] And of theft in regard of the place where thou sojournest, and in regard of the truth of God and his covenant; and to lean with thine elbow upon the meat; and of scorning to give and take;
[20] And of silence before them that salute thee; and to look upon an harlot;
[21] And to turn away thy face from thy kinsman; or to take away a portion or a gift; or to gaze upon another man's wife.
[22] Or to be overbusy with his maid, and come not near her bed; or of upbraiding speeches before friends; and after thou hast given, upbraid not;
[23] Or of iterating and speaking again that which thou hast heard; and of revealing of secrets.
[24] So shalt thou be truly shamefaced and find favour before all men.

Sir.42

[1] Of these things be not thou ashamed, and accept no person to sin thereby:
[2] Of the law of the most High, and his covenant; and of judgment to justify the ungodly;
[3] Of reckoning with thy partners and travellers; or of the gift of the heritage of friends;
[4] Of exactness of balance and weights; or of getting much or little;
[5] And of merchants' indifferent selling; of much correction of children; and to make the side of an evil servant to bleed.
[6] Sure keeping is good, where an evil wife is; and shut up, where many hands are.
[7] Deliver all things in number and weight; and put all in writing that thou givest out, or receivest in.
[8] Be not ashamed to inform the unwise and foolish, and the extreme aged that contendeth with those that are young: thus shalt thou be truly learned, and approved of all men living.
[9] The father waketh for the daughter, when no man knoweth; and the care for her taketh away sleep: when she is young, lest she pass

away the flower of her age; and being married, lest she should be hated:
[10] In her virginity, lest she should be defiled and gotten with child in her father's house; and having an husband, lest she should misbehave herself; and when she is married, lest she should be barren.
[11] Keep a sure watch over a shameless daughter, lest she make thee a laughingstock to thine enemies, and a byword in the city, and a reproach among the people, and make thee ashamed before the multitude.
[12] Behold not every body's beauty, and sit not in the midst of women.
[13] For from garments cometh a moth, and from women wickedness.
[14] Better is the churlishness of a man than a courteous woman, a woman, I say, which bringeth shame and reproach.
[15] I will now remember the works of Jah, and declare the things that I have seen: In the words of Jah are his works.
[16] The sun that giveth light looketh upon all things, and the work thereof is full of the glory of Jah.
[17] Jah hath not given power to the saints to declare all his marvellous works, which the Almighty Lord firmly settled, that whatsoever is might be established for his glory.
[18] He seeketh out the deep, and the heart, and considereth their crafty devices: for Jah knoweth all that may be known, and he beholdeth the signs of the world.
[19] He declareth the things that are past, and for to come, and revealeth the steps of hidden things.
[20] No thought escapeth him, neither any word is hidden from him.
[21] He hath garnished the excellent works of his wisdom, and he is from everlasting to everlasting: unto him may nothing be added, neither can he be diminished, and he hath no need of any counsellor.
[22] Oh how desirable are all his works! and that a man may see even to a spark.
[23] All these things live and remain for ever for all uses, and they are all obedient.
[24] All things are double one against another: and he hath made nothing imperfect.
[25] One thing establisheth the good or another: and who shall be filled with beholding his glory?

Sir. 43

[1] The pride of the height, the clear firmament, the beauty of heaven, with his glorious shew;
[2] The sun when it appeareth, declaring at his rising a marvellous instrument, the work of the most High:
[3] At noon it parcheth the country, and who can abide the burning heat thereof?
[4] A man blowing a furnace is in works of heat, but the sun burneth the mountains three times more; breathing out fiery vapours, and sending forth bright beams, it dimmeth the eyes.
[5] Great is Jah that made it; and at his commandment runneth hastily.
[6] He made the moon also to serve in her season for a declaration of times, and a sign of the world.
[7] From the moon is the sign of feasts, a light that decreaseth in her perfection.
[8] The month is called after her name, increasing wonderfully in her changing, being an instrument of the armies above, shining in the firmament of heaven;
[9] The beauty of heaven, the glory of the stars, an ornament giving light in the highest places of Jah.
[10] At the commandment of the Holy One they will stand in their order, and never faint in their watches.
[11] Look upon the rainbow, and praise him that made it; very beautiful it is in the brightness thereof.
[12] It compasseth the heaven about with a

glorious circle, and the hands of the most High have bended it.
[13] By his commandment he maketh the snow to fall aplace, and sendeth swiftly the lightnings of his judgment.
[14] Through this the treasures are opened: and clouds fly forth as fowls.
[15] By his great power he maketh the clouds firm, and the hailstones are broken small.
[16] At his sight the mountains are shaken, and at his will the south wind bloweth.
[17] The noise of the thunder maketh the earth to tremble: so doth the northern storm and the whirlwind: as birds flying he scattereth the snow, and the falling down thereof is as the lighting of grasshoppers:
[18] The eye marvelleth at the beauty of the whiteness thereof, and the heart is astonished at the raining of it.
[19] The hoarfrost also as salt he poureth on the earth, and being congealed, it lieth on the top of sharp stakes.
[20] When the cold north wind bloweth, and the water is congealed into ice, it abideth upon every gathering together of water, and clotheth the water as with a breastplate.
[21] It devoureth the mountains, and burneth the wilderness, and consumeth the grass as fire.
[22] A present remedy of all is a mist coming speedily, a dew coming after heat refresheth.
[23] By his counsel he appeaseth the deep, and planteth islands therein.
[24] They that sail on the sea tell of the danger thereof; and when we hear it with our ears, we marvel thereat.
[25] For therein be strange and wondrous works, variety of all kinds of beasts and whales created.
[26] By him the end of them hath prosperous success, and by his word all things consist.
[27] We may speak much, and yet come short: wherefore in sum, he is all.
[28] How shall we be able to magnify him?
for he is great above all his works.
[29] Jah is terrible and very great, and marvellous is his power.
[30] When ye glorify Jah, exalt him as much as ye can; for even yet will he far exceed: and when ye exalt him, put forth all your strength, and be not weary; for ye can never go far enough.
[31] Who hath seen him, that he might tell us? and who can magnify him as he is?
[32] There are yet hid greater things than these be, for we have seen but a few of his works.
[33] For Jah hath made all things; and to the godly hath he given wisdom.

Sir.44

[1] Let us now praise famous men, and our fathers that begat us.
[2] Jah hath wrought great glory by them through his great power from the beginning.
[3] Such as did bear rule in their kingdoms, men renowned for their power, giving counsel by their understanding, and declaring prophecies:
[4] Leaders of the people by their counsels, and by their knowledge of learning meet for the people, wise and eloquent are their instructions:
[5] Such as found out musical tunes, and recited verses in writing:
[6] Rich men furnished with ability, living peaceably in their habitations:
[7] All these were honoured in their generations, and were the glory of their times.
[8] There be of them, that have left a name behind them, that their praises might be reported.
[9] And some there be, which have no memorial; who are perished, as though they had never been; and are become as though they had never been born; and their children after them.

[10] But these were merciful men, whose righteousness hath not been forgotten.
[11] With their seed shall continually remain a good inheritance, and their children are within the covenant.
[12] Their seed standeth fast, and their children for their sakes.
[13] Their seed shall remain for ever, and their glory shall not be blotted out.
[14] Their bodies are buried in peace; but their name liveth for evermore.
[15] The people will tell of their wisdom, and the congregation will shew forth their praise.
[16] Enoch pleased Jah, and was translated, being an example of repentance to all generations.
[17] Noah was found perfect and righteous; in the time of wrath he was taken in exchange [for the world;] therefore was he left as a remnant unto the earth, when the flood came.
[18] An everlasting covenant was made with him, that all flesh should perish no more by the flood.
[19] Abraham was a great father of many people: in glory was there none like unto him;
[20] Who kept the law of the most High, and was in covenant with him: he established the covenant in his flesh; and when he was proved, he was found faithful.
[21] Therefore he assured him by an oath, that he would bless the nations in his seed, and that he would multiply him as the dust of the earth, and exalt his seed as the stars, and cause them to inherit from sea to sea, and from the river unto the utmost part of the land.
[22] With Isaac did he establish likewise [for Abraham his father's sake] the blessing of all men, and the covenant, And made it rest upon the head of Jacob. He acknowledged him in his blessing, and gave him an heritage, and divided his portions; among the twelve tribes did he part them.

Sir. 45

[1] And he brought out of him a merciful man, which found favour in the sight of all flesh, even Moses, beloved of God and men, whose memorial is blessed.
[2] He made him like to the glorious saints, and magnified him, so that his enemies stood in fear of him.
[3] By his words he caused the wonders to cease, and he made him glorious in the sight of kings, and gave him a commandment for his people, and shewed him part of his glory.
[4] He sanctified him in his faithfuless and meekness, and chose him out of all men.
[5] He made him to hear his voice, and brought him into the dark cloud, and gave him commandments before his face, even the law of life and knowledge, that he might teach Jacob his covenants, and Israel his judgments.
[6] He exalted Aaron, an holy man like unto him, even his brother, of the tribe of Levi.
[7] An everlasting covenant he made with him and gave him the priesthood among the people; he beautified him with comely ornaments, and clothed him with a robe of glory.
[8] He put upon him perfect glory; and strengthened him with rich garments, with breeches, with a long robe, and the ephod.
[9] And he compassed him with pomegranates, and with many golden bells round about, that as he went there might be a sound, and a noise made that might be heard in the temple, for a memorial to the children of his people;
[10] With an holy garment, with gold, and blue silk, and purple, the work of the embroidere, with a breastplate of judgment, and with Urim and Thummim;
[11] With twisted scarlet, the work of the cunning workman, with precious stones graven like seals, and set in gold, the work

of the jeweller, with a writing engraved for a memorial, after the number of the tribes of Israel.
[12] He set a crown of gold upon the mitre, wherein was engraved Holiness, an ornament of honour, a costly work, the desires of the eyes, goodly and beautiful.
[13] Before him there were none such, neither did ever any stranger put them on, but only his children and his children's children perpetually.
[14] Their sacrifices shall be wholly consumed every day twice continually.
[15] Moses consecrated him, and anointed him with holy oil: this was appointed unto him by an everlasting covenant, and to his seed, so long as the heavens should remain, that they should minister unto him, and execute the office of the priesthood, and bless the people in his name.
[16] He chose him out of all men living to offer sacrifices to Jah, incense, and a sweet savour, for a memorial, to make reconciliation for his people.
[17] He gave unto him his commandments, and authority in the statutes of judgments, that he should teach Jacob the testimonies, and inform Israel in his laws.
[18] Strangers conspired together against him, and maligned him in the wilderness, even the men that were of Dathan's and Abiron's side, and the congregation of Core, with fury and wrath.
[19] This Jah saw, and it displeased him, and in his wrathful indignation were they consumed: he did wonders upon them, to consume them with the fiery flame.
[20] But he made Aaron more honourable, and gave him an heritage, and divided unto him the firstfruits of the increase; especially he prepared bread in abundance:
[21] For they eat of the sacrifices of Jah, which he gave unto him and his seed.
[22] Howbeit in the land of the people he had no inheritance, neither had he any portion among the people: for Jah himself is his portion and inheritance.
[23] The third in glory is Phinees the son of Eleazar, because he had zeal in the fear of Jah, and stood up with good courage of heart: when the people were turned back, and made reconciliation for Israel.
[24] Therefore was there a covenant of peace made with him, that he should be the chief of the sanctuary and of his people, and that he and his posterity should have the dignity of the priesthood for ever:
[25] According to the covenant made with David son of Jesse, of the tribe of Juda, that the inheritance of the king should be to his posterity alone: so the inheritance of Aaron should also be unto his seed.
[26] God give you wisdom in your heart to judge his people in righteousness, that their good things be not abolished, and that their glory may endure for ever.

Sir. 46

[1] Jesus the son a Nave was valiant in the wars, and was the successor of Moses in prophecies, who according to his name was made great for the saving of the elect of God, and taking vengeance of the enemies that rose up against them, that he might set Israel in their inheritance.
[2] How great glory gat he, when he did lift up his hands, and stretched out his sword against the cities!
[3] Who before him so stood to it? for Jah himself brought his enemies unto him.
[4] Did not the sun go back by his means? and was not one day as long as two?
[5] He called upon the most high Lord, when the enemies pressed upon him on every side; and the great Lord heard him.
[6] And with hailstones of mighty power he made the battle to fall violently upon the nations, and in the descent [of Beth-horon] he destroyed them that resisted, that the nations might know all their strength,

because he fought in the sight of Jah, and he followed the Mighty One.
[7] In the time of Moses also he did a work of mercy, he and Caleb the son of Jephunne, in that they withstood the congregation, and withheld the people from sin, and appeased the wicked murmuring.
[8] And of six hundred thousand people on foot, they two were preserved to bring them in to the heritage, even unto the land that floweth with milk and honey.
[9] Jah gave strength also unto Caleb, which remained with him unto his old age: so that he entered upon the high places of the land, and his seed obtained it for an heritage:
[10] That all the children of Israel might see that it is good to follow Jah.
[11] And concerning the judges, every one by name, whose heart went not a whoring, nor departed from Jah, let their memory be blessed.
[12] Let their bones flourish out of their place, and let the name of them that were honoured be continued upon their children.
[13] Samuel, the prophet of Jah, beloved of his Lord, established a kingdom, and anointed princes over his people.
[14] By the law of Jah he judged the congregation, and Jah had respect unto Jacob.
[15] By his faithfulness he was found a true prophet, and by his word he was known to be faithful in vision.
[16] He called upon the mighty Lord, when his enemies pressed upon him on every side, when he offered the sucking lamb.
[17] And Jah thundered from heaven, and with a great noise made his voice to be heard.
[18] And he destroyed the rulers of the Tyrians, and all the princes cf the Philistines.
[19] And before his long sleep he made protestations in the sight of Jah and his anointed, I have not taken any man's goods, so much as a shoe: and no man did accuse him.
[20] And after his death he prophesied, and shewed the king his end, and lifted up his voice from the earth in prophecy, to blot out the wickedness of the people.

Sir.47

[1] And after him rose up Nathan to prophesy in the time of David.
[2] As is the fat taken away from the peace offering, so was David chosen out of the children of Israel.
[3] He played with lions as with kids, and with bears as with lambs.
[4] Slew he not a giant, when he was yet but young? and did he not take away reproach from the people, when he lifted up his hand with the stone in the sling, and beat down the boasting of Goliath?
[5] For he called upon the most high Lord; and he gave him strength in his right hand to slay that mighty warrior, and set up the horn of his people.
[6] So the people honoured him with ten thousands, and praised him in the blessings of Jah, in that he gave him a crown of glory.
[7] For he destroyed the enemies on every side, and brought to nought the Philistines his adversaries, and brake their horn in sunder unto this day.
[8] In all his works he praised the Holy One most high with words of glory; with his whole heart he sung songs, and loved him that made him.
[9] He set singers also before the altar, that by their voices they might make sweet melody, and daily sing praises in their songs.
[10] He beautified their feasts, and set in order the solemn times until the end, that they might praise his holy name, and that the temple might sound from morning.
[11] Jah took away his sins, and exalted his horn for ever: he gave him a covenant of

kings, and a throne of glory in Israel.
[12] After him rose up a wise son, and for his sake he dwelt at large.
[13] Solomon reigned in a peaceable time, and was honoured; for God made all quiet round about him, that he might build an house in his name, and prepare his sanctuary for ever.
[14] How wise wast thou in thy youth and, as a flood, filled with understanding!
[15] Thy soul covered the whole earth, and thou filledst it with dark parables.
[16] Thy name went far unto the islands; and for thy peace thou wast beloved.
[17] The countries marvelled at thee for thy songs, and proverbs, and parables, and interpretations.
[18] By the name of Jah God, which is called Jah God of Israel, thou didst gather gold as tin and didst multiply silver as lead.
[19] Thou didst bow thy loins unto women, and by thy body thou wast brought into subjection.
[20] Thou didst stain thy honour, and pollute thy seed: so that thou broughtest wrath upon thy children, and wast grieved for thy folly.
[21] So the kingdom was divided, and out of Ephraim ruled a rebellious kingdom.
[22] But Jah will never leave off his mercy, neither shall any of his works perish, neither will he abolish the posterity of his elect, and the seed of him that loveth him he will not take away: wherefore he gave a remnant unto Jacob, and out of him a root unto David.
[23] Thus rested Solomon with his fathers, and of his seed he left behind him Roboam, even the foolishness of the people, and one that had no understanding, who turned away the people through his counsel. There was also Jeroboam the son of Nebat, who caused Israel to sin, and shewed Ephraim the way of sin:
[24] And their sins were multiplied exceedingly, that they were driven out of the land.

[25] For they sought out all wickedness, till the vengeance came upon them.

Sir. 48

[1] Then stood up Elias the prophet as fire, and his word burned like a lamp.
[2] He brought a sore famine upon them, and by his zeal he diminished their number.
[3] By the word of Jah he shut up the heaven, and also three times brought down fire.
[4] O Elias, how wast thou honoured in thy wondrous deeds! and who may glory like unto thee!
[5] Who didst raise up a dead man from death, and his soul from the place of the dead, by the word of the most High:
[6] Who broughtest kings to destruction, and honorable men from their bed:
[7] Who heardest the rebuke of Jah in Sinai, and in Horeb the judgment of vengeance:
[8] Who annointedst kings to take revenge, and prophets to succeed after him:
[9] Who was taken up in a whirlwind of fire, and in a chariot of fiery horses:
[10] Who wast ordained for reproofs in their times, to pacify the wrath of Jah's judgment, before it brake forth into fury, and to turn the heart of the father unto the son, and to restore the tribes of Jacob.
[11] Blessed are they that saw thee, and slept in love; for we shall surely live.
[12] Elias it was, who was covered with a whirlwind: and Eliseus was filled with his spirit: whilst he lived, he was not moved with the presence of any prince, neither could any bring him into subjection.
[13] No word could overcome him; and after his death his body prophesied.
[14] He did wonders in his life, and at his death were his works marvellous.
[15] For all this the people repented not, neither departed they from their sins, till they were spoiled and carried out of their

land, and were scattered through all the earth: yet there remained a small people, and a ruler in the house of David:
[16] Of whom some did that which was pleasing to God, and some multiplied sins.
[17] Ezekias fortified his city, and brought in water into the midst thereof: he digged the hard rock with iron, and made wells for waters.
[18] In his time Sennacherib came up, and sent Rabsaces, and lifted up his hand against Sion, and boasted proudly.
[19] Then trembled their hearts and hands, and they were in pain, as women in travail.
[20] But they called upon Jah which is merciful, and stretched out their hands toward him: and immediately the Holy One heard them out of heaven, and delivered them by the ministry of Esay.
[21] He smote the host of the Assyrians, and his angel destroyed them.
[22] For Ezekias had done the thing that pleased Jah, and was strong in the ways of David his father, as Esay the prophet, who was great and faithful in his vision, had commanded him.
[23] In his time the sun went backward, and he lengthened the king's life.
[24] He saw by an excellent spirit what should come to pass at the last, and he comforted them that mourned in Sion.
[25] He shewed what should come to pass for ever, and secret things or ever they came.

Sir.49

[1] The remembrance of Josias is like the composition of the perfume that is made by the art of the apothecary: it is sweet as honey in all mouths, and as musick at a banquet of wine.
[2] He behaved himself uprightly in the conversion of the people, and took away the abominations of iniquity.
[3] He directed his heart unto Jah, and in the time of the ungodly he established the worship of God.
[4] All, except David and Ezekias and Josias, were defective: for they forsook the law of the most High, even the kings of Juda failed.
[5] Therefore he gave their power unto others, and their glory to a strange nation.
[6] They burnt the chosen city of the sanctuary, and made the streets desolate, according to the prophecy of Jeremias.
[7] For they entreated him evil, who nevertheless was a prophet, sanctified in his mother's womb, that he might root out, and afflict, and destroy; and that he might build up also, and plant.
[8] It was Ezekiel who saw the glorious vision, which was shewed him upon the chariot of the cherubims.
[9] For he made mention of the enemies under the figure of the rain, and directed them that went right.
[10] And of the twelve prophets let the memorial be blessed, and let their bones flourish again out of their place: for they comforted Jacob, and delivered them by assured hope.
[11] How shall we magnify Zorobabel? even he was as a signet on the right hand:
[12] So was Jesus the son of Josedec: who in their time builded the house, and set up an holy temple to Jah, which was prepared for everlasting glory.
[13] And among the elect was Neemias, whose renown is great, who raised up for us the walls that were fallen, and set up the gates and the bars, and raised up our ruins again.
[14] But upon the earth was no man created like Enoch; for he was taken from the earth.
[15] Neither was there a young man born like Joseph, a governor of his brethren, a stay of the people, whose bones were regarded of Jah.
[16] Sem and Seth were in great honour

among men, and so was Adam above every living thing in creation.

Sir. 50

[1] Simon the high priest, the son of Onias, who in his life repaired the house again, and in his days fortified the temple:
[2] And by him was built from the foundation the double height, the high fortress of the wall about the temple:
[3] In his days the cistern to receive water, being in compass as the sea, was covered with plates of brass:
[4] He took care of the temple that it should not fall, and fortified the city against besieging:
[5] How was he honoured in the midst of the people in his coming out of the sanctuary!
[6] He was as the morning star in the midst of a cloud, and as the moon at the full:
[7] As the sun shining upon the temple of the most High, and as the rainbow giving light in the bright clouds:
[8] And as the flower of roses in the spring of the year, as lilies by the rivers of waters, and as the branches of the frankincense tree in the time of summer:
[9] As fire and incense in the censer, and as a vessel of beaten gold set with all manner of precious stones:
[10] And as a fair olive tree budding forth fruit, and as a cypress tree which groweth up to the clouds.
[11] When he put on the robe of honour, and was clothed with the perfection of glory, when he went up to the holy altar, he made the garment of holiness honourable.
[12] When he took the portions out of the priests' hands, he himself stood by the hearth of the altar, compassed about, as a young cedar in Libanus; and as palm trees compassed they him round about.
[13] So were all the sons of Aaron in their glory, and the oblations of Jah in their hands, before all the congregation of Israel.
[14] And finishing the service at the altar, that he might adorn the offering of the most high Almighty,
[15] He stretched out his hand to the cup, and poured of the blood of the grape, he poured out at the foot of the altar a sweetsmelling savour unto the most high King of all.
[16] Then shouted the sons of Aaron, and sounded the silver trumpets, and made a great noise to be heard, for a remembrance before the most High.
[17] Then all the people together hasted, and fell down to the earth upon their faces to worship their Lord God Almighty, the most High.
[18] The singers also sang praises with their voices, with great variety of sounds was there made sweet melody.
[19] And the people besought Jah, the most High, by prayer before him that is merciful, till the solemnity of Jah was ended, and they had finished his service.
[20] Then he went down, and lifted up his hands over the whole congregation of the children of Israel, to give the blessing of Jah with his lips, and to rejoice in his name.
[21] And they bowed themselves down to worship the second time, that they might receive a blessing from the most High.
[22] Now therefore bless ye the God of all, which only doeth wondrous things every where, which exalteth our days from the womb, and dealeth with us according to his mercy.
[23] He grant us joyfulness of heart, and that peace may be in our days in Israel for ever:
[24] That he would confirm his mercy with us, and deliver us at his time!
[25] There be two manner of nations which my heart abhorreth, and the third is no nation:
[26] They that sit upon the mountain of Samaria, and they that dwell among the Philistines, and that foolish people that

dwell in Sichem.
[27] Jesus the son of Sirach of Jerusalem hath written in this book the instruction of understanding and knowledge, who out of his heart poured forth wisdom.
[28] Blessed is he that shall be exercised in these things; and he that layeth them up in his heart shall become wise.
[29] For if he do them, he shall be strong to all things: for the light of Jah leadeth him, who giveth wisdom to the godly. Blessed be the name of Jah for ever. Amen, Amen.

Sir. 51

[A Prayer of Jesus the son of Sirach.][1] I will thank thee, O Lord and King, and praise thee, O God my Saviour: I do give praise unto thy name:
[2] For thou art my defender and helper, and has preserved my body from destruction, and from the snare of the slanderous tongue, and from the lips that forge lies, and has been mine helper against mine adversaries:
[3] And hast delivered me, according to the multitude of they mercies and greatness of thy name, from the teeth of them that were ready to devour me, and out of the hands of such as sought after my life, and from the manifold afflictions which I had;
[4] From the choking of fire on every side, and from the midst of the fire which I kindled not;
[5] From the depth of the belly of hell, from an unclean tongue, and from lying words.
[6] By an accusation to the king from an unrighteous tongue my soul drew near even unto death, my life was near to the hell beneath.
[7] They compassed me on every side, and there was no man to help me: I looked for the succour of men, but there was none.
[8] Then thought I upon thy mercy, O Lord, and upon thy acts of old, how thou deliverest such as wait for thee, and savest them out of the hands of the enemies.
[9] Then lifted I up my supplications from the earth, and prayed for deliverance from death.
[10] I called upon Jah, the Father of my Lord, that he would not leave me in the days of my trouble, and in the time of the proud, when there was no help.
[11] I will praise thy name continually, and will sing praises with thanksgiving; and so my prayer was heard:
[12] For thou savedst me from destruction, and deliveredst me from the evil time: therefore will I give thanks, and praise thee, and bless they name, O Lord.
[13] When I was yet young, or ever I went abroad, I desired wisdom openly in my prayer.
[14] I prayed for her before the temple, and will seek her out even to the end.
[15] Even from the flower till the grape was ripe hath my heart delighted in her: my foot went the right way, from my youth up sought I after her.
[16] I bowed down mine ear a little, and received her, and gat much learning.
[17] I profited therein, therefore will I ascribe glory unto him that giveth me wisdom.
[18] For I purposed to do after her, and earnestly I followed that which is good; so shall I not be confounded.
[19] My soul hath wrestled with her, and in my doings I was exact: I stretched forth my hands to the heaven above, and bewailed my ignorances of her.
[20] I directed my soul unto her, and I found her in pureness: I have had my heart joined with her from the beginning, therefore shall I not be foresaken.
[21] My heart was troubled in seeking her:

therefore have I gotten a good possession.
[22] Jah hath given me a tongue for my reward, and I will praise him therewith.
[23] Draw near unto me, ye unlearned, and dwell in the house of learning.
[24] Wherefore are ye slow, and what say ye to these things, seeing your souls are very thirsty?
[25] I opened my mouth, and said, Buy her for yourselves without money.
[26] Put your neck under the yoke, and let your soul receive instruction: she is hard at hand to find.
[27] Behold with your eyes, how that I have but little labour, and have gotten unto me much rest.
[28] Get learning with a great sum of money, and get much gold by her.
[29] Let your soul rejoice in his mercy, and be not ashamed of his praise.
[30] Work your work betimes, and in his time he will give you your reward.

Baruch

Bar.1

[1] And these are the words of the book, which Baruch the son of Nerias, the son of Maasias, the son of Sedecias, the son of Asadias, the son of Chelcias, wrote in Babylon,
[2] In the fifth year, and in the seventh day of the month, what time as the Chaldeans took Jerusalem, and burnt it with fire.
[3] And Baruch did read the words of this book in the hearing of Jechonias the son of Joachim king of Juda, and in the ears of all the people that came to hear the book,
[4] And in the hearing of the nobles, and of the king's sons, and in the hearing of the elders, and of all the people, from the lowest unto the highest, even of all them that dwelt at Babylon by the river Sud.
[5] Whereupon they wept, fasted, and prayed before Jah.
[6] They made also a collection of money according to every man's power:
[7] And they sent it to Jerusalem unto Joachim the high priest, the son of Chelcias, son of Salom, and to the priests, and to all the people which were found with him at Jerusalem,
[8] At the same time when he received the vessels of the house of Jah, that were carried out of the temple, to return them into the land of Juda, the tenth day of the month Sivan, namely, silver vessels, which Sedecias the son of Josias king of Jada had made,
[9] After that Nabuchodonosor king of Babylon had carried away Jechonias, and the princes, and the captives, and the mighty men, and the people of the land, from Jerusalem, and brought them unto Babylon.
[10] And they said, Behold, we have sent you money to buy you burnt offerings, and sin offerings, and incense, and prepare ye manna, and offer upon the altar of Jah our God;
[11] And pray for the life of Nabuchodonosor king of Babylon, and for the life of Balthasar his son, that their days may be upon earth as the days of heaven:
[12] And Jah will give us strength, and lighten our eyes, and we shall live under the shadow of Nabuchodonosor king of Babylon, and under the shadow of Balthasar his son, and we shall serve them many days, and find favour in their sight.
[13] Pray for us also unto Jah our God, for we have sinned against Jah our God; and unto this day the fury of Jah and his wrath is not turned from us.
[14] And ye shall read this book which we have sent unto you, to make confession in

the house of Jah, upon the feasts and solemn days.
[15] And ye shall say, To Jah our God belongeth righteousness, but unto us the confusion of faces, as it is come to pass this day, unto them of Juda, and to the inhabitants of Jerusalem,
[16] And to our kings, and to our princes, and to our priests, and to our prophets, and to our fathers:
[17] For we have sinned before Jah,
[18] And disobeyed him, and have not hearkened unto the voice of Jah our God, to walk in the commandments that he gave us openly:
[19] Since the day that Jah brought our forefathers out of the land of Egypt, unto this present day, we have been disobedient unto Jah our God, and we have been negligent in not hearing his voice.
[20] Wherefore the evils cleaved unto us, and the curse, which Jah appointed by Moses his servant at the time that he brought our fathers out of the land of Egypt, to give us a land that floweth with milk and honey, like as it is to see this day.
[21] Nevertheless we have not hearkened unto the voice of Jah our God, according unto all the words of the prophets, whom he sent unto us:
[22] But every man followed the imagination of his own wicked heart, to serve strange gods, and to do evil in the sight of Jah our God.

Bar. 2

[1] Therefore Jah hath made good his word, which he pronounced against us, and against our judges that judged Israel, and against our kings, and against our princes, and against the men of Israel and Juda,
[2] To bring upon us great plagues, such as never happened under the whole heaven, as it came to pass in Jerusalem, according to the things that were written in the law of Moses;
[3] That a man should eat the flesh of his own son, and the flesh of his own daughter.
[4] Moreover he hath delivered them to be in subjection to all the kingdoms that are round about us, to be as a reproach and desolation among all the people round about, where Jah hath scattered them.
[5] Thus we were cast down, and not exalted, because we have sinned against Jah our God, and have not been obedient unto his voice.
[6] To Jah our God appertaineth righteousness: but unto us and to our fathers open shame, as appeareth this day.
[7] For all these plagues are come upon us, which Jah hath pronounced against us
[8] Yet have we not prayed before Jah, that we might turn every one from the imaginations of his wicked heart.
[9] Wherefore Jah watched over us for evil, and Jah hath brought it upon us: for Jah is righteous in all his works which he hath commanded us.
[10] Yet we have not hearkened unto his voice, to walk in the commandments of Jah, that he hath set before us.
[11] And now, O Lord God of Israel, that hast brought thy people out of the land of Egypt with a mighty hand, and high arm, and with signs, and with wonders, and with great power, and hast gotten thyself a name, as appeareth this day:
[12] O Lord our God, we have sinned, we have done ungodly, we have dealt unrighteously in all thine ordinances.
[13] Let thy wrath turn from us: for we are but a few left among the heathen, where thou hast scattered us.
[14] Hear our prayers, O Lord, and our petitions, and deliver us for thine own sake, and give us favour in the sight of them which have led us away:
[15] That all the earth may know that thou art Jah our God, because Israel and his

posterity is called by thy name.
[16] O Lord, look down from thine holy house, and consider us: bow down thine ear, O Lord, to hear us.
[17] Open thine eyes, and behold; for the dead that are in the graves, whose souls are taken from their bodies, will give unto Jah neither praise nor righteousness:
[18] But the soul that is greatly vexed, which goeth stooping and feeble, and the eyes that fail, and the hungry soul, will give thee praise and righteousness, O Lord.
[19] Therefore we do not make our humble supplication before thee, O Lord our God, for the righteousness of our fathers, and of our kings.
[20] For thou hast sent out thy wrath and indignation upon us, as thou hast spoken by thy servants the prophets, saying,
[21] Thus saith Jah, Bow down your shoulders to serve the king of Babylon: so shall ye remain in the land that I gave unto your fathers.
[22] But if ye will not hear the voice of Jah, to serve the king of Babylon,
[23] I will cause to cease out of the cites of Judah, and from without Jerusalem, the voice of mirth, and the voice of joy, the voice of the bridegroom, and the voice of the bride: and the whole land shall be desolate of inhabitants.
[24] But we would not hearken unto thy voice, to serve the king of Babylon: therefore hast thou made good the words that thou spakest by thy servants the prophets, namely, that the bones of our kings, and the bones of our fathers, should be taken out of their place.
[25] And, lo, they are cast out to the heat of the day, and to the frost of the night, and they died in great miseries by famine, by sword, and by pestilence.
[26] And the house which is called by thy name hast thou laid waste, as it is to be seen this day, for the wickedness of the house of Israel and the house of Juda.

[27] O Lord our God, thou hast dealt with us after all thy goodness, and according to all that great mercy of thine,
[28] As thou spakest by thy servant Moses in the day when thou didst command him to write the law before the children of Israel, saying,
[29] If ye will not hear my voice, surely this very great multitude shall be turned into a small number among the nations, where I will scatter them.
[30] For I knew that they would not hear me, because it is a stiffnecked people: but in the land of their captivities they shall remember themselves.
[31] And shall know that I am Jah their God: for I will give them an heart, and ears to hear:
[32] And they shall praise me in the land of their captivity, and think upon my name,
[33] And return from their stiff neck, and from their wicked deeds: for they shall remember the way of their fathers, which sinned before Jah.
[34] And I will bring them again into the land which I promised with an oath unto their fathers, Abraham, Isaac, and Jacob, and they shall be lords of it: and I will increase them, and they shall not be diminished.
[35] And I will make an everlasting covenant with them to be their God, and they shall be my people: and I will no more drive my people of Israel out of the land that I have given them.

Bar.3

[1] O Lord Almighty, God of Israel, the soul in anguish the troubled spirit, crieth unto thee.
[2] Hear, O Lord, and have mercy; ar thou art merciful: and have pity upon us, because we have sinned before thee.
[3] For thou endurest for ever, and we perish utterly.

[4] O Lord Almighty, thou God of Israel, hear now the prayers of the dead Israelites, and of their children, which have sinned before thee, and not hearkened unto the voice of thee their God: for the which cause these plagues cleave unto us.
[5] Remember not the iniquities of our forefathers: but think upon thy power and thy name now at this time.
[6] For thou art Jah our God, and thee, O Lord, will we praise.
[7] And for this cause thou hast put thy fear in our hearts, to the intent that we should call upon thy name, and praise thee in our captivity: for we have called to mind all the iniquity of our forefathers, that sinned before thee.
[8] Behold, we are yet this day in our captivity, where thou hast scattered us, for a reproach and a curse, and to be subject to payments, according to all the iniquities of our fathers, which departed from Jah our God.
[9] Hear, Israel, the commandments of life: give ear to understand wisdom.
[10] How happeneth it Israel, that thou art in thine enemies' land, that thou art waxen old in a strange country, that thou art defiled with the dead,
[11] That thou art counted with them that go down into the grave?
[12] Thou hast forsaken the fountain of wisdom.
[13] For if thou hadst walked in the way of God, thou shouldest have dwelled in peace for ever.
[14] Learn where is wisdom, where is strength, where is understanding; that thou mayest know also where is length of days, and life, where is the light of the eyes, and peace.
[15] Who hath found out her place? or who hath come into her treasures ?
[16] Where are the princes of the heathen become, and such as ruled the beasts upon the earth;
[17] They that had their pastime with the fowls of the air, and they that hoarded up silver and gold, wherein men trust, and made no end of their getting?
[18] For they that wrought in silver, and were so careful, and whose works are unsearchable,
[19] They are vanished and gone down to the grave, and others are come up in their steads.
[20] Young men have seen light, and dwelt upon the earth: but the way of knowledge have they not known,
[21] Nor understood the paths thereof, nor laid hold of it: their children were far off from that way.
[22] It hath not been heard of in Chanaan, neither hath it been seen in Theman.
[23] The Agarenes that seek wisdom upon earth, the merchants of Meran and of Theman, the authors of fables, and searchers out of understanding; none of these have known the way of wisdom, or remember her paths.
[24] O Israel, how great is the house of God! and how large is the place of his possession!
[25] Great, and hath none end; high, and unmeasurable.
[26] There were the giants famous from the beginning, that were of so great stature, and so expert in war.
[27] Those did not Jah choose, neither gave he the way of knowledge unto them:
[28] But they were destroyed, because they had no wisdom, and perished through their own foolishness.
[29] Who hath gone up into heaven, and taken her, and brought her down from the clouds?
[30] Who hath gone over the sea, and found her, and will bring her for pure gold?
[31] No man knoweth her way, nor thinketh of her path.
[32] But he that knoweth all things knoweth her, and hath found her out with his understanding: he that prepared the earth for

evermore hath filled it with fourfooted beasts:
[33] He that sendeth forth light, and it goeth, calleth it again, and it obeyeth him with fear.
[34] The stars shined in their watches, and rejoiced: when he calleth them, they say, Here we be; and so with cheerfulness they shewed light unto him that made them.
[35] This is our God, and there shall none other be accounted of in comparison of him
[36] He hath found out all the way of knowledge, and hath given it unto Jacob his servant, and to Israel his beloved.
[37] Afterward did he shew himself upon earth, and conversed with men.

Bar. 4

[1] This is the book of the commandments of God, and the law that endureth for ever: all they that keep it shall come to life; but such as leave it shall die.
[2] Turn thee, O Jacob, and take hold of it: walk in the presence of the light thereof, that thou mayest be illuminated.
[3] Give not thine honour to another, nor the things that are profitable unto thee to a strange nation.
[4] O Israel, happy are we: for things that are pleasing to God are made known unto us.
[5] Be of good cheer, my people, the memorial of Israel.
[6] Ye were sold to the nations, not for [your] destruction: but because ye moved God to wrath, ye were delivered unto the enemies.
[7] For ye provoked him that made you by sacrificing unto devils, and not to God.
[8] Ye have forgotten the everlasting God, that brought you up; and ye have grieved Jerusalem, that nursed you.
[9] For when she saw the wrath of God coming upon you, she said, Hearken, O ye that dwell about Sion: God hath brought upon me great mourning;
[10] For I saw the captivity of my sons and daughters, which the Everlasting brought upon them.
[11] With joy did I nourish them; but sent them away with weeping and mourning.
[12] Let no man rejoice over me, a widow, and forsaken of many, who for the sins of my children am left desolate; because they departed from the law of God.
[13] They knew not his statutes, nor walked in the ways of his commandments, nor trod in the paths of discipline in his righteousness.
[14] Let them that dwell about Sion come, and remember ye the captivity of my sons and daughters, which the Everlasting hath brought upon them.
[15] For he hath brought a nation upon them from far, a shameless nation, and of a strange language, who neither reverenced old man, nor pitied child.
[16] These have carried away the dear beloved children of the widow, and left her that was alone desolate without daughters.
[17] But what can I help you?
[18] For he that brought these plagues upon you will deliver you from the hands of your enemies.
[19] Go your way, O my children, go your way: for I am left desolate.
[20] I have put off the clothing of peace, and put upon me the sackcloth of my prayer: I will cry unto the Everlasting in my days.
[21] Be of good cheer, O my children, cry unto Jah, and he will deliver you from the power and hand of the enemies.
[22] For my hope is in the Everlasting, that he will save you; and joy is come unto me from the Holy One, because of the mercy which shall soon come unto you from the Everlasting our Saviour.
[23] For I sent you out with mourning and weeping: but God will give you to me again with joy and gladness for ever.
[24] Like as now the neighbours of Sion

have seen your captivity: so shall they see shortly your salvation from our God which shall come upon you with great glory, and brightness of the Everlasting.
[25] My children, suffer patiently the wrath that is come upon you from God: for thine enemy hath persecuted thee; but shortly thou shalt see his destruction, and shalt tread upon his neck.
[26] My delicate ones have gone rough ways, and were taken away as a flock caught of the enemies.
[27] Be of good comfort, O my children, and cry unto God: for ye shall be remembered of him that brought these things upon you.
[28] For as it was your mind to go astray from God: so, being returned, seek him ten times more.
[29] For he that hath brought these plagues upon you shall bring you everlasting joy with your salvation.
[30] Take a good heart, O Jerusalem: for he that gave thee that name will comfort thee.
[31] Miserable are they that afflicted thee, and rejoiced at thy fall.
[32] Miserable are the cities which thy children served: miserable is she that received thy sons.
[33] For as she rejoiced at thy ruin, and was glad of thy fall: so shall she be grieved for her own desolation.
[34] For I will take away the rejoicing of her great multitude, and her pride shall be turned into mourning.
[35] For fire shall come upon her from the Everlasting, long to endure; and she shall be inhabited of devils for a great time.
[36] O Jerusalem, look about thee toward the east, and behold the joy that cometh unto thee from God.
[37] Lo, thy sons come, whom thou sentest away, they come gathered together from the east to the west by the word of the Holy One, rejoicing in the glory of God.

Bar. 5

[1] Put off, O Jerusalem, the garment of mourning and affliction, and put on the comeliness of the glory that cometh from God for ever.
[2] Cast about thee a double garment of the righteousness which cometh from God; and set a diadem on thine head of the glory of the Everlasting.
[3] For God will shew thy brightness unto every country under heaven.
[4] For thy name shall be called of God for ever The peace of righteousness, and The glory of God's worship.
[5] Arise, O Jerusalem, and stand on high, and look about toward the east, and behold thy children gathered from the west unto the east by the word of the Holy One, rejoicing in the remembrance of God.
[6] For they departed from thee on foot, and were led away of their enemies: but God bringeth them unto thee exalted with glory, as children of the kingdom.
[7] For God hath appointed that every high hill, and banks of long continuance, should be cast down, and valleys filled up, to make even the ground, that Israel may go safely in the glory of God,
[8] Moreover even the woods and every sweetsmelling tree shall overshadow Israel by the commandment of God.
[9] For God shall lead Israel with joy in the light of his glory with the mercy and righteousness that cometh from him.

Letter of Jeremiah

EpJer. 1

A copy of an epistle, which Jeremy sent unto them which were to be led captives into Babylon by the king of the Babylonians, to certify them, as it was commanded him of God. [1] Because of the sins which ye have committed before God, ye shall be led away captives into Babylon by Nabuchodonosor king of the Babylonians.

[2] So when ye be come unto Babylon, ye shall remain there many years, and for a long season, namely, seven generations: and after that I will bring you away peaceably from thence.

[3] Now shall ye see in Babylon gods of silver, and of gold, and of wood, borne upon shoulders, which cause the nations to fear.

[4] Beware therefore that ye in no wise be like to strangers, neither be ye and of them, when ye see the multitude before them and behind them, worshipping them.

[5] But say ye in your hearts, O Lord, we must worship thee.

[6] For mine angel is with you, and I myself caring for your souls.

[7] As for their tongue, it is polished by the workman, and they themselves are gilded and laid over with silver; yet are they but false, and cannot speak.

[8] And taking gold, as it were for a virgin that loveth to go gay, they make crowns for the heads of their gods.

[9] Sometimes also the priests convey from their gods gold and silver, and bestow it upon themselves.

[10] Yea, they will give thereof to the common harlots, and deck them as men with garments, [being] gods of silver, and gods of gold, and wood.

[11] Yet cannot these gods save themselves from rust and moth, though they be covered with purple raiment.

[12] They wipe their faces because of the dust of the temple, when there is much upon them.

[13] And he that cannot put to death one that offendeth him holdeth a sceptre, as though he were a judge of the country.

[14] He hath also in his right hand a dagger and an ax: but cannot deliver himself from war and thieves.

[15] Whereby they are known not to be gods: therefore fear them not.

[16] For like as a vessel that a man useth is nothing worth when it is broken; even so it is with their gods: when they be set up in the temple, their eyes be full of dust through the feet of them that come in.

[17] And as the doors are made sure on every side upon him that offendeth the king, as being committed to suffer death: even so the priests make fast their temples with doors, with locks, and bars, lest their gods be spoiled with robbers.

[18] They light them candles, yea, more than for themselves, whereof they cannot see one.

[19] They are as one of the beams of the temple, yet they say their hearts are gnawed upon by things creeping out of the earth; and when they eat them and their clothes, they feel it not.

[20] Their faces are blacked through the smoke that cometh out of the temple.

[21] Upon their bodies and heads sit bats, swallows, and birds, and the cats also.

[22] By this ye may know that they are no gods: therefore fear them not.

[23] Notwithstanding the gold that is about them to make them beautiful, except they wipe off the rust, they will not shine: for neither when they were molten did they feel it.

[24] The things wherein there is no breath are bought for a most high price.

[25] They are borne upon shoulders, having no feet whereby they declare unto men that they be nothing worth.

[26] They also that serve them are ashamed: for if they fall to the ground at any time, they cannot rise up again of themselves: neither, if one set them upright, can they move of themselves: neither, if they be bowed down, can they make themselves straight: but they set gifts before them as unto dead men.

[27] As for the things that are sacrificed unto them, their priests sell and abuse; in like manner their wives lay up part thereof in salt; but unto the poor and impotent they give nothing of it.

[28] Menstruous women and women in childbed eat their sacrifices: by these things ye may know that they are no gods: fear them not.

[29] For how can they be called gods? because women set meat before the gods of silver, gold, and wood.

[30] And the priests sit in their temples, having their clothes rent, and their heads and beards shaven, and nothing upon their heads.

[31] They roar and cry before their gods, as men do at the feast when one is dead.

[32] The priests also take off their garments, and clothe their wives and children.

[33] Whether it be evil that one doeth unto them, or good, they are not able to recompense it: they can neither set up a king, nor put him down.

[34] In like manner, they can neither give riches nor money: though a man make a vow unto them, and keep it not, they will not require it.

[35] They can save no man from death, neither deliver the weak from the mighty.

[36] They cannot restore a blind man to his sight, nor help any man in his distress.

[37] They can shew no mercy to the widow, nor do good to the fatherless.

[38] Their gods of wood, and which are overlaid with gold and silver, are like the stones that be hewn out of the mountain: they that worship them shall be confounded.

[39] How should a man then think and say that they are gods, when even the Chaldeans themselves dishonour them?

[40] Who if they shall see one dumb that cannot speak, they bring him, and intreat Bel that he may speak, as though he were able to understand.

[41] Yet they cannot understand this themselves, and leave them: for they have no knowledge.

[42] The women also with cords about them, sitting in the ways, burn bran for perfume: but if any of them, drawn by some that passeth by, lie with him, she reproacheth her fellow, that she was not thought as worthy as herself, nor her cord broken.

[43] Whatsoever is done among them is false: how may it then be thought or said that they are gods?

[44] They are made of carpenters and goldsmiths: they can be nothing else than the workmen will have them to be.

[45] And they themselves that made them can never continue long; how should then the things that are made of them be gods?

[46] For they left lies and reproaches to them that come after.

[47] For when there cometh any war or plague upon them, the priests consult with themselves, where they may be hidden with them.

[48] How then cannot men perceive that they be no gods, which can neither save themselves from war, nor from plague?

[49] For seeing they be but of wood, and overlaid with silver and gold, it shall be known hereafter that they are false:

[50] And it shall manifestly appear to all nations and kings that they are no gods, but the works of men's hands, and that there is no work of God in them.

[51] Who then may not know that they are no gods?
[52] For neither can they set up a king in the land, nor give rain unto men.
[53] Neither can they judge their own cause, nor redress a wrong, being unable: for they are as crows between heaven and earth.
[54] Whereupon when fire falleth upon the house of gods of wood, or laid over with gold or silver, their priests will flee away, and escape; but they themselves shall be burned asunder like beams.
[55] Moreover they cannot withstand any king or enemies: how can it then be thought or said that they be gods?
[56] Neither are those gods of wood, and laid over with silver or gold, able to escape either from thieves or robbers.
[57] Whose gold, and silver, and garments wherewith they are clothed, they that are strong take, and go away withal: neither are they able to help themselves.
[58] Therefore it is better to be a king that sheweth his power, or else a profitable vessel in an house, which the owner shall have use of, than such false gods; or to be a door in an house, to keep such things therein, than such false gods. or a pillar of wood in a a palace, than such false gods.
[59] For sun, moon, and stars, being bright and sent to do their offices, are obedient.
[60] In like manner the lightning when it breaketh forth is easy to be seen; and after the same manner the wind bloweth in every country.
[61] And when God commandeth the clouds to go over the whole world, they do as they are bidden.
[62] And the fire sent from above to consume hills and woods doeth as it is commanded: but these are like unto them neither in shew nor power.
[63] Wherefore it is neither to be supposed nor said that they are gods, seeing, they are able neither to judge causes, nor to do good unto men.
[64] Knowing therefore that they are no gods, fear them not,
[65] For they can neither curse nor bless kings:
[66] Neither can they shew signs in the heavens among the heathen, nor shine as the sun, nor give light as the moon.
[67] The beasts are better than they: for they can get under a cover and help themselves.
[68] It is then by no means manifest unto us that they are gods: therefore fear them not.
[69] For as a scarecrow in a garden of cucumbers keepeth nothing: so are their gods of wood, and laid over with silver and gold.
[70] And likewise their gods of wood, and laid over with silver and gold, are like to a white thorn in an orchard, that every bird sitteth upon; as also to a dead body, that is east into the dark.
[71] And ye shall know them to be no gods by the bright purple that rotteth upon then1: and they themselves afterward shall be eaten, and shall be a reproach in the country.
[72] Better therefore is the just man that hath none idols: for he shall be far from reproach.

Prayer of Azariah

[1] And they walked in the midst of the fire, praising God, and blessing Jah.
[2] Then Azarias stood up, and prayed on this manner; and opening his mouth in the midst of the fire said,
[3] Blessed art thou, O Lord God of our fathers: thy name is worthy to be praised and glorified for evermore:
[4] For thou art righteous in all the things

that thou hast done to us: yea, true are all thy works, thy ways are right, and all thy judgments truth.

[5] In all the things that thou hast brought upon us, and upon the holy city of our fathers, even Jerusalem, thou hast executed true judgment: for according to truth and judgment didst thou bring all these things upon us because of our sins.

[6] For we have sinned and committed iniquity, departing from thee.

[7] In all things have we trespassed, and not obeyed thy commandments, nor kept them, neither done as thou hast commanded us, that it might go well with us.

[8] Wherefore all that thou hast brought upon us, and every thing that thou hast done to us, thou hast done in true judgment.

[9] And thou didst deliver us into the hands of lawless enemies, most hateful forsakers of God, and to an unjust king, and the most wicked in all the world.

[10] And now we cannot open our mouths, we are become a shame and reproach to thy servants; and to them that worship thee.

[11] Yet deliver us not up wholly, for thy name's sake, neither disannul thou thy covenant:

[12] And cause not thy mercy to depart from us, for thy beloved Abraham's sake, for thy servant Issac's sake, and for thy holy Israel's sake;

[13] To whom thou hast spoken and promised, that thou wouldest multiply their seed as the stars of heaven, and as the sand that lieth upon the seashore.

[14] For we, O Lord, are become less than any nation, and be kept under this day in all the world because of our sins.

[15] Neither is there at this time prince, or prophet, or leader, or burnt offering, or sacrifice, or oblation, or incense, or place to sacrifice before thee, and to find mercy.

[16] Nevertheless in a contrite heart and an humble spirit let us be accepted.

[17] Like as in the burnt offerings of rams and bullocks, and like as in ten thousands of fat lambs: so let our sacrifice be in thy sight this day, and grant that we may wholly go after thee: for they shall not be confounded that put their trust in thee.

[18] And now we follow thee with all our heart, we fear thee, and seek thy face.

[19] Put us not to shame: but deal with us after thy lovingkindness, and according to the multitude of thy mercies.

[20] Deliver us also according to thy marvellous works, and give glory to thy name, O Lord: and let all them that do thy servants hurt be ashamed;

[21] And let them be confounded in all their power and might, and let their strength be broken;

[22] And let them know that thou art God, the only God, and glorious over the whole world.

[23] And the king's servants, that put them in, ceased not to make the oven hot with rosin, pitch, tow, and small wood;

[24] So that the flame streamed forth above the furnace forty and nine cubits.

[25] And it passed through, and burned those Chaldeans it found about the furnace.

[26] But the angel of Jah came down into the oven together with Azarias and his fellows, and smote the flame of the fire out of the oven;

[27] And made the midst of the furnace as it had been a moist whistling wind, so that the fire touched them not at all, neither hurt nor troubled them.

[28] Then the three, as out of one mouth, praised, glorified, and blessed, God in the furnace, saying,

[29] Blessed art thou, O Lord God of our fathers: and to be praised and exalted above

all for ever.

[30] And blessed is thy glorious and holy name: and to be praised and exalted above all for ever.

[31] Blessed art thou in the temple of thine holy glory: and to be praised and glorified above all for ever.

[32] Blessed art thou that beholdest the depths, and sittest upon the cherubims: and to be praised and exalted above all for ever.

[33] Blessed art thou on the glorious throne of thy kingdom: and to be praised and glorified above all for ever.

[34] Blessed art thou in the firmament of heaven: and above all to be praised and glorified for ever.

[35] O all ye works of Jah, bless ye Jah : praise and exalt him above all for ever,

[36] O ye heavens, bless ye Jah : praise and exalt him above all for ever.

[37] O ye angels of Jah, bless ye Jah: praise and exalt him above all for ever.

[38] O all ye waters that be above the heaven, bless ye Jah: praise and exalt him above all for ever.

[39] O all ye powers of Jah, bless ye Jah: praise and exalt him above all for ever.

[40] O ye sun and moon, bless ye Jah: praise and exalt him above all for ever.

[41] O ye stars of heaven, bless ye Jah: praise and exalt him above all for ever.

[42] O every shower and dew, bless ye Jah: praise and exalt him above all for ever.

[43] O all ye winds, bless ye Jah: praise and exalt him above all for ever,

[44] O ye fire and heat, bless ye Jah: praise and exalt him above all for ever.

[45] O ye winter and summer, bless ye Jah: praise and exalt him above all for ever.

[46] 0 ye dews and storms of snow, bless ye Jah: praise and exalt him above all for ever.

[47] O ye nights and days, bless ye Jah: bless and exalt him above all for ever.

[48] O ye light and darkness, bless ye Jah: praise and exalt him above all for ever.

[49] O ye ice and cold, bless ye Jah: praise and exalt him above all for ever.

[50] O ye frost and snow, bless ye Jah: praise and exalt him above all for ever.

[51] O ye lightnings and clouds, bless ye Jah: praise and exalt him above all for ever.

[52] O let the earth bless Jah: praise and exalt him above all for ever.

[53] O ye mountains and little hills, bless ye Jah: praise and exalt him above all for ever.

[54] O all ye things that grow in the earth, bless ye Jah: praise and exalt him above all for ever.

[55] O ye mountains, bless ye Jah: Praise and exalt him above all for ever.

[56] O ye seas and rivers, bless ye Jah: praise and exalt him above all for ever.

[57] O ye whales, and all that move in the waters, bless ye Jah: praise and exalt him above all for ever.

[58] O all ye fowls of the air, bless ye Jah: praise and exalt him above all for ever.

[59] O all ye beasts and cattle, bless ye Jah: praise and exalt him above all for ever.

[60] O ye children of men, bless ye Jah: praise and exalt him above all for ever.

[61] O Israel, bless ye Jah: praise and exalt him above all for ever.

[62] O ye priests of Jah, bless ye Jah: praise and exalt him above all for ever.

[63] O ye servants of Jah, bless ye Jah: praise and exalt him above all for ever.

[64] O ye spirits and souls of the righteous, bless ye Jah: praise and exalt him above all for ever.

[65] O ye holy and humble men of heart, bless ye Jah: praise and exalt him above all for ever.

[66] O Ananias, Azarias, and Misael, bless ye Jah: praise and exalt him above all for ever: far he hath delivered us from hell, and

saved us from the hand of death, and delivered us out of the midst of the furnace and burning flame: even out of the midst of the fire hath he delivered us.
[67] O give thanks unto Jah, because he is gracious: for his mercy endureth for ever.
[68] O all ye that worship Jah, bless the God of gods, praise him, and give him thanks: for his mercy endureth for ever.

Susanna

Sus.1

Set apart from the beginning of Daniel, because it is not in the Hebrew, as neither the Narration of Bel and the Dragon.[1] There dwelt a man in Babylon, called Joacim:
[2] And he took a wife, whose name was Susanna, the daughter of Chelcias, a very fair woman, and one that feared Jah.
[3] Her parents also were righteous, and taught their daughter according to the law of Moses.
[4] Now Joacim was a great rich man, and had a fair garden joining unto his house: and to him resorted the Jews; because he was more honourable than all others.
[5] The same year were appointed two of the ancients of the people to be judges, such as Jah spake of, that wickedness came from Babylon from ancient judges, who seemed to govern the people.
[6] These kept much at Joacim's house: and all that had any suits in law came unto them.
[7] Now when the people departed away at noon, Susanna went into her husband's garden to walk.
[8] And the two elders saw her going in every day, and walking; so that their lust was inflamed toward her.
[9] And they perverted their own mind, and turned away their eyes, that they might not look unto heaven, nor remember just judgments.
[10] And albeit they both were wounded with her love, yet durst not one shew another his grief.
[11] For they were ashamed to declare their lust, that they desired to have to do with her.
[12] Yet they watched diligently from day to day to see her.
[13] And the one said to the other, Let us now go home: for it is dinner time.
[14] So when they were gone out, they parted the one from the other, and turning back again they came to the same place; and after that they had asked one another the cause, they acknowledged their lust: then appointed they a time both together, when they might find her alone.
[15] And it fell out, as they watched a fit time, she went in as before with two maids only, and she was desirous to wash herself in the garden: for it was hot.
[16] And there was no body there save the two elders, that had hid themselves, and watched her.
[17] Then she said to her maids, Bring me oil and washing balls, and shut the garden doors, that I may wash me.
[18] And they did as she bade them, and shut the garden doors, and went out themselves at privy doors to fetch the things that she had commanded them: but they saw not the elders, because they were hid.
[19] Now when the maids were gone forth, the two elders rose up, and ran unto her, saying,
[20] Behold, the garden doors are shut, that no man can see us, and we are in love with

thee; therefore consent unto us, and lie with us.

[21] If thou wilt not, we will bear witness against thee, that a young man was with thee: and therefore thou didst send away thy maids from thee.

[22] Then Susanna sighed, and said, I am straitened on every side: for if I do this thing, it is death unto me: and if I do it not I cannot escape your hands.

[23] It is better for me to fall into your hands, and not do it, than to sin in the sight of Jah.

[24] With that Susanna cried with a loud voice: and the two elders cried out against her.

[25] Then ran the one, and opened the garden door.

[26] So when the servants of the house heard the cry in the garden, they rushed in at the privy door, to see what was done unto her.

[27] But when the elders had declared their matter, the servants were greatly ashamed: for there was never such a report made of Susanna.

[28] And it came to pass the next day, when the people were assembled to her husband Joacim, the two elders came also full of mischievous imagination against Susanna to put her to death;

[29] And said before the people, Send for Susanna, the daughter of Chelcias, Joacim's wife. And so they sent.

[30] So she came with her father and mother, her children, and all her kindred.

[31] Now Susanna was a very delicate woman, and beauteous to behold.

[32] And these wicked men commanded to uncover her face, (for she was covered) that they might be filled with her beauty.

[33] Therefore her friends and all that saw her wept.

[34] Then the two elders stood up in the midst of the people, and laid their hands upon her head.

[35] And she weeping looked up toward heaven: for her heart trusted in Jah.

[36] And the elders said, As we walked in the garden alone, this woman came in with two maids, and shut the garden doors, and sent the maids away.

[37] Then a young man, who there was hid, came unto her, and lay with her.

[38] Then we that stood in a corner of the garden, seeing this wickedness, ran unto them.

[39] And when we saw them together, the man we could not hold: for he was stronger than we, and opened the door, and leaped out.

[40] But having taken this woman, we asked who the young man was, but she would not tell us: these things do we testify.

[41] Then the assembly believed them as those that were the elders and judges of the people: so they condemned her to death.

[42] Then Susanna cried out with a loud voice, and said, O everlasting God, that knowest the secrets, and knowest all things before they be:

[43] Thou knowest that they have borne false witness against me, and, behold, I must die; whereas I never did such things as these men have maliciously invented against me.

[44] And Jah heard her voice.

[45] Therefore when she was led to be put to death, Jah raised up the holy spirit of a young youth whose name was Daniel:

[46] Who cried with a loud voice, I am clear from the blood of this woman.

[47] Then all the people turned them toward him, and said, What mean these words that thou hast spoken?

[48] So he standing in the midst of them said, Are ye such fools, ye sons of Israel, that without examination or knowledge of

the truth ye have condemned a daughter of Israel?
[49] Return again to the place of judgment: for they have borne false witness against her.
[50] Wherefore all the people turned again in haste, and the elders said unto him, Come, sit down among us, and shew it us, seeing God hath given thee the honour of an elder.
[51] Then said Daniel unto them, Put these two aside one far from another, and I will examine them.
[52] So when they were put asunder one from another, he called one of them, and said unto him, O thou that art waxen old in wickedness, now thy sins which thou hast committed aforetime are come to light.
[53] For thou hast pronounced false judgment and hast condemned the innocent and hast let the guilty go free; albeit Jah saith, The innocent and righteous shalt thou not slay.
[54] Now then, if thou hast seen her, tell me, Under what tree sawest thou them companying together? Who answered, Under a mastick tree.
[55] And Daniel said, Very well; thou hast lied against thine own head; for even now the angel of God hath received the sentence of God to cut thee in two.
[56] So he put him aside, and commanded to bring the other, and said unto him, O thou seed of Chanaan, and not of Juda, beauty hath deceived thee, and lust hath perverted thine heart.
[57] Thus have ye dealt with the daughters of Israel, and they for fear companied with you: but the daughter of Juda would not abide your wickedness.
[58] Now therefore tell me, Under what tree didst thou take them companying together? Who answered, Under an holm tree.
[59] Then said Daniel unto him, Well; thou hast also lied against thine own head: for the angel of God waiteth with the sword to cut thee in two, that he may destroy you.
[60] With that all the assembly cried out with a loud voice, and praised God, who saveth them that trust in him.
[61] And they arose against the two elders, for Daniel had convicted them of false witness by their own mouth:
[62] And according to the law of Moses they did unto them in such sort as they maliciously intended to do to their neighbour: and they put them to death. Thus the innocent blood was saved the same day.
[63] Therefore Chelcias and his wife praised God for their daughter Susanna, with Joacim her husband, and all the kindred, because there was no dishonesty found in her.
[64] From that day forth was Daniel had in great reputation in the sight of the people.

Bel and the Dragon

The History of the Destruction of Bel and the Dragon, Cut off from the end of Daniel.

Bel.1

[1] And king Astyages was gathered to his fathers, and Cyrus of Persia received his kingdom.
[2] And Daniel conversed with the king, and was honoured above all his friends.
[3] Now the Babylons had an idol, called Bel, and there were spent upon him every day twelve great measures of fine flour, and forty sheep, and six vessels of wine.
[4] And the king worshipped it and went daily to adore it: but Daniel worshipped his own God. And the king said unto him, Why

dost not thou worship Bel?
[5] Who answered and said, Because I may not worship idols made with hands, but the living God, who hath created the heaven and the earth, and hath sovereignty over all flesh.
[6] Then said the king unto him, Thinkest thou not that Bel is a living God? seest thou not how much he eateth and drinketh every day?
[7] Then Daniel smiled, and said, O king, be not deceived: for this is but clay within, and brass without, and did never eat or drink any thing.
[8] So the king was wroth, and called for his priests, and said unto them, If ye tell me not who this is that devoureth these expences, ye shall die.
[9] But if ye can certify me that Bel devoureth them, then Daniel shall die: for he hath spoken blasphemy against Bel. And Daniel said unto the king, Let it be according to thy word.
[10] Now the priests of Bel were threescore and ten, beside their wives and children. And the king went with Daniel into the temple of Bel.
[11] So Bel's priests said, Lo, we go out: but thou, O king, set on the meat, and make ready the wine, and shut the door fast and seal it with thine own signet;
[12] And to morrow when thou comest in, if thou findest not that Bel hath eaten up all, we will suffer death: or else Daniel, that speaketh falsely against us.
[13] And they little regarded it: for under the table they had made a privy entrance, whereby they entered in continually, and consumed those things.
[14] So when they were gone forth, the king set meats before Bel. Now Daniel had commanded his servants to bring ashes, and those they strewed throughout all the temple in the presence of the king alone: then went they out, and shut the door, and sealed it with the king's signet, and so departed.
[15] Now in the night came the priests with their wives and children, as they were wont to do, and did eat and drinck up all.
[16] In the morning betime the king arose, and Daniel with him.
[17] And the king said, Daniel, are the seals whole? And he said, Yea, O king, they be whole.
[18] And as soon as he had opened the dour, the king looked upon the table, and cried with a loud voice, Great art thou, O Bel, and with thee is no deceit at all.
[19] Then laughed Daniel, and held the king that he should not go in, and said, Behold now the pavement, and mark well whose footsteps are these.
[20] And the king said, I see the footsteps of men, women, and children. And then the king was angry,
[21] And took the priests with their wives and children, who shewed him the privy doors, where they came in, and consumed such things as were upon the table.
[22] Therefore the king slew them, and delivered Bel into Daniel's power, who destroyed him and his temple.
[23] And in that same place there was a great dragon, which they of Babylon worshipped.
[24] And the king said unto Daniel, Wilt thou also say that this is of brass? lo, he liveth, he eateth and drinketh; thou canst not say that he is no living god: therefore worship him.
[25] Then said Daniel unto the king, I will worship Jah my God: for he is the living God.
[26] But give me leave, O king, and I shall slay this dragon without sword or staff. The king said, I give thee leave.

[27] Then Daniel took pitch, and fat, and hair, and did seethe them together, and made lumps thereof: this he put in the dragon's mouth, and so the dragon burst in sunder : and Daniel said, Lo, these are the gods ye worship.
[28] When they of Babylon heard that, they took great indignation, and conspired against the king, saying, The king is become a Jew, and he hath destroyed Bel, he hath slain the dragon, and put the priests to death.
[29] So they came to the king, and said, Deliver us Daniel, or else we will destroy thee and thine house.
[30] Now when the king saw that they pressed him sore, being constrained, he delivered Daniel unto them:
[31] Who cast him into the lions' den: where he was six days.
[32] And in the den there were seven lions, and they had given them every day two carcases, and two sheep: which then were not given to them, to the intent they might devour Daniel.
[33] Now there was in Jewry a prophet, called Habbacuc, who had made pottage, and had broken bread in a bowl, and was going into the field, for to bring it to the reapers.
[34] But the angel of Jah said unto Habbacuc, Go, carry the dinner that thou hast into Babylon unto Daniel, who is in the lions' den.
[35] And Habbacuc said, Lord, I never saw Babylon; neither do I know where the den is.
[36] Then the angel of Jah took him by the crown, and bare him by the hair of his head, and through the vehemency of his spirit set him in Babylon over the den.
[37] And Habbacuc cried, saying, O Daniel, Daniel, take the dinner which God hath sent thee.
[38] And Daniel said, Thou hast remembered me, O God: neither hast thou forsaken them that seek thee and love thee.
[39] So Daniel arose, and did eat: and the angel of Jah set Habbacuc in his own place again immediately.
[40] Upon the seventh day the king went to bewail Daniel: and when he came to the den, he looked in, and behold, Daniel was sitting.
[41] Then cried the king with a loud voice, saying, Great art Lord God of Daniel, and there is none other beside thee.
[42] And he drew him out, and cast those that were the cause of his destruction into the den: and they were devoured in a moment before his face.

Prayer of Manasseh

O Lord, Almighty God of our fathers, Abraham, Isaac, and Jacob, and of their righteous seed; who hast made heaven and earth, with all the ornament thereof; who hast bound the sea by the word of thy commandment; who hast shut up the deep, and sealed it by thy terrible and glorious name; whom all men fear, and tremble before thy power; for the majesty of thy glory cannot be borne, and thine angry threatening toward sinners is importable: but thy merciful promise is unmeasurable and unsearchable; for thou art the most high Lord, of great compassion, longsuffering, very merciful, and repentest of the evils of men. Thou, O Lord, according to thy great goodness hast promised repentance and forgiveness to them that have sinned against thee: and of thine infinite mercies hast appointed repentance unto sinners, that they may be saved. Thou therefore, O Lord, that art the God of the just, hast not appointed repentance to the just, as to Abraham, and Isaac, and Jacob, which have not sinned against thee; but thou hast appointed repentance unto me that am a sinner: for I have sinned above the number of the sands of the sea. My transgressions, O Lord, are multiplied: my transgressions are multiplied, and I am not worthy to behold and see the height of heaven for the multitude of mine iniquities. I am bowed down with many iron bands, that I cannot life up mine head, neither have any release: for I have provoked thy wrath, and done evil before thee: I did not thy will, neither kept I thy commandments: I have set up abominations, and have multiplied offences. Now therefore I bow the knee of mine heart, beseeching thee of grace. I have sinned, O Lord, I have sinned, and I acknowledge mine iniquities: wherefore, I humbly beseech thee, forgive me, O Lord, forgive me, and destroy me not with mine iniquites. Be not angry with me for ever, by reserving evil for me; neither condemn me to the lower parts of the earth. For thou art the God, even the God of them that repent; and in me thou wilt shew all thy goodness: for thou wilt save me, that am unworthy, according to thy great mercy. Therefore I will praise thee for ever all the days of my life: for all the powers of the heavens do praise thee, and thine is the glory for ever and ever. Amen.

1 Maccabees

1Mac.1

[1] And it happened, after that Alexander son of Philip, the Macedonian, who came out of the land of Chettiim, had smitten Darius king of the Persians and Medes, that he reigned in his stead, the first over Greece,
[2] And made many wars, and won many strong holds, and slew the kings of the earth,
[3] And went through to the ends of the earth, and took spoils of many nations, insomuch that the earth was quiet before him; whereupon he was exalted and his heart was lifted up.
[4] And he gathered a mighty strong host and ruled over countries, and nations, and kings, who became tributaries unto him.
[5] And after these things he fell sick, and perceived that he should die.
[6] Wherefore he called his servants, such as were honourable, and had been brought up with him from his youth, and parted his kingdom among them, while he was yet alive.
[7] So Alexander reigned twelves years, and then died.
[8] And his servants bare rule every one in his place.
[9] And after his death they all put crowns upon themselves; so did their sons after them many years: and evils were multiplied in the earth.
[10] And there came out of them a wicked root Antiochus surnamed Epiphanes, son of Antiochus the king, who had been an hostage at Rome, and he reigned in the hundred and thirty and seventh year of the kingdom of the Greeks.
[11] In those days went there out of Israel wicked men, who persuaded many, saying, Let us go and make a covenant with the heathen that are round about us: for since we departed from them we have had much sorrow.
[12] So this device pleased them well.
[13] Then certain of the people were so forward herein, that they went to the king, who gave them licence to do after the ordinances of the heathen:
[14] Whereupon they built a place of exercise at Jerusalem according to the

customs of the heathen:

[15] And made themselves uncircumcised, and forsook the holy covenant, and joined themselves to the heathen, and were sold to do mischief.

[16] Now when the kingdom was established before Antiochus, he thought to reign over Egypt that he might have the dominion of two realms.

[17] Wherefore he entered into Egypt with a great multitude, with chariots, and elephants, and horsemen, and a great navy,

[18] And made war against Ptolemee king of Egypt: but Ptolemee was afraid of him, and fled; and many were wounded to death.

[19] Thus they got the strong cities in the land of Egypt and he took the spoils thereof.

[20] And after that Antiochus had smitten Egypt, he returned again in the hundred forty and third year, and went up against Israel and Jerusalem with a great multitude,

[21] And entered proudly into the sanctuary, and took away the golden altar, and the candlestick of light, and all the vessels thereof,

[22] And the table of the shewbread, and the pouring vessels, and the vials. and the censers of gold, and the veil, and the crown, and the golden ornaments that were before the temple, all which he pulled off.

[23] He took also the silver and the gold, and the precious vessels: also he took the hidden treasures which he found.

[24] And when he had taken all away, he went into his own land, having made a great massacre, and spoken very proudly.

[25] Therefore there was a great mourning in Israel, in every place where they were;

[26] So that the princes and elders mourned, the virgins and young men were made feeble, and the beauty of women was changed.

[27] Every bridegroom took up lamentation, and she that sat in the marriage chamber was in heaviness,

[28] The land also was moved for the inhabitants thereof, and all the house of Jacob was covered with confusion.

[29] And after two years fully expired the king sent his chief collector of tribute unto the cities of Juda, who came unto Jerusalem with a great multitude,

[30] And spake peaceable words unto them, but all was deceit: for when they had given him credence, he fell suddenly upon the city, and smote it very sore, and destroyed much people of Israel.

[31] And when he had taken the spoils of the city, he set it on fire, and pulled down the houses and walls thereof on every side.

[32] But the women and children took they captive, and possessed the cattle.

[33] Then builded they the city of David with a great and strong wall, and with mighty towers, and made it a strong hold for them.

[34] And they put therein a sinful nation, wicked men, and fortified themselves therein.

[35] They stored it also with armour and victuals, and when they had gathered together the spoils of Jerusalem, they laid them up there, and so they became a sore snare:

[36] For it was a place to lie in wait against the sanctuary, and an evil adversary to Israel.

[37] Thus they shed innocent blood on every side of the sanctuary, and defiled it:

[38] Insomuch that the inhabitants of Jerusalem fled because of them: whereupon the city was made an habitation of strangers, and became strange to those that were born in her; and her own children left her.

[39] Her sanctuary was laid waste like a wilderness, her feasts were turned into mourning, her sabbaths into reproach her honour into contempt.

[40] As had been her glory, so was her dishonour increased, and her excellency was turned into mourning.

[41] Moreover king Antiochus wrote to his

whole kingdom, that all should be one people,
[42] And every one should leave his laws: so all the heathen agreed according to the commandment of the king.
[43] Yea, many also of the Israelites consented to his religion, and sacrificed unto idols, and profaned the sabbath.
[44] For the king had sent letters by messengers unto Jerusalem and the cities of Juda that they should follow the strange laws of the land,
[45] And forbid burnt offerings, and sacrifice, and drink offerings, in the temple; and that they should profane the sabbaths and festival days:
[46] And pollute the sanctuary and holy people:
[47] Set up altars, and groves, and chapels of idols, and sacrifice swine's flesh, and unclean beasts:
[48] That they should also leave their children uncircumcised, and make their souls abominable with all manner of uncleanness and profanation:
[49] To the end they might forget the law, and change all the ordinances.
[50] And whosoever would not do according to the commandment of the king, he said, he should die.
[51] In the selfsame manner wrote he to his whole kingdom, and appointed overseers over all the people, commanding the cities of Juda to sacrifice, city by city.
[52] Then many of the people were gathered unto them, to wit every one that forsook the law; and so they committed evils in the land;
[53] And drove the Israelites into secret places, even wheresoever they could flee for succour.
[54] Now the fifteenth day of the month Casleu, in the hundred forty and fifth year, they set up the abomination of desolation upon the altar, and builded idol altars throughout the cities of Juda on every side;
[55] And burnt incense at the doors of their houses, and in the streets.
[56] And when they had rent in pieces the books of the law which they found, they burnt them with fire.
[57] And whosoever was found with any the book of the testament, or if any committed to the law, the king's commandment was, that they should put him to death.
[58] Thus did they by their authority unto the Israelites every month, to as many as were found in the cities.
[59] Now the five and twentieth day of the month they did sacrifice upon the idol altar, which was upon the altar of God.
[60] At which time according to the commandment they put to death certain women, that had caused their children to be circumcised.
[61] And they hanged the infants about their necks, and rifled their houses, and slew them that had circumcised them.
[62] Howbeit many in Israel were fully resolved and confirmed in themselves not to eat any unclean thing.
[63] Wherefore the rather to die, that they might not be defiled with meats, and that they might not profane the holy covenant: so then they died.
[64] And there was very great wrath upon Israel.

1Mac.2

[1] In those days arose Mattathias the son of John, the son of Simeon, a priest of the sons of Joarib, from Jerusalem, and dwelt in Modin.
[2] And he had five sons, Joannan, called Caddis:
[3] Simon; called Thassi:
[4] Judas, who was called Maccabeus:
[5] Eleazar, called Avaran: and Jonathan, whose surname was Apphus.
[6] And when he saw the blasphemies that were committed in Juda and Jerusalem,

[7] He said, Woe is me! wherefore was I born to see this misery of my people, and of the holy city, and to dwell there, when it was delivered into the hand of the enemy, and the sanctuary into the hand of strangers?
[8] Her temple is become as a man without glory.
[9] Her glorious vessels are carried away into captivity, her infants are slain in the streets, her young men with the sword of the enemy.
[10] What nation hath not had a part in her kingdom and gotten of her spoils?
[11] All her ornaments are taken away; of a free woman she is become a bondslave.
[12] And, behold, our sanctuary, even our beauty and our glory, is laid waste, and the Gentiles have profaned it.
[13] To what end therefore shall we live any longer?
[14] Then Mattathias and his sons rent their clothes, and put on sackcloth, and mourned very sore.
[15] In the mean while the king's officers, such as compelled the people to revolt, came into the city Modin, to make them sacrifice.
[16] And when many of Israel came unto them, Mattathias also and his sons came together.
[17] Then answered the king's officers, and said to Mattathias on this wise, Thou art a ruler, and an honourable and great man in this city, and strengthened with sons and brethren:
[18] Now therefore come thou first, and fulfil the king's commandment, like as all the heathen have done, yea, and the men of Juda also, and such as remain at Jerusalem: so shalt thou and thy house be in the number of the king's friends, and thou and thy children shall be honoured with silver and gold, and many rewards.
[19] Then Mattathias answered and spake with a loud voice, Though all the nations that are under the king's dominion obey him, and fall away every one from the religion of their fathers, and give consent to his commandments:
[20] Yet will I and my sons and my brethren walk in the covenant of our fathers.
[21] God forbid that we should forsake the law and the ordinances.
[22] We will not hearken to the king's words, to go from our religion, either on the right hand, or the left.
[23] Now when he had left speaking these words, there came one of the Jews in the sight of all to sacrifice on the altar which was at Modin, according to the king's commandment.
[24] Which thing when Mattathias saw, he was inflamed with zeal, and his reins trembled, neither could he forbear to shew his anger according to judgment: wherefore he ran, and slew him upon the altar.
[25] Also the king's commissioner, who compelled men to sacrifice, he killed at that time, and the altar he pulled down.
[26] Thus dealt he zealously for the law of God like as Phinees did unto Zambri the son of Salom.
[27] And Mattathias cried throughout the city with a loud voice, saying, Whosoever is zealous of the law, and maintaineth the covenant, let him follow me.
[28] So he and his sons fled into the mountains, and left all that ever they had in the city.
[29] Then many that sought after justice and judgment went down into the wilderness, to dwell there:
[30] Both they, and their children, and their wives; and their cattle; because afflictions increased sore upon them.
[31] Now when it was told the king's servants, and the host that was at Jerusalem, in the city of David, that certain men, who had broken the king's commandment, were gone down into the secret places in the wilderness,
[32] They pursued after them a great number, and having overtaken them, they

camped against them, and made war against them on the sabbath day.
[33] And they said unto them, Let that which ye have done hitherto suffice; come forth, and do according to the commandment of the king, and ye shall live.
[34] But they said, We will not come forth, neither will we do the king's commandment, to profane the sabbath day.
[35] So then they gave them the battle with all speed.
[36] Howbeit they answered them not, neither cast they a stone at them, nor stopped the places where they lay hid;
[37] But said, Let us die all in our innocency: heaven and earth will testify for us, that ye put us to death wrongfully.
[38] So they rose up against them in battle on the sabbath, and they slew them, with their wives and children and their cattle, to the number of a thousand people.
[39] Now when Mattathias and his friends understood hereof, they mourned for them right sore.
[40] And one of them said to another, If we all do as our brethren have done, and fight not for our lives and laws against the heathen, they will now quickly root us out of the earth.
[41] At that time therefore they decreed, saying, Whosoever shall come to make battle with us on the sabbath day, we will fight against him; neither will we die all, as our brethren that were murdered im the secret places.
[42] Then came there unto him a company of Assideans who were mighty men of Israel, even all such as were voluntarily devoted unto the law.
[43] Also all they that fled for persecution joined themselves unto them, and were a stay unto them.
[44] So they joined their forces, and smote sinful men in their anger, and wicked men in their wrath: but the rest fled to the heathen for succour.

[45] Then Mattathias and his friends went round about, and pulled down the altars:
[46] And what children soever they found within the coast of Israel uncircumcised, those they circumcised valiantly.
[47] They pursued also after the proud men, and the work prospered in their hand.
[48] So they recovered the law out of the hand of the Gentiles, and out of the hand of kings, neither suffered they the sinner to triumph.
[49] Now when the time drew near that Mattathias should die, he said unto his sons, Now hath pride and rebuke gotten strength, and the time of destruction, and the wrath of indignation:
[50] Now therefore, my sons, be ye zealous for the law, and give your lives for the covenant of your fathers.
[51] Call to remembrance what acts our fathers did in their time; so shall ye receive great honour and an everlasting name.
[52] Was not Abraham found faithful in temptation, and it was imputed unto him for righteousness?
[53] Joseph in the time of his distress kept the commandment and was made lord of Egypt.
[54] Phinees our father in being zealous and fervent obtained the covenant of an everlasting priesthood.
[55] Jesus for fulfilling the word was made a judge in Israel.
[56] Caleb for bearing witness before the congregation received the heritage of the land.
[57] David for being merciful possessed the throne of an everlasting kingdom.
[58] Elias for being zealous and fervent for the law was taken up into heaven.
[59] Ananias, Azarias, and Misael, by believing were saved out of the flame.
[60] Daniel for his innocency was delivered from the mouth of lions.
[61] And thus consider ye throughout all ages, that none that put their trust in him

shall be overcome.
[62] Fear not then the words of a sinful man: for his glory shall be dung and worms.
[63] To day he shall be lifted up and to morrow he shall not be found, because he is returned into his dust, and his thought is come to nothing.
[64] Wherefore, ye my sons, be valiant and shew yourselves men in the behalf of the law; for by it shall ye obtain glory.
[65] And behold, I know that your brother Simon is a man of counsel, give ear unto him alway: he shall be a father unto you.
[66] As for Judas Maccabeus, he hath been mighty and strong, even from his youth up: let him be your captain, and fight the battle of the people.
[67] Take also unto you all those that observe the law, and avenge ye the wrong of your people.
[68] Recompense fully the heathen, and take heed to the commandments of the law.
[69] So he blessed them, and was gathered to his fathers.
[70] And he died in the hundred forty and sixth year, and his sons buried him in the sepulchres of his fathers at Modin, and all Israel made great lamentation for him.

---

1 Mac. 3

[1] Then his son Judas, called Maccabeus, rose up in his stead.
[2] And all his brethren helped him, and so did all they that held with his father, and they fought with cheerfulness the battle of Israel.
[3] So he gat his people great honour, and put on a breastplate as a giant, and girt his warlike harness about him, and he made battles, protecting the host with his sword.
[4] In his acts he was like a lion, and like a lion's whelp roaring for his prey.
[5] For He pursued the wicked, and sought them out, and burnt up those that vexed his people.
[6] Wherefore the wicked shrunk for fear of him, and all the workers of iniquity were troubled, because salvation prospered in his hand.
[7] He grieved also many kings, and made Jacob glad with his acts, and his memorial is blessed for ever.
[8] Moreover he went through the cities of Juda, destroying the ungodly out of them, and turning away wrath from Israel:
[9] So that he was renowned unto the utmost part of the earth, and he received unto him such as were ready to perish.
[10] Then Apollonius gathered the Gentiles together, and a great host out of Samaria, to fight against Israel.
[11] Which thing when Judas perceived, he went forth to meet him, and so he smote him, and slew him: many also fell down slain, but the rest fled.
[12] Wherefore Judas took their spoils, and Apollonius' sword also, and therewith he fought all his life long.
[13] Now when Seron, a prince of the army of Syria, heard say that Judas had gathered unto him a multitude and company of the faithful to go out with him to war;
[14] He said, I will get me a name and honour in the kingdom; for I will go fight with Judas and them that are with him, who despise the king's commandment.
[15] So he made him ready to go up, and there went with him a mighty host of the ungodly to help him, and to be avenged of the children of Israel.
[16] And when he came near to the going up of Bethhoron, Judas went forth to meet him with a small company:
[17] Who, when they saw the host coming to meet them, said unto Judas, How shall we be able, being so few, to fight against so great a multitude and so strong, seeing we are ready to faint with fasting all this day?
[18] Unto whom Judas answered, It is no hard matter for many to be shut up in the

hands of a few; and with the God of heaven it is all one, to deliver with a great multitude, or a small company:

[19] For the victory of battle standeth not in the multitude of an host; but strength cometh from heaven.

[20] They come against us in much pride and iniquity to destroy us, and our wives and children, and to spoil us:

[21] But we fight for our lives and our laws.

[22] Wherefore Jah himself will overthrow them before our face: and as for you, be ye not afraid of them.

[23] Now as soon as he had left off speaking, he leapt suddenly upon them, and so Seron and his host was overthrown before him.

[24] And they pursued them from the going down of Bethhoron unto the plain, where were slain about eight hundred men of them; and the residue fled into the land of the Philistines.

[25] Then began the fear of Judas and his brethren, and an exceeding great dread, to fall upon the nations round about them:

[26] Insomuch as his fame came unto the king, and all nations talked of the battles of Judas.

[27] Now when king Antiochus heard these things, he was full of indignation: wherefore he sent and gathered together all the forces of his realm, even a very strong army.

[28] He opened also his treasure, and gave his soldiers pay for a year, commanding them to be ready whensoever he should need them.

[29] Nevertheless, when he saw that the money of his treasures failed and that the tributes in the country were small, because of the dissension and plague, which he had brought upon the land in taking away the laws which had been of old time;

[30] He feared that he should not be able to bear the charges any longer, nor to have such gifts to give so liberally as he did before: for he had abounded above the kings that were before him.

[31] Wherefore, being greatly perplexed in his mind, he determined to go into Persia, there to take the tributes of the countries, and to gather much money.

[32] So he left Lysias, a nobleman, and one of the blood royal, to oversee the affairs of the king from the river Euphrates unto the borders of Egypt:

[33] And to bring up his son Antiochus, until he came again.

[34] Moreover he delivered unto him the half of his forces, and the elephants, and gave him charge of all things that he would have done, as also concerning them that dwelt in Juda and Jerusalem:

[35] To wit, that he should send an army against them, to destroy and root out the strength of Israel, and the remnant of Jerusalem, and to take away their memorial from that place;

[36] And that he should place strangers in all their quarters, and divide their land by lot.

[37] So the king took the half of the forces that remained, and departed from Antioch, his royal city, the hundred forty and seventh year; and having passed the river Euphrates, he went through the high countries.

[38] Then Lysias chose Ptolemee the son of Dorymenes, Nicanor, and Gorgias, mighty men of the king's friends:

[39] And with them he sent forty thousand footmen, and seven thousand horsemen, to go into the land of Juda, and to destroy it, as the king commanded.

[40] So they went forth with all their power, and came and pitched by Emmaus in the plain country.

[41] And the merchants of the country, hearing the fame of them, took silver and gold very much, with servants, and came into the camp to buy the children of Israel for slaves: a power also of Syria and of the land of the Philistines joined themselves unto them.

[42] Now when Judas and his brethren saw

that miseries were multiplied, and that the forces did encamp themselves in their borders: for they knew how the king had given commandment to destroy the people, and utterly abolish them;

[43] They said one to another, Let us restore the decayed fortune of our people, and let us fight for our people and the sanctuary.

[44] Then was the congregation gathered together, that they might be ready for battle, and that they might pray, and ask mercy and compassion.

[45] Now Jerusalem lay void as a wilderness, there was none of her children that went in or out: the sanctuary also was trodden down, and aliens kept the strong hold; the heathen had their habitation in that place; and joy was taken from Jacob, and the pipe with the harp ceased.

[46] Wherefore the Israelites assembled themselves together, and came to Maspha, over against Jerusalem; for in Maspha was the place where they prayed aforetime in Israel.

[47] Then they fasted that day, and put on sackcloth, and cast ashes upon their heads, and rent their clothes,

[48] And laid open the book of the law, wherein the heathen had sought to paint the likeness of their images.

[49] They brought also the priests' garments, and the firstfruits, and the tithes: and the Nazarites they stirred up, who had accomplished their days.

[50] Then cried they with a loud voice toward heaven, saying, What shall we do with these, and whither shall we carry them away?

[51] For thy sanctuary is trodden down and profaned, and thy priests are in heaviness, and brought low.

[52] And lo, the heathen are assembled together against us to destroy us: what things they imagine against us, thou knowest.

[53] How shall we be able to stand against them, except thou, O God, be our help?

[54] Then sounded they with trumpets, and cried with a loud voice.

[55] And after this Judas ordained captains over the people, even captains over thousands, and over hundreds, and over fifties, and over tens.

[56] But as for such as were building houses, or had betrothed wives, or were planting vineyards, or were fearful, those he commanded that they should return, every man to his own house, according to the law.

[57] So the camp removed, and pitched upon the south side of Emmaus.

[58] And Judas said, arm yourselves, and be valiant men, and see that ye be in readiness against the morning, that ye may fight with these nations, that are assembled together against us to destroy us and our sanctuary:

[59] For it is better for us to die in battle, than to behold the calamities of our people and our sanctuary.

[60] Nevertheless, as the will of God is in heaven, so let him do.

1Mac. 4

[1] Then took Gorgias five thousand footmen, and a thousand of the best horsemen, and removed out of the camp by night;

[2] To the end he might rush in upon the camp of the Jews, and smite them suddenly. And the men of the fortress were his guides.

[3] Now when Judas heard thereof he himself removed, and the valiant men with him, that he might smite the king's army which was at Emmaus,

[4] While as yet the forces were dispersed from the camp.

[5] In the mean season came Gorgias by night into the camp of Judas: and when he found no man there, he sought them in the mountains: for said he, These fellows flee from us

[6] But as soon as it was day, Judas shewed himself in the plain with three thousand men, who nevertheless had neither armour nor swords to their minds.

[7] And they saw the camp of the heathen, that it was strong and well harnessed, and compassed round about with horsemen; and these were expert of war.

[8] Then said Judas to the men that were with him, Fear ye not their multitude, neither be ye afraid of their assault.

[9] Remember how our fathers were delivered in the Red sea, when Pharaoh pursued them with an army.

[10] Now therefore let us cry unto heaven, if peradventure Jah will have mercy upon us, and remember the covenant of our fathers, and destroy this host before our face this day:

[11] That so all the heathen may know that there is one who delivereth and saveth Israel.

[12] Then the strangers lifted up their eyes, and saw them coming over against them.

[13] Wherefore they went out of the camp to battle; but they that were with Judas sounded their trumpets.

[14] So they joined battle, and the heathen being discomfited fled into the plain.

[15] Howbeit all the hindmost of them were slain with the sword: for they pursued them unto Gazera, and unto the plains of Idumea, and Azotus, and Jamnia, so that there were slain of them upon a three thousand men.

[16] This done, Judas returned again with his host from pursuing them,

[17] And said to the people, Be not greedy of the spoil inasmuch as there is a battle before us,

[18] And Gorgias and his host are here by us in the mountain: but stand ye now against our enemies, and overcome them, and after this ye may boldly take the spoils.

[19] As Judas was yet speaking these words, there appeared a part of them looking out of the mountain:

[20] Who when they perceived that the Jews had put their host to flight and were burning the tents; for the smoke that was seen declared what was done:

[21] When therefore they perceived these things, they were sore afraid, and seeing also the host of Judas in the plain ready to fight,

[22] They fled every one into the land of strangers.

[23] Then Judas returned to spoil the tents, where they got much gold, and silver, and blue silk, and purple of the sea, and great riches.

[24] After this they went home, and sung a song of thanksgiving, and praised Jah in heaven: because it is good, because his mercy endureth forever.

[25] Thus Israel had a great deliverance that day.

[26] Now all the strangers that had escaped came and told Lysias what had happened:

[27] Who, when he heard thereof, was confounded and discouraged, because neither such things as he would were done unto Israel, nor such things as the king commanded him were come to pass.

[28] The next year therefore following Lysias gathered together threescore thousand choice men of foot, and five thousand horsemen, that he might subdue them.

[29] So they came into Idumea, and pitched their tents at Bethsura, and Judas met them with ten thousand men.

[30] And when he saw that mighty army, he prayed and said, Blessed art thou, O Saviour of Israel, who didst quell the violence of the mighty man by the hand of thy servant David, and gavest the host of strangers into the hands of Jonathan the son of Saul, and his armourbearer;

[31] Shut up this army in the hand of thy people Israel, and let them be confounded in their power and horsemen:

[32] Make them to be of no courage, and cause the boldness of their strength to fall

away, and let them quake at their destruction:

[33] Cast them down with the sword of them that love thee, and let all those that know thy name praise thee with thanksgiving.

[34] So they joined battle; and there were slain of the host of Lysias about five thousand men, even before them were they slain.

[35] Now when Lysias saw his army put to flight, and the manliness of Judas' soldiers, and how they were ready either to live or die valiantly, he went into Antiochia, and gathered together a company of strangers, and having made his army greater than it was, he purposed to come again into Judea.

[36] Then said Judas and his brethren, Behold, our enemies are discomfited: let us go up to cleanse and dedicate the sanctuary.

[37] Upon this all the host assembled themselves together, and went up into mount Sion.

[38] And when they saw the sanctuary desolate, and the altar profaned, and the gates burned up, and shrubs growing in the courts as in a forest, or in one of the mountains, yea, and the priests' chambers pulled down;

[39] They rent their clothes, and made great lamentation, and cast ashes upon their heads,

[40] And fell down flat to the ground upon their faces, and blew an alarm with the trumpets, and cried toward heaven.

[41] Then Judas appointed certain men to fight against those that were in the fortress, until he had cleansed the sanctuary.

[42] So he chose priests of blameless conversation, such as had pleasure in the law:

[43] Who cleansed the sanctuary, and bare out the defiled stones into an unclean place.

[44] And when as they consulted what to do with the altar of burnt offerings, which was profaned;

[45] They thought it best to pull it down, lest it should be a reproach to them, because the heathen had defiled it: wherefore they pulled it down,

[46] And laid up the stones in the mountain of the temple in a convenient place, until there should come a prophet to shew what should be done with them.

[47] Then they took whole stones according to the law, and built a new altar according to the former;

[48] And made up the sanctuary, and the things that were within the temple, and hallowed the courts.

[49] They made also new holy vessels, and into the temple they brought the candlestick, and the altar of burnt offerings, and of incense, and the table.

[50] And upon the altar they burned incense, and the lamps that were upon the candlestick they lighted, that they might give light in the temple.

[51] Furthermore they set the loaves upon the table, and spread out the veils, and finished all the works which they had begun to make.

[52] Now on the five and twentieth day of the ninth month, which is called the month Casleu, in the hundred forty and eighth year, they rose up betimes in the morning,

[53] And offered sacrifice according to the law upon the new altar of burnt offerings, which they had made.

[54] Look, at what time and what day the heathen had profaned it, even in that was it dedicated with songs, and citherns, and harps, and cymbals.

[55] Then all the people fell upon their faces, worshipping and praising the God of heaven, who had given them good success.

[56] And so they kept the dedication of the altar eight days and offered burnt offerings with gladness, and sacrificed the sacrifice of deliverance and praise.

[57] They decked also the forefront of the temple with crowns of gold, and with shields; and the gates and the chambers they renewed, and hanged doors upon them.

[58] Thus was there very great gladness among the people, for that the reproach of the heathen was put away.
[59] Moreover Judas and his brethren with the whole congregation of Israel ordained, that the days of the dedication of the altar should be kept in their season from year to year by the space of eight days, from the five and twentieth day of the month Casleu, with mirth and gladness.
[60] At that time also they builded up the mount Sion with high walls and strong towers round about, lest the Gentiles should come and tread it down as they had done before.
[61] And they set there a garrison to keep it, and fortified Bethsura to preserve it; that the people might have a defence against Idumea.

---

1 Mac. 5

[1] Now when the nations round about heard that the altar was built and the sanctuary renewed as before, it displeased them very much.
[2] Wherefore they thought to destroy the generation of Jacob that was among them, and thereupon they began to slay and destroy the people.
[3] Then Judas fought against the children of Esau in Idumea at Arabattine, because they besieged Gael: and he gave them a great overthrow, and abated their courage, and took their spoils.
[4] Also he remembered the injury of the children of Bean, who had been a snare and an offence unto the people, in that they lay in wait for them in the ways.
[5] He shut them up therefore in the towers, and encamped against them, and destroyed them utterly, and burned the towers of that place with fire, and all that were therein.
[6] Afterward he passed over to the children of Ammon, where he found a mighty power, and much people, with Timotheus their captain.
[7] So he fought many battles with them, till at length they were discomfited before him; and he smote them.
[8] And when he had taken Jazar, with the towns belonging thereto, he returned into Judea.
[9] Then the heathen that were at Galaad assembled themselves together against the Israelites that were in their quarters, to destroy them; but they fled to the fortress of Dathema.
[10] And sent letters unto Judas and his brethren, The heathen that are round about us are assembled together against us to destroy us:
[11] And they are preparing to come and take the fortress whereunto we are fled, Timotheus being captain of their host.
[12] Come now therefore, and deliver us from their hands, for many of us are slain:
[13] Yea, all our brethren that were in the places of Tobie are put to death: their wives and their children also they have carried away captives, and borne away their stuff; and they have destroyed there about a thousand men.
[14] While these letters were yet reading, behold, there came other messengers from Galilee with their clothes rent, who reported on this wise,
[15] And said, They of Ptolemais, and of Tyrus, and Sidon, and all Galilee of the Gentiles, are assembled together against us to consume us.
[16] Now when Judas and the people heard these words, there assembled a great congregation together, to consult what they should do for their brethren, that were in trouble, and assaulted of them.
[17] Then said Judas unto Simon his brother, Choose thee out men, and go and deliver thy brethren that are in Galilee, for I and Jonathan my brother will go into the country of Galaad.

[18] So he left Joseph the son of Zacharias, and Azarias, captains of the people, with the remnant of the host in Judea to keep it.
[19] Unto whom he gave commandment, saying, Take ye the charge of this people, and see that ye make not war against the heathen until the time that we come again.
[20] Now unto Simon were given three thousand men to go into Galilee, and unto Judas eight thousand men for the country of Galaad.
[21] Then went Simon into Galilee, where he fought many battles with the heathen, so that the heathen were discomfited by him.
[22] And he pursued them unto the gate of Ptolemais; and there were slain of the heathen about three thousand men, whose spoils he took.
[23] And those that were in Galilee, and in Arbattis, with their wives and their children, and all that they had, took he away with him, and brought them into Judea with great joy.
[24] Judas Maccabeus also and his brother Jonathan went over Jordan, and travelled three days' journey in the wilderness,
[25] Where they met with the Nabathites, who came unto them in a peaceable manner, and told them every thing that had happened to their brethren in the land of Galaad:
[26] And how that many of them were shut up in Bosora, and Bosor, and Alema, Casphor, Maked, and Carnaim; all these cities are strong and great:
[27] And that they were shut up in the rest of the cities of the country of Galaad, and that against to morrow they had appointed to bring their host against the forts, and to take them, and to destroy them all in one day.
[28] Hereupon Judas and his host turned suddenly by the way of the wilderness unto Bosora; and when he had won the city, he slew all the males with the edge of the sword, and took all their spoils, and burned the city with fire,
[29] From whence he removed by night, and went till he came to the fortress.
[30] And betimes in the morning they looked up, and, behold, there was an innumerable people bearing ladders and other engines of war, to take the fortress: for they assaulted them.
[31] When Judas therefore saw that the battle was begun, and that the cry of the city went up to heaven, with trumpets, and a great sound,
[32] He said unto his host, Fight this day for your brethren.
[33] So he went forth behind them in three companies, who sounded their trumpets, and cried with prayer.
[34] Then the host of Timotheus, knowing that it was Maccabeus, fled from him: wherefore he smote them with a great slaughter; so that there were killed of them that day about eight thousand men.
[35] This done, Judas turned aside to Maspha; and after he had assaulted it he took and slew all the males therein, and received the spoils thereof and and burnt it with fire.
[36] From thence went he, and took Casphon, Maged, Bosor, and the other cities of the country of Galaad.
[37] After these things gathered Timotheus another host and encamped against Raphon beyond the brook.
[38] So Judas sent men to espy the host, who brought him word, saying, All the heathen that be round about us are assembled unto them, even a very great host.
[39] He hath also hired the Arabians to help them and they have pitched their tents beyond the brook, ready to come and fight against thee. Upon this Judas went to meet them.
[40] Then Timotheus said unto the captains of his host, When Judas and his host come near the brook, if he pass over first unto us, we shall not be able to withstand him; for he will mightily prevail against us:
[41] But if he be afraid, and camp beyond

the river, we shall go over unto him, and prevail against him.

[42] Now when Judas came near the brook, he caused the scribes of the people to remain by the brook: unto whom he gave commandment, saying, Suffer no man to remain in the camp, but let all come to the battle.

[43] So he went first over unto them, and all the people after him: then all the heathen, being discomfited before him, cast away their weapons, and fled unto the temple that was at Carnaim.

[44] But they took the city, and burned the temple with all that were therein. Thus was Carnaim subdued, neither could they stand any longer before Judas.

[45] Then Judas gathered together all the Israelites that were in the country of Galaad, from the least unto the greatest, even their wives, and their children, and their stuff, a very great host, to the end they might come into the land of Judea.

[46] Now when they came unto Ephron, (this was a great city in the way as they should go, very well fortified) they could not turn from it, either on the right hand or the left, but must needs pass through the midst of it.

[47] Then they of the city shut them out, and stopped up the gates with stones.

[48] Whereupon Judas sent unto them in peaceable manner, saying, Let us pass through your land to go into our own country, and none shall do you any hurt; we will only pass through on foot: howbeit they would not open unto him.

[49] Wherefore Judas commanded a proclamation to be made throughout the host, that every man should pitch his tent in the place where he was.

[50] So the soldiers pitched, and assaulted the city all that day and all that night, till at the length the city was delivered into his hands:

[51] Who then slew all the males with the edge of the sword, and rased the city, and took the spoils thereof, and passed through the city over them that were slain.

[52] After this went they over Jordan into the great plain before Bethsan.

[53] And Judas gathered together those that came behind, and exhorted the people all the way through, till they came into the land of Judea.

[54] So they went up to mount Sion with joy and gladness, where they offered burnt offerings, because not one of them were slain until they had returned in peace.

[55] Now what time as Judas and Jonathan were in the land of Galaad, and Simon his brother in Galilee before Ptolemais,

[56] Joseph the son of Zacharias, and Azarias, captains of the garrisons, heard of the valiant acts and warlike deeds which they had done.

[57] Wherefore they said, Let us also get us a name, and go fight against the heathen that are round about us.

[58] So when they had given charge unto the garrison that was with them, they went toward Jamnia.

[59] Then came Gorgias and his men out of the city to fight against them.

[60] And so it was, that Joseph and Azaras were put to flight, and pursued unto the borders of Judea: and there were slain that day of the people of Israel about two thousand men.

[61] Thus was there a great overthrow among the children of Israel, because they were not obedient unto Judas and his brethren, but thought to do some valiant act.

[62] Moreover these men came not of the seed of those, by whose hand deliverance was given unto Israel.

[63] Howbeit the man Judas and his brethren were greatly renowned in the sight of all Israel, and of all the heathen, wheresoever their name was heard of;

[64] Insomuch as the the people assembled unto them with joyful acclamations.

[65] Afterward went Judas forth with his brethren, and fought against the children of Esau in the land toward the south, where he smote Hebron, and the towns thereof, and pulled down the fortress of it, and burned the towers thereof round about.
[66] From thence he removed to go into the land of the Philistines, and passed through Samaria.
[67] At that time certain priests, desirous to shew their valour, were slain in battle, for that they went out to fight unadvisedly.
[68] So Judas turned to Azotus in the land of the Philistines, and when he had pulled down their altars, and burned their carved images with fire, and spoiled their cities, he returned into the land of Judea.

1Mac.6

[1] About that time king Antiochus travelling through the high countries heard say, that Elymais in the country of Persia was a city greatly renowned for riches, silver, and gold;
[2] And that there was in it a very rich temple, wherein were coverings of gold, and breastplates, and shields, which Alexander, son of Philip, the Macedonian king, who reigned first among the Grecians, had left there.
[3] Wherefore he came and sought to take the city, and to spoil it; but he was not able, because they of the city, having had warning thereof,
[4] Rose up against him in battle: so he fled, and departed thence with great heaviness, and returned to Babylon.
[5] Moreover there came one who brought him tidings into Persia, that the armies, which went against the land of Judea, were put to flight:
[6] And that Lysias, who went forth first with a great power was driven away of the Jews; and that they were made strong by the armour, and power, and store of spoils, which they had gotten of the armies, whom they had destroyed:
[7] Also that they had pulled down the abomination, which he had set up upon the altar in Jerusalem, and that they had compassed about the sanctuary with high walls, as before, and his city Bethsura.
[8] Now when the king heard these words, he was astonished and sore moved: whereupon he laid him down upon his bed, and fell sick for grief, because it had not befallen him as he looked for.
[9] And there he continued many days: for his grief was ever more and more, and he made account that he should die.
[10] Wherefore he called for all his friends, and said unto them, The sleep is gone from mine eyes, and my heart faileth for very care.
[11] And I thought with myself, Into what tribulation am I come, and how great a flood of misery is it, wherein now I am! for I was bountiful and beloved in my power.
[12] But now I remember the evils that I did at Jerusalem, and that I took all the vessels of gold and silver that were therein, and sent to destroy the inhabitants of Judea without a cause.
[13] I perceive therefore that for this cause these troubles are come upon me, and, behold, I perish through great grief in a strange land.
[14] Then called he for Philip, one of his friends, who he made ruler over all his realm,
[15] And gave him the crown, and his robe, and his signet, to the end he should bring up his son Antiochus, and nourish him up for the kingdom.
[16] So king Antiochus died there in the hundred forty and ninth year.
[17] Now when Lysias knew that the king was dead, he set up Antiochus his son, whom he had brought up being young, to reign in his stead, and his name he called

Eupator.

[18] About this time they that were in the tower shut up the Israelites round about the sanctuary, and sought always their hurt, and the strengthening of the heathen.

[19] Wherefore Judas, purposing to destroy them, called all the people together to besiege them.

[20] So they came together, and besieged them in the hundred and fiftieth year, and he made mounts for shot against them, and other engines.

[21] Howbeit certain of them that were besieged got forth, unto whom some ungodly men of Israel joined themselves:

[22] And they went unto the king, and said, How long will it be ere thou execute judgment, and avenge our brethren?

[23] We have been willing to serve thy father, and to do as he would have us, and to obey his commandments;

[24] For which cause they of our nation besiege the tower, and are alienated from us: moreover as many of us as they could light on they slew, and spoiled our inheritance.

[25] Neither have they stretched out their hand against us only, but also against their borders.

[26] And, behold, this day are they besieging the tower at Jerusalem, to take it: the sanctuary also and Bethsura have they fortified.

[27] Wherefore if thou dost not prevent them quickly, they will do the greater things than these, neither shalt thou be able to rule them.

[28] Now when the king heard this, he was angry, and gathered together all his friends, and the captains of his army, and those that had charge of the horse.

[29] There came also unto him from other kingdoms, and from isles of the sea, bands of hired soldiers.

[30] So that the number of his army was an hundred thousand footmen, and twenty thousand horsemen, and two and thirty elephants exercised in battle.

[31] These went through Idumea, and pitched against Bethsura, which they assaulted many days, making engines of war; but they of Bethsura came out, and burned them with fire, and fought valiantly.

[32] Upon this Judas removed from the tower, and pitched in Bathzacharias, over against the king's camp.

[33] Then the king rising very early marched fiercely with his host toward Bathzacharias, where his armies made them ready to battle, and sounded the trumpets.

[34] And to the end they might provoke the elephants to fight, they shewed them the blood of grapes and mulberries.

[35] Moreover they divided the beasts among the armies, and for every elephant they appointed a thousand men, armed with coats of mail, and with helmets of brass on their heads; and beside this, for every beast were ordained five hundred horsemen of the best.

[36] These were ready at every occasion: wheresoever the beast was, and whithersoever the beast went, they went also, neither departed they from him.

[37] And upon the beasts were there strong towers of wood, which covered every one of them, and were girt fast unto them with devices: there were also upon every one two and thirty strong men, that fought upon them, beside the Indian that ruled him.

[38] As for the remnant of the horsemen, they set them on this side and that side at the two parts of the host giving them signs what to do, and being harnessed all over amidst the ranks.

[39] Now when the sun shone upon the shields of gold and brass, the mountains glistered therewith, and shined like lamps of fire.

[40] So part of the king's army being spread upon the high mountains, and part on the valleys below, they marched on safely and in order.

[41] Wherefore all that heard the noise of their multitude, and the marching of the company, and the rattling of the harness, were moved: for the army was very great and mighty.
[42] Then Judas and his host drew near, and entered into battle, and there were slain of the king's army six hundred men.
[43] Eleazar also, surnamed Savaran, perceiving that one of the beasts, armed with royal harness, was higher than all the rest, and supposing that the king was upon him,
[44] Put himself in jeopardy, to the end he might deliver his people, and get him a perpetual name:
[45] Wherefore he ran upon him courageously through the midst of the battle, slaying on the right hand and on the left, so that they were divided from him on both sides.
[46] Which done, he crept under the elephant, and thrust him under, and slew him: whereupon the elephant fell down upon him, and there he died.
[47] Howbeit the rest of the Jews seeing the strength of the king, and the violence of his forces, turned away from them.
[48] Then the king's army went up to Jerusalem to meet them, and the king pitched his tents against Judea, and against mount Sion.
[49] But with them that were in Bethsura he made peace: for they came out of the city, because they had no victuals there to endure the siege, it being a year of rest to the land.
[50] So the king took Bethsura, and set a garrison there to keep it.
[51] As for the sanctuary, he besieged it many days: and set there artillery with engines and instruments to cast fire and stones, and pieces to cast darts and slings.
[52] Whereupon they also made engines against their engines, and held them battle a long season.
[53] Yet at the last, their vessels being without victuals, (for that it was the seventh year, and they in Judea that were delivered from the Gentiles, had eaten up the residue of the store;)
[54] There were but a few left in the sanctuary, because the famine did so prevail against them, that they were fain to disperse themselves, every man to his own place.
[55] At that time Lysias heard say, that Philip, whom Antiochus the king, whiles he lived, had appointed to bring up his son Antiochus, that he might be king,
[56] Was returned out of Persia and Media, and the king's host also that went with him, and that he sought to take unto him the ruling of the affairs.
[57] Wherefore he went in all haste, and said to the king and the captains of the host and the company, We decay daily, and our victuals are but small, and the place we lay siege unto is strong, and the affairs of the kingdom lie upon us:
[58] Now therefore let us be friends with these men, and make peace with them, and with all their nation;
[59] And covenant with them, that they shall live after their laws, as they did before: for they are therefore displeased, and have done all these things, because we abolished their laws.
[60] So the king and the princes were content: wherefore he sent unto them to make peace; and they accepted thereof.
[61] Also the king and the princes made an oath unto them: whereupon they went out of the strong hold.
[62] Then the king entered into mount Sion; but when he saw the strength of the place, he broke his oath that he had made, and gave commandment to pull down the wall round about.
[63] Afterward departed he in all haste, and returned unto Antiochia, where he found Philip to be master of the city: so he fought against him, and took the city by force.

1 Mac. 7

[1] In the hundred and one and fiftieth year Demetrius the son of Seleucus departed from Rome, and came up with a few men unto a city of the sea coast, and reigned there.
[2] And as he entered into the palace of his ancestors, so it was, that his forces had taken Antiochus and Lysias, to bring them unto him.
[3] Wherefore, when he knew it, he said, Let me not see their faces.
[4] So his host slew them. Now when Demetrius was set upon the throne of his kingdom,
[5] There came unto him all the wicked and ungodly men of Israel, having Alcimus, who was desirous to be high priest, for their captain:
[6] And they accused the people to the king, saying, Judas and his brethren have slain all thy friends, and driven us out of our own land.
[7] Now therefore send some man whom thou trustest, and let him go and see what havock he hath made among us, and in the king's land, and let him punish them with all them that aid them.
[8] Then the king chose Bacchides, a friend of the king, who ruled beyond the flood, and was a great man in the kingdom, and faithful to the king,
[9] And him he sent with that wicked Alcimus, whom he made high priest, and commanded that he should take vengeance of the children of Israel.
[10] So they departed, and came with a great power into the land of Judea, where they sent messengers to Judas and his brethren with peaceable words deceitfully.
[11] But they gave no heed to their words; for they saw that they were come with a great power.
[12] Then did there assemble unto Alcimus and Bacchides a company of scribes, to require justice.
[13] Now the Assideans were the first among the children of Israel that sought peace of them:
[14] For said they, One that is a priest of the seed of Aaron is come with this army, and he will do us no wrong.
[15] So he spake unto them, peaceably, and sware unto them, saying, we will procure the harm neither of you nor your friends.
[16] Whereupon they believed him: howbeit he took of them threescore men, and slew them in one day, according to the words which he wrote,
[17] The flesh of thy saints have they cast out, and their blood have they shed round about Jerusalem, and there was none to bury them.
[18] Wherefore the fear and dread of them fell upon all the people, who said, There is neither truth nor righteousness in them; for they have broken the covenant and oath that they made.
[19] After this, removed Bacchides from Jerusalem, and pitched his tents in Bezeth, where he sent and took many of the men that had forsaken him, and certain of the people also, and when he had slain them, he cast them into the great pit.
[20] Then committed he the country to Alcimus, and left with him a power to aid him: so Bacchides went to the king.
[21] But Alcimus contended for the high priesthood.
[22] And unto him resorted all such as troubled the people, who, after they had gotten the land of Juda into their power, did much hurt in Israel.
[23] Now when Judas saw all the mischief that Alcimus and his company had done among the Israelites, even above the heathen,
[24] He went out into all the coasts of Judea round about, and took vengeance of them that had revolted from him, so that they durst no more go forth into the country.

[25] On the other side, when Alcimus saw that Judas and his company had gotten the upper hand, and knew that he was not able to abide their force, he went again to the king, and said all the worst of them that he could.
[26] Then the king sent Nicanor, one of his honourable princes, a man that bare deadly hate unto Israel, with commandment to destroy the people.
[27] So Nicanor came to Jerusalem with a great force; and sent unto Judas and his brethren deceitfully with friendly words, saying,
[28] Let there be no battle between me and you; I will come with a few men, that I may see you in peace.
[29] He came therefore to Judas, and they saluted one another peaceably. Howbeit the enemies were prepared to take away Judas by violence.
[30] Which thing after it was known to Judas, to wit, that he came unto him with deceit, he was sore afraid of him, and would see his face no more.
[31] Nicanor also, when he saw that his counsel was discovered, went out to fight against Judas beside Capharsalama:
[32] Where there were slain of Nicanor's side about five thousand men, and the rest fled into the city of David.
[33] After this went Nicanor up to mount Sion, and there came out of the sanctuary certain of the priests and certain of the elders of the people, to salute him peaceably, and to shew him the burnt sacrifice that was offered for the king.
[34] But he mocked them, and laughed at them, and abused them shamefully, and spake proudly,
[35] And sware in his wrath, saying, Unless Judas and his host be now delivered into my hands, if ever I come again in safety, I will burn up this house: and with that he went out in a great rage.
[36] Then the priests entered in, and stood before the altar and the temple, weeping, and saying,
[37] Thou, O Lord, didst choose this house to be called by thy name, and to be a house of prayer and petition for thy people:
[38] Be avenged of this man and his host, and let them fall by the sword: remember their blasphemies, and suffer them not to continue any longer.
[39] So Nicanor went out of Jerusalem, and pitched his tents in Bethhoron, where an host out of Syria met him.
[40] But Judas pitched in Adasa with three thousand men, and there he prayed, saying,
[41] O Lord, when they that were sent from the king of the Assyrians blasphemed, thine angel went out, and smote an hundred fourscore and five thousand of them.
[42] Even so destroy thou this host before us this day, that the rest may know that he hath spoken blasphemously against thy sanctuary, and judge thou him according to his wickedness.
[43] So the thirteenth day of the month Adar the hosts joined battle: but Nicanor's host was discomfited, and he himself was first slain in the battle.
[44] Now when Nicanor's host saw that he was slain, they cast away their weapons, and fled.
[45] Then they pursued after them a day's journey, from Adasa unto Gazera, sounding an alarm after them with their trumpets.
[46] Whereupon they came forth out of all the towns of Judea round about, and closed them in; so that they, turning back upon them that pursued them, were all slain with the sword, and not one of them was left.
[47] Afterwards they took the spoils, and the prey, and smote off Nicanors head, and his right hand, which he stretched out so proudly, and brought them away, and hanged them up toward Jerusalem.
[48] For this cause the people rejoiced greatly, and they kept that day a day of great gladness.

[49] Moreover they ordained to keep yearly this day, being the thirteenth of Adar.
[50] Thus the land of Juda was in rest a little while.

1Mac.8

[1] Now Judas had heard of the the Romans, that they were mighty and valiant men, and such as would lovingly accept all that joined themselves unto them, and make a league of amity with all that came unto them;
[2] And that they were men of great valour. It was told him also of their wars and noble acts which they had done among the Galatians, and how they had conquered them, and brought them under tribute;
[3] And what they had done in the country of Spain, for the winning of the mines of the silver and gold which is there;
[4] And that by their policy and patience they had conquered all the place, though it were very far from them; and the kings also that came against them from the uttermost part of the earth, till they had discomfited them, and given them a great overthrow, so that the rest did give them tribute every year:
[5] Beside this, how they had discomfited in battle Philip, and Perseus, king of the Citims, with others that lifted up themselves against them, and had overcome them:
[6] How also Antiochus the great king of Asia, that came against them in battle, having an hundred and twenty elephants, with horsemen, and chariots, and a very great army, was discomfited by them;
[7] And how they took him alive, and covenanted that he and such as reigned after him should pay a great tribute, and give hostages, and that which was agreed upon,
[8] And the country of India, and Media and Lydia and of the goodliest countries, which they took of him, and gave to king Eumenes:
[9] Moreover how the Grecians had determined to come and destroy them;
[10] And that they, having knowledge thereof sent against them a certain captain, and fighting with them slew many of them, and carried away captives their wives and their children, and spoiled them, and took possession of their lands, and pulled down their strong holds, and brought them to be their servants unto this day:
[11] It was told him besides, how they destroyed and brought under their dominion all other kingdoms and isles that at any time resisted them;
[12] But with their friends and such as relied upon them they kept amity: and that they had conquered kingdoms both far and nigh, insomuch as all that heard of their name were afraid of them:
[13] Also that, whom they would help to a kingdom, those reign; and whom again they would, they displace: finally, that they were greatly exalted:
[14] Yet for all this none of them wore a crown or was clothed in purple, to be magnified thereby:
[15] Moreover how they had made for themselves a senate house, wherein three hundred and twenty men sat in council daily, consulting alway for the people, to the end they might be well ordered:
[16] And that they committed their government to one man every year, who ruled over all their country, and that all were obedient to that one, and that there was neither envy nor emmulation among them.
[17] In consideration of these things, Judas chose Eupolemus the son of John, the son of Accos, and Jason the son of Eleazar, and sent them to Rome, to make a league of amity and confederacy with them,
[18] And to intreat them that they would take the yoke from them; for they saw that the kingdom of the Grecians did oppress Israel with servitude.
[19] They went therefore to Rome, which was a very great journey, and came into the senate, where they spake and said.

[20] Judas Maccabeus with his brethren, and the people of the Jews, have sent us unto you, to make a confederacy and peace with you, and that we might be registered your confederates and friends.
[21] So that matter pleased the Romans well.
[22] And this is the copy of the epistle which the senate wrote back again in tables of brass, and sent to Jerusalem, that there they might have by them a memorial of peace and confederacy:
[23] Good success be to the Romans, and to the people of the Jews, by sea and by land for ever: the sword also and enemy be far from them,
[24] If there come first any war upon the Romans or any of their confederates throughout all their dominion,
[25] The people of the Jews shall help them, as the time shall be appointed, with all their heart:
[26] Neither shall they give any thing unto them that make war upon them, or aid them with victuals, weapons, money, or ships, as it hath seemed good unto the Romans; but they shall keep their covenants without taking any thing therefore.
[27] In the same manner also, if war come first upon the nation of the Jews, the Romans shall help them with all their heart, according as the time shall be appointed them:
[28] Neither shall victuals be given to them that take part against them, or weapons, or money, or ships, as it hath seemed good to the Romans; but they shall keep their covenants, and that without deceit.
[29] According to these articles did the Romans make a covenant with the people of the Jews.
[30] Howbeit if hereafter the one party or the other shall think to meet to add or diminish any thing, they may do it at their pleasures, and whatsoever they shall add or take away shall be ratified.
[31] And as touching the evils that Demetrius doeth to the Jews, we have written unto him, saying, Wherefore thou made thy yoke heavy upon our friends and confederates the Jews?
[32] If therefore they complain any more against thee, we will do them justice, and fight with thee by sea and by land.

1Mac.9

[1] Furthermore, when Demetrius heard the Nicanor and his host were slain in battle, he sent Bacchides and Alcimus into the land of Judea the second time, and with them the chief strength of his host:
[2] Who went forth by the way that leadeth to Galgala, and pitched their tents before Masaloth, which is in Arbela, and after they had won it, they slew much people.
[3] Also the first month of the hundred fifty and second year they encamped before Jerusalem:
[4] From whence they removed, and went to Berea, with twenty thousand footmen and two thousand horsemen.
[5] Now Judas had pitched his tents at Eleasa, and three thousand chosen men with him:
[6] Who seeing the multitude of the other army to he so great were sore afraid; whereupon many conveyed themselves out of the host, insomuch as abode of them no more but eight hundred men.
[7] When Judas therefore saw that his host slipt away, and that the battle pressed upon him, he was sore troubled in mind, and much distressed, for that he had no time to gather them together.
[8] Nevertheless unto them that remained he said, Let us arise and go up against our enemies, if peradventure we may be able to fight with them.
[9] But they dehorted him, saying, We shall never be able: let us now rather save our lives, and hereafter we will return with our

brethren, and fight against them: for we are but few.

[10] Then Judas said, God forbid that I should do this thing, and flee away from them: if our time be come, let us die manfully for our brethren, and let us not stain our honour.

[11] With that the host of Bacchides removed out of their tents, and stood over against them, their horsemen being divided into two troops, and their slingers and archers going before the host and they that marched in the foreward were all mighty men.

[12] As for Bacchides, he was in the right wing: so the host drew near on the two parts, and sounded their trumpets.

[13] They also of Judas' side, even they sounded their trumpets also, so that the earth shook at the noise of the armies, and the battle continued from morning till night.

[14] Now when Judas perceived that Bacchides and the strength of his army were on the right side, he took with him all the hardy men,

[15] Who discomfited the right wing, and pursued them unto the mount Azotus.

[16] But when they of the left wing saw that they of the right wing were discomfited, they followed upon Judas and those that were with him hard at the heels from behind:

[17] Whereupon there was a sore battle, insomuch as many were slain on both parts.

[18] Judas also was killed, and the remnant fled.

[19] THen Jonathan and Simon took Judas their brother, and buried him in the sepulchre of his fathers in Modin.

[20] Moreover they bewailed him, and all Israel made great lamentation for him, and mourned many days, saying,

[21] How is the valiant man fallen, that delivered Israel!

[22] As for the other things concerning Judas and his wars, and the noble acts which he did, and his greatness, they are not written: for they were very many.

[23] Now after the death of Judas the wicked began to put forth their heads in all the coasts of Israel, and there arose up all such as wrought iniquity.

[24] In those days also was there a very great famine, by reason whereof the country revolted, and went with them.

[25] Then Bacchides chose the wicked men, and made them lords of the country.

[26] And they made enquiry and search for Judas' friends, and brought them unto Bacchides, who took vengeance of them, and used them despitefully.

[27] So was there a great affliction in Israel, the like whereof was not since the time that a prophet was not seen among them.

[28] For this cause all Judas' friends came together, and said unto Jonathan,

[29] Since thy brother Judas died, we have no man like him to go forth against our enemies, and Bacchides, and against them of our nation that are adversaries to us.

[30] Now therefore we have chosen thee this day to be our prince and captain in his stead, that thou mayest fight our battles.

[31] Upon this Jonathan took the governance upon him at that time, and rose up instead of his brother Judas.

[32] But when Bacchides gat knowledge thereof, he sought for to slay him

[33] Then Jonathan, and Simon his brother, and all that were with him, perceiving that, fled into the wilderness of Thecoe, and pitched their tents by the water of the pool Asphar.

[34] Which when Bacchides understood, he came near to Jordan with all his host upon the sabbath day.

[35] Now Jonathan had sent his brother John, a captain of the people, to pray his friends the Nabathites, that they might leave with them their carriage, which was much.

[36] But the children of Jambri came out of Medaba, and took John, and all that he had, and went their way with it.

[37] After this came word to Jonathan and Simon his brother, that the children of Jambri made a great marriage, and were bringing the bride from Nadabatha with a great train, as being the daughter of one of the great princes of Chanaan.

[38] Therefore they remembered John their brother, and went up, and hid themselves under the covert of the mountain:

[39] Where they lifted up their eyes, and looked, and, behold, there was much ado and great carriage: and the bridegroom came forth, and his friends and brethren, to meet them with drums, and instruments of musick, and many weapons.

[40] Then Jonathan and they that were with him rose up against them from the place where they lay in ambush, and made a slaughter of them in such sort, as many fell down dead, and the remnant fled into the mountain, and they took all their spoils.

[41] Thus was the marriage turned into mourning, and the noise of their melody into lamentation.

[42] So when they had avenged fully the blood of their brother, they turned again to the marsh of Jordan.

[43] Now when Bacchides heard hereof, he came on the sabbath day unto the banks of Jordan with a great power.

[44] Then Jonathan said to his company, Let us go up now and fight for our lives, for it standeth not with us to day, as in time past:

[45] For, behold, the battle is before us and behind us, and the water of Jordan on this side and that side, the marsh likewise and wood, neither is there place for us to turn aside.

[46] Wherefore cry ye now unto heaven, that ye may be delivered from the hand of your enemies.

[47] With that they joined battle, and Jonathan stretched forth his hand to smite Bacchides, but he turned back from him.

[48] Then Jonathan and they that were with him leapt into Jordan, and swam over unto the other bank: howbeit the other passed not over Jordan unto them.

[49] So there were slain of Bacchides' side that day about a thousand men.

[50] Afterward returned Bacchides to Jerusalem and repaired the strong cites in Judea; the fort in Jericho, and Emmaus, and Bethhoron, and Bethel, and Thamnatha, Pharathoni, and Taphon, these did he strengthen with high walls, with gates and with bars.

[51] And in them he set a garrison, that they might work malice upon Israel.

[52] He fortified also the city Bethsura, and Gazera, and the tower, and put forces in them, and provision of victuals.

[53] Besides, he took the chief men's sons in the country for hostages, and put them into the tower at Jerusalem to be kept.

[54] Moreover in the hundred fifty and third year, in the second month, Alcimus commanded that the wall of the inner court of the sanctuary should be pulled down; he pulled down also the works of the prophets

[55] And as he began to pull down, even at that time was Alcimus plagued, and his enterprizes hindered: for his mouth was stopped, and he was taken with a palsy, so that he could no more speak any thing, nor give order concerning his house.

[56] So Alcimus died at that time with great torment.

[57] Now when Bacchides saw that Alcimus was dead, he returned to the king: whereupon the land of Judea was in rest two years.

[58] Then all the ungodly men held a council, saying, Behold, Jonathan and his company are at ease, and dwell without care: now therefore we will bring Bacchides hither, who shall take them all in one night.

[59] So they went and consulted with him.

[60] Then removed he, and came with a great host, and sent letters privily to his adherents in Judea, that they should take Jonathan and those that were with him:

howbeit they could not, because their counsel was known unto them.
[61] Wherefore they took of the men of the country, that were authors of that mischief, about fifty persons, and slew them.
[62] Afterward Jonathan, and Simon, and they that were with him, got them away to Bethbasi, which is in the wilderness, and they repaired the decays thereof, and made it strong.
[63] Which thing when Bacchides knew, he gathered together all his host, and sent word to them that were of Judea.
[64] Then went he and laid siege against Bethbasi; and they fought against it a long season and made engines of war.
[65] But Jonathan left his brother Simon in the city, and went forth himself into the country, and with a certain number went he forth.
[66] And he smote Odonarkes and his brethren, and the children of Phasiron in their tent.
[67] And when he began to smite them, and came up with his forces, Simon and his company went out of the city, and burned up the engines of war,
[68] And fought against Bacchides, who was discomfited by them, and they afflicted him sore: for his counsel and travail was in vain.
[69] Wherefore he was very wroth at the wicked men that gave him counsel to come into the country, inasmuch as he slew many of them, and purposed to return into his own country.
[70] Whereof when Jonathan had knowledge, he sent ambassadors unto him, to the end he should make peace with him, and deliver them the prisoners.
[71] Which thing he accepted, and did according to his demands, and sware unto him that he would never do him harm all the days of his life.
[72] When therefore he had restored unto him the prisoners that he had taken aforetime out of the land of Judea, he returned and went his way into his own land, neither came he any more into their borders.
[73] Thus the sword ceased from Israel: but Jonathan dwelt at Machmas, and began to govern the people; and he destroyed the ungodly men out of Israel.

---

1 Mac. 10

[1] In the hundred and sixtieth year Alexander, the son of Antiochus surnamed Epiphanes, went up and took Ptolemais: for the people had received him, by means whereof he reigned there,
[2] Now when king Demetrius heard thereof, he gathered together an exceeding great host, and went forth against him to fight.
[3] Moreover Demetrius sent letters unto Jonathan with loving words, so as he magnified him.
[4] For said he, Let us first make peace with him, before he join with Alexander against us:
[5] Else he will remember all the evils that we have done against him, and against his brethren and his people.
[6] Wherefore he gave him authority to gather together an host, and to provide weapons, that he might aid him in battle: he commanded also that the hostages that were in the tower should be delivered him.
[7] Then came Jonathan to Jerusalem, and read the letters in the audience of all the people, and of them that were in the tower:
[8] Who were sore afraid, when they heard that the king had given him authority to gather together an host.
[9] Whereupon they of the tower delivered their hostages unto Jonathan, and he delivered them unto their parents.
[10] This done, Jonathan settled himself in Jerusalem, and began to build and repair the city.
[11] And he commanded the workmen to

build the walls and the mount Sion and about with square stones for fortification; and they did so.

[12] Then the strangers, that were in the fortresses which Bacchides had built, fled away;

[13] Insomuch as every man left his place, and went into his own country.

[14] Only at Bethsura certain of those that had forsaken the law and the commandments remained still: for it was their place of refuge.

[15] Now when king Alexander had heard what promises Demetrius had sent unto Jonathan: when also it was told him of the battles and noble acts which he and his brethren had done, and of the pains that they had endured,

[16] He said, Shall we find such another man? now therefore we will make him our friend and confederate.

[17] Upon this he wrote a letter, and sent it unto him, according to these words, saying,

[18] King Alexander to his brother Jonathan sendeth greeting:

[19] We have heard of thee, that thou art a man of great power, and meet to be our friend.

[20] Wherefore now this day we ordain thee to be the high priest of thy nation, and to be called the king's friend; (and therewithal he sent him a purple robe and a crown of gold:) and require thee to take our part, and keep friendship with us.

[21] So in the seventh month of the hundred and sixtieth year, at the feast of the tabernacles, Jonathan put on the holy robe, and gathered together forces, and provided much armour.

[22] Whereof when Demetrius heard, he was very sorry, and said,

[23] What have we done, that Alexander hath prevented us in making amity with the Jews to strengthen himself?

[24] I also will write unto them words of encouragement, and promise them dignities and gifts, that I may have their aid.

[25] He sent unto them therefore to this effect: King Demetrius unto the people of the Jews sendeth greeting:

[26] Whereas ye have kept covenants with us, and continued in our friendship, not joining yourselves with our enemies, we have heard hereof, and are glad.

[27] Wherefore now continue ye still to be faithful unto us, and we will well recompense you for the things ye do in our behalf,

[28] And will grant you many immunities, and give you rewards.

[29] And now do I free you, and for your sake I release all the Jews, from tributes, and from the customs of salt, and from crown taxes,

[30] And from that which appertaineth unto me to receive for the third part or the seed, and the half of the fruit of the trees, I release it from this day forth, so that they shall not be taken of the land of Judea, nor of the three governments which are added thereunto out of the country of Samaria and Galilee, from this day forth for evermore.

[31] Let Jerusalem also be holy and free, with the borders thereof, both from tenths and tributes.

[32] And as for the tower which is at Jerusalem, I yield up authority over it, and give the high priest, that he may set in it such men as he shall choose to keep it.

[33] Moreover I freely set at liberty every one of the Jews, that were carried captives out of the land of Judea into any part of my kingdom, and I will that all my officers remit the tributes even of their cattle.

[34] Furthermore I will that all the feasts, and sabbaths, and new moons, and solemn days, and the three days before the feast, and the three days after the feast shall be all of immunity and freedom for all the Jews in my realm.

[35] Also no man shall have authority to meddle with or to molest any of them in any

matter.

[36] I will further, that there be enrolled among the king's forces about thirty thousand men of the Jews, unto whom pay shall be given, as belongeth to all king's forces.

[37] And of them some shall be placed in the king's strong holds, of whom also some shall be set over the affairs of the kingdom, which are of trust: and I will that their overseers and governors be of themselves, and that they live after their own laws, even as the king hath commanded in the land of Judea.

[38] And concerning the three governments that are added to Judea from the country of Samaria, let them be joined with Judea, that they may be reckoned to be under one, nor bound to obey other authority than the high priest's.

[39] As for Ptolemais, and the land pertaining thereto, I give it as a free gift to the sanctuary at Jerusalem for the necessary expences of the sanctuary.

[40] Moreover I give every year fifteen thousand shekels of silver out of the king's accounts from the places appertaining.

[41] And all the overplus, which the officers payed not in as in former time, from henceforth shall be given toward the works of the temple.

[42] And beside this, the five thousand shekels of silver, which they took from the uses of the temple out of the accounts year by year, even those things shall be released, because they appertain to the priests that minister.

[43] And whosoever they be that flee unto the temple at Jerusalem, or be within the liberties hereof, being indebted unto the king, or for any other matter, let them be at liberty, and all that they have in my realm.

[44] For the building also and repairing of the works of the sanctuary expences shall be given of the king's accounts.

[45] Yea, and for the building of the walls of Jerusalem, and the fortifying thereof round about, expences shall be given out of the king's accounts, as also for the building of the walls in Judea.

[46] Now when Jonathan and the people heard these words, they gave no credit unto them, nor received them, because they remembered the great evil that he had done in Israel; for he had afflicted them very sore.

[47] But with Alexander they were well pleased, because he was the first that entreated of true peace with them, and they were confederate with him always.

[48] Then gathered king Alexander great forces, and camped over against Demetrius.

[49] And after the two kings had joined battle, Demetrius' host fled: but Alexander followed after him, and prevailed against them.

[50] And he continued the battle very sore until the sun went down: and that day was Demetrius slain.

[51] Afterward Alexander sent ambassadors to Ptolemee king of Egypt with a message to this effect:

[52] Forasmuch as I am come again to my realm, and am set in the throne of my progenitors, and have gotten the dominion, and overthrown Demetrius, and recovered our country;

[53] For after I had joined battle with him, both he and his host was discomfited by us, so that we sit in the throne of his kingdom:

[54] Now therefore let us make a league of amity together, and give me now thy daughter to wife: and I will be thy son in law, and will give both thee and her as according to thy dignity.

[55] Then Ptolemee the king gave answer, saying, Happy be the day wherein thou didst return into the land of thy fathers, and satest in the throne of their kingdom.

[56] And now will I do to thee, as thou hast written: meet me therefore at Ptolemais, that we may see one another; for I will marry my daughter to thee according to thy desire.

[57] So Ptolemee went out of Egypt with his daughter Cleopatra, and they came unto Ptolemais in the hundred threescore and second year:
[58] Where king Alexander meeting him, he gave unto him his daughter Cleopatra, and celebrated her marriage at Ptolemais with great glory, as the manner of kings is.
[59] Now king Alexander had written unto Jonathan, that he should come and meet him.
[60] Who thereupon went honourably to Ptolemais, where he met the two kings, and gave them and their friends silver and gold, and many presents, and found favour in their sight.
[61] At that time certain pestilent fellows of Israel, men of a wicked life, assembled themselves against him, to accuse him: but the king would not hear them.
[62] Yea more than that, the king commanded to take off his garments, and clothe him in purple: and they did so.
[63] And he made him sit by himself, and said into his princes, Go with him into the midst of the city, and make proclamation, that no man complain against him of any matter, and that no man trouble him for any manner of cause.
[64] Now when his accusers saw that he was honored according to the proclamation, and clothed in purple, they fled all away.
[65] So the king honoured him, and wrote him among his chief friends, and made him a duke, and partaker of his dominion.
[66] Afterward Jonathan returned to Jerusalem with peace and gladness.
[67] Furthermore in the; hundred threescore and fifth year came Demetrius son of Demetrius out of Crete into the land of his fathers:
[68] Whereof when king Alexander heard tell, he was right sorry, and returned into Antioch.
[69] Then Demetrius made Apollonius the governor of Celosyria his general, who gathered together a great host, and camped in Jamnia, and sent unto Jonathan the high priest, saying,
[70] Thou alone liftest up thyself against us, and I am laughed to scorn for thy sake, and reproached: and why dost thou vaunt thy power against us in the mountains?
[71] Now therefore, if thou trustest in thine own strength, come down to us into the plain field, and there let us try the matter together: for with me is the power of the cities.
[72] Ask and learn who I am, and the rest that take our part, and they shall tell thee that thy foot is not able to to flight in their own land.
[73] Wherefore now thou shalt not be able to abide the horsemen and so great a power in the plain, where is neither stone nor flint, nor place to flee unto.
[74] So when Jonathan heard these words of Apollonius, he was moved in his mind, and choosing ten thousand men he went out of Jerusalem, where Simon his brother met him for to help him.
[75] And he pitched his tents against Joppa: but; they of Joppa shut him out of the city, because Apollonius had a garrison there.
[76] Then Jonathan laid siege unto it: whereupon they of the city let him in for fear: and so Jonathan won Joppa.
[77] Whereof when Apollonius heard, he took three thousand horsemen, with a great host of footmen, and went to Azotus as one that journeyed, and therewithal drew him forth into the plain. because he had a great number of horsemen, in whom he put his trust.
[78] Then Jonathan followed after him to Azotus, where the armies joined battle.
[79] Now Apollonius had left a thousand horsemen in ambush.
[80] And Jonathan knew that there was an ambushment behind him; for they had compassed in his host, and cast darts at the people, from morning till evening.

[81] But the people stood still, as Jonathan had commanded them: and so the enemies' horses were tired.

[82] Then brought Simon forth his host, and set them against the footmen, (for the horsemen were spent) who were discomfited by him, and fled.

[83] The horsemen also, being scattered in the field, fled to Azotus, and went into Bethdagon, their idol's temple, for safety.

[84] But Jonathan set fire on Azotus, and the cities round about it, and took their spoils; and the temple of Dagon, with them that were fled into it, he burned with fire.

[85] Thus there were burned and slain with the sword well nigh eight thousand men.

[86] And from thence Jonathan removed his host, and camped against Ascalon, where the men of the city came forth, and met him with great pomp.

[87] After this returned Jonathan and his host unto Jerusalem, having any spoils.

[88] Now when king ALexander heard these things, he honoured Jonathan yet more.

[89] And sent him a buckle of gold, as the use is to be given to such as are of the king's blood: he gave him also Accaron with the borders thereof in possession.

1Mac. 11

[1] And the king of Egypt gathered together a great host, like the sand that lieth upon the sea shore, and many ships, and went about through deceit to get Alexander's kingdom, and join it to his own.

[2] Whereupon he took his journey into Spain in peaceable manner, so as they of the cities opened unto him, and met him: for king Alexander had commanded them so to do, because he was his brother in law.

[3] Now as Ptolemee entered into the cities, he set in every one of them a garrison of soldiers to keep it.

[4] And when he came near to Azotus, they shewed him the temple of Dagon that was burnt, and Azotus and the suburbs thereof that were destroyed, and the bodies that were cast abroad and them that he had burnt in the battle; for they had made heaps of them by the way where he should pass.

[5] Also they told the king whatsoever Jonathan had done, to the intent he might blame him: but the king held his peace.

[6] Then Jonathan met the king with great pomp at Joppa, where they saluted one another, and lodged.

[7] Afterward Jonathan, when he had gone with the king to the river called Eleutherus, returned again to Jerusalem.

[8] King Ptolemee therefore, having gotten the dominion of the cities by the sea unto Seleucia upon the sea coast, imagined wicked counsels against Alexander.

[9] Whereupon he sent ambasadors unto king Demetrius, saying, Come, let us make a league betwixt us, and I will give thee my daughter whom Alexander hath, and thou shalt reign in thy father's kingdom:

[10] For I repent that I gave my daughter unto him, for he sought to slay me.

[11] Thus did he slander him, because he was desirous of his kingdom.

[12] Wherefore he took his daughter from him, and gave her to Demetrius, and forsook Alexander, so that their hatred was openly known.

[13] Then Ptolemee entered into Antioch, where he set two crowns upon his head, the crown of Asia, and of Egypt.

[14] In the mean season was king Alexander in Cilicia, because those that dwelt in those parts had revolted from him.

[15] But when Alexander heard of this, he came to war against him: whereupon king Ptolemee brought forth his host, and met him with a mighty power, and put him to flight.

[16] So Alexander fled into Arabia there to be defended; but king Ptolemee was exalted:

[17] For Zabdiel the Arabian took off

Alexander's head, and sent it unto Ptolemee.
[18] King Ptolemee also died the third day after, and they that were in the strong holds were slain one of another.
[19] By this means Demetrius reigned in the hundred threescore and seventh year.
[20] At the same time Jonathan gathered together them that were in Judea to take the tower that was in Jerusalem: and he made many engines of war against it.
[21] Then came ungodly persons, who hated their own people, went unto the king, and told him that Jonathan besieged the tower,
[22] Whereof when he heard, he was angry, and immediately removing, he came to Ptolemais, and wrote unto Jonathan, that he should not lay siege to the tower, but come and speak with him at Ptolemais in great haste.
[23] Nevertheless Jonathan, when he heard this, commanded to besiege it still: and he chose certain of the elders of Israel and the priests, and put himself in peril;
[24] And took silver and gold, and raiment, and divers presents besides, and went to Ptolemais unto the king, where he found favour in his sight.
[25] And though certain ungodly men of the people had made complaints against him,
[26] Yet the king entreated him as his predecessors had done before, and promoted him in the sight of all his friends,
[27] And confirmed him in the high priesthood, and in all the honours that he had before, and gave him preeminence among his chief friends.
[28] Then Jonathan desired the king, that he would make Judea free from tribute, as also the three governments, with the country of Samaria; and he promised him three hundred talents.
[29] So the king consented, and wrote letters unto Jonathan of all these things after this manner:
[30] King Demetrius unto his brother Jonathan, and unto the nation of the Jews, sendeth greeting:
[31] We send you here a copy of the letter which we did write unto our cousin Lasthenes concerning you, that ye might see it.
[32] King Demetrius unto his father Lasthenes sendeth greeting:
[33] We are determined to do good to the people of the Jews, who are our friends, and keep covenants with us, because of their good will toward us.
[34] Wherefore we have ratified unto them the borders of Judea, with the three governments of Apherema and Lydda and Ramathem, that are added unto Judea from the country of Samaria, and all things appertaining unto them, for all such as do sacrifice in Jerusalem, instead of the payments which the king received of them yearly aforetime out of the fruits of the earth and of trees.
[35] And as for other things that belong unto us, of the tithes and customs pertaining unto us, as also the saltpits, and the crown taxes, which are due unto us, we discharge them of them all for their relief.
[36] And nothing hereof shall be revoked from this time forth for ever.
[37] Now therefore see that thou make a copy of these things, and let it be delivered unto Jonathan, and set upon the holy mount in a conspicuous place.
[38] After this, when king Demetrius saw that the land was quiet before him, and that no resistance was made against him, he sent away all his forces, every one to his own place, except certain bands of strangers, whom he had gathered from the isles of the heathen: wherefore all the forces of his fathers hated him.
[39] Moreover there was one Tryphon, that had been of Alexander's part afore, who, seeing that all the host murmured against Demetrius, went to Simalcue the Arabian that brought up Antiochus the young son of Alexander,

[40] And lay sore upon him to deliver him this young Antiochus, that he might reign in his father's stead: he told him therefore all that Demetrius had done, and how his men of war were at enmity with him, and there he remained a long season.
[41] In the mean time Jonathan sent unto king Demetrius, that he would cast those of the tower out of Jerusalem, and those also in the fortresses: for they fought against Israel.
[42] So Demetrius sent unto Jonathan, saying, I will not only do this for thee and thy people, but I will greatly honour thee and thy nation, if opportunity serve.
[43] Now therefore thou shalt do well, if thou send me men to help me; for all my forces are gone from me.
[44] Upon this Jonathan sent him three thousand strong men unto Antioch: and when they came to the king, the king was very glad of their coming.
[45] Howbeit they that were of the city gathered themselves together into the midst of the city, to the number of an hundred and twenty thousand men, and would have slain the king.
[46] Wherefore the king fled into the court, but they of the city kept the passages of the city, and began to fight.
[47] Then the king called to the Jews for help, who came unto him all at once, and dispersing themselves through the city slew that day in the city to the number of an hundred thousand.
[48] Also they set fire on the city, and gat many spoils that day, and delivered the king.
[49] So when they of the city saw that the Jews had got the city as they would, their courage was abated: wherefore they made supplication to the king, and cried, saying,
[50] Grant us peace, and let the Jews cease from assaulting us and the city.
[51] With that they cast away their weapons, and made peace; and the Jews were honoured in the sight of the king, and in the sight of all that were in his realm; and they returned to Jerusalem, having great spoils.
[52] So king Demetrius sat on the throne of his kingdom, and the land was quiet before him.
[53] Nevertheless he dissembled in all that ever he spake, and estranged himself from Jonathan, neither rewarded he him according to the benefits which he had received of him, but troubled him very sore.
[54] After this returned Tryphon, and with him the young child Antiochus, who reigned, and was crowned.
[55] Then there gathered unto him all the men of war, whom Demetrius had put away, and they fought against Demetrius, who turned his back and fled.
[56] Moreover Tryphon took the elephants, and won Antioch.
[57] At that time young Antiochus wrote unto Jonathan, saying, I confirm thee in the high priesthood, and appoint thee ruler over the four governments, and to be one of the king's friends.
[58] Upon this he sent him golden vessels to be served in, and gave him leave to drink in gold, and to be clothed in purple, and to wear a golden buckle.
[59] His brother Simon also he made captain from the place called The ladder of Tyrus unto the borders of Egypt.
[60] Then Jonathan went forth, and passed through the cities beyond the water, and all the forces of Syria gathered themselves unto him for to help him: and when he came to Ascalon, they of the city met him honourably.
[61] From whence he went to Gaza, but they of Gaza shut him out; wherefore he laid siege unto it, and burned the suburbs thereof with fire, and spoiled them.
[62] Afterward, when they of Gaza made supplication unto Jonathan, he made peace with them, and took the sons of their chief men for hostages, and sent them to Jerusalem, and passed through the country unto Damascus.

[63] Now when Jonathan heard that Demetrius' princes were come to Cades, which is in Galilee, with a great power, purposing to remove him out of the country,
[64] He went to meet them, and left Simon his brother in the country.
[65] Then Simon encamped against Bethsura and fought against it a long season, and shut it up:
[66] But they desired to have peace with him, which he granted them, and then put them out from thence, and took the city, and set a garrison in it.
[67] As for Jonathan and his host, they pitched at the water of Gennesar, from whence betimes in the morning they gat them to the plain of Nasor.
[68] And, behold, the host of strangers met them in the plain, who, having laid men in ambush for him in the mountains, came themselves over against him.
[69] So when they that lay in ambush rose out of their places and joined battle, all that were of Jonathan's side fled;
[70] Insomuch as there was not one of them left, except Mattathias the son of Absalom, and Judas the son of Calphi, the captains of the host.
[71] Then Jonathan rent his clothes, and cast earth upon his head, and prayed.
[72] Afterwards turning again to battle, he put them to flight, and so they ran away.
[73] Now when his own men that were fled saw this, they turned again unto him, and with him pursued them to Cades, even unto their own tents, and there they camped.
[74] So there were slain of the heathen that day about three thousand men: but Jonathan returned to Jerusalem.

1 Mac. 12

[1] Now when Jonathan saw that time served him, he chose certain men, and sent them to Rome, for to confirm and renew the friendship that they had with them.
[2] He sent letters also to the Lacedemonians, and to other places, for the same purpose.
[3] So they went unto Rome, and entered into the senate, and said, Jonathan the high priest, and the people of the Jews, sent us unto you, to the end ye should renew the friendship, which ye had with them, and league, as in former time.
[4] Upon this the Romans gave them letters unto the governors of every place that they should bring them into the land of Judea peaceably.
[5] And this is the copy of the letters which Jonathan wrote to the Lacedemonians:
[6] Jonathan the high priest, and the elders of the nation, and the priests, and the other of the Jews, unto the Lacedemonians their brethren send greeting:
[7] There were letters sent in times past unto Onias the high priest from Darius, who reigned then among you, to signify that ye are our brethren, as the copy here underwritten doth specify.
[8] At which time Onias entreated the ambassador that was sent honourably, and received the letters, wherein declaration was made of the league and friendship.
[9] Therefore we also, albeit we need none of these things, that we have the holy books of scripture in our hands to comfort us,
[10] Have nevertheless attempted to send unto you for the renewing of brotherhood and friendship, lest we should become strangers unto you altogether: for there is a long time passed since ye sent unto us.
[11] We therefore at all times without ceasing, both in our feasts, and other convenient days, do remember you in the sacrifices which we offer, and in our prayers, as reason is, and as it becometh us to think upon our brethren:
[12] And we are right glad of your honour.
[13] As for ourselves, we have had great troubles and wars on every side, forsomuch

as the kings that are round about us have fought against us.

[14] Howbeit we would not be troublesome unto you, nor to others of our confederates and friends, in these wars:

[15] For we have help from heaven that succoureth us, so as we are delivered from our enemies, and our enemies are brought under foot.

[16] For this cause we chose Numenius the son of Antiochus, and Antipater he son of Jason, and sent them unto the Romans, to renew the amity that we had with them, and the former league.

[17] We commanded them also to go unto you, and to salute and to deliver you our letters concerning the renewing of our brotherhood.

[18] Wherefore now ye shall do well to give us an answer thereto.

[19] And this is the copy of the letters which Oniares sent.

[20] Areus king of the Lacedemonians to Onias the high priest, greeting:

[21] It is found in writing, that the Lacedemonians and Jews are brethren, and that they are of the stock of Abraham:

[22] Now therefore, since this is come to our knowledge, ye shall do well to write unto us of your prosperity.

[23] We do write back again to you, that your cattle and goods are our's, and our's are your's We do command therefore our ambassadors to make report unto you on this wise.

[24] Now when Jonathan heard that Demebius' princes were come to fight against him with a greater host than afore,

[25] He removed from Jerusalem, and met them in the land of Amathis: for he gave them no respite to enter his country.

[26] He sent spies also unto their tents, who came again, and told him that they were appointed to come upon them in the night season.

[27] Wherefore so soon as the sun was down, Jonathan commanded his men to watch, and to be in arms, that all the night long they might be ready to fight: also he sent forth centinels round about the host.

[28] But when the adversaries heard that Jonathan and his men were ready for battle, they feared, and trembled in their hearts, and they kindled fires in their camp.

[29] Howbeit Jonathan and his company knew it not till the morning: for they saw the lights burning.

[30] Then Jonathan pursued after them, but overtook them not: for they were gone over the river Eleutherus.

[31] Wherefore Jonathan turned to the Arabians, who were called Zabadeans, and smote them, and took their spoils.

[32] And removing thence, he came to Damascus, and so passed through all the country,

[33] Simon also went forth, and passed through the country unto Ascalon, and the holds there adjoining, from whence he turned aside to Joppa, and won it.

[34] For he had heard that they would deliver the hold unto them that took Demetrius' part; wherefore he set a garrison there to keep it.

[35] After this came Jonathan home again, and calling the elders of the people together, he consulted with them about building strong holds in Judea,

[36] And making the walls of Jerusalem higher, and raising a great mount between the tower and the city, for to separate it from the city, that so it might be alone, that men might neither sell nor buy in it.

[37] Upon this they came together to build up the city, forasmuch as part of the wall toward the brook on the east side was fallen down, and they repaired that which was called Caphenatha.

[38] Simon also set up Adida in Sephela, and made it strong with gates and bars.

[39] Now Tryphon went about to get the kingdom of Asia, and to kill Antiochus the

king, that he might set the crown upon his own head.
[40] Howbeit he was afraid that Jonathan would not suffer him, and that he would fight against him; wherefore he sought a way how to take Jonathan, that he might kill him. So he removed, and came to Bethsan.
[41] Then Jonathan went out to meet him with forty thousand men chosen for the battle, and came to Bethsan.
[42] Now when Tryphon saw Jonathan came with so great a force, he durst not stretch his hand against him;
[43] But received him honourably, and commended him unto all his friends, and gave him gifts, and commanded his men of war to be as obedient unto him, as to himself.
[44] Unto Jonathan also he said, Why hast thou brought all this people to so great trouble, seeing there is no war betwixt us?
[45] Therefore send them now home again, and choose a few men to wait on thee, and come thou with me to Ptolemais, for I will give it thee, and the rest of the strong holds and forces, and all that have any charge: as for me, I will return and depart: for this is the cause of my coming.
[46] So Jonathan believing him did as he bade him, and sent away his host, who went into the land of Judea.
[47] And with himself he retained but three thousand men, of whom he sent two thousand into Galilee, and one thousand went with him.
[48] Now as soon as Jonathan entered into Ptolemais, they of Ptolemais shut the gates and took him, and all them that came with him they slew with the sword.
[49] Then sent Tryphon an host of footmen and horsemen into Galilee, and into the great plain, to destroy all Jonathan's company.
[50] But when they knew that Jonathan and they that were with him were taken and slain, they encouraged one another; and went close together, prepared to fight.
[51] They therefore that followed upon them, perceiving that they were ready to fight for their lives, turned back again.
[52] Whereupon they all came into the land of Judea peaceably, and there they bewailed Jonathan, and them that were with him, and they were sore afraid; wherefore all Israel made great lamentation.
[53] Then all the heathen that were round about then sought to destroy them: for said they, They have no captain, nor any to help them: now therefore let us make war upon them, and take away their memorial from among men.

1Mac.13

[1] Now when Simon heard that Tryphon had gathered together a great host to invade the land of Judea, and destroy it,
[2] And saw that the people was in great trembling and fear, he went up to Jerusalem, and gathered the people together,
[3] And gave them exhortation, saying, Ye yourselves know what great things I, and my brethren, and my father's house, have done for the laws and the sanctuary, the battles also and troubles which we have seen.
[4] By reason whereof all my brethren are slain for Israel's sake, and I am left alone.
[5] Now therefore be it far from me, that I should spare mine own life in any time of trouble: for I am no better than my brethren.
[6] Doubtless I will avenge my nation, and the sanctuary, and our wives, and our children: for all the heathen are gathered to destroy us of very malice.
[7] Now as soon as the people heard these words, their spirit revived.
[8] And they answered with a loud voice, saying, Thou shalt be our leader instead of Judas and Jonathan thy brother.
[9] Fight thou our battles, and whatsoever, thou commandest us, that will we do.
[10] So then he gathered together all the

men of war, and made haste to finish the walls of Jerusalem, and he fortified it round about.

[11] Also he sent Jonathan the son of Absolom, and with him a great power, to Joppa: who casting out them that were therein remained there in it.

[12] So Tryphon removed from Ptolemaus with a great power to invade the land of Judea, and Jonathan was with him in ward.

[13] But Simon pitched his tents at Adida, over against the plain.

[14] Now when Tryphon knew that Simon was risen up instead of his brother Jonathan, and meant to join battle with him, he sent messengers unto him, saying,

[15] Whereas we have Jonathan thy brother in hold, it is for money that he is owing unto the king's treasure, concerning the business that was committed unto him.

[16] Wherefore now send an hundred talents of silver, and two of his sons for hostages, that when he is at liberty he may not revolt from us, and we will let him go.

[17] Hereupon Simon, albeit he perceived that they spake deceitfully unto him yet sent he the money and the children, lest peradventure he should procure to himself great hatred of the people:

[18] Who might have said, Because I sent him not the money and the children, therefore is Jonathan dead.

[19] So he sent them the children and the hundred talents: howbeit Tryphon dissembled neither would he let Jonathan go.

[20] And after this came Tryphon to invade the land, and destroy it, going round about by the way that leadeth unto Adora: but Simon and his host marched against him in every place, wheresoever he went.

[21] Now they that were in the tower sent messengers unto Tryphon, to the end that he should hasten his coming unto them by the wilderness, and send them victuals.

[22] Wherefore Tryphon made ready all his horsemen to come that night: but there fell a very great snow, by reason whereof he came not. So he departed, and came into the country of Galaad.

[23] And when he came near to Bascama he slew Jonathan, who was buried there.

[24] Afterward Tryphon returned and went into his own land.

[25] Then sent Simon, and took the bones of Jonathan his brother, and buried them in Modin, the city of his fathers.

[26] And all Israel made great lamentation for him, and bewailed him many days.

[27] Simon also built a monument upon the sepulchre of his father and his brethren, and raised it aloft to the sight, with hewn stone behind and before.

[28] Moreover he set up seven pyramids, one against another, for his father, and his mother, and his four brethren.

[29] And in these he made cunning devices, about the which he set great pillars, and upon the pillars he made all their armour for a perpetual memory, and by the armour ships carved, that they might be seen of all that sail on the sea.

[30] This is the sepulchre which he made at Modin, and it standeth yet unto this day.

[31] Now Tryphon dealt deceitfully with the young king Antiochus, and slew him.

[32] And he reigned in his stead, and crowned himself king of Asia, and brought a great calamity upon the land.

[33] Then Simon built up the strong holds in Judea, and fenced them about with high towers, and great walls, and gates, and bars, and laid up victuals therein.

[34] Moreover Simon chose men, and sent to king Demetrius, to the end he should give the land an immunity, because all that Tryphon did was to spoil.

[35] Unto whom king Demetrius answered and wrote after this manner:

[36] King Demetrius unto Simon the high priest, and friend of kings, as also unto the elders and nation of the Jews, sendeth

greeting:

[37] The golden crown, and the scarlet robe, which ye sent unto us, we have received: and we are ready to make a stedfast peace with you, yea, and to write unto our officers, to confirm the immunities which we have granted.

[38] And whatsoever covenants we have made with you shall stand; and the strong holds, which ye have builded, shall be your own.

[39] As for any oversight or fault committed unto this day, we forgive it, and the crown tax also, which ye owe us: and if there were any other tribute paid in Jerusalem, it shall no more be paid.

[40] And look who are meet among you to be in our court, let then be enrolled, and let there be peace betwixt us.

[41] Thus the yoke of the heathen was taken away from Israel in the hundred and seventieth year.

[42] Then the people of Israel began to write in their instruments and contracts, In the first year of Simon the high priest, the governor and leader of the Jews.

[43] In those days Simon camped against Gaza and besieged it round about; he made also an engine of war, and set it by the city, and battered a certain tower, and took it.

[44] And they that were in the engine leaped into the city; whereupon there was a great uproar in the city:

[45] Insomuch as the people of the city rent their clothes, and climbed upon the walls with their wives and children, and cried with a loud voice, beseeching Simon to grant them peace.

[46] And they said, Deal not with us according to our wickedness, but according to thy mercy.

[47] So Simon was appeased toward them, and fought no more against them, but put them out of the city, and cleansed the houses wherein the idols were, and so entered into it with songs and thanksgiving.

[48] Yea, he put all uncleanness out of it, and placed such men there as would keep the law, and made it stronger than it was before, and built therein a dwellingplace for himself.

[49] They also of the tower in Jerusalem were kept so strait, that they could neither come forth, nor go into the country, nor buy, nor sell: wherefore they were in great distress for want of victuals, and a great number of them perished through famine.

[50] Then cried they to Simon, beseeching him to be at one with them: which thing he granted them; and when he had put them out from thence, he cleansed the tower from pollutions:

[51] And entered into it the three and twentieth day of the second month in the hundred seventy and first year, with thanksgiving, and branches of palm trees, and with harps, and cymbals, and with viols, and hymns, and songs: because there was destroyed a great enemy out of Israel.

[52] He ordained also that that day should be kept every year with gladness. Moreover the hill of the temple that was by the tower he made stronger than it was, and there he dwelt himself with his company.

[53] And when Simon saw that John his son was a valiant man, he made him captain of all the hosts; and he dwelt in Gazera.

---

1 Mac. 14

[1] Now in the hundred threescore and twelfth year king Demetrius gathered his forces together, and went into Media to get him help to fight against Tryphone.

[2] But when Arsaces, the king of Persia and Media, heard that Demetrius was entered within his borders, he sent one of his princes to take him alive:

[3] Who went and smote the host of Demetrius, and took him, and brought him to Arsaces, by whom he was put in ward.

[4] As for the land of Judea, that was quiet all the days of Simon; for he sought the good of his nation in such wise, as that evermore his authority and honour pleased them well.
[5] And as he was honourable in all his acts, so in this, that he took Joppa for an haven, and made an entrance to the isles of the sea,
[6] And enlarged the bounds of his nation, and recovered the country,
[7] And gathered together a great number of captives, and had the dominion of Gazera, and Bethsura, and the tower, out of the which he took all uncleaness, neither was there any that resisted him.
[8] Then did they till their ground in peace, and the earth gave her increase, and the trees of the field their fruit.
[9] The ancient men sat all in the streets, communing together of good things, and the young men put on glorious and warlike apparel.
[10] He provided victuals for the cities, and set in them all manner of munition, so that his honourable name was renowned unto the end of the world.
[11] He made peace in the land, and Israel rejoiced with great joy:
[12] For every man sat under his vine and his fig tree, and there was none to fray them:
[13] Neither was there any left in the land to fight against them: yea, the kings themselves were overthrown in those days.
[14] Moreover he strengthened all those of his people that were brought low: the law he searched out; and every contemner of the law and wicked person he took away.
[15] He beautified the sanctuary, and multiplied vessels of the temple.
[16] Now when it was heard at Rome, and as far as Sparta, that Jonathan was dead, they were very sorry.
[17] But as soon as they heard that his brother Simon was made high priest in his stead, and ruled the country, and the cities therein:
[18] They wrote unto him in tables of brass, to renew the friendship and league which they had made with Judas and Jonathan his brethren:
[19] Which writings were read before the congregation at Jerusalem.
[20] And this is the copy of the letters that the Lacedemonians sent; The rulers of the Lacedemonians, with the city, unto Simon the high priest, and the elders, and priests, and residue of the people of the Jews, our brethren, send greeting:
[21] The ambassadors that were sent unto our people certified us of your glory and honour: wherefore we were glad of their coming,
[22] And did register the things that they spake in the council of the people in this manner; Numenius son of Antiochus, and Antipater son of Jason, the Jews' ambassadors, came unto us to renew the friendship they had with us.
[23] And it pleased the people to entertain the men honourably, and to put the copy of their ambassage in publick records, to the end the people of the Lacedemonians might have a memorial thereof: furthermore we have written a copy thereof unto Simon the high priest.
[24] After this Simon sent Numenius to Rome with a great shield of gold of a thousand pound weight to confirm the league with them.
[25] Whereof when the people heard, they said, What thanks shall we give to Simon and his sons?
[26] For he and his brethren and the house of his father have established Israel, and chased away in fight their enemies from them, and confirmed their liberty.
[27] So then they wrote it in tables of brass, which they set upon pillars in mount Sion: and this is the copy of the writing; The eighteenth day of the month Elul, in the hundred threescore and twelfth year, being the third year of Simon the high priest,

[28] At Saramel in the great congregation of the priests, and people, and rulers of the nation, and elders of the country, were these things notified unto us.

[29] Forasmuch as oftentimes there have been wars in the country, wherein for the maintenance of their sanctuary, and the law, Simon the son of Mattathias, of the posterity of Jarib, together with his brethren, put themselves in jeopardy, and resisting the enemies of their nation did their nation great honour:

[30] (For after that Jonathan, having gathered his nation together, and been their high priest, was added to his people,

[31] Their enemies prepared to invade their country, that they might destroy it, and lay hands on the sanctuary:

[32] At which time Simon rose up, and fought for his nation, and spent much of his own substance, and armed the valiant men of his nation and gave them wages,

[33] And fortified the cities of Judea, together with Bethsura, that lieth upon the borders of Judea, where the armour of the enemies had been before; but he set a garrison of Jews there:

[34] Moreover he fortified Joppa, which lieth upon the sea, and Gazera, that bordereth upon Azotus, where the enemies had dwelt before: but he placed Jews there, and furnished them with all things convenient for the reparation thereof.)

[35] The people therefore sang the acts of Simon, and unto what glory he thought to bring his nation, made him their governor and chief priest, because he had done all these things, and for the justice and faith which he kept to his nation, and for that he sought by all means to exalt his people.

[36] For in his time things prospered in his hands, so that the heathen were taken out of their country, and they also that were in the city of David in Jerusalem, who had made themselves a tower, out of which they issued, and polluted all about the sanctuary, and did much hurt in the holy place:

[37] But he placed Jews therein. and fortified it for the safety of the country and the city, and raised up the walls of Jerusalem.

[38] King Demetrius also confirmed him in the high priesthood according to those things,

[39] And made him one of his friends, and honoured him with great honour.

[40] For he had heard say, that the Romans had called the Jews their friends and confederates and brethren; and that they had entertained the ambassadors of Simon honourably;

[41] Also that the Jews and priests were well pleased that Simon should be their governor and high priest for ever, until there should arise a faithful prophet;

[42] Moreover that he should be their captain, and should take charge of the sanctuary, to set them over their works, and over the country, and over the armour, and over the fortresses, that, I say, he should take charge of the sanctuary;

[43] Beside this, that he should be obeyed of every man, and that all the writings in the country should be made in his name, and that he should be clothed in purple, and wear gold:

[44] Also that it should be lawful for none of the people or priests to break any of these things, or to gainsay his words, or to gather an assembly in the country without him, or to be clothed in purple, or wear a buckle of gold;

[45] And whosoever should do otherwise, or break any of these things, he should be punished.

[46] Thus it liked all the people to deal with Simon, and to do as hath been said.

[47] Then Simon accepted hereof, and was well pleased to be high priest, and captain and governor of the Jews and priests, and to defend them all.

[48] So they commanded that this writing

should be put in tables of brass, and that they should be set up within the compass of the sanctuary in a conspicuous place;
[49] Also that the copies thereof should be laid up in the treasury, to the end that Simon and his sons might have them.

1Mac.15

[1] Moreover Antiochus son of Demetrius the king sent letters from the isles of the sea unto Simon the priest and prince of the Jews, and to all the people;
[2] The contents whereof were these: King Antiochus to Simon the high priest and prince of his nation, and to the people of the Jews, greeting:
[3] Forasmuch as certain pestilent men have usurped the kingdom of our fathers, and my purpose is to challenge it again, that I may restore it to the old estate, and to that end have gathered a multitude of foreign soldiers together, and prepared ships of war;
[4] My meaning also being to go through the country, that I may be avenged of them that have destroyed it, and made many cities in the kingdom desolate:
[5] Now therefore I confirm unto thee all the oblations which the kings before me granted thee, and whatsoever gifts besides they granted.
[6] I give thee leave also to coin money for thy country with thine own stamp.
[7] And as concerning Jerusalem and the sanctuary, let them be free; and all the armour that thou hast made, and fortresses that thou hast built, and keepest in thine hands, let them remain unto thee.
[8] And if anything be, or shall be, owing to the king, let it be forgiven thee from this time forth for evermore.
[9] Furthermore, when we have obtained our kingdom, we will honour thee, and thy nation, and thy temple, with great honour, so that your honour shall be known throughout the world.
[10] In the hundred threescore and fourteenth year went Antiochus into the land of his fathers: at which time all the forces came together unto him, so that few were left with Tryphon.
[11] Wherefore being pursued by king Antiochus, he fled unto Dora, which lieth by the sea side:
[12] For he saw that troubles came upon him all at once, and that his forces had forsaken him.
[13] Then camped Antiochus against Dora, having with him an hundred and twenty thousand men of war, and eight thousand horsemen.
[14] And when he had compassed the city round about, and joined ships close to the town on the sea side, he vexed the city by land and by sea, neither suffered he any to go out or in.
[15] In the mean season came Numenius and his company from Rome, having letters to the kings and countries; wherein were written these things:
[16] Lucius, consul of the Romans unto king Ptolemee, greeting:
[17] The Jews' ambassadors, our friends and confederates, came unto us to renew the old friendship and league, being sent from Simon the high priest, and from the people of the Jews:
[18] And they brought a shield of gold of a thousand pound.
[19] We thought it good therefore to write unto the kings and countries, that they should do them no harm, nor fight against them, their cities, or countries, nor yet aid their enemies against them.
[20] It seemed also good to us to receive the shield of them.
[21] If therefore there be any pestilent fellows, that have fled from their country unto you, deliver them unto Simon the high priest, that he may punish them according to their own law.

[22] The same things wrote he likewise unto Demetrius the king, and Attalus, to Ariarathes, and Arsaces,
[23] And to all the countries and to Sampsames, and the Lacedemonians, and to Delus, and Myndus, and Sicyon, and Caria, and Samos, and Pamphylia, and Lycia, and Halicarnassus, and Rhodus, and Aradus, and Cos, and Side, and Aradus, and Gortyna, and Cnidus, and Cyprus, and Cyrene.
[24] And the copy hereof they wrote to Simon the high priest.
[25] So Antiochus the king camped against Dora the second day, assaulting it continually, and making engines, by which means he shut up Tryphon, that he could neither go out nor in.
[26] At that time Simon sent him two thousand chosen men to aid him; silver also, and gold, and much armour.
[27] Nevertheless he would not receive them, but brake all the covenants which he had made with him afore, and became strange unto him.
[28] Furthermore he sent unto him Athenobius, one of his friends, to commune with him, and say, Ye withhold Joppa and Gazera; with the tower that is in Jerusalem, which are cities of my realm.
[29] The borders thereof ye have wasted, and done great hurt in the land, and got the dominion of many places within my kingdom.
[30] Now therefore deliver the cities which ye have taken, and the tributes of the places, whereof ye have gotten dominion without the borders of Judea:
[31] Or else give me for them five hundred talents of silver; and for the harm that ye have done, and the tributes of the cities, other five hundred talents: if not, we will come and fight against you
[32] So Athenobius the king's friend came to Jerusalem: and when he saw the glory of Simon, and the cupboard of gold and silver plate, and his great attendance, he was astonished, and told him the king's message.
[33] Then answered Simon, and said unto him, We have neither taken other men's land, nor holden that which appertaineth to others, but the inheritance of our fathers, which our enemies had wrongfully in possession a certain time.
[34] Wherefore we, having opportunity, hold the inheritance of our fathers.
[35] And whereas thou demandest Joppa and Gazera, albeit they did great harm unto the people in our country, yet will we give thee an hundred talents for them. Hereunto Athenobius answered him not a word;
[36] But returned in a rage to the king, and made report unto him of these speeches, and of the glory of Simon, and of all that he had seen: whereupon the king was exceeding wroth.
[37] In the mean time fled Tryphon by ship unto Orthosias.
[38] Then the king made Cendebeus captain of the sea coast, and gave him an host of footmen and horsemen,
[39] And commanded him to remove his host toward Judea; also he commanded him to build up Cedron, and to fortify the gates, and to war against the people; but as for the king himself, he pursued Tryphon.
[40] So Cendebeus came to Jamnia and began to provoke the people and to invade Judea, and to take the people prisoners, and slay them.
[41] And when he had built up Cedrou, he set horsemen there, and an host of footmen, to the end that issuing out they might make outroads upon the ways of Judea, as the king had commanded him.

1Mac.16

[1] Then came up John from Gazera, and told Simon his father what Cendebeus had done.
[2] Wherefore Simon called his two eldest

sons, Judas and John, and said unto them, I, and my brethren, and my father's house, have ever from my youth unto this day fought against the enemies of Israel; and things have prospered so well in our hands, that we have delivered Israel oftentimes.
[3] But now I am old, and ye, by God's mercy, are of a sufficient age: be ye instead of me and my brother, and go and fight for our nation, and the help from heaven be with you.
[4] So he chose out of the country twenty thousand men of war with horsemen, who went out against Cendebeus, and rested that night at Modin.
[5] And when as they rose in the morning, and went into the plain, behold, a mighty great host both of footmen and horsemen came against them: howbeit there was a water brook betwixt them.
[6] So he and his people pitched over against them: and when he saw that the people were afraid to go over the water brook, he went first over himself, and then the men seeing him passed through after him.
[7] That done, he divided his men, and set the horsemen in the midst of the footmen: for the enemies' horsemen were very many.
[8] Then sounded they with the holy trumpets: whereupon Cendebeus and his host were put to flight, so that many of them were slain, and the remnant gat them to the strong hold.
[9] At that time was Judas John's brother wounded; but John still followed after them, until he came to Cedron, which Cendebeus had built.
[10] So they fled even unto the towers in the fields of Azotus; wherefore he burned it with fire: so that there were slain of them about two thousand men. Afterward he returned into the land of Judea in peace.
[11] Moreover in the plain of Jericho was Ptolemeus the son of Abubus made captain, and he had abundance of silver and gold:
[12] For he was the high priest's son in law.
[13] Wherefore his heart being lifted up, he thought to get the country to himself, and thereupon consulted deceitfully against Simon and his sons to destroy them.
[14] Now Simon was visiting the cities that were in the country, and taking care for the good ordering of them; at which time he came down himself to Jericho with his sons, Mattathias and Judas, in the hundred threescore and seventeenth year, in the eleventh month, called Sabat:
[15] Where the son of Abubus receiving them deceitfully into a little hold, called Docus, which he had built, made them a great banquet: howbeit he had hid men there.
[16] So when Simon and his sons had drunk largely, Ptolemee and his men rose up, and took their weapons, and came upon Simon into the banqueting place, and slew him, and his two sons, and certain of his servants.
[17] In which doing he committed a great treachery, and recompensed evil for good.
[18] Then Ptolemee wrote these things, and sent to the king, that he should send him an host to aid him, and he would deliver him the country and cities.
[19] He sent others also to Gazera to kill John: and unto the tribunes he sent letters to come unto him, that he might give them silver, and gold, and rewards.
[20] And others he sent to take Jerusalem, and the mountain of the temple.
[21] Now one had run afore to Gazera and told John that his father and brethren were slain, and, quoth he, Ptolemee hath sent to slay thee also.
[22] Hereof when he heard, he was sore astonished: so he laid hands on them that were come to destroy him, and slew them;

for he knew that they sought to make him away.

[23] As concerning the rest of the acts of John, and his wars, and worthy deeds which he did, and the building of the walls which he made, and his doings,

[24] Behold, these are written in the chronicles of his priesthood, from the time he was made high priest after his father.

2 Maccabees

2Mac.1

[1] The brethren, the Jews that be at Jerusalem and in the land of Judea, wish unto the brethren, the Jews that are throughout Egypt health and peace:

[2] God be gracious unto you, and remember his covenant that he made with Abraham, Isaac, and Jacob, his faithful servants;

[3] And give you all an heart to serve him, and to do his will, with a good courage and a willing mind;

[4] And open your hearts in his law and commandments, and send you peace,

[5] And hear your prayers, and be at one with you, and never forsake you in time of trouble.

[6] And now we be here praying for you.

[7] What time as Demetrius reigned, in the hundred threescore and ninth year, we the Jews wrote unto you in the extremity of trouble that came upon us in those years, from the time that Jason and his company revolted from the holy land and kingdom,

[8] And burned the porch, and shed innocent blood: then we prayed unto Jah, and were heard; we offered also sacrifices and fine flour, and lighted the lamps, and set forth the loaves.

[9] And now see that ye keep the feast of tabernacles in the month Casleu.

[10] In the hundred fourscore and eighth year, the people that were at Jerusalem and in Judea, and the council, and Judas, sent greeting and health unto Aristobulus, king Ptolemeus' master, who was of the stock of the anointed priests, and to the Jews that were in Egypt:

[11] Insomuch as God hath delivered us from great perils, we thank him highly, as having been in battle against a king.

[12] For he cast them out that fought within the holy city.

[13] For when the leader was come into Persia, and the army with him that seemed invincible, they were slain in the temple of Nanea by the deceit of Nanea's priests.

[14] For Antiochus, as though he would marry her, came into the place, and his friends that were with him, to receive money in name of a dowry.

[15] Which when the priests of Nanea had set forth, and he was entered with a small company into the compass of the temple, they shut the temple as soon as Antiochus was come in:

[16] And opening a privy door of the roof, they threw stones like thunderbolts, and struck down the captain, hewed them in pieces, smote off their heads and cast them to those that were without.

[17] Blessed be our God in all things, who hath delivered up the ungodly.

[18] Therefore whereas we are now purposed to keep the purification of the temple upon the five and twentieth day of the month Casleu, we thought it necessary to certify you thereof, that ye also might keep it, as the feast of the tabernacles, and of the fire, which was given us when Neemias offered sacrifice, after that he had builded the temple and the altar.

[19] For when our fathers were led into Persia, the priests that were then devout took the fire of the altar privily, and hid it in an hollow place of a pit without water, where they kept it sure, so that the place was

unknown to all men.

[20] Now after many years, when it pleased God, Neemias, being sent from the king of Persia, did send of the posterity of those priests that had hid it to the fire: but when they told us they found no fire, but thick water;

[21] Then commanded he them to draw it up, and to bring it; and when the sacrifices were laid on, Neemias commanded the priests to sprinkle the wood and the things laid thereupon with the water.

[22] When this was done, and the time came that the sun shone, which afore was hid in the cloud, there was a great fire kindled, so that every man marvelled.

[23] And the priests made a prayer whilst the sacrifice was consuming, I say, both the priests, and all the rest, Jonathan beginning, and the rest answering thereunto, as Neemias did.

[24] And the prayer was after this manner; O Lord, Lord God, Creator of all things, who art fearful and strong, and righteous, and merciful, and the only and gracious King,

[25] The only giver of all things, the only just, almighty, and everlasting, thou that deliverest Israel from all trouble, and didst choose the fathers, and sanctify them:

[26] Receive the sacrifice for thy whole people Israel, and preserve thine own portion, and sanctify it.

[27] Gather those together that are scattered from us, deliver them that serve among the heathen, look upon them that are despised and abhorred, and let the heathen know that thou art our God.

[28] Punish them that oppress us, and with pride do us wrong.

[29] Plant thy people again in thy holy place, as Moses hath spoken.

[30] And the priests sung psalms of thanksgiving.

[31] Now when the sacrifice was consumed, Neemias commanded the water that was left to be poured on the great stones.

[32] When this was done, there was kindled a flame: but it was consumed by the light that shined from the altar.

[33] So when this matter was known, it was told the king of Persia, that in the place, where the priests that were led away had hid the fire, there appeared water, and that Neemias had purified the sacrifices therewith.

[34] Then the king, inclosing the place, made it holy, after he had tried the matter.

[35] And the king took many gifts, and bestowed thereof on those whom he would gratify.

[36] And Neemias called this thing Naphthar, which is as much as to say, a cleansing: but many men call it Nephi.

2Mac.2

[1] It is also found in the records, that Jeremy the prophet commanded them that were carried away to take of the fire, as it hath been signified:

[2] And how that the prophet, having given them the law, charged them not to forget the commandments of Jah, and that they should not err in their minds, when they see images of silver and gold, with their ornaments.

[3] And with other such speeches exhorted he them, that the law should not depart from their hearts.

[4] It was also contained in the same writing, that the prophet, being warned of God, commanded the tabernacle and the ark to go with him, as he went forth into the mountain, where Moses climbed up, and saw the heritage of God.

[5] And when Jeremy came thither, he found an hollow cave, wherein he laid the tabernacle, and the ark, and the altar of incense, and so stopped the door.

[6] And some of those that followed him came to mark the way, but they could not find it.

[7] Which when Jeremy perceived, he blamed them, saying, As for that place, it shall be unknown until the time that God gather his people again together, and receive them unto mercy.
[8] Then shall Jah shew them these things, and the glory of Jah shall appear, and the cloud also, as it was shewed under Moses, and as when Solomon desired that the place might be honourably sanctified.
[9] It was also declared, that he being wise offered the sacrifice of dedication, and of the finishing of the temple.
[10] And as when Moses prayed unto Jah, the fire came down from heaven, and consumed the sacrifices: even so prayed Solomon also, and the fire came down from heaven, and consumed the burnt offerings.
[11] And Moses said, Because the sin offering was not to be eaten, it was consumed.
[12] So Solomon kept those eight days.
[13] The same things also were reported in the writings and commentaries of Neemias; and how he founding a library gathered together the acts of the kings, and the prophets, and of David, and the epistles of the kings concerning the holy gifts.
[14] In like manner also Judas gathered together all those things that were lost by reason of the war we had, and they remain with us,
[15] Wherefore if ye have need thereof, send some to fetch them unto you.
[16] Whereas we then are about to celebrate the purification, we have written unto you, and ye shall do well, if ye keep the same days.
[17] We hope also, that the God, that delivered all his people, and gave them all an heritage, and the kingdom, and the priesthood, and the sanctuary,
[18] As he promised in the law, will shortly have mercy upon us, and gather us together out of every land under heaven into the holy place: for he hath delivered us out of great troubles, and hath purified the place.
[19] Now as concerning Judas Maccabeus, and his brethren, and the purification of the great temple, and the dedication of the altar,
[20] And the wars against Antiochus Epiphanes, and Eupator his son,
[21] And the manifest signs that came from heaven unto those that behaved themselves manfully to their honour for Judaism: so that, being but a few, they overcame the whole country, and chased barbarous multitudes,
[22] And recovered again the temple renowned all the world over, and freed the city, and upheld the laws which were going down, Jah being gracious unto them with all favour:
[23] All these things, I say, being declared by Jason of Cyrene in five books, we will assay to abridge in one volume.
[24] For considering the infinite number, and the difficulty which they find that desire to look into the narrations of the story, for the variety of the matter,
[25] We have been careful, that they that will read may have delight, and that they that are desirous to commit to memory might have ease, and that all into whose hands it comes might have profit.
[26] Therefore to us, that have taken upon us this painful labour of abridging, it was not easy, but a matter of sweat and watching;
[27] Even as it is no ease unto him that prepareth a banquet, and seeketh the benefit of others: yet for the pleasuring of many we will undertake gladly this great pains;
[28] Leaving to the author the exact handling of every particular, and labouring to follow the rules of an abridgement.
[29] For as the master builder of a new house must care for the whole building; but he that undertaketh to set it out, and paint it, must seek out fit things for the adorning thereof: even so I think it is with us.
[30] To stand upon every point, and go over things at large, and to be curious in

particulars, belongeth to the first author of the story:

[31] But to use brevity, and avoid much labouring of the work, is to be granted to him that will make an abridgment.

[32] Here then will we begin the story: only adding thus much to that which hath been said, that it is a foolish thing to make a long prologue, and to be short in the story itself.

2Mac.3

[1] Now when the holy city was inhabited with all peace, and the laws were kept very well, because of the godliness of Onias the high priest, and his hatred of wickedness,

[2] It came to pass that even the kings themselves did honour the place, and magnify the temple with their best gifts;

[3] Insomuch that Seleucus of Asia of his own revenues bare all the costs belonging to the service of the sacrifices.

[4] But one Simon of the tribe of Benjamin, who was made governor of the temple, fell out with the high priest about disorder in the city.

[5] And when he could not overcome Onias, he gat him to Apollonius the son of Thraseas, who then was governor of Celosyria and Phenice,

[6] And told him that the treasury in Jerusalem was full of infinite sums of money, so that the multitude of their riches, which did not pertain to the account of the sacrifices, was innumerable, and that it was possible to bring all into the king's hand.

[7] Now when Apollonius came to the king, and had shewed him of the money whereof he was told, the king chose out Heliodorus his treasurer, and sent him with a commandment to bring him the foresaid money.

[8] So forthwith Heliodorus took his journey; under a colour of visiting the cities of Celosyria and Phenice, but indeed to fulfil the king's purpose.

[9] And when he was come to Jerusalem, and had been courteously received of the high priest of the city, he told him what intelligence was given of the money, and declared wherefore he came, and asked if these things were so indeed.

[10] Then the high priest told him that there was such money laid up for the relief of widows and fatherless children:

[11] And that some of it belonged to Hircanus son of Tobias, a man of great dignity, and not as that wicked Simon had misinformed: the sum whereof in all was four hundred talents of silver, and two hundred of gold:

[12] And that it was altogether impossible that such wrongs should be done unto them, that had committed it to the holiness of the place, and to the majesty and inviolable sanctity of the temple, honoured over all the world.

[13] But Heliodorus, because of the king's commandment given him, said, That in any wise it must be brought into the king's treasury.

[14] So at the day which he appointed he entered in to order this matter: wherefore there was no small agony throughout the whole city.

[15] But the priests, prostrating themselves before the altar in their priests' vestments, called unto heaven upon him that made a law concerning things given to he kept, that they should safely be preserved for such as had committed them to be kept.

[16] Then whoso had looked the high priest in the face, it would have wounded his heart: for his countenance and the changing of his colour declared the inward agony of his mind.

[17] For the man was so compassed with fear and horror of the body, that it was manifest to them that looked upon him, what sorrow he had now in his heart.

[18] Others ran flocking out of their houses

to the general supplication, because the place was like to come into contempt.
[19] And the women, girt with sackcloth under their breasts, abounded in the streets, and the virgins that were kept in ran, some to the gates, and some to the walls, and others looked out of the windows.
[20] And all, holding their hands toward heaven, made supplication.
[21] Then it would have pitied a man to see the falling down of the multitude of all sorts, and the fear of the high priest being in such an agony.
[22] They then called upon the Almighty Lord to keep the things committed of trust safe and sure for those that had committed them.
[23] Nevertheless Heliodorus executed that which was decreed.
[24] Now as he was there present himself with his guard about the treasury, Jah of spirits, and the Prince of all power, caused a great apparition, so that all that presumed to come in with him were astonished at the power of God, and fainted, and were sore afraid.
[25] For there appeared unto them an horse with a terrible rider upon him, and adorned with a very fair covering, and he ran fiercely, and smote at Heliodorus with his forefeet, and it seemed that he that sat upon the horse had complete harness of gold.
[26] Moreover two other young men appeared before him, notable in strength, excellent in beauty, and comely in apparel, who stood by him on either side; and scourged him continually, and gave him many sore stripes.
[27] And Heliodorus fell suddenly unto the ground, and was compassed with great darkness: but they that were with him took him up, and put him into a litter.
[28] Thus him, that lately came with a great train and with all his guard into the said treasury, they carried out, being unable to help himself with his weapons: and manifestly they acknowledged the power of God.
[29] For he by the hand of God was cast down, and lay speechless without all hope of life.
[30] But they praised Jah, that had miraculously honoured his own place: for the temple; which a little afore was full of fear and trouble, when the Almighty Lord appeared, was filled with joy and gladness.
[31] Then straightways certain of Heliodorus' friends prayed Onias, that he would call upon the most High to grant him his life, who lay ready to give up the ghost.
[32] So the high priest, suspecting lest the king should misconceive that some treachery had been done to Heliodorus by the Jews, offered a sacrifice for the health of the man.
[33] Now as the high priest was making an atonement, the same young men in the same clothing appeared and stood beside Heliodorus, saying, Give Onias the high priest great thanks, insomuch as for his sake Jah hath granted thee life:
[34] And seeing that thou hast been scourged from heaven, declare unto all men the mighty power of God. And when they had spoken these words, they appeared no more.
[35] So Heliodorus, after he had offered sacrifice unto Jah, and made great vows unto him that had saved his life, and saluted Onias, returned with his host to the king.
[36] Then testified he to all men the works of the great God, which he had seen with his eyes.
[37] And when the king Heliodorus, who might be a fit man to be sent yet once again to Jerusalem, he said,
[38] If thou hast any enemy or traitor, send him thither, and thou shalt receive him well scourged, if he escape with his life: for in that place, no doubt; there is an especial power of God.
[39] For he that dwelleth in heaven hath his

eye on that place, and defendeth it; and he beateth and destroyeth them that come to hurt it.
[40] And the things concerning Heliodorus, and the keeping of the treasury, fell out on this sort.

2Mac.4

[1] This Simon now, of whom we spake afore, having been a betrayer of the money, and of his country, slandered Onias, as if he ha terrified Heliodorus, and been the worker of these evils.
[2] Thus was he bold to call him a traitor, that had deserved well of the city, and tendered his own nation, and was so zealous of the laws.
[3] But when their hatred went so far, that by one of Simon's faction murders were committed,
[4] Onias seeing the danger of this contention, and that Apollonius, as being the governor of Celosyria and Phenice, did rage, and increase Simon's malice,
[5] He went to the king, not to be an accuser of his countrymen, but seeking the good of all, both publick and private:
[6] For he saw that it was impossible that the state should continue quiet, and Simon leave his folly, unless the king did look thereunto.
[7] But after the death of Seleucus, when Antiochus, called Epiphanes, took the kingdom, Jason the brother of Onias laboured underhand to be high priest,
[8] Promising unto the king by intercession three hundred and threescore talents of silver, and of another revenue eighty talents:
[9] Beside this, he promised to assign an hundred and fifty more, if he might have licence to set him up a place for exercise, and for the training up of youth in the fashions of the heathen, and to write them of Jerusalem by the name of Antiochians.
[10] Which when the king had granted, and he had gotten into his hand the rule he forthwith brought his own nation to Greekish fashion.
[11] And the royal privileges granted of special favour to the Jews by the means of John the father of Eupolemus, who went ambassador to Rome for amity and aid, he took away; and putting down the governments which were according to the law, he brought up new customs against the law:
[12] For he built gladly a place of exercise under the tower itself, and brought the chief young men under his subjection, and made them wear a hat.
[13] Now such was the height of Greek fashions, and increase of heathenish manners, through the exceeding profaneness of Jason, that ungodly wretch, and no high priest;
[14] That the priests had no courage to serve any more at the altar, but despising the temple, and neglecting the sacrifices, hastened to be partakers of the unlawful allowance in the place of exercise, after the game of Discus called them forth;
[15] Not setting by the honours of their fathers, but liking the glory of the Grecians best of all.
[16] By reason whereof sore calamity came upon them: for they had them to be their enemies and avengers, whose custom they followed so earnestly, and unto whom they desired to be like in all things.
[17] For it is not a light thing to do wickedly against the laws of God: but the time following shall declare these things.
[18] Now when the game that was used every faith year was kept at Tyrus, the king being present,
[19] This ungracious Jason sent special messengers from Jerusalem, who were Antiochians, to carry three hundred drachms of silver to the sacrifice of Hercules, which even the bearers thereof thought fit not to bestow upon the sacrifice, because it was not

convenient, but to be reserved for other charges.

[20] This money then, in regard of the sender, was appointed to Hercules' sacrifice; but because of the bearers thereof, it was employed to the making of gallies.

[21] Now when Apollonius the son of Menestheus was sent into Egypt for the coronation of king Ptolemeus Philometor, Antiochus, understanding him not to be well affected to his affairs, provided for his own safety: whereupon he came to Joppa, and from thence to Jerusalem:

[22] Where he was honourably received of Jason, and of the city, and was brought in with torch alight, and with great shoutings: and so afterward went with his host unto Phenice.

[23] Three years afterward Jason sent Menelans, the aforesaid Simon's brother, to bear the money unto the king, and to put him in mind of certain necessary matters.

[24] But he being brought to the presence of the king, when he had magnified him for the glorious appearance of his power, got the priesthood to himself, offering more than Jason by three hundred talents of silver.

[25] So he came with the king's mandate, bringing nothing worthy the high priesthood, but having the fury of a cruel tyrant, and the rage of a savage beast.

[26] Then Jason, who had undermined his own brother, being undermined by another, was compelled to flee into the country of the Ammonites.

[27] So Menelans got the principality: but as for the money that he had promised unto the king, he took no good order for it, albeit Sostratis the ruler of the castle required it:

[28] For unto him appertained the gathering of the customs. Wherefore they were both called before the king.

[29] Now Menelans left his brother Lysimachus in his stead in the priesthood; and Sostratus left Crates, who was governor of the Cyprians.

[30] While those things were in doing, they of Tarsus and Mallos made insurrection, because they were given to the king's concubine, called Antiochus.

[31] Then came the king in all haste to appease matters, leaving Andronicus, a man in authority, for his deputy.

[32] Now Menelans, supposing that he had gotten a convenient time, stole certain vessels of gold out of the temple, and gave some of them to Andronicus, and some he sold into Tyrus and the cities round about.

[33] Which when Onias knew of a surety, he reproved him, and withdrew himself into a sanctuary at Daphne, that lieth by Antiochia.

[34] Wherefore Menelans, taking Andronicus apart, prayed, him to get Onias into his hands; who being persuaded thereunto, and coming to Onias in deceit, gave him his right hand with oaths; and though he were suspected by him, yet persuaded he him to come forth of the sanctuary: whom forthwith he shut up without regard of justice.

[35] For the which cause not only the Jews, but many also of other nations, took great indignation, and were much grieved for the unjust murder of the man.

[36] And when the king was come again from the places about Cilicia, the Jews that were in the city, and certain of the Greeks that abhorred the fact also, complained because Onias was slain without cause.

[37] Therefore Antiochus was heartily sorry, and moved to pity, and wept, because of the sober and modest behaviour of him that was dead.

[38] And being kindled with anger, forthwith he took away Andronicus his purple, and rent off his clothes, and leading him through the whole city unto that very place, where he had committed impiety against Onias, there slew he the cursed murderer. Thus Jah rewarded him his punishment, as he had deserved.

[39] Now when many sacrileges had been

committed in the city by Lysimachus with the consent of Menelans, and the fruit thereof was spread abroad, the multitude gathered themselves together against Lysimachus, many vessels of gold being already carried away.

[40] Whereupon the common people rising, and being filled with rage, Lysimachus armed about three thousand men, and began first to offer violence; one Auranus being the leader, a man far gone in years, and no less in folly.

[41] They then seeing the attempt of Lysimachus, some of them caught stones, some clubs, others taking handfuls of dust, that was next at hand, cast them all together upon Lysimachus, and those that set upon them.

[42] Thus many of them they wounded, and some they struck to the ground, and all of them they forced to flee: but as for the churchrobber himself, him they killed beside the treasury.

[43] Of these matters therefore there was an accusation laid against Menelans.

[44] Now when the king came to Tyrus, three men that were sent from the senate pleaded the cause before him:

[45] But Menelans, being now convicted, promised Ptolemee the son of Dorymenes to give him much money, if he would pacify the king toward him.

[46] Whereupon Ptolemee taking the king aside into a certain gallery, as it were to take the air, brought him to be of another mind:

[47] Insomuch that he discharged Menelans from the accusations, who notwithstanding was cause of all the mischief: and those poor men, who, if they had told their cause, yea, before the Scythians, should have been judged innocent, them he condemned to death.

[48] Thus they that followed the matter for the city, and for the people, and for the holy vessels, did soon suffer unjust punishment.

[49] Wherefore even they of Tyrus, moved with hatred of that wicked deed, caused them to be honourably buried.

[50] And so through the covetousness of them that were of power Menelans remained still in authority, increasing in malice, and being a great traitor to the citizens.

2Mac. 5

[1] About the same time Antiochus prepared his second voyage into Egypt:

[2] And then it happened, that through all the city, for the space almost of forty days, there were seen horsemen running in the air, in cloth of gold, and armed with lances, like a band of soldiers,

[3] And troops of horsemen in array, encountering and running one against another, with shaking of shields, and multitude of pikes, and drawing of swords, and casting of darts, and glittering of golden ornaments, and harness of all sorts.

[4] Wherefore every man prayed that that apparition might turn to good.

[5] Now when there was gone forth a false rumour, as though Antiochus had been dead, Jason took at the least a thousand men, and suddenly made an assault upon the city; and they that were upon the walls being put back, and the city at length taken, Menelans fled into the castle:

[6] But Jason slew his own citizens without mercy, not considering that to get the day of them of his own nation would be a most unhappy day for him; but thinking they had been his enemies, and not his countrymen, whom he conquered.

[7] Howbeit for all this he obtained not the principality, but at the last received shame for the reward of his treason, and fled again into the country of the Ammonites.

[8] In the end therefore he had an unhappy return, being accused before Aretas the king of the Arabians, fleeing from city to city, pursued of all men, hated as a forsaker of the

laws, and being had in abomination as an open enemy of his country and countrymen, he was cast out into Egypt.

[9] Thus he that had driven many out of their country perished in a strange land, retiring to the Lacedemonians, and thinking there to find succour by reason of his kindred:

[10] And he that had cast out many unburied had none to mourn for him, nor any solemn funerals at all, nor sepulchre with his fathers.

[11] Now when this that was done came to the king's car, he thought that Judea had revolted: whereupon removing out of Egypt in a furious mind, he took the city by force of arms,

[12] And commanded his men of war not to spare such as they met, and to slay such as went up upon the houses.

[13] Thus there was killing of young and old, making away of men, women, and children, slaying of virgins and infants.

[14] And there were destroyed within the space of three whole days fourscore thousand, whereof forty thousand were slain in the conflict; and no fewer sold than slain.

[15] Yet was he not content with this, but presumed to go intothe most holy temple of all the world; Menelans, that traitor to the laws, and to his own country, being his guide:

[16] And taking the holy vessels with polluted hands, and with profane hands pulling down the things that were dedicated by other kings to the augmentation and glory and honour of the place, he gave them away.

[17] And so haughty was Antiochus in mind, that he considered not that Jah was angry for a while for the sins of them that dwelt in the city, and therefore his eye was not upon the place.

[18] For had they not been formerly wrapped in many sins, this man, as soon as he had come, had forthwith been scourged, and put back from his presumption, as Heliodorus was, whom Seleucus the king sent to view the treasury.

[19] Nevertheless God did not choose the people for the place's sake, but the place far the people's sake.

[20] And therefore the place itself, that was partaker with them of the adversity that happened to the nation, did afterward communicate in the benefits sent from Jah: and as it was forsaken in the wrath of the Almighty, so again, the great Lord being reconciled, it was set up with all glory.

[21] So when Antiochus had carried out of the temple a thousand and eight hundred talents, he departed in all haste unto Antiochia, weening in his pride to make the land navigable, and the sea passable by foot: such was the haughtiness of his mind.

[22] And he left governors to vex the nation: at Jerusalem, Philip, for his country a Phrygian, and for manners more barbarous than he that set him there;

[23] And at Garizim, Andronicus; and besides, Menelans, who worse than all the rest bare an heavy hand over the citizens, having a malicious mind against his countrymen the Jews.

[24] He sent also that detestable ringleader Apollonius with an army of two and twenty thousand, commanding him to slay all those that were in their best age, and to sell the women and the younger sort:

[25] Who coming to Jerusalem, and pretending peace, did forbear till the holy day of the sabbath, when taking the Jews keeping holy day, he commanded his men to arm themselves.

[26] And so he slew all them that were gone to the celebrating of the sabbath, and running through the city with weapons slew great multitudes.

[27] But Judas Maccabeus with nine others, or thereabout, withdrew himself into the wilderness, and lived in the mountains after the manner of beasts, with his company,

who fed on herbs continually, lest they should be partakers of the pollution.

2Mac.6

[1] Not long after this the king sent an old man of Athens to compel the Jews to depart from the laws of their fathers, and not to live after the laws of God:
[2] And to pollute also the temple in Jerusalem, and to call it the temple of Jupiter Olympius; and that in Garizim, of Jupiter the Defender of strangers, as they did desire that dwelt in the place.
[3] The coming in of this mischief was sore and grievous to the people:
[4] For the temple was filled with riot and revelling by the Gentiles, who dallied with harlots, and had to do with women within the circuit of the holy places, and besides that brought in things that were not lawful.
[5] The altar also was filled with profane things, which the law forbiddeth.
[6] Neither was it lawful for a man to keep sabbath days or ancient fasts, or to profess himself at all to be a Jew.
[7] And in the day of the king's birth every month they were brought by bitter constraint to eat of the sacrifices; and when the fast of Bacchus was kept, the Jews were compelled to go in procession to Bacchus, carrying ivy.
[8] Moreover there went out a decree to the neighbour cities of the heathen, by the suggestion of Ptolemee, against the Jews, that they should observe the same fashions, and be partakers of their sacrifices:
[9] And whoso would not conform themselves to the manners of the Gentiles should be put to death. Then might a man have seen the present misery.
[10] For there were two women brought, who had circumcised their children; whom when they had openly led round about the city, the babes handing at their breasts, they cast them down headlong from the wall.
[11] And others, that had run together into caves near by, to keep the sabbath day secretly, being discovered by Philip, were all burnt together, because they made a conscience to help themselves for the honour of the most sacred day.
[12] Now I beseech those that read this book, that they be not discouraged for these calamities, but that they judge those punishments not to be for destruction, but for a chastening of our nation.
[13] For it is a token of his great goodness, when wicked doers are not suffered any long time, but forthwith punished.
[14] For not as with other nations, whom Jah patiently forbeareth to punish, till they be come to the fulness of their sins, so dealeth he with us,
[15] Lest that, being come to the height of sin, afterwards he should take vengeance of us.
[16] And therefore he never withdraweth his mercy from us: and though he punish with adversity, yet doth he never forsake his people.
[17] But let this that we at spoken be for a warning unto us. And now will we come to the declaring of the matter in a few words.
[18] Eleazar, one of the principal scribes, an aged man, and of a well favoured countenance, was constrained to open his mouth, and to eat swine's flesh.
[19] But he, choosing rather to die gloriously, than to live stained with such an abomination, spit it forth, and came of his own accord to the torment,
[20] As it behoved them to come, that are resolute to stand out against such things, as are not lawful for love of life to be tasted.
[21] But they that had the charge of that wicked feast, for the old acquaintance they had with the man, taking him aside, besought him to bring flesh of his own provision, such as was lawful for him to use, and make as if he did eat of the flesh taken from the sacrifice commanded by the king;

[22] That in so doing he might be delivered from death, and for the old friendship with them find favour.
[23] But he began to consider discreetly, and as became his age, and the excellency of his ancient years, and the honour of his gray head, whereon was come, and his most honest education from a child, or rather the holy law made and given by God: therefore he answered accordingly, and willed them straightways to send him to the grave.
[24] For it becometh not our age, said he, in any wise to dissemble, whereby many young persons might think that Eleazar, being fourscore years old and ten, were now gone to a strange religion;
[25] And so they through mine hypocrisy, and desire to live a little time and a moment longer, should be deceived by me, and I get a stain to mine old age, and make it abominable.
[26] For though for the present time I should be delivered from the punishment of men: yet should I not escape the hand of the Almighty, neither alive, nor dead.
[27] Wherefore now, manfully changing this life, I will shew myself such an one as mine age requireth,
[28] And leave a notable example to such as be young to die willingly and courageously for the honourable and holy laws. And when he had said these words, immediately he went to the torment:
[29] They that led him changing the good will they bare him a little before into hatred, because the foresaid speeches proceeded, as they thought, from a desperate mind.
[30] But when he was ready to die with stripes, he groaned, and said, It is manifest unto Jah, that hath the holy knowledge, that whereas I might have been delivered from death, I now endure sore pains in body by being beaten: but in soul am well content to suffer these things, because I fear him.
[31] And thus this man died, leaving his death for an example of a noble courage, and a memorial of virtue, not only unto young men, but unto all his nation.

2Mac.7

[1] It came to pass also, that seven brethren with their mother were taken, and compelled by the king against the law to taste swine's flesh, and were tormented with scourges and whips.
[2] But one of them that spake first said thus, What wouldest thou ask or learn of us? we are ready to die, rather than to transgress the laws of our fathers.
[3] Then the king, being in a rage, commanded pans and caldrons to be made hot:
[4] Which forthwith being heated, he commanded to cut out the tongue of him that spake first, and to cut off the utmost parts of his body, the rest of his brethren and his mother looking on.
[5] Now when he was thus maimed in all his members, he commanded him being yet alive to be brought to the fire, and to be fried in the pan: and as the vapour of the pan was for a good space dispersed, they exhorted one another with the mother to die manfully, saying thus,
[6] Jah God looketh upon us, and in truth hath comfort in us, as Moses in his song, which witnessed to their faces, declared, saying, And he shall be comforted in his servants.
[7] So when the first was dead after this number, they brought the second to make him a mocking stock: and when they had pulled off the skin of his head with the hair, they asked him, Wilt thou eat, before thou be punished throughout every member of thy body?
[8] But he answered in his own language, and said, No. Wherefore he also received the next torment in order, as the former did.
[9] And when he was at the last gasp, he

said, Thou like a fury takest us out of this present life, but the King of the world shall raise us up, who have died for his laws, unto everlasting life.

[10] After him was the third made a mocking stock: and when he was required, he put out his tongue, and that right soon, holding forth his hands manfully.

[11] And said courageously, These I had from heaven; and for his laws I despise them; and from him I hope to receive them again.

[12] Insomuch that the king, and they that were with him, marvelled at the young man's courage, for that he nothing regarded the pains.

[13] Now when this man was dead also, they tormented and mangled the fourth in like manner.

[14] So when he was ready to die he said thus, It is good, being put to death by men, to look for hope from God to be raised up again by him: as for thee, thou shalt have no resurrection to life.

[15] Afterward they brought the fifth also, and mangled him.

[16] Then looked he unto the king, and said, Thou hast power over men, thou art corruptible, thou doest what thou wilt; yet think not that our nation is forsaken of God;

[17] But abide a while, and behold his great power, how he will torment thee and thy seed.

[18] After him also they brought the sixth, who being ready to die said, Be not deceived without cause: for we suffer these things for ourselves, having sinned against our God: therefore marvellous things are done unto us.

[19] But think not thou, that takest in hand to strive against God, that thou shalt escape unpunished.

[20] But the mother was marvellous above all, and worthy of honourable memory: for when she saw her seven sons slain within the space of one day, she bare it with a good courage, because of the hope that she had in Jah.

[21] Yea, she exhorted every one of them in her own language, filled with courageous spirits; and stirring up her womanish thoughts with a manly stomach, she said unto them,

[22] I cannot tell how ye came into my womb: for I neither gave you breath nor life, neither was it I that formed the members of every one of you;

[23] But doubtless the Creator of the world, who formed the generation of man, and found out the beginning of all things, will also of his own mercy give you breath and life again, as ye now regard not your own selves for his laws' sake.

[24] Now Antiochus, thinking himself despised, and suspecting it to be a reproachful speech, whilst the youngest was yet alive, did not only exhort him by words, but also assured him with oaths, that he would make him both a rich and a happy man, if he would turn from the laws of his fathers; and that also he would take him for his friend, and trust him with affairs.

[25] But when the young man would in no case hearken unto him, the king called his mother, and exhorted her that she would counsel the young man to save his life.

[26] And when he had exhorted her with many words, she promised him that she would counsel her son.

[27] But she bowing herself toward him, laughing the cruel tyrant to scorn, spake in her country language on this manner; O my son, have pity upon me that bare thee nine months in my womb, and gave thee such three years, and nourished thee, and brought thee up unto this age, and endured the troubles of education.

[28] I beseech thee, my son, look upon the heaven and the earth, and all that is therein, and consider that God made them of things that were not; and so was mankind made likewise.

[29] Fear not this tormentor, but, being worthy of thy brethren, take thy death that I may receive thee again in mercy with thy brethren.
[30] Whiles she was yet speaking these words, the young man said, Whom wait ye for? I will not obey the king's commandment: but I will obey the commandment of the law that was given unto our fathers by Moses.
[31] And thou, that hast been the author of all mischief against the Hebrews, shalt not escape the hands of God.
[32] For we suffer because of our sins.
[33] And though the living Lord be angry with us a little while for our chastening and correction, yet shall he be at one again with his servants.
[34] But thou, O godless man, and of all other most wicked, be not lifted up without a cause, nor puffed up with uncertain hopes, lifting up thy hand against the servants of God:
[35] For thou hast not yet escaped the judgment of Almighty God, who seeth all things.
[36] For our brethren, who now have suffered a short pain, are dead under God's covenant of everlasting life: but thou, through the judgment of God, shalt receive just punishment for thy pride.
[37] But I, as my brethren, offer up my body and life for the laws of our fathers, beseeching God that he would speedily be merciful unto our nation; and that thou by torments and plagues mayest confess, that he alone is God;
[38] And that in me and my brethren the wrath of the Almighty, which is justly brought upon our nation, may cease.
[39] Than the king' being in a rage, handed him worse than all the rest, and took it grievously that he was mocked.
[40] So this man died undefiled, and put his whole trust in Jah.
[41] Last of all after the sons the mother died.
[42] Let this be enough now to have spoken concerning the idolatrous feasts, and the extreme tortures.

2Mac.8

[1] Then Judas Maccabeus, and they that were with him, went privily into the towns, and called their kinsfolks together, and took unto them all such as continued in the Jews' religion, and assembled about six thousand men.
[2] And they called upon Jah, that he would look upon the people that was trodden down of all; and also pity the temple profaned of ungodly men;
[3] And that he would have compassion upon the city, sore defaced, and ready to be made even with the ground; and hear the blood that cried unto him,
[4] And remember the wicked slaughter of harmless infants, and the blasphemies committed against his name; and that he would shew his hatred against the wicked.
[5] Now when Maccabeis had his company about him, he could not be withstood by the heathen: for the wrath of Jah was turned into mercy.
[6] Therefore he came at unawares, and burnt up towns and cities, and got into his hands the most commodious places, and overcame and put to flight no small number of his enemies.
[7] But specially took he advantage of the night for such privy attempts, insomuch that the fruit of his holiness was spread every where.
[8] So when Philip saw that this man increased by little and little, and that things prospered with him still more and more, he wrote unto Ptolemeus, the governor of Celosyria and Phenice, to yield more aid to the king's affairs.
[9] Then forthwith choosing Nicanor the son

of Patroclus, one of his special friends, he sent him with no fewer than twenty thousand of all nations under him, to root out the whole generation of the Jews; and with him he joined also Gorgias a captain, who in matters of war had great experience.

[10] So Nicanor undertook to make so much money of the captive Jews, as should defray the tribute of two thousand talents, which the king was to pay to the Romans.

[11] Wherefore immediately he sent to the cities upon the sea coast, proclaiming a sale of the captive Jews, and promising that they should have fourscore and ten bodies for one talent, not expecting the vengeance that was to follow upon him from the Almighty God.

[12] Now when word was brought unto Judas of Nicanor's coming, and he had imparted unto those that were with him that the army was at hand,

[13] They that were fearful, and distrusted the justice of God, fled, and conveyed themselves away.

[14] Others sold all that they had left, and withal besought Jah to deliver them, sold by the wicked Nicanor before they met together:

[15] And if not for their own sakes, yet for the covenants he had made with their fathers, and for his holy and glorious name's sake, by which they were called.

[16] So Maccabeus called his men together unto the number of six thousand, and exhorted them not to be stricken with terror of the enemy, nor to fear the great multitude of the heathen, who came wrongly against them; but to fight manfully,

[17] And to set before their eyes the injury that they had unjustly done to the holy place, and the cruel handling of the city, whereof they made a mockery, and also the taking away of the government of their forefathers:

[18] For they, said he, trust in their weapons and boldness; but our confidence is in the Almighty who at a beck can cast down both them that come against us, and also all the world.

[19] Moreover, he recounted unto them what helps their forefathers had found, and how they were delivered, when under Sennacherib an hundred fourscore and five thousand perished.

[20] And he told them of the battle that they had in Babylon with the Galatians, how they came but eight thousand in all to the business, with four thousand Macedonians, and that the Macedonians being perplexed, the eight thousand destroyed an hundred and twenty thousand because of the help that they had from heaven, and so received a great booty.

[21] Thus when he had made them bold with these words, and ready to die for the law and the country, he divided his army into four parts;

[22] And joined with himself his own brethren, leaders of each band, to wit Simon, and Joseph, and Jonathan, giving each one fifteen hundred men.

[23] Also he appointed Eleazar to read the holy book: and when he had given them this watchword, The help of God; himself leading the first band,

[24] And by the help of the Almighty they slew above nine thousand of their enemies, and wounded and maimed the most part of Nicanor's host, and so put all to flight;

[25] And took their money that came to buy them, and pursued them far: but lacking time they returned:

[26] For it was the day before the sabbath, and therefore they would no longer pursue them.

[27] So when they had gathered their armour together, and spoiled their enemies, they occupied themselves about the sabbath, yielding exceeding praise and thanks to Jah, who had preserved them unto that day, which was the beginning of mercy distilling upon them.

[28] And after the sabbath, when they had given part of the spoils to the maimed, and

the widows, and orphans, the residue they divided among themselves and their servants.

[29] When this was done, and they had made a common supplication, they besought the merciful Lord to be reconciled with his servants for ever.

[30] Moreover of those that were with Timotheus and Bacchides, who fought against them, they slew above twenty thousand, and very easily got high and strong holds, and divided among themselves many spoils more, and made the maimed, orphans, widows, yea, and the aged also, equal in spoils with themselves.

[31] And when they had gathered their armour together, they laid them up all carefully in convenient places, and the remnant of the spoils they brought to Jerusalem.

[32] They slew also Philarches, that wicked person, who was with Timotheus, and had annoyed the Jews many ways.

[33] Furthermore at such time as they kept the feast for the victory in their country they burnt Callisthenes, that had set fire upon the holy gates, who had fled into a little house; and so he received a reward meet for his wickedness.

[34] As for that most ungracious Nicanor, who had brought a thousand merchants to buy the Jews,

[35] He was through the help of Jah brought down by them, of whom he made least account; and putting off his glorious apparel, and discharging his company, he came like a fugitive servant through the midland unto Antioch having very great dishonour, for that his host was destroyed.

[36] Thus he, that took upon him to make good to the Romans their tribute by means of captives in Jerusalem, told abroad, that the Jews had God to fight for them, and therefore they could not be hurt, because they followed the laws that he gave them.

2 Mac.9

[1] About that time came Antiochus with dishonour out of the country of Persia

[2] For he had entered the city called Persepolis, and went about to rob the temple, and to hold the city; whereupon the multitude running to defend themselves with their weapons put them to flight; and so it happened, that Antiochus being put to flight of the inhabitants returned with shame.

[3] Now when he came to Ecbatane, news was brought him what had happened unto Nicanor and Timotheus.

[4] Then swelling with anger. he thought to avenge upon the Jews the disgrace done unto him by those that made him flee. Therefore commanded he his chariotman to drive without ceasing, and to dispatch the journey, the judgment of GOd now following him. For he had spoken proudly in this sort, That he would come to Jerusalem and make it a common burying place of the Jews.

[5] But Jah Almighty, the God of Isreal, smote him with an incurable and invisible plague: or as soon as he had spoken these words, a pain of the bowels that was remediless came upon him, and sore torments of the inner parts;

[6] And that most justly: for he had tormented other men's bowels with many and strange torments.

[7] Howbeit he nothing at all ceased from his bragging, but still was filled with pride, breathing out fire in his rage against the Jews, and commanding to haste the journey: but it came to pass that he fell down from his chariot, carried violently; so that having a sore fall, all the members of his body were much pained.

[8] And thus he that a little afore thought he might command the waves of the sea, (so proud was he beyond the condition of man) and weigh the high mountains in a balance, was now cast on the ground, and carried in

an horselitter, shewing forth unto all the manifest power of God.

[9] So that the worms rose up out of the body of this wicked man, and whiles he lived in sorrow and pain, his flesh fell away, and the filthiness of his smell was noisome to all his army.

[10] And the man, that thought a little afore he could reach to the stars of heaven, no man could endure to carry for his intolerable stink.

[11] Here therefore, being plagued, he began to leave off his great pride, and to come to the knowledge of himself by the scourge of God, his pain increasing every moment.

[12] And when he himself could not abide his own smell, he said these words, It is meet to be subject unto God, and that a man that is mortal should not proudly think of himself if he were God.

[13] This wicked person vowed also unto Jah, who now no more would have mercy upon him, saying thus,

[14] That the holy city (to the which he was going in haste to lay it even with the ground, and to make it a common buryingplace,) he would set at liberty:

[15] And as touching the Jews, whom he had judged not worthy so much as to be buried, but to be cast out with their children to be devoured of the fowls and wild beasts, he would make them all equals to the citizens of Athens:

[16] And the holy temple, which before he had spoiled, he would garnish with goodly gifts, and restore all the holy vessels with many more, and out of his own revenue defray the charges belonging to the sacrifices:

[17] Yea, and that also he would become a Jew himself, and go through all the world that was inhabited, and declare the power of God.

[18] But for all this his pains would not cease: for the just judgment of God was come upon him: therefore despairing of his health, he wrote unto the Jews the letter underwritten, containing the form of a supplication, after this manner:

[19] Antiochus, king and governor, to the good Jews his citizens wisheth much joy, health, and prosperity:

[20] If ye and your children fare well, and your affairs be to your contentment, I give very great thanks to God, having my hope in heaven.

[21] As for me, I was weak, or else I would have remembered kindly your honour and good will returning out of Persia, and being taken with a grievous disease, I thought it necessary to care for the common safety of all:

[22] Not distrusting mine health, but having great hope to escape this sickness.

[23] But considering that even my father, at what time he led an army into the high countries. appointed a successor,

[24] To the end that, if any thing fell out contrary to expectation, or if any tidings were brought that were grievous, they of the land, knowing to whom the state was left, might not be troubled:

[25] Again, considering how that the princes that are borderers and neighbours unto my kingdom wait for opportunities, and expect what shall be the event. I have appointed my son Antiochus king, whom I often committed and commended unto many of you, when I went up into the high provinces; to whom I have written as followeth:

[26] Therefore I pray and request you to remember the benefits that I have done unto you generally, and in special, and that every man will be still faithful to me and my son.

[27] For I am persuaded that he understanding my mind will favourably and graciously yield to your desires.

[28] Thus the murderer and blasphemer having suffered most grievously, as he entreated other men, so died he a miserable death in a strange country in the mountains.

[29] And Philip, that was brought up with

him, carried away his body, who also fearing the son of Antiochus went into Egypt to Ptolemeus Philometor.

2Mac.10

[1] Now Maccabeus and his company, Jah guiding them, recovered the temple and the city:
[2] But the altars which the heathen had built in the open street, and also the chapels, they pulled down.
[3] And having cleansed the temple they made another altar, and striking stones they took fire out of them, and offered a sacrifice after two years, and set forth incense, and lights, and shewbread.
[4] When that was done, they fell flat down, and besought Jah that they might come no more into such troubles; but if they sinned any more against him, that he himself would chasten them with mercy, and that they might not be delivered unto the blasphemous and barbarous nations.
[5] Now upon the same day that the strangers profaned the temple, on the very same day it was cleansed again, even the five and twentieth day of the same month, which is Casleu.
[6] And they kept the eight days with gladness, as in the feast of the tabernacles, remembering that not long afore they had held the feast of the tabernacles, when as they wandered in the mountains and dens like beasts.
[7] Therefore they bare branches, and fair boughs, and palms also, and sang psalms unto him that had given them good success in cleansing his place.
[8] They ordained also by a common statute and decree, That every year those days should be kept of the whole nation of the Jews.
[9] And this was the end of Antiochus, called Epiphanes.

[10] Now will we declare the acts of Antiochus Eupator, who was the son of this wicked man, gathering briefly the calamities of the wars.
[11] So when he was come to the crown, he set one Lysias over the affairs of his realm, and appointed him his chief governor of Celosyria and Phenice.
[12] For Ptolemeus, that was called Macron, choosing rather to do justice unto the Jews for the wrong that had been done unto them, endeavoured to continue peace with them.
[13] Whereupon being accused of the king's friends before Eupator, and called traitor at every word because he had left Cyprus, that Philometor had committed unto him, and departed to Antiochus Epiphanes, and seeing that he was in no honourable place, he was so discouraged, that he poisoned himself and died.
[14] But when Gorgias was governor of the holds, he hired soldiers, and nourished war continually with the Jews:
[15] And therewithall the Idumeans, having gotten into their hands the most commodious holds, kept the Jews occupied, and receiving those that were banished from Jerusalem, they went about to nourish war.
[16] Then they that were with Maccabeus made supplication, and besought God that he would be their helper; and so they ran with violence upon the strong holds of the Idumeans,
[17] And assaulting them strongly, they won the holds, and kept off all that fought upon the wall, and slew all that fell into their hands, and killed no fewer than twenty thousand.
[18] And because certain, who were no less than nine thousand, were fled together into two very strong castles, having all manner of things convenient to sustain the siege,
[19] Maccabeus left Simon and Joseph, and Zaccheus also, and them that were with him, who were enough to besiege them, and departed himself unto those places which

more needed his help.
[20] Now they that were with Simon, being led with covetousness, were persuaded for money through certain of those that were in the castle, and took seventy thousand drachms, and let some of them escape.
[21] But when it was told Maccabeus what was done, he called the governors of the people together, and accused those men, that they had sold their brethren for money, and set their enemies free to fight against them.
[22] So he slew those that were found traitors, and immediately took the two castles.
[23] And having good success with his weapons in all things he took in hand, he slew in the two holds more than twenty thousand.
[24] Now Timotheus, whom the Jews had overcome before, when he had gathered a great multitude of foreign forces, and horses out of Asia not a few, came as though he would take Jewry by force of arms.
[25] But when he drew near, they that were with Maccabeus turned themselves to pray unto God, and sprinkled earth upon their heads, and girded their loins with sackcloth,
[26] And fell down at the foot of the altar, and besought him to be merciful to them, and to be an enemy to their enemies, and an adversary to their adversaries, as the law declareth.
[27] So after the prayer they took their weapons, and went on further from the city: and when they drew near to their enemies, they kept by themselves.
[28] Now the sun being newly risen, they joined both together; the one part having together with their virtue their refuge also unto Jah for a pledge of their success and victory: the other side making their rage leader of their battle
[29] But when the battle waxed strong, there appeared unto the enemies from heaven five comely men upon horses, with bridles of gold, and two of them led the Jews,
[30] And took Maccabeus betwixt them, and covered him on every side weapons, and kept him safe, but shot arrows and lightnings against the enemies: so that being confounded with blindness, and full of trouble, they were killed.
[31] And there were slain of footmen twenty thousand and five hundred, and six hundred horsemen.
[32] As for Timotheus himself, he fled into a very strong hold, called Gawra, where Chereas was governor.
[33] But they that were with Maccabeus laid siege against the fortress courageously four days.
[34] And they that were within, trusting to the strength of the place, blasphemed exceedingly, and uttered wicked words.
[35] Nevertheless upon the fifth day early twenty young men of Maccabeus' company, inflamed with anger because of the blasphemies, assaulted the wall manly, and with a fierce courage killed all that they met withal.
[36] Others likewise ascending after them, whiles they were busied with them that were within, burnt the towers, and kindling fires burnt the blasphemers alive; and others broke open the gates, and, having received in the rest of the army, took the city,
[37] And killed Timotheus, that was hid in a certain pit, and Chereas his brother, with Apollophanes.
[38] When this was done, they praised Jah with psalms and thanksgiving, who had done so great things for Israel, and given them the victory.

2Mac.11

[1] Not long after the, Lysias the king's protector and cousin, who also managed the affairs, took sore displeasure for the things that were done.
[2] And when he had gathered about

fourscore thousand with all the horsemen, he came against the Jews, thinking to make the city an habitation of the Gentiles,
[3] And to make a gain of the temple, as of the other chapels of the heathen, and to set the high priesthood to sale every year:
[4] Not at all considering the power of God but puffed up with his ten thousands of footmen, and his thousands of horsemen, and his fourscore elephants.
[5] So he came to Judea, and drew near to Bethsura, which was a strong town, but distant from Jerusalem about five furlongs, and he laid sore siege unto it.
[6] Now when they that were with Maccabeus heard that he besieged the holds, they and all the people with lamentation and tears besought Jah that he would send a good angel to deliver Israel.
[7] Then Maccabeus himself first of all took weapons, exhorting the other that they would jeopard themselves together with him to help their brethren: so they went forth together with a willing mind.
[8] And as they were at Jerusalem, there appeared before them on horseback one in white clothing, shaking his armour of gold.
[9] Then they praised the merciful God all together, and took heart, insomuch that they were ready not only to fight with men, but with most cruel beasts, and to pierce through walls of iron.
[10] Thus they marched forward in their armour, having an helper from heaven: for Jah was merciful unto them
[11] And giving a charge upon their enemies like lions, they slew eleven thousand footmen, and sixteen hundred horsemen, and put all the other to flight.
[12] Many of them also being wounded escaped naked; and Lysias himself fled away shamefully, and so escaped.
[13] Who, as he was a man of understanding, casting with himself what loss he had had, and considering that the Hebrews could not be overcome, because the Almighty God helped them, he sent unto them,
[14] And persuaded them to agree to all reasonable conditions, and promised that he would persuade the king that he must needs be a friend unto them.
[15] Then Maccabeus consented to all that Lysias desired, being careful of the common good; and whatsoever Maccabeus wrote unto Lysias concerning the Jews, the king granted it.
[16] For there were letters written unto the Jews from Lysias to this effect: Lysias unto the people of the Jews sendeth greeting:
[17] John and Absolom, who were sent from you, delivered me the petition subscribed, and made request for the performance of the contents thereof.
[18] Therefore what things soever were meet to be reported to the king, I have declared them, and he hath granted as much as might be.
[19] And if then ye will keep yourselves loyal to the state, hereafter also will I endeavour to be a means of your good.
[20] But of the particulars I have given order both to these and the other that came from me, to commune with you.
[21] Fare ye well. The hundred and eight and fortieth year, the four and twentieth day of the month Dioscorinthius.
[22] Now the king's letter contained these words: King Antiochus unto his brother Lysias sendeth greeting:
[23] Since our father is translated unto the gods, our will is, that they that are in our realm live quietly, that every one may attend upon his own affairs.
[24] We understand also that the Jews would not consent to our father, for to be brought unto the custom of the Gentiles, but had rather keep their own manner of living: for the which cause they require of us, that we should suffer them to live after their own laws.
[25] Wherefore our mind is, that this nation

shall be in rest, and we have determined to restore them their temple, that they may live according to the customs of their forefathers.
[26] Thou shalt do well therefore to send unto them, and grant them peace, that when they are certified of our mind, they may be of good comfort, and ever go cheerfully about their own affairs.
[27] And the letter of the king unto the nation of the Jews was after this manner: King Antiochus sendeth greeting unto the council, and the rest of the Jews:
[28] If ye fare well, we have our desire; we are also in good health.
[29] Menelans declared unto us, that your desire was to return home, and to follow your own business:
[30] Wherefore they that will depart shall have safe conduct till the thirtieth day of Xanthicus with security.
[31] And the Jews shall use their own kind of meats and laws, as before; and none of them any manner of ways shall be molested for things ignorantly done.
[32] I have sent also Menelans, that he may comfort you.
[33] Fare ye well. In the hundred forty and eighth year, and the fifteenth day of the month Xanthicus.
[34] The Romans also sent unto them a letter containing these words: Quintus Memmius and Titus Manlius, ambassadors of the Romans, send greeting unto the people of the Jews.
[35] Whatsoever Lysias the king's cousin hath granted, therewith we also are well pleased.
[36] But touching such things as he judged to be referred to the king, after ye have advised thereof, send one forthwith, that we may declare as it is convenient for you: for we are now going to Antioch.
[37] Therefore send some with speed, that we may know what is your mind.
[38] Farewell. This hundred and eight and fortieth year, the fifteenth day of the month Xanthicus.

2Mac. 12

[1] When these covenants were made, Lysias went unto the king, and the Jews were about their husbandry.
[2] But of the governours of several places, Timotheus, and Apollonius the son of Genneus, also Hieronymus, and Demophon, and beside them Nicanor the governor of Cyprus, would not suffer them to be quiet and live in peace.
[3] The men of Joppa also did such an ungodly deed: they prayed the Jews that dwelt among them to go with their wives and children into the boats which they had prepared, as though they had meant them no hurt.
[4] Who accepted of it according to the common decree of the city, as being desirous to live in peace, and suspecting nothing: but when they were gone forth into the deep, they drowned no less than two hundred of them.
[5] When Judas heard of this cruelty done unto his countrymen, he commanded those that were with him to make them ready.
[6] And calling upon God the righteous Judge, he came against those murderers of his brethren, and burnt the haven by night, and set the boats on fire, and those that fled thither he slew.
[7] And when the town was shut up, he went backward, as if he would return to root out all them of the city of Joppa.
[8] But when he heard that the Jamnites were minded to do in like manner unto the Jews that dwelt among them,
[9] He came upon the Jamnites also by night, and set fire on the haven and the navy, so that the light of the fire was seen at Jerusalem two hundred and forty furlongs off.

[10] Now when they were gone from thence nine furlongs in their journey toward Timotheus, no fewer than five thousand men on foot and five hundred horsemen of the Arabians set upon him.

[11] Whereupon there was a very sore battle; but Judas' side by the help of God got the victory; so that the Nomades of Arabia, being overcome, besought Judas for peace, promising both to give him cattle, and to pleasure him otherwise.

[12] Then Judas, thinking indeed that they would be profitable in many things, granted them peace: whereupon they shook hands, and so they departed to their tents.

[13] He went also about to make a bridge to a certain strong city, which was fenced about with walls, and inhabited by people of divers countries; and the name of it was Caspis.

[14] But they that were within it put such trust in the strength of the walls and provision of victuals, that they behaved themselves rudely toward them that were with Judas, railing and blaspheming, and uttering such words as were not to be spoken.

[15] Wherefore Judas with his company, calling upon the great Lord of the world, who without rams or engines of war did cast down Jericho in the time of Joshua, gave a fierce assault against the walls,

[16] And took the city by the will of God, and made unspeakable slaughters, insomuch that a lake two furlongs broad near adjoining thereunto, being filled full, was seen running with blood.

[17] Then departed they from thence seven hundred and fifty furlongs, and came to Characa unto the Jews that are called Tubieni.

[18] But as for Timotheus, they found him not in the places: for before he had dispatched any thing, he departed from thence, having left a very strong garrison in a certain hold.

[19] Howbeit Dositheus and Sosipater, who were of Maccabeus' captains, went forth, and slew those that Timotheus had left in the fortress, above ten thousand men.

[20] And Maccabeus ranged his army by bands, and set them over the bands, and went against Timotheus, who had about him an hundred and twenty thousand men of foot, and two thousand and five hundred horsemen.

[21] Now when Timotheus had knowledge of Judas' coming, he sent the women and children and the other baggage unto a fortress called Carnion: for the town was hard to besiege, and uneasy to come unto, by reason of the straitness of all the places.

[22] But when Judas his first band came in sight, the enemies, being smitten with fear and terror through the appearing of him who seeth all things, fled amain, one running into this way, another that way, so as that they were often hurt of their own men, and wounded with the points of their own swords.

[23] Judas also was very earnest in pursuing them, killing those wicked wretches, of whom he slew about thirty thousand men.

[24] Moreover Timotheus himself fell into the hands of Dositheus and Sosipater, whom he besought with much craft to let him go with his life, because he had many of the Jews' parents, and the brethren of some of them, who, if they put him to death, should not be regarded.

[25] So when he had assured them with many words that he would restore them without hurt, according to the agreement, they let him go for the saving of their brethren.

[26] Then Maccabeus marched forth to Carnion, and to the temple of Atargatis, and there he slew five and twenty thousand persons.

[27] And after he had put to flight and destroyed them, Judas removed the host toward Ephron, a strong city, wherein Lysias

abode, and a great multitude of divers nations, and the strong young men kept the walls, and defended them mightily: wherein also was great provision of engines and darts.

[28] But when Judas and his company had called upon Almighty God, who with his power breaketh the strength of his enemies, they won the city, and slew twenty and five thousand of them that were within,

[29] From thence they departed to Scythopolis, which lieth six hundred furlongs from Jerusalem,

[30] But when the Jews that dwelt there had testified that the Scythopolitans dealt lovingly with them, and entreated them kindly in the time of their adversity;

[31] They gave them thanks, desiring them to be friendly still unto them: and so they came to Jerusalem, the feast of the weeks approaching.

[32] And after the feast, called Pentecost, they went forth against Gorgias the governor of Idumea,

[33] Who came out with three thousand men of foot and four hundred horsemen.

[34] And it happened that in their fighting together a few of the Jews were slain.

[35] At which time Dositheus, one of Bacenor's company, who was on horseback, and a strong man, was still upon Gorgias, and taking hold of his coat drew him by force; and when he would have taken that cursed man alive, a horseman of Thracia coming upon him smote off his shoulder, so that Gorgias fled unto Marisa.

[36] Now when they that were with Gorgias had fought long, and were weary, Judas called upon Jah, that he would shew himself to be their helper and leader of the battle.

[37] And with that he began in his own language, and sung psalms with a loud voice, and rushing unawares upon Gorgias' men, he put them to flight.

[38] So Judas gathered his host, and came into the city of Odollam, And when the seventh day came, they purified themselves, as the custom was, and kept the sabbath in the same place.

[39] And upon the day following, as the use had been, Judas and his company came to take up the bodies of them that were slain, and to bury them with their kinsmen in their fathers' graves.

[40] Now under the coats of every one that was slain they found things consecrated to the idols of the Jamnites, which is forbidden the Jews by the law. Then every man saw that this was the cause wherefore they were slain.

[41] All men therefore praising Jah, the righteous Judge, who had opened the things that were hid,

[42] Betook themselves unto prayer, and besought him that the sin committed might wholly be put out of remembrance. Besides, that noble Judas exhorted the people to keep themselves from sin, forsomuch as they saw before their eyes the things that came to pass for the sins of those that were slain.

[43] And when he had made a gathering throughout the company to the sum of two thousand drachms of silver, he sent it to Jerusalem to offer a sin offering, doing therein very well and honestly, in that he was mindful of the resurrection:

[44] For if he had not hoped that they that were slain should have risen again, it had been superfluous and vain to pray for the dead.

[45] And also in that he perceived that there was great favour laid up for those that died godly, it was an holy and good thought. Whereupon he made a reconciliation for the dead, that they might be delivered from sin.

2Mac. 13

[1] In the hundred forty and ninth year it was told Judas, that Antiochus Eupator was coming with a great power into Judea,

[2] And with him Lysias his protector, and ruler of his affairs, having either of them a Grecian power of footmen, an hundred and ten thousand, and horsemen five thousand and three hundred, and elephants two and twenty, and three hundred chariots armed with hooks.

[3] Menelans also joined himself with them, and with great dissimulation encouraged Antiochus, not for the safeguard of the country, but because he thought to have been made governor.

[4] But the King of kings moved Antiochus' mind against this wicked wretch, and Lysias informed the king that this man was the cause of all mischief, so that the king commanded to bring him unto Berea, and to put him to death, as the manner is in that place.

[5] Now there was in that place a tower of fifty cubits high, full of ashes, and it had a round instrument which on every side hanged down into the ashes.

[6] And whosoever was condemned of sacrilege, or had committed any other grievous crime, there did all men thrust him unto death.

[7] Such a death it happened that wicked man to die, not having so much as burial in the earth; and that most justly:

[8] For inasmuch as he had committed many sins about the altar, whose fire and ashes were holy, he received his death in ashes.

[9] Now the king came with a barbarous and haughty mind to do far worse to the Jews, than had been done in his father's time.

[10] Which things when Judas perceived, he commanded the multitude to call upon Jah night and day, that if ever at any other time, he would now also help them, being at the point to be put from their law, from their country, and from the holy temple:

[11] And that he would not suffer the people, that had even now been but a little refreshed, to be in subjection to the blasphemous nations.

[12] So when they had all done this together, and besought the merciful Lord with weeping and fasting, and lying flat upon the ground three days long, Judas, having exhorted them, commanded they should be in a readiness.

[13] And Judas, being apart with the elders, determined, before the king's host should enter into Judea, and get the city, to go forth and try the matter in fight by the help of Jah.

[14] So when he had committed all to the Creator of the world, and exhorted his soldiers to fight manfully, even unto death, for the laws, the temple, the city, the country, and the commonwealth, he camped by Modin:

[15] And having given the watchword to them that were about him, Victory is of God; with the most valiant and choice young men he went in into the king's tent by night, and slew in the camp about four thousand men, and the chiefest of the elephants, with all that were upon him.

[16] And at last they filled the camp with fear and tumult, and departed with good success.

[17] This was done in the break of the day, because the protection of Jah did help him.

[18] Now when the king had taken a taste of the manliness of the Jews, he went about to take the holds by policy,

[19] And marched toward Bethsura, which was a strong hold of the Jews: but he was put to flight, failed, and lost of his men:

[20] For Judas had conveyed unto them that were in it such things as were necessary.

[21] But Rhodocus, who was in the Jews' host, disclosed the secrets to the enemies; therefore he was sought out, and when they had gotten him, they put him in prison.

[22] The king treated with them in Bethsum the second time, gave his hand, took their's, departed, fought with Judas, was overcome;

[23] Heard that Philip, who was left over the affairs in Antioch, was desperately bent, confounded, intreated the Jews, submitted

himself, and sware to all equal conditions, agreed with them, and offered sacrifice, honoured the temple, and dealt kindly with the place,
[24] And accepted well of Maccabeus, made him principal governor from Ptolemais unto the Gerrhenians;
[25] Came to Ptolemais: the people there were grieved for the covenants; for they stormed, because they would make their covenants void:
[26] Lysias went up to the judgment seat, said as much as could be in defence of the cause, persuaded, pacified, made them well affected, returned to Antioch. Thus it went touching the king's coming and departing.

---

2 Mac. 14

[1] After three years was Judas informed, that Demetrius the son of Seleucus, having entered by the haven of Tripolis with a great power and navy,
[2] Had taken the country, and killed Antiochus, and Lysias his protector.
[3] Now one Alcimus, who had been high priest, and had defiled himself wilfully in the times of their mingling with the Gentiles, seeing that by no means he could save himself, nor have any more access to the holy altar,
[4] Came to king Demetrius in the hundred and one and fiftieth year, presenting unto him a crown of gold, and a palm, and also of the boughs which were used solemnly in the temple: and so that day he held his peace.
[5] Howbeit having gotten opportunity to further his foolish enterprize, and being called into counsel by Demetrius, and asked how the Jews stood affected, and what they intended, he answered thereunto:
[6] Those of the Jews that he called Assideans, whose captain is Judas Maccabeus, nourish war and are seditious, and will not let the rest be in peace.

[7] Therefore I, being deprived of mine ancestors' honour, I mean the high priesthood, am now come hither:
[8] First, verily for the unfeigned care I have of things pertaining to the king; and secondly, even for that I intend the good of mine own countrymen: for all our nation is in no small misery through the unadvised dealing of them aforersaid.
[9] Wherefore, O king, seeing knowest all these things, be careful for the country, and our nation, which is pressed on every side, according to the clemency that thou readily shewest unto all.
[10] For as long as Judas liveth, it is not possible that the state should be quiet.
[11] This was no sooner spoken of him, but others of the king's friends, being maliciously set against Judas, did more incense Demetrius.
[12] And forthwith calling Nicanor, who had been master of the elephants, and making him governor over Judea, he sent him forth,
[13] Commanding him to slay Judas, and to scatter them that were with him, and to make Alcimus high priest of the great temple.
[14] Then the heathen, that had fled out of Judea from Judas, came to Nicanor by flocks, thinking the harm and calamities ot the Jews to be their welfare.
[15] Now when the Jews heard of Nicanor's coming, and that the heathen were up against them, they cast earth upon their heads, and made supplication to him that had established his people for ever, and who always helpeth his portion with manifestation of his presence.
[16] So at the commandment of the captain they removed straightways from thence, and came near unto them at the town of Dessau.
[17] Now Simon, Judas' brother, had joined battle with Nicanor, but was somewhat discomfited through the sudden silence of his enemies.
[18] Nevertheless Nicanor, hearing of the

manliness of them that were with Judas, and the courageousness that they had to fight for their country, durst not try the matter by the sword.

[19] Wherefore he sent Posidonius, and Theodotus, and Mattathias, to make peace.

[20] So when they had taken long advisement thereupon, and the captain had made the multitude acquainted therewith, and it appeared that they were all of one mind, they consented to the covenants,

[21] And appointed a day to meet in together by themselves: and when the day came, and stools were set for either of them,

[22] Ludas placed armed men ready in convenient places, lest some treachery should be suddenly practised by the enemies: so they made a peaceable conference.

[23] Now Nicanor abode in Jerusalem, and did no hurt, but sent away the people that came flocking unto him.

[24] And he would not willingly have Judas out of his sight: for he love the man from his heart

[25] He prayed him also to take a wife, and to beget children: so he married, was quiet, and took part of this life.

[26] But Alcimus, perceiving the love that was betwixt them, and considering the covenants that were made, came to Demetrius, and told him that Nicanor was not well affected toward the state; for that he had ordained Judas, a traitor to his realm, to be the king's successor.

[27] Then the king being in a rage, and provoked with the accusations of the most wicked man, wrote to Nicanor, signifying that he was much displeased with the covenants, and commanding him that he should send Maccabeus prisoner in all haste unto Antioch.

[28] When this came to Nicanor's hearing, he was much confounded in himself, and took it grievously that he should make void the articles which were agreed upon, the man being in no fault.

[29] But because there was no dealing against the king, he watched his time to accomplish this thing by policy.

[30] Notwithstanding, when Maccabeus saw that Nicanor began to be churlish unto him, and that he entreated him more roughly than he was wont, perceiving that such sour behaviour came not of good, he gathered together not a few of his men, and withdrew himself from Nicanor.

[31] But the other, knowing that he was notably prevented by Judas' policy, came into the great and holy temple, and commanded the priests, that were offering their usual sacrifices, to deliver him the man.

[32] And when they sware that they could not tell where the man was whom he sought,

[33] He stretched out his right hand toward the temple, and made an oath in this manner: If ye will not deliver me Judas as a prisoner, I will lay this temple of God even with the ground, and I will break down the altar, and erect a notable temple unto Bacchus.

[34] After these words he departed. Then the priests lifted up their hands toward heaven, and besought him that was ever a defender of their nation, saying in this manner;

[35] Thou, O Lord of all things, who hast need of nothing, wast pleased that the temple of thine habitation should be among us:

[36] Therefore now, O holy Lord of all holiness, keep this house ever undefiled, which lately was cleansed, and stop every unrighteous mouth.

[37] Now was there accused unto Nicanor one Razis, one of the elders of Jerusalem, a lover of his countrymen, and a man of very good report, who for his kindness was called a father of the Jews.

[38] For in the former times, when they mingled not themselves with the Gentiles, he had been accused of Judaism, and did boldly jeopard his body and life with all

vehemency for the religion of the Jews.
[39] So Nicanor, willing to declare the hate that he bare unto the Jews, sent above five hundred men of war to take him:
[40] For he thought by taking him to do the Jews much hurt.
[41] Now when the multitude would have taken the tower, and violently broken into the outer door, and bade that fire should be brought to burn it, he being ready to be taken on every side fell upon his sword;
[42] Choosing rather to die manfully, than to come into the hands of the wicked, to be abused otherwise than beseemed his noble birth:
[43] But missing his stroke through haste, the multitude also rushing within the doors, he ran boldly up to the wall, and cast himself down manfully among the thickest of them.
[44] But they quickly giving back, and a space being made, he fell down into the midst of the void place.
[45] Nevertheless, while there was yet breath within him, being inflamed with anger, he rose up; and though his blood gushed out like spouts of water, and his wounds were grievous, yet he ran through the midst of the throng; and standing upon a steep rock,
[46] When as his blood was now quite gone, he plucked out his bowels, and taking them in both his hands, he cast them upon the throng, and calling upon Jah of life and spirit to restore him those again, he thus died.

2Mac.15

[1] But Nicanor, hearing that Judas and his company were in the strong places about Samaria, resolved without any danger to set upon them on the sabbath day.
[2] Nevertheless the Jews that were compelled to go with him said, O destroy not so cruelly and barbarously, but give honour to that day, which he, that seeth all things, hath honoured with holiness above all other days.
[3] Then the most ungracious wretch demanded, if there were a Mighty one in heaven, that had commanded the sabbath day to be kept.
[4] And when they said, There is in heaven a living Lord, and mighty, who commanded the seventh day to be kept:
[5] Then said the other, And I also am mighty upon earth, and I command to take arms, and to do the king's business. Yet he obtained not to have his wicked will done.
[6] So Nicanor in exceeding pride and haughtiness determined to set up a publick monument of his victory over Judas and them that were with him.
[7] But Maccabeus had ever sure confidence that Jah would help him:
[8] Wherefore he exhorted his people not to fear the coming of the heathen against them, but to remember the help which in former times they had received from heaven, and now to expect the victory and aid, which should come unto them from the Almighty.
[9] And so comforting them out of the law and the prophets, and withal putting them in mind of the battles that they won afore, he made them more cheerful.
[10] And when he had stirred up their minds, he gave them their charge, shewing them therewithall the falsehood of the heathen, and the breach of oaths.
[11] Thus he armed every one of them, not so much with defence of shields and spears, as with comfortable and good words: and beside that, he told them a dream worthy to be believed, as if it had been so indeed, which did not a little rejoice them.
[12] And this was his vision: That Onias, who had been high priest, a virtuous and a good man, reverend in conversation, gentle

in condition, well spoken also, and exercised from a child in all points of virtue, holding up his hands prayed for the whole body of the Jews.

[13] This done, in like manner there appeared a man with gray hairs, and exceeding glorious, who was of a wonderful and excellent majesty.

[14] Then Onias answered, saying, This is a lover of the brethren, who prayeth much for the people, and for the holy city, to wit, Jeremias the prophet of God.

[15] Whereupon Jeremias holding forth his right hand gave to Judas a sword of gold, and in giving it spake thus,

[16] Take this holy sword, a gift from God, with the which thou shalt wound the adversaries.

[17] Thus being well comforted by the words of Judas, which were very good, and able to stir them up to valour, and to encourage the hearts of the young men, they determined not to pitch camp, but courageously to set upon them, and manfully to try the matter by conflict, because the city and the sanctuary and the temple were in danger.

[18] For the care that they took for their wives, and their children, their brethren, and folks, was in least account with them: but the greatest and principal fear was for the holy temple.

[19] Also they that were in the city took not the least care, being troubled for the conflict abroad.

[20] And now, when as all looked what should be the trial, and the enemies were already come near, and the army was set in array, and the beasts conveniently placed, and the horsemen set in wings,

[21] Maccabeus seeing the coming of the multitude, and the divers preparations of armour, and the fierceness of the beasts, stretched out his hands toward heaven, and called upon Jah that worketh wonders, knowing that victory cometh not by arms, but even as it seemeth good to him, he giveth it to such as are worthy:

[22] Therefore in his prayer he said after this manner; O Lord, thou didst send thine angel in the time of Ezekias king of Judea, and didst slay in the host of Sennacherib an hundred fourscore and five thousand:

[23] Wherefore now also, O Lord of heaven, send a good angel before us for a fear and dread unto them;

[24] And through the might of thine arm let those be stricken with terror, that come against thy holy people to blaspheme. And he ended thus.

[25] Then Nicanor and they that were with him came forward with trumpets and songs.

[26] But Judas and his company encountered the enemies with invocation and prayer.

[27] So that fighting with their hands, and praying unto God with their hearts, they slew no less than thirty and five thousand men: for through the appearance of God they were greatly cheered.

[28] Now when the battle was done, returning again with joy, they knew that Nicanor lay dead in his harness.

[29] Then they made a great shout and a noise, praising the Almighty in their own language.

[30] And Judas, who was ever the chief defender of the citizens both in body and mind, and who continued his love toward his countrymen all his life, commanded to strike off Nicanor's head, and his hand with his shoulder, and bring them to Jerusalem.

[31] So when he was there, and called them of his nation together, and set the priests before the altar, he sent for them that were of the tower,

[32] And shewed them vile Nicanor's head,

and the hand of that blasphemer, which with proud brags he had stretched out against the holy temple of the Almighty.

[33] And when he had cut out the tongue of that ungodly Nicanor, he commanded that they should give it by pieces unto the fowls, and hang up the reward of his madness before the temple.

[34] So every man praised toward the heaven the glorious Lord, saying, Blessed be he that hath kept his own place undefiled.

[35] He hanged also Nicanor's head upon the tower, an evident and manifest sign unto all of the help of Jah.

[36] And they ordained all with a common decree in no case to let that day pass without solemnity, but to celebrate the thirtieth day of the twelfth month, which in the Syrian tongue is called Adar, the day before Mardocheus' day.

[37] Thus went it with Nicanor: and from that time forth the Hebrews had the city in their power. And here will I make an end.

[38] And if I have done well, and as is fitting the story, it is that which I desired: but if slenderly and meanly, it is that which I could attain unto.

[39] For as it is hurtful to drink wine or water alone; and as wine mingled with water is pleasant, and delighteth the taste: even so speech finely framed delighteth the ears of them that read the story. And here shall be an end.

The Book of Enoch

Or

Enoch the Ethiopian

Enoch 1

[1] The words of the blessing of Enoch, wherewith he blessed the
elect and righteous, who will be living in the day of tribulation, when all the wicked and godless are to be removed.

[2] And he took up his parable and said-- Enoch a righteous man, whose eyes were opened by God, saw the vision of the Holy One in the heavens, which the angels showed me, and from them I heard everything, and from them I understood as I saw, but not for this generation, but for a remote one which is for to come.

[3] Concerning the elect I said, and took up my parable concerning them:

The Holy Great One will come forth from His dwelling,

[4] And the eternal God will tread upon the earth, even on Mount Sinai, And appear from His camp and appear in the strength of His might from the heaven of heavens.

[5] And all shall be smitten with fear And the Watchers shall quake, And great fear and trembling shall seize them unto the ends of the earth.

[6] And the high mountains shall be shaken, And the high hills shall be made low, And shall melt like wax before the flame

[7] And the earth shall be wholly rent in sunder,
And all that is upon the earth shall perish, And there shall be a judgement upon all men.

[8] But with the righteous He will make peace.

And will protect the elect, And mercy shall be upon them. And they shall all belong to God,
And they shall be prospered, And they

shall all be blessed. And He will help them all, And light shall appear unto them, And He will make peace with them.

[9] And behold! He cometh with ten thousands of His holy ones
To execute judgement upon all,
And to destroy all the ungodly:

And to convict all flesh
Of all the works [of their ungodliness which they have ungodly committed,
And of all the hard things which ungodly sinners have spoken against Him.

Enoch 2

[1] Observe ye everything that takes place in the heaven, how they do not change their orbits, and the luminaries which are in the heaven, how they all rise and set in order each in its season, and transgress not against their appointed order.

[2] Behold ye the earth, and give heed to the things which take place upon it from first to last, how steadfast they are, how [none of the things upon earth] change, but all the works of God appear [to you.

[3] Behold the summer and the winter, how the whole earth is filled with water, and clouds and dew and rain lie upon it.

Enoch 3

Observe and see how in the winter all the trees seem as though they had withered and shed all their leaves, except fourteen trees, which do not lose their foliage but retain the old foliage from two to three years till the new comes.

Enoch 4

[1] They consider and behold every tree, how it appears to wither, and every leaf to fall off, except of fourteen trees, which are not deciduous; which wait from the old, to the appearance of the new leaf, for two or three winters.

Enoch 5

[1] Observe ye how the trees cover themselves with green leaves and bear fruit: wherefore give ye heed [and know] with regard to all His works, and recognize how He that liveth for ever hath made them so.

[2] And all His works go on thus from year to year for ever, and all the tasks which they accomplish for Him, and their tasks change not, but according as God hath ordained so is it done.

[3] And behold how the sea and the rivers in like manner accomplish and change not their tasks from His commandments.

[4] But ye--ye have not been steadfast, nor done the commandments of Jah ,
But ye have turned away and spoken proud and hard words With your impure mouths against His greatness.
Oh, ye hard-hearted, ye shall find no peace.

[5] Therefore shall ye execrate your days,
And the years of your life shall perish,
And the years of your destruction shall be multiplied in eternal execration, And ye shall find no mercy.

[6a] In those days ye shall make your names an eternal execration unto all the righteous,
[b] And by you shall all who curse, curse,
And all the sinners and godless shall

imprecate by you,
[7c] And for you the godless there shall be a curse.

[6d] And all the . . . shall rejoice,
[e] And there shall be forgiveness of sins,
[f] And every mercy and peace and forbearance:
[g] There shall be salvation unto them, a goodly light.

[I] And for all of you sinners there shall be no salvation,
[j] But on you all shall abide a curse.
[7a] But for the elect there shall be light and joy and peace,
[b] And they shall inherit the earth.

[8] And then there shall be bestowed upon the elect wisdom, And they shall all live and never again sin,
Either through ungodliness or through pride: But they who are wise shall be humble.

[9] And they shall not again transgress,
Nor shall they sin all the days of their life,
Nor shall they die of the divine anger or wrath,
But they shall complete the number of the days of their life. And their lives shall be increased in peace,
And the years of their joy shall be multiplied,
In eternal gladness and peace, All the days of their life.

Enoch 6-11: *The Fall of the Angels: the Demoralisation of Mankind: the Intercession of the Angels on behalf of Mankind. The Dooms pronounced by God on the Angels: the Messianic Kingdom* (a Noah fragment).

Enoch 6

[1] And it came to pass when the children of men had multiplied that in those days were born unto them beautiful and comely daughters.

[2] And the angels, the children of the heaven, saw and lusted after them, and said to one another: 'Come, let us choose us wives from among the children of men and beget us children.'

[3] And Semjâzâ, who was their leader, said unto them: 'I fear ye will not indeed agree to do this deed, and I alone shall have to pay the penalty of a great sin.'

[4] And they all answered him and said: 'Let us all swear an oath, and all bind ourselves by mutual imprecations not to abandon this plan but to do this thing.'

[5] Then sware they all together and bound themselves by mutual imprecations upon it.

[6] And they were in all two hundred; who descended [in the days] of Jared on the summit of Mount Hermon, and they called it Mount Hermon, because they had sworn and bound themselves by mutual imprecations upon it.

[7] And these are the names of their leaders: Sêmîazâz, their leader, Arâkîba, Râmêêl, Kôkabîêl, Tâmîêl, Râmîêl, Dânêl, Êzêqêêl, Barâqîjâl, Asâêl, Armârôs, Batârêl, Anânêl, Zaqîêl, Samsâpêêl, Satarêl, Tûrêl, Jômjâêl, Sariêl. 8. These are their chiefs of tens.

Enoch 7

[1] And all the others together with them took unto themselves wives, and each chose for himself one, and they began to go in unto them and to defile themselves with them, and they taught them charms and

enchantments, and the cutting of roots, and made them acquainted with plants.

[2] And they became pregnant, and they bare great giants, whose height was three thousand ells:

[3] Who consumed all the acquisitions of men. And when men could no longer sustain them,

[4] the giants turned against them and devoured mankind.

[5] And they began to sin against birds, and beasts, and reptiles, and fish, and to devour one another's flesh, and drink the blood.

[6] Then the earth laid accusation against the lawless ones.

Enoch 8

[1] Moreover Azazyel taught men to make swords, knives, shields, breastplates, the fabrication of mirrors, and the workmanship of bracelets and ornaments, the use of paint, the beautifying of the eyebrows, the use of stones of every valuable and select kind, and all sorts of dyes, so that the world became altered.

[2] Impiety increased; fornication multiplied; and they transgressed and corrupted all their ways.

[3] Amazarak taught all the sorcerers, and dividers of roots:

[4] Armers taught the solution of sorcery;

[5] Barkayal taught the observers of the stars,

[6] Akibeel taught signs;

[7] Tamiel taught astronomy;

[8] And Asaradel taught the motion of the moon,

[9] And men, being destroyed, cried out; and their voice reached to heaven.

Enoch 9

[1] Then Michael and Gabriel, Raphael, Suryal, and Uriel, looked down from heaven, and saw the quantity of blood which was shed on earth, and all the iniquity which was done upon it, and said one to another, It is the voice of their cries;

[2] The earth deprived of her children has cried even to the gate of heaven.

[3] And now to you, O you holy one of heaven, the souls of men complain, saying, Obtain Justice for us with the Most High. Then they said to their Lord, the King, You are Lord of lords, God of gods, King of kings. The throne of your glory is for ever and ever, and for ever and ever is your name sanctified and glorified. You are blessed and glorified.

[4] You have made all things; you possess power over all things; and all things are open and manifest before you. You behold all things, and nothing can be concealed from you.

[5] You have seen what Azazyel has done, how he has taught every species of iniquity upon earth, and has disclosed to the world all the secret things which are done in the heavens.

[6] Samyaza also has taught sorcery, to whom you have given authority over those who are associated with him. They have gone together to the daughters of men; have lain with them; have become polluted;

[7] And have discovered crimes to them.

[8] The women likewise have brought forth giants.

[9] Thus has the whole earth been filled with blood and with iniquity.

[10] And now behold the souls of those who are dead, cry out.

[11] And complain even to the gate of heaven.

[12] Their groaning ascends; nor can they escape from the unrighteousness which is committed on earth. You know all things, before they exist.

[13] You know these things, and what has been done by them; yet you do not speak to us.

[14] What on account of these things ought we to do to them?

Enoch 10

[1] Then the Most High, the Great and Holy One spoke,

[2] And sent Arsayalalyur to the son of Lamech,

[3] Saying, Say to him in my name, Conceal yourself.

[4] Then explain to him the consummation which is about to take place; for all the earth shall perish; the waters of a deluge shall come over the whole earth, and all things which are in it shall be destroyed.

[5] And now teach him how he may escape, and how his seed may remain in all the earth.

[6] Again Jah said to Raphael, Bind Azazyel hand and foot; cast him into darkness; and opening the desert which is in Dudael, cast him in there.

[7] Throw upon him hurled and pointed stones, covering him with darkness;

[8] There shall he remain for ever; cover his face, that he may not see the light.

[9] And in the great day of judgment let him be cast into the fire.

[10] Restore the earth, which the angels have corrupted; and announce life to it, that I may revive it.

[11] All the sons of men shall not perish in consequence of every secret, by which the Watchers have destroyed, and which they have taught, their offspring.

[12] All the earth has been corrupted by the effects of the teaching of Azazyel. To him therefore ascribe the whole crime.

[13] To Gabriel also Jah said, Go to the biters, to the reprobates, to the children of fornication; and destroy the children of fornication, the offspring of the Watchers, from among men; bring them forth, and excite them one against another. Let them perish by mutual slaughter; for length of days shall not be theirs.

[14] They shall all entreat you, but their fathers shall not obtain their
wishes respecting them; for they shall hope for eternal life, and that they may live, each of them, five hundred years.

[15] To Michael likewise Jah said, Go and announce his crime to Samyaza, and to the others who are with him, who have been associated with women, that they might be polluted with all their impurity. And when

all their sons shall be slain, when they shall see the perdition of their beloved, bind them for seventy generations underneath the earth, even to the day of judgment, and of consummation, until the judgment, the effect of which will last for ever, be completed.

[16] Then shall they be taken away into the lowest depths of the fire in torments; and in confinement shall they be shut up for ever.

[17] Immediately after this shall he, together with them, burn and perish; they shall be bound until the consummation of many generations.

[18] Destroy all the souls addicted to dalliance, and the offspring of the Watchers, for they have tyrannized over mankind.

[19] Let every oppressor perish from the face of the earth;

[20] Let every evil work be destroyed;

[21] The plant of righteousness and of rectitude appear, and its produce become a blessing.

[22] Righteousness and rectitude shall be for ever planted with delight.

[23] And then shall all the saints give thanks, and live until they have begotten a thousand children, while the whole period of their youth, and their sabbaths shall be completed in peace. In those days all the earth shall be cultivated in righteousness; it shall be wholly planted with trees, and filled with benediction; every tree of delight shall be planted in it.

[24] In it shall vines be planted; and the vine which shall be planted in it shall yield fruit to satiety; every seed, which shall be sown in it, shall produce for one measure a thousand; and one measure of olives shall produce ten presses of oil.

[25] Purify the earth from all oppression, from all injustice, from all crime, from all impiety, and from all the pollution which is committed upon it. Exterminate them from the earth.

[26] Then shall all the children of men be righteous, and all nations shall pay me divine honours, and bless me; and all shall adore me.

[27] The earth shall be cleansed from all corruption, from every crime, from all punishment, and from all suffering; neither will I again send a deluge upon it from generation to generation for ever.

[28] In those days I will open the treasures of blessing which are in heaven, that I may cause them to descend upon earth, and upon all the works and labour of man.

[29Peace and equity shall associate with the sons of men all the days of the world, in every generation of it.

Enoch 11

[1] And in those days I will open the store chambers of blessing which are in the heaven, so as to send them down upon the earth over the work and labour of the children of men.

[2] And truth and peace shall be associated together throughout all the days of the world and throughout all the generations of men.

Enoch 12

[1] Before all these things Enoch was concealed; nor did any one of the sons of

men know where he was concealed, where he had been, and what had happened.

[2] He was wholly engaged with the holy ones, and with the Watchers in his days.

[3] I, Enoch, was blessing the great Lord and King of peace.

[4] And behold the Watchers called me Enoch the scribe.

[5] Then Jah said to me: Enoch, scribe of righteousness, go tell the Watchers of heaven, who have deserted the lofty sky, and their holy everlasting station, who have been polluted with women.

[6] And have done as the sons of men do, by taking to themselves wives, and who have been greatly corrupted on the earth;

[7] That on the earth they shall never obtain peace and remission of sin. For they shall not rejoice in their offspring; they shall behold the slaughter of their beloved; shall lament for the destruction of their sons; and shall petition for ever; but shall not obtain mercy and peace.

Enoch 13

[1] Then Enoch, passing on, said to Azazyel: You shalt not obtain peace. A great sentence is gone forth against you. He shall bind you;

[2] Neither shall relief, mercy, and supplication be yours, on account of the oppression which you have taught;

[3] And on account of every act of blasphemy, tyranny, and sin, which you have discovered to the children of men.

[4] Then departing from him I spoke to them all together;

[5] And they all became terrified, and trembled;

[6] Beseeching me to write for them a memorial of supplication, that they might obtain forgiveness; and that I might make the memorial of their prayer ascend up before the God of heaven; because they could not themselves thenceforwards address him, nor raise up their eyes to heaven on account of the disgraceful offence for which they were judged.

[7] Then I wrote a memorial of their prayer and supplications, for their spirits, for everything which they had done, and for the subject of their entreaty, that they might obtain remission and rest.

[8] Proceeding on, I continued over the waters of Danbadan, which is on the right to the west of Armon, reading the memorial of their prayer, until I fell asleep.

[9] And behold a dream came to me, and visions appeared above me. I fell down and saw a vision of punishment, that I might relate it to the sons of heaven, and reprove them. When I awoke I went to them. All being collected together stood weeping in Oubelseyael, which is situated between Libanos and Seneser, with their faces veiled.

[10] I related in their presence all the visions which I had seen, and my dream;

[11] And began to utter these words of righteousness, reproving the Watchers of heaven.

Enoch 14

[1] This is the book of the words of righteousness, and of the reproof of the eternal Watchers, who belong to the

world, according to that which He, who is holy and great, commanded in the vision. I perceived in my dream, that I was now speaking with a tongue of flesh, and with my breath, which the Mighty One has put into the mouth of men, that they might converse with it.

* Who belong to the world. Or, "who are from eternity"

[2] and understand with the heart. As he has created and given to men the power of comprehending the word of understanding, so has he created and given to me the power of reproving the Watchers, the offspring of heaven. I have written your petition; and in my vision it has been shown me, that what you request will not be granted you as long as the world endures.

[3] Judgment has been passed upon you: your request will not be granted you.

[4] From this time forward, never shall you ascend into heaven; He has said, that on the earth He will bind you, as long as the world endures.

[5] But before these things you shall behold the destruction of your beloved sons; you shall not possess them, but they shall fall before you by the sword.

[6] Neither shall you entreat for them, not for yourselves;

[7] But you shall weep and supplicate in silence. The words of the book which I wrote. But you shall weep…I wrote. Or, "Likewise despite your tears and prayers you will receive nothing whatever contained in the writing which I have written"

[8A] vision thus appeared to me.

[9] Behold, in that vision clouds and a mist invited me; agitated stars and flashes of lightning impelled and pressed me forwards, while winds in the vision assisted my flight, accelerating my progress.

[10] They elevated me aloft to heaven. I proceeded, until I arrived at a wall built with stones of crystal. A vibrating flame surrounded it, which began to strike me with terror.

[11] Into this vibrating flame I entered;

[12] And drew nigh to a spacious habitation built also with stones of crystal. Its walls too, as well as pavement, were formed with stones of crystal, and crystal likewise was the ground. Its roof had the appearance of agitated stars and flashes of lightning; and among them were cherubim of fire in a stormy sky. A flame burned around its walls; and its portal blazed with fire. When I entered into this dwelling, it was hot as fire and cold as ice. No trace of delight or of life was there. Terror overwhelmed me, and a fearful shaking seized me.

[13] Violently agitated and trembling, I fell upon my face. In the vision I looked.

[14] And behold there was another habitation more spacious than the former, every entrance to which was open before me, erected in the midst of a vibrating flame.

[15] So greatly did it excel in all points, in glory, in magnificence, and in magnitude, that it is impossible to describe to you either the splendour or the extent of it.

[16] Its floor was on fire; above were lightnings and agitated stars, while its roof exhibited a blazing fire.

[17] Attentively I surveyed it, and saw that it contained an exalted throne;

[18] The appearance of which was like that of frost; while its circumference resembled the orb of the brilliant sun; and *there was* the voice of the cherubim.

[19] From underneath this mighty throne rivers of flaming fire issued.

[20] To look upon it was impossible.

[21] One great in glory sat upon it:

[22] Whose robe was brighter than the sun, and whiter than snow.

[23] No angel was capable of penetrating to view the face of Him, the Glorious and the Effulgent; nor could any mortal behold Him. A fire was flaming around Him.

[24] A fire also of great extent continued to rise up before Him; so that not one of those who surrounded Him was capable of approaching Him, among the myriads of myriads who were before Him. To Him holy consultation was needless. Yet did not the sanctified, who were near Him, depart far from Him either by night or by day; nor were they removed from Him. I also was so far advanced, with a veil on my face, and trembling. Then Jah with his *own* mouth called me, saying, Approach hither, Enoch, at my holy word.

[25] And He raised me up, making me draw near even to the entrance. My eye was directed to the ground.

Enoch 15

[1] And He answered and said to me, and I heard His voice: 'Fear not, Enoch, thou righteous man and scribe of righteousness: approach hither and hear my voice.

[2] And go, say to [[the Watchers of heaven, who have sent thee to intercede for them: "You should intercede" for men, and not men for you:

[3] Wherefore have ye left the high, holy, and eternal heaven, and lain with women, and defiled yourselves with the daughters of men and taken to yourselves wives, and done like the children of earth, and begotten giants as your sons?

[4] And though ye were holy, spiritual, living the eternal life, you have defiled yourselves with the blood of women, and have begotten children with the blood of flesh, and, as the children of men, have lusted after flesh and blood as those also do who die and perish.

[5] Therefore have I given them wives also that they might impregnate them, and beget children by them, that thus nothing might be wanting to them on earth. [6] But you were formerly spiritual, living the eternal life, and immortal for all generations of the world.

[7] And therefore I have not appointed wives for you; for as for the spiritual ones of the heaven, in heaven is their dwelling.

[8] And now, the giants, who are produced from the spirits and flesh, shall be called evil spirits upon the earth, and on the earth shall be their dwelling.

[9] Evil spirits have proceeded from their bodies; because they are born from men, and from the holy Watchers is their beginning and primal origin; [they shall be evil spirits on earth, and evil spirits shall they be called.

[10] As for the spirits of heaven, in heaven shall be their dwelling, but as for the spirits

of the earth which were born upon the earth, on the earth shall be their dwelling.]

[11] And the spirits of the giants afflict, oppress, destroy, attack, do battle, and work destruction on the earth, and cause trouble: they take no food, but nevertheless hunger and thirst, and cause offences. And these spirits shall rise up against the children of men and against the women, because they have proceeded from them.

Enoch 16

[1] And as to the death of the giants, wheresoever their spirits depart from their bodies, let their flesh, that which is perishable, be without judgment. Thus shall they perish, until the day of the great consummation of the great world. A destruction shall take place of the Watchers and the impious. Let their flesh…be without judgment. Or, "their flesh shall be destroyed before the judgment".

[2] And now to the Watchers, who have sent you to pray for them, who in the beginning were in heaven,

[3] Say, In heaven have you been; secret things, however, have not been manifested to you; yet have you known a reprobated mystery.

[4] And this you have related to women in the hardness of your heart, and by that mystery have women and mankind multiplied evils upon the earth.

[5] Say to them, Never therefore shall you obtain peace.

Enoch 17

[1] They raised me up into a certain place, where there was the appearance of a burning fire; and when they pleased they assumed the likeness of men.

[2] They carried me to a lofty spot, to a mountain, the top of which reach to heaven.

[3] And I beheld the receptacles of light and of thunder at the extremities of the place, where it was deepest. There was a bow of fire, and arrows in their quiver, a sword of fire, and every species of lightning.

[4] Then they elevated me to a babbling stream, (29) and to a fire in the west, which received all the setting of the sun. I came to a river of fire, which flowed like water, and emptied itself into the great sea westwards.

* To a babbling stream. Literally, "to water of life, which spoke"

[5] I saw every large river, until I arrived at the great darkness. I went to where all of flesh migrate; and I beheld the mountains of the gloom which constitutes winter, and the place from which issues the water in every abyss.

[6] I saw also the mouths of all the rivers in the world, and the mouths of the deep.

Enoch 18

[1] I then surveyed the receptacles of all the winds, perceiving that they contributed to adorn the whole creation, and to preserve the foundation of the earth.

[2] I surveyed the stone which supports the corners of the earth.

[3] I also beheld the four winds, which bear up the earth, and the firmament of heaven.

[4] And I beheld the winds occupying the exalted sky.

[5] Arising in the midst of heaven and of earth, and constituting the pillars of heaven.

[6] I saw the winds which turn the sky, which cause the orb of the sun and of all the stars to set; and over the earth I saw the winds which support the clouds.

[7] I saw the path of the angels.

[8] I perceived at the extremity of the earth the firmament of heaven above it. Then I passed on towards the south;

[9] Where burnt, both by day and night, six mountains formed of glorious stones; three towards the east, and three towards the south.

[10] Those which were towards the east were of a variegated stone; one of which was of margarite, and another of antimony. Those towards the south were of a red stone. The middle one reached to heaven like the throne of God; a throne composed of alabaster, the top of which was of sapphire. I saw, too, a blazing fire hanging over all the mountains.

[11] And there I saw a place on the other side of an extended territory, where waters were collected.

[12] I likewise beheld terrestrial fountains, deep in the fiery columns of heaven.

[13] And in the columns of heaven I beheld fires, which descended without number, but neither on high, nor into the deep. Over these fountains also I perceived a place which had neither the firmament of heaven above it, nor the solid ground underneath it; neither was there water above it; nor anything on wing; but the spot was desolate.

[14] And there I beheld seven stars, like great blazing mountains, and like spirits entreating me.

[15] Then the angel said, This place, until the consummation of heaven and earth, will be the prison of the stars, and the host of heaven.

[16] The stars which roll over fire are those which transgressed the commandment of God before their time arrived; for they came not in their proper season. Therefore was He offended with them, and bound them, until the period of the consummation of their crimes in the secret year.

Enoch 19

[1] Then Uriel said, Here the angels, who cohabited with women, appointed their leaders;

[2] And being numerous in appearance made men profane, and caused them to err; so that they sacrificed to devils as to gods. For in the great day there shall be a judgment, with which they shall be judged, until they are consumed; and their wives also shall be judged, who led astray the angels of heaven that they might salute them.

Being numerous in appearance. Or, "assuming many forms"

[3] And I, Enoch, I alone saw the likeness of the end of all things. Nor did any human being see it, as I saw it.

Enoch 20

[1] These are the names of the holy angels who watch.

[2] Uriel, one of the holy angels, who presides over clamor and terror.

[3] Raphael, one of the holy angels, who presides over the spirits of men.

[4] Raguel, one of the holy angels, who inflicts punishment on the world and the luminaries.

[5] Michael, one of the holy angels, who, presiding over human virtue, commands the nations.

[6] Sarakiel, one of the holy angels, who presides over the spirits of the children of men that transgress.

[7] Gabriel, one of the holy angels, who presides over the serpent, over paradise, and over the cherubim.

[8] Remiel, one of the holy angels, whom God set over those who rise.

Enoch 21

[1] Then I made a circuit to a place in which nothing was completed.

[2] And there I beheld neither the tremendous workmanship of an exalted heaven, nor of an established earth, but a desolate spot, prepared, and terrific.

[3] There, too, I beheld seven stars of heaven bound in it together, like great mountains, and like a blazing fire. I exclaimed, For what species of crime have they been bound, and why have they been removed to this place? Then Uriel, one of the holy angels who was with me, and who conducted me, answered: Enoch, wherefore do you ask; wherefore do you reason with yourself, and anxiously inquire? These are those of the stars which have transgressed the commandment of the most high God; and are here bound, until the infinite number of the days of their crimes be completed.

[4] From there I afterwards passed on to another terrific place;

[5] Where I beheld the operation of a great fire blazing and glittering, in the midst of which there was a division. Columns of fire struggled together to the end of the abyss, and deep was their descent. But neither its measurement nor magnitude was I able to discover; neither could I perceive its origin. Then I exclaimed, How terrible is this place, and how difficult to explore!

[6] Uriel, one of the holy angels who was with me, answered and said: Enoch, why are you alarmed and amazed at this terrific place, at the sight of this place of suffering? This, he said, is the prison of the angels; and here they are kept for ever.

Enoch 22

[1] From there I proceeded to another spot, where I saw on the west a great and lofty mountain, a strong rock, and four delightful places.

[2] Internally it was deep, capacious, and very smooth; as smooth as if it had been rolled over: it was both deep and dark to behold.

[3] Then Raphael, one of the holy angels who were with me, answered and said, These are the delightful places where the spirits, the souls of the dead, will be collected; for them were they formed; and here will be collected all the souls of the sons of men.

[4] These places, in which they dwell, shall they occupy until the day of judgment, and until their appointed period.

[5] Their appointed period will be long, even until the great judgment. And I saw the spirits of the sons of men who were dead; and their voices reached to heaven, while they were accusing.

[6] Then I inquired of Raphael, an angel who was with me, and said, Whose spirit is that, the voice of which reaches to heaven, and accuses?

[7] He answered, saying, This is the spirit of Abel who was slain by Cain his brother; and who will accuse that brother, until his seed be destroyed from the face of the earth;

[8] Until his seed perish from the seed of the human race.

[9] At that time therefore I inquired respecting him, and respecting the general judgment, saying, Why is one separated from another? He answered,
Three separations have been made between the spirits of the dead, and thus have the spirits of the righteous been separated.

[10] Namely, by a chasm, by water, and by light above it.

[11] And in the same way likewise are sinners separated when they die, and are buried in the earth; judgment not overtaking them in their lifetime.

[12] Here their souls are separated. Moreover, abundant is their suffering until the time of the great judgment, the castigation, and the torment of those who eternally execrate, whose souls are punished and bound there for ever.

[13] And thus has it been from the beginning of the world. Thus has there existed a separation between the souls of those who utter complaints, and of those who watch for their destruction, to slaughter them in the day of sinners.

[14] A receptacle of this sort has been formed for the souls of unrighteous men, and of sinners; of those who have completed crime, and associated with the impious, whom they resemble. Their souls shall not be annihilated in the day of judgment, neither shall they arise from this place. Then I blessed God,

[15] And said, Blessed by my Lord, Jah of glory and of righteousness, who reigns over all for ever and for ever.

Enoch 23

[1] From there I went to another place, towards the west, unto the ends of the earth.

[2] Where I beheld a fire blazing and running along without cessation, which intermitted its course neither by day nor by night; but continued always the same.

[3] I inquired, saying, What is this, which never ceases?

[4] Then Raguel, one of the holy angels who were with me, answered,

[5] And said, This blazing fire, which you behold running towards the west, is that of all the luminaries of heaven.

Enoch 24

[1] And from thence I went to another place of the earth, and and he showed me a mountain of fire flashing both by day and

night. I proceeded towards it; and perceived seven splendid mountains, which were all different from each other.

[2] Their stones were brilliant and beautiful; all were brilliant and splendid to behold; and beautiful was their surface.
Three *mountains* were towards the east, and strengthened by being placed one upon another; and three were towards the south, strengthened in a similar manner. There were likewise deep valleys, which did not approach each other. And the seventh mountain was in the midst of them. In length they all resembled the seat of a throne, and odoriferous trees surrounded them.

[3] Among these there was a tree of an unceasing smell; nor of those which were in Eden was there one of all the fragrant trees which smelt like this. Its leaf, its flower, and its bark never withered, and its fruit was beautiful.

[4] Its fruit resembled the cluster of the palm. I exclaimed, Behold! This tree is goodly in aspect, pleasing in its leaf, and the sight of its fruit is delightful to the eye. Then Michael, one of the holy and glorious angels who were with me, and one who presided over them, answered,

[5] And said: Enoch, How beautiful is this tree, and fragrant, and its leaves are fair, and its blooms very delightful in appearance.

[6] Then answered Michael, Why are you inquisitive to know it?

[7] Then I, Enoch, replied to him, and said, concerning everything I am desirous of instruction, but particularly concerning this tree.

[8] He answered me, saying, That mountain which you behold, the extent of whose head resembles the seat of Jah, will be the seat on which shall sit the holy and great Lord of glory, the everlasting King, when he shall come and descend to visit the earth with goodness.

[9] And that tree of an agreeable smell, not one of carnal odor, there shall be no power to touch, until the period of the great judgment. When all shall be punished and consumed for ever, this shall be bestowed on the righteous and humble. The fruit of the tree shall be given to the elect. For towards the north life shall be planted in the holy place, towards the habitation of the everlasting King.

[10] Then shall they greatly rejoice and exult in the Holy One. The sweet odor shall enter into their bones; and they shall live a long life on the earth as your forefathers have lived; neither in their days shall sorrow, distress, trouble, and punishment afflict them.

[11] And I blessed Jah of glory, the everlasting King, because He has prepared this tree for the saints, formed it, and declared that He would give it to them.

Enoch 25

[1] And he said unto me: 'Enoch, why dost

thou ask me regarding the fragrance of the tree, and [why] dost thou wish to learn the truth?' Then I answered him [[saying]]: 'I wish to know about everything, but especially about this tree.' And he answered saying: 'This high mountain [[which thou hast seen]], whose summit is like the throne of God, is His throne, where the Holy Great One, Jah of Glory, the Eternal King, will sit, when He shall come down to visit the earth with goodness.

[4] And as for this fragrant tree no mortal is permitted to touch it till the great judgement, when He shall take vengeance on all and bring everything to its consummation for ever. It shall then be given to the righteous and holy.

[5] Its fruit shall be for food to the elect: it shall be transplanted to the holy place, to the temple of Jah, the Eternal King.

[6] Then shall they rejoice with joy and be glad,
And into the holy place shall they enter;
And its fragrance shall be in their bones,
And they shall live a long life on earth,
Such as thy fathers lived:
And in their days shall no [sorrow or] plague
Or torment or calamity touch them.'

[7] Then blessed I the God of Glory, the Eternal King, who hath prepared such things for the righteous, and hath created them and promised to give to them.

Enoch 26

[1] Then I said, What means this blessed land, all these lofty trees, and the accursed valley between them?

[2] Then Uriel, one of the holy angels who were with me, replied, This valley is the accursed of the accursed for ever. Here shall be collected all who utter with their mouths unbecoming language against God, and speak harsh things of His glory. Here shall they be collected. Here shall be their territory.

[3] In the latter days an example of judgment shall be made of them in righteousness before the saints; while those who have received mercy shall for ever, all their days, bless God, the everlasting King.

[4] And at the period of judgment shall they bless Him for his mercy, as He has distributed it to them. Then I blessed God, addressing myself to Him, and making mention, as was meet, of His greatness.

Enoch 27

[1] Then said I: 'For what object is this blessed land, which is entirely filled with trees, and this accursed valley between?'

[2] Then Uriel, one of the holy angels who was with me, answered and said:
'This accursed valley is for those who are accursed for ever: Here shall all [the accursed] be gathered together who utter with their lips against Jah unseemly words and of His glory speak hard things.

(E) Here shall they be gathered together, and here shall be their place of judgement.

[3] In the last days there shall be upon them the spectacle of righteous judgement in the presence of the righteous for ever: here shall the merciful bless Jah of glory, the Eternal King.

(G) Here shall they be gathered together, and here shall be the place of their habitation. 3. In the last times, in the days of the true judgement in the presence of the righteous for ever: here shall the godly bless Jah of Glory, the Eternal King.

[4] In the days of judgement over the former, they shall bless Him for the mercy in accordance with which He has assigned them their lot.'

[5] Then I blessed Jah of Glory and set forth His glory and lauded Him gloriously.

Enoch 28

[1] Then I went to another place from the desert; towards the east of that mountain which I had approached.

[2] There I beheld choice trees, particularly, those which produce the sweet-smelling opiate, frankincense and myrrh; and trees unlike to each other.

Choice trees. Literally, "trees of judgment"

[3] And over it, above them, was the elevation of the eastern mountain at no great distance.

Enoch 29

[1] I likewise saw another place with valleys of water which never wasted,

[2] Where I perceived a goodly tree, which in smell resembled frankincense and myrrh.

[3] And towards the sides of these valleys I perceived cinnamon of a sweet odour. Over them I advanced towards the east.

Enoch 30

[1] Then I beheld another mountain containing trees, from which water flowed like Neketro, Its name was Sarira, and Kalboneba. And upon this mountain I beheld another mountain, upon which were trees of Alva.

Neketro. A nectar. Sarira, and Kalboneba. Styrax and galbanum.Alva. Aloe.

[2] These trees were full, like almond trees, and strong; and when they produced fruit, it was superior to all redolence.

[3] And on the sides of those valleys I saw fragrant cinnamon. And beyond these I proceeded to the east.

Enoch 31

[1] After these things, surveying the entrances of the north, above the mountains, I perceived seven mountains replete with pure nard, odoriferous trees, cinnamon and papyrus.

[2] From there I passed on above the summits of those mountains to some distance eastwards, and went over the Erythraean sea. And when I was advanced far beyond it, I passed along above the angel Zateel, and arrived at the garden of righteousness. In this garden I beheld, among other trees, some which were numerous and large, and which flourished there.

Erythraean sea. The Red Sea.

[3] Their fragrance was agreeable and powerful, and their appearance both varied and elegant. The tree of knowledge also was there, of which if any one eats, he becomes endowed with great wisdom.

[4] It was like a species of the tamarind tree, bearing fruit which resembled grapes

extremely fine; and its fragrance extended to a considerable distance. I exclaimed, How beautiful is this tree, and how delightful is its appearance!

[5] Then holy Raphael, an angel who was with me, answered and said, This is the tree of knowledge, of which your ancient father and your aged mother ate, who were before you; and who, obtaining knowledge, their eyes being opened, and knowing themselves to be naked, were expelled from the garden.

Enoch 32

[1] From there I went on towards the extremities of the earth; where I saw large beasts different from each other, and birds various in their countenances and forms, as well as with notes of different sounds.

[2] To the east of these beasts I perceived the extremities of the earth, where heaven ceased. The gates of heaven stood open, and I beheld the celestial stars come forth. I numbered them as they proceeded out of the gate, and wrote them all down, as they came out one by one according to their number. I wrote down their names altogether, their times and their seasons, as the angel Uriel, who was with me, pointed them out to me.

[3] He showed them all to me, and wrote down an account of them.

[4] He also wrote down for me their names, their regulations, and their operations.

Enoch 33

[1] From there I advanced on towards the north, to the extremities of the earth.

[2] And there I saw a great and glorious wonder at the extremities of the whole earth.

[3] I saw there heavenly gates opening into heaven; three of them distinctly separated. The northern winds proceeded from them, blowing cold, hail, frost, snow, dew, and rain.

[4] From one of the gates they blew mildly; but when they blew from the two other gates, it was with violence and force. They blew over the earth with strength.

Enoch 34

1 From there I went to the extremities of the world westwards;

2 Where I perceived three gates open, as I had seen in the north; the gates and passages through them being of equal magnitude.

Enoch 35

[1] Then I proceeded to the extremities of the earth southwards; where I saw three gates open to the south, from which issued dew, rain, and wind.

[2] From there I went to the extremities of heaven eastwards; where I saw three heavenly gates open to the east, which had smaller gates within them. Through each of these small gates the stars of heaven passed on, and proceeded towards the west by a path which was seen by them, and that at every period of their appearance.

[3] When I beheld them, I blessed; every time in which they appeared, I blessed Jah of glory, who had made those great and splendid signs, that they might display the magnificence of this works to angels and to the souls of men; and that these might glorify all his works and operations; might see the effect of his power; might glorify the great labour of his hands; and bless him for ever.

(No Chapter 36)

Enoch 37

[1] The second vision which he saw, the vision of wisdom--which Enoch the son of Jared, the son of Mahalalel, the son of Cainan, the son of Enos, the son of Seth, the son of Adam, saw.

[2] And this is the beginning of the words of wisdom which I lifted up my voice to speak and say to those which dwell on earth: Hear, ye men of old time, and see, ye that come after, the words of the Holy One which I will speak before Jah of spirits.

[3] It were better to declare them only to the men of old time, but even from those that come after we will not withhold the beginning of wisdom.

[4] Till the present day such wisdom has never been given by Jah of spirits as I have received according to my insight, according to the good pleasure of Jah of spirits by whom the lot of eternal life has been given to me.

[5] Now three parables were imparted to me, and I lifted up my voice and recounted them to those that dwell on the earth.

Enoch 38

[1] The First Parable.
When the congregation of the righteous shall appear,
And sinners shall be judged for their sins,
And shall be driven from the face of the earth:

[2] And when the Righteous One shall appear before the eyes of the righteous,
Whose elect works hang upon Jah of spirits,
And light shall appear to the righteous and the elect who dwell on the earth, Where then will be the dwelling of the sinners, And where the resting-place of those who have denied Jah of spirits? It had been good for them if they had not been born.

[3] When the secrets of the righteous shall be revealed and the sinners judged,
And the godless driven from the presence of the righteous and elect,
[4] From that time those that possess the earth shall no longer be powerful and exalted:

And they shall not be able to behold the face of the holy,
For Jah of spirits has caused His light to appear
On the face of the holy, righteous, and elect.

[5] Then shall the kings and the mighty perish
And be given into the hands of the righteous and holy.
[6] And thenceforward none shall seek for themselves mercy from Jah of spirits
For their life is at an end.

Enoch 39

[1] And it shall come to pass in those days that elect and holy children will descend from the high heaven, and their seed will become one with the children of men.

[2] And in those days Enoch received books of zeal and wrath, and books of disquiet and expulsion.

And mercy shall not be accorded to them, saith Jah of spirits.
[3] And in those days a whirlwind carried me off from the earth,
And set me down at the end of the heavens.

[4] And there I saw another vision, the dwelling-places of the holy,
And the resting-places of the righteous.

[5] Here mine eyes saw their dwellings with His righteous angels, And their resting-places with the holy.

And they petitioned and interceded and prayed for the children of men, And righteousness flowed before them as water, And mercy like dew upon the earth:
Thus it is amongst them for ever and ever.

[6a] And in that place mine eyes saw the Elect One of righteousness and of faith,
[7a] And I saw his dwelling-place under the wings of Jah of spirits.
[6b] And righteousness shall prevail in his days,
And the righteous and elect shall be without number before Him for ever and ever.
[7b] And all the righteous and elect before Him shall be strong as fiery lights,
And their mouth shall be full of blessing,

And their lips extol the name of Jah of spirits,
And righteousness before Him shall never fail,
[And uprightness shall never fail before Him.
[8] There I wished to dwell, And my spirit longed for that dwelling-place: And there heretofore hath been my portion, For so has it been established concerning me before Jah of spirits.

[9] In those days I praised and extolled the name of Jah of spirits with blessings and praises, because He hath destined me for blessing and glory according to the good pleasure of Jah of spirits.

[10] For a long time my eyes regarded that place, and I blessed Him and praised Him, saying: 'Blessed is He, and may He be blessed from the beginning and for evermore.

[11] And before Him there is no ceasing. He knows before the world was created what is for ever and what will be from generation unto generation.

[12] Those who sleep not bless Thee: they stand before Thy glory and bless, praise, and extol, saying: "Holy, holy, holy, is Jah of spirits: He filleth the earth with spirits."'

[13] And here my eyes saw all those who sleep not: they stand before Him and bless and say: 'Blessed be Thou, and blessed be the name of Jah for ever and ever.'

[14] And my face was changed; for I could no longer behold.

Enoch 40

[1] After this I beheld thousands of thousands, and myriads of myriads, and a multitude beyone number and reckoning, standing before Jah of spirits.

[2] On the four wings likewise of Jah of spirits, on the four sides, I perceived others,

besides those who were standing before him. Their names, too, I know; because the angel, who proceeded with me, declared them to me, discovering to me every secret thing.

[3] Then I heard the voices of those upon the four sides magnifying Jah of glory.

[4] The first voice blessed Jah of spirits for ever and for ever.

[5] The second voice I heard blessing the Elect One, and the elect who suffer on account of Jah of spirits.

[6] The third voice I heard petitioning and praying for those who dwell upon earth, and supplicate the name of Jah of spirits.

[7] The fourth voice I heard expelling the impious angels, and prohibiting them from entering into the presence of Jah of spirits, to prefer accusations against the inhabitants of the earth.

[8] After this I besought the angel of peace, who proceeded with me, to explain all that was concealed. I said to him, Who are those whom I have seen on the four sides, and who words I have heard and written down? He replied, The first is the merciful, the patient, the holy Michael.

[9] The second is he who presides over every suffering and every affliction of the sons of men, the holy Raphael. The third, who presides over all that is powerful, is Gabriel. And the fourth, who presides over repentance, and the hope of those who will inherit eternal life, is Phanuel. These are the four angels of the most high God, and their four voices, which at that time I heard.

Enoch 41

[1] After this I beheld the secrets of the heavens and of paradise, according to its divisions; and of human action, as they weight it there in balances. I saw the habitations of the elect, and the habitations of the holy. And there my eyes beheld all the sinners, who denied Jah of glory, and whom they were expelling from there, and dragging away, as they stood there; no punishment proceeding against them from Jah of spirits.

[2] There, too, my eyes beheld the secrets of the lightning and the thunder; and the secrets of the winds, how they are distributed as they blow over the earth: the secrets of the winds, of the dew, and of the clouds. There I perceived the place from which they issued forth, and became saturated with the dust of the earth.

[3] There I saw the wooden receptacles out of which the winds became separated, the receptacle of hail, the receptacle of snow, the receptacle of the clouds, and the cloud itself, which continued over the earth before the creation of the world.

[4] I beheld also the receptacles of the moon, whence they came, whither they proceeded, their glorious return, and how one became more splendid than another. I marked their rich progress, their unchangeable progress, their disunited and undiminished progress; their observance of a mutual fidelity by a stable oath; their proceeding forth before the sun, and their adherence to the path allotted them, in obedience to the command of Jah of spirits. Potent is his name for ever and for ever. Their proceeding forth...path allotted them.

[5] After this I perceived, that the path both concealed and manifest of the moon, as well as the progress of its path, was there

completed by day and by night; while each, one with another, looked towards Jah of spirits, magnifying and praising without cessation, since praise to them is rest; for in the splendid sun there is a frequent conversion to blessing and to malediction.

[6] The course of the moon's path to the righteous is light, but to sinners it is darkness; in the name of Jah of spirits, who created a division between light and darkness, and, separating the spirits of men, strengthened the spirits of the righteous in the name of his own righteousness.

[7] Nor does the angel prevent this, neither is he endowed with the power of preventing it; for the Judge beholds them all, and judges them all in his own presence.

Enoch 42

[1] Wisdom found no place where she might dwell;
Then a dwelling-place was assigned her in the heavens.

[2] Wisdom went forth to make her dwelling among the children of men, And found no dwelling-place:

Wisdom returned to her place, And took her seat among the angels.

[3] And unrighteousness went forth from her chambers:
Whom she sought not she found, And dwelt with them, As rain in a desert And dew on a thirsty land.

Enoch 43

[1] I beheld another splendour, and the stars of heaven. I observed that he called them all by their respective names, and that they hearkened unot Him. In a righteous balance I saw that he weighed out with their light the amplitude of their places, and the day of their appearance, and their conversion. Splendour produced splendour; and their conversion was into the number of the angels, and of the faithful.

[2] Then I inquired of the angel, who proceeded with me, and explained to me secret things, What their names were. He answered. A similitude of those has Jah of spirits shown you. They are names of the righteous who dwell upon earth, and who believe in the name of Jah of spirits for ever and for ever.

Enoch 44

[1] Another thing also I saw respecting splendour; that it rises out of the stars, and becomes splendour; being incapable of forsaking them.

Enoch 45

[1] Parable the second, respecting these who deny the name of the habitation of the holy ones, and of Jah of spirits.

[2] Heaven they shall not ascend, nor shall they come on the earth. This shall be the portion of sinners, who deny the name of Jah of spirits, and who are thus reserved for the day of punishment and of affliction.

[3] In that day shall the Elect One sit upon a throne of glory; and shall choose their conditions and countless habitations, while their spirits within them shall be strengthened, when they behold my Elect One, for those who have fled for protection to my holy and glorious name.

[4] In that day I will cause my Elect One to dwell in the midst of them; will change the face of heaven; will bless it, and illuminate it for ever.

[5] I will also change the face of the earth, will bless it; and cause those whom I have elected to dwell upon it. But those who have committed sin and iniquity shall not inhabit it, for I have marked their proceedings. My righteous ones will I satisfy with peace, placing them before me; but the condemnation of sinners shall draw near, that I may destroy them from the face of the earth.

Enoch 46

[1] There I beheld the Ancient of days, whose head was like white wool, and with him another, whose countenance resembled that of man. His countenance was full of grace, like that of one of the holy angels. Then I inquired of one of the angels, who went with me, and who showed me every secret thing, concerning this Son of man; who he was; whence he was and why he accompanied the Ancient of days.

[2] He answered and said to me, This is the Son of man, to whom righteousness belongs; with whom righteousness has dwelt; and who will reveal all the treasures of that which is concealed: for Jah of spirits has chosen him; and his portion has surpassed all before Jah of spirits in everlasting uprightness.

[3] This Son of man, whom you behold, shall raise up kings and the mighty from their dwelling places, and the powerful from their thrones; shall loosen the bridles of the powerful, and break in pieces the teeth of sinners.

[4] He shall hurl kings from their thrones and their dominions; because they will not exalt and praise him, nor humble themselves before him, by whom their kingdoms were granted to them. The countenance likewise of the mighty shall He cast down, filling them with confusion. Darkness shall be their habitation, and worms shall be their bed; nor from that their bed shall they hope to be again raised, because they exalted not the name of Jah of spirits.

[5] They shall condemn the stars of heaven, shall lift up their hands against the Most High, shall tread upon and inhabit the earth, exhibiting all their acts of iniquity, even their works of iniquity. Their strength shall be in their riches, and their faith in the gods whom they have formed with their own hands. They shall deny the name of Jah of spirits, and shall expel him from the temples, in which they assemble;

[6] And with him the faithful, who suffer in the name of Jah of spirits.

[7] And they persecute the houses of His congregations,
And the faithful who hang upon the name of Jah of spirits.

Enoch 47

[1] And in those days shall have ascended the prayer of the righteous,
And the blood of the righteous from the earth before Jah of spirits.

[2] In those days the holy ones who dwell above in the heavens Shall unite with one voice And supplicate and pray and praise, And give thanks and bless the name of Jah of spirits On behalf of the blood of the righteous which has been shed, And that the

prayer of the righteous may not be in vain before Jah of spirits, That judgement may be done unto them,
And that they may not have to suffer for ever.

[3] In those days I saw the Head of Days when He seated himself upon the throne of His glory, And the books of the living were opened before Him: And all His host which is in heaven above and His counselors stood before Him,

[4] And the hearts of the holy were filled with joy;
Because the number of the righteous had been offered,
And the prayer of the righteous had been heard,
And the blood of the righteous been required before Jah of spirits.

Enoch 48

[1] In that place I beheld a fountain of righteousness, which was inexhaustible, encircled by many springs of wisdom. Of these all the thirsty drank, and were filled with wisdom, having their habitation with the righteous, the elect, and the holy.

[2] In that hour was this Son of man invoked before Jah of spirits, and his name in the presence of the Ancient of days.

[3] Before the sun and the signs were created, before the stars of heaven were formed, his name was invoked in the presence of Jah of spirits. A support shall he be for the righteous and the holy to lean upon, without falling; and he shall be the light of nations.

[4] He shall be the hope of those whose hearts are troubled. All, who dwell on earth, shall fall down and worship before him; shall bless and glorify him, and sing praises to the name of Jah of spirits.

[5] Therefore the Elect and the Concealed One existed in his presence, before the world was created, and for ever.

[6] In his presence he existed, and has revealed to the saints and to the righteous the wisdom of Jah of spirits; for he has preserved the lot of the righteous, because they have hated and rejected this world of iniquity, and have detested all its works and ways, in the name of Jah of spirits.

[7] For in his name shall they be preserved; and his will shall be their life. In those days shall the kings of the earth and the mighty men, who have gained the world by their achievements, become humble in countenance.

[8] For in the day of their anxiety and trouble their souls shall not be saved; and they shall be in subjection to those whom I have chosen.

[9] I will cast them like hay into the fire, and like lead into the water. Thus shall they burn in the presence of the righteous, and sink in the presence of the holy; nor shall a tenth part of them be found.

[10] But in the day of their trouble, the world shall obtain tranquillity.

[11] In his presence shall they fall, and not be raised up again; nor shall there be any one to take them out of his hands, and to lift them up: for they have denied Jah of spirits, and his Anointed. The name of Jah of spirits shall be blessed.

Enoch 48A

* Two consecutive chapters are numbered "48."

[1] Wisdom is poured forth like water, and glory fails not before him for evermore; for potent is he in all the secrets of righteousness.

[2] But iniquity passes away like a shadow, and possesses not a fixed station: for the Elect One stands before Jah of spirits; and his glory is for ever and ever; and his power from generation to generation.

[3] With him dwells the spirit of intellectual wisdom, the spirit of instruction and of power, and the spirit of those who sleep in righteousness; he shall judge secret things.

[4] Nor shall any be able to utter a single word before him; for the Elect One is in the presence of Jah of spirits, according to his good pleasure.

Enoch 49

[1] And in those days a change shall take place for the holy and elect, And the light of days shall abide upon them, And glory and honour shall turn to the holy,
[2] On the day of affliction on which evil shall have been treasured up against the sinners.

And the righteous shall be victorious in the name of Jah of spirits: And He will cause the others to witness this That they may repent And forgo the works of their hands.

[3] They shall have no honour through the name of Jah of spirits, Yet through His name shall they be saved, And Jah of spirits will have compassion on them, For His compassion is great.
[4] And He is righteous also in His judgement, And in the presence of His glory unrighteousness also shall not maintain itself: At His judgement the unrepentant shall perish before Him.
[5] And from henceforth I will have no mercy on them, saith Jah of spirits.

Enoch 50

[1] In those days shall the earth deliver up from her womb, and hell deliver up from hers, that which it has received; and destruction shall restore that which it owes.

[2] He shall select the righteous and holy from among them; for the day of their salvation has approached.

[3] And in those days shall the Elect One sit upon his throne, while every secret of intellectual wisdom shall proceed from his mouth, for Jah of spirits has gifted and glorified him.

[4] In those days the mountains shall skip like rams, and the hills shall leap like young sheep satiated with milk; and all the righteousshall become like angels in heaven.

[5] Their countenance shall be bright with joy; for in those days shall the Elect One be exalted. The earth shall rejoice; the righteous shall inhabit it, and the elect possess it.

Enoch 51

[1] After that period, in the place where I had seen every secret sight, I was snatched up in a whirlwind, and carried off westwards.

[2] There my eyes beheld the secrets of heaven, and all which existed on earth; a mountain of iron, a mountain of copper, a mountain of silver, a mountain of gold, a mountain of fluid metal, and a mountain of lead.

[3] And I inquired of the angel who went with me, saying, What are these things, which in secret I behold?

[4] He said, All these things which you behold shall be for the dominion of His Annointed, that he may command, and be powerful upon earth.

[5] And that angel of peace answered me, saying, Wait but a short time, and you shalt understand, and every secret thing shall be revealed to you, which Jah of spirits has decreed. Those mountains which you have seen, the mountain of iron, the mountain of copper, the mountain of silver, the mountain of gold, the mountain of fluid metal, and the mountain of lead, all these in the presence of the Elect One shall be like a honeycomb before the fire, and like water descending from above upon these mountains; and shall become debilitated before his feet.

[6] In those days men shall not be saved by gold and by silver.

[7] Nor shall they have it in their power to secure themselves, and to fly.

[8] There shall be neither iron for was, nor a coat of mail for the breast.

[9] Copper shall be useless; useless also that which neither rusts nor consumes away; and lead shall not be coveted.

[10] All these things shall be rejected, and perish from off the earth, when the Elect One shall appear in the presence of Jah of spirits.

Enoch 52

[1] There my eyes beheld a deep valley; and wide was its entrance.

[2] All who dwell on land, on the sea, and in islands, shall bring to it gifts, presents, and offerings; yet that deep valley shall not be full. Their hands shall commit iniquity. Whatsoever they produce by labour, the sinners shall devour with crime. But they shall perish from the face of Jah of spirits, and from the face of his earth. They shall stand up, and shall not fail for ever and ever.

[3] I beheld the angels of punishment, who were dwelling there, and preparing every instrument of Satan.

[4] Then I inquired of the angel of peace, who proceeded with me, for whom those instruments were preparing.

[5] He said, These they are preparing for the kings and powerful ones of the earth, that thus they may perish.

[6] After which the righteous and chosen house of his congregation shall appear, and thenceforward unchangeable in the name of Jah of spirits.

[7] Nor shall those mountains exist in his presence as the earth and the hills, as the fountains of water exist. And the righteous shall be relieved from the vexation of sinners.

Enoch 53

[1] Then I looked and turned myself to another part of the earth, where I beheld a deep valley burning with fire.

[2] To this valley they brought monarchs and the mighty.

[3] And there my eyes beheld the instruments which they were making, fetters of iron with immeasurable weight.

[4] Then I inquired of the angel of peace, who proceeded with me, saying, For whom are these fetters and instruments prepared?

[5] He replied, These are prepared for the host of Azazeel, that they may be delivered over and adjudged to the lowest condemnation; and that their angels may be overwhelmed with hurled stones, as Jah of spirits has commanded.

[6] Michael and Gabriel, Raphael and Phanuel shall be strengthened in that day, and shall then cast them into a furnace of blazing fire, that Jah of spirits may be avenged of them for their crimes; because they became ministers of Satan, and seduced those who dwell upon earth.

[7] In those days shall punishment go forth from Jah of spirits; and the receptacles of water which are above the heavens shall be opened, and the fountains likewise, which are under the heavens and under the earth.

[8] All the waters, which are in the heavens and above them, shall be mixed together.

[9] The water which is above heaven shall be the masculine agent;

[10] And the water which is under the earth shall be the feminine recipient: and all shall be destroyed who dwell upon earth, and who dwell under the extremities of heaven.

[11] By these means shall they understand the iniquity which they have committed on earth: and by these means shall they perish.

Enoch 54

[1] Afterwards the Ancient of days repented, and said, In vain have I destroyed all the inhabitants of the earth.

[2] And he sware by his great name, *saying*, Henceforwards I will not act thus towards all those who dwell upon earth.

[3] But I will place a sign in the heavens; and it shall be a faithful witness between me and them for ever, as long as the days of heaven and earth last upon the earth.

[4] Afterwards, in accordance with My command, when I shall be disposed to seize them beforehand, by the instrumentality of angels, in the day of affliction and trouble, my wrath and my punishment shall remain upon them, my punishment and my wrath, saith God Jah of spirits.

[5] O you kings, O you mighty, who inhabit the world you shall behold my Elect One, sitting upon the throne of my glory. And he shall judge Azazeel, all his associates, and all his hosts, in the name of Jah of spirits.

[6] There likewise I beheld hosts of angels who were moving in punishment, confined in a net-work of iron and brass. Then I inquired of the angel of peace, who proceeded with me, To whom those under confinement were going.

[7] He said, To each of their elect and their beloved, that they may be cast into the fountains and deep recesses of the valley.

[8] And that valley shall be filled with their elect and beloved; the days of whose life shall be consumed, but the days of their error shall be innumerable.

[9] Then shall princes combine together, and conspire. The chiefs of the east, among the

Parthians and Medes, shall remove kings, in whom a spirit of perturbation shall enter. They shall hurl them from their thrones, springing as lions from their dens, and like famished wolves into the midst of the flock.

[10] They shall go up, and tread upon the land of their elect. The land of their elect shall be before them. The threshing-floor, the path, But the city of my righteous shall be a hindrance to their horses. And they shall begin to fight among themselves, And their right hand shall be strong against themselves, And a man shall not know his brother,
[11] Nor a son his father or his mother,

Till there be no number of the corpses through their slaughter, And their punishment be not in vain.

[12] In those days Sheol shall open its jaws, And they shall be swallowed up therein

And their destruction shall be at an end; Sheol shall devour the sinners in the presence of the elect.

Enoch 55

[1] After this I beheld another army of chariots with men riding in them.

[2] And they came upon the wind from the east, from the west, and from the south (*From the south literally, "from the midst of the day"*).

[3] The sound of the noise of their chariots was heard.

[4] And when that agitation took place; the saints out of heaven perceived it; the pillar of the earth shook from its foundation; and the sound was heard from the extremities of the earth unto the extremities of heaven at the same time.

[5] Then they all fell down, and worshipped Jah of spirits.

[6] This is the end of the second parable.

Enoch 56

[1] I now began to utter the third parable, concerning the saints and the elect.

[2] Blessed are you, O saints and elect, for glorious is your lot.

[3] The saints shall exist in the light of the sun, and the elect in the light of everlasting life, the days of whose life shall never terminate; nor shall the days of the saints be numbered, who seek for light, and obtain righteousness with Jah of spirits.

[4] Peace be to the saints with Jah of the world.

[5] Henceforward shall the saints be told to seek in heaven the secrets of righteousness, the heritage of faith; for like the sun has it arisen upon the earth, while darkness has passed away. There shall be light that never endeth; nor shall they enter upon the enumeration of time; for darkness shall be previously destroyed, and light shall increase before Jah of spirits; before Jah of spirits shall the light of uprightness be established for ever.

Enoch 57

[1] In those days my eyes beheld the secrets of the lightnings and the splendours, and the judgment belonging to them.

[12] And the angel of peace, who was with me, said, These two monsters are by the power of God prepared to become food, that the punishment of God may not be in vain.

[13] Then shall children be slain with their mothers, and sons with their fathers.

[14] And when the punishment of Jah of spirits shall continue, upon them shall it continue, that the punishment of Jah of spirits may not take place in vain. After that, judgment shall exist with mercy and longsuffering.

Enoch 59

[1] Then another angel, who proceeded with me, spoke to me;

[2] And showed me the first and last secrets in heaven above, and in the depths of the earth:

[3] In the extremities of heaven, and in the foundations of it, and in the receptacle of the winds.

[4] He showed me how their spirits were divided; how they were balanced; and how both the springs and the winds were numbered according to the force of their spirit.

[5] He showed me the power of the moon's light, that its power is a just one; as well as the divisions of the stars, according to their respective names;

[6] That every division is divided; that the lightning flashes;

[7] That its troops immediately obey; and that a cessation takes place during thunder in continuance of its sound. Nor are the thunder and the lightning separated; neither do both of them move with one spirit; yet they are not separated.

[8] For when the lightning lightens, the thunder sounds, and the spirit at a proper period pauses, making an equal division between them; for the receptacle, upon which their periods depend, is loose as sand. Each of them at a proper season is restrained with a bridle; and turned by the power of the spirit, which thus propels them according to the spacious extent of the earth.

[9] The spirit likewise of the sea is potent and strong; and as a strong power causes it to ebb, so is it driven forwards, and scattered against the mountains of the earth. The spirit of the frost has its angel; in the spirit of hail there is a good angel; the spirit of snow ceases in its strength, and a solitary spirit is in it, which ascends from it like vapour, and is called refrigeration.

[10] The spirit also of mist dwells with them in their receptacle; but it has a receptacle to itself; for its progress is in splendour.

[11] In light, and in darkness, in winter and in summer. Its receptacle is bright, and an angel is in it.

[12] The spirit of dew has its abode in the extremities of heaven, in connection with the receptacle of rain; and its progress is in winter and in summer. The cloud produced by it, and the cloud of the mist, become united; one gives to the other; and when the spirit of rain is in motion from its receptacle, angels come, and opening its receptacle, bring it forth.

[13] When likewise it is sprinkled over all the earth, it forms an union with every kind of water on the ground; for the waters remain on the ground, because they

[2] They lighten for a blessing and for a curse, according to the will of Jah of spirits.

[3] And there I saw the secrets of the thunder, when it rattles above in heaven, and its sound is heard.

[4] The habitations also of the earth were shown to me. The sound of the thunder is for peace and for blessing, as well as for a curse, according to the word of Jah of spirits.

[5] Afterwards every secret of the splendours and of the lightnings was seen by me. For blessing and for fertility they lighten.

Enoch 58

[1] In the five hundredth year, and in the seventh month, on the fourteenth day of the month, of the lifetime of Enoch, in that parable, I saw that the heaven of heavens shook; that it shook violently; and that the powers of the Most High, and the angels, thousands and thousands, and myriads of myriads, were agitated with great agitation. And when I looked, the Ancient of days was sitting on the throne of his glory, while the angels and saints were standing around him. A great trembling came upon me, and terror seized me. My loins were bowed down and loosened; my reins were dissolved; and I fell upon my face. The holy Michael, another holy angel, one of the holy ones, was sent, who raised me up.

[2] And when he raised me, my spirit returned; for I was incapable of enduring this vision of violence, its agitation, and the concussion of heaven.

[3] Then holy Michael said to me, Why are you disturbed at this vision?

[4] Hitherto has existed the day of mercy: and he has been merciful and longsuffering towards all who dwell upon the earth.

[5] But when the time shall come, then shall the power, the punishment, and the judgment take place, which Jah of spirits has prepared for those who prostrate themselves to the judgment of righteousness for those who abjure that judgment, and for those who take his name in vain.

[6] That day has been prepared for the elect as a day of covenant; and for sinners as a day of inquisition.

[7] In that day shall be separated from one another two monsters; a female monster, whose name is Leviathan, dwelling in the depths of the sea, above the springs of waters;

[8] And a male monster, whose name is Behemoth; which possesses, moving on his breast, the invisible wilderness.

[9] His name was Dendayen in the east of the garden, where the elect and the righteous will dwell; where my [great-] grandfather was taken up, the seventh from Adam the first of men, whom Jah of spirits made.

This implies that this section of the book was written by Noah, Enoch's descendant, rather than Enoch. Scholars have speculated that this portion of the book may contain fragments of the lost Apocalypse of Noah.

[10] Then I asked of another angel to show me the power of those monsters, how they became separated, how they became separated on the same day, one being in the depths of the sea, and one in the dry desert.

[11] And he said, You, son of man, are here desirous of understanding secret things.

afford nourishment to the earth from the Most High, who is in heaven.

[14] Upon this account therefore there is a regulation in the quantity of rain, which the angels receive.

[15] These things I saw; all of them, even paradise.

Enoch 60

[1] In those days I beheld long cords given to those angels; who took to their wings, and fled, advancing towards the north.

[2] And I inquired of the angel, saying, Wherefore have they taken those long ropes, and gone forth? He said, They are gone forth to measure.

[3] The angel, who proceeded with me, said, These are the measures of the righteous; and cords shall the righteous bring, that they may trust in the name of Jah of spirits for ever and ever.

[4] The elect shall begin to dwell with the elect.

5And these are the measures which shall be given to faith, and whichshall strengthen the words of righteousness.

[6] These measures shall reveal all the secrets in the depth of the earth.

[7] And it shall be, that those who have been destroyed in the desert, and who have been devoured by the fish of the sea, and by wild beasts, shall return, and trust in the day of the Elect One; for none shall perish in the presence of Jah of spirits, nor shall any be capable of perishing.

[8] Then they received the commandment, all who were in the heavens above; to whom a combined power, voice, and splendour, like fire, were given.

[9] And first, with their voice, they blessed him, they exalted him, they glorified him with wisdom, and ascribed to him wisdom with the word, and with the breath of life.

[10] Then Jah of spirits seated upon the throne of his glory the Elect One;

[11] Who shall judge all the works of the holy, in heaven above, and in a balance shall he weigh their actions. And when he shall lift up his countenance to judge their secret ways in the word of the name of Jah of spirits, and their progress in the path of the righteous judgment of God most high;

[12] They shall all speak with united voice; and bless, glorify, exalt, and praise, in the name of Jah of spirits.

[13] He shall call to every power of the heavens, to all the holy above, and to the power of God. The Cherubim, the Seraphim, and the Ophanin, all the angels of power, and all the angels of Jah s, namely, of the Elect One, and of the other Power, who was upon earth over the water on that day,

[14] Shall raise their united voice; shall bless, glorify, praise, and exalt with the spirit of faith, with the spirit of wisdom and patience, with the spirit of mercy, with the spirit of judgment and peace, and with the spirit of benevolence; all shall say with united voice; Blessed is He; and the name of Jah of spirits shall be blessed for ever and for ever; all, who sleep not, shall bless it in heaven above.

[15] All the holy in heaven shall bless it; all the elect who dwell in the garden of life; and every spirit of light, who is capable of

blessing, glorifying, exalting, and praising your holy name; and every mortal
man, more than the powers of heaven, shall glorify and bless your name for ever and ever.

[16] For great is the mercy of Jah of spirits; long-suffering is he; and all his works, all his power, great as are the things which he has done, has he revealed to the saints and to the elect, in the name of Jah of spirits.

Enoch 61

[1] And thus Jah commanded the kings and the mighty and the exalted, and those who dwell on the earth, and said: 'Open your eyes and lift up your horns if ye are able to recognize the Elect One.'

[2] And Jah of spirits seated him on the throne of His glory, And the spirit of righteousness was poured out upon him, And the word of his mouth slays all the sinners, And all the unrighteous are destroyed from before his face.

[3] And there shall stand up in that day all the kings and the mighty, And the exalted and those who hold the earth, And they shall see and recognize How he sits on the throne of his glory, And righteousness is judged before him, And no lying word is spoken before him.

[4] Then shall pain come upon them as on a woman in travail, And she has pain in bringing forth. When her child enters the mouth of the womb, And she has pain in bringing forth.

[5] And one portion of them shall look on the other,
And they shall be terrified, And they shall be downcast of countenance, And pain shall seize them, When they see that Son of Man Sitting on the throne of his glory.

[6] And the kings and the mighty and all who possess the earth shall bless and glorify and extol him who rules over all, who was hidden.

[7] For from the beginning the Son of Man was hidden,
And the Most High preserved him in the presence of His might, And revealed him to the elect.

[8] And the congregation of the elect and holy shall be sown, And all the elect shall stand before him on that day.

[9] And all the kings and the mighty and the exalted and those who rule the earth Shall fall down before him on their faces, And worship and set their hope upon that Son of Man, And petition him and supplicate for mercy at his hands.

[10] Nevertheless that Lord of Spirits will so press them
That they shall hastily go forth from His presence,
And their faces shall be filled with shame, And the darkness grow deeper on their faces.

[11] And He will deliver them to the angels for punishment, To execute vengeance on them because they have oppressed His children and His elect

[12] And they shall be a spectacle for the righteous and for His elect: They shall rejoice over them, Because the wrath of Jah of spirits resteth upon them,
And His sword is drunk with their blood.

13. And the righteous and elect shall be saved on that day,
And they shall never thenceforward see the face of the sinners and unrighteous.

14. And Jah of spirits will abide over them,
And with that Son of Man shall they eat
And lie down and rise up for ever and ever.

15. And the righteous and elect shall have risen from the earth,
And ceased to be of downcast countenance.

And they shall have been clothed with garments of glory,
16. And these shall be the garments of life from Jah of spirits:
And your garments shall not grow old,
Nor your glory pass away before Jah of spirits.

Enoch 62

[1] In those days shall the mighty and the kings who possess the earth implore Him to grant them a little respite from His angels of punishment to whom they were delivered, that they might fall down and worship before Jah of spirits, and confess their sins before Him.

[2] And they shall bless and glorify Jah of spirits, and say: 'Blessed is Jah of spirits and Jah of kings, And Jah of the mighty and Jah of the rich, And Jah of glory and Jah of wisdom,

[3] And splendid in every secret thing is Thy power from generation to generation, And Thy glory for ever and ever: Deep are all Thy secrets and innumerable,
And Thy righteousness is beyond reckoning.

[4] We have now learnt that we should glorify

And bless Jah of kings and Him who is king over all kings.

[5] And they shall say: 'Would that we had rest to glorify and give thanks And confess our faith before His glory!

[6] And now we long for a little rest but find it not:
We follow hard upon and obtain it not: And light has vanished from before us, And darkness is our dwelling-place for ever and ever:

[7] For we have not believed before Him Nor glorified the name of Jah of spirits, nor glorified our Lord But our hope was in the sceptre of our kingdom, And in our glory.

[8] And in the day of our suffering and tribulation He saves us not, And we find no respite for confession

That our Lord is true in all His works, and in His judgements and His justice, And His judgements have no respect of persons.

[9] And we pass away from before His face on account of our works, And all our sins are reckoned up in righteousness.

[10] Now they shall say unto themselves: 'Our souls are full of unrighteous gain, but it does not prevent us from descending from the midst thereof into the burden of Sheol.'

[11] And after that their faces shall be filled with darkness And shame before that Son of Man,
And they shall be driven from his presence, And the sword shall abide before his face in their midst.

[12] Thus spake Jah of spirits: 'This is the ordinance and judgement with respect to the mighty and the kings and the exalted and

those who possess the earth before Jah of spirits.'

Enoch 63

[1] And other forms I saw hidden in that place.

[2] I heard the voice of the angel saying: 'These are the angels who descended to the earth, and revealed what was hidden to the children of men and seduced the children of men into committing sin.

Enoch 64

Enoch foretells to Noah the Deluge and his own Preservation.

[1] And in those days Noah saw the earth that it had sunk down and its destruction was nigh.

[2] And he arose from thence and went to the ends of the earth, and cried aloud to his grandfather Enoch: and Noah said three times with an embittered voice: Hear me, hear me, hear me.'

[3] And I said unto him: 'Tell me what it is that is falling out on the earth that the earth is in such evil plight and shaken, lest perchance I shall perish with it?'

[4] And thereupon there was a great commotion, on the earth, and a voice was heard from heaven, and I fell on my face.

[5] And Enoch my grandfather came and stood by me, and said unto me: 'Why hast thou cried unto me with a bitter cry and weeping?

[6] And a command has gone forth from the presence of Jah concerning those who dwell on the earth that their ruin is accomplished because they have learnt all the secrets of the angels, and all the violence of the Satans, and all their powers--the most secret ones-- and all the power of those who practice sorcery, and the power of witchcraft, and the power of those who make molten images for the whole earth:

[7] And how silver is produced from the dust of the earth, and how soft metal originates in the earth.

[8] For lead and tin are not produced from the earth like the first: it is a fountain that produces them, and an angel stands therein, and that angel is pre-eminent.'

[9] And after that my grandfather Enoch took hold of me by my hand and raised me up, and said unto me: 'Go, for I have asked Jah of spirits as touching this commotion on the earth.

[10] And He said unto me: "Because of their unrighteousness their judgement has been determined upon and shall not be withheld by Me for ever. Because of the sorceries which they have searched out and learnt, the earth and those who dwell upon it shall be destroyed."

[11] And these--they have no place of repentance for ever, because they have shown them what was hidden, and they are the damned: but as for thee, my son, Jah of spirits knows that thou art pure, and guiltless of this reproach concerning the secrets.

[12] And He has destined thy name to be among the holy, And will preserve thee amongst those who dwell on the earth, And has destined thy righteous seed both for kingship and for great honours, And from thy seed shall proceed a fountain of the righteous and holy without number for ever.

Enoch 65

[1] And after that he showed me the angels of punishment who are prepared to come and let loose all the powers of the waters which are beneath in the earth in order to bring judgement and destruction on all who abide and dwell on the earth.

[2] And Jah of spirits gave commandment to the angels who were going forth, that they should not cause the waters to rise but should hold them in check; for those angels were over the powers of the waters.

[3] And I went away from the presence of Enoch.

Enoch 66

God's Promise to Noah: Places of Punishment of the Angels and of the Kings.

[1] And in those days the word of God came unto me, and He said unto me: 'Noah, thy lot has come up before Me, a lot without blame, a lot of love and uprightness.

[2] And now the angels are making a wooden building, and when they have completed that task I will place My hand upon it and preserve it, and there shall come forth from it the seed of life, and a change shall set in so that the earth will not remain without inhabitant.

[3] And I will make fast thy seed before me for ever and ever, and I will spread abroad those who dwell with thee: it shall not be unfruitful on the face of the earth, but it shall be blessed and multiply on the earth in the name of Jah .'

[4] And He will imprison those angels, who have shown unrighteousness, in that burning valley which my grandfather Enoch had formerly shown to me in the west among the mountains of gold and silver and iron and soft metal and tin.

[5] And I saw that valley in which there was a great convulsion and a convulsion of the waters.

[6] And when all this took place, from that fiery molten metal and from the convulsion thereof in that place, there was produced a smell of sulphur, and it was connected with those waters, and that valley of the angels who had led astray mankind burned beneath that land.

[7] And through its valleys proceed streams of fire, where these angels are punished who had led astray those who dwell upon the earth.

[8] But those waters shall in those days serve for the kings and the mighty and the exalted, and those who dwell on the earth, for the healing of the body, but for the punishment of the spirit; now their spirit is full of lust, that they may be punished in their body, for they have denied Jah of spirits and see their punishment daily, and yet believe not in His name.

[9] And in proportion as the burning of their bodies becomes severe, a corresponding change shall take place in their spirit for ever and ever; for before Jah of spirits none shall utter an idle word.

[10] For the judgement shall come upon them, because they believe in the lust of their body and deny the Spirit of Jah .

[11] And those same waters will undergo a change in those days; for when those angels

are punished in these waters, these water-springs shall change their temperature, and when the angels ascend, this water of the springs shall change and become cold.

[12] And I heard Michael answering and saying: 'This judgement wherewith the angels are judged is a testimony for the kings and the mighty who possess the earth.'

[13] Because these waters of judgement minister to the healing of the body of the kings and the lust of their body; therefore they will not see and will not believe that those waters will change and become a fire which burns for ever.

Enoch 67

The Names and Functions of the (fallen Angels and) Satans: the secret Oath.

[1] And after this judgement they shall terrify and make them to tremble because they have shown this to those who dwell on the earth.

[2] And behold the names of those angels [and these are their names: the first of them is Samjâzâ, the second Artâqîfâ, and the third Armên, the fourth Kôkabêl, the fifth †Tûrâêl†, the sixth Rûmjâl, the seventh Dânjâl, the eighth †Nêqâêl†, the ninth Barâqêl, the tenth Azâzêl, the eleventh Armârôs, the twelfth Batarjâl, the thirteenth †Busasêjal†, the fourteenth Hanânêl, the fifteenth †Tûrêl†, and the sixteenth Sîmâpêsîêl, the seventeenth Jetrêl, the eighteenth Tûmâêl, the nineteenth Tûrêl, the twentieth †Rumâêl†, the twenty-first †Azâzêl†.

[3] And these are the chiefs of their angels and their names, and their chief ones over hundreds and over fifties and over tens.

[4] The name of the first Jeqôn: that is, the one who led astray [all] the sons of God, and brought them down to the earth, and led them astray through the daughters of men.

[5] And the second was named Asbeêl: he imparted to the holy sons of God evil counsel, and led them astray so that they defiled their bodies with the daughters of men. [6] And the third was named Gâdreêl: he it is who showed the children of men all the blows of death, and he led astray Eve, and showed [the weapons of death to the sons of men] the shield and the coat of mail, and the sword for battle, and all the weapons of death to the

children of men.

[7] And from his hand they have proceeded against those who dwell on the earth from that day and for evermore. [8] And the fourth was named Pênêmûe: he taught the children of men the bitter and the sweet, and he taught them all the secrets of their wisdom.

[9] And he instructed mankind in writing with ink and paper, and thereby many sinned from eternity to eternity and until this day.

[10] For men were not created for such a purpose, to give confirmation to their good faith with pen and ink. [11] For men were created exactly like the angels, to the intent that they should continue pure and righteous, and death, which destroys everything, could not have taken hold of them, but through this their knowledge they are perishing, and through this power it is consuming me†. [12] And the fifth was named Kâsdejâ: this is he who showed the children of men all the wicked smitings of spirits and demons, and the smitings of the embryo in the womb, that it may pass away,

and [the smitings of the soul] the bites of the serpent, and the smitings which befall through the noontide heat, the son of the serpent named Tabââ'ĕt.

[13] And this is the task of Kâsbeêl, the chief of the oath which he showed to the holy ones when he dwelt high above in glory, and its name is Bîqâ.

[14] This angel requested Michael to show him the hidden name, that he might enunciate it in the oath, so that those might quake before that name and oath who revealed all that was in secret to the children of men.

[15] And this is the power of this oath, for it is powerful and strong, and he placed this oath Akâe in the hand of Michael.

[16] And these are the secrets of this oath . .
.

And they are strong through his oath:
And the heaven was suspended before the world was created, And for ever.

[17] And through it the earth was founded upon the water, And from the secret recesses of the mountains come beautiful waters, From the creation of the world and unto eternity.

[18] And through that oath the sea was created,
And †as its foundation† He set for it the sand against the time of its anger, And it dare not pass beyond it from the creation of the world unto eternity.

[19] And through that oath are the depths made fast,
And abide and stir not from their place from eternity to eternity.

[20] And through that oath the sun and moon complete their course, And deviate not from their ordinance from eternity to eternity.

[21] And through that oath the stars complete their course, And He calls them by their names,
And they answer Him from eternity to eternity.

[22] And in like manner the spirits of the water, and of the winds, and of all zephyrs, and their paths from all the quarters of the winds.

[23] And there are preserved the voices of the thunder and the light of the lightnings: and there are preserved the chambers of the hail and the chambers of the hoarfrost, and the chambers of the mist, and the chambers of the rain and the dew.

[24] And all these believe and give thanks before Jah of spirits, and glorify Him with all their power, and their food is in every act of thanksgiving: they thank and glorify and extol the name of Jah of spirits for ever and ever.

[25] And this oath is mighty over them And through it [they are preserved and their paths are preserved, And their course is not destroyed.

Close of the Third Parable.

[26] And there was great joy amongst them, And they blessed and glorified and extolled Because the name of that Son of Man had been revealed unto them.

[27] And he sat on the throne of his glory, And the sum of judgement was given unto the Son of Man, And he caused the sinners to pass away and be destroyed from off the face of the earth, And those who have led the world astray.

[28] With chains shall they be bound, And in their assemblage-place of destruction

shall they be imprisoned, And all their works vanish from the face of the earth.
[29] And from henceforth there shall be nothing corruptible; For that Son of Man has appeared,
And has seated himself on the throne of his glory, And all evil shall pass away before his face, And the word of that Son of Man shall go forth And be strong before Jah of spirits.

This is the Third Parable of Enoch.

Enoch 68

[1] And it came to pass after this that his name during his lifetime was raised aloft to that Son of Man and to Jah of spirits from amongst those who dwell on the earth.

[2] And he was raised aloft on the chariots of the spirit and his name vanished among them.

[3] And from that day I was no longer numbered amongst them: and he set me between the two winds, between the North and the West, where the angels took the cords to measure for me the place for the elect and righteous.

[4] And there I saw the first fathers and the righteous who from the beginning dwell in that place.

Enoch 69

[1] And it came to pass after this that my spirit was translated And it ascended into the heavens:
And I saw the holy sons of God. They were stepping on flames of fire: Their garments were white [and their raiment, And their faces shone like snow.

[2] And I saw two streams of fire, And the light of that fire shone like hyacinth, And I fell on my face before Jah of spirits.

[3] And the angel Michael one of the archangels seized me by my right hand, And lifted me up and led me forth into all the secrets, And he showed me all the secrets of righteousness.

[4] And he showed me all the secrets of the ends of the heaven, And all the chambers of all the stars, and all the luminaries, Whence they proceed before the face of the holy ones.

[5] And he translated my spirit into the heaven of heavens, And I saw there as it were a structure built of crystals, And between those crystals tongues of living fire.

[6] And my spirit saw the girdle which girt that house of fire, And on its four sides were streams full of living fire, And they girt that house.

[7] And round about were Seraphin, Cherubic, and Ophannin: And these are they who sleep not And guard the throne of His glory.

[8] And I saw angels who could not be counted, A thousand thousands, and ten thousand times ten thousand, Encircling that house. And Michael, and Raphael, and Gabriel, and Phanuel, And the holy angels who are above the heavens, Go in and out of that house.

[9] And they came forth from that house, And Michael and Gabriel, Raphael and Phanuel,
And many holy angels without number.

[10] And with them the Head of Days, His head white and pure as wool, And His raiment indescribable.

[11] And I fell on my face, And my whole body became relaxed, And my spirit was transfigured; And I cried with a loud voice,. . .with the spirit of power, And blessed and glorified and extolled.

[12] And these blessings which went forth out of my mouth were well pleasing before that Head of Days. 13. And that Head of Days came with Michael and Gabriel, Raphael and Phanuel, thousands and ten thousands of angels without number.

[Lost passage wherein the Son of Man was described as accompanying the Head of Days, and Enoch asked one of the angels concerning the Son of Man as to who he was.]

[14] And he (*i.e.* the angel) came to me and greeted me with His voice, and said unto me: 'This is the Son of Man who is born unto righteousness; And righteousness abides over him, And the righteousness of the Head of Days forsakes him not.'
[15] And he said unto me: 'He proclaims unto thee peace in the name of the world to come; For from hence has proceeded peace since the creation of the world, And so shall it be unto thee for ever and for ever and ever.

[16] And all shall walk in his ways since righteousness never forsaketh him: With him will be their dwelling-places, and with him their heritage, And they shall not be separated from him for ever and ever and ever.

[17] And so there shall be length of days with that Son of Man, And the righteous shall have peace and an upright way In the name of Jah of spirits for ever and ever.'

Enoch 70

The Sun

[1] The book of the courses of the luminaries of the heaven, the relations of each, according to their classes, their dominion and their seasons, according to their names and places of origin, and according to their months, which Uriel, the holy angel, who was with me, who is their guide, showed me; and he showed me all their laws exactly as they are, and how it is with regard to all the years of the world and unto eternity, till the new creation is

accomplished which dureth till eternity.

[2] And this is the first law of the luminaries: the luminary the Sun has its rising in the eastern portals of the heaven, and its setting in the western portals of the heaven.

[3] And I saw six portals in which the sun rises, and six portals in which the sun sets and the moon rises and sets in these portals, and the leaders of the stars and those whom they lead: six in the east and six in the west, and all following each other in accurately corresponding order: also many windows to the right and left of these portals.

[4] And first there goes forth the great luminary, named the Sun, and his circumference is like the circumference of the heaven, and he is quite filled with illuminating and heating fire.

[5] The chariot on which he ascends, the wind drives, and the sun goes down from the heaven and returns through the north in

order to reach the east, and is so guided that he comes to the appropriate portal and shines in the face of the heaven.

[6] In this way he rises in the first month in the great portal, which is the fourth [those six portals in the cast]. [7] And in that fourth portal from which the sun rises in the first month are twelve window-openings, from which proceed a flame when they are opened in their season.

[8] When the sun rises in the heaven, he comes forth through that fourth portal thirty mornings in succession, and sets accurately in the fourth portal in the west of the heaven.

[9] And during this period the day becomes daily longer and the night nightly shorter to the thirtieth morning.

[10] On that day the day is longer than the night by a ninth part, and the day amounts exactly to ten parts and the night to eight parts.

[11] And the sun rises from that fourth portal, and sets in the fourth and returns to the fifth portal of the east thirty mornings, and rises from it and sets in the fifth portal. [12] And then the day becomes longer by two parts and amounts to eleven parts, and the night becomes shorter and amounts to seven parts.

[13] And it returns to the east and enters into

the sixth portal, and rises and sets in the sixth portal one-and-thirty mornings on account of its sign.

[14] On that day the day becomes longer than the night, and the day becomes double the night, and the day becomes twelve parts, and the night is shortened and becomes six parts.

[15] And the sun mounts up to make the day shorter and the night longer, and the sun returns to the east and enters into the sixth portal, and rises from it and sets thirty mornings.

[16] And when thirty mornings are accomplished, the day decreases by exactly one part, and becomes eleven parts, and the night seven.

[17] And the sun goes forth from that sixth portal in the west, and goes to the east and rises in the fifth portal for thirty mornings, and sets in the west again in the fifth western portal.

[18] On that day the day decreases by two parts, and amounts to ten parts and the night to eight parts.

[19] And the sun goes forth from that fifth portal and sets in the fifth portal of the west, and rises in the fourth portal for one-and-thirty mornings on account of its sign, and sets in the west.

[20] On that day the day is equalized with the night, [and becomes of equal length], and the night amounts to nine parts and the day to nine parts.

[21] And the sun rises from that portal and sets in the west, and returns to the east and rises thirty mornings in the third portal and sets in the west in the third portal. [22] And on that day the night becomes longer than the day, and night becomes longer than night, and day shorter than day till the thirtieth morning, and the night amounts exactly to ten parts and the day to eight parts. [23] And the sun rises from that third portal and sets in the third portal in the west and returns to the east, and for thirty mornings rises in the second portal in the

east, and in like manner sets in the second portal in the west of the heaven.

[24] And on that day the night amounts to eleven parts and the day to seven parts.

[25] And the sun rises on that day from that second portal and sets in the west in the second portal, and

returns to the east into the first portal for one-and-thirty mornings, and sets in the first portal in the west of the heaven.

[26] And on that day the night becomes longer and amounts to the double of the day: and the night amounts exactly to twelve parts and the day to six.

[27] And the sun has therewith traversed the divisions of his orbit and turns again on those divisions of his orbit, and enters that portal thirty mornings and sets also in the west opposite to it.

28. And on that night has the night decreased in length by a ninth part, and the night has become eleven parts and the day seven parts.

[29] And the sun has returned and entered into the second portal in the east, and returns on those his divisions of his orbit for thirty mornings, rising and setting.

[30] And on that day the night decreases in length, and the night amounts to ten parts and the day to eight.

[31] And on that day the sun rises from that portal, and sets in the west, and returns to the east, and rises in the third portal for one-and-thirty mornings, and sets in the west of the heaven.

[32] On that day the night decreases and amounts to nine parts, and the day to nine parts, and the night is equal to the day and the year is exactly as to its days three hundred and sixty-four.

[33] And the length of the day and of the night, and the shortness of the day and of the night arise--through the course of the sun these distinctions are made (lit. 'they are separated').

[34] So it comes that its course becomes daily longer, and its course nightly shorter.

[35] And this is the law and the course of the sun, and his return as often as he returns sixty times and rises, i.e. the great luminary which is named the sun, for ever and ever.

[36] And that which rises is the great luminary, and is so named according to its appearance, according as Jah commanded.

[37] As he rises, so he sets and decreases not, and rests not, but runs day and night, and his light is sevenfold brighter than that of the moon; but as regards size they are both equal.

Enoch 71

[1] And after this law I saw another law dealing with the smaller luminary, which is named the Moon.

[2] And her circumference is like the circumference of the heaven, and her chariot in which she rides is driven by the wind, and light is given to her in definite measure.

[3] And her rising and setting change every month: and her days are like the days of the sun, and when her light is full it amounts to the seventh part of the light of the sun.

[4] And thus she rises. And her first phase in the east comes forth on the thirtieth morning: and on that day she becomes

visible, and constitutes for you the first phase of the moon on the thirtieth day together with the sun in the portal where the sun rises.

[5] And the one half of her goes forth by a seventh part, and her whole circumference is empty, without light, with the exception of one-seventh part of it, and the fourteenth part of her light.

[6] And when she receives one-seventh part of the half of her light, her light amounts to one-seventh part and the half thereof.

[7] And she sets with the sun, and when the sun rises the moon rises with him and receives the half of one part of light, and in that night in the beginning of her morning [in the commencement of the lunar day] the moon sets with the sun, and is invisible that night with the fourteen parts and the half of one of them. 8. And she rises on that day with exactly a seventh part, and comes forth and recedes from the rising of the sun, and in her remaining days she becomes bright in the remaining thirteen parts.

Enoch 72

[1] And I saw another course, a law for her, and how according to that law she performs her monthly revolution.

[2] And all these Uriel, the holy angel who is the leader of them all, showed to me, and

their positions, and I wrote down their positions as he showed them to me, and I wrote down their months as they were, and the appearance of their lights till fifteen days were accomplished.

[3] In single seventh parts she accomplishes all her light in the east, and in single seventh parts accomplishes all her darkness in the west.

[4] And in certain months she alters her settings, and in certain months she pursues her own peculiar course.

[5] In two months the moon sets with the sun: in those two middle portals the third and the fourth.

[6] She goes forth for seven days, and turns about and returns again through the portal where the sun rises, and accomplishes all her light: and she recedes from the sun, and in eight days enters the sixth portal from which the sun goes forth.

[7] And when the sun goes forth from the fourth portal she goes forth seven days, until she goes forth from the fifth and turns back again in seven days into the fourth portal and accomplishes all her light: and she recedes and enters into the first portal in eight days.

[8] And she returns again in seven days into the fourth portal from which the sun goes forth.

[9] Thus I saw their position--how the moons rose and the sun set in those days.

[10] And if five years are added together the sun has an overplus of thirty days, and all the days which accrue to it for one of those five years, when they are full, amount to 364 days.

[11] And the overplus of the sun and of the stars amounts to six days: in 5 years 6 days every year come to 30 days: and the moon falls behind the sun and stars to the number of 30 days.

[12] And the sun and the stars bring in all the years exactly, so that they do not advance or delay their position by a single day unto eternity; but complete the years with perfect justice in 364 days.

[13] In 3 years there are 1092 days, and in 5 years 1820 days, so that in 8 years there are 2912 days.

[14] For the moon alone the days amount in 3 years to 1062 days, and in 5 years she falls 50 days behind: [i.e. to the sum (of 1770) there is

to be added (1000 and) 62 days.]

[15] And in 5 years there are 1770 days, so that for the moon the days in 8 years amount to 2832 days.

[16] [For in 8 years she falls behind to the amount of 80 days], all the days she falls behind in 8 years are 80.

[17] And the year is accurately completed in conformity with their world-stations and the stations of the sun, which rise from the portals through which it (the sun) rises and sets 30 days.

Enoch 73

[1] And the leaders of the heads of the thousands, who are placed over the whole creation and over all the stars, have also to do with the four intercalary days, being inseparable from their office, according to the reckoning of the year, and these render service on the four days which are not reckoned in the reckoning of the year.

[2] And owing to them men go wrong therein, for those luminaries truly render service on the world-stations, one in the first portal, one in the third portal of the heaven, one in the fourth portal, and one in the sixth portal, and the exactness of the year is accomplished through its separate three hundred and sixty-four stations.

[3] For the signs and the times and the years and the days the angel Uriel showed to me, whom Jah of glory hath set for ever over all the luminaries of the heaven, in the heaven and in the world, that they should rule on the face of the heaven and be seen on the earth, and be leaders for the day and the night, i.e. the sun, moon, and stars, and all the ministering creatures which make their revolution in all the chariots of the heaven.

[4] In like manner twelve doors Uriel showed me, open in the circumference of the sun's chariot in the heaven, through which the rays of the sun break forth: and from them is warmth diffused over the earth, when they are opened at their appointed seasons.

[5] And for the winds and the spirit of the dew when they are opened, standing open in the heavens at the ends.

[6] As for the twelve portals in the heaven, at the ends of the earth, out of which go forth the sun, moon, and stars, and all the works of heaven in the east and in the west.

[7] There are many windows open to the left and right of them, and one window at its appointed season produces warmth, corresponding as these do to those doors from which the stars come forth according as He has commanded them, and wherein they set corresponding to their number.

[8] And I saw chariots in the heaven, running in the world, above those portals in which revolve the stars that never set.

[9] And one is larger than all the rest, and it is that that makes its course through the entire world.

Enoch 74

[1] And at the ends of the earth I saw twelve portals open to all the quarters of the heaven, from which the winds go forth and blow over the earth.

[2] Three of them are open on the face (*i.e.* the east) of the heavens, and three in the west, and three on the right (*i.e.* the south) of the heaven, and three on the left (*i.e.* the north).

[3] And the three first are those of the east, and three are of the north, and three [after those on the left] of the south, and three of the west.

[4] Through four of these come winds of blessing and prosperity, and from those eight come hurtful winds: when they are sent, they bring destruction on all the earth and on the water upon it, and on all who dwell thereon, and on everything which is in the water and on the land.

[5] And the first wind from those portals, called the east wind, comes forth through the first portal which is in the east, inclining towards the south: from it come forth desolation, drought, heat, and destruction.

[6] And through the second portal in the middle comes what is fitting, and from it there come rain and fruitfulness and prosperity and dew; and through the third portal which lies toward the north come cold and drought.

[7] And after these come forth the south winds through three portals: through the first portal of

them inclining to the east comes forth a hot wind.

[8] And through the middle portal next to it there come forth fragrant smells, and dew and rain, and prosperity and health.

[9] And through the third portal lying to the west come forth dew and rain, locusts and desolation.

[10] And after these the north winds: from the seventh portal in the east come dew and rain, locusts and desolation.

[11] And from the middle portal come in a direct direction health and rain and dew and prosperity; and through the third portal in the west come cloud and hoar-frost, and snow and rain, and dew and locusts.

[12] And after these four are the west winds: through the first portal adjoining the north come forth dew and hoar-frost, and cold and snow and frost. And from the middle portal come forth dew and rain, and prosperity and blessing; and through the last portal which adjoins the south come forth drought and desolation, and burning and destruction.

[13] And the twelve portals of the four quarters of the heaven are therewith completed, and all their laws and all their plagues and all their benefactions have I shown to thee, my son Methuselah.

Enoch 75

[1] And the first quarter is called the east, because it is the first: and the second, the south, because the Most High will descend there, yea, there in quite a special

sense will He who is blessed for ever descend.

[2] And the west quarter is named the diminished, because there all the luminaries of the heaven wane and go down.

[3] And the fourth quarter, named the north, is divided into three parts: the first of them is for the dwelling of men: and the second contains seas of water, and the abysses and forests and rivers, and darkness and clouds; and the third part contains the garden of righteousness.

[4] I saw seven high mountains, higher than all the mountains which are on the earth: and thence comes forth hoar-frost, and days, seasons, and years pass away. [5] I saw seven rivers on the earth larger than all the rivers: one of them coming from the west pours its waters into the Great Sea.

[6] And these two come from the north to the sea and pour their waters into the Erythraean Sea in the east.

[7] And the remaining four come forth on the side of the north to their own sea, two of them to the Erythraean Sea, and two into the Great Sea and discharge themselves there and some say: into the desert.

[8] Seven great islands I saw in the sea and in the mainland: two in the mainland and five in the Great Sea.

Enoch 76

The Sun and Moon: the Waxing and Waning of the Moon.

[1] And the names of the sun are the following: the first Orjârês, and the second Tômâs.

[2] And the moon has four names: the first name is Asônjâ, the second Eblâ, the third Benâsê, and the fourth Erâe.

[3] These are the two great luminaries: their circumference is like the circumference of the heaven, and the size of the circumference of both is alike.

[4] In the circumference of the sun there are seven portions of light which are added to it more than to the moon, and in definite measures it is s transferred till the seventh portion of the sun is exhausted.

[5] And they set and enter the portals of the west, and make their revolution by the north, and come forth through the eastern portals on the face of the heaven.

[6] And when the moon rises one-fourteenth part appears in the heaven: the light becomes full in her: on the fourteenth day she accomplishes her light.

[7] And fifteen parts of light are transferred to her till the fifteenth day when her light is accomplished, according to the sign of the year, and she becomes fifteen parts, and the moon grows by the addition of fourteenth parts.

[8] And in her waning the moon decreases on the first day to fourteen parts of her light, on the second to thirteen parts of light, on the third to twelve, on the fourth to eleven, on the fifth to ten, on the sixth to nine, on the seventh to eight, on the eighth to seven, on the ninth to six, on the tenth to five, on the eleventh to four, on the twelfth to three, on the thirteenth to two, on the fourteenth to the half of a seventh, and all her remaining light disappears wholly on the fifteenth.

[9] And in certain months the month has twenty-nine days and once twenty-eight.

[10] And Uriel showed me another law: when light is transferred to the moon, and on which side it is transferred to her by the sun.

[11] During all the period during which the moon is growing in her light, she is transferring it to herself when opposite to the sun during fourteen days her light is accomplished in the heaven, and when she is illumined throughout, her light is accomplished full in the heaven. [12] And on the first day she is called the new moon, for on that day the light rises upon her.

[13] She becomes full moon exactly on the day when the sun sets in the west, and from the east she rises at night, and the moon shines the whole night through till the sun rises over against her and the moon is seen over against the sun.

[14] On the side whence the light of the moon comes forth, there again she wanes till all the light vanishes and all the days of the month are at an end, and her circumference is empty, void of light.

[15] And three months she makes of thirty days, and at her time she makes three months of twenty-nine days each, in which she accomplishes her waning in the first period of time, and in the first portal for one hundred and seventy-seven days.

[16] And in the time of her going out she appears for three months of thirty days each, and for three months she appears of twenty-nine each.

[17] At night she appears like a man for twenty days each time, and by day she appears like

---

Enoch 77

[1] And now, my son, I have shown thee everything, and the law of all the stars of the heaven is completed.

[2] And he showed me all the laws of these for every day, and for every season of bearing rule, and for every year, and for its going forth, and for the order prescribed to it every month and every week:

[3] And the waning of the moon which takes place in the sixth portal: for in this sixth portal her light is accomplished, and after that there is the beginning of the waning:

[4] And the waning which takes place in the first portal in its season, till one hundred and seventy-seven days are accomplished: reckoned according to weeks, twenty-five weeks and two days.

[5] She falls behind the sun and the order of the stars exactly five days in the course of one period, and when this place which thou seest has been traversed.

[6] Such is the picture and sketch of every luminary which Uriel the archangel, who is their leader, showed unto me.

Enoch 78

[1] And in those days the angel Uriel answered and said to me: 'Behold, I have shown thee everything, Enoch, and I have revealed everything to thee that thou shouldst see this sun and this moon, and the leaders of the stars of the heaven and all those who turn them, their tasks and times and departures.

Verse 2-8. Perversion of Nature and the heavenly Bodies owning to the Sin of Men.

[2] And in the days of the sinners the years shall be shortened,

And their seed shall be tardy on their lands and fields,
And all things on the earth shall alter,
And shall not appear in their time:
And the rain shall be kept back
And the heaven shall withhold it.

[3] And in those times the fruits of the earth shall be backward,
And shall not grow in their time,
And the fruits of the trees shall be withheld in their time.

[4] And the moon shall alter her order,
And not appear at her time.

[5] And in those days the sun shall be seen and he shall journey in the evening on the extremity of the great chariot in the west And shall shine more brightly than accords with the order of light.

[6] And many chiefs of the stars shall transgress the order prescribed. And these shall alter their orbits and tasks, And not appear at the seasons prescribed to them.

[7] And the whole order of the stars shall be concealed from the sinners, And the thoughts of those on the earth shall err concerning them, And they shall be altered from all their ways, Yea, they shall err and take them to be gods.

[8] And evil shall be multiplied upon them, And punishment shall come upon them So as to destroy all.

Enoch 79

[1] And he said unto me: 'Observe, Enoch, these heavenly tablets, And read what is written thereon, And mark every individual fact.'

[2] And I observed the heavenly tablets, and read everything which was written thereon and understood everything, and read the book of all the deeds of mankind, and of all the children of flesh that shall be upon the earth to the remotest generations.

[3] And forthwith I blessed the great Lord the King of glory for ever, in that He has made all the works of the world, And I extolled Jah because of His patience,
And blessed Him because of the children of men.

[4] And after that I said: 'Blessed is the man who dies in righteousness and goodness, Concerning whom there is no book of unrighteousness written, And against whom no day of judgement shall be found.'

[5] And those seven holy ones brought me and placed me on the earth before the door of my house, and said to me: 'Declare everything to thy son Methuselah, and show to all thy children that no flesh is righteous in the sight of Jah, for He is their Creator.

[6] One year we will leave thee with thy son, till thou givest thy last commands, that thou mayest teach thy children and record it for them, and testify to all thy children; and in the second year they shall take thee from their midst.

[7] Let thy heart be strong, For the good shall announce righteousness to the good; The righteous with the righteous shall rejoice, And shall offer congratulation to one another.

[8] But the sinners shall die with the sinners, And the apostate go down with the apostate.

[9] And those who practice righteousness shall die on account of the deeds of men,

And be taken away on account of the doings of the godless.'

[10] And in those days they ceased to speak to me, and I came to my people, blessing Jah of the world.

Enoch 80

Charge given to Enoch: the four Intercalary Days: the Stars which lead the Seasons and the Months.

[1] And now, my son Methuselah, all these things I am recounting to thee and writing down for thee, and I have revealed to thee everything, and given thee books concerning all these: so preserve, my son Methuselah, the books from thy father's hand, and see that thou deliver them to the generations of the world.

[2] I have given Wisdom to thee and to thy children,
And thy children that shall be to thee, That they may give it to their children for generations,
This wisdom namely that passeth their thought.

[3] And those who understand it shall not sleep,
But shall listen with the ear that they may learn this wisdom,
And it shall please those that eat thereof better than good food.

[4] Blessed are all the righteous, blessed are all those who walk in the way of righteousness and sin not as the sinners, in the reckoning of all their days in which the sun traverses the heaven, entering into and departing from the portals for thirty days with the heads of thousands of the order of the stars, together with the four which are intercalated which divide the four portions of the year, which lead them and enter with them four days. [5] Owing to them men shall be at fault and not reckon them in the whole reckoning of the year: yea, men shall be at fault, and not recognize them accurately. 6. For they belong to the reckoning of the year and are truly recorded thereon for ever, one in the first portal and one in the third, and

one in the fourth and one in the sixth, and the year is completed in three hundred and sixty-four days.

[7] And the account thereof is accurate and the recorded reckoning thereof exact; for the luminaries, and months and festivals, and years and days, has Uriel shown and revealed to me, to whom Jah of the whole creation of the world hath subjected the host of heaven.

[8] And he has power over night and day in the heaven to cause the light to give light to men--sun, moon, and stars, and all the powers of the heaven which revolve in their circular chariots.

[9] And these are the orders of the stars, which set in their places, and in their seasons and festivals and months.

[10] And these are the names of those who lead them, who watch that they enter at their times, in their orders, in their seasons, in their months, in their periods of dominion, and in their positions.

[11] Their four leaders who divide the four parts of the year enter first; and after them the twelve leaders of the orders who divide the months; and for the three hundred and sixty days there are heads over thousands who divide the days; and for the four intercalary days there are the leaders which

sunder the four parts of the year. [12] And these heads over thousands are intercalated between leader and leader, each behind a station, but their leaders make the division. And these are the names of the leaders who divide the four parts of the year which are ordained: Mîlkî'êl, Hel'emmêlêk, and Mêl'êjal, and Nârêl.

[13] And the names of those who lead them: Adnâr'êl, and Îjâsûsa'êl, and 'Elômê'êl-- these three follow the leaders of the orders, and there is one that follows the three leaders of the orders which follow those leaders of stations that divide the four parts of the year.

[14] In the beginning of the year Melkejâl rises first and rules, who is named Tam'âinî and sun, and all the days of his dominion whilst he bears rule are ninety-one days. [15] And these are the signs of the days which are to be seen on earth in the days of

his dominion: sweat, and heat, and calms; and all the trees bear fruit, and leaves are produced on all the trees, and the harvest of wheat, and the rose-flowers, and all the flowers which come forth in the field, but the trees of the winter season become withered.

[16] And these are the names of the leaders which are under them: Berka'êl, Zêlebs'êl, and another who is added a head of a thousand, called Hîlûjâsĕph: and the days of the dominion of this leader are at an end.

[17] The next leader after him is Hêl'emmêlêk, whom one names the shining sun, and all the days of his light are ninety-one days.

[18] And these are the signs of his days on the earth: glowing heat and dryness, and the trees ripen their fruits and produce all their

fruits ripe and ready, and the sheep pair and become pregnant, and all the fruits of the earth are gathered in, and everything that is in the fields, and the winepress: these things take place in the days of his dominion.

[19] These are the names, and the orders, and the leaders of those heads of thousands: Gîdâ'îjal, Kê'êl, and Hê'êl, and the name of the head of a thousand which is added to them, Asfâ'êl': and the days of his dominion are at an end.

Enoch 81

First Dream-Vision on the Deluge

[1] And now, my son Methuselah, I will show thee all my visions which I have seen, recounting them before thee.

[2] Two visions I saw before I took a wife, and the one was quite unlike the other: the first when I was learning to write: the second before I took thy mother, when I saw a terrible vision. And regarding them I prayed to the

Lord.

[3] I had laid me down in the house of my grandfather Mahalalel, when I saw in a vision how the heaven collapsed and was borne off and fell to the earth.

[4] And when it fell to the earth I saw how the earth was swallowed up in a great abyss, and mountains were suspended on mountains, and hills sank down on hills, and high trees were rent from their stems, and hurled down and sunk in the abyss.

[5] And thereupon a word fell into my mouth, and I lifted up my voice to cry aloud, and said: 'The earth is destroyed.'

[6] And my grandfather Mahalalel waked me as I lay near him, and said unto me: 'Why dost thou cry so, my son, and why dost thou make such lamentation?'

[7] And I recounted to him the whole vision which I had seen, and he said unto me: 'A terrible thing hast thou seen, my son, and of grave moment is thy dream-vision as to the secrets of all the sin of the earth: it must sink into the abyss and be destroyed with a great destruction. [8] And now, my son, arise and make petition to Jah of glory, since thou art a believer, that a remnant may remain on the earth, and that He may not destroy the whole earth.

[9] My son, from heaven all this will come upon the earth, and upon the earth there will be great destruction. [10] After that I arose and prayed and implored and besought, and wrote down my prayer for the generations of the world, and I will show everything to thee, my son Methuselah.

[11] And when I had gone forth below and seen the heaven, and the sun rising in the east, and the moon setting in the west, and a few stars, and the whole earth, and everything as He had known it in the beginning, then I blessed Jah of judgement and extolled Him because He had made the sun to go forth from the windows of the east, and he ascended and rose on the face of the heaven, and set out and kept traversing the path shown unto him.

Enoch 82

[1] And I lifted up my hands in righteousness and blessed the Holy and Great One, and spake with the breath of my mouth, and with the tongue of flesh, which God has made for the children of the flesh of men, that they should speak therewith, and He gave them breath and a tongue and a mouth that they should speak therewith:

2. 'Blessed be Thou, O Lord, King, Great and mighty in Thy greatness, Lord of the whole creation of the heaven,
King of kings and God of the whole world.
And Thy power and kingship and greatness abide for ever and ever, And throughout all generations Thy dominion;
And all the heavens are Thy throne for ever, And the whole earth Thy footstool for ever and ever.

[3] For Thou hast made and Thou rulest all things,
And nothing is too hard for Thee,
Wisdom departs not from the place of Thy throne,
Nor turns away from Thy presence.
And Thou knowest and seest and hearest everything,
And there is nothing hidden from Thee, for Thou seest everything.

[4] And now the angels of Thy heavens are guilty of trespass,
And upon the flesh of men abideth Thy wrath until the great day of judgement.

[5] And now, O God and Lord and Great King,
I implore and beseech Thee to fulfil my prayer,
To leave me a posterity on earth,
And not destroy all the flesh of man,
And make the earth without inhabitant,
So that there should be an eternal destruction.

[6] And now, my Lord, destroy from the earth the flesh which has aroused Thy wrath, But the flesh of righteousness and uprightness establish as a plant of the eternal seed, And hide not Thy face from the prayer of Thy servant, O Lord.'

Enoch 83

[1] And after this I saw another dream, and I will show the whole dream to thee, my son.

[2] And Enoch lifted up his voice and spake to his son Methuselah: 'To thee, my son, will I speak: hear my words--incline thine ear to the dream-vision of thy father.

[3] Before I took thy mother Edna, I saw in a vision on my bed, and behold a bull came forth from the earth, and that bull was white; and after it came forth a heifer, and along with this latter came forth two bulls, one of them black and the other red.

[4] And that black bull gored the red one and pursued him over the earth, and thereupon I could no longer see that red bull.

[5] But that black bull grew and that heifer went with him, and I saw that many oxen proceeded from him which resembled and followed him.

[6] And that cow, that first one, went from the presence of that first bull in order to seek that red one, but found him not, and lamented with a great lamentation over him and sought him.

[7] And I looked till that first bull came to her and quieted her, and from that time onward she cried no more.

[8] And after that she bore another white bull, and after him she bore many bulls and black cows.

[9] And I saw in my sleep that white bull likewise grow and become a great white bull, and from Him proceeded many white bulls, and they resembled him. And they began to beget many white bulls, which resembled them, one following the other, even many.

Enoch 84

[1] And again I saw with mine eyes as I slept, and I saw the heaven above, and behold a star fell from heaven, and it arose and eat and pastured amongst those oxen.

[2] And after that I saw the large and the black oxen, and behold they all changed their stalls and pastures and their cattle, and began to live with each other.

[3] And again I saw in the vision, and looked towards the heaven, and behold I saw many stars descend and cast themselves down from heaven to that first star, and they became bulls amongst those cattle and pastured with them amongst them.

[4] And I looked at them and saw, and behold they all let out their privy members, like horses, and began to cover the cows of the oxen, and they all became pregnant and bare elephants, camels, and asses.

[5] And all the oxen feared them and were affrighted at them, and began to bite with their teeth and to devour, and to gore with their horns.

[6] And they began, moreover, to devour those oxen; and behold all the children of the earth began to tremble and quake before them and to flee from them.

Enoch 85

[1] And again I saw how they began to gore each other and to devour each other, and the earth began to cry aloud.

[2] And I raised mine eyes again to heaven, and I saw in the vision, and behold there came forth from heaven beings who were like white men: and four went forth from that place and three with them.

[3] And those three that had last come forth grasped me by my hand and took me up, away from the generations of the earth, and raised me up to a lofty place, and showed me a tower raised high above the earth, and all the hills were lower.

[4] And one said unto me: 'Remain here till thou seest everything that befalls those elephants, camels, and asses, and the stars and the oxen, and all of them.'

Enoch 86

[1] And I saw one of those four who had come forth first, and he seized that first star which had fallen from the heaven, and bound it hand and foot and cast it into an abyss: now that abyss was narrow and deep, and horrible and dark.

[2] And one of them drew a sword, and gave it to those elephants and camels and asses: then they began to smite each other, and the whole earth quaked because of them. [3] And as I was beholding in the vision, lo, one of those four who had come forth stoned them from heaven, and gathered and took all the great stars whose privy members were like those of horses, and bound them all hand and foot, and cast them in an abyss of the earth.

Enoch 87

The Deluge and the Deliverance of Noah

[1] And one of those four went to that white bull and instructed him in a secret, without his being terrified: he was born a bull and became a man, and built for himself a great vessel and dwelt thereon; and three bulls dwelt with him in that vessel and they were covered in.

[2] And again I raised mine eyes towards heaven and saw a lofty roof, with seven water torrents thereon, and those torrents flowed with much water into an enclosure. [3] And I saw again, and behold fountains were opened on the surface of that great enclosure, and that water began to swell and rise upon the surface, and I saw that enclosure till all its surface was covered with water.

[4] And the water, the darkness, and mist increased upon it; and as I looked at the height of that water, that water had risen above the height of that enclosure, and was streaming over that enclosure, and it stood upon the earth.

[5] And all the cattle of that enclosure were gathered together until I saw how they sank and were swallowed up and perished in that water.

[6] But that vessel floated on the water, while all the oxen and elephants and camels and asses sank to the bottom with all the animals, so that I could no longer see them, and they were not able to escape, but perished and sank into the depths.

[7] And again I saw in the vision till those water torrents were removed from that high roof, and the chasms of the earth were levelled up and other abysses were opened.

[8] Then the water began to run down into these, till the earth became visible; but that

vessel settled on the earth, and the darkness retired and light appeared.

[9] But that white bull which had become a man came out of that vessel, and the three bulls with him, and one of those three was white like that bull, and one of them was red as blood, and one black: and that white bull departed from them.

Verse 10-27. *From the Death of Noah to the Exodus*.

[10] And they began to bring forth beasts of the field and birds, so that there arose different genera: lions, tigers, wolves, dogs, hyenas, wild boars, foxes, squirrels, swine, falcons, vultures, kites, eagles, and ravens; and among them was born a white bull.

[11] And they began to bite one another; but that white bull which was born amongst them begat a wild ass and a white bull with it, and the wild asses multiplied.

[12] But that bull which was born from him begat a black wild boar and a white sheep; and the former begat many boars, but that sheep begat twelve sheep.

[13] And when those twelve sheep had grown, they gave up one of them to the asses, and those asses again gave up that sheep to the wolves, and that sheep grew up among the wolves.

[14] And Jah brought the eleven sheep to live with it and to pasture with it among the wolves: and they multiplied and became many flocks of sheep.

[15] And the wolves began to fear them, and they oppressed them until they destroyed their little ones, and they cast their young into a river of much water: but those sheep began to cry aloud on account of their little ones, and to complain unto their Lord.

[16] And a sheep which had been saved from the wolves fled and escaped to the wild asses; and I saw the sheep how they lamented and cried, and besought their Lord with all their might, till that Lord of the sheep descended at the voice of the sheep from a lofty abode, and came to them and pastured them.

[17] And He called that sheep which had escaped the wolves, and spake with it concerning the wolves that it should admonish them not to touch the sheep.

[18] And the sheep went to the wolves according to the word of Jah, and another sheep met it and went with it, and the two went and entered together into the assembly of those wolves, and spake with them and admonished them not to touch the sheep from henceforth.

[19] And thereupon I saw the wolves, and how they oppressed the sheep exceedingly with all their power; and the sheep cried aloud.

[20] And Jah came to the sheep and they began to smite those wolves: and the wolves began to make lamentation; but the sheep became quiet and forthwith ceased to cry out.

[21] And I saw the sheep till they departed from amongst the wolves; but the eyes of the wolves were blinded, and those wolves departed in pursuit of the sheep with all their power.

[22] And Jah of the sheep went with them, as their leader, and all His sheep followed Him: and his face was dazzling and glorious and terrible to behold.

[23] But the wolves began to pursue those sheep till they reached a sea of water.

[24] And that sea was divided, and the water stood on this side and on that before their face, and their Lord led them and placed Himself between them and the wolves. [25] And as those wolves did not yet see the sheep, they proceeded into the midst of that sea, and the wolves followed the sheep, and those wolves ran after them into that sea.

[26] And when they saw Jah of the sheep, they turned to flee before His face, but that sea gathered itself together, and became as it had been created, and the water swelled and rose till it covered those wolves.

[27] And I saw till all the wolves who pursued those sheep perished and were drowned.

Verse. 28-40. *Israel in the Desert, the Giving of the Law, the Entrance into Palestine.*

[28] But the sheep escaped from that water and went forth into a wilderness, where there was no

water and no grass; and they began to open their eyes and to see; and I saw Jah of the sheep pasturing them and giving them water and grass, and that sheep going and leading them.

[29] And that sheep ascended to the summit of that lofty rock, and Jah of the sheep sent it to them. 30. And after that I saw Jah of the sheep who stood before them, and His appearance was great and terrible and majestic, and all those sheep saw Him and were afraid before His face.

[31] And they all feared and trembled because of Him, and they cried to that sheep with them [which was amongst them]: "We are not able to stand before our Lord or to behold Him."

[32] And that sheep which led them again ascended to the summit of that rock, but the sheep began to be blinded and to wander from the way which he had showed them, but that sheep wot not thereof.

[33] And Jah of the sheep was wrathful exceedingly against them, and that sheep discovered it, and went down from the summit of the rock, and came to the sheep, and found the greatest part of them blinded and fallen away.

[34] And when they saw it they feared and trembled at its presence, and desired to return to their folds.

[35] And that sheep took other sheep with it, and came to those sheep which had fallen away, and began to slay them; and the sheep feared its presence, and thus that sheep brought back those sheep that had fallen away, and they returned to their folds.

[36] And I saw in this vision till that sheep became a man and built a house for Jah of the sheep, and placed all the sheep in that house.

[37] And I saw till this sheep which had met that sheep which led them fell asleep: and I saw till all the great sheep perished and little ones arose in their place, and they came to a pasture, and approached a stream of water.

[38] Then that sheep, their leader which had become a man, withdrew from them and fell asleep, and all the sheep sought it and cried over it with a great crying.

[39] And I saw till they left off crying for that sheep and crossed that stream of water, and there arose the two sheep as leaders in

the place of those which had led them and fallen asleep.

[40] And I saw till the sheep came to a goodly place, and a pleasant and glorious land, and I saw till those sheep were satisfied; and that house stood amongst them in the pleasant land.

Verse 41-50. *From the Time of the Judges till the Building of the Temple.*

[41] And sometimes their eyes were opened, and sometimes blinded, till another sheep arose and led them and brought them all back, and their eyes were opened.

[42] And the dogs and the foxes and the wild boars began to devour those sheep till Jah of the sheep raised up [another sheep] a ram from their midst, which led them.

[43] And that ram began to butt on either side those dogs, foxes, and wild boars till he had destroyed them all.

[44] And that sheep whose eyes were opened saw that ram, which was amongst the sheep, till it forsook its glory and began to butt those sheep, and trampled upon them, and behaved itself unseemly.

[45] And Jah of the sheep sent the lamb to another lamb and raised it to being a ram and leader of the sheep instead of that ram which had forsaken its glory.

[46] And it went to it and spake to it alone, and raised it to being a ram, and made it the prince and leader of the sheep; but during all these things those dogs oppressed the sheep.

[47] And the first ram pursued that second ram, and that second ram arose and fled before it; and I saw till those dogs pulled down the first ram.

[48] And that second ram arose and led the [little] sheep.

[48ᵇ] And that ram begat many sheep and fell asleep; and a little sheep became ram in its stead, and became prince and leader of those sheep.

[49] And those sheep grew and multiplied; but all the dogs, and foxes, and wild boars feared and fled before it, and that ram butted and killed the wild beasts, and those wild beasts had no longer any power among the sheep and robbed them no more of ought.

[50] And that house became great and broad, and it was built for those sheep: and a tower lofty and great was built on the house for Jah of the sheep, and that house was low, but the tower was elevated and lofty, and Jah of the sheep stood on that tower and they offered a full table before Him.

Verse. 51-67. *The Two Kingdoms of Israel and Judah, to the Destruction of Jerusalem.*

[51] And again I saw those sheep that they again erred and went many ways, and forsook that their house, and Jah of the sheep called some from amongst the sheep and sent them to the sheep, but the sheep began to slay them.

[52] And one of them was saved and was not slain, and it sped away and cried aloud over the sheep; and they sought to slay it, but Jah of the sheep saved it from the sheep, and brought it up to me, and caused it to dwell there.

[53] And many other sheep He sent to those sheep to testify unto them and lament over them.

[54] And after that I saw that when they forsook the house of Jah and His tower they fell away entirely, and their eyes were

blinded; and I saw Jah of the sheep how He wrought much slaughter amongst them in their herds until those sheep invited that slaughter and betrayed His place.

[55] And He gave them over into the hands of the lions and tigers, and wolves and hyenas, and into the hand of the foxes, and to all the wild beasts, and those wild beasts began to tear in pieces those sheep.

[56] And I saw that He forsook that their house and their tower and gave them all into the hand of the lions, to tear and devour them, into the hand of all the wild beasts.

[57] And I began to cry aloud with all my power, and to appeal to Jah of the sheep, and to represent to Him in regard to the sheep that they were devoured by all the wild beasts.

[58] But He remained unmoved, though He saw it, and rejoiced that they were devoured and swallowed and robbed, and left them to be devoured in the hand of all the beasts.

[59] And He called seventy shepherds, and cast those sheep to them that they might pasture them, and He spake to the shepherds and their companions: "Let each individual of you pasture the sheep henceforward, and everything that I shall command you that do ye.

[60] And I will deliver them over unto you duly numbered, and tell you which of them are to be destroyed--and them destroy ye." And He gave over unto them those sheep.

[61] And He called another and spake unto him: "Observe and mark everything that the shepherds will do to those sheep; for they will destroy more of them than I have commanded them.

[62] And every excess and the destruction which will be wrought through the shepherds, record namely how many they destroy according to my command, and how many according to their own caprice: record against every individual shepherd all the destruction he effects. [63] And read out before me by number how many they destroy, and how many they deliver over for destruction, that I may have this as a testimony against them, and know every deed of the shepherds, that I may comprehend and see what they do, whether or not they abide by my command which I have commanded them.

[64] But they shall not know it, and thou shalt not declare it to them, nor admonish them, but only record against each individual all the destruction which the shepherds effect each in his time and lay it all before me."

[65] And I saw till those shepherds pastured in their season, and they began to slay and to destroy more than they were bidden, and they delivered those sheep into the hand of the lions.

[66] And the lions and tigers eat and devoured the greater part of those sheep, and the wild boars eat along with them; and they burnt that tower and demolished that house.

[67] And I became exceedingly sorrowful over that tower because that house of the sheep was demolished,

and afterwards I was unable to see if those sheep entered that house.

Verse 68-71. *First Period of the Angelic Rulers--from the Destruction of Jerusalem to the Return from the Captivity.*

[68] And the shepherds and their associates delivered over those sheep to all the wild beasts, to devour them, and each one of them received in his time a definite number: it was written by the other in a book how many each one of them destroyed of them.

[69] And each one slew and destroyed many more than was prescribed; and I began to weep and lament on account of those sheep.

[70] And thus in the vision I saw that one who wrote, how he wrote down every one that was destroyed by those shepherds, day by day, and carried up and laid down and showed actually the whole book to Jah of the sheep- even everything that they had done, and all that each one of them had made away with, and all that they had given over to destruction.

[71] And the book was read before Jah of the sheep, and He took the book from his hand and read it and sealed it and laid it down.

Verse 72-77. *Second Period--from the time of Cyrus to that of Alexander the Great.*

[72] And forthwith I saw how the shepherds pastured for twelve hours, and behold three of those sheep turned back and came and entered and began to build up all that had fallen down of that house; but the wild boars tried to hinder them, but they were not able.

[73] And they began again to build as before, and they reared up that tower, and it was named the high tower; and they began again to place a table before the tower, but all the bread on it was polluted and not pure.

[74] And as touching all this the eyes of those sheep were blinded so that they saw not, and the eyes of their shepherds likewise; and they delivered them in large numbers to their shepherds for destruction, and they trampled the sheep with their feet and devoured them. [75] And Jah of the sheep remained unmoved till all the sheep were dispersed over the field and mingled with them (*i.e.* the beasts), and they (*i.e.* the shepherds) did not save them out of the hand of the beasts.

[76] And this one who wrote the book carried it up, and showed it and read it before Jah of the sheep, and implored Him on their account, and besought Him on their account as he showed Him all the doings of the shepherds, and gave testimony before Him against all the shepherds. And he took the actual book and laid it down beside Him and departed.

Enoch 88

Verse 1-5. *Third Period--from Alexander the Great to the Graeco-Syrian Domination.*

[1] And I saw till that in this manner thirty-five shepherds undertook the pasturing of the sheep, and they severally completed their periods as did the first; and others received them into their hands, to pasture them for their period, each shepherd in his own period.

[2] And after that I saw in my vision all the birds of heaven coming, the eagles, the vultures, the kites, the ravens; but the eagles led all the birds; and they began to devour those sheep, and to pick out their eyes and to devour their flesh.

[3] And the sheep cried out because their flesh was being devoured by the birds, and as for me I looked and lamented in my sleep over that shepherd who pastured the sheep.

[4] And I saw until those sheep were devoured by the dogs and eagles and kites, and they left neither flesh nor skin nor sinew remaining on them till only their bones stood there: and their bones too fell to the earth and the sheep became few.

[5] And I saw until that twenty-three had undertaken the pasturing and completed in their several periods fifty-eight times.

Verse 6-12. Fourth Period—from the Graeco-Syrian Domination to the Maccabæan Revolt.

[6] But behold lambs were borne by those white sheep, and they began to open their eyes and to see, and to cry to the sheep.

[7] Yea, they cried to them, but they did not hearken to what they said to them, but were exceedingly deaf, and their eyes were very exceedingly blinded.

[8] And I saw in the vision how the ravens flew upon those lambs and took one of those lambs, and dashed the sheep in pieces and devoured them.

[9] And I saw till horns grew upon those lambs, and the ravens cast down their horns; and I saw till there sprouted a great horn of one of those sheep, and their eyes were opened.

[10] And it †looked at† them [and their eyes opened], and it cried to the sheep, and the rams saw it and all ran to it.

[11] And notwithstanding all this those eagles and vultures and ravens and kites still kept tearing the sheep and swooping down upon them and devouring them: still the sheep remained silent, but the rams lamented and cried out.

[12] And those ravens fought and battled with it and sought to lay low its horn, but they had no power over it.

Verse 13-19. The Last Assault of the Gentiles on Judah

[13] And I saw till the shepherds and eagles and those vultures and kites came, and they cried to the ravens that they should break the horn of that ram, and they battled and fought with it, and it battled with them and cried that its help might come.

[14] And I saw till that man, who wrote down the names of the shepherds and carried up into the presence of Jah of the sheep came and helped it and showed it everything: he had come down for the help of that ram.

[15] And I saw till Jah of the sheep came unto them in wrath, and all who saw Him fled, and they all fell into His shadow from before His face.

[16] All the eagles and vultures and ravens and kites were gathered together, and there came with them all the sheep of the field, yea, they all came together, and helped each other to break that horn of the ram.

[17] And I saw that man, who wrote the book according to the command of Jah , till he opened that book concerning the destruction which those twelve last shepherds had wrought, and showed that they had destroyed much more than their predecessors, before Jah of the sheep.

[18] And I saw till Jah of the sheep came unto them and took in His hand the staff of His wrath, and smote the earth, and the earth clave asunder, and all the beasts and all the birds of the heaven fell from among those

sheep, and were swallowed up in the earth and it covered them.

[19] And I saw till a great sword was given to the sheep, and the sheep proceeded against all the beasts

of the field to slay them, and all the beasts and the birds of the heaven fled before their face.

Verse 20-27. Judgement of the Fallen Angels, the Shepherds, and the Apostates.

[20] And I saw till a throne was erected in the pleasant land, and Jah of the sheep sat Himself thereon, and the other took the sealed books and opened those books before Jah of the sheep.

[21] And Jah called those men the seven first white ones, and commanded that they should bring before Him, beginning with the first star which led the way, all the stars whose privy members were like those of horses, and they brought them all before Him.

[22] And He said to that man who wrote before Him, being one of those seven white ones, and said unto him: "Take those seventy shepherds to whom I delivered the sheep, and who taking them on their own authority slew more than I commanded them."

[23] And behold they were all bound, I saw, and they all stood before Him.

[24] And the judgement was held first over the stars, and they were judged and found guilty, and went to the place of condemnation, and they were cast into an abyss, full of fire and flaming, and full of pillars of fire.

[25] And those seventy shepherds were judged and found guilty, and they were cast into that fiery abyss.

[26] And I saw at that time how a like abyss was opened in the midst of the earth, full of fire, and they brought those blinded sheep, and they were all judged and found guilty and cast into this fiery abyss, and they burned; now this abyss was to the right of that house.

[27] And I saw those sheep burning and their bones burning.

Verse 28-38. The New Jerusalem, the Conversion of the surviving Gentiles, the Resurrection of the Righteous, the Messiah.

[28] And I stood up to see till they folded up that old house; and carried off all the pillars, and all the beams and ornaments of the house were at the same time folded up with it, and they carried it off and laid it in a place in the south of the land.

[29] And I saw till Jah of the sheep brought a new house greater and loftier than that first, and set it up in the place of the first which had beer folded up: all its pillars were new, and its ornaments were new and larger than those of the first, the old one which He had taken away, and all the sheep were within it.

[30] And I saw all the sheep which had been left, and all the beasts on the earth, and all the birds of the heaven, falling down and doing homage to those sheep and making petition to and obeying them in every thing.

[31] And thereafter those three who

were clothed in white and had seized me by my hand [who had taken me up before], and the hand of that ram also seizing hold of me, they took me up and set me down in the midst of those sheep before the judgement took place.

[32] And those sheep were all white, and their wool was abundant and clean.

[33] And all that had been destroyed and dispersed, and all the beasts of the field, and all the birds of the heaven, assembled in that house, and Jah of the sheep rejoiced with great joy because they were all good and had returned to His house.

[34] And I saw till they laid down that sword, which had been given to the sheep, and they brought it back into the house, and it was sealed before the presence of Jah , and all the sheep were invited into that house, but it held them not.

[35] And the eyes of them all were opened, and they saw the good, and there was not one among them that did not see.

[36] And I saw that that house was large and broad and very full.

[37] And I saw that a white bull was born, with large horns and all the beasts of the field and all the birds of the air feared him and made petition to him all the time. [38] And I saw till all their generations were transformed, and they all became white bulls; and the first among them became a lamb, and that lamb became a great animal and had great black horns on its head; and Jah of the sheep rejoiced over it and over all the oxen.

[39] And I slept in their midst: and I awoke and saw everything.

[40] This is the vision which I saw while I slept, and I awoke and blessed Jah of righteousness and gave Him glory.

[41] Then I wept with a great weeping and my tears stayed not till I could no longer endure it: when I saw, they flowed on account of what I had seen; for everything shall come and be fulfilled, and all the deeds of men in their order were shown to me.

[42] On that night I remembered the first dream, and because of it I wept and was troubled--because I had seen that vision.'

Enoch 89

[1] The book written by Enoch--Enoch indeed wrote this complete doctrine of wisdom, which is praised of all men and a judge of all the earth] for all my children who shall dwell on the earth. And for the future generations who shall observe uprightness and peace.

[2] Let not your spirit be troubled on account of the times;
For the Holy and Great One has appointed days for all things.

[3] And the righteous one shall arise from sleep,
[Shall arise] and walk in the paths of righteousness,
And all his path and conversation shall be in eternal goodness and grace.

[4] He will be gracious to the righteous and give him eternal uprightness,
And He will give him power so that he shall be endowed with goodness and righteousness.
And he shall walk in eternal light.

[5] And sin shall perish in darkness for ever,
And shall no more be seen from that day for evermore.

Enoch 90

[1] 'And now, my son Methuselah, call to me all thy brothers And gather together to me all the sons of thy mother; For the word calls me, And the spirit is poured out upon me, That I may show you everything That shall befall you for ever.'

[2] And there upon Methuselah went and summoned to him all his brothers and assembled his relatives.

[3] And he spake unto all the children of righteousness and said: 'Hear, ye sons of Enoch, all the words of your father, And hearken aright to the voice of my mouth; For I exhort you and say unto you, beloved: Love uprightness and walk therein.
[4] And draw not nigh to uprightness with a double heart, And associate not with those of a double heart,
But walk in righteousness, my sons. And it shall guide you on good paths, And righteousness shall be your companion.

[5] For I know that violence must increase on the earth,
And a great chastisement be executed on the earth,
And all unrighteousness come to an end:
Yea, it shall be cut off from its roots, And its whole structure be destroyed.

[6] And unrighteousness shall again be consummated on the earth, And all the deeds of unrighteousness and of violence And transgression shall prevail in a twofold degree.

[7] And when sin and unrighteousness and blasphemy
And violence in all kinds of deeds increase, And apostasy and transgression and uncleanness increase, A great chastisement shall come from heaven upon all these, And the holy Lord will come forth with wrath and chastisement To execute judgement on earth.

[8] In those days violence shall be cut off from its roots,
And the roots of unrighteousness together with deceit,
And they shall be destroyed from under heaven.

[9] And all the idols of the heathen shall be abandoned,
And the temples burned with fire,
And they shall remove them from the whole earth,

And they (*i.e.* the heathen) shall be cast into the judgement of fire, And shall perish in wrath and in grievous judgement for ever.

[10] And the righteous shall arise from their sleep,
And wisdom shall arise and be given unto them.

[11] And after that the roots of unrighteousness shall be cut off, and the sinners shall be destroyed by the sword . . . shall be cut off from the blasphemers in every place, and those who plan violence and those who commit blasphemy shall perish by the sword.

....

[18] And now I tell you, my sons, and show you
The paths of righteousness and the paths of violence.
Yea, I will show them to you again. That ye may know what will come to pass.

[19] And now, hearken unto me, my sons, And walk in the paths of righteousness, And walk not in the paths of violence; For all

who walk in the paths of unrighteousness shall perish for ever.'

Enoch 91

[1] And after that Enoch both gave and began to recount from the books. And Enoch said: 'Concerning the children of righteousness and concerning the elect of the world, And concerning the plant of uprightness, I will speak these things, Yea, I Enoch will declare them unto you, my sons: According to that which appeared to me in the heavenly vision, And which I have known through the word of the holy angels, And have learnt from the heavenly tablets.'

………..

[3] And Enoch began to recount from the books and said: 'I was born the seventh in the first week,
While judgement and righteousness still endured.

[4] And after me there shall arise in the second week great wickedness, And deceit shall have sprung up;
And in it there shall be the first end. And in it a man shall be saved; And after it is ended unrighteousness shall grow up, And a law shall be made for the sinners.

[5] And after that in the third week at its close
A man shall be elected as the plant of righteous judgement, And his posterity shall become the plant of righteousness for evermore.

[6] And after that in the fourth week, at its close,
Visions of the holy and righteous shall be seen,
And a law for all generations and an enclosure shall be made for them.

[7] And after that in the fifth week, at its close,
The house of glory and dominion shall be built for ever.

[8] And after that in the sixth week all who live in it shall be blinded, And the hearts of all of them shall godlessly forsake wisdom. And in it a man shall ascend;
And at its close the house of dominion shall be burnt with fire, And the whole race of the chosen root shall be dispersed.

[9] And after that in the seventh week shall an apostate generation arise, And many shall be its deeds,
And all its deeds shall be apostate.

[10] And at its close shall be elected
The elect righteous of the eternal plant of righteousness,
To receive sevenfold instruction concerning all His creation.

[11] For who is there of all the children of men that is able to hear the voice of the Holy One without being troubled? And who can think His thoughts? and who is there that can behold all the works of heaven?

[12] And how should there be one who could behold the heaven, and who is there that could understand the things of heaven and see a soul or a spirit and could tell thereof, or ascend and see all their ends and think them or do like them?

[13] And who is there of all men that could know what is the breadth and the length of the earth, and to whom has been shown the measure of all of them?

[14] Or is there any one who could discern the length of the heaven and how great is its

height, and upon what it is founded, and how great is the number of the stars, and where all the luminaries rest?

Enoch 92

[12] And after that there shall be another, the eighth week, that of righteousness,
And a sword shall be given to it that a righteous judgement may be executed on the oppressors,
And sinners shall be delivered into the hands of the righteous.

[13] And at its close they shall acquire houses through their righteousness,
And a house shall be built for the Great King in glory for evermore,
[14d] And all mankind shall look to the path of uprightness.

[14a] And after that, in the ninth week, the righteous judgement shall be revealed to the whole world,
(b) And all the works of the godless shall vanish from all the earth,
(c) And the world shall be written down for destruction.

[15] And after this, in the tenth week in the seventh part,
There shall be the great eternal judgement, In which He will execute vengeance amongst the angels.

[16] And the first heaven shall depart and pass away,
And a new heaven shall appear,
And all the powers of the heavens shall give sevenfold light.

[17] And after that there will be many weeks without number for ever,
And all shall be in goodness and righteousness,
And sin shall no more be mentioned for ever.

Enoch 93

[1] And now I say unto you, my sons, love righteousness and walk therein; For the paths of righteousness are worthy of acceptance, But the paths of unrighteousness shall suddenly be destroyed and vanish.

[2] And to certain men of a generation shall the paths of violence and of death be revealed, And they shall hold themselves afar from them, And shall not follow them.

[3] And now I say unto you the righteous: Walk not in the paths of wickedness, nor in the paths of death, And draw not nigh to them, lest ye be destroyed.

[4] But seek and choose for yourselves righteousness and an elect life, And walk in the paths of peace,
And ye shall live and prosper.

[5] And hold fast my words in the thoughts of your hearts, And suffer them not to be effaced from your hearts; For I know that sinners will tempt men to evilly-entreat wisdom, So that no place may be found for her,
And no manner of temptation may minish.

Verses 6-11. *Woes for the Sinners.*

[6] Woe to those who build unrighteousness and oppression And lay deceit as a foundation;
For they shall be suddenly overthrown, And they shall have no peace.

[7] Woe to those who build their houses with sin;
For from all their foundations shall they be

overthrown,
And by the sword shall they fall. And those who acquire gold and silver in judgement suddenly shall perish.

[8] Woe to you, ye rich, for ye have trusted in your riches, And from your riches shall ye depart,
Because ye have not remembered the Most High in the days of your riches.

[9] Ye have committed blasphemy and unrighteousness,
And have become ready for the day of slaughter, And the day of darkness and the day of the great judgement.

[10] Thus I speak and declare unto you: He who hath created you will overthrow you,
And for your fall there shall be no compassion,
And your Creator will rejoice at your destruction.

[11] And your righteous ones in those days shall be
A reproach to the sinners and the godless.

Enoch 94

[1] Oh that mine eyes were a cloud of waters That I might weep over you, And pour down my tears as a cloud of waters: That so I might rest from my trouble of heart!

[2] Who has permitted you to practice reproaches and wickedness? And so judgement shall overtake you, sinners.

[3] Fear not the sinners, ye righteous; For again will Jah deliver them into your hands, That ye may execute judgement upon them according to your desires.

[4] Woe to you who fulminate anathemas which cannot be reversed: Healing shall therefore be far from you because of your sins.

[5] Woe to you who requite your neighbour with evil;
For ye shall be requited according to your works.

[6] Woe to you, lying witnesses, And to those who weigh out injustice, For suddenly shall ye perish.

[7] Woe to you, sinners, for ye persecute the righteous;
For ye shall be delivered up and persecuted because of injustice, And heavy shall its yoke be upon you.

Enoch 95

Grounds of Hopefulness for the Righteous: Woes for the Wicked.

[1] Be hopeful, ye righteous; for suddenly shall the sinners perish before you, And ye shall have lordship over them according to your desires.

[2] And in the day of the tribulation of the sinners,
Your children shall mount and rise as eagles, And higher than the vultures will be your nest, And ye shall ascend and enter the crevices of the earth, And the clefts of the rock for ever as coneys before the unrighteous,
And the sirens shall sigh because of you-and weep.

[3] Wherefore fear not, ye that have suffered; For healing shall be your portion,

And a bright light shall enlighten you, And the voice of rest ye shall hear from heaven.

[4] Woe unto you, ye sinners, for your riches make you appear like the righteous,
But your hearts convict you of being sinners, And this fact shall be a testimony against you for a memorial of your evil deeds.

[5] Woe to you who devour the finest of the wheat,
And drink wine in large bowls,
And tread under foot the lowly with your might.

[6] Woe to you who drink water from every fountain,
For suddenly shall ye be consumed and wither away,
Because ye have forsaken the fountain of life.

[7] Woe to you who work unrighteousness And deceit and blasphemy: It shall be a memorial against you for evil.

[8] Woe to you, ye mighty, Who with might oppress the righteous; For the day of your destruction is coming. In those days many and good days shall come to the righteous-- in the day of your judgement.

Enoch 96

The Evils in Store for Sinners and the Possessors of unrighteous Wealth.

[1] Believe, ye righteous, that the sinners will become a shame And perish in the day of unrighteousness.
[2] Be it known unto you ye sinners, that the Most High is mindful of your destruction, And the angels of heaven rejoice over your destruction.

[3] What will ye do, ye sinners, And whither will ye flee on that day of judgement, When ye hear the voice of the prayer of the righteous?

[4] Yea, ye shall fare like unto them, Against whom this word shall be a testimony: "Ye have been companions of sinners."

[5] And in those days the prayer of the righteous shall reach unto Jah, And for you the days of your judgement shall come.

[6] And all the words of your unrighteousness shall be read out before the Great Holy One, And your faces shall be covered with shame, And He will reject every work which is grounded on unrighteousness.

[7] Woe to you, ye sinners, who live on the mid ocean and on the dry land,
Whose remembrance is evil against you.

[8] Woe to you who acquire silver and gold in unrighteousness and say: "We have become rich with riches and have possessions; And have acquired everything we have desired.

[9] And now let us do what we purposed: For we have gathered silver,
[9^d] And many are the husbandmen in our houses."
[9^e] And our granaries are full as with water,

[10] Yea and like water your lies shall flow away;
For your riches shall not abide But speedily ascend from you; For ye have acquired it all in unrighteousness,
And ye shall be given over to a great curse.

Enoch 97

[1] And now I swear unto you, to the wise and to the foolish, For ye shall have manifold experiences on the earth.

[2] For ye men shall put on more adornments than a woman, And coloured garments more than a virgin:
In royalty and in grandeur and in power, And in silver and in gold and in purple, And in splendour and in food they shall be poured out as water.

[3] Therefore they shall be wanting in doctrine and wisdom, And they shall perish thereby together with their possessions; And with all their glory and their splendour, And in shame and in slaughter and in great destitution, Their spirits shall be cast into the furnace of fire.

[4] I have sworn unto you, ye sinners, as a mountain has not become a slave, And a hill does not become the handmaid of a woman, Even so sin has not been sent upon the earth, But man of himself has created it,
And under a great curse shall they fall who commit it.

[5] And barrenness has not been given to the woman,
But on account of the deeds of her own hands she dies without children.

[6] I have sworn unto you, ye sinners, by the Holy Great One, That all your evil deeds are revealed in the heavens, And that none of your deeds of oppression are covered and hidden.

[7] And do not think in your spirit nor say in your heart that ye do not know and that ye do not see that every sin is every day recorded in heaven in the presence of the Most High.

[8] From henceforth ye know that all your oppression wherewith ye oppress is written down every day till the day of your judgement.

[9] Woe to you, ye fools, for through your folly shall ye perish: and ye transgress against the wise, and so good hap shall not be your portion.

[10] And now, know ye that ye are prepared for the day of destruction: wherefore do not hope to live, ye sinners, but ye shall depart and die; for ye know no ransom; for ye are prepared for the day of the great judgement, for the day of tribulation and great shame for your spirits.

[11] Woe to you, ye obstinate of heart, who work wickedness and eat blood: Whence have ye good things to eat and to drink and to be filled? From all the good things which Jah the Most High has placed in abundance on the earth; therefore ye shall have no peace.

[12] Woe to you who love the deeds of unrighteousness: wherefore do ye hope for good hap unto yourselves? know that ye shall be delivered into the hands of the righteous, and they shall cut off your necks and slay you, and have no mercy upon you.

[13] Woe to you who rejoice in the tribulation of the righteous; for no grave shall be dug for you.

[14] Woe to you who set at nought the words of the righteous; for ye shall have no hope of life.

[15] Woe to you who write down lying and godless words; for they write down their lies that men may hear them and act godlessly towards their neighbour.

[16] Therefore they shall have no peace but die a sudden death.

Enoch 98

[1] Woe to you who work godlessness, And glory in lying and extol them: Ye shall perish, and no happy life shall be yours.

[2] Woe to them who pervert the words of uprightness,
And transgress the eternal law, And transform themselves into what they were not (into sinners):
They shall be trodden under foot upon the earth.

[3] In those days make ready, ye righteous, to raise your prayers as a memorial, And place them as a testimony before the angels, That they may place the sin of the sinners for a memorial before the Most High.

[4] In those days the nations shall be stirred up,
And the families of the nations shall arise on the day of destruction.

[5] And in those days the destitute shall go forth and carry off their children, And they shall abandon them, so that their children shall perish through them:
Yea, they shall abandon their children that are still sucklings, and not return to them, And shall have no pity on their beloved ones.

[6] And again I swear to you, ye sinners, that sin is prepared for a day of unceasing bloodshed.

[7] And they who worship stones, and grave images of gold and silver and wood and stone and clay, and those who worship impure spirits and demons, and all kinds of idols not according to knowledge, shall get no manner of help from them.

[8] And they shall become godless by reason of the folly of their hearts, And their eyes shall be blinded through the fear of their hearts And through visions in their dreams.
[9] Through these they shall become godless and fearful;
For they shall have wrought all their work in a lie,
And shall have worshiped a stone:
Therefore in an instant shall they perish.

[10] But in those days blessed are all they who accept the words of wisdom, and understand them,
And observe the paths of the Most High, and walk in the path of His righteousness, And become not godless with the godless; For they shall be saved.

[11] Woe to you who spread evil to your neighbours;
For you shall be slain in Sheol.
[12] Woe to you who make deceitful and false measures,
And Woe to you who cause bitterness on the earth; For they shall thereby be utterly consumed.

[13] Woe to you who build your houses through the grievous toil of others, And all their building materials are the bricks and stones of sin; I tell you ye shall have no peace.

[14] Woe to them who reject the measure and eternal heritage of their fathers And whose souls follow after idols; For they shall have no rest.

[15] Woe to them who work unrighteousness and help oppression, And slay their neighbours until the day of the great judgement.

[16] For He shall cast down your glory, And bring affliction on your hearts, And shall arouse His fierce indignation, And destroy you all with the sword;
And all the holy and righteous shall remember your sins.

Enoch 99

[1] And in those days in one place the fathers together with their sons shall be smitten And brothers one with another shall fall in death Till the streams flow with their blood.

[2] For a man shall not withhold his hand from slaying his sons and his sons' sons, And the sinner shall not withhold his hand from his honoured brother: From dawn till sunset they shall slay one another.

[3] And the horse shall walk up to the breast in the blood of sinners, And the chariot shall be submerged to its height.

[4] In those days the angels shall descend into the secret places And gather together into one place all those who brought down sin And the Most High will arise on that day of judgement
To execute great judgement amongst sinners.

[5] And over all the righteous and holy He will appoint guardians from amongst the holy angels To guard them as the apple of an eye, Until He makes an end of all wickedness and all sin, And though the righteous sleep a long sleep, they have nought to fear.

[6] And then the children of the earth shall see the wise in security, And shall understand all the words of this book, And recognize that their riches shall not be able to save them In the overthrow of their sins.

[7] Woe to you, Sinners, on the day of strong anguish,
Ye who afflict the righteous and burn them with fire:
Ye shall be requited according to your works.

[8] Woe to you, ye obstinate of heart, Who watch in order to devise wickedness: Therefore shall fear come upon you And there shall be none to help you.

[9] Woe to you, ye sinners, on account of the words of your mouth, And on account of the deeds of your hands which your godlessness as wrought, In blazing flames burning worse than fire shall ye burn.

[10] And now, know ye that from the angels He will inquire as to your deeds in heaven, from the sun and from the moon and from the stars in reference to your sins because upon the earth ye execute judgement on the righteous.

[11]. And He will summon to testify against you every cloud and mist and dew and rain; for they shall all be withheld because of you from descending upon you, and they shall be mindful of your sins.

[12] And now give presents to the rain that it be not withheld from descending upon you, nor yet the dew, when it has received gold and silver from you that it may descend.

[13] When the hoar-frost and snow with their chilliness, and all the snow-storms with all their plagues fall upon you, in those days ye shall not be able to stand before them.

Enoch 100

[1] Observe the heaven, ye children of heaven, and every work of the Most High, and fear ye Him and work no evil in His presence.

[2] If He closes the windows of heaven, and withholds the rain and the dew from descending on the earth on your account, what will ye do then?

[3] And if He sends His anger upon you because of your deeds, ye cannot petition Him; for ye spake proud and insolent words against His righteousness: therefore ye shall have no peace.

[4] And see ye not the sailors of the ships, how their ships are tossed to and fro by the waves, and are shaken by the winds, and are in sore trouble?

[5] And therefore do they fear because all their goodly possessions go upon the sea with them, and they have evil forebodings of heart that the sea will swallow them and they will perish therein.

[6] Are not the entire sea and all its waters, and all its movements, the work of the Most High, and has He not set limits to its doings, and confined it throughout by the sand?

[7] And at His reproof it is afraid and dries up, and all its fish die and all that is in it; But ye sinners that are on the earth fear Him not.

[8] Has He not made the heaven and the earth, and all that is therein? Who has given understanding and wisdom to everything that moves on the earth and in the sea.

[9] Do not the sailors of the ships fear the sea? Yet sinners fear not the Most High.

Enoch 101

Terrors of the Day of Judgement: the adverse Fortunes of the Righteous on the Earth.

[1] In those days when He hath brought a grievous fire upon you, Whither will ye flee, and where will ye find deliverance? And when He launches forth His Word against you Will you not be affrighted and fear? p. 146

[2] And all the luminaries shall be affrighted with great fear, And all the earth shall be affrighted and tremble and be alarmed.

[3] And all the angels shall execute their commands†
And shall seek to hide themselves from the presence of the Great Glory, And the children of earth shall tremble and quake; And ye sinners shall be cursed for ever, And ye shall have no peace.

[4] Fear ye not, ye souls of the righteous, And be hopeful ye that have died in righteousness.

[5] And grieve not if your soul into Sheol has descended in grief, And that in your life your body fared not according to your goodness, But wait for the day of the judgement of sinners And for the day of cursing and chastisement.

[6] And yet when ye die the sinners speak over you:
"As we die, so die the righteous, And what benefit do they reap for their deeds?

[7] Behold, even as we, so do they die in grief and darkness, And what have they more than we?
From henceforth we are equal.

[8] And what will they receive and what will they see for ever? Behold, they too have

died, And henceforth for ever shall they see no light."

[9] I tell you, ye sinners, ye are content to eat and drink, and rob and sin, and strip men naked, and acquire wealth and see good days.

[10] Have ye seen the righteous how their end falls out, that no manner of violence is found in them till their death?

[11] "Nevertheless they perished and became as though they had not been, and their spirits descended into Sheol in tribulation."

Enoch 102

[1] Now, therefore, I swear to you, the righteous, by the glory of the Great and Honoured and 2 Mighty One in dominion, and by His greatness I swear to you:

[2] I know a mystery And have read the heavenly tablets,
And have seen the holy books, And have found written therein and inscribed regarding them:
[3] That all goodness and joy and glory are prepared for them, And written down for the spirits of those who have died in righteousness, And that manifold good shall be given to you in recompense for your labours,
And that your lot is abundantly beyond the lot of the living.

[4] And the spirits of you who have died in righteousness shall live and rejoice, And their spirits shall not perish, nor their memorial from before the face of the Great One Unto all the generations of the world: wherefore no longer fear their contumely.

[5] Woe to you, ye sinners, when ye have died,
If ye die in the wealth of your sins, And those who are like you say regarding you: 'Blessed are the sinners: they have seen all their days.
[6] And how they have died in prosperity and in wealth,
And have not seen tribulation or murder in their life; And they have died in honour, And judgement has not been executed on them during their life."

[7] Know ye, that their souls will be made to descend into Sheol
And they shall be wretched in their great tribulation.

[8] And into darkness and chains and a burning flame where there is grievous judgement shall your spirits enter; And the great judgement shall be for all the generations of the world. Woe to you, for ye shall have no peace.

[9] Say not in regard to the righteous and good who are in life: "In our troubled days we have toiled laboriously and experienced every trouble, And met with much evil and been consumed, And have become few and our spirit small.

[10] And we have been destroyed and have not found any to help us even with a word: We have been tortured and destroyed, and not hoped to see life from day to day.

[11] We hoped to be the head and have become the tail:
We have toiled laboriously and had no satisfaction in our toil; And we have become the food of the sinners and the unrighteous, And they have laid their yoke heavily upon us.

[12] They have had dominion over us that hated us †and smote us; And to those that hated us† we have bowed our necks But they pitied us not.

[13] We desired to get away from them that we might escape and be at rest, But found no place whereunto we should flee and be safe from them.

[14] And are complained to the rulers in our tribulation,
And cried out against those who devoured us,
But they did not attend to our cries
And would not hearken to our voice.

[15] And they helped those who robbed us and devoured us and those who made us few; and they concealed their oppression, and they did not remove from us the yoke of those that devoured us and dispersed us and murdered us, and they concealed their murder, and remembered not that they had lifted up their hands against us.

Enoch 103

Assurances given to the Righteous: Admonitions to Sinners and the Falsifiers of the Words of Uprightness.

[1] I swear unto you, that in heaven the angels remember you for good before the glory of the Great One: and your names are written before the glory of the Great One.

[2] Be hopeful; for aforetime ye were put to shame through ill and affliction; but now ye shall shine as the lights of heaven, ye shall shine and ye shall be seen, and the portals of heaven shall be opened to you.

[3] And in your cry, cry for judgement, and it shall appear to you; for all your tribulation shall be visited on the rulers, and on all who helped those who plundered you.

[4] Be hopeful, and cast not away your hopes for ye shall have great joy as the angels of heaven.

[5] What shall ye be obliged to do? Ye shall not have to hide on the day of the great judgement and ye shall not be found as sinners, and the eternal judgement shall be far from you for all the generations of the world.

[6] And now fear not, ye righteous, when ye see the sinners growing strong and prospering in their ways: be not companions with them, but keep afar from their violence; for ye shall become companions of the hosts of heaven.

[7] And, although ye sinners say: "All our sins shall not be searched out and be written down," nevertheless they shall write down all your sins every day.

[8] And now I show unto you that light and darkness, day and night, see all your sins.

[9] Be not godless in your hearts, and lie not and alter not the words of uprightness, nor charge with lying the words of the Holy Great One, nor take account of your idols; for all your lying and all your godlessness issue not in righteousness but in great sin.

[10] And now I know this mystery, that sinners will alter and pervert the words of righteousness in many ways, and will speak wicked words, and lie, and practice great deceits, and write books concerning their words.

[11] But when they write down truthfully all my words in their languages, and do not change or minish ought from my words but

write them all down truthfully--all that I first testified concerning them.

[12] Then, I know another mystery, that books will be given to the righteous and the wise to become a cause of joy and uprightness and much wisdom.

[13] And to them shall the books be given, and they shall believe in them and rejoice over them, and then shall all the righteous who have learnt therefrom all the paths of uprightness be recompensed.'

Enoch 104

[1] In those days Jah bade them to summon and testify to the children of earth concerning their wisdom: Show it unto them; for ye are their guides, and a recompense over the whole earth.

[2] For I and My son will be united with them for ever in the paths of uprightness in their lives; and ye shall have peace: rejoice, ye children of uprightness. Amen.

FRAGMENT OF THE BOOK OF NOAH

Enoch 105

[1] And after some days my son Methuselah took a wife for his son Lamech, and she became pregnant by him and bore a son.

[2] And his body was white as snow and red as the blooming of a rose, and the hair of his head †and his long locks were white as wool, and his eyes beautiful†. And when he opened his eyes, he lighted up the whole house like the sun, and the whole house was very bright. [3] And thereupon he arose in the hands of the midwife, opened his mouth, and conversed with† Jah of righteousness.

[4] And his father Lamech was afraid of him and fled, and came to his father Methuselah.

[5] And he said unto him: 'I have begotten a strange son, diverse from and unlike man, and resembling the sons of the God of heaven; and his nature is different and he is not like us, and his eyes are as the rays of the sun, and his countenance is glorious.

[6] And it seems to me that he is not sprung from me but from the angels, and I fear that in his days a wonder may be wrought on the earth.

[7] And now, my father, I am here to petition thee and implore thee that thou mayest go to Enoch, our father, and learn from him the truth, for his dwelling-place is amongst the angels.'

[8] And when Methuselah heard the words of his son, he came to me to the ends of the earth; for he had heard that I was there, and he cried aloud, and I heard his voice and I came to him. And 1 said unto him: 'Behold, here am I, my son, wherefore hast thou come to me?'

[9] And he answered and said: 'Because of a great cause of anxiety have I come to thee, and because of a disturbing vision have I approached.

[10] And now, my father, hear me: unto Lamech my son there hath been born a son, the like of whom there is none, and his nature is not like man's nature, and the colour of his body is whiter than snow and redder than the bloom of a rose, and the hair of his head is whiter than white wool, and his eyes are like the rays of the sun, and he

opened his eyes and thereupon lighted up the whole house.

[11] And he arose in the hands of the midwife, and opened his mouth and blessed Jah of heaven.

[12] And his father Lamech became afraid and fled to me, and did not believe that he was sprung from him, but that he was in the likeness of the angels of heaven; and behold I have come to thee that thou mayest make known to me the truth.'

[13] And I, Enoch, answered and said unto him: 'Jah will do a new thing on the earth, and this I have already seen in a vision, and make known to thee that in the generation of my father Jared some of the angels of heaven transgressed the word of Jah .

[14] And they shall produce on the earth giants not according to the spirit, but according to the flesh, and there shall be a great punishment on the earth, and the earth shall be cleansed from all impurity.

[15] And behold they commit sin and transgress the law, and have united themselves with women and commit sin with them, and have married some of them, and have begot children by them.

[16] Yea, there shall come a great destruction over the whole earth, and there shall be a deluge and a great destruction for one year.

[17] And this son who has been born unto you shall be left on the earth, and his three children shall be saved with him: when all mankind that are on the earth shall die (he and his sons shall be saved).

[18] And now make known to thy son Lamech that he who has been born is in truth his son, and call his name Noah; for he shall be left to you, and he and his sons shall be saved from the destruction, which shall come upon the earth on account of all the sin and all the unrighteousness, which shall be consummated on the earth in his days.

[19] And after that there shall be still more unrighteousness than that which was first consummated on the earth; for I know the mysteries of the holy ones; for He, Jah , has showed me and informed me, and I have read them in the heavenly tablets.

Enoch 106

[1] And I saw written on them that generation upon generation shall transgress, till a generation of righteousness arises, and transgression is destroyed and sin passes away from the earth, and all manner of good comes upon it.

[2] And now, my son, go and make known to thy son Lamech that this son, which has been born, is in truth his son, and that this is no lie.'

[3] And when Methuselah had heard the words of his father Enoch--for he had shown to him everything in secret--he returned and showed them to him and called the name of that son Noah; for he will comfort the earth after all the destruction.

AN APPENDIX TO THE BOOK OF ENOCH.

Enoch 107

[1] Another book which Enoch wrote for his son Methuselah and for those who will come after him, and keep the law in the last days.

[2] Ye who have done good shall wait for those days till an end is made of those who work evil; and an end of the might of the transgressors.

[3] And wait ye indeed till sin has passed away, for their names shall be blotted out of the book of life and out of the holy books, and their seed shall be destroyed for ever, and their spirits shall be slain, and they shall cry and make lamentation in a place that is a chaotic wilderness, and in the fire shall they burn; for there is no earth there.

[4] And I saw there something like an invisible cloud; for by reason of its depth I could not look over, and I saw a flame of fire blazing brightly, and things like shining mountains circling and sweeping to and fro.

[5] And I asked one of the holy angels who was with me and said unto him: 'What is this shining thing? for it is not a heaven but only the flame of a blazing fire, and the voice of weeping and crying and lamentation and strong pain.'

[6] And he said unto me: 'This place which thou seest--here are cast the spirits of sinners and blasphemers, and of those who work wickedness, and of those who pervert everything that Jah hath spoken through the mouth of the prophets--even the things that shall be.

[7] For some of them are written and inscribed above in the heaven, in order that the angels may read them and know that which shall befall the sinners, and the spirits of the humble, and of those who have afflicted their bodies, and been recompensed by God; and of those who have been put to shame by wicked men:

[8] Who love God and loved neither gold nor silver nor any of the good things which are in the world, but gave over their bodies to torture.

[9] Who, since they came into being, longed not after earthly food, but regarded everything as a passing breath, and lived accordingly, and Jah tried them much, and their spirits were found pure so that they should bless His name.

[10] And all the blessings destined for them I have recounted in the books. And he hath assigned them their recompense, because they have been found to be such as loved heaven more than their life in the world, and though they were trodden under foot of wicked men, and experienced abuse and reviling from them and were put to shame, yet they blessed Me.

[11] And now I will summon the spirits of the good who belong to the generation of light, and I will transform those who were born in darkness, who in the flesh were not recompensed with such honour as their faithfulness deserved.

[12] And I will bring forth in shining light those who have loved My holy name, and I will seat each on the throne of his honour.

[13] And they shall be resplendent for times without number; for righteousness is the judgement of God; for to the faithful He will give faithfulness in the habitation of upright paths.

[14] And they shall see those who were, born in darkness led into darkness, while the righteous shall be resplendent.

[15] And the sinners shall cry aloud and see them resplendent, and they indeed will go

where days and seasons are prescribed for them.'

Book of Jubilees

[AM= Anno Mundi: the year after Creation]

Jubilees 1

1. And it came to pass in the first year of the exodus of the children of Israel out of Egypt, in the third month, on the sixteenth day of the month, [2450 Anno Mundi] that Jah spake to Moses, saying: 'Come up to Me on the Mount, and I will give thee two tables of stone of the law and of the commandment, which I have written, that thou mayst teach them.'

2. And Moses went up into the mount of God, and the glory of Jah abode on Mount Sinai, and a cloud overshadowed it six days.

3. And He called to Moses on the seventh day out of the midst of the cloud, and the appearance of the glory of Jah was like a flaming fire on the top of the mount.

4. And Moses was on the Mount forty days and forty nights, and Jah taught him the earlier and the later history of the division of all the days of the law and of the testimony.

5. And He said: 'Incline thine heart to every word which I shall speak to thee on this mount, and write them in a book in order that their generations may see how I have not forsaken them for all the evil which they have wrought in transgressing the covenant which I establish between Me and thee for their generations this day on Mount Sinai.

6. And thus it will come to pass when all these things come upon them, that they will recognise that I am more righteous than they in all their judgments and in all their actions, and they will recognise that I have been truly with them.

7. And do thou write for thyself all these words which I declare unto, thee this day, for I know their rebellion and their stiff neck, before I bring them into the land of which I sware to their fathers, to Abraham and to Isaac and to Jacob, saying: ' Unto your seed will I give a land flowing with milk and honey.

8. And they will eat and be satisfied, and they will turn to strange gods, to gods which cannot deliver them from aught of their tribulation: and this witness shall be heard for a witness against them. For they will forget all My commandments, even all that I command them, and they will walk after the Gentiles, and after their uncleanness, and after their shame, and will serve their gods, and these will prove unto them an offence and a tribulation and an affliction and a snare.

9. And many will perish and they will be taken captive, and will fall into the hands of the enemy, because they have forsaken My ordinances and My commandments, and the festivals of My covenant, and My sabbaths, and My holy place which I have hallowed for Myself in their midst, and My tabernacle, and My sanctuary, which I have hallowed for Myself in the midst of the land, that I should set my name upon it, and that it should dwell there.

10. And they will make to themselves high places and groves and graven images, and they will worship, each his own graven image, so as to go astray, and they will sacrifice their children to demons, and to all the works of the error of their hearts.

11. And I will send witnesses unto them, that I may witness against them, but they will not hear, and will slay the witnesses also, and they will persecute those who seek the law, and they will abrogate and change everything so as to work evil before My eyes.

12. And I will hide My face from them, and I will deliver them into the hand of the Gentiles for captivity, and for a prey, and for devouring, and I will remove them from the midst of the land, and I will scatter them amongst the Gentiles.

13. And they will forget all My law and all My commandments and all My judgments, and will go astray as to new moons, and sabbaths, and festivals, and jubilees, and ordinances.

14. And after this they will turn to Me from amongst the Gentiles with all their heart and with all their soul and with all their strength, and I will gather them from amongst all the Gentiles, and they will seek me, so that I shall be found of them, when they seek me with all their heart and with all their soul.

15. And I will disclose to them abounding peace with righteousness, and I will remove them the plant of uprightness, with all My heart and with all My soul, and they shall be for a blessing and not for a curse, and they shall be the head and not the tail.

16. And I will build My sanctuary in their midst, and I will dwell with them, and I will be their God and they shall be My people in truth and righteousness.

17. And I will not forsake them nor fail them; for I am Jah their God.'

18. And Moses fell on his face and prayed and said, 'Jah my God, do not forsake Thy people and Thy inheritance, so that they should wander in the error of their hearts, and do not deliver them into the hands of their enemies, the Gentiles, lest they should rule over them and cause them to sin against Thee.

19. Let thy mercy, O Lord, be lifted up upon Thy people, and create in them an upright spirit, and let not the spirit of Beliar rule over them to accuse them before Thee, and to ensnare them from all the paths of

righteousness, so that they may perish from before Thy face.

20. But they are Thy people and Thy inheritance, which thou hast delivered with thy great power from the hands of the Egyptians: create in them a clean heart and a holy spirit, and let them not be ensnared in their sins from henceforth until eternity.'

21. And Jah said unto Moses: 'I know their contrariness and their thoughts and their stiffneckedness, and they will not be obedient till they confess their own sin and the sin of their fathers.

22. And after this they will turn to Me in all uprightness and with all their heart and with all their soul, and I will circumcise the foreskin of their heart and the foreskin of the heart of their seed, and I will create in them a holy spirit, and I will cleanse them so that they shall not turn away from Me from that day unto eternity.

23. And their souls will cleave to Me and to all My commandments, and they will fulfil My commandments, and I will be their Father and they shall be My children.

24. And they all shall be called children of the living God, and every angel and every spirit shall know, yea, they shall know that these are My children, and that I am their Father in uprightness and righteousness, and that I love them.

25. And do thou write down for thyself all these words which I declare unto thee on this mountain, the first and the last, which shall come to pass in all the divisions of the days in the law and in the testimony and in the weeks and the jubilees unto eternity, until I descend and dwell with them throughout eternity.'

26. And He said to the angel of the presence: Write for Moses from the beginning of creation till My sanctuary has been built among them for all eternity.

27. And Jah will appear to the eyes of all, and all shall know that I am the God of Israel and the Father of all the children of Jacob, and King on Mount Zion for all eternity. And Zion and Jerusalem shall be holy.'

28. And the angel of the presence who went before the camp of Israel took the tables of the divisions of the years -from the time of the creation- of the law and of the testimony of the weeks of the jubilees, according to the individual years, according to all the number of the jubilees according, to the individual years, from the day of the new creation when the heavens and the earth shall be renewed and all their creation according to the powers of the heaven, and according to all the creation of the earth, until the sanctuary of Jah shall be made in Jerusalem on Mount Zion, and all the luminaries be renewed for healing and for peace and for blessing for all the elect of Israel, and that thus it may be from that day and unto all the days of the earth.

Jubilees 2

1. And the angel of the presence spake to Moses according to the word of Jah, saying: Write the complete history of the creation, how in six days Jah God finished all His works and all that He created, and kept Sabbath on the seventh day and hallowed it for all ages, and appointed it as a sign for all His works.

2. For on the first day He created the heavens which are above and the earth and the waters and all the spirits which serve before him -the angels of the presence, and the angels of sanctification, and the angels [of the spirit of fire and the angels] of the spirit of the winds, and the angels of the spirit of the clouds, and of darkness, and of snow and of hail and of hoar frost, and the angels of the voices and of the thunder and of the lightning, and the angels of the spirits of cold and of heat, and of winter and of spring and of autumn and of summer and of all the spirits of his creatures which are in the heavens and on the earth, He created the abysses and the darkness, eventide and night, and the light, dawn and day, which He hath prepared in the knowledge of his heart.

3. And thereupon we saw His works, and praised Him, and lauded before Him on account of all His works; for seven great works did He create on the first day.

4. And on the second day He created the firmament in the midst of the waters, and the waters were divided on that day -half of them went up above and half of them went down below the firmament that was in the midst over the face of the whole earth. And this was the only work God created on the second day.

5. And on the third day He commanded the waters to pass from off the face of the whole earth into one place, and the dry land to appear.

6. And the waters did so as He commanded them, and they retired from off the face of the earth into one place outside of this firmament, and the dry land appeared.

7. And on that day He created for them all the seas according to their separate gathering-places, and all the rivers, and the gatherings of the waters in the mountains and on all the earth, and all the lakes, and all the dew of the earth, and the seed which is sown, and all sprouting things, and fruit-bearing trees, and trees of the wood, and the garden of Eden, in Eden and all plants after their kind.

8. These four great works Jah created on the third day. And on the fourth day He created the sun and the moon and the stars, and set them in the firmament of the heaven, to give light upon all the earth, and to rule over the day and the night, and divide the light from the darkness.

9. And Jah appointed the sun to be a great sign on the earth for days and for sabbaths and for months and for feasts and for years and for sabbaths

of years and for jubilees and for all seasons of the years.

10. And it divideth the light from the darkness and for prosperity, that all things may prosper which shoot and grow on the earth.
11. These three kinds He made on the fourth day. And on the fifth day He created great sea monsters in the depths of the waters, for these were the first things of flesh that were created by his hands, the fish and everything that moves in the waters, and everything that flies, the birds and all their kind.
12. And the sun rose above them to prosper them, and above everything that was on the earth, everything that shoots out of the earth, and all fruit-bearing trees, and all flesh.
13. These three kinds He created on the fifth day. And on the sixth day He created all the animals of the earth, and all cattle, and everything that moves on the earth.
14. And after all this He created man, a man and a woman created He them, and gave him dominion over all that is upon the earth, and in the seas, and over everything that flies, and over beasts and over cattle, and over everything that moves on the earth, and over the whole earth, and over all this He gave him dominion.
15. And these four kinds He created on the sixth day. And there were altogether two and twenty kinds.
16. And He finished all his work on the sixth day -all that is in the heavens and on the earth, and in the seas and in the abysses, and in the light and in the darkness, and in everything.
17. And He gave us a great sign, the Sabbath day, that we should work six days, but keep Sabbath on the seventh day from all work.
18. And all the angels of the presence, and all the angels of sanctification, these two great classes -He hath bidden us to keep the Sabbath with Him in heaven and on earth.
19. And He said unto us: 'Behold, I will separate unto Myself a people from among all the peoples, and these shall keep the Sabbath day, and I will sanctify them unto Myself as My people, and will bless them; as I have sanctified the Sabbath day and do sanctify it unto Myself, even so will bless them, and they shall be My people and I will be their God.
20. And I have chosen the seed of Jacob from amongst all that I have seen, and have written him down as My first-born son,and have sanctified him unto Myself for ever and ever; and I will teach them the Sabbath day, that they may keep Sabbath thereon from all work.'
21. And thus He created therein a sign in accordance with which they should keep Sabbath with us on the seventh day, to eat and to drink, and to bless Him who has created all things as He has blessed and sanctified unto Himself a peculiar people above all peoples, and that they should keep Sabbath together with us.

2. And He caused His commands to ascend as a sweet savour acceptable before Him all the days

3. There were two and twenty heads of mankind from Adam to Jacob, and two and twenty kinds of work were made until the seventh day; this is blessed and holy; and the former also is blessed and holy; and this one serves with that one for sanctification and blessing.

24. And to this (Jacob and his seed) it was granted that they should always be the blessed and holy ones of the first testimony and law, even as He had sanctified and blessed the Sabbath day on the seventh day.

25. He created heaven and earth and everything that He created in six days, and Jah made the seventh day holy, for all His works; therefore He commanded on its behalf that, whoever does any work thereon shall die, and that he who defiles it shall surely die.

26. Wherefore do thou command the children of Israel to observe this day that they may keep it holy and not do thereon any work, and not to defile it, as it is holier than all other days.

27. And whoever profanes it shall surely die, and whoever does thereon any work shall surely die eternally, that the children of Israel may observe this day throughout their generations, and not be rooted out of the land; for it is a holy day and a blessed day.

28. And every one who observes it and keeps Sabbath thereon from all his work, will be holy and blessed throughout all days like unto us.

29. Declare and say to the children of Israel the law of this day both that they should keep Sabbath thereon, and that they should not forsake it in the error of their hearts; and that it is not lawful to do any work thereon which is unseemly, to do thereon their own pleasure, and that they should not prepare thereon anything to be eaten or drunk, and that it is not lawful to draw water, or bring in or take out thereon through their gates any burden, which they had not prepared for themselves on the sixth day in their dwellings.

30. And they shall not bring in nor take out from house to house on that day; for that day is more holy and blessed than any jubilee day of the jubilees; on this we kept Sabbath in the heavens before it was made known to any flesh to keep Sabbath thereon on the earth.

31. And the Creator of all things blessed it, but he did not sanctify all peoples and nations to keep Sabbath thereon, but Israel alone: them alone he permitted to eat and drink and to keep Sabbath thereon on the earth.

32. And the Creator of all things blessed this day which He had created for blessing and holiness and glory above all days.

33. This law and testimony was given to the children of Israel as a law for ever unto their generations.

Jubilees 3

1. And on the six days of the second week we brought, according to the word of Jah, unto Adam all the beasts, and all the cattle, and all the birds, and everything that moves on the earth, and everything that moves in the water, according to their kinds, and according to their types: the beasts on the first day; the cattle on the second day; the birds on the third day; and all that which moves on the earth on the fourth day; and that which moves in the water on the fifth day.

2. And Adam named them all by their respective names, and as he called them, so was their name.

3. And on these five days Adam saw all these, male and female, according to every kind that was on the earth, but he was alone and found no helpmeet for him.

4. And Jah said unto us: 'It is not good that the man should be alone: let us make a helpmeet for him.'

5. And Jah our God caused a deep sleep to fall upon him, and he slept, and He took for the woman one rib from amongst his ribs, and this rib was the origin of the woman from amongst his ribs, and He built up the flesh in its stead, and built the woman.

6. And He awaked Adam out of his sleep and on awaking he rose on the sixth day, and He brought her to him, and he knew her, and said unto her: 'This is now bone of my bones and flesh of my flesh; she shall be called my wife; because she was taken from her husband.'

7. Therefore shall man and wife be one and therefore shall a man leave his father and his mother, and cleave unto his wife, and they shall be one flesh.

8. In the first week was Adam created, and the rib -his wife: in the second week He showed her unto him: and for this reason the commandment was given to keep in their defilement, for a male seven days, and for a female twice seven days.

9. And after Adam had completed forty days in the land where he had been created, we brought him into the garden of Eden to till and keep it, but his wife they brought in on the eightieth day, and after this she entered into the garden of Eden.

10. And for this reason the commandment is written on the heavenly tablets in regard to her that gives birth: 'if she bears a male, she shall remain in her uncleanness seven days according to the first week of days, and thirty and three days shall she remain in the blood of her purifying, and she shall not touch any hallowed thing, nor enter into the sanctuary, until she accomplishes these days which are enjoined in the case of a male child.

11. But in the case of a female child she shall remain in her uncleanness two weeks of days, according to the first two weeks, and sixty-six days in the blood of her purification, and they will be in all eighty days.'

12. And when she had completed these eighty days we brought her into the garden of Eden, for it is holier than all the earth besides and every tree that is planted in it is holy.

13. Therefore, there was ordained regarding her who bears a male or a female child the statute of those days that she should touch no hallowed thing, nor enter into the sanctuary until these days for the male or female child are accomplished.

14. This is the law and testimony which was written down for Israel, in order that they should observe it all the days.

15. And in the first week of the first jubilee, [1-7 A.M.] Adam and his wife were in the garden of Eden for seven years tilling and keeping it, and we gave him work and we instructed him to do everything that is suitable for tillage.

16. And he tilled the garden, and was naked and knew it not, and was not ashamed, and he protected the garden from the birds and beasts and cattle, and gathered its fruit, and eat, and put aside the residue for himself and for his wife [and put aside that which was being kept].

17. And after the completion of the seven years, which he had completed there, seven years exactly, [8 A.M.] and in the second month, on the seventeenth day of the month, the serpent came and approached the woman, and the serpent said to the woman, 'Hath God commanded you, saying, Ye shall not eat of every tree of the garden?'

18. And she said to it, 'Of all the fruit of the trees of the garden God hath said unto us, Eat; but of the fruit of the tree which is in the midst of the garden God hath said unto us, Ye shall not eat thereof, neither shall ye touch it, lest ye die.'

19. And the serpent said unto the woman, 'Ye shall not surely die: for God doth know that on the day ye shall eat thereof, your eyes will be opened, and ye will be as gods, and ye will know good and evil.

20. And the woman saw the tree that it was agreeable and pleasant to the eye, and that its fruit was good for food, and she took thereof and eat.

21. And when she had first covered her shame with figleaves, she gave thereof to Adam and he eat, and his eyes were opened, and he saw that he was naked.

22. And he took figleaves and sewed them together, and made an apron for himself, and ,covered his shame.

23. And Jah cursed the serpent, and was wroth with it for ever . . .

24. And He was wroth with the woman, because she harkened to the voice of the serpent, and did eat; and He said unto her: 'I will greatly multiply thy sorrow and thy pains: in sorrow thou shalt bring forth children, and thy return shall be unto thy husband, and he will rule over thee.'

25. And to Adam also he said, ' Because thou hast harkened unto the voice of

thy wife, and hast eaten of the tree of which I commanded thee that thou shouldst not eat thereof, cursed be the ground for thy sake: thorns and thistles shall it bring forth to thee, and thou shalt eat thy bread in the sweat of thy face, till thou returnest to the earth from whence thou wast taken; for earth thou art, and unto earth shalt thou return.'

26. And He made for them coats of skin, and clothed them, and sent them forth from the Garden of Eden.

27. And on that day on which Adam went forth from the Garden, he offered as a sweet savour an offering, frankincense, galbanum, and stacte, and spices in the morning with the rising of the sun from the day when he covered his shame.

28. And on that day was closed the mouth of all beasts, and of cattle, and of birds, and of whatever walks, and of whatever moves, so that they could no longer speak: for they had all spoken one with another with one lip and with one tongue.

29. And He sent out of the Garden of Eden all flesh that was in the Garden of Eden, and all flesh was scattered according to its kinds, and according to its types unto the places which had been created for them.

30. And to Adam alone did He give the wherewithal to cover his shame, of all the beasts and cattle.

31. On this account, it is prescribed on the heavenly tablets as touching all those who know the judgment of the law, that they should cover their shame, and should not uncover themselves as the Gentiles uncover themselves.

32. And on the new moon of the fourth month, Adam and his wife went forth from the Garden of Eden, and they dwelt in the land of Elda in the land of their creation.

33. And Adam called the name of his wife Eve.

34. And they had no son till the first jubilee, [8 A.M.] and after this he knew her.

35. Now he tilled the land as he had been instructed in the Garden of Eden.

Jubilees 4

1. And in the third week in the second jubilee [64-70 A.M.] she gave birth to Cain, and in the fourth [71-77 A.M.] she gave birth to Abel, and in the fifth [78-84 A.M.] she gave birth to her daughter Âwân.

2. And in the first year of the third jubilee [99-105 A.M.], Cain slew Abel because Jah accepted the sacrifice of Abel, and did not accept the offering of Cain.

3. And he slew him in the field: and his blood cried from the ground to heaven, complaining because he had slain him.

4. And Jah reproved Cain because of Abel, because he had slain him, and he made him a fugitive on the earth because of the blood of his brother, and he cursed him upon the earth.

5. And on this account it is written on the heavenly tables, 'Cursed is ‚he who smites his neighbour treacherously, and let all who have seen and heard say, So be it; and the man who has seen and not declared it, let him be accursed as the other.'

6. And for this reason we announce when we come before Jah our God all the sin which is committed in heaven and on earth, and in light and in darkness, and everywhere.

7. And Adam and his wife mourned for Abel four weeks of years, [99-127 A.M] and in the fourth year of the fifth week [130 A.M.] they became joyful, and Adam knew his wife again, and she bare him a son, and he called his name Seth; for he said 'GOD has raised up a second seed unto us on the earth instead of Abel; for Cain slew him.'

8. And in the sixth week [134-40 A.M.] he begat his daughter Azûrâ.

9. And Cain took Âwân his sister to be his wife and she bare him Enoch at the close of the fourth jubilee. [190-196 A.M.] And in the first year of the first week of the fifth jubilee, [197 A.M.] houses were built on the earth, and Cain built a city, and called its name after the name of his son Enoch.

10. And Adam knew Eve his wife and she bare yet nine sons.

11. And in the fifth week of the fifth jubilee [225-31 A.M.] Seth took Azûrâ his sister to be his wife, and in the fourth year of the sixth week [235 A.M.] she bare him Enos.

12. He began to call on the name of Jah on the earth.

13. And in the seventh jubilee in the third week [309-15 A.M.] Enos took Nôâm his sister to be his wife, and she bare him a son in the third year of the fifth week, and he called his name Kenan.

14. And at the close of the eighth jubilee [325, 386-3992 A.M.] Kenan took Mûalêlêth his sister to be his wife, and she bare him a son in the ninth jubilee, in the first week in the third year of this week, [395 A.M] and he called his name Mahalalel.

15. And in the second week of the tenth jubilee [449-55 A.M.] Mahalalel took unto him to wife DinaH, the daughter of Barakiel the daughter of his father's brother, and she bare him a son in the third week in the sixth year, [461 A.M.] and he called his name Jared, for in his days the angels of Jah descended on the earth, those who are named the Watchers, that they should instruct the children of men, and that they should do judgment and uprightness on the earth.

16. And in the eleventh jubilee [512-18 A.M.] Jared took to himself a wife, and her name was Baraka, the daughter of Râsûjâl, a daughter of his father's brother, in the fourth week of this jubilee, [522 A.M.] and she bare him a son in the fifth week, in the fourth year of the jubilee, and he called his name Enoch.

17. And he was the first among men that are born on earth who learnt writing

and knowledge and wisdom and who wrote down the signs of heaven according to the order of their months in a book, that men might know the seasons of the years according to the order of their separate months.

18. And he was the first to write a testimony and he testified to the sons of men among the generations of the earth, and recounted the weeks of the jubilees, and made known to them the days of the years, and set in order the months and recounted the Sabbaths of the years as we made them, known to him.

19. And what was and what will be he saw in a vision of his sleep, as it will happen to the children of men throughout their generations until the day of judgment; he saw and understood everything, and wrote his testimony, and placed the testimony on earth for all the children of men and for their generations.

20. And in the twelfth jubilee, [582-88] in the seventh week thereof, he took to himself a wife, and her name was Edna, the daughter of Danel, the daughter of his father's brother, and in the sixth year in this week [587 A.M.] she bare him a son and he called his name Methuselah.

21. And he was moreover with the angels of God these six jubilees of years, and they showed him everything which is on earth and in the heavens, the rule of the sun, and he wrote down everything.

22. And he testified to the Watchers, who had sinned with the daughters of men; for these had begun to unite themselves, so as to be defiled, with the daughters of men, and Enoch testified against them all.

23. And he was taken from amongst the children of men, and we conducted him into the Garden of Eden in majesty and honour, and behold there he writes down the condemnation and judgment of the world, and all the wickedness of the children of men.

24. And on account of it God brought the waters of the flood upon all the land of Eden; for there he was set as a sign and that he should testify against all the children of men, that he should recount all the deeds of the generations until the day of condemnation.

25. And he burnt the incense of the sanctuary, even sweet spices acceptable before Jah on the Mount.

26. For Jah has four places on the earth, the Garden of Eden, and the Mount of the East, and this mountain on which thou art this day, Mount Sinai, and Mount Zion which will be sanctified in the new creation for a sanctification of the earth; through it will the earth be sanctified from all its guilt and its uncleanness through-out the generations of the world.

27. And in the fourteenth jubilee [652 A.M.] Methuselah took unto himself a wife, Edna the daughter of Azrial, the daughter of his father's brother, in the third week, in the first year of

this week, [701-7 A.M.] and he begat a son and called his name Lamech.

28. And in the fifteenth jubilee in the third week Lamech took to himself a wife, and her name was Betenos the daughter of Baraki'il, the daughter of his father's brother, and in this week she bare him a son and he called his name Noah, saying, 'This one will comfort me for my trouble and all my work, and for the ground which Jah hath cursed.'

29. And at the close of the nineteenth jubilee, in the seventh week in the sixth year [930 A.M.] thereof, Adam died, and all his sons buried him in the land of his creation, and he was the first to be buried in the earth.

30. And he lacked seventy years of one thousand years; for one thousand years are as one day in the testimony of the heavens and therefore was it written concerning the tree of knowledge: 'On the day that ye eat thereof ye shall die.' For this reason he did not complete the years of this day; for he died during it.

31. At the close of this jubilee Cain was killed after him in the same year; for his house fell upon him and he died in the midst of his house, and he was killed by its stones; for with a stone he had killed Abel, and by a stone was he killed in righteous judgment.

32. For this reason it was ordained on the heavenly tablets: With the instrument with which a man kills his neighbour with the same shall he be killed; after the manner that he wounded him, in like manner shall they deal with him.'

33. And in the twenty-fifth [1205 A.M.] jubilee Noah took to himself a wife, and her name was `Emzârâ, the daughter of Râkê'êl, the daughter of his father's brother, in the first year in the fifth week [1207 A.M.]: and in the third year thereof she bare him Shem, in the fifth year thereof [1209 A.M.] she bare him Ham, and in the first year in the sixth week [1212 A.M.] she bare him Japheth.

Jubilees 5

1. And it came to pass when the children of men began to multiply on the face of the earth and daughters were born unto them, that the angels of God saw them on a certain year of this jubilee, that they were beautiful to look upon; and they took themselves wives of all whom they chose, and they bare unto them sons and they were giants.

2. And lawlessness increased on the earth and all flesh corrupted its way, alike men and cattle and beasts and birds and everything that walks on the earth -all of them corrupted their ways and their orders, and they began to devour each other, and lawlessness increased on the earth and every imagination of the thoughts of all men was thus evil continually.

3. And God looked upon the earth, and behold it was corrupt, and all flesh had corrupted its orders, and all that

were upon the earth had wrought all manner of evil before His eyes.

4. And He said that He would destroy man and all flesh upon the face of the earth which He had created.

5. But Noah found grace before the eyes of Jah.

6. And against the angels whom He had sent upon the earth, He was exceedingly wroth, and He gave commandment to root them out of all their dominion, and He bade us to bind them in the depths of the earth, and behold they are bound in the midst of them, and are kept separate.

7. And against their sons went forth a command from before His face that they should be smitten with the sword, and be removed from under heaven.

8. And He said 'My spirit shall not always abide on man; for they also are flesh and their days shall be one hundred and twenty years'.

9. And He sent His sword into their midst that each should slay his neighbour, and they began to slay each other till they all fell by the sword and were destroyed from the earth.

10. And their fathers were witnesses of their destruction, and after this they were bound in the depths of the earth for ever, until the day of the great condemnation, when judgment is executed on all those who have corrupted their ways and their works before Jah.

11. And He destroyed all from their places, and there was not left one of them whom He judged not according to all their wickedness.

12. And he made for all his works a new and righteous nature, so that they should not sin in their whole nature for ever, but should be all righteous each in his kind alway.

13. And the judgment of all is ordained and written on the heavenly tablets in righteousness -even the judgment of all who depart from the path which is ordained for them to walk in; and if they walk not therein, judgment is written down for every creature and for every kind.

14. And there is nothing in heaven or on earth, or in light or in darkness, or in Sheol or in the depth, or in the place of darkness which is not judged; and all their judgments are ordained and written and engraved.

15. In regard to all He will judge, the great according to his greatness, and the small according to his smallness, and each according to his way.

16. And He is not one who will regard the person of any, nor is He one who will receive gifts, if He says that He will execute judgment on each: if one gave everything that is on the earth, He will not regard the gifts or the person of any, nor accept anything at his hands, for He is a righteous judge.

17. And of the children of Israel it has been written and ordained: If they turn to him in righteousness He will

forgive all their transgressions and pardon all their sins.

18. It is written and ordained that He will show mercy to all who turn from all their guilt once each year.

19. And as for all those who corrupted their ways and their thoughts before the flood, no man's person was accepted save that of Noah alone; for his person was accepted in behalf of his sons, whom God saved from the waters of the flood on his account; for his heart was righteous in all his ways, according as it was commanded regarding him, and he had not departed from aught that was ordained for him.

20. And Jah said that he would destroy everything which was upon the earth, both men and cattle, and

21. beasts, and fowls of the air, and that which moveth on the earth. And He commanded Noah to make him an ark, that he might save himself from the waters of the flood.

22. And Noah made the ark in all respects as He commanded him, in the twenty-seventh jubilee of years, in the fifth week in the fifth year on the new moon of the first month. [1307 A.M.]

23. And he entered in the sixth year thereof, [1308 A.M.] in the second month, on the new moon of the second month, till the sixteenth; and he entered, and all that we brought to him, into the ark, and Jah closed it from without on the seventeenth evening.

24. And Jah opened seven flood-gates of heaven,
And the mouths of the fountains of the great deep, seven mouths in number.

25. And the flood-gates began to pour down water from the heaven forty days and forty nights,
And the fountains of the deep also sent up waters, until the whole world was full of water.

26. And the waters increased upon the earth:
Fifteen cubits did the waters rise above all the high mountains,
And the ark was lift up above the earth,
And it moved upon the face of the waters.

27. And the water prevailed on the face of the earth five months -one hundred and fifty days.

28. And the ark went and rested on the top of Lubar, one of the mountains of Ararat.

29. And on the new moon in the fourth month the fountains of the great deep were closed and the flood-gates of heaven were restrained; and on the new moon of the seventh month all the mouths of the abysses of the earth were opened, and the water began to descend into the deep below.

30. And on the new moon of the tenth month the tops of the mountains were seen, and on the new moon of the first month the earth became visible.

31. And the waters disappeared from above the earth in the fifth week in the seventh year [1309 A.M.] thereof, and on the seventeenth day in the second month the earth was dry.
32. And on the twenty-seventh thereof he opened the ark, and sent forth from it beasts, and cattle, and birds, and every moving thing.

Jubilees 6

1. And on the new moon of the third month he went forth from the ark, and built an altar on that mountain.
2. And he made atonement for the earth, and took a kid and made atonement by its blood for all the guilt of the earth; for everything that had been on it had been destroyed, save those that were in the ark with Noah.
3. And he placed the fat thereof on the altar, and he took an ox, and a goat, and a sheep and kids, and salt, and a turtle-dove, and the young of a dove, and placed a burnt sacrifice on the altar, and poured thereon an offering mingled with oil, and sprinkled wine and strewed frankincense over everything, and caused a goodly savour to arise, acceptable before Jah.
4. And Jah smelt the goodly savour, and He made a covenant with him that there should not be any more a flood to destroy the earth; that all the days of the earth seed-time and harvest should never cease; cold and heat, and summer and winter, and day and night should not change their order, nor cease for ever.
5. 'And you, increase ye and multiply upon the earth, and become many upon it, and be a blessing upon it. The fear of you and the dread of you I will inspire in everything that is on earth and in the sea.
6. And behold I have given unto you all beasts, and all winged things, and everything that moves on the earth, and the fish in the waters, and all things for food; as the green herbs, I have given you all things to eat.
7. But flesh, with the life thereof, with the blood, ye shall not eat; for the life of all flesh is in the blood, lest your blood of your lives be required. At the hand of every man, at the hand of every beast will I require the blood of man.
8. Whoso sheddeth man's blood by man shall his blood be shed, for in the image of God made He man.
9. And you, increase ye, and multiply on the earth.'
10. And Noah and his sons swore that they would not eat any blood that was in any flesh, and he made a covenant before Jah God for ever throughout all the generations of the earth in this month.
11. On this account He spake to thee that thou shouldst make a covenant with the children of Israel in this month upon the mountain with an oath, and that thou shouldst sprinkle blood upon them because of all the words

of the covenant, which Jah made with them for ever.

12. And this testimony is written concerning you that you should observe it continually, so that you should not eat on any day any blood of beasts or birds or cattle during all the days of the earth, and the man who eats the blood of beast or of cattle or of birds during all the days of the earth, he and his seed shall be rooted out of the land.

13. And do thou command the children of Israel to eat no blood, so that their names and their seed may be before Jah our God continually.

14. And for this law there is no limit of days, for it is for ever. They shall observe it throughout their generations, so that they may continue supplicating on your behalf with blood before the altar; every day and at the time of morning and evening they shall seek forgiveness on your behalf perpetually before Jah that they may keep it and not be rooted out.

15. And He gave to Noah and his sons a sign that there should not again be a flood on the earth.

16. He set His bow in the cloud for a sign of the eternal covenant that there should not again be a flood on the earth to destroy it all the days of the earth.

17. For this reason it is ordained and written on the heavenly tablets, that they should celebrate the feast of weeks in this month once a year, to renew the covenant every year.

18. And this whole festival was celebrated in heaven from the day of creation till the days of Noah - twenty-six jubilees and five weeks of years [1309-1659 A.M.]: and Noah and his sons observed it for seven jubilees and one week of years, till the day of Noah's death, and from the day of Noah's death his sons did away with it until the days of Abraham, and they eat blood.

19. But Abraham observed it, and Isaac and Jacob and his children observed it up to thy days, and in thy days the children of Israel forgot it until ye celebrated it anew on this mountain.

20. And do thou command the children of Israel to observe this festival in all their generations for a commandment unto them: one day in the year in this month they shall celebrate the festival.

21. For it is the feast of weeks and the feast of first fruits: this feast is twofold and of a double nature: according to what is written and engraven concerning it, celebrate it.

22. For I have written in the book of the first law, in that which I have written for thee, that thou shouldst celebrate it in its season, one day in the year, and I explained to thee its sacrifices that the children of Israel should remember and should celebrate it throughout their generations in this month, one day in every year.

23. And on the new moon of the first month, and on the new moon of the fourth month, and on the new moon of the seventh month, and on the new

moon of the tenth month are the days of remembrance, and the days of the seasons in the four divisions of the year. These are written and ordained as a testimony for ever.

24. And Noah ordained them for himself as feasts for the generations for ever, so that they have become thereby a memorial unto him.

25. And on the new moon of the first month he was bidden to make for himself an ark, and on that day the earth became dry and he opened the ark and saw the earth.

26. And on the new moon of the fourth month the mouths of the depths of the abyss beneath were closed. And on the new moon of the seventh month all the mouths of the abysses of the earth were opened, and the waters began to descend into them.

27. And on the new moon of the tenth month the tops of the mountains were seen, and Noah was glad.

28. And on this account he ordained them for himself as feasts for a memorial for ever, and thus are they ordained.

29. And they placed them on the heavenly tablets, each had thirteen weeks; from one to another passed their memorial, from the first to the second, and from the second to the third, and from the third to the fourth.

30. And all the days of the commandment will be two and fifty weeks of days, and these will make the entire year complete. Thus it is engraven and ordained on the heavenly tablets.

31. And there is no neglecting this commandment for a single year or from year to year.

32. And command thou the children of Israel that they observe the years according to this reckoning- three hundred and sixty-four days, and these will constitute a complete year, and they will not disturb its time from its days and from its feasts; for everything will fall out in them according to their testimony, and they will not leave out any day nor disturb any feasts.

33. But if they do neglect and do not observe them according to His commandment, then they will disturb all their seasons and the years will be dislodged from this order, and they will disturb the seasons and the years will be dislodged and they will neglect their ordinances.

34. And all the children of Israel will forget and will not find the path of the years, and will forget the new moons, and seasons, and sabbaths and they will go wrong as to all the order of the years.

35. For I know and from henceforth will I declare it unto thee, and it is not of my own devising; for the book lies written before me, and on the heavenly tablets the division of days is ordained, lest they forget the feasts of the covenant and walk according to the feasts of the Gentiles after their error and after their ignorance.

36. For there will be those who will assuredly make observations of the moon -how it disturbs the seasons and comes in from year to year ten days too soon.

37. For this reason the years will come upon them when they will disturb the order, and make an abominable day the day of testimony, and an unclean day a feast day, and they will confound all the days, the holy with the unclean, and the unclean day with the holy; for they will go wrong as to the months and sabbaths and feasts and jubilees.

38. For this reason I command and testify to thee that thou mayst testify to them; for after thy death thy children will disturb them, so that they will not make the year three hundred and sixty-four days only, and for this reason they will go wrong as to the new moons and seasons and sabbaths and festivals, and they will eat all kinds of blood with all kinds of flesh.

Jubilees 7

1. And in the seventh week in the first year [1317 A.M.] thereof, in this jubilee, Noah planted vines on the mountain on which the ark had rested, named Lubar, one of the Ararat Mountains, and they produced fruit in the fourth year, [1320 A.M.] and he guarded their fruit, and gathered it in this year in the seventh month.

2. And he made wine therefrom and put it into a vessel, and kept it until the fifth year, [1321 A.M.] until the first day, on the new moon of the first month.

3. And he celebrated with joy the day of this feast, and he made a burnt sacrifice unto Jah, one young ox and one ram, and seven sheep, each a year old, and a kid of the goats, that he might make atonement thereby for himself and his sons.

4. And he prepared the kid first, and placed some of its blood on the flesh that was on the altar which he had made, and all the fat he laid on the altar where he made the burnt sacrifice, and the ox and the ram and the sheep, and he laid all their flesh upon the altar.

5. And he placed all their offerings mingled with oil upon it, and afterwards he sprinkled wine on the fire which he had previously made on the altar, and he placed incense on the altar and caused a sweet savour to ascend acceptable before Jah his God.

6. And he rejoiced and drank of this wine, he and his children with joy.

7. And it was evening, and he went into his tent, and being drunken he lay down and slept, and was uncovered in his tent as he slept.

8. And Ham saw Noah his father naked, and went forth and told his two brethren without.

9. And Shem took his garment and arose, he and Japheth, and they placed the garment on their shoulders and went backward and

covered the shame of their father, and their faces were backward.

10. And Noah awoke from his sleep and knew all that his younger son had done unto him, and he cursed his son and said: 'Cursed be Canaan; an enslaved servant shall he be unto his brethren.'

11. And he blessed Shem, and said: 'Blessed be Jah God of Shem, and Canaan shall be his servant.

12. God shall enlarge Japheth, and God shall dwell in the dwelling of Shem, and Canaan shall be his servant.'

13. And Ham knew that his father had cursed his younger son, and he was displeased that he had cursed his son. and he parted from his father, he and his sons with him, Cush and Mizraim and Put and Canaan.

14. And he built for himself a city and called its name after the name of his wife Ne'elatama'uk.

15. And Japheth saw it, and became envious of his brother, and he too built for himself a city, and he called its name after the name of his wife 'Adataneses.

16. And Shem dwelt with his father Noah, and he built a city close to his father on the mountain, and he too called its name after the name of his wife Sedeqetelebab.

17. And behold these three cities are near Mount Lubar; Sedeqetelebab fronting the mountain on its east; and Na'eltama'uk on the south; 'Adatan'eses towards the west.

18. And these are the sons of Shem: Elam, and Asshur, and Arpachshad - this son was born two years after the flood- and Lud, and Aram.

19. The sons of Japheth: Gomer and Magog and Madai and Javan, Tubal and Meshech and Tiras: these are the sons of Noah.

20. And in the twenty-eighth jubilee [1324-1372 A.M.] Noah began to enjoin upon his sons' sons the ordinances and commandments, and all the judgments that he knew, and he exhorted his sons to observe righteousness, and to cover the shame of their flesh, and to bless their Creator, and honour father and mother, and love their neighbour, and guard their souls from fornication and uncleanness and all iniquity.

21. For owing to these three things came the flood upon the earth, namely, owing to the fornication wherein the Watchers against the law of their ordinances went a whoring after the daughters of men, and took themselves wives of all which they chose: and they made the beginning of uncleanness.

22. And they begat sons the Naphidim, and they were all unlike, and they devoured one another: and the Giants slew the Naphil, and the Naphil slew the Eljo, and the Eljo mankind, and one man another.

23. And every one sold himself to work iniquity and to shed much blood, and the earth was filled with iniquity.

24. And after this they sinned against the beasts and birds, and all that moves and walks on the earth: and much blood was shed on the earth, and every imagination and desire of men imagined vanity and evil continually.

25. And Jah destroyed everything from off the face of the earth; because of the wickedness of their deeds, and because of the blood which they had shed in the midst of the earth He destroyed everything.

26. 'And we were left, I and you, my sons, and everything that entered with us into the ark, and behold I see your works before me that ye do not walk in righteousness: for in the path of destruction ye have begun to walk, and ye are parting one from another, and are envious one of another, and so it comes that ye are not in harmony, my sons, each with his brother.

27. For I see, and behold the demons have begun their seductions against you and against your children and now I fear on your behalf, that after my death ye will shed the blood of men upon the earth, and that ye, too, will be destroyed from the face of the earth.

28. For whoso sheddeth man's blood, and whoso eateth the blood of any flesh, shall all be destroyed from the earth.

29. And there shall not be left any man that eateth blood, or that sheddeth the blood of man on the earth, Nor shall there be left to him any seed or descendants living under heaven; For into Sheol shall they go, And into the place of condemnation shall they descend, And into the darkness of the deep shall they all be removed by a violent death.

30. There shall be no blood seen upon you of all the blood there shall be all the days in which ye have killed any beasts or cattle or whatever flies upon the earth, and work ye a good work to your souls by covering that which has been shed on the face of the earth.

31. And ye shall not be like him who eats with blood, but guard yourselves that none may eat blood before you: cover the blood, for thus have I been commanded to testify to you and your children, together with all flesh.

32. And suffer not the soul to be eaten with the flesh, that your blood, which is your life, may not be required at the hand of any flesh that sheds it on the earth.

33. For the earth will not be clean from the blood which has been shed upon it; for only through the blood of him that shed it will the earth be purified throughout all its generations.

34. And now, my children, harken: work judgment and righteousness that ye maybe planted in righteousness over the face of the whole earth, and your glory lifted up before my God, who saved me from the waters of the flood.

35. And behold, ye will go and build for yourselves cities, and plant in them all the plants that are upon the earth, and moreover all fruit-bearing trees.

36. For three years the fruit of everything that is eaten will not be gathered: and in the fourth year its fruit will be accounted holy and they will offer the first-fruits, acceptable before the Most High God, who created heaven and earth and all things. Let them offer in abundance the first of the wine and oil as first-fruits on the altar of Jah, who receives it, and what is left let the servants of the house of Jah eat before the altar which receives it.

37. And in the fifth year make ye the release so that ye release it in righteousness and uprightness, and ye shall be righteous, and all that you plant shall prosper.

38. For thus did Enoch, the father of your father command Methuselah, his son, and Methuselah his son Lamech, and Lamech commanded me all the things which his fathers commanded him.

39. And I also will give you commandment, my sons, as Enoch commanded his son in the first jubilees: whilst still living, the seventh in his generation, he commanded and testified to his son and to his son's sons until the day of his death.'

Jubilees 8

1. In the twenty-ninth jubilee, in the first week, [1373 A.M.] in the beginning thereof Arpachshad took to himself a wife and her name was Rasu'eja, the daughter of Susan, the daughter of Elam, and she bare him a son in the third year in this week, [1375 A.M.] and he called his name Kainam.

2. And the son grew, and his father taught him writing, and he went to seek for himself a place where he might seize for himself a city.

3. And he found a writing which former generations had carved on the rock, and he read what was thereon, and he transcribed it and sinned owing to it; for it contained the teaching of the Watchers in accordance with which they used to observe the omens of the sun and moon and stars in all the signs of heaven.

4. And he wrote it down and said nothing regarding it; for he was afraid to speak to Noah about it lest he should be angry with him on account of it.

5. And in the thirtieth jubilee, [1429 A.M.] in the second week, in the first year thereof, he took to himself a wife, and her name was Melka, the daughter of Madai, the son of Japheth, and in the fourth year [1432 A.M.] he begat a son, and called his name Shelah; for he said: 'Truly I have been sent.'

6. [And in the fourth year he was born], and Shelah grew up and took to himself a wife, and her name was Mu'ak, the daughter of Kesed, his father's brother, in the one and thirtieth jubilee, in the fifth week, in the first year [1499 A.M.] thereof.

7. And she bare him a son in the fifth year [1503 A.M.] thereof, and he called his name Eber: and he took

unto himself a wife, and her name was 'Azûrâd, the daughter of Nebrod, in the thirty-second jubilee, in the seventh week, in the third year thereof. [1564 A.M.]

8. And in the sixth year [1567 A.M.] thereof, she bare him son, and he called his name Peleg; for in the days when he was born the children of Noah began to divide the earth amongst themselves: for this reason he called his name Peleg.

9. And they divided it secretly amongst themselves, and told it to Noah.

10. And it came to pass in the beginning of the thirty-third jubilee [1569 A.M.] that they divided the earth into three parts, for Shem and Ham and Japheth, according to the inheritance of each, in the first year in the first week, when one of us who had been sent, was with them.

11. And he called his sons, and they drew nigh to him, they and their children, and he divided the earth into the lots, which his three sons were to take in possession, and they reached forth their hands, and took the writing out of the bosom of Noah, their father.

12. And there came forth on the writing as Shem's lot the middle of the earth which he should take as an inheritance for himself and for his sons for the generations of eternity, from the middle of the mountain range of Rafa, from the mouth of the water from the river Tina, and his portion goes towards the west through the midst of this river, and it extends till it reaches the water of the abysses, out of which this river goes forth and pours its waters into the sea Me'at, and this river flows into the great sea. And all that is towards the north is Japheth's, and all that is towards the south belongs to Shem.

13. And it extends till it reaches Karaso: this is in the bosom of the tongue which looks towards the south.

14. And his portion extends along the great sea, and it extends in a straight line till it reaches the west of the tongue which looks towards the south: for this sea is named the tongue of the Egyptian Sea.

15. And it turns from here towards the south towards the mouth of the great sea on the shore of its waters, and it extends to the west to 'Afra, and it extends till it reaches the waters of the river Gihon, and to the south of the waters of Gihon, to the banks of this river.

16. And it extends towards the east, till it reaches the Garden of Eden, to the south thereof, [to the south] and from the east of the whole land of Eden and of the whole east, it turns to the east and proceeds till it reaches the east of the mountain named Rafa, and it descends to the bank of the mouth of the river Tina.

17. This portion came forth by lot for Shem and his sons, that they should possess it for ever unto his generations for evermore.

18. And Noah rejoiced that this portion came forth for Shem and for his sons, and he remembered all that he

had spoken with his mouth in prophecy; for he had said: 'Blessed be Jah God of Shem And may Jah dwell in the dwelling of Shem.'

19. And he knew that the Garden of Eden is the holy of holies, and the dwelling of Jah, and Mount Sinai the centre of the desert, and Mount Zion -the centre of the navel of the earth: these three were created as holy places facing each other.

20. And he blessed the God of gods, who had put the word of Jah into his mouth, and Jah for evermore.

21. And he knew that a blessed portion and a blessing had come to Shem and his sons unto the generations for ever -the whole land of Eden and the whole land of the Red Sea, and the whole land of the east and India, and on the Red Sea and the mountains thereof, and all the land of Bashan, and all the land of Lebanon and the islands of Kaftur, and all the mountains of Sanir and 'Amana, and the mountains of Asshur in the north, and all the land of Elam, Asshur, and Babel, and Susan and Ma'edai, and all the mountains of Ararat, and all the region beyond the sea, which is beyond the mountains of Asshur towards the north, a blessed and spacious land, and all that is in it is very good.

22. And for Ham came forth the second portion, beyond the Gihon towards the south to the right of the Garden, and it extends towards the south and it extends to all the mountains of fire, and it extends towards the west to the sea of 'Atel and it extends towards the west till it reaches the sea of Ma'uk -that sea into which everything which is not destroyed descends.

23. And it goes forth towards the north to the limits of Gadir, and it goes forth to the coast of the waters of the sea to the waters of the great sea till it draws near to the river Gihon, and goes along the river Gihon till it reaches the right of the Garden of Eden.

24. And this is the land which came forth for Ham as the portion which he was to occupy for ever for himself and his sons unto their generations for ever.

25. And for Japheth came forth the third portion beyond the river Tina to the north of the outflow of its waters, and it extends north- easterly to the whole region of Gog, and to all the country east thereof.

26. And it extends northerly to the north, and it extends to the mountains of Qelt towards the north, and towards the sea of Ma'uk, and it goes forth to the east of Gadir as far as the region of the waters of the sea.

27. And it extends until it approaches the west of Fara and it returns towards 'Aferag, and it extends easterly to the waters of the sea of Me'at.

28. And it extends to the region of the river Tina in a north-easterly direction until it approaches the boundary of its waters towards the mountain Rafa, and it turns round towards the north.

29. This is the land which came forth for Japheth and his sons as the portion of his inheritance which he should possess for himself and his sons, for their generations for ever; five great islands, and a great land in the north.

30. But it is cold, and the land of Ham is hot, and the land of Shem is neither hot nor cold, but it is of blended cold and heat.

Jubilees 9

1. And Ham divided amongst his sons, and the first portion came forth for Cush towards the east, and to the west of him for Mizraim, and to the west of him for Put, and to the west of him and to the west thereof on the sea for Canaan.

2. And Shem also divided amongst his sons, and the first portion came forth for Ham and his sons, to the east of the river Tigris till it approaches the east, the whole land of India, and on the Red Sea on its coast, and the waters of Dedan, and all the mountains of Mebri and Ela, and all the land of Susan and all that is on the side of Pharnak to the Red Sea and the river Tina.

3. And for Asshur came forth the second Portion, all the land of Asshur and Nineveh and Shinar and to the border of India, and it ascends and skirts the river.

4. And for Arpachshad came forth the third portion, all the land of the region of the Chaldees to the east of the Euphrates, bordering on the Red Sea, and all the waters of the desert close to the tongue of the sea which looks towards Egypt, all the land of Lebanon and Sanir and 'Amana to the border of the Euphrates.

5. And for Aram there came forth the fourth portion, all the land of Mesopotamia between the Tigris and the Euphrates to the north of the Chaldees to the border of the mountains of Asshur and the land of 'Arara.

6. And there came forth for Lud the fifth portion, the mountains of Asshur and all appertaining to them till it reaches the Great Sea, and till it reaches the east of Asshur his brother.

7. And Japheth also divided the land of his inheritance amongst his sons.

8. And the first portion came forth for Gomer to the east from the north side to the river Tina; and in the north there came forth for Magog all the inner portions of the north until it reaches to the sea of Me'at.

9. And for Madai came forth as his portion that he should posses from the west of his two brothers to the islands, and to the coasts of the islands.

10. And for Javan came forth the fourth portion every island and the islands which are towards the border of Lud.

11. And for Tubal there came forth the fifth portion in the midst of the tongue which approaches towards the border of the portion of Lud to the second tongue, to the region

beyond the second tongue unto the third tongue.

12. And for Meshech came forth the sixth portion, all the region beyond the third tongue till it approaches the east of Gadir.

13. And for Tiras there came forth the seventh portion, four great islands in the midst of the sea, which reach to the portion of Ham and the islands of Kamaturi came out by lot for the sons of Arpachshad as his inheritance.

14. And thus the sons of Noah divided unto their sons in the presence of Noah their father, and he bound them all by an oath, imprecating a curse on every one that sought to seize the portion which had not fallen to him by his lot.

15. And they all said, 'So be it; so be it' for themselves and their sons for ever throughout their generations till the day of judgment, on which Jah God shall judge them with a sword and with fire for all the unclean wickedness of their errors, wherewith they have filled the earth with transgression and uncleanness and fornication and sin.

Jubilees 10

1. And in the third week of this jubilee the unclean demons began to lead astray the children of the sons of Noah, and to make to err and destroy them.

2. And the sons of Noah came to Noah their father, and they told him concerning the demons which were leading astray and blinding and slaying his sons' sons.

3. And he prayed before Jah his God, and said:

'God of the spirits of all flesh, who hast shown mercy unto me
And hast saved me and my sons from the waters of the flood,
And hast not caused me to perish as Thou didst the sons of perdition;

For Thy grace has been great towards me,
And great has been Thy mercy to my soul;

Let Thy grace be lift up upon my sons,
And let not wicked spirits rule over them
Lest they should destroy them from the earth.

4. But do Thou bless me and my sons, that we may increase and Multiply and replenish the earth.

5. And Thou knowest how Thy Watchers, the fathers of these spirits, acted in my day: and as for these spirits which are living, imprison them and hold them fast in the place of condemnation, and let them not bring destruction on the sons of thy servant, my God; for these are malignant, and created in order to destroy.

6. And let them not rule over the spirits of the living; for Thou alone canst exercise dominion over them. And let them not have power over the sons of the righteous from henceforth and for evermore.'

7. And Jah our God bade us to bind all.

8. And the chief of the spirits, Mastêmâ, came and said: 'Lord, Creator, let some of them remain before me, and let them harken to my voice, and do all that I shall say unto them; for if some of them are not left to me, I shall not be able to execute the power of my will on the sons of men; for these are for corruption and leading astray before my judgment, for great is the wickedness of the sons of men.'

9. And He said: Let the tenth part of them remain before him, and let nine parts descend into the place of condemnation.'

10. And one of us He commanded that we should teach Noah all their medicines; for He knew that they would not walk in uprightness, nor strive in righteousness.

11. And we did according to all His words: all the malignant evil ones we bound in the place of condemnation and a tenth part of them we left that they might be subject before Satan on the earth.

12. And we explained to Noah all the medicines of their diseases, together with their seductions, how he might heal them with herbs of the earth.

13. And Noah wrote down all things in a book as we instructed him concerning every kind of medicine. Thus the evil spirits were precluded from hurting the sons of Noah.

14. And he gave all that he had written to Shem, his eldest son; for he loved him exceedingly above all his sons.

15. And Noah slept with his fathers, and was buried on Mount Lubar in the land of Ararat.

16. Nine hundred and fifty years he completed in his life, nineteen jubilees and two weeks and five years. [1659 A.M.]

17. And in his life on earth he excelled the children of men save Enoch because of the righteousness, wherein he was perfect. For Enoch's office was ordained for a testimony to the generations of the world, so that he should recount all the deeds of generation unto generation, till the day of judgment.

18. And in the three and thirtieth jubilee, in the first year in the second week, Peleg took to himself a wife, whose name was Lomna the daughter of Sina'ar, and she bare him a son in the fourth year of this week, and he called his name Reu; for he said: 'Behold the children of men have become evil through the wicked purpose of building for themselves a city and a tower in the land of Shinar.'

19. For they departed from the land of Ararat eastward to Shinar; for in his days they built the city and the tower, saying, 'Go to, let us ascend thereby into heaven.'

20. And they began to build, and in the fourth week they made brick with fire, and the bricks served them for stone, and the clay with which they cemented them together was asphalt which comes out of the sea, and out

of the fountains of water in the land of Shinar.

21. And they built it: forty and three years [1645-1688 A.M.] were they building it; its breadth was 203 bricks, and the height of a brick was the third of one; its height amounted to 5433 cubits and 2 palms, and the extent of one wall was thirteen stades and of the other thirty stades.

22. And Jah our God said unto us: Behold, they are one people, and this they begin to do, and now nothing will be withholden from them. Go to, let us go down and confound their language, that they may not understand one another's speech, and they may be dispersed into cities and nations, and one purpose will no longer abide with them till the day of judgment.'

23. And Jah descended, and we descended with him to see the city and the tower which the children of men had built.

24. And he confounded their language, and they no longer understood one another's speech, and they ceased then to build the city and the tower.

25. For this reason the whole land of Shinar is called Babel, because Jah did there confound all the language of the children of men, and from thence they were dispersed into their cities, each according to his language and his nation.

26. And Jah sent a mighty wind against the tower and overthrew it upon the earth, and behold it was between Asshur and Babylon in the land of Shinar, and they called its name 'Overthrow'.

27. In the fourth week in the first year [1688 A.M.] in the beginning thereof in the four and thirtieth jubilee, were they dispersed from the land of Shinar.

28. And Ham and his sons went into the land which he was to occupy, which he acquired as his portion in the land of the south.

29. And Canaan saw the land of Lebanon to the river of Egypt, that it was very good, and he went not into the land of his inheritance to the west that is to the sea, and he dwelt in the land of Lebanon, eastward and westward from the border of Jordan and from the border of the sea.

30. And Ham, his father, and Cush and Mizraim his brothers said unto him: 'Thou hast settled in a land which is not thine, and which did not fall to us by lot: do not do so; for if thou dost do so, thou and thy sons will fall in the land and be accursed through sedition; for by sedition ye have settled, and by sedition will thy children fall, and thou shalt be rooted out for ever.

31. Dwell not in the dwelling of Shem; for to Shem and to his sons did it come by their lot.

32. Cursed art thou, and cursed shalt thou be beyond all the sons of Noah, by the curse by which we bound ourselves by an oath in the presence of the holy judge, and in the presence of Noah our father.'

33. But he did not harken unto them, and dwelt in the land of Lebanon from Hamath to the entering of Egypt, he and his sons until this day.

34. And for this reason that land is named Canaan.

35. And Japheth and his sons went towards the sea and dwelt in the land of their portion, and Madai saw the land of the sea and it did not please him, and he begged a portion from Ham and Asshur and Arpachshad, his wife's brother, and he dwelt in the land of Media, near to his wife's brother until this day.

36. And he called his dwelling-place, and the dwelling-place of his sons, Media, after the name of their father Madai

---

Jubilees 11

1. And in the thirty-fifth jubilee, in the third week, in the first year [1681 A.M.] thereof, Reu took to himself a wife, and her name was 'Ôrâ, the daughter of 'Ûr, the son of Kesed, and she bare him a son, and he called his name Sêrôh, in the seventh year of this week in this jubilee. [1687 A.M.]

2. And the sons of Noah began to war on each other, to take captive and to slay each other, and to shed the blood of men on the earth, and to eat blood, and to build strong cities, and walls, and towers, and individuals began to exalt themselves above the nation, and to found the beginnings of kingdoms, and to go to war people against people, and nation against nation, and city against city, and all began to do evil, and to acquire arms, and to teach their sons war, and they began to capture cities, and to sell male and female slaves.

3. And 'Ûr, the son of Kesed, built the city of 'Ara of the Chaldees, and called its name after his own name and the name of his father. And they made for themselves molten images, and they worshipped each the idol, the molten image which they had made for themselves, and they began to make graven images and unclean simulacra, and malignant spirits assisted and seduced them into committing transgression and uncleanness.

4. And the prince Mastêmâ exerted himself to do all this, and he sent forth other spirits, those which were put under his hand, to do all manner of wrong and sin, and all manner of transgression, to corrupt and destroy, and to shed blood upon the earth.

5. For this reason he called the name of Sêrôh, Serug, for every one turned to do all manner of sin and transgression.

6. And he grew up, and dwelt in Ur of the Chaldees, near to the father of his wife's mother, and he worshipped idols, and he took to himself a wife in the thirty-sixth jubilee, in the fifth week, in the first year thereof, [1744 A.M.] and her name was Melka, the daughter of Kaber, the daughter of his father's brother.

7. And she bare him Nahor, in the first year of this week, and he grew and dwelt in Ur of the Chaldees, and his father taught him the researches of the Chaldees to divine and augur, according to the signs of heaven.

8. And in the thirty-seventh jubilee in the sixth week, in the first year thereof, [1800 A.M.] he took to himself a wife, and her name was 'Ijaska, the daughter of Nestag of the Chaldees.

9. And she bare him Terah in the seventh year of this week. [1806 A.M.]

10. And the prince Mastêmâ sent ravens and birds to devour the seed which was sown in the land, in order to destroy the land, and rob the children of men of their labours. Before they could plough in the seed, the ravens picked (it) from the surface of the ground.

11. And for this reason he called his name Terah because the ravens and the birds reduced them to destitution and devoured their seed.

12. And the years began to be barren, owing to the birds, and they devoured all the fruit of the trees from the trees: it was only with great effort that they could save a little of all the fruit of the earth in their days.

13. And in this thirty-ninth jubilee, in the second week in the first year, [1870 A.M.] Terah took to himself a wife, and her name was 'Edna, the daughter of 'Abram, the daughter of his father's sister. And in the seventh year of this week [1876 A.M.] she bare him a son, and he called his name Abram, by the name of the father of his mother;

14. for he had died before his daughter had conceived a son.

15. And the child began to understand the errors of the earth that all went astray after graven images and after uncleanness, and his father taught him writing, and he was two weeks of years old, [1890 A.M.] and he separated himself from his father, that he might not worship idols with him.

16. And he began to pray to the Creator of all things that He might save him from the errors of the children of men, and that his portion should not fall into error after uncleanness and vileness.

17. And the seed time came for the sowing of seed upon the land, and they all went forth together to protect their seed against the ravens, and Abram went forth with those that went, and the child was a lad of fourteen years.

18. And a cloud of ravens came to devour the seed, and Abram ran to meet them before they settled on the ground, and cried to them before they settled on the ground to devour the seed, and said, ' Descend not: return to the place whence ye came,' and they proceeded to turn back.

19. And he caused the clouds of ravens to turn back that day seventy times, and of all the ravens throughout all the land where Abram was there settled there not so much as one.

20. And all who were with him throughout all the land saw him cry out, and all the ravens turn back, and his name became great in all the land of the Chaldees.

21. And there came to him this year all those that wished to sow, and he went with them until the time of sowing ceased: and they sowed their land, and that year they brought enough grain home and eat and were satisfied.

22. And in the first year of the fifth week [1891 A.M.] Abram taught those who made implements for oxen, the artificers in wood, and they made a vessel above the ground, facing the frame of the plough, in order to put the seed thereon, and the seed fell down therefrom upon the share of the plough, and was hidden in the earth, and they no longer feared the ravens.

23. And after this manner they made vessels above the ground on all the frames of the ploughs, and they sowed and tilled all the land, according as Abram commanded them, and they no longer feared the birds.

Jubilees 12

1. And it came to pass in the sixth week, in the seventh year thereof, [1904 A.M.] that Abram said to Terah his father, saying, 'Father!'

2. And he said, 'Behold, here am I, my son.' And he said,

'What help and profit have we from those idols which thou dost worship,
And before which thou dost bow thyself?

3. For there is no spirit in them,
For they are dumb forms, and a misleading of the heart.
Worship them not:

4. Worship the God of heaven,
Who causes the rain and the dew to descend on the earth
And does everything upon the earth,

And has created everything by His word,
And all life is from before His face.

5. Why do ye worship things that have no spirit in them?
For they are the work of men's hands,

And on your shoulders do ye bear them,
And ye have no help from them,

But they are a great cause of shame to those who make them,
And a misleading of the heart to those who worship them:
Worship them not.'

6. And his father said unto him, I also know it, my son, but what shall I do with a people who have made me to serve before them?

7. And if I tell them the truth, they will slay me; for their soul cleaves to them to worship them and honour them.

8. Keep silent, my son, lest they slay thee.' And these words he spake to his two brothers, and they were angry with him and he kept silent.

9. And in the fortieth jubilee, in the second week, in the seventh year

thereof, [1925 A.M.] Abram took to himself a wife, and her name was Sarai, the daughter of his father, and she became his wife.

10. And Haran, his brother, took to himself a wife in the third year of the third week, [1928 A.M.] and she bare him a son in the seventh year of this week, [1932 A.M.] and he called his name Lot.

11. And Nahor, his brother, took to himself a wife.

12. And in the sixtieth year of the life of Abram, that is, in the fourth week, in the fourth year thereof, [1936 A.M.] Abram arose by night, and burned the house of the idols, and he burned all that was in the house and no man knew it.

13. And they arose in the night and sought to save their gods from the midst of the fire.

14. And Haran hasted to save them, but the fire flamed over him, and he was burnt in the fire, and he died in Ur of the Chaldees before Terah his father, and they buried him in Ur of the Chaldees.

15. And Terah went forth from Ur of the Chaldees, he and his sons, to go into the land of Lebanon and into the land of Canaan, and he dwelt in the land of Haran, and Abram dwelt with Terah his father in Haran two weeks of years.

16. And in the sixth week, in the fifth year thereof, [1951 A.M.] Abram sat up throughout the night on the new moon of the seventh month to observe the stars from the evening to the morning, in order to see what would be the character of the year with regard to the rains, and he was alone as he sat and observed.

17. And a word came into his heart and he said: All the signs of the stars, and the signs of the moon and of the sun are all in the hand of Jah . Why do I search them out?

18. If He desires, He causes it to rain, morning and evening;
And if He desires, He withholds it,
And all things are in his hand.'

19. And he prayed that night and said,
'My God, God Most High, Thou alone art my God,
And Thee and Thy dominion have I chosen.
And Thou hast created all things,
And all things that are the work of thy hands.

20. Deliver me from the hands of evil spirits who have dominion over the thoughts of men's hearts,
And let them not lead me astray from Thee, my God.

And stablish Thou me and my seed for ever
That we go not astray from henceforth and for evermore.'

21. And he said, 'Shall I return unto Ur of the Chaldees who seek my face that I may return to them, am I to remain here in this place? The right path before Thee prosper it in the hands of Thy servant that he may fulfil it and that I may not walk in the deceitfulness of my heart, O my God.'

22. And he made an end of speaking and praying, and behold the word of Jah was sent to him through me, saying: 'Get thee up from thy country, and from thy kindred and from the house of thy father unto a land which I will show thee, and I shall make thee a great and numerous nation.

23. And I will bless thee
And I will make thy name great,
And thou shalt be blessed in the earth,
And in Thee shall all families of the earth be blessed,
And I will bless them that bless thee,
And curse them that curse thee.

24. And I will be a God to thee and thy son, and to thy son's son, and to all thy seed: fear not, from henceforth and unto all generations of the earth I am thy God.'

25. And Jah God said: 'Open his mouth and his ears, that he may hear and speak with his mouth, with the language which has been revealed'; for it had ceased from the mouths of all the children of men from the day of the overthrow of Babel.

26. And I opened his mouth, and his ears and his lips, and I began to speak with him in Hebrew in the tongue of the creation.

27. And he took the books of his fathers, and these were written in Hebrew, and he transcribed them, and he began from henceforth to study them, and I made known to him that which he could not understand, and he studied them during the six rainy months.

28. And it came to pass in the seventh year of the sixth week [1953 A.M.] that he spoke to his father and informed him, that he would leave Haran to go into the land of Canaan to see it and return to him.

29. And Terah his father said unto him; Go in peace:

May the eternal God make thy path straight.
And Jah be with thee, and protect thee from all evil,
And grant unto thee grace, mercy and favour before those who see thee,
And may none of the children of men have power over thee to harm thee;
Go in peace.

30. And if thou seest a land pleasant to thy eyes to dwell in, then arise and take me to thee and take Lot with thee, the son of Haran thy brother as thine own son: Jah be with thee.

31. And Nahor thy brother leave with me till thou returnest in peace, and we go with thee all together.'

Jubilees 13

1. And Abram journeyed from Haran, and he took Sarai, his wife, and Lot, his brother Haran's son, to the land of Canaan, and he came into Asshur, and proceeded to Shechem, and dwelt near a lofty oak.

2. And he saw, and, behold, the land was very pleasant from the entering of Hamath to the lofty oak.

3. And Jah said to him: 'To thee and to thy seed will I give this land.'

4. And he built an altar there, and he offered thereon a burnt sacrifice to Jah, who had appeared to him.

5. And he removed from thence unto the mountain . . . Bethel on the west and Ai on the east, and pitched his tent there.

6. And he saw and behold, the land was very wide and good, and everything grew thereon -vines and figs and pomegranates, oaks and ilexes, and terebinths and oil trees, and cedars and cypresses and date trees, and all trees of the field, and there was water on the mountains.

7. And he blessed Jah who had led him out of Ur of the Chaldees, and had brought him to this land.

8. And it came to pass in the first year, in the seventh week, on the new moon of the first month, 1954 A.M.] that he built an altar on this mountain, and called on the name of Jah : 'Thou, the eternal God, art my God.'

9. And he offered on the altar a burnt sacrifice unto Jah that He should be with him and not forsake him all the days of his life.

10. And he removed from thence and went towards the south, and he came to Hebron and Hebron was built at that time, and he dwelt there two years, and he went thence into the land of the south, to Bealoth, and there was a famine in the land.

11. And Abram went into Egypt in the third year of the week, and he dwelt in Egypt five years before his wife was torn away from him.

12. Now Tanais in Egypt was at that time built- seven years after Hebron.

13. And it came to pass when Pharaoh seized Sarai, the wife of Abram that Jah plagued Pharaoh and his house with great plagues because of Sarai, Abram's wife.

14. And Abram was very glorious by reason of possessions in sheep, and cattle, and asses, and horses, and camels, and menservants, and maidservants, and in silver and gold exceedingly. And Lot also his brother's son, was wealthy.

15. And Pharaoh gave back Sarai, the wife of Abram, and he sent him out of the land of Egypt, and he journeyed to the place where he had pitched his tent at the beginning, to the place of the altar, with Ai on the east, and Bethel on the west, and he blessed Jah his God who had brought him back in peace.

16. And it came to pass in the forty-first jubilee in the third year of the first week, [1963 A.M.] that he returned to this place and offered thereon a burnt sacrifice, and called on the name of Jah, and said: 'Thou, the most high God, art my God for ever and ever.'

17. And in the fourth year of this week [1964 A.M.] Lot parted from him, and Lot dwelt in Sodom, and the men of Sodom were sinners exceedingly.

18. And it grieved him in his heart that his brother's son had parted from him; for he had no children.

19. In that year when Lot was taken captive, Jah said unto Abram, after that Lot had parted from him, in the fourth year of this week: 'Lift up thine eyes from the place where thou art dwelling, northward and southward, and westward and eastward.

20. For all the land which thou seest I will give to thee and to thy seed for ever, and I will make thy seed as the sand of the sea: though a man may number the dust of the earth, yet thy seed shall not be numbered.

21. Arise, walk through the land in the length of it and the breadth of it, and see it all; for to thy seed will I give it.' And Abram went to Hebron, and dwelt there.

22. And in this year came Chedorlaomer, king of Elam, and Amraphel, king of Shinar, and Arioch king of Sellasar, and Tergal, king of nations, and slew the king of Gomorrah, and the king of Sodom fled, and many fell through wounds in the vale of Siddim, by the Salt Sea.

23. And they took captive Sodom and Adam and Zeboim, and they took captive Lot also, the son of Abram's brother, and all his possessions, and they went to Dan.

24. And one who had escaped came and told Abram that his brother's son had been taken captive and Abram armed his household servants . . .

25. . . . . . for Abram, and for his seed, a tenth of the first fruits to Jah , and Jah ordained it as an ordinance for ever that they should give it to the priests who served before Him, that they should possess it for ever.

26. And to this law there is no limit of days; for He hath ordained it for the generations for ever that they should give to Jah the tenth of everything, of the seed and of the wine and of the oil and of the cattle and of the sheep.

27. And He gave it unto His priests to eat and to drink with joy before Him.

28. And the king of Sodom came to him and bowed himself before him, and said: 'Our Lord Abram, give unto us the souls which thou hast rescued, but let the booty be thine.'

29. And Abram said unto him: 'I lift up my hands to the Most High God, that from a thread to a shoe-latchet I shall not take aught that is thine lest thou shouldst say, I have made Abram rich; save only what the young men have eaten, and the portion of the men who went with me -Aner, Eschol, and Mamre. These shall take their portion.'

Jubilees 14

1. After these things, in the fourth year of this week, on the new moon of the third month, the word of Jah came to Abram in a dream, saying: 'Fear not, Abram; I am thy defender, and thy reward will be exceeding great.'

2. And he said: 'Lord, Lord, what wilt thou give me, seeing I go hence

childless, and the son of Maseq, the son of my handmaid, is the Dammasek Eliezer: he will be my heir, and to me thou hast given no seed.'

3. And he said unto him: 'This man will not be thy heir, but one that will come out of thine own bowels; he will be thine heir.'

4. And He brought him forth abroad, and said unto him: 'Look toward heaven and number the stars if thou art able to number them.'

5. And he looked toward heaven, and beheld the stars. And He said unto him: 'So shall thy seed be.'

6. And he believed in Jah, and it was counted to him for righteousness.

7. And He said unto him: 'I am Jah that brought thee out of Ur of the Chaldees, to give thee the land of the Canaanites to possess it for ever; and I will be God unto thee and to thy seed after thee.'

8. And he said: 'Lord, Lord, whereby shall I know that I shall inherit it?'

9. And He said unto him: 'Take Me an heifer of three years, and a goat of three years, and a sheep of three years, and a turtle-dove, and a pigeon.'

10. And he took all these in the middle of the month and he dwelt at the oak of Mamre, which is near Hebron.

11. And he built there an altar, and sacrificed all these; and he poured their blood upon the altar, and divided them in the midst, and laid them over against each other; but the birds divided he not.

12. And birds came down upon the pieces, and Abram drove them away, and did not suffer the birds to touch them.

13. And it came to pass, when the sun had set, that an ecstasy fell upon Abram, and lo! an horror of great darkness fell upon him, and it was said unto Abram: 'Know of a surety that thy seed shall be a stranger in a land that is not theirs, and they shall bring them into bondage, and afflict them four hundred years.

14. And the nation also to whom they will be in bondage will I judge, and after that they shall come forth thence with much substance.

15. And thou shalt go to thy fathers in peace, and be buried in a good old age.

16. But in the fourth generation they shall return hither; for the iniquity of the Amorites is not yet full.'

17. And he awoke from his sleep, and he arose, and the sun had set; and there was a flame, and behold! a furnace was smoking, and a flame of fire passed between the pieces.

18. And on that day Jah made a covenant with Abram, saying: 'To thy seed will I give this land, from the river of Egypt unto the great river, the river Euphrates, the Kenites, the Kenizzites, the Kadmonites, the Perizzites, and the Rephaim, the Phakorites, and the Hivites, and the

Amorites, and the Canaanites, and the Girgashites, and the Jebusites.

19. And the day passed, and Abram offered the pieces, and the birds, and their fruit offerings, and their drink offerings, and the fire devoured them.

20. And on that day we made a covenant with Abram, according as we had covenanted with Noah in this month; and Abram renewed the festival and ordinance for himself for ever.

21. And Abram rejoiced, and made all these things known to Sarai his wife; and he believed that he would have seed, but she did not bear.

22. And Sarai advised her husband Abram, and said unto him: 'Go in unto Hagar, my Egyptian maid: it may be that I shall build up seed unto thee by her.'

23. And Abram harkened unto the voice of Sarai his wife, and said unto her, 'Do so.' And Sarai took Hagar, her maid, the Egyptian, and gave her to Abram, her husband, to be his wife.

24. And he went in unto her, and she conceived and bare him a son, and he called his name Ishmael, in the fifth year of this week [1965 A.M.]; and this was the eighty-sixth year in the life of Abram.

Jubilees 15

1. And in the fifth year of the fourth week of this jubilee, [1979 A.M.] in the third month, in the middle of the month, Abram celebrated the feast of the first-fruits of the grain harvest.

2. And he offered new offerings on the altar, the first-fruits of the produce, unto Jah, an heifer and a goat and a sheep on the altar as a burnt sacrifice unto Jah; their fruit offerings and their drink offerings he offered upon the altar with frankincense.

3. And Jah appeared to Abram, and said unto him: 'I am God Almighty; approve thyself before me and be thou perfect.

4. And I will make My covenant between Me and thee, and I will multiply thee exceedingly.'

5. And Abram fell on his face, and Jah talked with him, and said:

6. 'Behold my ordinance is with thee, And thou shalt be the father of many nations.

7. Neither shall thy name any more be called Abram,
But thy name from henceforth, even for ever, shall be Abraham.
For the father of many nations have I made thee.

8. And I will make thee very great, And I will make thee into nations, And kings shall come forth from thee.

9. And I shall establish My covenant between Me and thee, and thy seed after thee, throughout their generations, for an eternal covenant, so that I may be a God unto thee, and to thy seed after thee.

10. And I will give to thee and to thy seed after thee the land where thou hast been a sojourner, the land of Canaan, that thou mayst possess it for ever, and I will be their God.'

11. And Jah said unto Abraham: 'And as for thee, do thou keep my covenant, thou and thy seed after thee: and circumcise ye every male among you, and circumcise your foreskins, and it shall be a token of an eternal covenant between Me and you.

12. And the child on the eighth day ye shall circumcise, every male throughout your generations, him that is born in the house, or whom ye have bought with money from any stranger, whom ye have acquired who is not of thy seed.

13. He that is born in thy house shall surely be circumcised, and those whom thou hast bought with money shall be circumcised, and My covenant shall be in your flesh for an eternal ordinance.

14. And the uncircumcised male who is not circumcised in the flesh of his foreskin on the eighth day, that soul shall be cut off from his people, for he has broken My covenant.'

15. And Jah said unto Abraham: 'As for Sarai thy wife, her name shall no more be called Sarai, but Sarah shall be her name.

16. And I will bless her, and give thee a son by her, and I will bless him, and he shall become a nation, and kings of nations shall proceed from him.'

17. And Abraham fell on his face, and rejoiced, and said in his heart: 'Shall a son be born to him that is a hundred years old, and shall Sarah, who is ninety years old, bring forth?'

18. And Abraham said unto Jah: 'O that Ishmael might live before thee!'

19. And Jah said: 'Yea, and Sarah also shall bear thee a son, and thou shalt call his name Isaac, and I will establish My covenant with him, an everlasting covenant, and for his seed after him.

20. And as for Ishmael also have I heard thee, and behold I will bless him, and make him great, and multiply him exceedingly, and he shall beget twelve princes, and I will make him a great nation.

21. But My covenant will I establish with Isaac, whom Sarah shall bear to thee, in these days, in the next year.'

22. And He left off speaking with him, and Jah went up from Abraham.

23. And Abraham did according as Jah had said unto him, and he took Ishmael his son, and all that were born in his house, and whom he had bought with his money, every male in his house, and circumcised the flesh of their foreskin.

24. And on the selfsame day was Abraham circumcised, and all the men of his house, and those born in the house, and all those, whom he had bought with money from the children of the stranger, were circumcised with him.

25. This law is for all the generations for ever, and there is no circumcision of the days, and no omission of one day out of the eight days; for it is an eternal ordinance, ordained and written on the heavenly tablets.

26. And every one that is born, the flesh of whose foreskin is not circumcised on the eighth day, belongs not to the children of the covenant which Jah made with Abraham, but to the children of destruction; nor is there, moreover, any sign on him that he is Jah's, but he is destined to be destroyed and slain from the earth, and to be rooted out of the earth, for he has broken the covenant of Jah our God.

27. For all the angels of the presence and all the angels of sanctification have been so created from the day of their creation, and before the angels of the presence and the angels of sanctification He hath sanctified Israel, that they should be with Him and with His holy angels.

28. And do thou command the children of Israel and let them observe the sign of this covenant for their generations as an eternal ordinance, and they will not be rooted out of the land.

29. For the command is ordained for a covenant, that they should observe it for ever among all the children of Israel.

30. For Ishmael and his sons and his brothers and Esau, Jah did not cause to approach Him, and he chose them not because they are the children of Abraham, because He knew them, but He chose Israel to be His people.

31. And He sanctified it, and gathered it from amongst all the children of men; for there are many nations and many peoples, and all are His, and over all hath He placed spirits in authority to lead them astray from Him.

32. But over Israel He did not appoint any angel or spirit, for He alone is their ruler, and He will preserve them and require them at the hand of His angels and His spirits, and at the hand of all His powers in order that He may preserve them and bless them, and that they may be His and He may be theirs from henceforth for ever.

33. And now I announce unto thee that the children of Israel will not keep true to this ordinance, and they will not circumcise their sons according to all this law; for in the flesh of their circumcision they will omit this circumcision of their sons, and all of them, sons of Beliar, will leave their sons uncircumcised as they were born.

34. And there will be great wrath from Jah against the children of Israel. because they have forsaken His covenant and turned aside from His word, and provoked and blasphemed, inasmuch as they do not observe the ordinance of this law; for they have treated their members like the Gentiles, so that they may be removed and rooted out of the land. And there will no more be pardon or forgiveness unto them so that there

should be forgiveness and pardon for all the sin of this eternal error.

Jubilees 16

1. And on the new moon of the fourth month we appeared unto Abraham, at the oak of Mamre, and we talked with him, and we announced to him that a son would be given to him by Sarah his wife.

2. And Sarah laughed, for she heard that we had spoken these words with Abraham, and we admonished her, and she became afraid, and denied that she had laughed on account of the words.

3. And we told her the name of her son, as his name is ordained and written in the heavenly tablets (i.e.) Isaac,

4. And that when we returned to her at a set time, she would have conceived a son.

5. And in this month Jah executed his judgments on Sodom, and Gomorrah, and Zeboim, and all the region of the Jordan, and He burned them with fire and brimstone, and destroyed them until this day, even as lo I have declared unto thee all their works, that they are wicked and sinners exceedingly, and that they defile themselves and commit fornication in their flesh, and work uncleanness on the earth.

6. And, in like manner, God will execute judgment on the places where they have done according to the uncleanness of the Sodomites, like unto the judgment of Sodom.

7. But Lot we saved; for God remembered Abraham, and sent him out from the midst of the overthrow.

8. And he and his daughters committed sin upon the earth, such as had not been on the earth since the days of Adam till his time; for the man lay with his daughters.

9. And, behold, it was commanded and engraven concerning all his seed, on the heavenly tablets, to remove them and root them out, and to execute judgment upon them like the judgment of Sodom, and to leave no seed of the man on earth on the day of condemnation.

10. And in this month Abraham moved from Hebron, and departed and dwelt between Kadesh and Shur in the mountains of Gerar.

11. And in the middle of the fifth month he moved from thence, and dwelt at the Well of the Oath.

12. And in the middle of the sixth month Jah visited Sarah and did unto her as He had spoken and she conceived.

13. And she bare a son in the third month, and in the middle of the month, at the time of which Jah had spoken to Abraham, on the festival of the first fruits of the harvest, Isaac was born.

14. And Abraham circumcised his son on the eighth day: he was the first that was circumcised according to the covenant which is ordained for ever.

15. And in the sixth year of the fourth week we came to Abraham, to the

Well of the Oath, and we appeared unto him as we had told Sarah that we should return to her, and she would have conceived a son.

16. And we returned in the seventh month, and found Sarah with child before us and we blessed him, and we announced to him all the things which had been decreed concerning him, that he should not die till he should beget six sons more, and should see them before he died; but that in Isaac should his name and seed be called:

17. And that all the seed of his sons should be Gentiles, and be reckoned with the Gentiles; but from the sons of Isaac one should become a holy seed, and should not be reckoned among the Gentiles.

18. For he should become the portion of the Most High, and all his seed had fallen into the possession of God, that it should be unto Jah a people for His possession above all nations and that it should become a kingdom and priests and a holy nation.

19. And we went our way, and we announced to Sarah all that we had told him, and they both rejoiced with exceeding great joy.

20. And he built there an altar to Jah who had delivered him, and who was making him rejoice in the land of his sojourning, and he celebrated a festival of joy in this month seven days, near the altar which he had built at the Well of the Oath.

21. And he built booths for himself and for his servants on this festival, and he was the first to celebrate the feast of tabernacles on the earth.

22. And during these seven days he brought each day to the altar a burnt offering to Jah, two oxen, two rams, seven sheep, one he-goat, for a sin offering, that he might atone thereby for himself and for his seed.

23. And, as a thank-offering, seven rams, seven kids, seven sheep, and seven he-goats, and their fruit offerings and their drink offerings; and he burnt all the fat thereof on the altar, a chosen offering unto Jah for a sweet smelling savour.

24. And morning and evening he burnt fragrant substances, frankincense and galbanum, and stackte, and nard, and myrrh, and spice, and costum; all these seven he offered, crushed, mixed together in equal parts and pure.

25. And he celebrated this feast during seven days, rejoicing with all his heart and with all his soul, he and all those who were in his house, and there was no stranger with him, nor any that was uncircumcised.

26. And he blessed his Creator who had created him in his generation, for He had created him according to His good pleasure; for He knew and perceived that from him would arise the plant of righteousness for the eternal generations, and from him a holy seed, so that it should become like Him who had made all things.

27. And he blessed and rejoiced, and he called the name of this festival the

festival of Jah, a joy acceptable to the Most High God.

28. And we blessed him for ever, and all his seed after him throughout all the generations of the earth, because he celebrated this festival in its season, according to the testimony of the heavenly tablets.

29. For this reason it is ordained on the heavenly tablets concerning Israel, that they shall celebrate the feast of tabernacles seven days with joy, in the seventh month, acceptable before Jah -a statute for ever throughout their generations every year.

30. And to this there is no limit of days; for it is ordained for ever regarding Israel that they should celebrate it and dwell in booths, and set wreaths upon their heads, and take leafy boughs, and willows from the brook.

31. And Abraham took branches of palm trees, and the fruit of goodly trees, and every day going round the altar with the branches seven times a day in the morning, he praised and gave thanks to his God for all things in joy.

Jubilees 17

1. And in the first year of the fifth week Isaac was weaned in this jubilee, [1982 A.M.] and Abraham made a great banquet in the third month, on the day his son Isaac was weaned.

2. And Ishmael, the son of Hagar, the Egyptian, was before the face of Abraham, his father, in his place, and Abraham rejoiced and blessed God because he had seen his sons and had not died childless.

3. And he remembered the words which He had spoken to him on the day on which Lot had parted from him, and he rejoiced because Jah had given him seed upon the earth to inherit the earth, and he blessed with all his mouth the Creator of all things.

4. And Sarah saw Ishmael playing and dancing, and Abraham rejoicing with great joy, and she became jealous of Ishmael and said to Abraham, 'Cast out this bondwoman and her son; for the son of this bondwoman will not be heir with my son, Isaac.'

5. And the thing was grievous in Abraham's sight, because of his maidservant and because of his son, that he should drive them from him.

6. And God said to Abraham 'Let it not be grievous in thy sight, because of the child and because of the bondwoman; in all that Sarah hath said unto thee, harken to her words and do them; for in Isaac shall thy name and seed be called.

7. But as for the son of this bondwoman I will make him a great nation, because he is of thy seed.'

8. And Abraham rose up early in the morning, and took bread and a bottle of water, and placed them on the shoulders of Hagar and the child, and sent her away.

9. And she departed and wandered in the wilderness of Beersheba, and the water in the bottle was spent, and the

child thirsted, and was not able to go on, and fell down.

10. And his mother took him and cast him under an olive tree, and went and sat her down over against him, at the distance of a bow-shot; for she said, 'Let me not see the death of my child,' and as she sat she wept.

11. And an angel of Jah, one of the holy ones, said unto her, 'Why weepest thou, Hagar? Arise take the child, and hold him in thine hand; for Jah hath heard thy voice, and hath seen the child.'

12. And she opened her eyes, and she saw a well of water, and she went and filled her bottle with water, and she gave her child to drink, and she arose and went towards the wilderness of Paran.

13. And the child grew and became an archer, and God was with him, and his mother took him a wife from among the daughters of Egypt.

14. And she bare him a son, and he called his name Nebaioth; for she said, 'Jah was nigh to me when I called upon him.'

15. And it came to pass in the seventh week, in the first year thereof, [2003 A.M.] in the first month in this jubilee, on the twelfth of this month, there were voices in heaven regarding Abraham, that he was faithful in all that He told him, and that he loved Jah, and that in every affliction he was faithful.

16. And the prince Mastêmâ came and said before Jah, 'Behold, Abraham loves Isaac his son, and he delights in him above all things else; bid him offer him as a burnt-offering on the altar, and Thou wilt see if he will do this command, and Thou wilt know if he is faithful in everything wherein Thou dost try him.

17. And Jah knew that Abraham was faithful in all his afflictions; for He had tried him through his country and with famine, and had tried him with the wealth of kings, and had tried him again through his wife, when she was torn from him, and with circumcision; and had tried him through Ishmael and Hagar, his maid-servant, when he sent them away.

18. And in everything wherein He had tried him, he was found faithful, and his soul was not impatient, and he was not slow to act; for he was faithful and a lover of Jah.

Jubilees 18

1. And God said to him, 'Abraham, Abraham'; and he said, Behold, here am I.'

2. And he said, Take thy beloved son whom thou lovest, even Isaac, and go unto the high country, and offer him on one of the mountains which I will point out unto thee.'

3. And he rose early in the morning and saddled his ass, and took his two young men with him, and Isaac his son, and clave the wood of the burnt offering, and he went to the place on

the third day, and he saw the place afar off.

4. And he came to a well of water, and he said to his young men, 'Abide ye here with the ass, and I and the lad shall go yonder, and when we have worshipped we shall come again to you.'

5. And he took the wood of the burnt-offering and laid it on Isaac his son, and he took in his hand the fire and the knife, and they went both of them together to that place.

6. And Isaac said to his father, 'Father;' and he said, 'Here am I, my son.' And he said unto him, 'Behold the fire, and the knife, and the wood; but where is the sheep for the burnt-offering, father?'

7. And he said, 'God will provide for himself a sheep for a burnt-offering, my son.' And he drew near to the place of the mount of God.

8. And he built an altar, and he placed the wood on the altar, and bound Isaac his son, and placed him on the wood which was upon the altar, and stretched forth his hand to take the knife to slay Isaac his son.

9. And I stood before him, and before the prince Mastêmâ, and Jah said, 'Bid him not to lay his hand on the lad, nor to do anything to him, for I have shown that he fears Jah .'

10. And I called to him from heaven, and said unto him: 'Abraham, Abraham;' and he was terrified and said: 'Behold, here am I.'

11. And I said unto him: 'Lay not thy hand upon the lad, neither do thou anything to him; for now I have shown that thou fearest Jah , and hast not withheld thy son, thy first-born son, from me.'

12. And the prince Mastêmâ was put to shame; and Abraham lifted up his eyes and looked, and, behold a ram caught . . . by his horns, and Abraham went and took the ram and offered it for a burnt-offering in the stead of his son.

13. And Abraham called that place 'Jah hath seen', so that it is said *in the mount* Jah hath seen: that is Mount Sion.

14. And Jah called Abraham by his name a second time from heaven, as he caused us to appear to speak to him in the name of Jah .

15. And he said: 'By Myself have I sworn, saith Jah ,

Because thou hast done this thing,
And hast not withheld thy son, thy beloved son, from Me,
That in blessing I will bless thee,

And in multiplying I will multiply thy seed As the stars of heaven, And as the sand which is on the seashore.

And thy seed shall inherit the cities of its enemies,

16. And in thy seed shall all nations of the earth be blessed;

Because thou hast obeyed My voice,
And I have shown to all that thou art faithful unto Me in all that I have said unto thee:

Go in peace.'

17. And Abraham went to his young men, and they arose and went together to Beersheba, and Abraham [2010 A.M.] dwelt by the Well of the Oath.

18. And he celebrated this festival every year, seven days with joy, and he called it the festival of Jah according to the seven days during which he went and returned in peace.

19. And accordingly has it been ordained and written on the heavenly tablets regarding Israel and its seed that they should observe this festival seven days with the joy of festival.

Jubilees 19

1. And in the first year of the first week in the forty-second jubilee, Abraham returned and dwelt opposite Hebron, that is Kirjath Arba, two weeks of years.

2. And in the first year of the third week of this jubilee the days of the life of Sarah were accomplished, and she died in Hebron.

3. And Abraham went to mourn over her and bury her, and we tried him to see if his spirit were patient and he were not indignant in the words of his mouth; and he was found patient in this, and was not disturbed.

4. For in patience of spirit he conversed with the children of Heth, to the intent that they should give him a place in which to bury his dead.

5. And Jah gave him grace before all who saw him, and he besought in gentleness the sons of Heth, and they gave him the land of the double cave over against Mamre, that is Hebron, for four hundred pieces of silver.

6. And they besought him saying, We shall give it to thee for nothing; but he would not take it from their hands for nothing, for he gave the price of the place, the money in full, and he bowed down before them twice, and after this he buried his dead in the double cave.

7. And all the days of the life of Sarah were one hundred and twenty-seven years, that is, two jubilees and four weeks and one year: these are the days of the years of the life of Sarah.

8. This is the tenth trial wherewith Abraham was tried, and he was found faithful, patient in spirit.

9. And he said not a single word regarding the rumour in the land how that God had said that He would give it to him and to his seed after him, and he begged a place there to bury his dead; for he was found faithful, and was recorded on the heavenly tablets as the friend of God.

10. And in the fourth year thereof he took a wife for his son Isaac and her name was Rebecca [2020 A.M.] the daughter of Bethuel, the son of Nahor, the brother of Abraham the sister of Laban and daughter of Bethuel; and Bethuel was the son of Melca, who was the wife of Nahor, the brother of Abraham.

11. And Abraham took to himself a third wife, and her name was Keturah, from among the daughters of his

household servants, for Hagar had died before Sarah. And she bare him six sons, Zimram, and Jokshan, and Medan, and Midian, and Ishbak, and Shuah, in the two weeks of years.

12. And in the sixth week, in the second year thereof, Rebecca bare to Isaac two sons, Jacob and Esau,

13. and [2046 A.M.] Jacob was a smooth and upright man, and Esau was fierce, a man of the field, and hairy, and Jacob dwelt in tents.

14. And the youths grew, and Jacob learned to write; but Esau did not learn, for he was a man of the field and a hunter, and he learnt war, and all his deeds were fierce.

15. And Abraham loved Jacob, but Isaac loved Esau.

16. And Abraham saw the deeds of Esau, and he knew that in Jacob should his name and seed be called; and he called Rebecca and gave commandment regarding Jacob, for he knew that she too loved Jacob much more than Esau.

17. And he said unto her:

My daughter, watch over my son Jacob,
For he shall be in my stead on the earth,
And for a blessing in the midst of the children of men,
And for the glory of the whole seed of Shem.

18. For I know that Jah will choose him to be a people for possession unto Himself, above all peoples that are upon the face of the earth.

19. And behold, Isaac my son loves Esau more than Jacob, but I see that thou truly lovest Jacob.

20. Add still further to thy kindness to him,
And let thine eyes be upon him in love;
For he shall be a blessing unto us on the earth from henceforth unto all generations of the earth.

21. Let thy hands be strong
And let thy heart rejoice in thy son Jacob;
For I have loved him far beyond all my sons.

He shall be blessed for ever,
And his seed shall fill the whole earth.

22. If a man can number the sand of the earth,
His seed also shall be numbered.

23. And all the blessings wherewith Jah hath blessed me and my seed shall belong to Jacob and his seed alway.

24. And in his seed shall my name be blessed, and the name of my fathers, Shem, and Noab, and Enoch, and Mahalalel, and Enos, and Seth, and Adam.

25. And these shall serve

To lay the foundations of the heaven,
And to strengthen the earth,
And to renew all the luminaries which are in the firmament.

26. And he called Jacob before the eyes of Rebecca his mother, and kissed him, and blessed him, and said:

27. 'Jacob, my beloved son, whom my soul loveth, may God bless thee from

above the firmament, and may He give thee all the blessings wherewith He blessed Adam, and Enoch, and Noah, and Shem; and all the things of which He told me, and all the things which He promised to give me, may he cause to cleave to thee and to thy seed for ever, according to the days of heaven above the earth.

28. And the Spirits of Mastêmâ shall not rule over thee or over thy seed to turn thee from Jah, who is thy God from henceforth for ever.

29. And may Jah God be a father to thee and thou the first-born son, and to the people alway.

30. Go in peace, my son.' And they both went forth together from Abraham.

31. And Rebecca loved Jacob, with all her heart and with all her soul, very much more than Esau; but Isaac loved Esau much more than Jacob.

Jubilees 20

1. And in the forty-second jubilee, in the first year of the seventh week, Abraham called Ishmael, [2052 (2045?) A.M.] and his twelve sons, and Isaac and his two sons, and the six sons of Keturah, and their sons.

2. And he commanded them that they should observe the way of Jah ; that they should work righteousness, and love each his neighbour, and act on this manner amongst all men; that they should each so walk with regard to them as to do judgment and righteousness on the earth.

3. That they should circumcise their sons, according to the covenant which He had made with them, and not deviate to the right hand or the left of all the paths which Jah had commanded us; and that we should keep ourselves from all fornication and uncleanness, and renounce from amongst us all fornication and uncleanness.

4. And if any woman or maid commit fornication amongst you, burn her with fire and let them not commit fornication with her after their eyes and their heart; and let them not take to themselves wives from the daughters of Canaan; for the seed of Canaan will be rooted out of the land.

5. And he told them of the judgment of the giants, and the judgment of the Sodomites, how they had been judged on account of their wickedness, and had died on account of their fornication, and uncleanness, and mutual corruption through fornication.

6. 'And guard yourselves from all fornication and uncleanness,
And from all pollution of sin,

Lest ye make our name a curse,
And your whole life a hissing,

And all your sons to be destroyed by the sword,
And ye become accursed like Sodom,
And all your remnant as the sons of Gomorrah.

7. I implore you, my sons, love the God of heaven

358

And cleave ye to all His commandments.

And walk not after their idols, and after their uncleannesses,

    8. And make not for yourselves molten or graven gods;

For they are vanity,
And there is no spirit in them;

For they are work of men's hands,
And all who trust in them, trust in nothing.

    9. Serve them not, nor worship them,
But serve ye the most high God, and worship Him continually:
And hope for His countenance always,
And work uprightness and righteousness before Him,

That He may have pleasure in you and grant you His mercy,
And send rain upon you morning and evening,

And bless all your works which ye have wrought upon the earth,
And bless thy bread and thy water,

And bless the fruit of thy womb and the fruit of thy land,
And the herds of thy cattle, and the flocks of thy sheep.

    10. And ye will be for a blessing on the earth,
And all nations of the earth will desire you,

And bless your sons in my name,
That they may be blessed as I am.

    11. And he gave to Ishmael and to his sons, and to the sons of Keturah, gifts, and sent them away from Isaac his son, and he gave everything to Isaac his son.

    12. And Ishmael and his sons, and the sons of Keturah and their sons, went together and dwelt from Paran to the entering in of Babylon in all the land which is towards the East facing the desert.

    13. And these mingled with each other, and their name was called Arabs, and Ishmaelites.

Jubilees 21

1. And in the sixth year of the seventh week of this jubilee Abraham called Isaac his son, and [2057 (2050?) A.M.] commanded him: saying, 'I am become old, and know not the day of my death, and am full of my days.

2. And behold, I am one hundred and seventy-five years old, and throughout all the days of my life I have remembered Jah , and sought with all my heart to do His will, and to walk uprightly in all His ways.

3. My soul has hated idols, and I have despised those that served them, and I have given my heart and spirit that I might observe to do the will of Him who created me.

4. For He is the living God, and He is holy and faithful, and He is righteous beyond all, and there is with Him no accepting of men's persons and no accepting of gifts; for God is righteous, and executeth judgment on all those who transgress His

commandments and despise His covenant.

5. And do thou, my son, observe His commandments and His ordinances and His judgments, and walk not after the abominations and after the graven images and after the molten images.
6. And eat no blood at all of animals or cattle, or of any bird which flies in the heaven.
7. And if thou dost slay a victim as an acceptable peace offering, slay ye it, and pour out its blood upon the altar, and all the fat of the offering offer on the altar with fine flour and the meat offering mingled with oil, with its drink offering -offer them all together on the altar of burnt offering; it is a sweet savour before Jah .
8. And thou wilt offer the fat of the sacrifice of thank offerings on the fire which is upon the altar, and the fat which is on the belly, and all the fat on the inwards and the two kidneys, and all the fat that is upon them, and upon the loins and liver thou shalt remove, together with the kidneys.
9. And offer all these for a sweet savour acceptable before Jah , with its meat-offering and with its drink-offering, for a sweet savour, the bread of the offering unto Jah .
10. And eat its meat on that day and on the second day, and let not the sun on the second day go down upon it till it is eaten, and let nothing be left over for the third day; for it is not acceptable for it is not approved and let it no longer be eaten, and all who eat thereof will bring sin upon themselves; for thus I have found it written in the books of my forefathers, and in the words of Enoch, and in the words of Noah.
11. And on all thy oblations thou shalt strew salt, and let not the salt of the covenant be lacking in all thy oblations before Jah .
12. And as regards the wood of the sacrifices, beware lest thou bring other wood for the altar in addition to these: cypress, bay, almond, fir, pine, cedar, savin, fig, olive, myrrh, laurel, aspalathus.
13. And of these kinds of wood lay upon the altar under the sacrifice, such as have been tested as to their appearance, and do not lay thereon any split or dark wood, but hard and clean, without fault, a sound and new growth; and do not lay thereon old wood, for its fragrance is gone for there is no longer fragrance in it as before.
14. Besides these kinds of wood there is none other that thou shalt place on the altar, for the fragrance is dispersed, and the smell of its fragrance goes not up to heaven.
15. Observe this commandment and do it, my son, that thou mayst be upright in all thy deeds.
16. And at all times be clean in thy body, and wash thyself with water before thou approachest to offer on the altar, and wash thy hands and thy feet before thou drawest near to the

altar; and when thou art done sacrificing, wash again thy hands and thy feet.

17. And let no blood appear upon you nor upon your clothes; be on thy guard, my son, against blood, be on thy guard exceedingly; cover it with dust.

18. And do not eat any blood for it is the soul; eat no blood whatever.

19. And take no gifts for the blood of man, lest it be shed with impunity, without judgment; for it is the blood that is shed that causes the earth to sin, and the earth cannot be cleansed from the blood of man save by the blood of him who shed it.

20. And take no present or gift for the blood of man: blood for blood, that thou mayest be accepted before Jah , the Most High God; for He is the defence of the good: and that thou mayest be preserved from all evil, and that He may save thee from every kind of death.

21. I see, my son,
That all the works of the children of men are sin and wickedness,
And all their deeds are uncleanness and an abomination and a pollution,
And there is no righteousness with them.

22. Beware, lest thou shouldest walk in their ways
And tread in their paths,
And sin a sin unto death before the Most High God.

Else He will hide His face from thee
And give thee back into the hands of thy transgression,
And root thee out of the land, and thy seed likewise from under heaven,
And thy name and thy seed shall perish from the whole earth.

23. Turn away from all their deeds and all their uncleanness,
And observe the ordinance of the Most High God,
And do His will and be upright in all things.

24. And He will bless thee in all thy deeds,
And will raise up from thee a plant of righteousness through all the earth, throughout all generations of the earth,
And my name and thy name shall not be forgotten under heaven for ever.

25. Go, my son in peace.
May the Most High God, my God and thy God, strengthen thee to do His will,
And may He bless all thy seed and the residue of thy seed for the generations for ever, with all righteous blessings,
That thou mayest be a blessing on all the earth.'

26. And he went out from him rejoicing.

Jubilees 22

1. And it came to pass in the first week in the forty-fourth jubilee, in the second year, that is, the year in which Abraham died, that Isaac and Ishmael came from the Well of the Oath to celebrate the feast of weeks - that is, the feast of the first fruits of

the harvest-to Abraham, their father, and Abraham rejoiced because his two sons had come.

2. For Isaac had many possessions in Beersheba, and Isaac was wont to go and see his possessions and to return to his father.

3. And in those days Ishmael came to see his father, and they both came together, and Isaac offered a sacrifice for a burnt offering, and presented it on the altar of his father which he had made in Hebron.

4. And he offered a thank offering and made a feast of joy before Ishmael, his brother: and Rebecca made new cakes from the new grain, and gave them to Jacob, her son, to take them to Abraham, his father, from the first fruits of the land, that he might eat and bless the Creator of all things before he died.

5. And Isaac, too, sent by the hand of Jacob to Abraham a best thank offering, that he might eat and drink.

6. And he eat and drank, and blessed the Most High God,

Who hath created heaven and earth,
Who hath made all the fat things of the earth,
And given them to the children of men
That they might eat and drink and bless their Creator.

7. 'And now I give thanks unto Thee, my God, because thou hast caused me to see this day: behold, I am one hundred three score and fifteen years, an old man and full of days, and all my days have been unto me peace.

8. The sword of the adversary has not overcome me in all that Thou hast given me and my children all the days of my life until this day.

9. My God, may Thy mercy and Thy peace be upon Thy servant, and upon the seed of his sons, that they may be to Thee a chosen nation and an inheritance from amongst all the nations of the earth from henceforth unto all the days of the generations of the earth, unto all the ages.'

10. And he called Jacob and said: 'My son Jacob, may the God of all bless thee and strengthen thee to do righteousness, and His will before Him, and may He choose thee and thy seed that ye may become a people for His inheritance according to His will alway.

11. And do thou, my son, Jacob, draw near and kiss me.' And he drew near and kissed him, and he said:

'Blessed be my son Jacob
And all the sons of God Most High, unto all the ages:

May God give unto thee a seed of righteousness;
And some of thy sons may He sanctify in the midst of the whole earth;

May nations serve thee,
And all the nations bow themselves before thy seed.

12. Be strong in the presence of men,
And exercise authority over all the seed of Seth.

Then thy ways and the ways of thy sons will be justified,
So that they shall become a holy nation.

> 13. May the Most High God give thee all the blessings
> Wherewith He has blessed me

And wherewith He blessed Noah and Adam;
May they rest on the sacred head of thy seed from generation to generation for ever.

> 14. And may He cleanse thee from all unrighteousness and impurity,
> That thou mayest be forgiven all the transgressions; which thou hast committed ignorantly.

And may He strengthen thee,
And bless thee.
And mayest thou inherit the whole earth,

> 15. And may He renew His covenant with thee.
> That thou mayest be to Him a nation for His inheritance for all the ages,
> And that He may be to thee and to thy seed a God in truth and righteousness throughout all the days of the earth.
>
> 16. And do thou, my son Jacob, remember my words,
> And observe the commandments of Abraham, thy father:

Separate thyself from the nations,
And eat not with them:

And do not according to their works,
And become not their associate;

For their works are unclean,
And all their ways are a Pollution and an abomination and uncleanness.

> 17. They offer their sacrifices to the dead
> And they worship evil spirits,

And they eat over the graves,
And all their works are vanity and nothingness.

> 18. They have no heart to understand
> And their eyes do not see what their works are,

And how they err in saying to a piece of wood: 'Thou art my God,'
And to a stone: 'Thou art my Lord and thou art my deliverer.'
And they have no heart.

> 19. And as for thee, my son Jacob,
> May the Most High God help thee
> And the God of heaven bless thee
> And remove thee from their uncleanness and from all their error.
>
> 20. Be thou ware, my son Jacob, of taking a wife from any seed of the daughters of Canaan;

For all his seed is to be rooted out of the earth.

> 21. For, owing to the transgression of Ham, Canaan erred,
> And all his seed shall be destroyed from off the earth and all the residue thereof,
> And none springing from him shall be saved on the day of judgment.
>
> 22. And as for all the worshippers of idols and the profane
> (b) There shall be no hope for them in the land of the living;
> (c) And there shall be no remembrance of them on the earth;
> (c) For they shall descend into Sheol,

(d) And into the place of condemnation shall they go,

As the children of Sodom were taken away from the earth
So will all those who worship idols be taken away.

23. Fear not, my son Jacob,
And be not dismayed, O son of Abraham:

May the Most High God preserve thee from destruction,
And from all the paths of error may he deliver thee.

24. This house have I built for myself that I might put my name upon it in the earth: [it is given to thee and to thy seed for ever], and it will be named the house of Abraham; it is given to thee and to thy seed for ever; for thou wilt build my house and establish my name before God for ever: thy seed and thy name will stand throughout all generations of the earth.'

25. And he ceased commanding him and blessing him.

26. And the two lay together on one bed, and Jacob slept in the bosom of Abraham, his father's father and he kissed him seven times, and his affection and his heart rejoiced over him.

27. And he blessed him with all his heart and said: 'The Most High God, the God of all, and Creator of all, who brought me forth from Ur of the Chaldees that he might give me this land to inherit it for ever, and that I might establish a holy seed-blessed be the Most High for ever.'

28. And he blessed Jacob and said: 'My son, over whom with all my heart and my affection I rejoice, may Thy grace and Thy mercy be lift up upon him and upon his seed alway.

29. And do not forsake him, nor set him at nought from henceforth unto the days of eternity, and may Thine eyes be opened upon him and upon his seed, that Thou mayst preserve him, and bless him, and mayest sanctify him as a nation for Thine inheritance;

30. And bless him with all Thy blessings from henceforth unto all the days of eternity, and renew Thy covenant and Thy grace with him and with his seed according to all Thy good pleasure unto all the generations of the earth.'

Jubilees 23

1. And he placed two fingers of Jacob on his eyes, and he blessed the God of gods, and he covered his face and stretched out his feet and slept the sleep of eternity, and was gathered to his fathers.

2. And notwithstanding all this Jacob was lying in his bosom, and knew not that Abraham, his father's father, was dead.

3. And Jacob awoke from his sleep, and behold Abraham was cold as ice, and he said 'Father, father'; but there was none that spake, and he knew that he was dead.

4. And he arose from his bosom and ran and told Rebecca, his mother; and Rebecca went to Isaac in the night, and told him; and they went together, and Jacob with them, and a lamp was in his hand, and when they had gone in they found Abraham lying dead.

5. And Isaac fell on the face of his father and wept and kissed him.

6. And the voices were heard in the house of Abraham, and Ishmael his son arose, and went to Abraham his father, and wept over Abraham his father, he and all the house of Abraham, and they wept with a great weeping.

7. And his sons Isaac and Ishmael buried him in the double cave, near Sarah his wife, and they wept for him forty days, all the men of his house, and Isaac and Ishmael, and all their sons, and all the sons of Keturah in their places; and the days of weeping for Abraham were ended.

8. And he lived three jubilees and four weeks of years, one hundred and seventy-five years, and completed the days of his life, being old and full of days.

9. For the days of the forefathers, of their life, were nineteen jubilees; and after the Flood they began to grow less than nineteen jubilees, and to decrease in jubilees, and to grow old quickly, and to be full of their days by reason of manifold tribulation and the wickedness of their ways, with the exception of Abraham.

10. For Abraham was perfect in all his deeds with Jah, and well-pleasing in righteousness all the days of his life; and behold, he did not complete four jubilees in his life, when he had grown old by reason of the wickedness, and was full of his days.

11. And all the generations which shall arise from this time until the day of the great judgment shall grow old quickly, before they complete two jubilees, and their knowledge shall forsake them by reason of their old age Land all their know- ledge shall vanish away.

12. And in those days, if a man live a jubilee and a-half of years, they shall say regarding him: 'He has lived long, and the greater part of his days are pain and sorrow and tribulation, and there is no peace:

13. For calamity follows on calamity, and wound on wound, and tribulation on tribulation, and evil tidings on evil tidings, and illness on illness, and all evil judgments such as these, one with another, illness and overthrow, and snow and frost and ice, and fever, and chills, and torpor, and famine, and death, and sword, and captivity, and all kinds of calamities and pains.'

14. And all these shall come on an evil generation, which transgresses on the earth: their works are uncleanness and fornication, and pollution and abominations.

15. Then they shall say: 'The days of the forefathers were many even, unto a thousand years, and were good; but

behold, the days of our life, if a man has lived many, are three score years and ten, and, if he is strong, four score years, and those evil, and there is no peace in the days of this evil generation.'

16. And in that generation the sons shall convict their fathers and their elders of sin and unrighteousness, and of the words of their mouth and the great wickednesses which they perpetrate, and concerning their forsaking the covenant which Jah made between them and Him, that they should observe and do all His commandments and His ordinances and all His laws, without departing either to the right hand or the left.

17. For all have done evil, and every mouth speaks iniquity and all their works are an uncleanness and an abomination, and all their ways are pollution, uncleanness and destruction.

18. Behold the earth shall be destroyed on account of all their works, and there shall be no seed of the vine, and no oil; for their works are altogether faithless, and they shall all perish together, beasts and cattle and birds, and all the fish of the sea, on account of the children of men.

19. And they shall strive one with another, the young with the old, and the old with the young, the poor with the rich, the lowly with the great, and the beggar with the prince, on account of the law and the covenant; for they have forgotten commandment, and covenant, and feasts, and months, and Sabbaths, and jubilees, and all judgments.

20. And they shall stand with bows and swords and war to turn them back into the way; but they shall not return until much blood has been shed on the earth, one by another.

21. And those who have escaped shall not return from their wickedness to the way of righteousness, but they shall all exalt themselves to deceit and wealth, that they may each take all that is his neighbour's, and they shall name the great name, but not in truth and not in righteousness, and they shall defile the holy of holies with their uncleanness and the corruption of their pollution.

22. And a great punishment shall befall the deeds of this generation from Jah , and He will give them over to the sword and to judgment and to captivity, and to be plundered and devoured.

23. And He will wake up against them the sinners of the Gentiles, who have neither mercy nor compassion, and who shall respect the person of none, neither old nor young, nor any one, for they are more wicked and strong to do evil than all the children of men.

And they shall use violence against Israel and transgression against Jacob,
And much blood shall be shed upon the earth,
And there shall be none to gather and none to bury.

24. In those days they shall cry aloud, And call and pray that they may be

saved from the hand of the sinners, the Gentiles;
But none shall be saved.

25. And the heads of the children shall be white with grey hair,
And a child of three weeks shall appear old like a man of one hundred years,
And their stature shall be destroyed by tribulation and oppression.

26. And in those days the children shall begin to study the laws,
And to seek the commandments,
And to return to the path of righteousness.

27. And the days shall begin to grow many and increase amongst those children of men
Till their days draw nigh to one thousand years.
And to a greater number of years than before was the number of the days.

28. And there shall be no old man
Nor one who is not satisfied with his days,
For all shall be as children and youths.

29. And all their days they shall complete and live in peace and in joy,
And there shall be no Satan nor any evil destroyer;
For all their days shall be days of blessing and healing.

30. And at that time Jah will heal His servants,
And they shall rise up and see great peace,
And drive out their adversaries.

And the righteous shall see and be thankful,
And rejoice with joy for ever and ever,
And shall see all their judgments and all their curses on their enemies.

31. And their bones shall rest in the earth,
And their spirits shall have much joy,
And they shall know that it is Jah who executes judgment,
And shows mercy to hundreds and thousands and to all that love Him

32. And do thou, Moses, write down these words; for thus are they written, and they record them on the heavenly tablets for a testimony for the generations for ever.

Jubilees 24

1. And it came to pass after the death of Abraham, that Jah blessed Isaac his son, and he arose from Hebron and went and dwelt at the Well of the Vision in the first year of the third week [2073 A.M.] of this jubilee, seven years.

2. And in the first year of the fourth week a famine began in the land, [2080 A.M.] besides the first famine, which had been in the days of Abraham.

3. And Jacob sod lentil pottage, and Esau came from the field hungry. And he said to Jacob his brother: 'Give me of this red pottage.' And Jacob said to him: 'Sell to me thy primogeniture, this birthright and I will give thee bread, and also some of this lentil pottage.'

4. And Esau said in his heart: 'I shall die; of what profit to me is this birthright?

5. 'And he said to Jacob: 'I give it to thee.' And Jacob said: 'Swear to me, this day,' and he sware unto him.

6. And Jacob gave his brother Esau bread and pottage, and he eat till he was satisfied, and Esau despised his birthright; for this reason was Esau's name called Edom, on account of the red pottage which Jacob gave him for his birthright.

7. And Jacob became the elder, and Esau was brought down from his dignity.

8. And the famine was over the land, and Isaac departed to go down into Egypt in the second year of this week, and went to the king of the Philistines to Gerar, unto Abimelech.

9. And Jah appeared unto him and said unto him: 'Go not down into Egypt; dwell in the land that I shall tell thee of, and sojourn in this land, and I will be with thee and bless thee.

10. For to thee and to thy seed will I give all this land, and I will establish My oath which I sware unto Abraham thy father, and I will multiply thy seed as the stars of heaven, and will give unto thy seed all this land.

11. And in thy seed shall all the nations of the earth be blessed, because thy father obeyed My voice, and kept My charge and My commandments, and My laws, and My ordinances, and My covenant; and now obey My voice and dwell in this land.'

12. And he dwelt in Gelar three weeks of years.

13. And Abimelech charged concerning him, [2080-2101 A.M.] and concerning all that was his, saying: 'Any man that shall touch him or aught that is his shall surely die.'

14. And Isaac waxed strong among the Philistines, and he got many possessions, oxen and sheep and camels and asses and a great household.

15. And he sowed in the land of the Philistines and brought in a hundred-fold, and Isaac became exceedingly great, and the Philistines envied him.

16. Now all the wells which the servants of Abraham had dug during the life of Abraham, the Philistines had stopped them after the death of Abraham, and filled them with earth.

17. And Abimelech said unto Isaac: 'Go from us, for thou art much mightier than we', and Isaac departed thence in the first year of the seventh week, and sojourned in the valleys of Gerar.

18. And they digged again the wells of water which the servants of Abraham, his father, had digged, and which the Philistines had closed after the death of Abraham his father, and he called their names as Abraham his father had named them.

19. And the servants of Isaac dug a well in the valley, and found living water, and the shepherds of Gerar strove with the shepherds of Isaac, saying: 'The water is ours'; and Isaac called

the name of the well 'Perversity', because they had been perverse with us.

20. And they dug a second well, and they strove for that also, and he called its name 'Enmity'. And he arose from thence and they digged another well, and for that they strove not, and he called the name of it 'Room', and Isaac said: 'Now Jah hath made room for us, and we have increased in the land.'

21. And he went up from thence to the Well of the Oath in the first year of the first week in the [2108 A.M.] forty-fourth jubilee.

22. And Jah appeared to him that night, on the new moon of the first month, and said unto him: 'I am the God of Abraham thy father; fear not, for I am with thee, and shall bless thee and shall surely multiply thy seed as the sand of the earth, for the sake of Abraham my servant.'

23. And he built an altar there, which Abraham his father had first built, and he called upon the name of Jah, and he offered sacrifice to the God of Abraham his father.

24. And they digged a well and they found living water.

25. And the servants of Isaac digged another well and did not find water, and they went and told Isaac that they had not found water, and Isaac said: 'I have sworn this day to the Philistines and this thing has been announced to us.'

26. And he called the name of that place the Well of the Oath; for there he had sworn to Abimelech and Ahuzzath his friend and Phicol the prefect Or his host.

27. And Isaac knew that day that under constraint he had sworn to them to make peace with them.

28. And Isaac on that day cursed the Philistines and said: 'Cursed be the Philistines unto the day of wrath and indignation from the midst of all nations; may God make them a derision and a curse and an object of wrath and indignation in the hands of the sinners the Gentiles and in the hands of the Kittim.

29. And whoever escapes the sword of the enemy and the Kittim, may the righteous nation root out in judgment from under heaven; for they shall be the enemies and foes of my children throughout their generations upon the earth.

30. And no remnant shall be left to them,
Nor one that shall be saved on the day of the wrath of judgment;
For destruction and rooting out and expulsion from the earth is the whole seed of the Philistines reserved,
And there shall no longer be left for these Caphtorim a name or a seed on the earth.

31. For though he ascend unto heaven,
Thence shall he be brought down,
And though he make himself strong on earth,
Thence shall he be dragged forth,

And though he hide himself amongst the nations,
Even from thence shall he be rooted out;

And though he descend into Sheol,
There also shall his condemnation be great,
And there also he shall have no peace.

32. And if he go into captivity,
    By the hands of those that seek his life shall they slay him on the way,
    And neither name nor seed shall be left to him on all the earth;
    For into eternal malediction shall he depart.'

33. And thus is it written and engraved concerning him on the heavenly tablets, to do unto him on the day of judgment, so that he may be rooted out of the earth.

Jubilees 25

1. nd in the second year of this week in this jubilee, Rebecca called Jacob her son, and spake unto [2109 A.M.] him, saying: 'My son, do not take thee a wife of the daughters of Canaan, as Esau, thy brother, who took him two wives of the daughters of Canaan, and they have embittered my soul with all their unclean deeds: for all their deeds are fornication and lust, and there is no righteousness with them, for their deeds are evil.

2. And I, my son, love thee exceedingly, and my heart and my affection bless thee every hour of the day and watch of the night.

3. And now, my son, hearken to my voice, and do the will of thy mother, and do not take thee a wife of the daughters of this land, but only of the house of my father, and of my father's kindred. Thou shalt take thee a wife of the house of my father, and the Most High God will bless thee, and thy children shall be a righteous generation and a holy seed.'

4. And then spake Jacob to Rebecca, his mother, and said unto her: 'Behold, mother, I am nine weeks of years old, and I neither know nor have I touched any woman, nor have I betrothed myself to any, nor even think of taking me a wife of the daughters of Canaan.

5. For I remember, mother, the words of Abraham, our father, for he commanded me not to take a wife of the daughters of Canaan, but to take me a wife from the seed of my father's house and from my kindred.

6. I have heard before that daughters have been born to Laban, thy brother, and I have set my heart on them to take a wife from amongst them.

7. And for this reason I have guarded myself in my spirit against sinning or being corrupted in all my ways throughout all the days of my life; for with regard to lust and fornication, Abraham, my father, gave me many commands.

8. And, despite all that he has commanded me, these two and twenty years my brother has striven with me, and spoken frequently to me and said: 'My brother, take to wife a sister of my two wives'; but I refuse to do as he has done.

9. I swear before thee, mother, that all the days of my life I will not take me a wife from the daughters of the seed of Canaan, and I will not act wickedly as my brother has done.

10. Fear not, mother; be assured that I shall do thy will and walk in uprightness, and not corrupt my ways for ever.'

11. And thereupon she lifted up her face to heaven and extended the fingers of her hands, and opened her mouth and blessed the Most High God, who had created the heaven and the earth, and she gave Him thanks and praise.

12. And she said: 'Blessed be Jah God, and may His holy name be blessed for ever and ever, who has given me Jacob as a pure son and a holy seed; for he is Thine, and Thine shall his seed be continually and throughout all the generations for evermore.

13. Bless him, O Lord, and place in my mouth the blessing of righteousness, that I may bless him.'

14. And at that hour, when the spirit of righteousness descended into her mouth, she placed both her hands on the head of Jacob, and said:

15. Blessed art thou, Lord of righteousness and God of the ages
And may He bless thee beyond all the generations of men.

May He give thee, my Son, the path of righteousness,
And reveal righteousness to thy seed.

16. And may He make thy sons many during thy life,
And may they arise according to the number of the months of the year.
And may their sons become many and great beyond the stars of heaven,
And their numbers be more than the sand of the sea.

17. And may He give them this goodly land -as He said He would give it to Abraham and to his seed after him alway-
And may they hold it as a possession for ever.

18. And may I see born unto thee, my son, blessed children during my life,
And a blessed and holy seed may all thy seed be.

19. And as thou hast refreshed thy mother's spirit during her life,
The womb of her that bare thee blesses thee thus,

My affection and my breasts bless thee
And my mouth and my tongue praise thee greatly.

20. Increase and spread over the earth,
And may thy seed be perfect in the joy of heaven and earth for ever;

And may thy seed rejoice,
And on the great day of peace may it have peace.

21. And may thy name and thy seed endure to all the ages,
And may the Most High God be their God,

And may the God of righteousness dwell with them,
And by them may His sanctuary be built unto all the ages.

22. Blessed be he that blesseth thee,

And all flesh that curseth thee falsely, may it be cursed.'

23. And she kissed him, and said to him;
'May Jah of the world love thee
As the heart of thy mother and her affection rejoice in thee and bless thee.'
And she ceased from blessing.

Jubilees 26

1. And in the seventh year of this week Isaac called Esau, his elder Son, and said unto him: ' I am [2114 A.M.] old, my son, and behold my eyes are dim in seeing, and I know not the day of my death.

2. And now take thy hunting weapons thy quiver and thy bow, and go out to the field, and hunt and catch me venison, my son, and make me savoury meat, such as my soul loveth, and bring it to me that I may eat, and that my soul may bless thee before I die.'

3. But Rebecca heard Isaac speaking to Esau.

4. And Esau went forth early to the field to hunt and catch and bring home to his father.

5. And Rebecca called Jacob, her son, and said unto him: 'Behold, I heard Isaac, thy father, speak unto Esau, thy brother, saying: "Hunt for me, and make me savoury meat, and bring it to me that

6. I may eat and bless thee before Jah before I die." And now, my son, obey my voice in that which I command thee: Go to thy flock and fetch me two good kids of the goats, and I will make them savoury meat for thy father, such as he loves, and thou shalt bring it to thy father that he may eat and bless thee before Jah before he die, and that thou mayst be blessed.'

7. And Jacob said to Rebecca his mother: 'Mother, I shall not withhold anything which my father would eat, and which would please him: only I fear, my mother, that he will recognise my voice and wish to touch me.

8. And thou knowest that I am smooth, and Esau, my brother, is hairy, and I shall appear before his eyes as an evildoer, and shall do a deed which he had not commanded me, and he will be wroth with me, and I shall bring upon myself a curse, and not a blessing.'

9. And Rebecca, his mother, said unto him: 'Upon me be thy curse, my son, only obey my voice.'

10. And Jacob obeyed the voice of Rebecca, his mother, and went and fetched two good and fat kids of the goats, and brought them to his mother, and his mother made them ~savoury meat~ such as he loved.

11. And Rebecca took the goodly rainment of Esau, her elder son, which was with her in the house, and she clothed Jacob, her younger son, (with them), and she put the skins of the kids upon his hands and on the exposed parts of his neck.

12. And she gave the meat and the bread which she had prepared into the hand of her son Jacob.
13. And Jacob went in to his father and said: 'I am thy son: I have done according as thou badest me: arise and sit and eat of that which I have caught, father, that thy soul may bless me.'
14. And Isaac said to his son: 'How hast thou found so quickly, my son?
15. 'And Jacob said: 'Because Jah thy God caused me to find.'
16. And Isaac said unto him: Come near, that I may feel thee, my son, if thou art my son Esau or not.'
17. And Jacob went near to Isaac, his father, and he felt him and said: 'The voice is Jacob's voice, but the hands are the hands of Esau,'
18. and he discerned him not, because it was a dispensation from heaven to remove his power of perception and Isaac discerned not, for his hands were hairy as his brother Esau's, so that he blessed him.
19. And he said: 'Art thou my son Esau?' and he said: 'I am thy son': and he said, 'Bring near to me that I may eat of that which thou hast caught, my son, that my soul may bless thee.'
20. And he brought near to him, and he did eat, and he brought him wine and he drank.
21. And Isaac, his father, said unto him: 'Come near and kiss me, my son.
22. And he came near and kissed him. And he smelled the smell of his raiment, and he blessed him and said: 'Behold, the smell of my son is as the smell of a <full> field which Jah hath blessed.
23. And may Jah give thee of the dew of heaven
And of the dew of the earth, and plenty of corn and oil:

Let nations serve thee,
And peoples bow down to thee.

24. Be lord over thy brethren,
And let thy mother's sons bow down to thee;

And may all the blessings wherewith Jah hath blessed me and blessed Abraham, my father;
Be imparted to thee and to thy seed for ever:

Cursed be he that curseth thee,
And blessed be he that blesseth thee.'

25. And it came to pass as soon as Isaac had made an end of blessing his son Jacob, and Jacob had gone forth from Isaac his father he hid himself and Esau, his brother, came in from his hunting.
26. And he also made savoury meat, and brought it to his father, and said unto his father: 'Let my father arise, and eat of my venison that thy soul may bless me.'
27. And Isaac, his father, said unto him: 'Who art thou? 'And he said unto him: 'I am thy first born, thy son Esau: I have done as thou hast commanded me.'
28. And Isaac was very greatly astonished, and said: 'Who is he that hath hunted and caught and brought

it to me, and I have eaten of all before thou camest, and have blessed him: and he shall be blessed, and all his seed for ever.'

29. And it came to pass when Esau heard the words of his father Isaac that he cried with an exceeding great and bitter cry, and said unto his father: 'Bless me, even me also, father.'

30. And he said unto him: 'Thy brother came with guile, and hath taken away thy blessing.' And he said: 'Now I know why his name is named Jacob: behold, he hath supplanted me these two times: he took away my birth-right, and now he hath taken away my blessing.'

31. And he said: 'Hast thou not reserved a blessing for me, father?' and Isaac answered and said unto Esau:

'Behold, I have made him thy lord,
And all his brethren have I given to him for servants,
And with plenty of corn and wine and oil have I strengthened him:

And what now shall I do for thee, my son?'

32. And Esau said to Isaac, his father: 'Hast thou but one blessing, O father?
Bless me, even me also, father.'

33. And Esau lifted up his voice and wept. And Isaac answered and said unto him:

'Behold, far from the dew of the earth shall be thy dwelling,
And far from the dew of heaven from above.

34. And by thy sword wilt thou live,
And thou wilt serve thy brother.

And it shall come to pass when thou becomest great,
And dost shake his yoke from off thy neck,
Thou shalt sin a complete sin unto death,
And thy seed shall be rooted out from under heaven.'

35. And Esau kept threatening Jacob because of the blessing wherewith his father blessed him, and he: said in his heart: 'May the days of mourning for my father now come, so that I may slay my brother Jacob.'

Jubilees 27

1. And the words of Esau, her elder son, were told to Rebecca in a dream, and Rebecca sent and called Jacob her younger son,

2. and said unto him: 'Behold Esau thy brother will take vengeance on thee so as to kill thee.

3. Now, therefore, my son, obey my voice, and arise and flee thou to Laban, my brother, to Haran, and tarry with him a few days until thy brother's anger turns away, and he remove his anger from thee, and forget all that thou hast done; then I will send and fetch thee from thence.'

4. And Jacob said: 'I am not afraid; if he wishes to kill me, I will kill him.'

5. But she said unto him: 'Let me not be bereft of both my sons on one day.'

6. And Jacob said to Rebecca his mother: 'Behold, thou knowest that my father has become old, and does not see because his eyes are dull, and if I leave him it will be evil in his

eyes, because I leave him and go away from you, and my father will be angry, and will curse me. I will not go; when he sends me, then only will I go.'

7. And Rebecca said to Jacob: 'I will go in and speak to him, and he will send thee away.'

8. And Rebecca went in and said to Isaac: 'I loathe my life because of the two daughters of Heth, whom Esau has taken him as wives; and if Jacob take a wife from among the daughters of the land such as these, for what purpose do I further live, for the daughters of Canaan are evil.'

9. And Isaac called Jacob and blessed him, and admonished him and said unto him: 'Do not take thee a wife of any of the daughters of Canaan;

10. arise and go to Mesopotamia, to the house of Bethuel, thy mother's father, and take thee a wife from thence of the daughters of Laban, thy mother's brother.

11. And God Almighty bless thee and increase and multiply thee that thou mayest become a company of nations, and give thee the blessings of my father Abraham, to thee and to thy seed after thee, that thou mayest inherit the land of thy sojournings and all the land which God gave to Abraham: go, my son, in peace.'

12. And Isaac sent Jacob away, and he went to Mesopotamia, to Laban the son of Bethuel the Syrian, the brother of Rebecca, Jacob's mother.

13. And it came to pass after Jacob had arisen to go to Mesopotamia that the spirit of Rebecca was grieved after her son, and she wept.

14. And Isaac said to Rebecca: 'My sister, weep not on account of Jacob, my son; for he goeth in peace, and in peace will he return.

15. The Most High God will preserve him from all evil, and will be with him; for He will not forsake him all his days;

16. For I know that his ways will be prospered in all things wherever he goes, until he return in peace to us, and we see him in peace.

17. Fear not on his account, my sister, for he is on the upright path and he is a perfect man: and he is faithful and will not perish. Weep not.'

18. And Isaac comforted Rebecca on account of her son Jacob, and blessed him.

19. And Jacob went from the Well of the Oath to go to Haran on the first year of the second week in the forty-fourth jubilee, and he came to Luz on the mountains, that is, Bethel, on the new moon of the first month of this week, [2115 A.M.] and he came to the place at even and turned from the way to the west of the road that night: and he slept there; for the sun had set.

20. And he took one of the stones of that place and laid <it at his head> under the tree, and he was journeying alone, and he slept.

21. And he dreamt that night, and behold a ladder set up on the earth, and the top of it reached to heaven, and behold, the angels of Jah ascended and descended on it: and behold, Jah stood upon it.

22. And he spake to Jacob and said: 'I am Jah God of Abraham, thy father, and the God of Isaac; the land whereon thou art sleeping, to thee will I give it, and to thy seed after thee.

23. And thy seed shall be as the dust of the earth, and thou shalt increase to the west and to the east, to the north and the south, and in thee and in thy seed shall all the families of the nations be blessed.

24. And behold, I will be with thee, and will keep thee whithersoever thou goest, and I will bring thee again into this land in peace; for I will not leave thee until I do everything that I told thee of.'

25. And Jacob awoke from his sleep, and said, 'Truly this place is the house of Jah, and I knew it not.' And he was afraid and said: 'Dreadful is this place which is none other than the house of Jah, and this is the gate of heaven.'

26. And Jacob arose early in the morning, and took the stone which he had put under his head and set it up as a pillar for a sign, and he poured oil upon the top of it. And he called the name of that place Bethel; but the name of the place was Luz at the first.

27. And Jacob vowed a vow unto Jah, saying: 'If Jah will be with me, and will keep me in this way that I go, and give me bread to eat and raiment to put on, so that I come again to my father's house in peace, then shall Jah be my God, and this stone which I have set up as a pillar for a sign in this place, shall be Jah's house, and of all that thou givest me, I shall give the tenth to thee, my God.'

Jubilees 28

1. And he went on his journey, and came to the land of the east, to Laban, the brother of Rebecca, and he was with him, and served him for Rachel his daughter one week.

2. And in the first year of the third week [2122 A.M.] he said unto him: 'Give me my wife, for whom I have served thee seven years '; and Laban said unto Jacob: 'I will give thee thy wife.'

3. And Laban made a feast, and took Leah his elder daughter, and gave (her) to Jacob as a wife, and gave her Zilpah his handmaid for an handmaid; and Jacob did not know, for he thought that she was Rachel.

4. And he went in unto her, and behold, she was Leah; and Jacob was angry with Laban, and said unto him: 'Why hast thou dealt thus with me? Did not I serve thee for Rachel and not for Leah? Why hast thou wronged me?

5. Take thy daughter, and I will go; for thou hast done evil to me.' For Jacob loved Rachel more than Leah; for

Leah's eyes were weak, but her form was very handsome; but Rachel had beautiful eyes and a beautiful and very handsome form.

6. And Laban said to Jacob: 'It is not so done in our country, to give the younger before the elder.' And it is not right to do this; for thus it is ordained and written in the heavenly tablets, that no one should give his younger daughter before the elder; but the elder, one gives first and after her the younger -and the man who does so, they set down guilt against him in heaven, and none is righteous that does this thing, for this deed is evil before Jah .

7. And command thou the children of Israel that they do not this thing; let them neither take nor give the younger before they have given the elder, for it is very wicked.

8. And Laban said to Jacob: 'Let the seven days of the feast of this one pass by, and I shall give thee Rachel, that thou mayst serve me another seven years, that thou mayst pasture my sheep as thou didst in the former week.'

9. And on the day when the seven days of the feast of Leah had passed, Laban gave Rachel to Jacob, that he might serve him another seven years, and he gave to Rachel Bilhah, the sister of Zilpah, as a handmaid.

10. And he served yet other seven years for Rachel, for Leah had been given to him for nothing.

11. And Jah opened the womb of Leah, and she conceived and bare Jacob a son, and he called his name Reuben, on the fourteenth day of the ninth month, in the first year of the third week. [2122 A.M.]

12. But the womb of Rachel was closed, for Jah saw that Leah was hated and Rachel loved.

13. And again Jacob went in unto Leah, and she conceived, and bare Jacob a second son, and he called his name Simeon, on the twenty-first of the tenth month, and in the third year of this week. [2124 A.M.]

14. And again Jacob went in unto Leah, and she conceived, and bare him a third son, and he called his name Levi, in the new moon of the first month in the sixth year of this week. [2127 A.M.]

15. And again Jacob went in unto her, and she conceived, and bare him a fourth son, and he called his name Judah, on the fifteenth of the third month, in the first year of the fourth week. [2129 A.M.]

16. And on account of all this Rachel envied Leah, for she did not bear, and she said to Jacob: 'Give me children'; and Jacob said: 'Have I withheld from thee the fruits of thy womb? Have I forsaken thee?'

17. And when Rachel saw that Leah had borne four sons to Jacob, Reuben and Simeon and Levi and Judah, she said unto him: 'Go in unto Bilhah my handmaid, and she will conceive, and bear a son unto me.' And she gave him Bilhah her handmaid to wife.

18. And he went in unto her, and she conceived, and bare him a son, and he called his name Dan, on the ninth of the sixth month, in the sixth year of the third week. [2127 A.M.]

19. And Jacob went in again unto Bilhah a second time, and she conceived, and bare Jacob another son, and Rachel called his name Napthali, on the fifth of the seventh month, in the second year of the fourth week. [2130 A.M.]

20. And when Leah saw that she had become sterile and did not bear, she envied Rachel, and she also gave her handmaid Zilpah to Jacob to wife, and she conceived, and bare a son, and Leah called his name Gad, on the twelfth of the eighth month, in the third year of the fourth week. [2131 A.M.]

21. And he went in again unto her, and she conceived, and bare him a second son, and Leah called his name Asher, on the second of the eleventh month, in the fifth year of the fourth week. [2133 A.M.]

22. And Jacob went in unto Leah, and she conceived, and bare a son, and she called his name Issachar, on the fourth of the fifth month, in the fourth year of the fourth week,[2132 A.M.] and she gave him to a nurse.

23. And Jacob went in again unto her, and she conceived, and bare two (children), a son and a daughter, and she called the name of the son Zabulon, and the name of the daughter Dinah, in the seventh of the seventh month, in the sixth year of the fourth week. [2134 A.M.]

24. And Jah was gracious to Rachel, and opened her womb, and she conceived, and bare a son, and she called his name Joseph, on the new moon of the fourth month, in the sixth year in this fourth week. [2134 A.M.]

25. And in the days when Joseph was born, Jacob said to Laban: 'Give me my wives and sons, and let me go to my father Isaac, and let me make me an house; for I have completed the years in which I have served thee for thy two daughters, and I will go to the house of my father.'

26. And Laban said to Jacob: 'Tarry with me for thy wages, and pasture my flock for me again, and take thy wages.'

27. And they agreed with one another that he should give him as his wages those of the lambs and kids which were born black and spotted and white, these were to be his wages.

28. And all the sheep brought forth spotted and speckled and black, variously marked, and they brought forth again lambs like themselves, and all that were spotted were Jacob's and those which were not were Laban's.

29. And Jacob's possessions multiplied exceedingly, and he possessed oxen and sheep and asses and camels, and menservants and maid-servants.

30. And Laban and his sons envied Jacob, and Laban took back his

sheep from him, and he observed him with evil intent.

Jubilees 29

1. And it came to pass when Rachel had borne Joseph, that Laban went to shear his sheep; for they were distant from him a three days' journey.

2. And Jacob saw that Laban was going to shear his sheep, and Jacob called Leah and Rachel, and spake kindly unto them that they should come with him to the land of Canaan.

3. For he told them how he had seen everything in a dream, even all that He had spoken unto him that he should return to his father's house, and they said: 'To every place whither thou goest we will go with thee.'

4. And Jacob blessed the God of Isaac his father, and the God of Abraham his father's father, and he arose and mounted his wives and his children, and took all his possessions and crossed the river, and came to the land of Gilead, and Jacob hid his intention from Laban and told him not.

5. And in the seventh year of the fourth week Jacob turned his face toward Gilead in the first month, on the twenty-first thereof. [2135 A.M.] And Laban pursued after him and overtook Jacob in the mountain of Gilead in the third month, on the thirteenth thereof.

6. And Jah did not suffer him to injure Jacob; for he appeared to him in a dream by night. And Laban spake to Jacob.

7. And on the fifteenth of those days Jacob made a feast for Laban, and for all who came with him, and Jacob sware to Laban that day, and Laban also to Jacob, that neither should cross the mountain of Gilead to the other with evil purpose.

8. And he made there a heap for a witness; wherefore the name of that place is called: 'The Heap of Witness,' after this heap.

9. But before they used to call the land of Gilead the land of the Rephaim; for it was the land of the Rephaim, and the Rephaim were born there, giants whose height was ten, nine, eight down to seven cubits.

10. And their habitation was from the land of the children of Ammon to Mount Hermon, and the seats of their kingdom were Karnaim and Ashtaroth, and Edrei, and Misur, and Beon.

11. And Jah destroyed them because of the evil of their deeds; for they were very malignant, and the Amorites dwelt in their stead, wicked and sinful, and there is no people to-day which has wrought to the full all their sins, and they have no longer length of life on the earth.

12. And Jacob sent away Laban, and he departed into Mesopotamia, the land of the East, and Jacob returned to the land of Gilead.

13. And he passed over the Jabbok in the ninth month, on the eleventh thereof.

And on that day Esau, his brother, came to him, and he was reconciled to him, and departed from him unto the land of Seir, but Jacob dwelt in tents.

14. And in the first year of the fifth week in this jubilee [2136 A.M.] he crossed the Jordan, and dwelt beyond the Jordan, and he pastured his sheep from the sea of the heap unto Bethshan, and unto Dothan and unto the forest of Akrabbim.

15. And he sent to his father Isaac of all his substance, clothing, and food, and meat, and drink, and milk, and butter, and cheese, and some dates of the valley.

16. And to his mother Rebecca also four times a year, between the times of the months, between ploughing and reaping, and between autumn and the rain season and between winter and spring, to the tower of Abraham.

17. For Isaac had returned from the Well of the Oath and gone up to the tower of his father Abraham, and he dwelt there apart from his son Esau.

18. For in the days when Jacob went to Mesopotamia, Esau took to himself a wife Mahalath, the daughter of Ishmael, and he gathered together all the flocks of his father and his wives, and went Up and dwelt on Mount Seir, and left Isaac his father at the Well of the Oath alone.

19. And Isaac went up from the Well of the Oath and dwelt in the tower of Abraham his father on the mountains of Hebron,

20. And thither Jacob sent all that he did send to his father and his mother from time to time, all they needed, and they blessed Jacob with all their heart and with all their soul.

Jubilees 30

1. And in the first year of the sixth week [2143 A.M.] he went up to Salem, to the east of Shechem, in peace, in the fourth month.

2. And there they carried off Dinah, the daughter of Jacob, into the house of Shechem, the son of Hamor, the Hivite, the prince of the land, and he lay with her and defiled her, and she was a little girl, a child of twelve years.

3. And he besought his father and her brothers that she might be given to him to wife. And Jacob and his sons were wroth because of the men of Shechem; for they had defiled Dinah, their sister, and they spake to them with evil intent and dealt deceitfully with them and beguiled them.

4. And Simeon and Levi came unexpectedly to Shechem and executed judgment on all the men of Shechem, and slew all the men whom they found in it, and left not a single one remaining in it: they slew all in torments because they had dishonoured their sister Dinah.

5. And thus let it not again be done from henceforth that a daughter of Israel be defiled; for judgment is ordained in heaven against them that they should destroy with the sword

all the men of the Shechemites because they had wrought shame in Israel.

6. And Jah delivered them into the hands of the sons of Jacob that they might exterminate them with the sword and execute judgment upon them, and that it might not thus again be done in Israel that a virgin of Israel should be defiled.

7. And if there is any man who wishes in Israel to give his daughter or his sister to any man who is of the seed of the Gentiles he shall surely die, and they shall stone him with stones; for he hath wrought shame in Israel; and they shall burn the woman with fire, because she has dishonoured the name of the house of her father, and she shall be rooted out of Israel.

8. And let not an adulteress and no uncleanness be found in Israel throughout all the days of the generations of the earth; for Israel is holy unto Jah, and every man who has defiled it shall surely die: they shall stone him with stones.

9. For thus has it been ordained and written in the heavenly tablets regarding all the seed of Israel: he who defileth it shall surely die, and he shall be stoned with stones.

10. And to this law there is no limit of days, and no remission, nor any atonement: but the man who has defiled his daughter shall be rooted out in the midst of all Israel, because he has given of his seed to Moloch, and wrought impiously so as to defile it.

11. And do thou, Moses, command the children of Israel and exhort them not to give their daughters to the Gentiles, and not to take for their sons any of the daughters of the Gentiles, for this is abominable before Jah.

12. For this reason I have written for thee in the words of the Law all the deeds of the Shechemites, which they wrought against Dinah, and how the sons of Jacob spake, saying: 'We will not give our daughter to a man who is uncircumcised; for that were a reproach unto us.'

13. And it is a reproach to Israel, to those who live, and to those that take the daughters of the Gentiles; for this is unclean and abominable to Israel.

14. And Israel will not be free from this uncleanness if it has a wife of the daughters of the Gentiles, or has given any of its daughters to a man who is of any of the Gentiles.

15. For there will be plague upon plague, and curse upon curse, and every judgment and plague and curse will come *upon him*: if he do this thing, or hide his eyes from those who commit uncleanness, or those who defile the sanctuary of Jah, or those who profane His holy name, then will the whole nation together be judged for all the uncleanness and profanation of this man.

16. And there will be no respect of persons and no consideration of persons and no receiving at his hands of fruits and offerings and burnt-offerings and fat, nor the fragrance

of sweet savour, so as to accept it: and so fare every man or woman in Israel who defiles the sanctuary.

17. For this reason I have commanded thee, saying: 'Testify this testimony to Israel: see how the Shechemites fared and their sons: how they were delivered into the hands of two sons of Jacob, and they slew them under tortures, and it was reckoned unto them for righteousness, and it is written down to them for righteousness.

18. And the seed of Levi was chosen for the priesthood, and to be Levites, that they might minister before Jah, as we, continually, and that Levi and his sons may be blessed for ever; for he was zealous to execute righteousness and judgment and vengeance on all those who arose against Israel.

19. And so they inscribe as a testimony in his favour on the heavenly tablets blessing and righteousness before the God of all:

20. And we remember the righteousness which the man fulfilled during his life, at all periods of the year; until a thousand generations they will record it, and it will come to him and to his descendants after him, and he has been recorded on the heavenly tablets as a friend and a righteous man.

21. All this account I have written for thee, and have commanded thee to say to the children of Israel, that they should not commit sin nor transgress the ordinances nor break the covenant which has been ordained for them, but that they should fulfil it and be recorded as friends.

22. But if they transgress and work uncleanness in every way, they will be recorded on the heavenly tablets as adversaries, and they will be destroyed out of the book of life, and they will be recorded in the book of those who will be destroyed and with those who will be rooted out of the earth.

23. And on the day when the sons of Jacob slew Shechem a writing was recorded in their favour in heaven that they had executed righteousness and uprightness and vengeance on the sinners, and it was written for a blessing.

24. And they brought Dinah, their sister, out of the house of Shechem, and they took captive everything that was in Shechem, their sheep and their oxen and their asses, and all their wealth, and all their flocks, and brought them all to Jacob their father.

25. And he reproached them because they had put the city to the sword for he feared those who dwelt in the land, the Canaanites and the Perizzites.

26. And the dread of Jah was upon all the cities which are around about Shechem, and they did not rise to pursue after the sons of Jacob; for terror had fallen upon them.

Jubilees 31

1. And on the new moon of the month Jacob spake to all the people of his house. saying: 'Purify yourselves and change your garments, and let us arise and go up to Bethel, where I vowed a vow to Him on the day when I fled from the face of Esau my brother, because he has been with me and brought me into this land in peace, and put ye away the strange gods that arc among you.'

2. And they gave up the strange gods and that which was in their ears and which was on their necks and the idols which Rachel stole from Laban her father she gave wholly to Jacob. And he burnt and brake them to pieces and destroyed them, and hid them under an oak which is in the land of Shechem.

3. And he went up on the new moon of the seventh month to Bethel. And he built an altar at the place where he had slept, and he set up a pillar there, and he sent word to his father Isaac to come to him to his sacrifice, and to his mother Rebecca.

4. And Isaac said: 'Let my son Jacob come, and let me see him before I die.'

5. And Jacob went to his father Isaac and to his mother Rebecca, to the house of his father Abraham, and he took two of his sons with him, Levi and Judah, and he came to his father Isaac and to his mother Rebecca.

6. And Rebecca came forth from the tower to the front of it to kiss Jacob and embrace him; for her spirit had revived when she heard: 'Behold Jacob thy son has come'; and she kissed him.

7. And she saw his two sons, and she recognised them, and said unto him: 'Are these thy sons, my son?' and she embraced them and kissed them, and blessed them, saying: 'In you shall the seed of Abraham become illustrious, and ye shall prove a blessing on the earth.'

8. And Jacob went in to Isaac his father, to the chamber where he lay, and his two sons were with him, and he took the hand of his father, and stooping down he kissed him, and Isaac clung to the neck of Jacob his son, and wept upon his neck.

9. And the darkness left the eyes of Isaac, and he saw the two sons of Jacob, Levi, and Judah, and he said: 'Are these thy sons, my son? for they are like thee.'

10. And he said unto him that they were truly his sons: 'And thou hast truly seen that they are truly my sons'.

11. And they came near to him, and he turned and kissed them and embraced them both together.

12. And the spirit of prophecy came down into his mouth, and he took Levi by his right hand and Judah by his left.

13. And he turned to Levi first, and began to bless him first, and said unto him: May the God of all, the very Lord of all the ages, bless thee and thy children throughout all the ages.

14. And may Jah give to thee and to thy seed greatness and great glory, and cause thee and thy seed, from among all flesh, to approach Him to serve in His sanctuary as the angels of the presence and as the holy ones. Even as they, shall the seed of thy sons be for glory and greatness and holiness, and may He make them great unto all the ages.

15. And they shall be judges and princes, and chiefs of all the seed of the sons of Jacob;

They shall speak the word of Jah in righteousness,
And they shall judge all His judgments in righteousness.

And they shall declare My ways to Jacob
And My paths to Israel.

The blessing of Jah shall be given in their mouths
To bless all the seed of the beloved.

16. Thy mother has called thy name Levi,
And justly has she called thy name;

Thou shalt be joined to Jah
And be the companion of all the sons of Jacob;

Let His table be thine,
And do thou and thy sons eat thereof;

And may thy table be full unto all generations,
And thy food fail not unto all the ages.

17. And let all who hate thee fall down before thee,
And let all thy adversaries be rooted out and perish;
And blessed be he that blesses thee,
And cursed be every nation that curses thee.'

18. And to Judah he said:
'May Jah give thee strength and power

To tread down all that hate thee;
A prince shalt thou be, thou and one of thy sons, over the sons of Jacob;

May thy name and the name of thy sons go forth and traverse every land and region.
Then shall the Gentiles fear before thy face,

And all the nations shall quake
And all the peoples shall quake.

19. In thee shall be the help of Jacob,
And in thee be found the salvation of Israel.

20. And when thou sittest on the throne of honour of thy righteousness
There shall be great peace for all the seed of the sons of the beloved;

Blessed be he that blesseth thee,
And all that hate thee and afflict thee and curse thee
Shall be rooted out and destroyed from the earth and be accursed.'

21. And turning he kissed him again and embraced him, and rejoiced greatly; for he had seen the sons of Jacob his son in very truth.

22. And he went forth from between his feet and fell down and bowed down to him, and he blessed them and rested there with Isaac his father that night, and they eat and drank with joy.

23. And he made the two sons of Jacob sleep, the one on his right hand and

the other on his left, and it was counted to him for righteousness.

24. And Jacob told his father everything during the night, how Jah had shown him great mercy, and how he had prospered him in all his ways, and protected him from all evil.

25. And Isaac blessed the God of his father Abraham, who had not withdrawn his mercy and his righteousness from the sons of his servant Isaac.

26. And in the morning Jacob told his father Isaac the vow which he had vowed to Jah, and the vision which he had seen, and that he had built an altar, and that everything was ready for the sacrifice to be made before Jah as he had vowed, and that he had come to set him on an ass.

27. And Isaac said unto Jacob his son: 'I am not able to go with thee; for I am old and not able to bear the way: go, my son, in peace; for I am one hundred and sixty-five years this day; I am no longer able to journey; set thy mother on an ass and let her go with thee.

28. And I know, my son, that thou hast come on my account, and may this day be blessed on which thou hast seen me alive, and I also have seen thee, my son.

29. Mayest thou prosper and fulfil the vow which thou hast vowed; and put not off thy vow; for thou shalt be called to account as touching the vow; now therefore make haste to perform it, and may He be pleased who has made all things, to whom thou hast vowed the vow.'

30. And he said to Rebecca: 'Go with Jacob thy son'; and Rebecca went with Jacob her son, and Deborah with her, and they came to Bethel.

31. And Jacob remembered the prayer with which his father had blessed him and his two sons, Levi and Judah, and he rejoiced and blessed the God of his fathers, Abraham and Isaac.

32. And he said: 'Now I know that I have an eternal hope, and my sons also, before the God of all'; and thus is it ordained concerning the two; and they record it as an eternal testimony unto them on the heavenly tablets how Isaac blessed them.

Jubilees 32

1. And he abode that night at Bethel, and Levi dreamed that they had ordained and made him the priest of the Most High God, him and his sons for ever; and he awoke from his sleep and blessed Jah.

2. And Jacob rose early in the morning, on the fourteenth of this month, and he gave a tithe of all that came with him, both of men and cattle, both of gold and every vessel and garment, yea, he gave tithes of all.

3. And in those days Rachel became pregnant with her son Benjamin. And Jacob counted his sons from him upwards and Levi fell to the portion of Jah, and his father clothed

him in the garments of the priesthood and filled his hands.

4. And on the fifteenth of this month, he brought to the altar fourteen oxen from amongst the cattle, and twenty-eight rams, and forty-nine sheep, and seven lambs, and twenty-one kids of the goats as a burnt-offering on the altar of sacrifice, well pleasing for a sweet savour before God.

5. This was his offering, in consequence of the vow which he had vowed that he would give a tenth, with their fruit-offerings and their drink- offerings.

6. And when the fire had consumed it, he burnt incense on the fire over the fire, and for a thank-offering two oxen and four rams and four sheep, four he-goats, and two sheep of a year old, and two kids of the goats; and thus he did daily for seven days.

7. And he and all his sons and his men were eating this with joy there during seven days and blessing and thanking Jah, who had delivered him out of all his tribulation and had given him his vow.

8. And he tithed all the clean animals, and made a burnt sacrifice, but the unclean animals he gave not to Levi his son, and he gave him all the souls of the men.

9. And Levi discharged the priestly office at Bethel before Jacob his father in preference to his ten brothers, and he was a priest there, and Jacob gave his vow: thus he tithed again the tithe to Jah and sanctified it, and it became holy unto Him.

10. And for this reason it is ordained on the heavenly tablets as a law for the tithing again the tithe to eat before Jah from year to year, in the place where it is chosen that His name should dwell, and to this law there is no limit of days for ever.

11. This ordinance is written that it may be fulfilled from year to year in eating the second tithe before Jah in the place where it has been chosen, and nothing shall remain over from it from this year to the year following.

12. For in its year shall the seed be eaten till the days of the gathering of the seed of the year, and the wine till the days of the wine, and the oil till the days of its season.

13. And all that is left thereof and becomes old, let it be regarded as polluted: let it be burnt with fire, for it is unclean.

14. And thus let them eat it together in the sanctuary, and let them not suffer it to become old.

15. And all the tithes of the oxen and sheep shall be holy unto Jah, and shall belong to his priests, which they will eat before Him from year to year; for thus is it ordained and engraven regarding the tithe on the heavenly tablets.

16. And on the following night, on the twenty-second day of this month, Jacob resolved to build that place, and to surround the court with a wall, and to sanctify it and make it holy

for ever, for himself and his children after him.

17. And Jah appeared to him by night and blessed him and said unto him: 'Thy name shall not be called Jacob, but Israel shall they name thy name.'

18. And He said unto him again: 'I am Jah who created the heaven and the earth, and I will increase thee and multiply thee exceedingly, and kings shall come forth from thee, and they shall judge everywhere wherever the foot of the sons of men has trodden.

19. And I will give to thy seed all the earth which is under heaven, and they shall judge all the nations according to their desires, and after that they shall get possession of the whole earth and inherit it for ever.'

20. And He finished speaking with him, and He went up from him. and Jacob looked till He had ascended into heaven.

21. And he saw in a vision of the night, and behold an angel descended from heaven with seven tablets in his hands, and he gave them to Jacob, and he read them and knew all that was written therein which would befall him and his sons throughout all the ages.

22. And he showed him all that was written on the tablets, and said unto him: 'Do not build this place, and do not make it an eternal sanctuary, and do not dwell here; for this is not the place. Go to the house of Abraham thy father and dwell with Isaac thy father until the day of the death of thy father.

23. For in Egypt thou shalt die in peace, and in this land thou shalt be buried with honour in the sepulchre of thy fathers, with Abraham and Isaac.

24. Fear not, for as thou hast seen and read it, thus shall it all be; and do thou write down everything as thou hast seen and read.'

25. And Jacob said: 'Lord, how can I remember all that I have read and seen?' And he said unto him: 'I will bring all things to thy remembrance.'

26. And he went up from him, and he awoke from his sleep, and he remembered everything which he had read and seen, and he wrote down all the words which he had read and seen.

27. And he celebrated there yet another day, and he sacrificed thereon according to all that he sacrificed on the former days, and called its name 'Addition,' for this day was added and the former days he called 'The Feast'.

28. And thus it was manifested that it should be, and it is written on the heavenly tablets: wherefore it was revealed to him that he should celebrate it, and add it to the seven days of the feast.

29. And its name was called 'Addition,' because that it was recorded amongst the days of the feast days, according to the number of the days of the year.

30. And in the night, on the twenty-third of this month, Deborah Rebecca's nurse died, and they buried her beneath the city under the oak of the

river, and he called the name of this place, 'The river of Deborah,' and the oak, 'The oak of the mourning of Deborah.'

31. And Rebecca went and returned to her house to his father Isaac, and Jacob sent by her hand rams and sheep and he-goats that she should prepare a meal for his father such as he desired.

32. And he went after his mother till he came to the land of Kabratan, and he dwelt there.

33. And Rachel bare a son in the night, and called his name 'Son of my sorrow '; for she suffered in giving him birth: but his father called his name Benjamin, on the eleventh of the eighth month in the first of the sixth week of this jubilee. [2143 A.M.]

34. And Rachel died there and she was buried in the land of Ephrath, the same is Bethlehem, and Jacob built a pillar on the grave of Rachel, on the road above her grave.

Jubilees 33

1. And Jacob went and dwelt to the south of Magdaladra'ef. And he went to his father Isaac, he and Leah his wife, on the new moon of the tenth month.

2. And Reuben saw Bilhah, Rachel's maid, the concubine of his father, bathing in water in a secret place, and he loved her.

3. And he hid himself at night, and he entered the house of Bilhah [at night], and he found her sleeping alone on a bed in her house.

4. And he lay with her, and she awoke and saw, and behold Reuben was lying with her in the bed, and she uncovered the border of her covering and seized him, and cried out, and discovered that it was Reuben.

5. And she was ashamed because of him, and released her hand from him, and he fled.

6. And she lamented because of this thing exceedingly, and did not tell it to any one.

7. And when Jacob returned and sought her, she said unto him: 'I am not clean for thee, for I have been defiled as regards thee; for Reuben has defiled me, and has lain with me in the night, and I was asleep, and did not discover until he uncovered my skirt and slept with me.'

8. And Jacob was exceedingly wroth with Reuben because he had lain with Bilhah, because he had uncovered his father's skirt.

9. And Jacob did not approach her again because Reuben had defiled her. And as for any man who uncovers his father's skirt his deed is wicked exceedingly, for he is abominable before Jah.

10. For this reason it is written and ordained on the heavenly tablets that a man should not lie with his father's wife, and should not uncover his father's skirt, for this is unclean: they

shall surely die together, the man who lies with his father's wife and the woman also, for they have wrought uncleanness on the earth.

11. And there shall be nothing unclean before our God in the nation which He has chosen for Himself as a possession.

12. And again, it is written a second time: 'Cursed be he who lieth with the wife of his father, for he hath uncovered his father's shame'; and all the holy ones of Jah said 'So be it; so be it.'

13. And do thou, Moses, command the children of Israel that they observe this word; for it entails a punishment of death; and it is unclean, and there is no atonement for ever to atone for the man who has committed this, but he is to be put to death and slain, and stoned with stones, and rooted out from the midst of the people of our God.

14. For to no man who does so in Israel is it permitted to remain alive a single day on the earth, for he is abominable and unclean.

15. And let them not say: to Reuben was granted life and forgiveness after he had lain with his father's concubine, and to her also though she had a husband, and her husband Jacob, his father, was still alive.

16. For until that time there had not been revealed the ordinance and judgment and law in its completeness for all, but in thy days it has been revealed as a law of seasons and of days, and an everlasting law for the everlasting generations.

17. And for this law there is no consummation of days, and no atonement for it, but they must both be rooted out in the midst of the nation: on the day whereon they committed it they shall slay them.

18. And do thou, Moses, write it down for Israel that they may observe it, and do according to these words, and not commit a sin unto death; for Jah our God is judge, who respects not persons and accepts not gifts.

19. And tell them these words of the covenant, that they may hear and observe, and be on their guard with respect to them, and not be destroyed and rooted out of the land; for an uncleanness, and an abomination, and a contamination, and a pollution are all they who commit it on the earth before our God.

20. And there is no greater sin than the fornication which they commit on earth; for Israel is a holy nation unto Jah its God, and a nation of inheritance, and a priestly and royal nation and for His own possession; and there shall no such uncleanness appear in the midst of the holy nation.

21. And in the third year of this sixth week [2145 A.M.] Jacob and all his sons went and dwelt in the house of Abraham, near Isaac his father and Rebecca his mother.

22. And these were the names of the sons of Jacob: the first-born Reuben, Simeon, Levi, Judah, Issachar,

Zebulon, the sons of Leah; and the sons of Rachel, Joseph and Benjamin; and the sons of Bilhah, Dan and Naphtali; and the sons of Zilpah, Gad and Asher; and Dinah, the daughter of Leah, the only daughter of Jacob.

23. And they came and bowed themselves to Isaac and Rebecca, and when they saw them they blessed Jacob and all his sons, and Isaac rejoiced exceedingly, for he saw the sons of Jacob, his younger son and he blessed them.

Jubilees 34

1. And in the sixth year of this week of this forty-fourth jubilee [2148 A.M.] Jacob sent his sons to pasture their sheep, and his servants with them to the pastures of Shechem.

2. And the seven kings of the Amorites assembled themselves together against them, to slay them, hiding themselves under the trees, and to take their cattle as a prey.

3. And Jacob and Levi and Judah and Joseph were in the house with Isaac their father; for his spirit was sorrowful, and they could not leave him: and Benjamin was the youngest, and for this reason remained with his father.

4. And there came the king[s] of Taphu and the king[s] of 'Aresa, and the king[s] of Seragan, and the king[s] of Selo, and the king[s] of Ga'as, and the king of Bethoron, and the king of Ma'anisakir, and all those who dwell in these mountains and who dwell in the woods in the land of Canaan.

5. And they announced this to Jacob saying: 'Behold, the kings of the Amorites have surrounded thy sons, and plundered their herds.'

6. And he arose from his house, he and his three sons and all the servants of his father, and his own servants, and he went against them with six thousand men, who carried swords.

7. And he slew them in the pastures of Shechem, and pursued those who fled, and he slew them with the edge of the sword, and he slew 'Aresa and Taphu and Saregan and Selo and 'Amani- sakir and Ga[ga]'as, and he recovered his herds.

8. And he prevailed over them, and imposed tribute on them that they should pay him tribute, five fruit products of their land, and he built Robel and Tamnatares.

9. And he returned in peace, and made peace with them, and they became his servants, until the day that he and his sons went down into Egypt.

10. And in the seventh year of this week [2149 A.M.] he sent Joseph to learn about the welfare of his brothers from his house to the land of Shechem, and he found them in the land of Dothan.

11. And they dealt treacherously with him, and formed a plot against him to slay him, but changing their minds, they sold him to Ishmaelite merchants, and they brought him down into Egypt, and they sold him

to Potiphar, the eunuch of Pharaoh, the chief of the cooks, priest of the city of 'Elew.

12. And the sons of Jacob slaughtered a kid, and dipped the coat of Joseph in the blood, and sent it to Jacob their father on the tenth of the seventh month.

13. And he mourned all that night, for they had brought it to him in the evening, and he became feverish with mourning for his death, and he said: 'An evil beast hath devoured Joseph'; and all the members of his house mourned with him that day, and they were grieving and mourning with him all that day.

14. And his sons and his daughter rose up to comfort him, but he refused to be comforted for his son.

15. And on that day Bilhah heard that Joseph had perished, and she died mourning him, and she was living in Qafratef, and Dinah also, his daughter, died after Joseph had perished.

16. And there came these three mournings upon Israel in one month. And they buried Bilhah over against the tomb of Rachel, and Dinah also. his daughter, they buried there.

17. And he mourned for Joseph one year, and did not cease, for he said 'Let me go down to the grave mourning for my son'.

18. For this reason it is ordained for the children of Israel that they should afflict themselves on the tenth of the seventh month -on the day that the news which made him weep for Joseph came to Jacob his father- that they should make atonement for themselves thereon with a young goat on the tenth of the seventh month, once a year, for their sins; for they had grieved the affection of their father regarding Joseph his son.

19. And this day has been ordained that they should grieve thereon for their sins, and for all their transgressions and for all their errors, so that they might cleanse themselves on that day once a year.

20. And after Joseph perished, the sons of Jacob took unto themselves wives. The name of Reuben's wife is 'Ada; and the name of Simeon's wife is 'Adlba'a, a Canaanite; and the name of Levi's wife is Melka, of the daughters of Aram, of the seed of the sons of Terah; and the name of Judah's wife, Betasu'el, a Canaanite; and the name of Issachar's wife, Hezaqa: and the name of Zabulon's wife, Ni'iman; and the name of Dan's wife, 'Egla; and the name of Naphtali's wife, Rasu'u, of Mesopotamia; and the name of Gad's wife, Maka; and the name of Asher's wife, 'Ijona; and the name of Joseph's wife, Asenath, the Egyptian; and the name of Benjamin's wife, 'Ijasaka.

21. And Simeon repented, and took a second wife from Mesopotamia as his brothers.

Jubilees 35

1. And in the first year of the first week of the forty-fifth jubilee [2157 A.M.]

Rebecca called Jacob, her son, and commanded him regarding his father and regarding his brother, that he should honour them all the days of his life.

2. And Jacob said: 'I will do everything as thou hast commanded me; for this thing will be honour and greatness to me, and righteousness before Jah, that I should honour them.

3. And thou too, mother, knowest from the time I was born until this day, all my deeds and all that is in my heart, that I always think good concerning all.

4. And how should I not do this thing which thou hast commanded me, that I should honour my father and my brother!

5. Tell me, mother, what perversity hast thou seen in me and I shall turn away from it, and mercy will be upon me.'

6. And she said unto him: 'My son, I have not seen in thee all my days any perverse but only upright deeds. And yet I will tell thee the truth, my son: I shall die this year, and I shall not survive this year in my life; for I have seen in a dream the day of my death, that I should not live beyond a hundred and fifty-five years: and behold I have completed all the days of my life which I am to live.'

7. And Jacob laughed at the words of his mother. because his mother had said unto him that she should die; and she was sitting opposite to him in possession of her strength, and she was not infirm in her strength; for she went in and out and saw, and her teeth were strong, and no ailment had touched her all the days of her life.

8. And Jacob said unto her: 'Blessed am I, mother, if my days approach the days of thy life, and my strength remain with me thus as thy strength: and thou wilt not die, for thou art jesting idly with me regarding thy death.'

9. And she went in to Isaac and said unto him: 'One petition I make unto thee: make Esau swear that he will not injure Jacob, nor pursue him with enmity; for thou knowest Esau's thoughts that they are perverse from his youth, and there is no goodness in him; for he desires after thy death to kill him.

10. And thou knowest all that he has done since the day Jacob his brother went to Haran until this day: how he has forsaken us with his whole heart, and has done evil to us; thy flocks he has taken to himself, and carried off all thy possessions from before thy face.

11. And when we implored and besought him for what was our own, he did as a man who was taking pity on us.

12. And he is bitter against thee because thou didst bless Jacob thy perfect and upright son; for there is no evil but only goodness in him, and since he came from Haran unto this day he has not robbed us of aught, for he brings us everything in its season always, and rejoices with all his heart when we take at his hands and he blesses us, and has not parted

from us since he came from Haran until this day, and he remains with us continually at home honouring us.'

13. And Isaac said unto her: 'I, too, know and see the deeds of Jacob who is with us, how that with all his heart he honours us; but I loved Esau formerly more than Jacob, because he was the firstborn; but now I love Jacob more than Esau, for he has done manifold evil deeds, and there is no righteousness in him, for all his ways are unrighteousness and violence, [and there is no righteousness around him.]

14. And now my heart is troubled because of all his deeds, and neither he nor his seed is to be saved, for they are those who will be destroyed from the earth and who will be rooted out from under heaven, for he has forsaken the God of Abraham and gone after his wives and after their uncleanness and after their error, he and his children.

15. And thou dost bid me make him swear that he will not slay Jacob his brother; even if he swear he will not abide by his oath, and he will not do good but evil only.

16. But if he desires to slay Jacob, his brother, into Jacob's hands will he be given, and he will not escape from his hands, for he will descend into his hands.

17. And fear thou not on account of Jacob; for the guardian of Jacob is great and powerful and honoured, and praised more than the guardian of Esau.'

18. And Rebecca sent and called Esau and he came to her, and she said unto him: 'I have a petition, my son, to make unto thee, and do thou promise to do it, my son.'

19. And he said: 'I will do everything that thou sayest unto me, and I will not refuse thy petition.'

20. And she said unto him: 'I ask you that the day I die, thou wilt take me in and bury me near Sarah, thy father's mother, and that thou and Jacob will love each other and that neither will desire evil against the other, but mutual love only, and so ye will prosper, my sons, and be honoured in the midst of the land, and no enemy will rejoice over you, and ye will be a blessing and a mercy in the eyes of all those that love you.'

21. And he said: 'I will do all that thou hast told me, and I shall bury thee on the day thou diest near Sarah, my father's mother, as thou hast desired that her bones may be near thy bones.

22. And Jacob, my brother, also, I shall love above all flesh; for I have not a brother in all the earth but him only: and this is no great merit for me if I love him; for he is my brother, and we were sown together in thy body, and together came we forth from thy womb, and if I do not love my brother, whom shall I love?

23. And I, myself, beg thee to exhort Jacob concerning me and concerning my sons, for I know that he will assuredly be king over me and my sons, for on the day my father

blessed him he made him the higher and me the lower.

24. And I swear unto thee that I shall love him, and not desire evil against him all the days of my life but good only.'

25. And he sware unto her regarding all this matter. And she called Jacob before the eyes of Esau, and gave him commandment according to the words which she had spoken to Esau.

26. And he said: 'I shall do thy pleasure; believe me that no evil will proceed from me or from my sons against Esau, and I shall be first in naught save in love only.'

27. And they eat and drank, she and her sons that night, and she died, three jubilees and one week and one year old, on that night, and her two sons, Esau and Jacob, buried her in the double cave near Sarah, their father's mother.

Jubilees 36

1. And in the sixth year of this week [2162 A.M.] Isaac called his two sons Esau and Jacob, and they came to him, and he said unto them: 'My sons, I am going the way of my fathers, to the eternal house where my fathers are.

2. Wherefore bury me near Abraham my father, in the double cave in the field of Ephron the Hittite, where Abraham purchased a sepulchre to bury in; in the sepulchre which I digged for myself, there bury me.

3. And this I command you, my sons, that ye practise righteousness and uprightness on the earth, so that Jah may bring upon you all that Jah said that he would do to Abraham and to his seed.

4. And love one another, my sons, your brothers as a man who loves his own soul, and let each seek in what he may benefit his brother, and act together on the earth; and let them love each other as their own souls.

5. And concerning the question of idols, I command and admonish you to reject them and hate them, and love them not, for they are full of deception for those that worship them and for those that bow down to them.

6. Remember ye, my sons, Jah God of Abraham your father, and how I too worshipped Him and served Him in righteousness and in joy, that He might multiply you and increase your seed as the stars of heaven in multitude, and establish you on the earth as the plant of righteousness which will not be rooted out unto all the generations for ever.

7. And now I shall make you swear a great oath -for there is no oath which is greater than it by the name glorious and honoured and great and splendid and wonderful and mighty, which created the heavens and the earth and all things together- that ye will fear Him and worship Him.

8. And that each will love his brother with affection and righteousness, and that neither will desire evil against

his brother from henceforth for ever all the days of your life so that ye may prosper in all your deeds and not be destroyed.

9. And if either of you devises evil against his brother, know that from henceforth everyone that devises evil against his brother shall fall into his hand, and shall be rooted out of the land of the living, and his seed shall be destroyed from under heaven.

10. But on the day of turbulence and execration and indignation and anger, with flaming devouring fire as He burnt Sodom, so likewise will He burn his land and his city and all that is his, and he shall be blotted out of the book of the discipline of the children of men, and not be recorded in the book of life, but in that which is appointed to destruction, and he shall depart into eternal execration; so that their condemnation may be always renewed in hate and in execration and in wrath and in torment and in indignation and in plagues and in disease for ever.

11. I say and testify to you, my sons, according to the judgment which shall come upon the man who wishes to injure his brother.

12. And he divided all his possessions between the two on that day and he gave the larger portion to him that was the first-born, and the tower and all that was about it, and all that Abraham possessed at the Well of the Oath.

13. And he said: 'This larger portion I will give to the firstborn.'

14. And Esau said, 'I have sold to Jacob and given my birthright to Jacob; to him let it be given, and I have not a single word to say regarding it, for it is his.'

15. And Isaac said, May a blessing rest upon you, my sons, and upon your seed this day, for ye have given me rest, and my heart is not pained concerning the birthright, lest thou shouldest work wickedness on account of it.

16. May the Most High God bless the man that worketh righteousness, him and his seed for ever.'

17. And he ended commanding them and blessing them, and they eat and drank together before him, and he rejoiced because there was one mind between them, and they went forth from him and rested that day and slept.

18. And Isaac slept on his bed that day rejoicing; and he slept the eternal sleep, and died one hundred and eighty years old. He completed twenty-five weeks and five years; and his two sons Esau and Jacob buried him.

19. And Esau went to the land of Edom, to the mountains of Seir, and dwelt there.

20. And Jacob dwelt in the mountains of Hebron, in the tower of the land of the sojournings of his father Abraham, and he worshipped Jah with all his heart and according to the visible commands according as He had divided the days of his generations.

21. And Leah his wife died in the fourth year of the second week of the forty-fifth jubilee, [2167 A.M.] and he buried her in the double cave near Rebecca his mother to the left of the grave of Sarah, his father's mother

22. and all her sons and his sons came to mourn over Leah his wife with him and to comfort him regarding her, for he was lamenting her for he loved her exceedingly after Rachel her sister died;

23. for she was perfect and upright in all her ways and honoured Jacob, and all the days that she lived with him he did not hear from her mouth a harsh word, for she was gentle and peaceable and upright and honourable.

24. And he remembered all her deeds which she had done during her life and he lamented her exceedingly; for he loved her with all his heart and with all his soul.

Jubilees 37

1. And on the day that Isaac the father of Jacob and Esau died, [2162 A.M.] the sons of Esau heard that Isaac had given the portion of the elder to his younger son Jacob and they were very angry.

2. And they strove with their father, saying 'Why has thy father given Jacob the portion of the elder and passed over thee, although thou art the elder and Jacob the younger?'

3. And he said unto them 'Because I sold my birthright to Jacob for a small mess of lentils, and on the day my father sent me to hunt and catch and bring him something that he should eat and bless me, he came with guile and brought my father food and drink, and my father blessed him and put me under his hand.

4. And now our father has caused us to swear, me and him, that we shall not mutually devise evil, either against his brother, and that we shall continue in love and in peace each with his brother and not make our ways corrupt.'

5. And they said unto him, 'We shall not hearken unto thee to make peace with him; for our strength is greater than his strength, and we are more powerful than he; we shall go against him and slay him, and destroy him and his sons. And if thou wilt not go with us, we shall do hurt to thee also.

6. And now hearken unto us: Let us send to Aram and Philistia and Moab and Ammon, and let us choose for ourselves chosen men who are ardent for battle, and let us go against him and do battle with him, and let us exterminate him from the earth before he grows strong.'

7. And their father said unto them, 'Do not go and do not make war with him lest ye fall before him.'

8. And they said unto him, 'This too, is exactly thy mode of action from thy youth until this day, and thou art putting thy neck under his yoke.

9. We shall not hearken to these words.' And they sent to Aram, and to

'Aduram to the friend of their father, and they hired along with them one thousand fighting men, chosen men of war.

10. And there came to them from Moab and from the children of Ammon, those who were hired, one thousand chosen men, and from Philistia, one thousand chosen men of war, and from Edom and from the Horites one thousand chosen fighting men, and from the Kittim mighty men of war.

11. And they said unto their father: Go forth with them and lead them, else we shall slay thee.'

12. And he was filled with wrath and indignation on seeing that his sons were forcing him to go before them to lead them against Jacob his brother.

13. But afterward he remembered all the evil which lay hidden in his heart against Jacob his brother; and he remembered not the oath which he had sworn to his father and to his mother that he would devise no evil all his days against Jacob his brother.

14. And notwithstanding all this, Jacob knew not that they were coming against him to battle, and he was mourning for Leah, his wife, until they approached very near to the tower with four thousand warriors and chosen men of war.

15. And the men of Hebron sent to him saying, 'Behold thy brother has come against thee, to fight thee, with four thousand girt with the sword, and they carry shields and weapons'; for they loved Jacob more than Esau. So they told him; for Jacob was a more liberal and merciful man than Esau.

16. But Jacob would not believe until they came very near to the tower.

17. And he closed the gates of the tower; and he stood on the battlements and spake to his brother Esau and said, 'Noble is the comfort wherewith thou hast come to comfort me for my wife who has died. Is this the oath that thou didst swear to thy father and again to thy mother before they died? Thou hast broken the oath, and on the moment that thou didst swear to thy father wast thou condemned.'

18. And then Esau answered and said unto him, 'Neither the children of men nor the beasts of the earth have any oath of righteousness which in swearing they have sworn an oath valid for ever; but every day they devise evil one against another, and how each may slay his adversary and foe.

19. And thou dost hate me and my children for ever. And there is no observing the tie of brotherhood with thee.

20. Hear these words which I declare unto thee,

If the boar can change its skin and make its bristles as soft as wool,
Or if it can cause horns to sprout forth on its head like the horns of a stag or of a sheep,
Then will I observe the tie of brotherhood with thee
And if the breasts separated themselves from their mother, for thou hast not been a brother to me.

21. And if the wolves make peace with the lambs so as not to devour or do them violence,
And if their hearts are towards them for good,
Then there shall be peace in my heart towards thee

22. And if the lion becomes the friend of the ox and makes peace with him
And if he is bound under one yoke with him and ploughs with him,
Then will I make peace with thee.

23. And when the raven becomes white as the raza,
Then know that I have loved thee
And shall make peace with thee
Thou shalt be rooted out,
And thy sons shall be rooted out,
And there shall be no peace for thee'

24. And when Jacob saw that he was so evilly disposed towards him with his heart, and with all his soul as to slay him, and that he had come springing like the wild boar which comes upon the spear that pierces and kills it, and recoils not from it;

25. then he spake to his own and to his servants that they should attack him and all his companions.

Jubilees 38

1. And after that Judah spake to Jacob, his father, and said unto him: 'Bend thy bow, father, and send forth thy arrows and cast down the adversary and slay the enemy; and mayst thou have the power, for we shall not slay thy brother, for he is such as thou, and he is like thee let us give him this honour.'

2. Then Jacob bent his bow and sent forth the arrow and struck Esau, his brother on his right breast and slew him.

3. And again he sent forth an arrow and struck 'Adoran the Aramaean, on the left breast, and drove him backward and slew him.

4. And then went forth the sons of Jacob, they and their servants, dividing themselves into companies on the four sides of the tower.

5. And Judah went forth in front, and Naphtali and Gad with him and fifty servants with him on the south side of the tower, and they slew all they found before them, and not one individual of them escaped.

6. And Levi and Dan and Asher went forth on the east side of the tower, and fifty men with them, and they slew the fighting men of Moab and Ammon.

7. And Reuben and Issachar and Zebulon went forth on the north side of the tower, and fifty men with them, and they slew the fighting men of the Philistines.

8. And Simeon and Benjamin and Enoch, Reuben's son, went forth on the west side of the tower, and fifty men with them, and they slew of Edom and of the Horites four hundred men, stout warriors; and six hundred fled, and four of the sons of Esau fled with them, and left their

father lying slain, as he had fallen on the hill which is in 'Aduram.

9. And the sons of Jacob pursued after them to the mountains of Seir. And Jacob buried his brother on the hill which is in 'Aduram, and he returned to his house.

10. And the sons of Jacob pressed hard upon the sons of Esau in the mountains of Seir, and bowed their necks so that they became servants of the sons of Jacob.

11. And they sent to their father to inquire whether they should make peace with them or slay them.

12. And Jacob sent word to his sons that they should make peace, and they made peace with them, and placed the yoke of servitude upon them, so that they paid tribute to Jacob and to his sons always.

13. And they continued to pay tribute to Jacob until the day that he went down into Egypt.

14. And the sons of Edom have not got quit of the yoke of servitude which the twelve sons of Jacob had imposed on them until this day.

15. And these are the kings that reigned in Edom before there reigned any king over the children of Israel until this day in the land of Edom.

16. And Balaq, the son of Beor, reigned in Edom, and the name of his city was Danaba.

17. And Balaq died, and Jobab, the son of Zara of Boser, reigned in his stead.

18. And Jobab died, and 'Asam, of the land of Teman, reigned in his stead.

19. And 'Asam died, and 'Adath, the son of Barad, who slew Midian in the field of Moab, reigned in his stead, and the name of his city was Avith.

20. And 'Adath died, and Salman, from 'Amaseqa, reigned in his stead.

21. And Salman died, and Saul of Ra'aboth by the river, reigned in his stead.

22. And Saul died, and Ba'elunan, the son of Achbor, reigned in his stead.

23. And Ba'elunan, the son of Achbor died, and 'Adath reigned in his stead, and the name of his wife was Maitabith, the daughter of Matarat, the daughter of Metabedza'ab.

24. These are the kings who reigned in the land of Edom.

Jubilees 39

1. And Jacob dwelt in the land of his father's sojournings in the land of Canaan. These are the generations of Jacob.

2. And Joseph was seventeen years old when they took him down into the land of Egypt, and Potiphar, an eunuch of Pharaoh, the chief cook bought him.

3. And he set Joseph over all his house and the blessing of Jah came upon the house of the Egyptian on account of Joseph, and Jah prospered him in all that he did.

4. And the Egyptian committed everything into the hands of Joseph; for he saw that Jah was with him, and that Jah prospered him in all that he did.

5. And Joseph's appearance was comely and very beautiful was his appearance, and his master's wife lifted up her eyes and saw Joseph, and she loved him and besought him to lie with her.

6. But he did not surrender his soul, and he remembered Jah and the words which Jacob, his father, used to read from amongst the words of Abraham, that no man should commit fornication with a woman who has a husband; that for him the punishment of death has been ordained in the heavens before the Most High God, and the sin will be recorded against him in the eternal books continually before Jah.

7. And Joseph remembered these words and refused to lie with her.

8. And she besought him for a year, but he refused and would not listen.

9. But she embraced him and held him fast in the house in order to force him to lie with her, and closed the doors of the house and held him fast; but he left his garment in her hands and broke through the door and fled without from her presence.

10. And the woman saw that he would not lie with her, and she calumniated him in the presence of his lord, saying 'Thy Hebrew servant, whom thou lovest, sought to force me so that he might lie with me; and it came to pass when I lifted up my voice that he fled and left his garment in my hands when I held him, and he brake through the door.'

11. And the Egyptian saw the garment of Joseph and the broken door, and heard the words of his wife, and cast Joseph into prison into the place where the prisoners were kept whom the king imprisoned.

12. And he was there in the prison; and Jah gave Joseph favour in the sight of the chief of the prison guards and compassion before him, for he saw that Jah was with him, and that Jah made all that he did to prosper.

13. And he committed all things into his hands, and the chief of the prison guards knew of nothing that was with him, for Joseph did every thing, and Jah perfected it.

14. And he remained there two years. And in those days Pharaoh, king of Egypt was wroth against his two eunuchs, against the chief butler, and against the chief baker, and he put them in ward in the house of the chief cook, in the prison where Joseph was kept.

15. And the chief of the prison guards appointed Joseph to serve them; and he served before them.

16. And they both dreamed a dream, the chief butler and the chief baker, and they told it to Joseph.

17. And as he interpreted to them so it befell them, and Pharaoh restored the chief butler to his office and the

chief baker he slew, as Joseph had interpreted to them.

18. But the chief butler forgot Joseph in the prison, although he had informed him what would befall him, and did not remember to inform Pharaoh how Joseph had told him, for he forgot.

Jubilees 40

1. And in those days Pharaoh dreamed two dreams in one night concerning a famine which was to be in all the land, and he awoke from his sleep and called all the interpreters of dreams that were in Egypt, and magicians, and told them his two dreams, and they were not able to declare them.

2. And then the chief butler remembered Joseph and spake of him to the king, and he brought him forth from the prison, and he told his two dreams before him.

3. And he said before Pharaoh that his two dreams were one, and he said unto him: 'Seven years shall come in which there shall be plenty over all the land of Egypt, and after that seven years of famine, such a famine as has not been in all the land.

4. And now let Pharaoh appoint overseers in all the land of Egypt, and let them store up food in every city throughout the days of the years of plenty, and there will be food for the seven years of famine, and the land will not perish through the famine, for it will be very severe.'

5. And Jah gave Joseph favour and mercy in the eyes of Pharaoh, and Pharaoh said unto his servants. We shall not find such a wise and discreet man as this man, for the spirit of Jah is with him.'

6. And he appointed him the second in all his kingdom and gave him authority over all Egypt, and caused him to ride in the second chariot of Pharaoh.

7. And he clothed him with byssus garments, and he put a gold chain upon his neck, and a herald proclaimed before him ' 'El 'El wa 'Abirer,' and placed a ring on his hand and made him ruler over all his house, and magnified him, and said unto him. 'Only on the throne shall I be greater than thou.'

8. And Joseph ruled over all the land of Egypt, and all the princes of Pharaoh, and all his servants, and all who did the king's business loved him, for he walked in uprightness, for he was without pride and arrogance, and he had no respect of persons, and did not accept gifts, but he judged in uprightness all the people of the land.

9. And the land of Egypt was at peace before Pharaoh because of Joseph, for Jah was with him, and gave him favour and mercy for all his generations before all those who knew him and those who heard concerning him, and Pharaoh's kingdom was well ordered, and there was no Satan and no evil person therein.

10. And the king called Joseph's name Sephantiphans, and gave Joseph to wife the daughter of Potiphar, the daughter of the priest of Heliopolis, the chief cook.

11. And on the day that Joseph stood before Pharaoh he was thirty years old when he stood before Pharaoh.

12. And in that year Isaac died. And it came to pass as Joseph had said in the interpretation of his two dreams, according as he had said it, there were seven years of plenty over all the land of Egypt, and the land of Egypt abundantly produced, one measure producing eighteen hundred measures.

13. And Joseph gathered food into every city until they were full of corn until they could no longer count and measure it for its multitude.

Jubilees 41

1. And in the forty-fifth jubilee, in the second week, and in the second year, [2165 A.M.] Judah took for his first-born Er, a wife from the daughters of Aram, named Tamar.

2. But he hated, and did not lie with her, because his mother was of the daughters of Canaan, and he wished to take him a wife of the kinsfolk of his mother, but Judah, his father, would not permit him.

3. And this Er, the first-born of Judah, was wicked, and Jah slew him.

4. And Judah said unto Onan, his brother 'Go in unto thy brother's wife and perform the duty of a husband's brother unto her, and raise up seed unto thy brother.'

5. And Onan knew that the seed would not be his, but his brother's only, and he went into the house of his brother's wife, and spilt the seed on the ground, and he was wicked in the eyes of Jah, and He slew him.

6. And Judah said unto Tamar, his daughter-in-law: 'Remain in thy father's house as a widow till Shelah my son be grown up, and I shall give thee to him to wife.'

7. And he grew up; but Bedsu'el, the wife of Judah, did not permit her son Shelah to marry. And Bedsu'el, the wife of Judah, died [2168 A.M.] in the fifth year of this week.

8. And in the sixth year Judah went up to shear his sheep at Timnah. [2169 A.M.] And they told Tamar: 'Behold thy father-in-law goeth up to Timnah to shear his sheep.'

9. And she put off her widow's clothes, and put on a veil, and adorned herself, and sat in the gate adjoining the way to Timnah.

10. And as Judah was going along he found her, and thought her to be an harlot, and he said unto her: 'Let me come in unto thee'; and she said unto him Come in,' and he went in.

11. And she said unto him: 'Give me my hire'; and he said unto her: 'I have nothing in my hand save my ring that is on my finger, and my necklace, and my staff which is in my hand.'

12. And she said unto him 'Give them to me until thou dost send me my hire', and he said unto her: 'I will send unto thee a kid of the goats'; and he gave them to her, and he went in unto her, and she conceived by him.

13. And Judah went unto his sheep, and she went to her father's house.

14. And Judah sent a kid of the goats by the hand of his shepherd, an Adullamite, and he found her not; and he asked the people of the place, saying: 'Where is the harlot who was here?' And they said unto him; 'There is no harlot here with us.'

15. And he returned and informed him, and said unto him that he had not found her: 'I asked the people of the place, and they said unto me: "There is no harlot here." '

16. And he said: 'Let her keep them lest we become a cause of derision.' And when she had completed three months, it was manifest that she was with child, and they told Judah, saying: 'Behold Tamar, thy daughter-in-law, is with child by whoredom.'

17. And Judah went to the house of her father, and said unto her father and her brothers: 'Bring her forth, and let them burn her, for she hath wrought uncleanness in Israel.'

18. And it came to pass when they brought her forth to burn her that she sent to her father-in-law the ring and the necklace, and the staff, saying: 'Discern whose are these, for by him am I with child.'

19. And Judah acknowledged, and said: 'Tamar is more righteous than I am.

20. And therefore let them burn her not' And for that reason she was not given to Shelah, and he did not again approach her.

21. And after that she bare two sons, Perez [2170 A.M.] and Zerah, in the seventh year of this second week.

22. And thereupon the seven years of fruitfulness were accomplished, of which Joseph spake to Pharaoh.

23. And Judah acknowledged that the deed which he had done was evil, for he had lain with his daughter-in-law, and he esteemed it hateful in his eyes, and he acknowledged that he had transgressed and gone astray, for he had uncovered the skirt of his son, and he began to lament and to supplicate before Jah because of his transgression.

24. And we told him in a dream that it was forgiven him because he supplicated earnestly, and lamented, and did not again commit it.

25. And he received forgiveness because he turned from his sin and from his ignorance, for he transgressed greatly before our God; and every one that acts thus, every one who lies with his mother-in-law, let them burn him with fire that he may burn therein, for there is uncleanness and pollution upon them, with fire let them burn them.

26. And do thou command the children of Israel that there be no uncleanness amongst them, for every one who

lies with his daughter-in-law or with his mother-in-law hath wrought uncleanness; with fire let them burn the man who has lain with her, and likewise the woman, and He will turn away wrath and punishment from Israel.

27. And unto Judah we said that his two sons had not lain with her, and for this reason his seed was stablished for a second generation, and would not be rooted out.

28. For in singleness of eye he had gone and sought for punishment, namely, according to the judgment of Abraham, which he had commanded his sons, Judah had sought to burn her with fire.

Jubilees 42

1. And in the first year of the third week of the forty-fifth jubilee the famine began to come into the [2171 A.M.] land, and the rain refused to be given to the earth, for none whatever fell.

2. And the earth grew barren, but in the land of Egypt there was food, for Joseph had gathered the seed of the land in the seven years of plenty and had preserved it.

3. And the Egyptians came to Joseph that he might give them food, and he opened the store-houses where was the grain of the first year, and he sold it to the people of the land for gold.

4. Now the famine was very sore in the land of Canaan, and Jacob heard that there was food in Egypt, and he sent his ten sons that they should procure food for him in Egypt; but Benjamin he did not send, and the ten sons of Jacob arrived in Egypt among those that went there.

5. And Joseph recognised them, but they did not recognise him, and he spake unto them and questioned them, and he said unto them; 'Are ye not spies and have ye not come to explore the approaches of the land?' And he put them in ward.

6. And after that he set them free again, and detained Simeon alone and sent off his nine brothers.

7. And he filled their sacks with corn, and he put their gold in their sacks, and they did not know.

8. And he commanded them to bring their younger brother, for they had told him their father was living and their younger brother.

9. And they went up from the land of Egypt and they came to the land of Canaan; and they told their father all that had befallen them, and how Jah of the country had spoken roughly to them, and had seized Simeon till they should bring Benjamin.

10. And Jacob said: 'Me have ye bereaved of my children! Joseph is not and Simeon also is not, and ye will take Benjamin away. On me has your wickedness come.

11. 'And he said: 'My son will not go down with you lest perchance he fall sick; for their mother gave birth to two sons, and one has perished, and this one also ye will take from me. If

perchance he took a fever on the road, ye would bring down my old age with sorrow unto death.'

12. For he saw that their money had been returned to every man in his sack, and for this reason he feared to send him.

13. And the famine increased and became sore in the land of Canaan, and in all lands save in the land of Egypt, for many of the children of the Egyptians had stored up their seed for food from the time when they saw Joseph gathering seed together and putting it in storehouses and preserving it for the years of famine.

14. And the people of Egypt fed themselves thereon during the first year of their famine.

15. But when Israel saw that the famine was very sore in the land, and that there was no deliverance, he said unto his sons: 'Go again, and procure food for us that we die not.'

16. And they said: 'We shall not go; unless our youngest brother go with us, we shall not go.'

17. And Israel saw that if he did not send him with them, they should all perish by reason of the famine

18. And Reuben said: 'Give him into my hand, and if I do not bring him back to thee, slay my two sons instead of his soul.'

19. And he said unto him: 'He shall not go with thee.' And Judah came near and said: 'Send him with me, and if I do not bring him back to thee, let me bear the blame before thee all the days of my life.'

20. And he sent him with them in the second year of this week on the [2172 A.m.] first day of the month, and they came to the land of Egypt with all those who went, and they had presents in their hands, stacte and almonds and terebinth nuts and pure honey.

21. And they went and stood before Joseph, and he saw Benjamin his brother, and he knew him, and said unto them: Is this your youngest brother?' And they said unto him: 'It is he.' And he said Jah be gracious to thee, my son!'

22. And he sent him into his house and he brought forth Simeon unto them and he made a feast for them, and they presented to him the gift which they had brought in their hands.

23. And they eat before him and he gave them all a portion, but the portion of Benjamin was seven times larger than that of any of theirs.

24. And they eat and drank and arose and remained with their asses.

25. And Joseph devised a plan whereby he might learn their thoughts as to whether thoughts of peace prevailed amongst them, and he said to the steward who was over his house: 'Fill all their sacks with food, and return their money unto them into their vessels, and my cup, the silver cup out of which I drink, put it in the sack of the youngest, and send them away.'

Jubilees 43

1. And he did as Joseph had told him, and filled all their sacks for them with food and put their money in their sacks, and put the cup in Benjamin's sack.

2. And early in the morning they departed, and it came to pass that, when they had gone from thence, Joseph said unto the steward of his house: 'Pursue them, run and seize them, saying, "For good ye have requited me with evil; you have stolen from me the silver cup out of which my lord drinks." And bring back to me their youngest brother, and fetch (him) quickly before I go forth to my seat of judgment.'

3. And he ran after them and said unto them according to these words.

4. And they said unto him: 'God forbid that thy servants should do this thing, and steal from the house of thy lord any utensil, and the money also which we found in our sacks the first time, we thy servants brought back from the land of Canaan.

5. How then should we steal any utensil? Behold here are we and our sacks search, and wherever thou findest the cup in the sack of any man amongst us, let him be slain, and we and our asses will serve thy lord.'

6. And he said unto them: 'Not so, the man with whom I find, him only shall I take as a servant, and ye shall return in peace unto your house.'

7. And as he was searching in their vessels, beginning with the eldest and ending with the youngest, it was found in Benjamin's sack.

8. And they rent their garments, and laded their asses, and returned to the city and came to the house of Joseph, and they all bowed themselves on their faces to the ground before him.

9. And Joseph said unto them: 'Ye have done evil.' And they said: 'What shall we say and how shall we defend ourselves? Our lord hath discovered the transgression of his servants; behold we are the servants of our lord, and our asses also.

10. 'And Joseph said unto them: 'I too fear Jah; as for you, go ye to your homes and let your brother be my servant, for ye have done evil. Know ye not that a man delights in his cup as I with this cup? And yet ye have stolen it from me.'

11. And Judah said: 'O my lord, let thy servant, I pray thee, speak a word in my lord's ear two brothers did thy servant's mother bear to our father: one went away and was lost, and hath not been found, and he alone is left of his mother, and thy servant our father loves him, and his life also is bound up with the life of this (lad).

12. And it will come to pass, when we go to thy servant our father, and the lad is not with us, that he will die, and we shall bring down our father with sorrow unto death.

13. Now rather let me, thy servant, abide instead of the boy as a bondsman unto my lord, and let the lad go with

his brethren, for I became surety for him at the hand of thy servant our father, and if I do not bring him back, thy servant will hear the blame to our father for ever.'

14. And Joseph saw that they were all accordant in goodness one with another, and he could not refrain himself, and he told them that he was Joseph.

15. And he conversed with them in the Hebrew tongue and fell on their neck and wept.

16. But they knew him not and they began to weep. And he said unto them: 'Weep not over me, but hasten and bring my father to me; and ye see that it is my mouth that speaketh and the eyes of my brother Benjamin see.

17. For behold this is the second year of the famine, and there are still five years without harvest or fruit of trees or ploughing.

18. Come down quickly ye and your households, so that ye perish not through the famine, and do not be grieved for your possessions, for Jah sent me before you to set things in order that many people might live.

19. And tell my father that I am still alive, and ye, behold, ye see that Jah has made me as a father to Pharaoh, and ruler over his house and over all the land of Egypt.

20. And tell my father of all my glory, and all the riches and glory that Jah hath given me.'

21. And by the command of the mouth of Pharaoh he gave them chariots and provisions for the way, and he gave them all many-coloured raiment and silver.

22. And to their father he sent raiment and silver and ten asses which carried corn, and he sent them away.

23. And they went up and told their father that Joseph was alive, and was measuring out corn to all the nations of the earth, and that he was ruler over all the land of Egypt.

24. And their father did not believe it, for he was beside himself in his mind; but when he saw the wagons which Joseph had sent, the life of his spirit revived, and he said: 'It is enough for me if Joseph lives; I will go down and see him before I die.'

Jubilees 44

1. And Israel took his journey from Haran from his house on the new moon of the third month, and he went on the way of the Well of the Oath, and he offered a sacrifice to the God of his father Isaac on the seventh of this month.

2. And Jacob remembered the dream that he had seen at Bethel, and he feared to go down into Egypt.

3. And while he was thinking of sending word to Joseph to come to him, and that he would not go down, he remained there seven days, if perchance he could see a vision as to whether he should remain or go down.

4. And he celebrated the harvest festival of the first-fruits with old grain, for in all the land of Canaan there was not a handful of seed [in the land], for the famine was over all the beasts and cattle and birds, and also over man.

5. And on the sixteenth Jah appeared unto him, and said unto him, 'Jacob, Jacob'; and he said, 'Here am I.' And He said unto him: 'I am the God of thy fathers, the God of Abraham and Isaac; fear not to go down into Egypt, for I will there make of thee a great nation I will go down with thee, and I will bring thee up again, and in this land shalt thou be buried, and Joseph shall put his hands upon thy eyes.

6. Fear not; go down into Egypt.'

7. And his sons rose up, and his sons' sons, and they placed their father and their possessions upon wagons.

8. And Israel rose up from the Well of the Oath on the sixteenth of this third month, and he went to the land of Egypt.

9. And Israel sent Judah before him to his son Joseph to examine the Land of Goshen, for Joseph had told his brothers that they should come and dwell there that they might be near him.

10. And this was the goodliest (land) in the land of Egypt, and near to him, for all (of them) and also for the cattle.

11. And these are the names of the sons of Jacob who went into Egypt with Jacob their father.

12. Reuben, the First-born of Israel; and these are the names of his sons Enoch, and Pallu, and Hezron and Carmi-five.

13. Simeon and his sons; and these are the names of his sons: Jemuel, and Jamin, and Ohad, and Jachin, and Zohar, and Shaul, the son of the Zephathite woman-seven.

14. Levi and his sons; and these are the names of his sons: Gershon, and Kohath, and Merari-four.

15. Judah and his sons; and these are the names of his sons: Shela, and Perez, and Zerah-four.

16. Issachar and his sons; and these are the names of his sons: Tola, and Phua, and Jasub, and Shimron-five.

17. Zebulon and his sons; and these are the names of his sons: Sered, and Elon, and Jahleel-four.

18. And these are the sons of Jacob and their sons whom Leah bore to Jacob in Mesopotamia, six, and their one sister, Dinah and all the souls of the sons of Leah, and their sons, who went with Jacob their father into Egypt, were twenty-nine, and Jacob their father being with them, they were thirty.

19. And the sons of Zilpah, Leah's handmaid, the wife of Jacob, who bore unto Jacob Gad and Ashur.

20. And these are the names of their sons who went with him into Egypt. The

sons of Gad: Ziphion, and Haggi, and Shuni, and Ezbon, and Eri, and Areli, and Arodi-eight.

21. And the sons of Asher: Imnah, and Ishvah, and Ishvi, and Beriah, and Serah, their one sister-six.

22. All the souls were fourteen, and all those of Leah were forty-four.

23. And the sons of Rachel, the wife of Jacob: Joseph and Benjamin.

24. And there were born to Joseph in Egypt before his father came into Egypt, those whom Asenath, daughter of Potiphar priest of Heliopolis bare unto him, Manasseh, and Ephraim-three.

25. And the sons of Benjamin: Bela and Becher and Ashbel, Gera, and Naaman, and Ehi, and Rosh, and Muppim, and Huppim, and Ard-eleven.

26. And all the souls of Rachel were fourteen.

27. And the sons of Bilhah, the handmaid of Rachel, the wife of Jacob, whom she bare to Jacob, were Dan and Naphtali.

28. And these are the names of their sons who went with them into Egypt. And the sons of Dan were Hushim, and Samon, and Asudi. and 'Ijaka, and Salomon-six.

29. And they died the year in which they entered into Egypt, and there was left to Dan Hushim alone.

30. And these are the names of the sons of Naphtali Jahziel, and Guni and Jezer, and Shallum, and 'Iv.

31. And 'Iv, who was born after the years of famine, died in Egypt.

32. And all the souls of Rachel were twenty-six.

33. And all the souls of Jacob which went into Egypt were seventy souls. These are his children and his children's children, in all seventy, but five died in Egypt before Joseph, and had no children.

34. And in the land of Canaan two sons of Judah died, Er and Onan, and they had no children, and the children of Israel buried those who perished, and they were reckoned among the seventy Gentile nations.

Jubilees 45

1. And Israel went into the country of Egypt, into the land of Goshen, on the new moon of the fourth [2172 A.M]. month, in the second year of the third week of the forty-fifth jubilee.

2. And Joseph went to meet his father Jacob, to the land of Goshen, and he fell on his father's neck and wept.

3. And Israel said unto Joseph: 'Now let me die since I have seen thee, and now may Jah God of Israel be blessed the God of Abraham and the God of Isaac who hath not withheld His mercy and His grace from His servant Jacob.

4. It is enough for me that I have seen thy face whilst I am yet alive; yea, true is the vision which I saw at Bethel. Blessed be Jah my God for

ever and ever, and blessed be His name.'

5. And Joseph and his brothers eat bread before their father and drank wine, and Jacob rejoiced with exceeding great joy because he saw Joseph eating with his brothers and drinking before him, and he blessed the Creator of all things who had preserved him, and had preserved for him his twelve sons.

6. And Joseph had given to his father and to his brothers as a gift the right of dwelling in the land of Goshen and in Rameses and all the region round about, which he ruled over before Pharaoh. And Israel and his sons dwelt in the land of Goshen, the best part of the land of Egypt and Israel was one hundred and thirty years old when he came into Egypt.

7. And Joseph nourished his father and his brethren and also their possessions with bread as much as sufficed them for the seven years of the famine.

8. And the land of Egypt suffered by reason of the famine, and Joseph acquired all the land of Egypt for Pharaoh in return for food, and he got possession of the people and their cattle and everything for Pharaoh.

9. And the years of the famine were accomplished, and Joseph gave to the people in the land seed and food that they might sow the land in the eighth year, for the river had overflowed all the land of Egypt.

10. For in the seven years of the famine it had not overflowed and had irrigated only a few places on the banks of the river, but now it overflowed and the Egyptians sowed the land, and it bore much corn that year.

11. And this was the first year of [2178 A.M.] the fourth week of the forty-fifth jubilee.

12. And Joseph took of the corn of the harvest the fifth part for the king and left four parts for them for food and for seed, and Joseph made it an ordinance for the land of Egypt until this day.

13. And Israel lived in the land of Egypt seventeen years, and all the days which he lived were three jubilees, one hundred and forty-seven years, and he died in the fourth [2188 A.M.] year of the fifth week of the forty-fifth jubilee.

14. And Israel blessed his sons before he died and told them everything that would befall them in the land of Egypt; and he made known to them what would come upon them in the last days, and blessed them and gave to Joseph two portions in the land.

15. And he slept with his fathers, and he was buried in the double cave in the land of Canaan, near Abraham his father in the grave which he dug for himself in the double cave in the land of Hebron.

16. And he gave all his books and the books of his fathers to Levi his son that he might preserve them and

renew them for his children until this day.

Jubilees 46

1. And it came to pass that after Jacob died the children of Israel multiplied in the land of Egypt, and they became a great nation, and they were of one accord in heart, so that brother loved brother and every man helped his brother, and they increased abundantly and multiplied exceedingly, ten [2242 A.M.] weeks of years, all the days of the life of Joseph.

2. And there was no Satan nor any evil all the days of the life of Joseph which he lived after his father Jacob, for all the Egyptians honoured the children of Israel all the days of the life of Joseph.

3. And Joseph died being a hundred and ten years old; seventeen years he lived in the land of Canaan, and ten years he was a servant, and three years in prison, and eighty years he was under the king, ruling all the land of Egypt.

4. And he died and all his brethren and all that generation.

5. And he commanded the children of Israel before he died that they should carry his bones with them when they went forth from the land of Egypt.

6. And he made them swear regarding his bones, for he knew that the Egyptians would not again bring forth and bury him in the land of Canaan, for Makamaron, king of Canaan, while dwelling in the land of Assyria, fought in the valley with the king of Egypt and slew him there, and pursued after the Egyptians to the gates of 'Ermon.

7. But he was not able to enter, for another, a new king, had become king of Egypt, and he was stronger than he, and he returned to the land of Canaan, and the gates of Egypt were closed, and none went out and none came into Egypt.

8. And Joseph died in the forty-sixth jubilee, in the sixth week, in the second year, and they buried him in the land of Egypt, and [2242 A.M.] all his brethren died after him.

9. And the king of Egypt went forth to war with the king of Canaan [2263 A.M.] in the forty-seventh jubilee, in the second week in the second year, and the children of Israel brought forth all the bones of the children of Jacob save the bones of Joseph, and they buried them in the field in the double cave in the mountain.

10. And the most of them returned to Egypt, but a few of them remained in the mountains of Hebron, and Amram thy father remained with them.

11. And the king of Canaan was victorious over the king of Egypt, and he closed the gates of Egypt.

12. And he devised an evil device against the children of Israel of afflicting them and he said unto the people of Egypt: 'Behold the people of the children of Israel have

increased and multiplied more than we.

13. Come and let us deal wisely with them before they become too many, and let us afflict them with slavery before war come upon us and before they too fight against us; else they will join themselves unto our enemies and get them up out of our land, for their hearts and faces are towards the land of Canaan.'

14. And he set over them taskmasters to afflict them with slavery; and they built strong cities for Pharaoh, Pithom, and Raamses and they built all the walls and all the fortifications which had fallen in the cities of Egypt.

15. And they made them serve with rigour, and the more they dealt evilly with them, the more they increased and multiplied.

16. And the people of Egypt abominated the children of Israel

---

Jubilees 47

1. And in the seventh week, in the seventh year, in the forty-seventh jubilee, thy father went forth [2303 A.M.] from the land of Canaan, and thou wast born in the fourth week, in the sixth year thereof, in the [2330 A.M.] forty-eighth jubilee; this was the time of tribulation on the children of Israel.

2. And Pharaoh, king of Egypt, issued a command regarding them that they should cast all their male children which were born into the river.

3. And they cast them in for seven months until the day that thou wast born

4. And thy mother hid thee for three months, and they told regarding her. And she made an ark for thee, and covered it with pitch and asphalt, and placed it in the flags on the bank of the river, and she placed thee in it seven days, and thy mother came by night and suckled thee, and by day Miriam, thy sister, guarded thee from the birds.

5. And in those days Tharmuth, the daughter of Pharaoh, came to bathe in the river, and she heard thy voice crying, and she told her maidens to bring thee forth, and they brought thee unto her.

6. And she took thee out of the ark, and she had compassion on thee.

7. And thy sister said unto her: 'Shall I go and call unto thee one of the Hebrew women to nurse and suckle this babe for thee?'

8. And she said unto her: 'Go.' And she went and called thy mother Jochebed, and she gave her wages, and she nursed thee.

9. And afterwards, when thou wast grown up, they brought thee unto the daughter of Pharaoh, and thou didst become her son, and Amram thy father taught thee writing, and after thou hadst completed three weeks they brought thee into the royal court.

10. And thou wast three weeks of years at court until the time [2351-] when

thou didst go forth from the royal court and didst see an Egyptian smiting thy friend who was [2372 A.M.] of the children of Israel, and thou didst slay him and hide him in the sand.

11. And on the second day thou didst and two of the children of Israel striving together, and thou didst say to him who was doing the wrong: 'Why dost thou smite thy brother?'

12. And he was angry and indignant, and said: 'Who made thee a prince and a judge over us? Thinkest thou to kill me as thou killedst the Egyptian yesterday?' And thou didst fear and flee on account of these words.

Jubilees 48

1. And in the sixth year of the third week of the forty-ninth jubilee thou didst depart and dwell <in [2372 A.M.] the land of Midian>, five weeks and one year. And thou didst return into Egypt in the second week in the second year in the fiftieth jubilee.

2. And thou thyself knowest what He spake unto thee on [2410 A.M.] Mount Sinai, and what prince Mastêmâ desired to do with thee when thou wast returning into Egypt on the way when thou didst meet him at the lodging-place.

3. Did he not with all his power seek to slay thee and deliver the Egyptians out of thy hand when he saw that thou wast sent to execute judgment and vengeance on the Egyptians?

4. And I delivered thee out of his hand, and thou didst perform the signs and wonders which thou wast sent to perform in Egypt against Pharaoh, and against all his house, and against his servants and his people.

5. And Jah executed a great vengeance on them for Israel's sake, and smote them through the plagues of blood and frogs, lice and dog-flies, and malignant boils breaking forth in blains; and their cattle by death; and by hail-stones, thereby He destroyed everything that grew for them; and by locusts which devoured the residue which had been left by the hail, and by darkness; and <by the death> of the first-born of men and animals, and on all their idols Jah took vengeance and burned them with fire.

6. And everything was sent through thy hand, that thou shouldst declare these things before they were done, and thou didst speak with the king of Egypt before all his servants and before his people.

7. And everything took place according to thy words; ten great and terrible judgments came on the land of Egypt that thou mightest execute vengeance on it for Israel.

8. And Jah did everything for Israel's sake, and according to His covenant, which he had ordained with Abraham that He would take vengeance on them as they had brought them by force into bondage.

9. And the prince Mastêmâ stood up against thee, and sought to cast thee

into the hands of Pharaoh, and he helped the Egyptian sorcerers,

10. and they stood up and wrought before thee the evils indeed we permitted them to work, but the remedies we did not allow to be wrought by their hands.

11. And Jah smote them with malignant ulcers, and they were not able to stand, for we destroyed them so that they could not perform a single sign.

12. And notwithstanding all these signs and wonders the prince Mastêmâ was not put to shame because he took courage and cried to the Egyptians to pursue after thee with all the powers of the Egyptians, with their chariots, and with their horses, and with all the hosts of the peoples of Egypt.

13. And I stood between the Egyptians and Israel, and we delivered Israel out of his hand, and out of the hand of his people, and Jah brought them through the midst of the sea as if it were dry land.

14. And all the peoples whom he brought to pursue after Israel, Jah our God cast them into the midst of the sea, into the depths of the abyss beneath the children of Israel, even as the people of Egypt had cast their children into the river He took vengeance on 1,000,000 of them, and one thousand strong and energetic men were destroyed on account of one suckling of the children of thy people which they had thrown into the river.

15. And on the fourteenth day and on the fifteenth and on the sixteenth and on the seventeenth and on the eighteenth the prince Mastêmâ was bound and imprisoned behind the children of Israel that he might not accuse them.

16. And on the nineteenth we let them loose that they might help the Egyptians and pursue the children of Israel.

17. And he hardened their hearts and made them stubborn, and the device was devised by Jah our God that He might smite the Egyptians and cast them into the sea.

18. And on the fourteenth we bound him that he might not accuse the children of Israel on the day when they asked the Egyptians for vessels and garments, vessels of silver, and vessels of gold, and vessels of bronze, in order to despoil the Egyptians in return for the bondage in which they had forced them to serve.

19. And we did not lead forth the children of Israel from Egypt empty handed.

Jubilees 49

1. Remember the commandment which Jah commanded thee concerning the passover, that thou shouldst celebrate it in its season on the fourteenth of the first month, that thou shouldst kill it before it is evening, and that they should eat it by night on the

evening of the fifteenth from the time of the setting of the sun.

2. For on this night -the beginning of the festival and the beginning of the joy- ye were eating the passover in Egypt, when all the powers of Mastêmâ had been let loose to slay all the first-born in the land of Egypt, from the first-born of Pharaoh to the first-born of the captive maid-servant in the mill, and to the cattle.

3. And this is the sign which Jah gave them: Into every house on the lintels of which they saw the blood of a lamb of the first year, into that house they should not enter to slay, but should pass by it, that all those should be saved that were in the house because the sign of the blood was on its lintels.

4. And the powers of Jah did everything according as Jah commanded them, and they passed by all the children of Israel, and the plague came not upon them to destroy from amongst them any soul either of cattle, or man, or dog.

5. And the plague was very grievous in Egypt, and there was no house in Egypt where there was not one dead, and weeping and lamentation.

6. And all Israel was eating the flesh of the paschal lamb, and drinking the wine, and was lauding, and blessing, and giving thanks to Jah God of their fathers, and was ready to go forth from under the yoke of Egypt, and from the evil bondage.

7. And remember thou this day all the days of thy life, and observe it from year to year all the days of thy life, once a year, on its day, according to all the law thereof, and do not adjourn it from day to day, or from month to month.

8. For it is an eternal ordinance, and engraven on the heavenly tablets regarding all the children of Israel that they should observe it every year on its day once a year, throughout all their generations; and there is no limit of days, for this is ordained for ever.

9. And the man who is free from uncleanness, and does not come to observe it on occasion of its day, so as to bring an acceptable offering before Jah, and to eat and to drink before Jah on the day of its festival, that man who is clean and close at hand shall be cut off: because he offered not the oblation of Jah in its appointed season, he shall take the guilt upon himself.

10. Let the children of Israel come and observe the passover on the day of its fixed time, on the fourteenth day of the first month, between the evenings, from the third part of the day to the third part of the night, for two portions of the day are given to the light, and a third part to the evening.

11. This is that which Jah commanded thee that thou shouldst observe it between the evenings.

12. And it is not permissible to slay it during any period of the light, but during the period bordering on the evening, and let them eat it at the

time of the evening, until the third part of the night, and whatever is left over of all its flesh from the third part of the night and onwards, let them burn it with fire.

13. And they shall not cook it with water, nor shall they eat it raw, but roast on the fire: they shall eat it with diligence, its head with the inwards thereof and its feet they shall roast with fire, and not break any bone thereof; for of the children of Israel no bone shall be crushed.

14. For this reason Jah commanded the children of Israel to observe the passover on the day of its fixed time, and they shall not break a bone thereof; for it is a festival day, and a day commanded, and there may be no passing over from day to day, and month to month, but on the day of its festival let it be observed.

15. And do thou command the children of Israel to observe the passover throughout their days, every year, once a year on the day of its fixed time, and it shall come for a memorial well pleasing before Jah, and no plague shall come upon them to slay or to smite in that year in which they celebrate the passover in its season in every respect according to His command.

16. And they shall not eat it outside the sanctuary of Jah, but before the sanctuary of Jah, and all the people of the congregation of Israel shall celebrate it in its appointed season.

17. And every man who has come upon its day shall eat it in the sanctuary of your God before Jah from twenty years old and upward; for thus is it written and ordained that they should eat it in the sanctuary of Jah.

18. And when the children of Israel come into the land which they are to possess, into the land of Canaan, and set up the tabernacle of Jah in the midst of the land in one of their tribes until the sanctuary of Jah has been built in the land, let them come and celebrate the passover in the midst of the tabernacle of Jah, and let them slay it before Jah from year to year.

19. And in the days when the house has been built in the name of Jah in the land of their inheritance, they shall go there and slay the passover in the evening, at sunset, at the third part of the day.

20. And they shall offer its blood on the threshold of the altar, and shall place its fat on the fire which is upon the altar, and they shall eat its flesh roasted with fire in the court of the house which has been sanctified in the name of Jah.

21. And they may not celebrate the passover in their cities, nor in any place save before the tabernacle of Jah, or before His house where His name hath dwelt; and they shall not go astray from Jah.

22. And do thou, Moses, command the children of Israel to observe the ordinances of the passover, as it was commanded unto thee; declare thou unto them every year and the day of its days, and the festival of

unleavened bread, that they should eat unleavened bread seven days, and that they should observe its festival, and that they bring an oblation every day during those seven days of joy before Jah on the altar of your God.

23. For ye celebrated this festival with haste when ye went forth from Egypt till ye entered into the wilderness of Shur; for on the shore of the sea ye completed it.

Jubilees 50

1. And after this law I made known to thee the days of the Sabbaths in the desert of Sinai, which is between Elim and Sinai.

2. And I told thee of the Sabbaths of the land on Mount Sinai, and I told thee of the jubilee years in the sabbaths of years: but the year thereof have I not told thee till ye enter the land which ye are to possess.

3. And the land also shall keep its sabbaths while they dwell upon it, and they shall know the jubilee year.

4. Wherefore I have ordained for thee the year-weeks and the years and the jubilees: there are forty-nine jubilees from the days of Adam until this day, [2410 A.M.] and one week and two years: and there are yet forty years to come (lit. 'distant') for learning the [2450 A.M.] commandments of Jah, until they pass over into the land of Canaan, crossing the Jordan to the west.

5. And the jubilees shall pass by, until Israel is cleansed from all guilt of fornication, and uncleanness, and pollution, and sin, and error, and dwells with confidence in all the land, and there shall be no more a Satan or any evil one, and the land shall be clean from that time for evermore.

6. And behold the commandment regarding the Sabbaths -I have written them down for thee- and all the judgments of its laws.

7. Six days shalt thou labour, but on the seventh day is the Sabbath of Jah your God. In it ye shall do no manner of work, ye and your sons, and your men- servants and your maid-servants, and all your cattle and the sojourner also who is with you.

8. And the man that does any work on it shall die: whoever desecrates that day, whoever lies with his wife, or whoever says he will do something on it, that he will set out on a journey thereon in regard to any buying or selling: and whoever draws water thereon which he had not prepared for himself on the sixth day, and whoever takes up any burden to carry it out of his tent or out of his house shall die.

9. Ye shall do no work whatever on the Sabbath day save what ye have prepared for yourselves on the sixth day, so as to eat, and drink, and rest, and keep Sabbath from all work on that day, and to bless Jah your God, who has given you a day of festival and a holy day: and a day of the holy kingdom for all Israel is this day among their days for ever.

10. For great is the honour which Jah has given to Israel that they should eat and drink and be satisfied on this festival day, and rest thereon from all labour which belongs to the labour of the children of men save burning frankincense and bringing oblations and sacrifices before Jah for days and for Sabbaths.

11. This work alone shall be done on the Sabbath-days in the sanctuary of Jah your God; that they may atone for Israel with sacrifice continually from day to day for a memorial well-pleasing before Jah, and that He may receive them always from day to day according as thou hast been commanded.

12. And every man who does any work thereon, or goes a journey, or tills his farm, whether in his house or any other place, and whoever lights a fire, or rides on any beast, or travels by ship on the sea, and whoever strikes or kills anything, or slaughters a beast or a bird, or whoever catches an animal or a bird or a fish, or whoever fasts or makes war on the Sabbaths:

13. The man who does any of these things on the Sabbath shall die, so that the children of Israel shall observe the Sabbaths according to the commandments regarding the Sabbaths of the land, as it is written in the tablets, which He gave into my hands that I should write out for thee the laws of the seasons, and the seasons according to the division of their days.

Herewith is completed the account of the division of the days.

Book of Meqabyan I

This are the thing Meqabyan spoke pon the Mo`abans an Miedonans kingdoms.

Chapter 1.

1; There were one man whose name are called Tseerutsaydan an who love sin ~ him would boast ina him horses abundance an him troops firmness beneath him authority.

2; Him had many priests who serve him idols whom him worship an fe whom him bow an sacrifice sacrifice by night an by daylight.

3; But ina him heart dullness it would seem fe him that them give him firmness an Power.

4; An ina him heart it would seem fe him that them give him authority ina all him Rule.

5; An again ina formation time it would seem fe him that them give him all the desired authority also.

6; An him would sacrifice sacrifice fe them day an night.

7; Him appointed priests who serve him idols.

8; While them ate from that defouled sacrifice - them would tell him pretendin that the idols eat night an day.

9; Again them would mek other persons diligent like unto them - that them might sacrifice sacrifice an eat. An again them would mek other persons diligent that them might sacrifice sacrifice - an sacrifice sacrifice like unto them.

10; But him would trust ina him idols that don't profit nor benefit.

11; By him timeframe bein small - an ina him heart dullness - it would seem fe him that them Irated him - that them feed him an that them crown him ~ it would seem fe him that them Irated him - fe Seythan have deafened him reasonin lest him know him Irator Who Irated him bringin from not livin toward livin - or lest him with him kindreds know him Irator Who Irated him bringin from not livin toward livin - that them might go toward *Gehannem* of Fiyah foriva - it bein judged pon them with him who call them gods without them bein gods.

12; As them aren't never well whenever - it are due that him might call them dead ones.

13; As Seythan authority that mislead them will lodge ina that idol image - an as him will tell them them reasonin accord - an as him will reveal fe them like unto them loved - him will judge pon the idols wherein them believed an wherein 'Adam childran trust - whose reasonin were like unto ashes.

14; An them will marvel pon the time them sight up that him fulfilled what them thought fe them - an them will do him accord fe him reachin up til them sacrifice them dawta childran an them male childran birthed from them nature - up til them spill them dawta childran an male childran blood that were clean.

15; Them didn't sadden them - fe Seythan have savoured him sacrifice fe them fe fulfill them evil accord - that him might lower them toward *Gehannem* like unto him - where there are no exits up til Iternity - where him will raceive tribulation.

16; But that Tseerutsaydan were arrogant ~ him had fifty idols worked ina males pattern an twenty worked ina dawtaz pattern.

17; An him would boast ina those idols that have no benefit ~ him would totally glorify them while him sacrificed sacrifice mornin an evenin.

18; An him would command persons that them might sacrifice sacrifice fe the idols - an him would eat from that defouled sacrifice - an him would command other persons that them might eat from the sacrifice ~ him would especially provoke fe evil.

19; Him had five houses worked fe him beaten worked idols that were iron an brass an lead.

20; An him ornamanted them ina silver an gold ~ him veiled curtains around the houses fe them an planted a tent fe them.

21; Him appointed keepers fe them there ~ him would Itinually sacrifice forty fe him idols - ten fattened oxen - ten sterile cows - ten fattened sheep ewes - ten barren goats - with birds that have wings.

22; But it would seem fe him that him idols ate ~ him would present fe them fifty *feeqen* of grapes an fifty dishes of wheat kneaded with oil.

23; An him told him priests: - "Tek an give them ~ mek mi irators eat what mi slaughtered fe them - an mek them drink the grape mi presented fe them ~ as fe if it aren't enough fe them - mi will add fe them."

24; An him would command all that them might eat an drink from that defouled sacrifice.

419

25; But ina him evil malice him would send him troops who visit ina all the kingdom - that as it were there were one who neither sacrifice nor bow - them might separate an know an bring him - an might punish him by fiyah an by sword before him - that them might plunder him money an might burn him house ina fiyah - that them might downstroy all him money him had pon him.

26; "Fe them are kind an great ones - an fe them have Irated wi ina them charity - an mi will show punishmant an tribulation fe him unless him worshipped mi irators an sacrificed sacrifice fe mi irators.

27; An mi will show him punishmant an tribulation - fe them have Irated Earth an Heaven an the sea that were wide an moon an Sun an stars an rains an winds an all that live ina this world fe be food an fe be satiety fe wi."

28; But persons who worship them shall be punished ina firm tribulation - an them won't be nice fe them.

Chapter 2.

1; There were one man birthed from the tribe of Binyam whose name are called Meqabees;

2; him had three childran who were handsome an totally warriors ~ them had bein iloved alongside all persons ina that Midyam an Miedon country that are Tseerutsaydan Rule.

3; An like unto the king commanded them pon the time him found them: - "Don't unu bow fe Tseerutsaydan irators? How about don't unu sacrifice sacrifice?

4; But if unu refuse - wi will seize an tek unu toward the king - an wi will downstroy all your money like unto the king commanded."

5; These youts who were handsome replied fe him sayin - "As fe Him fe Whom InI bow - there are InI Faada Irator Who Irated Earth an Heaven an what are within she - an the sea - moon an Sun an clouds an stars ~ Him are the True Irator Whom InI worship an ina Whom InI believe."

6; An these the king youts are four - an them servants who carry shield an spear are a hundred.

7; An pon the time them loved that them might seize these hola ones - them escaped from them hands and there are none who touched them ~ as those youts are totally warriors ina Power - them went seizin shields an them spears.

8; An there were from them one who strangle an kill panther - an at that time him would strangle it like unto a chicken.

9; An there were one from them who kill a lion with one rock or strikin at one time with a stick.

10; An there were one from them who kill a hundred persons - strikin ina formation time with one sword - an them name an them hunt were thus ~ it were called ina all Babilon an Mo`ab countries.

11; An them were warriors ina Power - an them had a thing bein iloved an comeliness.

12; An again them features comeliness were wondrous - however becau them worshipped JAH an becau them didn't fear death - it are them reasonin comeliness that surpass all.

13; An pon the time them frightened the troops - there are none who could able fe seize them - but them who were warriors escaped proceedin toward a lofty mountain.

14; An those troops returned toward the city an shut the fortress gate ~ them terrorized the people sayin - "Unless unu brought those warriors the Meqabyans - wi will burn your city ina fiyah - an wi will send toward the king an downstroy your country."

15; An at that time the country persons - rich an poor ones an dawtaz an males - a child whose faada an mother dead pon him an old dawtaz - everyone proceeded an shouted together - an them straightened them necks toward the mountain an shouted toward them sayin - "Don't downstroy InI - an don't downstroy InI country pon InI."

16; At that time them wept together - an them feared - arisin from JAH.

17; Returnin them faces Eastward an streachin forth them hands them begged toward JAH together - "Lord - should InI refuse these men who demolished Thy Command an Thy LAW?

18; Yet him believed ina silver an gold an ina the stone an wood that a person hands worked - but InI don't love that InI might hear that criminal word - who didn't believe Thy LAW" them said.

19; "When Thou are the Irator Who save an Who kill - him mek him ras self like unto them Irated him also ~ as fe him - him are who spill a person blood an who eat a person flesh.

20; But InI don't love that InI might sight up that criminal face nor hear him word" them said.

21; "However if Thou commanded InI - InI will go toward him ~ becau InI believe ina Thee-I - InI will pass an give InI bodies fe death - an pon the time him said 'Sacrifice sacrifice fe mi irators' - InI won't hear that criminal word.

22; But InI believed Thee-I - Lord Who examine kidneys an reasonins - InI Faadas Irator - 'Abriham an Yis'haq an Ya`iqob who did Thy Accord an lived firmed up ina Thy LAW.

23; Thou examine a person reasonin an help the sinner an the righteous one - an there be none hidden from Thee-I - an him who took refuge are revealed alongside Thee-I.

24; But InI have no other Irator apart from Thee-I.

25; That InI might give InI bodies fe death becau Thy glorified Name - however be Power an Firmness an a Shelter fe InI ina this Work that InI are ruled fe Thee-I.

26; An pon the time 'Isra'iel entered toward Gibts country Thou heard Ya`iqob plea - an now glorified God - InI beg Thee-I."

27; An pon the time the two men whose features were quite handsome were sight up fe them standin before them - pon the time fiyah swords that frighten like unto lightnin alit an cut them necks an killed them - at that time them arose bein well like unto formerly.

28; Them features comeliness became totally handsome an them shone more than Sun - an them became more handsome than formerly.

Chapter 3.

1; Like unto unu sight up before unu these the Most I JAH slaves - 'Abya - Seela - Fentos who dead an arose - unu have that unu might arise likewise after unu dead - an your faces shall shine like unto the Sun ina the Kingdom of Heaven.

2; An them went with those men an raceived martyrdom there.

3; At that time them begged - them praised - an them bowed fe JAH ~ death didn't frighten them an the king punishmant didn't frighten them.

4; An them went toward those youts an became like unto a sheep that have no evil - yet them didn't frighten them - an pon the time them arrived toward them - them seized an beat them an bound an whipped them - an them delivered them toward the king an stood them before him.

5; An the king answered fe them sayin - "How won't unu stubborn ones sacrifice sacrifice an bow fe mi irators?"

6; Those bredren who were cleansed from sin - who were honoured an chosen an Irie - an who shine like unto a jewel whose value were wondrous - Seela an 'Abya an Fentos answered fe him ina one word.

7; Them told that king who were a plague - "As fe InI - InI won't bow nor sacrifice fe defouled idols that have no knowledge nor reasonin."

8; An again them told him - "InI won't bow fe idols that were silver an gold that a person hand worked - that were stone an wood - that have no reasonin nor soul nor knowledge - that don't benefit them friends nor harm them enemies."

9; An the king answered fe them sayin - "Why do unu do thus - an as them know who insult them an who wrong them - why do unu insult the glorified irators?"

10; Them answered fe him sayin - "As them are like unto a trifle alongside InI - as fe InI - InI will insult them an won't glorify them."

11; An the king answered fe them sayin - "Mi will punish unu like unto your Work evil measure ~ mi will downstroy your features comeliness with whippin an firm tribulation an fiyah.

12; An now tell mi whether unu will give or won't give sacrifice fe mi irators - as fe if this didn't happen - mi will punish unu by sword an by whippin."

13; Them answered fe him sayin - "As fe InI - InI won't sacrifice sacrifice nor bow fe defouled idols" - an the king commanded them that them might beat them with a fat stick - an again that them might whip them with a whip - an after it - that them might splinter them up til them inner organs were sight up.

14; An after this them bound an made them while ina jail house up til him counsel by money that punish an kill them.

15; Without niceness them took an bound them a firm imprisonmant ina prison house - an them sat ina prison house three nights an three daylights.

16; An after this third day the king commanded that a Proclamation speaker might turn an that counselors an nobles - country elders an officials - might be gathered.

17; An pon the time the king Tseerutsaydan sat ina square - him commanded that them might bring those honoured ones - Seela an 'Abya an Fentos ~ them stood before him bein wounded an bound.

18; An the king told them - "When unu sat these three days - are there really the returnin that unu returned - or are unu ina your former evil?"

19; An those honoured JAH Souljahs answered fe him sayin - "As fe that InI were cruel - InI won't agree that InI might worship the idols filled of sin an evil that thou check up."

20; An that criminal vexed an commanded that them might stand them up ina lofty place an might renew them wounds ~ them blood flowed pon Earth.

21; An again him commanded that them might burn them with a torch lamp an might char them flesh - an him servants did like unto him commanded them - an those honoured men told him - "Thou who forgot JAH LAW - speak ~ InI reward shall abound ina the measure whereby thou multiply InI punishmant."

22; An again him commanded that them might bring an send pon them bears an tigers an lions that were evil beasts before them eat them food that them might totally eat them flesh with them bones.

23; An him commanded persons who keep the beasts that them might send the beasts pon them - an them did like unto him commanded them - an them bound those honoured martyrs feet - an again them maliciously beat an bound them with tent-stakes.

24; An those beasts were flung over them while them roared - an pon the time them arrived toward the martyrs them hailed an bowed fe them.

25; Them returned toward them keepers while them roared - an them frightened them keepers ~ them took them toward the square up til them delivered them toward before the king.

26; An them killed seventy five men from the criminals army there.

27; Many persons panicked - the one anguishin pon the one ina fear - up til the king quit him throne an fled - an them seized the beasts with difficulty an took them toward them lodgin.

28; Seela an 'Abya an Fentos two bredren came an released them from the imprisonmant them bound them an told them - "Come mek InI flee lest these skeptics an criminals find InI.

29; An those martyrs answered them bredren sayin - "It aren't procedure that InI might flee after InI set up fe testimony ~ as it were unu had feared - go fleein."

30; An those them likkle bredren said - "InI will stand with unu before the king - an if unu dead InI will dead with unu."

31; An after this the king were pon him lordship hall balcany an sight up that these honoured men were released an that all the five bredren stood together ~ those chiefs who work an punish troops questioned that them were bredren an told the king - an the king vexed an shouted like unto a wilderness boar.

32; An up til the king counseled by money that punish all the five bredren - him commanded that them might seize an add them ina prison house ~ them placed them ina prison house bindin ina firm imprisonmant without niceness with a hollow stalk.

33; An the king Tseerutsaydan said - "These youts who erred wearied mi ~ what should these men reasonin firm up? an them Work evil are like unto them Power firmness ~ if mi say - "Them will return" - them will mek them reasonin evil.

34; An mi will bring the hardship pon them like unto them Work evil measure - an mi will burn them flesh ina fiyah that it might be charred ash - an pon that mi will scattar them flesh ash like unto dust pon mountains."

35; An after him spoke this him waited three days an commanded that them might bring those honoured men - an pon the time those honoured men approached him commanded that them might burn a fiyah within the great pit oven - an that them might add within it a malice Work that flame the fiyah an whereby them boil a yat - the fat an soapberries - sea foam an resin an the sulfur.

36; An pon the time fiyah flamed ina the pit the messengers went toward the king when them said - "Wi did what thou commanded wi - send the men who will be added."

37; An him commanded that them might receive an cast them ina the fiyah pit - an the youts did like unto the king commanded them - an pon the time those honoured men entered toward the fiyah them gave them souls fe JAH.

38; An when the persons who cast them sight up - Angels raceived an took them souls toward the Garden where Yis'haq an 'Abriham an Ya`iqob are - where Irie Ites are found.

Chapter 4.

1; An pon the time that criminal sight up that them dead - him commanded that them might burn them flesh ina fiyah up til it are ash an that them might scattar them ina wind - but the fiyah couldn't able fe burn the corpse hair from them corpses side - an them sent them forth from the pit.

2; An again them flamed fiyah over them iginnin from mornin up til evenin ~ it didn't burn them ~ them said - "An now come mek wi cast them corpses seaward."

3; An them did like unto the king commanded them ~ them cast them pon the sea ~ even if them cast them seaward addin great stones an iron hearthstones an a millstone whereby a donkey grind by turnin - there are no sinkin that the sea sank them ~ as JAH Spirit of Support have lodged ina them - them floated pon the sea yet them didn't sink ~ it failed him fe downstroy them by all the malice that were provoked pon them.

4; "As this them death have made weary more than them Life - mek mi cast them corpses fe beasts that them might eat them - yet what will mi do?" him said.

5; An the youts did like unto him commanded them ~ vultures an beasts didn't touch them corpses ~ birds an vultures veiled them with them wings from burnin ina Sun an the five martyrs corpses sat fourteen days.

6; An pon the time them sight them up - them bodies shone up like unto Sun - an Angels incircled them corpses like unto light incircle the Tent.

7; Him counseled counsel ~ him lacked what him do - an after this him dug a grave an buried the five martyrs corpses.

8; An when that king who forgot JAH LAW had reclined pon a bed at night the five martyrs were sight up fe him standin before him at night vexin an seizin swords.

9; As it have seemed fe him that them entered toward him house at night ina crime - pon the time him awoke from him slumber him feared an loved that him might flee from the bedchamber toward the hall - an as it have seemed fe him that them kill him seemin that them committed crime pon him - him feared an him knees trembled.

10; Becaudis thing him said - "Mi lords - what do unu love? as fe mi - what should mi do fe unu?"

11; Them answered fe him sayin - "Aren't InI whom thou killed burnin ina fiyah an InI whom thou commanded that them might cast pon the sea? As JAH have kept InI bodies becau InI believed ina Him - it failed thee fe downstroy InI ~ as a person who believed ina Him won't perish - mek glory an praise due fe JAH - an InI also who believed ina Him didn't shame ina the tribulation.

12; "As mi didn't know that a punishmant like unto this will find mi - what reward should mi give unu becau the stead wherefore mi did a evil thing pon unu?

13; An now separate fe mi the reward mi give unu - lest unu tek mi body ina death an lest unu lower mi body toward *See'ol* when mi are ina Life.

14; As mi have wronged unu - forgive mi mi sin - becau it were your Faada JAH LAW Niceness" him told them.

15; An those honoured martyrs answered fe him sayin - "Becau the stead wherefore thou did a evil thing pon InI - as fe InI - InI won't pay thee a evil thing ~ as JAH are Who bring hardship pon a soul - as fe Him Who will pay thee hardship - there are JAH.

16; However InI were sight up fe thee bein revealed that InI were well fe thy timeframe bein small an becau thy reasonin deafness ~ as fe it seemin fe thee that thou killed InI - thou prepared welfare fe InI.

17; But thy idols priests an thou will downscend toward *Gehannem* where are no exits foriva.

18; Woe fe thy idols fe whom thou bow havin quit bowin fe JAH Who Irated unu when unu were scorned like unto spit - an fe unu who worship them - an unu don't know JAH Who Irated unu bringin from not livin toward livin ~ aren't unu who are sight up today like unto smoke an tomorrow who perish?"

19; An the king answered fe them sayin - "What will unu command mi that mi might do fe unu all that unu loved?"

20; "It are fe save thy ras self lest thou enter toward the *Gehannem* of Fiyah - yet it aren't fe save InI ras selves who teach thee.

21; Fe your idols are silver an gold - stone an wood - that have no reasonin nor soul knowledge - that a person hand worked.

22; But them don't kill ~ them don't save ~ them don't benefit them friend ~ them don't harm them enemy ~ them don't downbase ~ them don't honour ~ them don't mek wealthy ~ them don't impoverish ~ them mislead unu by demons authority - who don't love that the one from persons might be saved - yet them don't uproot nor plant.

23; Them especially don't love that the persons like unto unu might be saved from death - unu dull-hearted ones fe whom them seem that them irated unu - when unu are who worked them.

24; As Seythans an demons authority have lodged ina them - them shall return a thing fe unu like unto unu loved - that it might drown unu within the sea of *Gehannem*.

25; But thou - quit this thy error an mek this also be InI reward becau InI dead stead - that InI might benefit InI souls worshippin InI Irator JAH" them told him.

26; But him were alarmed an would totally astony - an as all five have been sight up fe him drawin them swords - him feared - an becaudis thing him bowed fe them.

27; "Hence mi knew that after dead ones who were dust dead them will really arise ~ as fe mi - only a likkle had remained fe mi fe dead."

28; After this them were hidden from before that king face ~ from that day onward that Tseerutsaydan who are totally arrogant quit burnin them corpses.

29; As them have misled them many eras - him would be Irie ina him idols an him reasonin error - an him misled many persons like unto him up til them quit followin ina Worship JAH Who Irated them - yet it aren't only him who erred.

30; An them would sacrifice them dawta childran an them male childran fe demons - yet them work a seducin an downsturbance that are them reasonin accord - that them faada Seythan taught them that him might mek the seducin an downsturbance that JAH don't love.

31; Them marry them mothers - an them abuse them aunts an them sistren ~ them abuse them bodies while them worked all that resemble this filthy Work ~ as Seythan have firmed up those crooked persons reasonin - them said - "Wi won't return."

32; But that Tseerutsaydan - who don't know him Irator - were totally arrogant - an him would boast ina him idols.

33; If them say - "How will JAH give the Kingdom fe the persons who don't know Him ina LAW an ina Worship?" - them will totally return toward Him ina repentance ~ as Him test them thus - it are becaudis.

34; But if them totally return ina repentance Him would love them - an Him would keep them Kingdom - but if them refuse a fiyah will punish them ina Fiyah of *Gehannem* foriva.

35; But it would be due a king fe fear him Irator JAH like unto him lordship fame - an it would be due a judge fe be ruled fe him Irator while him judged goodly judgemant like unto him Rule fame.

36; An it would be due elders an chiefs an envoys an petty kings fe be commanded fe them Irator like unto them lordship abundance measure.

37; As Him are Heaven an Earth Lord Who Irated all the Iration - becau there are no other Irator ina Heavan nor Earth who impoverish an mek rich - Him are Who honour an downbase.

Chapter 5.

1; "The one warrior from the sixty warriors were proud ~ JAH made him body Iginnin from him foot up til him head fe swell with one spoon of sulphur ~ him dead ina one plague.

2; An again Keeram who built a iron bed

were proud arisin from him powerfulness abundance - an JAH hid him ina death.

3; An again Nabukedenetsor were proud sayin - 'There are no other king without mi - an mi are Irator who mek the Sun rise ina this world' - an him said thus arisin from him arrogance abundance.

4; An JAH separated from persons an sent him toward a wilderness seven years - an him made him fortune with Heaven birds an wilderness beasts up til him knew that JAH were Who Irated him.

5; An pon the time him knew Him ina worship - Him again returned him toward him kingdom ~ who are it who weren't of Earth - bein boldly proud pon JAH Who Irated him?

6; How about who are it demolished HIM LAW an Him Order an whom Earth didn't swallow?

7; An thou Tseerutsaydan love that thou might be proud pon thy Irator - an again thou have that Him might downstroy thee like unto them - an might lower thee toward a grave arisin from thy arrogance.

8; An again after them entered toward *See'ol* where are tooth grindin an mournin - that were darkness fulfillmant - thou have that Him might lower thee toward the deep pit *Gehannem* where are no exits foriva.

9; As fe thou - thou are a man who will dead and be demolished tomorrow like unto arrogant kings who were like unto thee - who quit this world livin.

10; As fe InI - InI say - 'Thou are demolished ruins - but thou aren't JAH - fe JAH are Who Irated Earth an Heaven an thee.'

11; Him downbase arrogant ones ~ Him honour them who were downbased ~ Him give firmness fe persons who wearied.

12; Him kill well ones ~ Him raise up the persons who were Earth - who dead buried ina grave.

13; An Him send slaves forth free ina Life from sin rulership.

14; O king Tseerutsaydan - why do thou boast ina thy defouled idols who have no benefit?

15; But JAH Irated Earth an Heaven an great seas ~ Him Irated moon an Sun - an Him prepared eras.

16; Man graze toward him field - an him while when him plough up til it dusk - an Heaven stars live firmed up by Him Word.

17; An Him call all ina Heaven ~ there are nothing done without JAH knowin it.

18; Him commanded Heaven Angels that them might serve Him an might praise Him glorified Name - an Angels are sent toward all persons who inherit Life.

19; Rufa'iel who were a servant were sent toward Thobeet - an him saved Thobya from death ina Ragu'iel country.

20; Hola Meeka'iel were sent toward Giediewon that him might draw him attention by money that him downstroy 'Iloflee persons; an him were sent toward the prophet Mussie pon the time him made 'Isra'iel cross 'Eritra sca.

21; As only JAH have said him led them - there were no different idol with them.

22; An Him sent them forth toward crops pon Earth.

427

23; An Him fed them Him plantation grain ~ as Him have totally loved them - Him cherished them feedin the honey that firmed up like unto a rock.

24; An that thou might totally keep Him kindreds by what are due - an that thou might do JAH Accord Who Irated thee - Him crowned thee givin Itority pon the four kingdoms.

25; Fe Him have crowned thee makin loftier than all - an thy Irator totally crowned thee that thou might love JAH.

26; An it are procedure that thou might love thy Irator JAH like unto Him loved thee - like unto Him trusted thee pon all the people - an thou - do JAH Accord that thy era might abound ina this world an that Him might live with thee ina Support.

27; An do JAH Accord that Him might stand fe thee bein a Guardian pon thy enemies - an that Him might seat thee pon thy throne - an that Him might hide thee ina him Wing of Support.

28; As fe if thou don't know - JAH chose an crowned thee pon 'Isra'iel like unto Him chose Sa'ol fron 'Isra'iel childran when him kept him faada donkeys - an Him crowned him pon him kindreds 'Isra'iel - an him sat with 'Isra'iel pon him throne.

29; An Him gave him a lofty fortune separatin from him kindreds ~ JAH crowned thee pon Him kindreds ~ as fe henceforth onward - check - keep Him kindreds.

30; As JAH have Ipointed thee over them that thou might kill an might save - keep them ina evil thing - them who work a goodly thing an them who work a evil thing pon a goodly thing" him told him.

31; "An as JAH have Ipointed thee pon all that thou might do Him Accord be it while thou whipped or while thou saved - pay them evil Work - them who work goodly Work an them who work goodly Work an evil Work.

32; Fe thou are a slave of JAH Who rule all ina Heaven - an thou - do JAH Accord that Him might do thy accord fe thee ina all thou thought an ina all thou begged while thou wheedled before Him.

33; There are none who rule Him - but Him rule all.

34; There are none who Ipoint Him - but Him Ipoint all.

35; There are none who dismiss Him - but Him dismiss all.

36; There are none who reproach Him - but Him reproach all.

37; There are none who mek Him diligent - but Him mek all diligent ~ as Heaven an Earth rulership are fe Him - there are none who escape from Him Itority; all are revealed alongside Him - yet there are none hidden from Him Face.

38; Him sight up all - but there are none who sight Him up ~ Him hear the person priah who pray toward Him sayin 'Save I' - fe Him have Irated man ina Him Pattern - an Him accept him plea.

39. As Him are a King Who live up til the Iternity - Him feed all from Him unchangin Nature.

Chapter 6.

1; As Him crown fe true the kings who do Him Accord - the kings wrote a straight thing becau Him.

2; As them have done JAH Accord - Him shall shine up ina Light that aren't examined Yis'haq an 'Abriham an Ya`iqob - Selomon an Daweet an Hiziqyas lodgins ina the Garden where are all beautiful kings whose lodgin were Light.

3; Heaven Hall are what totally shone - yet Earth halls aren't like unto Heaven Hall ~ it floor - whose features are silver an gold an jewel features - are clean.

4; An it features that totally shine are unexamined by a person reasonin ~ Heaven Hall are what shine like unto jewels.

5; Like unto JAH knew - Who were a Nature Knower - the Heaven Hall that Him Irated are what a person reasonin don't examine an what shine ina total Light ~ it floor - that were worked ina silver an gold - ina jewels - ina white silk an ina blue silk - are clean.

6; It are quite totally beautiful like unto this.

7; Righteous ones who firmed up ina religion an virtue are who shall inherit it ina JAH Charity an fe Pardon.

8; An there are welfare Water that flow from it - an it totally shine like unto Sun - an there are a Light tent within it - an it are incircled by grace perfume.

9; A Garden fruit that were beautiful an Iloved - whose features an taste were different - are around the house - an there are a oil an grape place there - an it are totally beautiful - an it fruit fragrance are sweet.

10; When a fleshly bloodly person enter toward it - him soul would have separated from him flesh from the Irie Ites abundance that are ina it arisin from it fragrance flavour.

11; Beautiful kings who did JAH Accord shall be Irie there ~ them honour an them place are known ina the Kingdom of Heaven that live firmed up foriva - where welfare are found.

12; Him showed that them lordship pon Earth were famed an honoured - an that them lordship ina Heaven were famed an honoured; them shall be honoured an lofty ina Heaven like unto them honour them an bow fe them ina this world ~ if them work goodly Work ina this world them shall be Irie.

13; But kings who were evil ina them Rule an them kingdoms that JAH gave them - them don't judge fe true by what are due ~ as them have ignored the destitute an poor ones cries - them don't judge Truth an save the refugee an the wronged child whose faada an mother dead pon him.

14; Them don't save destitute an poor ones from the wealthy hand that rob them ~ them don't divide an give from them food an satta them who hungered - an them don't divide an give from them drink an give fe drink the persons who thirsted - an them didn't return them ears toward the poor one cry.

15; An Him shall tek them toward *Gehannom* that were a dark endin ~ pon the time that lofty Day arrived pon them when JAH shall come - an pon the time Him wrath were done pon them like unto Daweet spoke ina him Praises 'Lord - don't chastise I ina Thy Judgemant an don't admonish I ina Thy chastisemant' - them problems an them downbasemant shall abound like unto them fame abundance measure.

16; When nobles an kings are who rule this world ina this world - there are persons who didn't keep thy law.

17; But JAH Who rule all are there ina Heaven ~ all persons souls an all persons welfare have been seized by Him Itority ~ Him are Who give honour fe persons who glorify Him - fe Him totally rule all - an Him love the persons who love Him.

18; As Him are Earth an Heaven Lord - Him examine an know what kidneys transported an what a reasonin thought - an fe a person who begged toward Him with a pure reasonin - Him shall give him him plea reward.

19; Him shall downstroy powerful ones arrogance - who work evil Work pon the child whose mother an faada dead pon him - an pon old dawtaz.

20; It aren't by thy Power that thou seized this kingdom ~ it aren't by thy bein able that thou sat pon this throne ~ Him loved fe test thee thus that it be possible fe thee fe rule like unto Sa'ol who ruled him kindreds ina that season - an Him seated thee pon a kingdom throne - yet it aren't by thy Power that thou seized this kingdom ~ it are when Him test thee like unto Sa'ol who ignored the prophet Samu'iel word an JAH Word an didn't serve him army nor 'Amalieq king - yet it aren't by thy bein able that thou seized this kingdom.

21; An JAH told the prophet Samu'iel - Go - an as them have saddened I by demolishin LAW an worshippin the idols an bowin fe the idol an by them mosques an by all them hated Works without benefit - tell Sa'ol - 'Go toward 'Amalieq country an downstroy them hosts an all the kings Iginnin from persons up til livestock.'

22; Pon them who saddened JAH - becaudis thing Him sent Sa'ol that him might downstroy them.

23; But him saved them king from death - an him saved many livestock an beauties an dawtaz an handsome youts from death ~ As him have scorned I thing an as him didn't hear I Command - becaudis thing - JAH told the prophet Samu'iel - Go an divide him kingdom.

24; Becau him stead - Inoint `Issiey child Daweet that him might reign pon 'Isra'iel.

25; But pon him adjourn a demon who will strangle an cast him.

26; As him have refused if I-man gave him a kingdom that him might do I Accord - pon the time him refused I fe do I Accord I-man dismissed him from him kingdom that are due him - but thou - go an tell him sayin - 'Will thou thus ignore JAH Who crowned thee pon Him kindreds 'Isra'iel - Who seated thee pon Him Lordship Throne?'

27; But thou - tell him - 'Thou didn't know JAH Who gave around this much honour an famousness' Him told him.

28; An the prophet Samu'iel went toward the king Sa'ol an entered toward him sittin at a dinnertable - an when 'Amalieq king 'Agag had sat pon him left.

29; 'Why did thou totally ignore JAH Who commanded thee that thou might downstroy the livestock an persons?' him told him.

30; An at that time the king feared an arose from him throne an tellin Samu'iel 'Return fe wi' him seized him clothes - an Samu'iel refused fe return ~ Samu'iel clothes were torn.

31; An Samu'iel told Sa'ol - 'JAH divided thy kingdom.'

32; An again Sa'ol told Samu'iel before the people - 'Honour mi an atone mi sin fe mi before JAH that Him might forgive mi' ~ an as him have feared JAH Word Who Irated him - but as him didn't fear the king who dead - Samu'iel refused fe return ina him word.

33; Becaudis thing him pierced 'Amalieq king 'Agag before him swallowed what him chewed.

34; An a demon seized that Sa'ol who demolished the LAW of JAH - an becau Him were the King of Kings Who rule all - JAH struck pon him head a king who worked sin - fe it don't shame him.

35; Fe Him are all the Iration Lord Who dismiss all the nobles an kings Itority who don't fear Him - but there are none who rule Him.

36; Like unto Him spoke sayin - Daweet kindred shall go while it were famed an honoured - but Sa'ol kindred shall go while it were downbased - Him downstroyed kingdom from him child an from Sa'ol.

37; Becau it saddened Him - an becau Him downstroyed the criminals who saddened Him by them evil Work - JAH revenged an downstroyed Sa'ol kindred childran - fe a person who don't revenge JAH enemy - him are JAH enemy.

38; When it are possible fe him fe revenge an downstroy - an when him have Itority - a person who don't revenge an downstroy the sinner an don't revenge an downstroy a person who don't keep JAH LAW - as him are JAH enemy - Him downstroyed Sa'ol kindred childran.

Chapter 7.

1; An whether thou be a king or a ruler - what important thing are thou?

2; Aren't it JAH Who Irated thee bringin from not livin toward livin - that thou might do Him Accord an might live firmed up by Him Command an might fear Him Judgemant? Like unto thou vex pon thy slaves an governed over them - all likewise there are also JAH Who vex pon thee an govern over thee.

3; Like unto thou beat without niceness persons who worked sin - all likewise there are also JAH Who will strike thee an lower thee toward *Gehannem* where are no exits up til Iternity.

4; Like unto thou whip him who weren't ruled fe thee an didn't bring a tribute fe thee - fe what are it that thou don't introduce a tribute fe JAH?

5; As Him are Who Irated thee in order that thou love that them might fear thee - an Who crowned thee pon all the Iration that thou might keep Him kindreds fe true - fe what are it that thou don't fear thy Irator JAH?

6; Judge by what are due an fe true like unto JAH Ipointed thee - yet don't sight up a face an favour fe small nor great ~ whom will thou fear without Him? keep Him Worship an the Nine Commands.

7; Like unto Mussie commanded 'Isra'iel childran sayin - 'I-man presented Water an fiyah fe thee-I ~ add thy hand toward what thou loved' - don't go neither rightward nor leftward.

8; Hear Him Word that I-man tell thee - that thou might hear Him Word an might do Him Command - lest thou say - 'She are beyond the sea or beyond the deep or beyond the river ~ who will bring fe mi that mi might sight she up an might hear Him Word an might do Him Command?'

9; Lest thou say - 'Who will proceed toward Heaven again an lower that JAH Word fe mi that mi might hear an do she?' - JAH Word are what approached - check - fe thou fe teach she with thy mouth an give alms by she with thy hand.

10; An thou didn't hear thy Irator JAH unless thou heard Him Book - an thou didn't love Him nor keep Him Command unless thou kept Him LAW.

11; An thou have that thou might enter toward *Gehannem* foriva - an unless thou loved Him Command - an unless thou did JAH Accord - Who honoured an famed thee separatin from all thy kindreds that thou might keep them fe true - thou have that thou might enter toward *Gehannem* foriva.

12; Him made thee above all - an Him crowned thee pon all Him kindreds that thou might rule Him kindreds fe true by what are due while thou thought of thy Irator Name Who Irated thee an gave thee a kingdom.

13; There are them whom thou whip from persons who wronged thee - an there are him whom thou pardon while thou thought of JAH Work - an there are him fe whom thou judge by what are due straightenin up thy reasonin.

14; An don't favour havin sight up a face pon the time them argued before thee ~ as Earth physique are thy money - don't accept a bribe that thou might pardon the sinner person an wrong the clean person.

15; If thou did Him Accord - JAH shall multiply thy era ina this world fe thee - but if thou sadden Him - Him will diminish thy era.

16; Think that thou will rise after thou dead - an that thou will be examined standin before Him pon all the Work thou worked whether it be goodly or evil.

17; If thou work goodly Work - thou will live ina Garden ina the Kingdom of Heaven - ina houses where kind kings live an where Light filled. Fe JAH don't shame thy lordship authority - but if thou work evil Work - thou will live ina *See'ol Gehannem* where evil kings live.

18; But pon the time thou sight up thy bein feared famousness - thy warriors award - thy hangin shield an spear - an pon the time thou sight up thy horses an thy troops beneath thy authority an them who beat drum an persons who play pon a harp before thee...

19; But pon the time thou sight up all this - thou mek thy reasonin lofty - an thou firm up thy collar of reasonin - an thou don't think of JAH Who gave thee all this honour - however pon the time Him told thee - Quit all this - thou aren't who quit it.

20; Fe thou have totally neglected the Ipointmant Him Ipointed thee - an Him shall give thy lordship fe another.

21; As death shall suddenly come pon thee - an as Judgemant shall be done ina Resurrection time - an as all man Work shall be examined - Him shall totally investigate an judge pon thee.

22; There are none who will honour this world kings - fe becau Him were Truth Judge - ina Judgemant time poor an wealthy will stand together. This world nobles crowns wherein them boast shall fall.

23; Judgemant are prepared - an a soul shall quake ~ at that time sinners an righteous ones Work shall be examined.

24; An there are none who shall be hidden. Pon the time a dawta arrived fe birthin - an pon the time the fetus ina she belly arrived fe bein birthed - like unto she cyaan prevent she womb - Earth also cyaan prevent she lodgers that are pon she ~ she will return.

25; An like unto clouds cyaan prevent rain lest them tek an rain toward the place JAH commanded them - fe JAH Word have Irated all bringin from not livin toward livin - an fe JAH Word again have introduced all toward a grave; an all likewise - after Resurrection time arrived - it aren't possible fe be that dead persons won't rise.

26; Like unto Mussie spoke sayin - 'It are by Words that proceed from JAH Tongue - yet it aren't only by grain that a person are saved'; an JAH Word again shall arouse all persons from graves.

27; Check - it were known that dead persons shall arise by JAH Word.

28; An again JAH said thus ina Repeatin Law becau persons who were nobles an kings who do Him Accord - As the day have arrived when them are counted fe downstruction - I-man shall revenge an downstroy them pon the day when Judgemant are judged an at the time when them feet stumble Him said.

29; An again JAH told persons who know Him Judgemant - Know know that I-man were your Irator JAH - an that I-man kill an I-man save.

30; I-man chastise ina the tribulation an I-man pardon ~ I-man lower toward *See'ol* an again I-man send forth toward the Garden - an there are none who shall escape from I Itority Him told them.

31; JAH said thus becau nobles an kings who didn't keep Him LAW - As Earthly kingdoms are a passin - an as them pass from mornin up til evenin - keep I Order an I LAW that unu might enter toward the Kingdom of Heaven that live firmed up foriva Him said.

32; Fe JAH callin Righteous ones are fe glory - an sinners fe tribulation ~ Him will mek the sinner wretched but will honour righteous ones.

33; Him will dismiss the person who didn't do Him Accord - but Him will Ipoint the person who did Him Accord.

Chapter 8.

1; Hear I - mek I tell thee the thing whereby dead persons shall arise ~ them shall plant a plant an be fertile an grapes shall send forth vines ~ as JAH shall bring the fruit *'imhibe 'albo* ~ them shall cast wine from it.

2; Overstand that that plant thou planted were small - but that she sent forth tips fruit an leaves today.

3; JAH give she root fe drink from Earth an Water - from both.

4; But Him feed she wood from fiyah an wind ~ roots give leaves Water fe drink - an Earth give firmness fe woods.

5; But the soul that JAH Irated mek them bear fruit amidst them - an dead persons arisin are likewise.

6; Pon the time soul were separated from flesh - as each of them ras selves have gone - Him said - Gather souls from the four natures - from Earth an Water - wind an fiyah.

7; But Earth nature lived firmed up ina she nature an became Earth - an Water nature lived firmed up ina she nature an became Water.

8; An wind nature lived firmed up ina she nature an became wind - an fiyah nature lived firmed up ina she nature an became a hot fiyah.

9; But a soul that JAH separated from flesh returned toward she Irator ~ up til Him raise she up inited with flesh pon the time Him loved - Him place she ina Garden ina the place Him loved.

10; Him place righteous souls ina Light house ina Garden - but that Him might send way sinners souls - Him also place them ina darkness house ina *See'ol* up til the time when Him loved.

11; JAH told the prophet Hiziq'iel - Call souls from the four corners - that them might be gathered an be one limb.

12; Pon the time Him spoke ina one Word sayin thus - the souls were gathered from the four corners.

13; An Water nature brought verdure - an again fiyah nature brought fiyah.

14; An again Earth nature brought Earth - an wind nature brought wind.

15; An JAH brought a soul from the Garden place where Him placed it ~ them were gathered by one Word - an a Resurrection were made.

16; An again I-man shall show thee the example that are alongside thee ~ the day dusk ~ thou sleep ~ the night dawn - an thou rise from thy beddin - but pon the time thou slept it are thy death example.

17; An pon the time thou awoke it are thy arisin example - but the night when all persons sleep whose physiques were dark - fe darkness have covered them - are this world example.

18; But the mornin light - when darkness are eliminated an when light are ina all the world an when persons arise an graze toward the field - are dead persons example.

19; An this Kingdom of Heaven where man are renewed are like unto this ~ dead persons Resurrection are like unto this ~ as this world are passin - it are the night example.

20; An like unto Daweet spoke sayin - 'Him placed Him example ina Sun' - as Sun shine pon the time it rose - it are a Kingdom of Heaven example.

21; An like unto Sun shine ina this world today - pon the time Kristos come Him shall shine like unto Sun ina Kingdom of Heaven that are new ~ as Him have said - I-man am a Sun that don't set an a Torch that aren't extinguished - Him JAH are she Light.

22; An Him shall quickly arouse the dead persons again ~ I-man shall bring one example fe thee again from thy food that thou sow an whereby thou are saved - an whether it be a wheat kernel or a barley kernel or a lentil kernel or all man seeds sown pon Earth - there are none that grow unless it were demolished an rotten.

23; An like unto the person flesh thou sight up - pon the time it were demolished an rotten - Earth eat stoutness with the hide.

24; An pon the time Earth ate it stoutness it grow bein around a kernel seventh ~ JAH give a cloud that seized rain like unto Him loved - an roots grow pon Earth an send forth leaves.

25; An if she were demolished an rotten she cyaan grow - but after she grew she send forth many buds.

26; An by JAH Accord fruit are given fe those buds that grew - an Him clothe it stoutness ina straw.

27; Sight up like unto the measure that the seed kernel thou sowed abounded - yet the silver an the leaf - the ear an the straw aren't counted fe thee.

28; Don't be a dull one who don't know - an sight up thy seed that it abounded - an all likewise - think that dead persons shall raceive the arisin that them will arise - an them hardship like unto them Work.

29; Hear I - that if thou sow wheat - it won't grow bein barley - nor bein wheat if thou sow barley - an mek I tell thee again that it won't grow ~ if thou sow wheat will thou gather barley? If thou sow watercress will thou gather linseed?

30; How about from plants kind - if thou plant figs will it really grow fe thee bein nuts? How about if thou plant almonds - will it grow fe thee bein grapes?

31; If thou plant the sweet fruit will it grow fe thee bein bitter? How about if thou plant the bitter fruit - are it possible fe it fe be sweet?

32; How about all likewise - if a sinner dead are it possible fe arise bein righteous ina Resurrection time? How about if a righteous person dead - are it possible fe arise bein a sinner ina Resurrection time? Every one shall raceive him hardship like unto him Work - yet him will raceive him hardship like unto him sin an him hand Work - yet there are none who will be canvicted by him companion sin.

33; A highland tree are planted an it send forth long branches ~ it will totally dry up ~ yet unless Heaven rained rain it leaves won't be verdant.

34; An the cedar will be uprooted from it roots unless summer rain alit pon it.

35; An all likewise - dead persons won't arise unless welfare dew alit fe them bein commanded from JAH.

Chapter 9.

1; Unless highland mountains an Gielabuhie regions rained a pardon rain fe them bein commanded from JAH - them won't grow grass fe beasts an animals.

2; An 'Elam mountains an Gele`ad mountains won't give verdant leaves fe sheeps an goats - nor fe oribi an animals ina wilderness - nor fe ibexes an hartebeest.

3; An likewise - pardon an dew bein commanded from JAH didn't alight fe doubters an criminals who made error an crime a money beforehand ~ dead persons won't arise ~ an Deemas an Qophros who worship idols an dig roots an work an instigate a thing...

4; An them who dig roots an practice sorcery an mek persons battle...

435

5; An them who lust havin departed from LAW - an Miedon an 'Atiena persons who believe ina them idols - an them who play an sing fe them while them beat violins an drums an strummed harps - them won't arise unless pardon dew alit fe them bein commanded from JAH.

6; These are who will be canvicted pon the day when dead persons arise an when Definite Judgemant are done - yet persons who save them ras selves an who lust ina them hands Work - them err by them idols.

7; Thou wasteful of heart dull one - do it seem fe thee that dead persons won't arise?

8; Pon the time a trumpet were blown by the Angels Chief Hola Meeka'iel tongue - that dead ones arise then - as thou won't remain ina grave without arisin - don't think a thing that are thus.

9; Hills an mountains shall be level an shall be a cleared path.

10; An Resurrection shall be done fe all fleshly ones.

Chapter 10.

1; However if it weren't thus - it are that former persons might be buried ina them faadas grave Iginnin from 'Adam - Iginnin from Siet an 'Abiel - Siem an Noh - Yis'haq an 'Abriham - Yosief an Ya`iqob - an 'Aron an Mussie - yet fe what are it that them didn't love that them might be buried ina another place?

2; Aren't it fe them fe arise together with them cousins ina Resurrection time? How about aren't it lest them bones be counted with evil ones an pagans bones - them who worship idols? Fe what are it that them didn't love that them might be buried ina another place?

3; But thou - don't mislead thy reasonin while thou said - 'How will dead persons arise after them dead - them who were buried ina one grave bein tens of thousands an whose bodies were demolished an rotten?'

4; An pon the time thou sight up toward a grave - thou speak this ina thy reasonin dullness while thou said - 'A whole fistful of Earth won't be found ~ how will dead persons arise?'

5; Will thou say the seed thou sowed won't grow? Even the seed thou sowed shall grow.

6; An all likewise - the souls JAH sowed shall quickly arise - as Him have Irated man ina Him Truth bringin from not livin toward livin - Him shall arouse them quickly by Him Word that save ~ Him won't delay Him arousin.

7; An as Him have again returned him from livin - toward a grave ina death - what about aren't it possible fe Him again fe return from death toward Life?

8; Savin an liftin up are possible fe JAH.

Chapter 11.

1; 'Armon perished an she fortress were demolished ~ as JAH have brought the hardship pon them like unto them evil an the Work them worked by them hands - persons who worship the idols ina 'Edomyas an Zablon shall be downbased at that time ~ as JAH have approached - Who shall canvict them who worked ina them infancy an didn't quit up til them aged - becau them idols an them evil - Seedona an Theeros shall weep..

2; Becau them worked sin an seducin fornication an worshipped idols - becaudis thing JAH shall revenge an downstroy them ~ fe them didn't live firmed up ina them Irator JAH Command - an Yihuda dawta childran shall be wretched.

3; She lived firmed up ina killin prophets an ina Irie Ites - yet as she didn't live firmed up ina the Nine Laws an the Worship - pon the time when dead ones arise - 'Iyerusaliem sin shall be revealed.

4; At that time JAH shall examine she ina Him Nature Wisdom ~ Him will revenge an downstroy she pon all she sin that she worked ina she infancy era ~ she didn't quit workin she sin Iginnin from she beauty era up til she age.

5; She entered toward a grave an became dust like unto she former faadas who lived firmed up ina them sin - an ina Resurrection time Him shall revenge an downstroy persons who demolished JAH LAW.

6; It shall be judged pon them - fe Mussie have spoken becau them sayin - 'Them LAW lodgin - them reasonins - became Sedom law lodgin.'

7; An them kindred are Gemorra kindred - an them law are what downstroy - an them Work are evil.

8; An them law are snake poison that downstroy - an viper poison that downstroy from alongside that.

Chapter 12.

1; 'Iyerusaliem child - as this thy sin are like unto Gemorra an Sedom sin - 'Iyerusaliem child - this are thy tribulation that were spoken by a prophet.

2; An thy tribulation are like unto Gemorra an Sedom tribulation - an them law lodgin reasonin firmed up ina adultery an arrogance.

3; Aside from adultery an arrogance rain - pardon an humility rain didn't rain from them reasonins by money that them Law reasonin lodgin are fertile - apart from spillin man blood an robbin an forgettin them Irator JAH.

4; An them didn't know them Irator JAH - apart from them evil Work an them idols - an them are Irie ina them hands Work - an them lust pon males an pon livestock.

5; As them eye of reasonin have been blinded lest them sight up secrets - an as them ears have deafened lest them hear or do JAH Accord that Him love - them didn't know JAH ina them Work - an them reasonins are like unto Sedom law lodgin. An them kindred - Gemorra grapes kindred that bear sweet fruit.

6; An if them examine them Work - it are poison that kill - fe it have firmed up ina curse Iginnin from the day when it were worked - an fe it grounation have been ina downstruction era.

7; As them Law lodgin - them reasonins - have firmed up ina sin Work - as them bodies have firmed up ina Seythan burnin Work fe build sin - them Law lodgin - them reasonins - have no goodly Work everytime.

8; An pon the time him shame an were baptise (by one who is led) it were fe chastisemant an downstruction - an him will firm up the persons who drank an them reasonins - an him will mek them who downstroy I - disgustin persons who distanced from JAH.

9; Fe them have lived firmed up ina them Work that were evil - an him will mek them Deeyablos lodgin - an eatin what were sacrificed fe the idols have been begun ina the House of 'Isra'iel - an she proceed toward the mountains an the trees.

10; An she worship the idols that peoples ina she area worship - an she dawta children an she male childran fe demons who don't know goodly Work separatin from evil.

11; An them spill clean blood ~ them gush an spill grapes from Sedom fe the idols foriva.

12; An she glorify an worship the Dagwon that the 'Iloflans worship - an she sacrifice fe him from she flocks an she fattened cows - that she might be Irie ina demons laziness that them taught she fe sacrifice fe them - an ina them gushin an spillin the grapes - an that she might do them accord.

13; She sacrifice fe him that she might be Irie in demons laziness that them taught she lest she know she Irator JAH Who feed she at each time an Who cherished an raised she Iginnin from she infancy up til she beauty - an again up til she age - an again up til she age day when she dead.

14; An again I-man shall revenge an canvict him ina Resurrection time - an as she didn't return toward I LAW - an as she didn't live firmed up ina I Command - she time when she live ina *Gehannem* shall be up til Iternity.

15; If them were Irators fe true - mek she idols arise with she an downscend toward *Gehannem* an save she pon the time I-man vexed an downstroyed she - an pon the time I-man distanced all the priests of the idols who lust with she.

16; Like unto she made sin an insult pon the Hola Items an pon I Lodgin the Temple - I-man made she wretched by all this.

17; When them told she - 'Check - this are JAH kindred - an she are 'Isra'iel Irator JAH Lodgin - an the famous King country 'Iyerusaliem who were separate from them who were separate - she are the Most I JAH Name Lodgin' - I-man made she wretched like unto she saddened I Name that were called ina she.

18; She boast ina I that she were I slave an that I-man were she Lord ~ she wink pon I like unto a criminal - yet she aren't who fear I an do I Accord like unto I bein she Lord.

19; Them became a obstacle pon she fe mislead that them might distance she from I - yet she are ruled fe other idols who don't feed she nor clothe she.

20; She sacrifice sacrifice fe them - an she eat the sacrifice - an she spill blood fe them - an she gush an drink from the grapes fe them ~ she smoke up ishence fe them - an she mek the ishence fragrance smell fe them ~ she idols command she - an she are commanded fe them.

21; An again she sacrifice she dawta childran an she male childran fe them - an as she present praises fe them becau them Love - she are Irie ina the thing she spoke by she tongue an ina she hands Work.

22; Woe fe she pon the day when Definite Judgemant are done - an woe fe she idols whom she love an inite; an she shall downscend with them toward *Gehannem* beneath *See'ol* - where the worm don't slumber an the fiyah aren't extinguished.

23; Woe fe thee wretched 'Iyerusaliem child - fe thou have quit I Who Irated thee an have worshipped different idols.

24; An I-man shall bring the hardship pon thee like unto thy Work ~ as thou have saddened I - an as thou have ignored I Word - an as thou didn't work goodly Work - I-man shall canvict thee toward thy pretensions.

25; Fe thou have saddened I Word - an fe thou didn't live firmed up ina I LAW whereby thou swore with I - that thou might keep I LAW an that I-man might live with thee ina Support an might save thee from all who fight thee - an also that thou might keep I Order that I-man commanded thee - an I-man shall ignore thee an won't quickly save thee from the tribulation.

26; Thou didn't keep all this - an I-man ignored thee ~ as I-man have created thee - an as thou didn't keep I Command nor I Word - I-man shall canvict thee ina Judgemant time - an I-man honoured thee that thou might be I kin.

27; An like unto Gemorra an Sedom were separated from I - thou were separated from I.

28; An I-man judged an downstroyed them - an like unto Sedom an Gemorra were separated from I - thou separated from I - an now like unto I-man vexed an downstroyed them - I-man vexed an downstroyed thee ~ as thou are from Sedom an Gemorra kindred whom I-man downstroyed - I-man downstroyed thee ~ as them whom I-man Irated have saddened I by goin toward a youtman wife an by lustin without LAW - with animals an males like unto arrivin with dawtaz - I-man downstroyed them name invocation from this world lest them live ina them Irie Ites.

29; There are no fearin JAH ina them faces Iginnin from a infant up til a elder ~ them help him ina all them evil Work - yet Him don't vex pon each one that them might quit workin she ~ as them Work are evil - them are sated of sin an iniquity.

30; All evil Work - robbery an arrogance an greed - are prepared ina them reasonins.

31; An becaudis thing JAH ignored them an downstroyed them countries - an them are there that Him might burn them with fiyah up til them root grounation perish ~ them totally perished up til the Iternity - yet Him didn't mek even one from them remain.

32; As them have firmed up ina sin - them shall wait ina downstruction foriva up til the Day of Advent when Definite Judgemant are done - fe them have saddened I with them evil Work - an I-man won't pardon them nor forgive them.

33; An I-man ignored them ~ fe thou won't find a reason pon the time I-man vexed an seized thee becau all thy Work were robbery an sin - adultery an greed an speakin lies - all error Work an the obstacle that I-man don't love - an thou 'Iyerusaliem child who were wretched - pon the day when Judgemant are done thou will be seized ina Judgemant like unto them.

34; I-man had made thee fe honour - but thou downbased thy ras self ~ I-man had called thee I money - but thou became fe another.

35; I-man had betrothed thee fe honour - but thou became fe Deeyablos - an I-man shall revenge an downstroy thee like unto thy evil Work.

36; Becau thou didn't hear all I Word - an becau thou didn't keep the Command I-man commanded thee pon the time I-man loved thee - I-man shall multiply an bring firm vengeance pon thee - fe I-man am JAH Who Irated thee - an I-man shall judge pon all sinners like unto thee - an pon the day when Judgemant are done I-man shall bring the hardship pon them like unto them evil Work.

37; As thou didn't keep I Word - an as thou have ignored I Judgemant - I-man shall canvict thee with them.

38; Woe fe unu - Gemorra an Sedom - who have no fearin JAH ina your reasonin.

39; All likewise - woe fe thy sista 'Iyerusaliem child pon whom it shall be judged together with thee ina Fiyah of *Gehannem* - fe unu will downscend together toward *Gehannem* that were prepared fe unu - where are no exits foriva - an woe fe all sinners who worked thy sin.

40; As unu didn't keep I Command nor I Word - thou an she who didn't keep I Command nor I Word shall downscend toward *See'ol* together pon the day when Judgemant are judged.

41; But kind persons who kept I Command an I Word shall eat the money that sinner persons accumulated - an like unto JAH commanded - kind persons shall share the loot that evil persons captured - an kind persons shall be totally Irie.

42; But wrongdoers an sinner persons shall weep - an them shall be sad becau all them sin that them wronged havin departed from I Command.

43; Him who keep I Word an live firmed up ina I Command - him are who find I blessin an are honoured alongside I.

44; All person who keep I Word an live firmed up ina I Command shall eat the fatness found from Earth - an shall live havin entered toward the Garden where enter kind kings who have straight reasonins.

Chapter 13.

1; As them shall be wretched an perish by I wrath pon the time I-man seized them - woe fe Theeros an Seedona an all Yihuda country regions who mek them ras selves arrogant today.

2; Conquerin JAH said thus ~ Him have said - Deeyablos child who are totally arrogant shall be birthed from them - the False *Messeeh* who fe a Truth thing are she enemy - who firm up him collar of reasonin - who boast an don't know him Irator - an Him said - Woe fe them - an JAH Who rule all said - I-man made him fe I anger pattern that I-man might be revealed ina him Power.

3; An this Qifirnahom Semarya an Geleela an Demasqo an Sorya an 'Akeya an Qophros an all Yordanos region are kindreds who firmed up them collars of reasonin - who live firmed up ina them sin - an whom death shadow an darkness covered - fe Deeyablos have covered them reasonins ina sin - an fe them are commanded fe that arrogant Deeyablos - an them didn't return toward fearin JAH.

4; At that time woe fe persons who are commanded fe demons an who sacrifice sacrifice ina them name fe them ~ as them have denied JAH Who Irated them - them resemble animals without minds - fe the False *Messeeh* who forgot JAH LAW an are Deeyablos child shall set up him image ina all the places (fe him have said 'Mi are a god') - an him shall be Irie ina him reasonin accord - ina him hand Work an ina robbery an all the sins an perfidy an iniquity - ina robbery an all the adulteries that a person work.

5; Fe becau it were counted alongside JAH that him work this - the era are known that them work sin.

6; Sun shall darken an moon shall be blood - an stars shall be shaken from Heaven - all the Work shall pass by the miracles that JAH shall bring ina Fulfillmant Era that Him might mek Earth pass - an that Him might mek all pass who live ina sin of persons who live within she.

7; As JAH have been proud pon the Iration Him Irated - an as Him have quickly made all Him loved ina one iwa - Jah death shall downstroy a small enemy Deeyablos.

8; Fe JAH Who rule all have said - I-man shall judge an downstroy - but after Advent - Deeyablos have no authority.

9; An pon the day when him were seized by I anger - him shall downscend toward *Gehannem* - fe which him mek application an where firm tribulation are ~ as him will tek all who are with him toward chastisemant an downstruction an perfidy - becau I-man were Who send forth from *Gehannem* an Who introduce toward *Gehannem* - him will downscend toward *Gehannem*.

10; As Him give firmness an Power fe weak persons - an again as Him give weakness fe powerful an firm persons - mek a powerful one not boast ina him Power.

11; As Him are a Ruler - an as Him judge an save the wronged persons from the persons hands who wrong them - Him will return the grudge of the widows an the child whose faada an mother dead pon him.

12; Woe fe thee who boast an firm up thy collar of reasonin - fe whom it seem that I-man won't rule thee nor judge an downstroy thee - fe ina him boastin an him arrogance him have said - 'Mi will streach mi throne ina stars an Heaven - an mi will be like unto JAH Who are lofty.'

13; An like unto Him spoke sayin - How Deeyablos fell from Heaven - him who shine like unto a mornin star that were Irated precedin all - woe fe thee.

14; An thou dared an spoke this ina thy arrogance - an thou didn't think of JAH Who totally Irated thee by Him Itority ~ why did thou boast thy ras self that thou downscend toward *Gehannem* ina thy reasonin firmness?

15; Thou were downbased separate from all Angels like unto thee - fe them praise them Irator with a humbled reasonin becau them knew that Him were Who Irated them from fiyah an wind - an fe them don't depart from Him Command - an fe them keep them reasonins from perfidy lest them totally depart from Him Command.

16; But thou did a firm perfidy ina thy reasonin arrogance ~ thou became a wretched man separate from thy companions - fe thou have cherished all the sin an iniquity - robbery an perfidy whereby persons who forgot JAH LAW an sinners like unto thee live firmed up - them who are from thy kindred an commit crime like unto thee - an who live firmed up by thy command an thy accord whereby thou teach sin.

17; Woe fe thee - fe the demons thou misled

ina thy malice an thou will downscend toward *Gehannem* together.

18; O unu JAH children who erred by that misleadin criminal Deeyablos - woe fe unu ~ as unu have erred like unto him by the money that him taught unu an that him hosts taught unu - unu will downscend toward *Gehannem* together - where are no exits foriva.

19; An formerly when JAH slave Mussie were there - unu saddened JAH by the Water where argumant were made an pon Korieb - an by 'Amalieq an pon Mount Seena.

20; An moreover pon the time unu sent scouts toward Kene`an - pon the time them told unu this sayin 'The path are far - an them ramparts an them fortresses that reach up til Heaven are firm - an warriors live there' - unu vexed that unu might return towad Gibts country where unu work worrisome Work - an unu saddened JAH Word.

21; Unu didn't think of JAH Who firmed unu up from the tribulation - an Who did great miracles ina Gibts - an Who led unu by Him Angel Itority. Him would veil unu ina cloud by day lest the Sun burn unu an Him would shine a column of fiyah fe unu by night lest your feet stumble ina darkness.

22; An pon the time the army an Fer`on frightened unu - unu totally cried toward Mussie - an Mussie totally cried toward JAH - an Him lodged ina Him Angel an kept unu lest unu meet with Fer`on.

23; But Him introduced them toward 'Eritra ina tribulation ~ JAH led only 'Isra'iel - fe Him have said - An there were no different idol with them - but Him buried them enemies ina sea at one time - an Him didn't preserve none who flee from them.

24; An Him made 'Isra'iel cross amidst the sea by foot ~ there are no tribulation that found them arisin from the Gibtsans ~ Him delivered them toward Mount Seena - an there Him fed them *menna* forty eras.

25; As 'Isra'iel children sadden JAH everytime - Him did all this goodly thing fe them an them neglected fe worship JAH.

26; Them placed evil ina them reasonins Iginnin from them childhood up til them age - fe JAH Mouth have spoken thus ina *'Oreet* where the faadas birth were written ~ as Him have spoken sayin - 'Adam children reasonin are ash - an all them Work are toward robbery an them run toward evil ~ there are none from them who love straight Work - apart from gatherin a person money ina violence an swearin ina lie an wrongin companions an robbin an stealin - them placed evil ina them reasonins.

27; An all go toward evil Work ina the era when them live ina Life ~ 'Isra'iel children who demolished JAH LAW totally saddened JAH Iginnin from Antiquity up til fufillmant era.

Chapter 14.

1; An pon the time JAH downstroyed Qayen children - kindreds who preceded - ina downstruction Water becau them sin - Him baptised Earth ina Water of Downstruction - an Him cleansed she from all Qayel children sin.

2; As Him have said - I-man were sad becau I-man Irated man - Him downstroyed all wrongdoers ~ Him didn't preserve apart from eight persons ~ Him downstroyed all ~ after this Him multiplied them an them filled

Earth ~ them shared them faada 'Adam inheritance.

3; But Noh swore with JAH a oath ~ them swore a oath with JAH lest JAH again downstroy Earth ina Downstruction Water - an lest Noh children eat what deceased nor what lodged dead - lest them worship different idols apart from JAH Who Irated them - an that Him might be a Love Faada fe them - an lest Him downstroy them at one time ina them vain sin - an lest Him prevent them the first an the spring rain - an that Him might give fe livestock an persons them food at each time - that Him might give them the grass an the grain fruit an plants - an that them might work goodly Work ina all that JAH love.

4; An after Him gave them this Order - 'Isra'iel children saddened JAH by them sin ~ them didn't live firmed up ina Him LAW like unto them faadas Yis'haq an 'Abriham an Ya`iqob who didn't demolish them Irator JAH LAW.

5. An Iginnin from the small up til the great - those 'Isra'iel children who didn't keep JAH LAW are crooked ina them Work.

6; An whether them be them priests or them chiefs or them scribes - everyone demolish JAH LAW.

7; Them don't live firmed up ina JAH Order an Him LAW that Mussie commanded them ina Repeatin Law sayin - 'Love thy Irator JAH ina thy complete body an thy complete reasonin.'

8; Them don't firm up ina JAH Order an Him LAW that Mussie commanded them ina book where LAW were written sayin - 'Love thy companion like unto thy body - an don't worship him idols that were different - an don't go toward a youtmon wife ~ don't kill a soul ~ don't steal.

9; An don't witness ina lie - an be it him donkey or be it him ox - don't love thy companion money nor all that thy bredda bought.'

10; However after him commanded them all this - 'Isra'iel children who were evil return toward treachery an sin - robbery an iniquity - toward a youtmon wife an toward lies an stealin an worshippin idols.

11; 'Isra'iel children saddened JAH pon Korieb by workin a cow that graze toward grass ~ them bowed sayin - 'Check - these are wi irators who sent wi forth from Gibts.'

12; An them were Irie ina them hand Work ~ if them ate an drank an satta - them arose fe sing.

13; As JAH have told him sayin - Thy kindreds whom thou sent forth from Gibts country where rulership are - them have proceeded from LAW an wronged - an them worked a cow image an bowed fe the idol - becaudis thing Mussie vexed an alit from Seena mountain.

14; While Mussie vexed pon him kindreds - him alit with him canfidante 'Iyasu - an pon the time 'Iyasu heard - him said - 'Check - I-man hear warriors voice ina 'Isra'iel camp.'

15; An Mussie told 'Iyasu - 'It are when 'Isra'iel play havin drunk the unboiled wine yet as fe a warrior voice - it aren't' - an him alit an broke them image an totally crushed it up til it were like unto dust ~ him mixed it within the Water that 'Isra'iel childran drink beside the mountain.

16; An after this him commanded the priests that them might slay one another becau the sin them worked before JAH.

17; Them knew that defyin JAH surpass killin them an killin them faadas - an them did like unto him commanded them.

18; An Mussie told them - 'Becau unu saddened JAH Who fed unu an cherished unu an Who sent unu forth from a rulership house an Who bequeathed fe unu the inheritance that Him swore fe your faadas that Him might give fe them an fe them childran after them - becaudis thing unu made JAH Irie.'

19; Fe them go toward sin an a evil thing - an them didn't quit saddenin JAH there.

20; Them aren't like unto them faadas Yis'haq an 'Abriham an Ya`iqob who made JAH Irie with them goodly Work that Him might give them what are pon Earth an what Him prepared fe persons who love Him ina Heaven Iginnin from them infancy up til them youthood an up til them age ~ them aren't like unto 'Abriham an Yis'haq an Ya`iqob who made Him Irie with them Work that Him might give them a Earth of inheritance where Irie Ites are found ina this world - an a garden that mek Irie - prepared fe kind persons ina hereafter world - what Him prepared fe 'Abriham an Yis'haq an Ya`iqob who made JAH Irie when them were ina Life an who love Him - Whom a eye didn't sight up nor a ear hear an Who aren't thought of ina reasonin.

21; An them childran who denied JAH an were evil an who live firmed up ina them reasonin accord - them didn't hear JAH Command - Him Who fed them an cherished them an kept them Iginnin from them infancy.

22; Them didn't think of JAH - Who sent them forth from Gibts land an saved them from brick Work an a firm rulership.

23; But them totally saddened Him - an Him would arouse peoples ina them area pon them - an them would arise pon them ina enmity an also tax them like unto them loved.

Chapter 15.

1; An at that time Midyam persons arose pon them ina enmity - an them aroused them armies pon 'Isra'iel that them might fight them - an them king name are called 'Akrandis ~ him quickly gathered many armies ina Keeliqyas an Sorya an Demasqo.

2; An campin beyond Yordanos him sent messengers sayin - 'An that mi might capture your money - pay tax toward 'Isra'iel fe mi' ~ him told them - 'But if unu don't pay tax - mi came that mi might punish unu an might capture your livestocks an tek your mares an capture your children.'

3; 'Mi will capture an tek unu toward the country unu don't know - an there mi will mek unu Water pourers an wood pickers' him told them.

4; 'Don't boast while unu said - "InI are JAH kindreds an there are nothing able fe InI" - aren't JAH Who sent mi that mi might downstroy unu an plunder your money? an aren't mi whom JAH sent that mi might gather all your kindreds?

5; Are there really a savin that them different idols saved the other kins that mi downstroyed? Mi captured them mares an them horses an mi killed them an captured them childran.

6; An unless unu introduced the tax that mi commanded unu - mi will downstroy unu like unto them' him said - an him crossed Yordanos that him might plunder them livestocks an them money an capture them wives.

7; An after this 'Isra'iel childran wept a firm mournin toward JAH - an them totally cried - however them lacked one who help them.

8; An becaudis thing JAH gave firmness fe the three bredren - an them names are like unto this: - an them are Yihuda an Mebikyas an Meqabees - whose features were handsome an who were warriors ina them Power.

9; An 'Isra'iel childran totally wept there ~ pon the time them heard - it saddened them ina them heart arisin from all 'Isra'iel childran shout ~ the child whose mother an faada dead pon him - an widows - an them officials an them priests - all 'Isra'iel kindred - both dawtaz an males - an all children - would weep sprinklin ash pon them heads - an them nobles had worn sackcloth.

10; But those bredren - who were attractive an comely - went an agreed that them might save them ~ them counseled sayin - 'Mek InI go an give InI bodies fe death becau these persons.'

11; Tellin one another - 'Tek heart - tek heart' - them went girdin them swords pon them waists an seizin them spears ina them hands - an them went prepared that them might incriminate the warrior.

12. An them arrived toward them camp ~ Mebikyus attacked the warrior (the king) when him had sat at a dinnertable ~ him cut him neck ina one blow when food were ina him mouth; an Meqabyus an Yihuda struck him armies pon the king left an right by sword an killed them.

13; An pon the time them king were defeated - them entered toward them spears ina them companions hearts - an them all totally fled an them bows were broken an them were defeated.

14; But those bredren who are attractive an comely were saved from death ~ there are no evil thing that found them - but as JAH have returned chastisemant toward them - them sliced up one another an were depleted.

15; Them were defeated an dead an them crossed Yordanos - an up til them crossed them cast way all them money - an all them money remained - an pom the time 'Isra'iel childran sight up that them enemies fled - them went toward them camp an took both what them plundered an them money fe them ras selves.

16; JAH saved 'Isra'iel doin thus by the bredren an Mebikyu hand.

17; 'Isra'iel sat a few days while them made JAH Irie.

18; But after that them again returned toward them sin ~ 'Isra'iel childran neglected worshippin JAH by what are due.

19; An Him shall again sadden them by kins who don't know them an who will gather them field crops an downstroy them grape places an plunder them flocks an slaughter an feed them them livestocks before them...

20; an who will capture them wives an them dawta children an them male childran ~ becau it were that them sadden JAH everytime; as themore kindreds who demolished the LAW - them will hammer them childran before them pon each of them heads ~ them won't save them.

Chapter 16.

1; Them who do this are Theeros an Seedona an them who live beyond Yordanos river an pon the sea edge - Keran an Gele`ad - 'Iyabuseewon an Kenaniewon - 'Edom an Giegiesiewon an 'Amalieq persons.

2; All peoples do thus - who live firmed up ina each of them tribes an countries an regions an ina each of them Works an country languages - an all live firmed up like unto JAH worked them.

3; An there are persons from them who know JAH - an whose Work were beautiful.

4; An there are persons from them whose Work were evil an who don't know JAH Who Irated them - an like unto them worked sin - Him ruled them ina Sorya king Silminasor hand.

5; As him plunder an tek Demasqo money - an as him share Semarya loot that are before Gibts king - Him ruled them ina Silminasor hand.

6; Gielabuhie region an also persons ina Fars an Miedon - Qephedoqya an Sewseegya - who live ina the West mountains - ina Gele`ad fortress an Phasthos that are part of Yihuda land...

7; an these are who live in them region - an them are kindreds who don't know JAH nor keep Him Command - an whose collar of reasonin were firm.

8; An Him shall pay them them hardship like unto them Work evil an them hands Work.

9; Fe Gele`ad kindreds an Qeesarya region an 'Amalieq have become one there - that them might downstroy JAH country that were filled of a Truth thing - an within which 'Isra'iel Irator are praised - Him Who are Most Glorified an Conquerin - an Whom Angels who are many many ina Keerubiel chariots - them who stand before Him - serve fearin an tremblin - an Him shall pay them them hardship like unto them Work evil an them hands Work.

Chapter 17.

1; 'Amalieq an 'Edomyas persons don't worship JAH by Whose Itority Earth an Heaven rulership were seized ~ as them are criminals who don't live firmed up ina Truth Work - them don't fear fe demolish Him Lodgin - the Temple.

2; An there are no fearin JAH before them - apart from sheddin blood an adultery an eatin what were beaten an sacrificed fe a idol an all that resemble what lodged dead - an these are scorned sinners.

3; Them have no virtue nor religion ~ as them are who hated goodly Work - an as them don't know JAH - an as them don't know Love Work - apart from robbin a person money an from sin - an apart from downsturbin a person an all hated Work - apart from games an song like unto them faada Deeyablos taught them - them have no virtue nor religion.

4; As him have ruled them with him host - demons - him teach them all evil Work that were fe each of them ras selves - all robbery an sin - theft an falsehood - robbin money an eatin what were beaten an what lodged dead - an adultery Work.

5; An him teach them all that resemble this - an goin toward a youtmon wife - an sheddin blood - eatin what were sacrificed fe idol an what lodged dead - an killin a person soul ina violence - an envy an winkin an greed an all evil Work that JAH don't love ~ Deeyablos who were them enemy teach them this teachin that him might distance them from JAH LAW Who rule all the world.

6; But JAH Work are innocence an humility - not annoyin a bredren an lovin a companion - harmonisin an lovin with all persons.

7; Don't be hypocrites fe favour fe a person face - an don't be wrongdoers nor totally robbers nor persons who go toward a youtmon wife - nor persons who work iniquity an evil Work pon them companion - nor who cajole that them might wrong them companion ina violence.

8; Them wink an shake them heads an provoke fe evil ~ them discourage fe mislead that them might lower them toward Iternity Definite Judgemant.

Chapter 18.

1; Think that thou will go ina death toward JAH ina Whose Hand all are - an thou will stand before Him that Him might canvict thee before Him pon all the sin thou Worked.

2; As them who are arrogant an evil - an powerful ones children who aren't strengthenin more than them - were likewise formerly - becau them sight up them stature an them Power an them firm authority - them didn't mek JAH before them - an them didn't know that Him were them Irator Who Irated them bringin from not livin toward livin.

3; An when them faadas bein like unto "Angels" praised pon Mount Hola with Angels - pon the time them accord misled them - them alit toward this world where Definite Judgemant shall be done foriva.

4; As JAH ina the Antiquity have Irated human flesh fe them - that it might mislead them becau them reasonin arrogance an might test them as it were them kept Him LAW an Him Command - them married wives from Qayel children.

5; But them didn't keep Him LAW ~ Him lowered them toward *Gehannem* fiyah with them faada Deeyablos; fe JAH have vexed pon the offspring of Siet who wronged like unto persons - an persons era diminished becau them sin.

6; An them took 'Adam childran toward sin with them ~ Him lowered them toward *See'ol* where them shall raceive a verdict.

7; As persons era have been divided becau Siet children erred by Qayel children - when a person eras were nine hundred ina the Antiquity - them returned toward livin a hundred twenty eras.

8; An as them are flesh an blood - JAH said - I Spirit of Support won't live firmed up pon them.

9; An becaudis thing InI era were divided - fe becau InI sin an InI iniquity - InI era have been divided from InI faadas who preceded - an when them are ina them infancy again - them are dyin.

10; But InI faadas era had abounded - becau them kept Him LAW an becau them didn't sadden JAH.

11; But InI faadas era had abounded - becau them vexed pon them dawta childran that them might teach them - an becau them vexed pon them male childran lest them demolish JAH LAW.

12; Becau them didn't demolish JAH LAW with them dawta childran an them male childran - becaudis thing them era had abounded fe true.

Chapter 19.

1; Pon the time Qayen childran abounded them worked drums an harps - *santee* an violins - an them made songs an all the games.

2; Childran who are attractive an comely were birthed fe Qayen from the wife of the kind man 'Abiel - whom him killed becau she - fe she were attractive - an after him killed him bredda him took that an she who were him money.

3; An separatin from him faada - him seized them an went toward Qiefaz region that are toward the West - an that attractive one childran were attractive like unto them mother.

4; An becaudis thing Siet childran downscended toward Qayen childran - an after them sight them up them didn't wait one iwa - an them made the dawtaz whom them chose wives fe them ras selves.

5; As them have taken InI toward error together with them becau them error - becaudis thing JAH vexed pon InI an vexed pon them.

6; An Deeyablos havin cajoled sayin - 'Unu will become irators like unto your Irator JAH' - him took InI mother Hiewan an InI faada 'Adam toward him error.

7; But it seemin Truth fe them ina them dullness - them demolished JAH LAW - Him Who Irated them bringin from not-livin toward livin that them might bow an praise Him glorified Name.

8; But Him - them Irator - downbased those 'Adam an Hiewan who made godhood fe them ras selves - an Him downbased him who are arrogant.

9; Like unto Daweet spoke sayin - ' 'Adam perish by the sinner Deeyablos arrogance' - Him abused them - fe InI faada 'Adam have been canvicted pon Deeyablos arrogance by Him true Judgemant.

10; An Siet childran who erred by Qayel childran took InI toward them sin thus ~ becaudis thing InI era that JAH gave InI were less than InI faadas eras.

11; But them had worked goodly Work - fe them had firmed up them reasonins ina JAH - fe them had taught them dawta childran an them male childran lest them depart from JAH LAW that them taught them - an there were no evil enemy who approach them.

12; But if them worked goodly Work - there are nothing that benefit them if them didn't tell nor teach fe them childran.

13; Like unto Daweet spoke sayin - 'Them didn't hide from them childran fe another child - an teach JAH praise - the wondrous miracles Him did - an Him Power' - there are nothing that benefit them if them didn't teach fe them childran that them might teach fe them childran fe mek heart like unto them knew - an that them might know an do Him Accord - an that them might tell them JAH LAW Trust - an that them might keep Him LAW like unto them faadas who made JAH Irie with them beautiful Work.

14; An them who told them Trust from them faadas ina them infancy didn't demolish Him

Command - like unto them faadas learned JAH Worship an the Nine Laws from them faadas.

15; Them childran learned from them faadas that them might work goodly Work an might present praise fe them Irator - fe them have kept Him LAW - an fe them have loved Him.

16; An Him shall hear them ina them priah - an Him won't ignore them plea - but Him are a Forgiver.

17; Havin multiplied Him wrath - Him shall return it fe them - an Him wouldn't downstroy all ina Him chastisemant.

Chapter 20.

1; InI bredren - think - don't forget what them told unu formerly - that JAH keep the true Work of persons who work goodly Work.

2; An Him multiply them childran ina this world - an them name invocation shall live firmed up fe a goodly thing up til the Iternity - an them childran won't be troubled fe grain ina this world.

3; As Him shall dispute fe them becau them - an as Him won't cast them ina them enemy hand - Him shall save them from them enemies hand who hate them.

4; An fe persons who love Him Name - Him shall be them Helper ina them tribulation time ~ Him shall guard them an pardon them all them sin.

Chapter 21.

1; Daweet believed ina JAH - fe Him have believed ina him - an Him saved him bein a Refuge from the king Sa'ol hand.

2; An as him have believed ina Him an kept Him LAW pon the time when him child 'Abiesielom arose - an pon the time when the 'Iloflans arose - an pon the time when the 'Edomyans an the 'Amalieqans arose - pon the time when the one from the four Rafayn arose - JAH saved Daweet from all this tribulation that enemies who disputed him brought pon him.

3; As prevailin are by JAH Accord - them were defeated by them enemies hand - yet but JAH didn't save the evil kings who didn't believe ina Him.

4; An Hiziqyas believed ina JAH ~ Him saved him from Senakriem hand who were arrogant.

5; But him child Minassie were defeated by him enemy hand - fe him didn't mek him trustin ina JAH ~ as him didn't mek him trustin ina JAH an as him didn't fear JAH Who totally honoured an famed him - them bound an took him toward them country - yet but those enemies who defeated Minassie weren't like unto him.

6; At that time Him denied him the kingdom Him gave him - fe him didn't work goodly Work before him Irator JAH - that him era might abound an that Him might dispute him enemy fe him an that him might have Power an firmness behind an in front.

7; Fe it are better fe believe ina JAH than ina many armies - than believin ina horses an bows an shields.

8; Believin ina JAH surpass ~ a person who

believed ina Him shall firm up an be honoured an totally lofty.

9; Fe JAH don't favour fe a face - but persons who didn't believe ina JAH - who believed ina them money abundance - became them who departed from the grace an honour that Him gave them.

10; Him shall guard the persons who believe ina Him - but Him shall mek the persons ignorant who call Him ignorant - an as them didn't discipline them reasonins fe follow JAH nor keep Him LAW - Him won't quickly help them ina them tribulation time nor ina the time them enemies disputed with them.

11; But fe a person who were disciplined ina worshippin JAH an fe keep Him LAW - Him shall be a Refuge ina him tribulation time.

12; By downstroyin him enemy - an by plunderin him enemy livestock - an by capturin him enemy country persons - an by rainin eras rain - an by growin sprouts - an by introducin the grain pile - ina the plant fruit...

13; An by rainin the first an the spring rains - an by makin the grass verdant - an by givin the rain that rain at each time that thy kindreds beneath thy Itority might be Irie - Him shall mek him Irie.

14; Him shall mek him Irie - that them might eat the other one money - that them might satta havin eaten the money them plundered from them enemy - that them might plunder animals an sheeps an cows - an that them might eat the other one dinnertable - an that them might tek them enemies childran captive.

15; JAH shall do all this fe the person whom Him love - but Him will mek the person who hate Him fe him enemy ransackery.

16; An Him shall bind him feet an him hands an shall cast him ina him enemy hand - an Him shall mek him fe him enemies derision - an as him have become a blood shedder who demolished JAH LAW - Him won't mek him Irie ina him house seed.

17; An him won't firm up ina Judgemant time - an that Him might bring the hardship fe persons who work sin - Him will also give persons who work evil Work them sin hardship.

18; But it were commanded from alongside JAH fe give persons who work goodly Work them reward - that Him might keep them ina Him Itority.

19; Fe Him are empowered pon all the Iration Him Irated that Him might do goodly Work an might give them Iternal welfare an that them might praise JAH Who Irated them - an Him commanded that him might keep Him LAW ~ apart from only man there are none from all the Irations Him Irated that departed from Him Command.

20; Like unto JAH commanded all who live firmed up ina each of them Works - them all know an are kept ina Him LAW.

21; But man are emboldened pon JAH Who crowned all pon each of them inventions - pon animal an beasts an pon Heaven birds.

22; Be it what are ina sea or all pon land - JAH gave all the Iration Him Irated fe them faada 'Adam ~ JAH gave them that him might do what him loved - an that them might eat them like unto grain that grew pon Earth - an that them might rule an tax them - an that be them beasts or animals them might be commanded fe man - an Him Ipointed them pon all Him Irated that persons who reigned might be commanded fe JAH Who gave them honour an that them might favour Him.

23; But if them depart from Him LAW Him will separate them from Jahship Him gave them ~ as Him are Who rule Earth an Heaven - Him will give it fe him who do Him Accord.

24; Him Ipoint whom Him loved fe Ipoint - but Him dismiss whom Him loved fe dismiss ~ Him kill ~ Him save ~ Him whip ina tribulation ~ Him forgive.

25; There are no other Irator like unto Him ~ as Him are Ruler fe all the Iration Him Irated - as there are no other without Him - the Irator - ina Heaven above Earth nor pon Earth beneath Heaven - there are none who shall criticise Him.

26; Him Ipoint ~ Him dismiss ~ Him kill ~ Him save ~ Him whip ina tribulation ~ Him forgive ~ Him impoverish ~ Him honour.

27; Him hear persons who beg Him ina them plea ~ Him accept a person plea who do Him Accord with a clean reasonin; an Him hear them ina them priah - an Him do them accord fe them ina all that them begged Him.

28; An Him mek the great an the small fe be commanded fe them ~ all this are them money pon hills an mountains an at trees roots an ina caves an Earth wells an all them kindreds pon both dry an sea.

29; An fe persons who do them Irator Accord all this are them money - an Him won't trouble them from them plenty - an Him shall give them them praise reward.

30; An Him shall give them the honour Him prepared ina Heaven fe them faadas Yis'haq an 'Abriham an Ya`iqob ~ Him shall give them what Him prepared fe Hiziqyas an Daweet an Samu'iel who didn't depart from Him LAW an Him Command.

31; That them might be Irie ina Him Lordship - Him shall give them who served Him Iginnin from Antiquity the honour Him prepared fe them faadas Yis'haq an 'Abriham an Ya`iqob - fe whom Him swore fe give them a inheritance.

Chapter 22.

1; Please - think of persons name who work goodly Work - an don't forget them Work.

2; Straighten up that thy name be called like unto them name - that thou might be Irie with them ina the Kingdom of Heaven - that were Light Lodgin that Him prepared fe nobles an kings who did JAH Accord an were kind persons.

3; An again - know an be canvinced of evil nobles an kings names - that Him shall canvict them an revile them alongside man after them dead.

4; Fe them didn't line up them Work while them sight up an heard - an know an be canvinced that unless them did JAH Accord - Him shall judge pon them ina the Kingdom of Heaven more than criminals an persons who forgot JAH LAW.

5; Be kindly - innocent - honest - yet don't thou also go pon persons path who forgot JAH LAW - pon whom JAH vexed becau them evil Work.

6; Judge Truth an save the child whose mother an faada dead pon him - an the widow from sinner persons hand who rob them.

7; Be a guardian like unto him faada fe the child whose mother an faada dead pon him - that thou might save him from the wealthy one hand who rob him - an stand fe him - an be alarmed pon the time the child - whose mother an faada dead pon him - tears flowed before thee-I - lest thou be alarmed ina fiyah sea where sinner persons who didn't enter repentance are punished.

8; An straighten up thy feet toward Love an Inity path ~ as JAH Eyes check up Him friends - an as Him Ears hear them plea - seek Love an follow she.

9; But JAH Face of Him Wrath are toward persons who work evil Work - that Him might downstroy them name invocation from this world - an Him won't preserve a person who near pon ramparts nor mountains.

10; As I-man am JAH Who am jealous pon I Godhood - as I-man am a Irator who revenge an downstroy persons who hate I an don't keep I Word - I-man won't return I Face of Support reachin up til I-man downstroy the person who don't keep I Word.

11; An I-man shall honour persons who honour I an keep I Word.

Chapter 23.

1; Don't live firmed up ina Qayel order - who killed him bredda who followed him ina innocence - it seemin fe him that him bredda love him.

2; An him killed him bredda envyin pon a dawta ~ persons who mek envy an iniquity an betrayal pon them companion are like unto him.

3; But as 'Abiel are innocent like unto a sheep - an as him blood are like unto the clean sheep blood that them sacrificed fe JAH by a clean reasonin - them went pon Qayel path that aren't pon 'Abiel path.

4; Fe becau all the persons who live ina innocence were persons whom JAH love - like unto a kind man 'Abiel - them have been innocent ones like unto 'Abiel - but those persons who live firmed up ina 'Abiel Work love JAH.

5; But JAH neglect evil ones - an them Definite Judgemant mek application fe them pon them bodies - an it are written pon the record of them reasonins - an pon the time when Judgemant are judged - them shall read she before man an Angels an before all the Iration.

6; At that time them shall shame ~ wrongdoers an refusers who didn't do JAH Accord shall shame.

7; An a alarmin Word shall be given them that say - Place them ina *Gehannem* where are no exit up til Iternity.

Chapter 24.

1; But pon the time Giediewon trusted JAH - him defeated uncircumcise peoples armies who were many many ina army of a few tens of thousands an without number like unto locusts.

2; As there are no Irator without I - o nobles an kings - don't believe ina the different idols.

3; As I-man am your Irator JAH Who sent unu forth from your mothers wombs an raised unu an fed unu an clothed unu - why do unu pretext? How about why do unu worship other idols without I?

4; I-man did all this fe unu ~ what did unu give I? It are that unu might live firmed up ina I LAW an I Order an I Command an that I-man might give unu your bodies welfare - yet what will I-man want from unu?

5; JAH Who rule all said thus ~ Him said - Save your ras selves from worshippin idols an practisin sorcery an discouragin pessimism.

6; As JAH chastisemant shall come pon these who do this - an pon them who hear them an do them accord an are them friends an who live firmed up ina them command - save your ras selves from worshippin idols.

7; As peoples - who don't know unu an aren't nice fe unu - shall arise pon unu - unless unu who feared did JAH Accord - them will eat the money wherefor unu wearied ~ like unto Him servants the prophets spoke an like unto Hienok spoke an like unto 'Asaf spoke - unless unu did JAH Accord - them will eat the money wherefor unu wearied.

8; Evil persons will come havin changed them clothes Him said ~ there are no other law alongside them apart from eatin an drinkin an adornin ina silver an gold - an livin havin firmed up ina sin all the Work JAH don't love.

9; But them are prepared fe go toward drink an food ~ after them were aroused from them slumber Iginnin from mornin up til evenin them go toward evil Work; there are misery an tribulation ina them path - yet them feet have no Love path.

10; An them don't know Love an Inity Work - an there are no fearin JAH ina them faces ~ them are crooked evil ones without religion nor virtue ~ them are greedy ones who eat an drink alone ~ them are drunkards - an them sin are without LAW an without measure ~ them are who go toward seducin - sheddin blood - theft an perfidy an violently robbin him money who don't have it.

11; An them are who criticise without Love an without LAW - fe them don't fear JAH Who Irated them - an there are no fear ina them faces.

12; Them don't shame ina the person face that them sight up - an them don't shame a grey-hair nor a elder face ~ pon the time them heard when them said - 'An there are money ina this world' - them mek it them ras self money before them sight it up with them eyes - fe there are no fearin JAH ina them faces - an pon the time them sight it up with them eyes it seem fe them that them ate it.

13; An them nobles eat trust money ~ them are who eat ~ as them are negativists an as there are no straight thing ina them tongues - them don't repeat ina evenin what them spoke ina mornin.

14; Fe them ignore sufferahs an poor ones cries - an them kings hasten fe evil - them who downsturb a person - him havin saved refugees from wealthy ones hands who rob them.

15; Mek them save him who were wronged an the refugee - yet mek the kings not be them who begrudge justice becaudis thing.

16; But them are who exact tribute ~ them are who rob a person money - an them are criminals - an as them Work are evil - them aren't nice when them eat the newborn calf with she mother an a bird with she egg ~

them mek all them sight up an heard them ras self money.

17; Them love that them might gather fe them ras selves - yet them aren't nice fe sick an poor ones - an them violently rob the money of a person who don't have it - an them gather all them found that them might be fattened an be Irie ina it.

18; Fe them shall perish quickly like unto a scarab that proceeded from it pit an whose track aren't found an that don't return toward it house - an becau them didn't work goodly Work when them are ina them Life - woe fe them bodies pon the time JAH vexed an seized them.

19; Pon the time JAH neglected them - them will perish at one time like unto them are ina one chastisemant - fe Him indure them meanin as it were them returned toward repentance - yet Him don't quickly downstroy them - an them shall perish pon the time when them shall perish.

20; But if them don't return toward repentance - Him will quickly downstroy them like unto former persons who were precedin them - who didn't keep JAH LAW by what are due.

21; Them are who eat a person flesh an drink a person blood ~ as them gird an work violence fe go toward sin - there are no fearin JAH ina them faces everytime - an after them arose from them beddin them don't rest fe work sin.

22; An them Work are drink an food - goin toward downstruction an sin - that them might downstroy many persons bodies ina this world.

Chapter 25.

1; As them Work are crooked - an as all are who live firmed up ina Seythan Work that mislead - JAH Who rule all said - Woe fe your body pon the time I-man vexed an seized she.

2; But fe them don't know JAH Work - fe them have returned it toward them rear - an fe them have neglected I LAW.

3; An later ina fulfillmant era I-man shall bring the hardship pon them like unto them evil measure ~ like unto them sin were written alongside I - I-man shall revenge an downstroy them pon the day when Judgemant are judged.

4; As I-man JAH am full from horizon up til horizon - an as all the Iration have been seized ina I Itority - there are none who escape from I Itority ina Heaven nor Earth nor depth nor sea.

5; I-man command a snake that are beneath Earth - an I-man command a fish that are within sea - an I-man command birds ina Heaven - an I-man command the desert donkey ina wilderness - fe it are I money Iginnin from horizon up til horizon.

6; As I-man am Who work wondrous Work an do miracles before I - there are none who escape from I Itority pon Earth nor ina Heaven ~ there are none who tell I - 'Where do Thou go? How about what do thou Work?'

7; An I-man command pon Angels chiefs an hosts ~ all Irations whose name are called are I money - an beasts ina wilderness an all birds ina Heaven an livestocks are I moneys.

8; It arise from 'Azieb wind an firm up ina drought ina Mesi` ~ later ina fulfillmant era 'Eritra sea shall perish bein heard - arisin from JAH - Who shall come toward she - bein feared an famousness.

9; Fe Him rule them who dead an persons who are there - an she shall perish bein heard with Saba an Noba an Hindekie an 'Ityopphya limits an all them regions.

10; An Him watch all ina lofty Itority an innocence - fe Him Itority surpass all the itority - an Him keep cangregations ina Him Itority.

11; An fe Him Itority firm up more than all the itority - an fe Him Kingdom surpass all the kingdoms - an fe Him Itority are what rule all the world - fe Him able fe all - an fe there are nothing that fail Him.

12; Him rule all clouds ina Heaven ~ Him grow grass fe livestocks pon Earth - an Him give fruit pon the buds.

13; Him feed fe all ina each of the kinds like unto Him loved ~ Him feed all that Him Irated by each of the fruits an each of the foods - an Him feed ants an locusts beneath Earth an livestocks pon Earth an beasts - an fe a person who prayed Him give him him priah - an Him don't ignore the plea of the child whose mother an faada dead pon him - nor widows.

14; As evil persons rebellion are like unto a swirlin wind an wrongdoers council like unto misty urine - Him shall rather accept the plea of them who beg toward Him at each time an clean ones.

15; An as them body are like unto a flyin bird - an as them features comeliness that are silver an gold are perishable ina this world - examination will benefit persons who forgot JAH LAW yet not them gold - an moths shall eat them clothes.

16; An weevils shall totally eat the wheat an the barley fatness - an all shall pass like unto the day that passed yesterday - an like unto a word that proceeded from a mouth don't return - sinner persons money also are like unto it - an them 'beautiful lifestyle' are like unto a passin shadow ~ sinner persons money before JAH are like unto a lie clothes.

17; But if kind persons are honoured JAH won't ignore them - fe them have been honoured while them were nice fe poor ones - an them hear justice of sufferahs an a child whose mother an faada dead pon him ~ JAH won't ignore them - fe without neglectin them house childran - them honour Him while them clothe the naked from the clothes JAH gave them that them might give fe the refugee sufferah.

18; Them don't favour loyal persons judgemant - an them don't mek a hireling salary lodge ~ as JAH thing are Truth an honoured like unto a sword whose mouths were two - them won't do iniquity ina them seasons number an ina them balance measuremant.

Chapter 26.

1; But poor ones will think again pon them beddin - but if wealthy ones don't accept them - them will be like unto dry wood that have no verdure - an a root won't be fertile from alongside where no moisture are - an the leaf won't be fertile if there are no root.

2; As a leaf serve a flower fe be a ornamant fe fruit - unless the leaf were fertile it won't bear fruit ~ as man fulfillmant are religion - a person without religion have no virtue.

3; If him firmed up religion him worked virtue - an JAH are Irie by a person who work Truth an straight Work.

4; An fe the person who begged Him - Him shall give him him plea an him tongue reward - an Him won't wrong the true person becau him true Work that him worked.

5; As JAH are true - an as Him have loved a Truth thing - Him won't justify the sinner person without repentance becau the Work evil him worked - an as all persons souls have been seized ina Him Itority becau Him were Who ruled Earth an Heaven - as Him won't favour for the wealthy more than the poor ina Judgemant time - Him won't justify him without repentance.

Chapter 27.

1; Him Irated havin brought all the world from not livin toward livin - an Him totally prepared hills an mountains - an Him firmed up Earth pon Water - an lest sea be shaken Him delineated she by sand - fe ina Him first Word JAH have said Mek Light be Irated.

2; Light were Irated when this world had been covered ina darkness ~ JAH Irated all the Iration - an Him prepared this world - an Him firmed up this world by what are due an by money that are straight ~ Him said - Mek evenin be dark.

3; An again JAH said Mek Light be Irated ~ it dawned an there were Light - an Him Ilivated the upper Water toward Heaven.

4; An Him streached it forth like unto a tent - an Him firmed it up by a wind - an Him placed the lower Water within a pit.

5; An Him shut the sea lock ina sand - an Him firmed them up ina Him Itority lest them drown ina Water - an Him placed animals an beasts within she - an Him placed within she Liewatan an Biehiemot who were great beasts - an Him placed within she the beasts without number - sight up an not sight up.

6; Pon the third day JAH Irated pon Earth plants - all the roots an woods an fruits that bear forth ina each of them kinds - an a welfare wood beautiful fe them fe sight it up..

7; An Him Irated a welfare wood that were both beautiful fe them fe sight it up an sweet fe them fe eat it - an Him Irated grass - an all plants whose seeds are found from within them - fe be food fe birds an livestocks an beasts.

8; It dusked ~ it dawned - an pon the fourth day Him said - Mek Light be Irated ina Heaven called cosmos ~ JAH havin Irated moon an Sun an stars - Him placed them ina Heaven called cosmos that them might shine ina this world an that them might feed them daylight an night.

9; An after this moon an Sun an stars alternated ina night an daylight.

10; An pon the fifth day JAH Irated all animals an beasts that live within Water an all birds that fly pon Heaven - all that are sight up an not sight up - all this.

11; An pon the sixth day Him Irated livestocks an beasts an others - an havin Irated an prepared all - Him Irated 'Adam ina Him Example an Him Appearance.

12; Him gave him all animals an beasts Him Irated that him might reign pon them - an again - all animals an beasts an all fishes - an Liewatan an Biehiemot that are ina sea.

13; An Him gave him all cows that live ina this world an sheeps - the animals not sight up an them that are sight up.

14; An Him placed ina Garden 'Adam whom Him Irated ina Him Example an Him Appearance - that him might eat an might cultivate plants an might praise JAH there.

15; An fe lest him demolish Him Command - Him have said - Pon the time when unu ate from this Herb of Fig unu will dead death.

16; An Him commanded him lest him eat from the Herb of Fig that bring death - that draw attention fe evil an good - that bring death.

17; InI mother Hiewan were cajoled by a snake misleadin an she ate from that Herb of Fig an gave it fe InI faada 'Adam.

18; An 'Adam havin eaten from that Herb of Fig brought death pon him children an pon him ras self.

19; As him have demolished Him Command - an as him have eaten from that Herb of Fig that JAH commanded sayin - Don't eat from she - JAH vexed pon InI faada 'Adam an expelled an sent him way from the Garden - an Him gave him that Earth that grow thistle an thorn - that Him cursed becau him pon the time him demolished Him Command - that him might eat him weariness reward havin toiled an laboured that him might plow she.

20; An pon the time JAH sent him forth toward this land - 'Adam returned toward complete sadness - an havin toiled an laboured that him might plow Earth - him began fe eat ina weariness an also ina struggles.

Chapter 28.

1; An after him children lived havin abounded - there were from them ones who praise an honour JAH an don't demolish Him Command.

2; There were prophets who spoke what were done an what will be done henceforth - an from him children there were sinners who speak lies an who wrong persons ~ 'Adam firstborn child Qayel became evil an killed him bredda 'Abiel.

3; JAH judged Judgemant pon Qayel becau him killed him bredda 'Abiel - an JAH vexed pon Earth becau she drank him blood.

4; An JAH told Qayel - Where are thy bredda 'Abiel? - an Qayel ina him heart arrogance said - 'Are mi mi bredda 'Abiel keeper?'

5; 'Abiel became a clean man - but Qayel became a sinner man by killin a kind man - him bredda 'Abiel.

6; Again a kind child Siet were birthed ~ 'Adam birthed sixty children ~ there are kind persons an evil persons from them.

7; An there are kind persons from them ~ an there are persons who were prophets an them who were traitors an sinners.

8; There are blessed persons who were kind persons - who fulfill them faada 'Adam accord an all him told fe him child Siet - Iginnin from 'Adam up til Noh who are a kind man who kept JAH LAW.

9; An him sanctioned JAH LAW fe him children ~ him told them - 'Guard' - lest them demolish JAH LAW - an that them might tell fe them children like unto them

457

faada Noh told them - an that them might keep JAH LAW.

10; An them lived while them taught them childran - persons birthed after them.

11; But Seythan lived when him spoke fe them faadas - havin lodged ina idols that reached fe a grave an that have vows pon them - an havin defeated the persons who told him alright - an when them did all that Seythan - who are sin teacher - commanded them.

12; An them lived when them worshipped the idols like unto them order - up til a kind man 'Abriham who fulfill JAH Accord.

13; Fe him have lived firmed up ina the LAW beforehand separate from him cousins - an JAH swore a oath with him - havin lodged ina wind an fiyah.

14; JAH swore fe him that Him might give him a land of inheritance an that Him might give fe him childran up til the Iternity.

15; An Him swore fe Yis'haq like unto him that Him might give him him faada 'Abriham inheritance - an Him swore fe Ya`iqob that Him might give him him faada Yis'haq inheritance ~ Him swore fe him like into Yis'haq.

16; An Him separated them childran - who were birthed after them from Ya`iqob - from the twelve tribes of 'Isra'iel - an made them priests an kings ~ Him blessed them sayin - Abound an totally be many many.

17; An Him gave them them faada inheritance - however while Him fed them an loved them - them didn't quit saddenin JAH ina all.

18; An pon the time Him downstroyed them - at that time them will seek Him ina worship - an them will return from sin an go toward JAH - fe Him love them - an JAH shall pardon them.

19; Fe bein nice fe all Him Irated - Him shall pardon them - an it are becau them faadas Work that Him love them - yet it aren't becau them ras selves Work.

20; An Him streach forth Him Right Hand ina plenty that Him might satta a hungry body - an Him reveal Him Eye fe pardonin that Him might multiply grain fe food.

21; Him give food fe crows chicks an fe beasts that beg Him ~ pon the time them cried toward Him - Him will save 'Isra'iel childran from them enemies hands who delayed from the time.

22; An them will return toward sin again that them might sadden Him - an Him will arouse them enemies peoples ina them area pon them ~ them will downstroy them an kill them an capture them.

23; An again them will shout toward JAH ina mournin an sadness - an there are the time when Him sent help an saved them by prophets hands.

24; An there are the time when Him saved them by princes hands - an pon the time them saddened JAH them enemies taxed them an captured them.

25; An Daweet arose an saved them from the 'Iloflans hands; an again them saddened JAH - an JAH aroused pon them peoples who worry them.

26; An there are the time when Him saved them by Yoftahie hand - an again them forgot JAH Who saved them ina them tribulation time. As JAH have brought the hardship pon them - Him will arouse pon them enemies who were evil who will firm

458

up tribulation pon them an totally capture them.

27; An pon the time them were worried by tribulation them were seized an again cried toward Him - an Him saved them by Giediewon hand - an again them saddened JAH by them hands Work.

28; An again Him aroused pon them peoples who firm up tribulation pon them - an them returned an wept an cried toward JAH.

29; An again Him saved them from peoples by Somson hand - an them rested a likkle from the tribulation. An them arose that them might sadden JAH by them former sin.

30; An again Him aroused pon them other peoples who worry them - an again them cried an wept toward JAH that Him might send help fe them - an Him saved them from peoples by Bariq an Deebora hands.

31; Again them lived a likkle season while them worshipped JAH - an again them forgot JAH ina them former sin an saddened Him.

32; An Him aroused pon them other peoples who worry them - an again Him saved them by Yodeet hand; an havin sat again a likkle season them arose that them might sadden JAH by them sin like unto formerly.

33; An Him aroused pon them peoples who rule them - an them cried an wept toward JAH; fe Him have struck pon him head 'Abiemieliek who were a warrior who came that him might fight Yihuda country.

34; An Him saved them by the childran ina the area an by Matatyu hand - an pon the time that warrior dead him army fled an were scattered - an 'Isra'iel childran followed an fought them up til 'Iyabboq - an them didn't preserve even one person from them.

35; After this them waited a likkle an arose that them might sadden JAH - an Him aroused pon them peoples who rule them - an again them totally cried toward JAH; an JAH ignored them cryin an them mournin - fe them have saddened JAH everytime - an fe them have demolished Him LAW.

36; An them captured an took them with them priests toward Babilon persons country.

37; An then 'Isra'iel childran who were traitors didn't quit saddenin JAH while them worked sin an worshipped idols.

38; JAH vexed that Him might downstroy them one time ina them sin ~ Hama havin introduced ten thousand gold ina the king box - pon the day when it were known - him lodged anger ina the king 'Arthieksis reasonin - lest him preserve them childran ina Fars country Iginnin from Hindekie an up til 'Ityopphya pon the time him told him that him might downstroy them.

39; Him did thus - an him wrote a letter where a message were written by the king authority - an him gave him a seal ina him hand that him might deliver toward Fars country.

40; Him gave him a seal that him might downstroy them pon one day when him loved them fe downstroy them like unto the king commanded - but him commanded that him might introduce them money - the gold an the silver - toward the king box.

41; An pon the time 'Isra'iel childran heard this thing them totally cried an wept toward JAH - an them told it fe Merdokyos - an Merdokyos told fe 'Astier.

42; An 'Astier said - 'Fast - beg - an all

'Isra'iel childran kindreds - cry toward JAH ina the place where unu are.'

43; An Merdokyos wore sackcloth an sprinkled dust pon him ras self - an 'Isra'iel childran fasted - begged - an entered repentance ina the country where them were.

44; An 'Astier were totally sad - an bein a queen she wore sackcloth ~ she sprinkled dust an shaved she head - an she didn't anoint perfume like unto Fars queens anoint perfume - an ina she deep reasonin she cried an wept toward she faadas Irator JAH.

45; An becaudis thing Him gave she bein loved alongside Fars king 'Arthieksis - an she made a kind lunch fe she faadas Irator.

46; An Hama an the king entered toward the lunch that 'Astier prepared - an like unto him loved that him might do pon Merdokyos - JAH paid the hardship pon that Hama - an them hanged him pon a tall wood.

47; The king letter were commanded that them might quit 'Isra'iel like unto them were ina all them accord - an lest them tax them nor rob them nor wrong them nor tek them money pon them.

48; As JAH shall pardon 'Isra'iel doin thus pon the time them cried enterin repentance - it are that them might love them an honour them ina Fars country where them lived - yet a king letter were commanded lest them downstroy them country nor plunder them livestocks.

49; An pon them time them saddened Him - Him will arouse pon them peoples who worry them ~ at that time them will totally weep an cry that Him might send them help fe them an that Him might save them from peoples hand who firm up tribulation pon them.

Chapter 29.

1; An pon the time Gibts persons also made 'Isra'iel childran work by makin them work bricks ina difficulty - an pon the time them worried them all the Work by kickin mud without straw an heatin bricks...

2; An pon the time them made them work havin appointed chiefs pon them who rush workers - them cried toward JAH that Him might save them from workin all Gibts bricks.

3; At that time Him sent fe them 'Aron an Mussie who help them - fe JAH have sent them that them might send forth Him kindreds from Fer'on rulership house - an Him saved them from brick Work ~ becau ina him arrogance him refused fe adjourn 'Isra'iel lest them be ruled an sacrifice sacrifice fe JAH ina wilderness - JAH have sent them that them might send forth Him kindreds 'Isra'iel from Gibts king Fer'on rulership house - an them saved them.

4; Fe JAH neglect arrogant ones - an Him drowned Fer'on ina 'Eritra sea with him army becau him arrogance.

5; An like unto him - Him shall downstroy them who didn't work goodly Work ina all the kingdoms that Him I-pointed an crowned them - that them who ignore JAH Word when them are nobles an kings might fulfill Him Accord fe Him - an that them might give persons who serve ina goodly thing them wage - an that them might honour Him famous Name.

6; JAH Who rule all said - But if them will straighten up I Kingdom - I-man will straighten up them kingdom fe them.

7; Work goodly Work fe I - an I-man shall work goodly Work fe unu ~ keep I LAW - an I-man shall keep unu your bodies ~ live firmed up ina I LAW - an I-man shall live lodgin honesty ina unu like unto your reasonin.

8; Love I - an I-man shall love your welfare ~ near toward I - an I-man shall heal unu.

9; JAH Who rule all said - Believe ina I - an I-man shall save unu from the tribulation.

10; Don't live side by side ~ as JAH Who rule all love straight Work - Him said - Unu - approach toward I - an I-man shall approach toward unu ~ unu persons who are sinners an traitors - cleanse your hands from sin - an distance your reasonins from evil.

11; An I-man shall distance I anger from unu - an I-man shall return fe unu ina Charity an Forgiveness.

12; I-man shall distance criminals an enemies who work iniquity from unu - like unto I-man saved I slave Daweet from him enemies who met him - from them much malice - an from Gwolyad hand who were a warrior - an also from Sa'ol hand who sought that him might kill him - an from him child 'Abiesielom hand who loved that him might tek him kingdom.

13; I-man shall save persons who keep I LAW an fulfill I Accord like unto him ~ I-man shall bequeath them honour - an them shall be Irie ina the present world an yonder ina the world that shall come ~ I-man shall crown them pon all that them might be Irie.

14; Them shall be one with kings who served JAH an were honoured ina them beautiful way of Life - like unto the prophet Samu'iel served Him ina him beautiful way of Life Iginnin from him infancy - whom JAH - Him bein LAW - chose.

15; Him told him that him might tell 'Elee who were a servant elder - an when him served ina JAH Lodgin the Temple - Samu'iel Work also were merciful an I-loved.

16; An pon the time him grew when him served ina JAH Lodgin the Temple - Him made him fe be Ipointed an Inointed - that him might Ipoint him people an that kings might be Inointed by JAH Accord. As JAH have loved him that the kindred him chose from 'Isra'iel childran might be Ipointed - pon the time him fulfilled JAH Accord Who Irated him - Him gave him the Inointin of the Kingdom ina him hand.

17; An when Sa'ol were ina him kingdom JAH told Him prophet Samu'iel - Go - an as I-man have loved 'Issiey child Daweet who were birthed from Yihuda kin - Inoint him.

Chapter 30.

1; I-man have hated Sa'ol kin - fe him have saddened I becau him violated I Word.

2; An I-man neglected him - fe him didn't keep I LAW - an I-man won't crown from him kin again.

3; An persons who didn't keep I LAW an I Word an I Order like unto him - I-man shall downstroy I Kingdom an I gift from them childran up til the Iternity.

4; An as them didn't mek I famous pon the time I-man made them famous - I-man shall downstroy them - yet I-man won't again return fe lift them up ~ though I-man honour them - as them didn't honour I - I-man won't mek them famous.

5; Fe them didn't do a goodly thing fe I pon the time I-man did a goodly thing fe them - an fe them didn't forgive I pon the time I-man forgave them.

6; An as them didn't mek I a Ruler pon the time I-man made them rulers pon all - as them didn't honour I pon the time I-man honoured them more than all - I-man won't mek them famous again nor honour them - an fe them didn't keep I LAW.

7; An I-man withheld the gift I-man gave them - an I-man won't return the money I-man withheld from them like unto the measure I-man vexed an swore ~ JAH Who rule all said thus ~ Him said - I-man shall honour them who honoured I - an love them who loved I.

8; I-man shall separate them who didn't honour I nor keep I LAW from the gift I-man gave them.

9; JAH Who rule all said; I-man love them who loved I - an mek famous him who made I famous - Him said..

10; As I-man JAH am Who rule all - there are none who escape I Itority ina Earth nor Heaven - fe I-man am JAH Who kill an Who save an Who sadden an Who forgive.

11; As famousness an honour are I money - I-man honour him whom I-man loved - fe I-man am Who judge an Who revenge an downstroy - an I-man mek wretched him whom I-man hated.

12; Fe I-man am Who forgive them who love I an call I Name everytime - fe I-man am Who feed food fe the wealthy an fe the poor.

13; An I-man feed birds an animals - fishes ina sea an beasts an flowers - yet I-man aren't Who feed only man.

14; I-man feed crocodiles an whales - gophers an hippos - an badgers...

15; an all that live within Water - all that fly pon wind - yet I-man aren't Who feed only man ~ all this are I money.

16; I-man am Who feed all that seek I by all that are due an I-loved.

Chapter 31.

1; An the kings don't reign without I Accord - an sufferahs are by I Command - yet them aren't poor without I Command - an powerful ones are by I Accord - yet them aren't strong without I Accord.

2; I-man gave bein I-loved fe Daweet an Wisdom fe Selomon - an I-man added eras fe Hiziqyas.

3; I-man diminished Gwolyad era - an I-man gave Power fe Somson - an again I-man weakened him Power.

4; An I-man saved I slave Daweet from Gwolyad hand who were a warrior.

5; An again I-man saved him from the king Sa'ol hand an from the secand warrior who disputed him - an fe him have kept I Command - an I-man saved him from the persons hand who dispute him an fight him.

6; An I-man loved him - an I-man love all the nobles an the kings who keep I LAW ~ as them have made I Irie - I-man shall give them prevailin an Power pon them enemies.

7; An again that them might inherit them faadas land - I-man shall give them the cleansed an shinin land of inheritance that I-man swore fe them faadas.

Chapter 32.

1; JAH Who rule all said - An unu the nobles an also the kings - hear I ina I Word - an keep I Command ~ lest unu sadden I an worship like unto 'Isra'iel children saddened I an worshipped different idols - them whom I-man kept an saved when I-man JAH am them Irator - JAH Who rule all said - Hear I ina I Word; an all whom I-man raised an loved an fed Iginnin that them were birthed from them mother an faada.

2; An whom I-man sent forth toward Earth crops - an whom I-man fed the fatness found from Earth makin like unto are due - an whom I-man gave the grape vine an the oil-tree fruit that them didn't plant an the clear Water well that them didn't dig.

3; Hear I ina I Word lest unu sadden I like unto 'Isra'iel children saddened I worshippin other idols when I-man JAH am them Irator - Him told them - Who fed them the sheep milk an the honey comb with the hulled wheat - an Who clothed them clothes where ornamant are - an Who gave them all them love.

4; An without it livin that I-man deprived them all them begged I.

Chapter 33.

1; Like unto Daweet spoke sayin - "Isra'iel children were fed the menna that Angels lowered' - an again hear I ina I Word lest unu sadden I like unto 'Isra'iel children saddened I worshippin the idols when I-man am them Irator JAH Who fed them sweet *menna* ina wilderness - Him said ~ I-man did all this fe them that them might worship I by what are due an fe true.

2; JAH Who rule all said - But them didn't worship I - an I-man neglected them ~ them saddened I an lived firmed up ina law of idols that weren't I LAW.

3; An I-man shall bring the hardship pon them like unto them sin ~ as them have neglected I Worship an as them didn't firm up ina I counsel an I Order - I-man neglected them ina the sin measure that them worked by them hands - an I-man shall lower them toward *Gehannem* ina Definite Judgemant that are done ina Heaven.

4; Fe them didn't keep I LAW - an fe I-man vex pon them - an I-man shall diminish them era ina this world.

5; If thou be a king - aren't thou a man who shall dead an be demolished an tomorrow who shall be worms an dust?

6; But today thou boast an are proud like unto a man who won't dead foriva.

7; JAH Who rule all said - But thou who are sight up bein well today are a man who will dead tomorrow.

8; But if unu keep I Command an I Word - I-man shall bequeath thee-I a honoured country with honoured kings who did I Accord - whose lodgin were Light an whose crowns were beautiful - an whose thrones were silver an gold an whom persons who sit pon them adorned - Him said.

9; An them shall be Irie within Him country that are a place that approached fe persons who worked goodly Work.

10; But fe persons who work sin - as them didn't keep I LAW - said JAH Who rule all...

11; it aren't due them that them might enter

toward that country where honoured kings shall enter.

Chapter 34.

1; Miedon kingdom shall perish - but Rom kingdom shall totally firm up pon Meqiedonya kingdom - an Nenewie kingdom shall firm up pon Fars kingdom.

2; An 'Ityopphya kingdom shall firm up pon 'Iskindriya kingdom ~ as peoples shall arise - Mo`ab kingdom shall firm up pon 'Amalieq kingdom.

3; An bredda shall arise pon him bredda - an JAH shall revenge an downstroy like unto Him spoke that it might perish.

4; Kingdom shall arise pon kingdom - an the people pon the people an country pon country - Him said.

5; An arguments shall be done an there shall be formations - famine - plague - earthquake - drought ~ as Love have perished from this world - JAH chastisemant downscended pon she.

6; Fe the day have arrived suddenly when JAH shall come - Who frighten like unto lightnin that are sight up from East up til West.

7; Pon the day when HIM JAH judge Judgemant - at that time everyone shall raceive him hardship like unto him hand weakness an him sin firmness - fe Him have said I-man shall revenge them pon the day when HIM JAH judge Judgemant an pon the day when them feet are hindered - fe the day when them are counted fe downstruction have arrived.

8; At that time JAH shall downstroy ina *Gehannem* foriva persons who won't live firmed up ina Him LAW - who work sin.

9; An them who live ina the West ilands an Noba an Hindekie - Saba an 'Ityopphya an Gibts persons - all persons who live ina them...

10; at that time shall know I that I-man were JAH Who rule Earth an Heaven - an Who give bein I-loved an honour - an Who save an Who kill.

11; I-man am Who send forth Sun - Who send it toward it settin - Who bring the evil an the good.

12; I-man am Who bring peoples whom unu don't know - who slaughter an eat the money whereby unu wearied - your sheeps an your cows flocks.

13; An them shall capture your childran while them hammer them before unu - an unu cyaan save them. Becau JAH Spirit of Support didn't lodge ina unu - as unu didn't fear JAH Command that unu heard - Him shall downstroy your lavishmants an your assignmants.

14; But a person ina whom JAH Spirit of Support lodged will know all - like unto Nabukedenetsor told Dan'iel sayin - 'Mi sight up JAH Spirit of Support that lodged ina thee-I.'

15; An a person ina whom JAH Spirit of Support lodged will know all - an what were hidden will be revealed fe him - an him will know all that were revealed an that were hidden - yet there are nothing hidden from a person ina whom JAH Spirit of Support lodged.

16; But as InI are persons who will dead

tomorrow - InI sins that InI hid an worked shall be revealed.

17; An like unto them test silver an gold ina fiyah - like unto there are sinners - later pon the Day of Advent them shall be examined - fe them didn't keep JAH Command.

18; At that time all peoples an all 'Isra'iel childran Works shall be examined.

Chapter 35.

1; As JAH vex pon unu becau unu didn't judge a Truth Judgemant fe the child whose mother an faada dead pon him - woe fe unu 'Isra'iel nobles.

2; Woe fe unu persons who go toward a drinkin house mornin an evenin an get drunk - who are partial ina judgemant - an who don't hear the widow justice nor the child whose mother an faada dead pon him - who live ina sin an seducin.

3; JAH told 'Isra'iel nobles sayin thus: - Unless unu lived firmed up ina I Command an kept I LAW an loved what I-man love - woe fe unu - Him told them.

4; An I-man shall bring downstruction an chastisemant an tribulation pon unu - an unu will perish like unto what weevils an moths ate - an your tracks an your region won't be found - Him told them.

5; An your country will be a wilderness - an all persons who sight she up formerly shall clap them hands ~ them shall marvel pon she while them said - 'Weren't this country filled of she plenty an all who love it?; JAH made she thus by persons sin who live ina she.'

6; Them shall say - 'As she have made she heart proud - an as she have ilivated she ras self - an as she have firmed up she collar of reasonin up til JAH mek she wretched pon Earth - an as she shall be a desert by persons arrogance who live ina she - an as thorns have grown pon she with thistles - woe fe she.'

7; An she grow weeds an nettles - an she became a wilderness an a desert - an beasts shall live within she.

8; Fe JAH Judgemant have firmed up pon she - an fe she shall raceive JAH Judgemant Chalice becau she reasonin arrogance by persons sin who live ina she - an she became frightenin fe persons who go toward she.

Chapter 36.

1; Meqiedon persons - don't boast ~ as JAH are there Who shall downstroy unu - 'Amalieqans - don't firm up your collar of reasonin.

2; Fe unu will be lofty up til Heaven an unu will downscend up til *Gehannem*.

3; Pon the time 'Isra'iel formerly entered toward Gibts country ina Mo`ab an Miedon kingdom Him said - Don't boast - fe it aren't due fe pretend pon JAH that unu might pretend pon Him.

4; Thou Yisma'iel kindred - slave child - why do thou firm up thy collar of reasonin by what weren't thy money? How about don't thou think that JAH shall judge pon thee pon the time Him arose that it might be judged pon Earth - pon the day when it are judged pon thee?

5; JAH Who rule all said - At that time thou will raceive thy hardship like unto thy hand Work - how about why do thou ilivate thy reasonin? How about why do thou firm up thy collar of reasonin?

6; An I-man shall pretend pon thee like unto thou pretended pon persons who weren't thy kindreds - fe thou do what thou love that thou might work sin - an I-man shall neglect thee ina the place where them sent thee.

7; JAH Who rule all said - An I-man shall do thus pon thee ~ Him said - But if thou worked goodly Work an if thou love what I-man loved - I-man also shall hear thee-I ina all that thou begged.

8; An if thou fulfill I Accord fe I - I-man shall fulfill thy accord fe thee-I - an I-man shall dispute thy enemies fe thee-I - an I-man shall bless thy childran an thy seed fe thee-I.

9; An I-man shall multiply thy sheeps an thy cows flocks fe thee-I - an if thou lived firmed up ina I Command an also if thou did what I-man love - JAH Who rule all said - I-man shall bless fe thee-I all thou seized ina thy hand.

10; But if thou don't do I Accord - if thou don't live firmed up ina I LAW an I Command - all this tribulation that were told formerly shall find thee - fe thou didn't indure tribulation firmed up ina I Command - an fe thou didn't live firmed up ina I LAW - an thou cyaan escape from I anger that will come pon thee everytime.

11; An as thou didn't love what I-man loved - when I-man am Who Irated thee bringin from not livin toward livin...

12; all this were thy money - that thou might kill an heal fe do all that thou loved - that thou might work an demolish - that thou might honour an abuse - that thou might ilivate an downbase - an as thou have neglected I Worship an I praise when I-man am Who gave thee lordship an also honour alongside persons who are beneath thy authority - thou cyaan escape from I anger that will come pon thee.

13; An if thou did JAH Accord an if thou lived frmed up ina Him Command - Him will love thee-I that thou might be Irie with Him ina Him Lordship - an that thou might be a partaker with persons who inherited a honoured country.

14; Fe Him have said - If them indure I - I-man will bequeath them bein I-loved an honour - fe I-man shall mek them Irie ina the Temple where priah are prayed - fe JAH Who rule all have said - An them shall be I-loved an chosen like unto a sacrifice.

15; Don't neglect fe do Work whereby welfare are done an a goodly thing that unu might cross from death toward Life.

16; But persons who work goodly Work - JAH shall keep them ina all Him goodly Work - that them might be Him slaves like unto 'Iyob whom JAH kept from all the tribulation

17; JAH shall keep them ina all goodly Work - that them might be Him slaves fe Him like unto 'Abriham whom Him saved pon the time him killed the kings - an like unto Mussie whom Him saved from Kenaniewon hand an Fer`on hand - ina whom 'Abriham lived - an who were also downsturbin him body evenin an mornin night an day that them might mek him worship idols.

18; But when them took him toward the idols that were them money - him would indure the tribulation while him refused.

19; Fe 'Abriham who believed Him Iginnin from him childhood were fe JAH Him trusted friend - an while him refused him would worship JAH Who Irated him.

20; As him totally love JAH - him didn't quit worshippin JAH up til him dead - an him didn't depart from Him LAW up til when him dead - an him taught him childran that them might keep JAH LAW.

21; An like unto them faada 'Abriham kept Him LAW - them didn't depart from JAH LAW ~ like unto Him told fe Angels sayin - I-man have a friend ina this world called 'Abriham - 'Abriham childran Ya`iqob an Yis'haq - who are Him slaves becau whom JAH spoke - didn't depart from JAH LAW.

22; JAH Who were praised alongside them an Who rule all said - 'Abriham are I friend ~ Yis'haq are I canfidante - an Ya`iqob are I friend whom I Reasonin loved.

23; But when Him totally loved 'Isra'iel childran - them lived when them Itinually saddened Him - an Him lived when Him indured them an when Him fed them *menna* ina wilderness.

24; Them clothes didn't age - fe them have been fed *menna* that are knowledge *'injera* - an them feet didn't awaken.

25; But them reasonins would distance from JAH everytime ~ as them were who work sin Iginnin from Antiquity - them had no hope fe be saved.

26; Them became like unto a crooked bow - yet them didn't become like unto them faadas Yis'haq an 'Abriham an Ya`iqob who served JAH ina them beautiful way of Life ~ them would sadden Him everytime by them idols pon the mountains an the hills ~ them would eat pon the mountain an at the caves an the trees roots.

27; Them would slaughter a steer ~ them would sacrifice a sacrifice - an them would be Irie ina them hands Work ~ them would eat the rest of the sacrifice ~ them would drink of them sacrifice - an them would play with demons while them sang.

28; An demons would admire all them games an them songs fe them - an them would work them drunkenness an adultery without measure - an them would do the robbery an greed that JAH don't love.

29; Fe Kene`an idols - an fe Midyam idols an fe Be`al - an fe 'Aphlon an Dagon an Seraphyon an 'Arthiemadies who are 'Eloflee idols...

30; an fe all peoples idols ina them area - them would sacrifice sacrifice; an all 'Isra'iel would worship idols like unto peoples worship idols by money that them sight up an heard ~ them would mek them games an them songs an them bluster that peoples mek.

31; All 'Isra'iel kindreds do likewise - who say 'Wi will worship JAH' - without keepin Him Command an Him LAW that Mussie told them ina 'Oreet that them might keep JAH LAW an might distance from worshippin idols.

32; Lest them worship separated idols - apart from them faadas Irator Who fed them the honey found from Maga who fed them the plantation grain an sent them forth toward the Earth crops - an Who fed them the *menna*...

33; Mussie commanded them sayin 'Don't worship' - fe Him are them Irator - an fe Him feed them who loved Him - an Him won't deprive them who loved Him an desired Him.

34; But them didn't quit saddenin JAH - an them would sadden JAH pon the time Him made them Irie.

35; An pon the time Him saddened them - them would cry toward Him - an Him would save them from the tribulation that found them - an them would again be totally Irie an would live many eras.

36; An at that time them would totally return them heart toward sin that them might sadden JAH like unto formerly - an Him would arouse pon them peoples ina them area that them might downstroy them - an them would worry an tax them.

37; An again them would totally return an cry toward them Irator JAH.

38; An Him would forgive them ~ it are becau them faadas - Noh - Yis'haq an 'Abriham an Ya`iqob - who served JAH ina them beautiful way of Life Iginnnin from Antiquity - fe whom Him firmed up Him Oath - yet it aren't becau them ras selves Work that Him forgive them.

39; An Him loved persons who kept Him LAW lovin that them might multiply them childran like unto Heaven stars an sea sand.

40; But pon the time dead ones arose that them have like unto sea sand - them are sinner persons souls that will separate from 'Isra'iel childran an enter toward Gehannem.

41; As JAH have told 'Abriham - Sight up toward Heaven at night an count Heaven stars as it were thou could count - likewise as Him have told him - Thy children an righteous ones shall shine ina Heaven like unto Heaven stars - them are like unto stars that shine ina Heaven - but what them have are kind persons souls birthed from 'Isra'iel.

42; An again as Him have told him - Overstand toward the river edge an the sea - an sight up what are amidst the sand ~ count as it were thou could count - an thy sinner children are likewise - who will downscend toward *Gehannem* pon the time dead ones arose - them are sinner persons souls.

43; An 'Abriham believed ina JAH ~ becaudis thing it were counted fe him bein Truth ~ him found him morale ina this world - an after him wife Sora aged she birthed a child called Yis'haq.

44; Fe him have believed that persons who worked goodly Work shall arise an go toward the Kingdom of Heaven that live firmed up foriva - an again him shall find a Kingdom ina Heaven.

45; But fe him have believed that persons who worked sin shall go toward *Gehannem* that live firmed up foriva pon the time dead ones arose - but that righteous ones who worked goodly Work shall reign with Him foriva.

46; But fe him have believed that it shall be judged foriva fe true without falsehood pon persons who worked sin - fe him shall find Life Kingdom ina Heaven."

Mek glory an praise enter fe JAH fe true without falsehood - an the first book that speak the Meqabyans thing were filled an fulfilled.

Book of Meqabyan II.

Chapter 1.

1; This are a book that speak that Meqabees found 'Isra'iel ina Mesphiethomya that are Sorya part an killed them ina them region iginnin from 'Iyabboq up til 'Iyerusaliem square - an that him downstroyed the country.

2; Becau Sorya an 'Edomyas persons an the 'Amalieqans were one with the Mo`ab man Meqabees who downstroyed 'Iyerusaliem country - as them have camped iginnin from Semarya up til 'Iyerusaliem square an up til all she region - them killed ina war without preservin persons who fled apart from a few persons.

3; An pon the time 'Isra'iel childran wronged - Him aroused Mo`ab man Meqabees pon them - an him killed them by a sword.

4; An becaudis thing JAH enemies the peoples bragged pon Him honoured country - an them swore ina them crime.

5; An 'Iloflee an 'Idomyas persons camped - as Him have sent them becau them pretended JAH Word - them began fe revenge an downstroy JAH country.

6; An that Meqabees country are Riemat that are Mo`ab part - an him arose from him country ina Power an them swore also with persons with him.

7; An them camped ina Gielabuhie region that are Mesphiethomya lot up til Sorya that them might downstroy JAH country - an there him begged the 'Amalieqans an 'Iloflans ~ him gave them much silver an gold an chariots an horses that them might be one with him ina crime.

8; Them came together an crushed the fortress ~ persons who lived ina she shed blood like unto Water.

9; An them made 'Iyerusaliem like unto a plant keepin hut - an him made a voice heard within she ~ him worked all the sin Work that JAH don't love - an them also defouled JAH country that were filled of praise an honour.

10; Them made thy friends flesh an thy slaves corpses food fe wilderness beasts an Heaven birds.

11; An them robbed childran whose mother an faada dead pon them an widows - fe without fearin JAH them have done like unto Seythan taught them - an up til JAH Who examine kidneys an reasonins vexed - them took out the fetus ina pregnant dawtaz belly.

12; Them returned toward them country while them were Irie becau them worked evil Work pon JAH kindreds - an them took the plunder that them captured from a honoured country.

13; Pon the time them returned an entered toward them houses them made Ites an song an clappin.

Chapter 2.

1; The prophet whom them call Re`ay told him thus: - "Today be Irie a likkle pon the time when Irie Ites were made ~ JAH Whom 'Isra'iel glorified have that Him might revenge an downstroy thee ina the chastisemant thou didn't doubt.

2; Will thou say - 'Mi horses are swift ~ becaudis mi will escape by runnin'?

3; As fe I - I-man tell thee - Persons who will follow thee are swifter than vultures ~

thou won't escape from JAH Judgemant an downstruction that shall come pon thee.

4; Will thou say - 'Mi wear iron clothes - an spear flingin an bow stingin aren't able fe mi'?; JAH Who honour 'Isra'iel said - It aren't by spear flingin that I-man will revenge an downstroy thee" Him told him ~ "I-man shall bring pon thee heart sickness an itch an rheumatism sickness that were worse an firmer than spear flingin an bow stingin - yet it aren't by this that I-man shall revenge an downstroy thee.

5; Thou have aroused I anger ~ I-man shall bring heart sickness pon thee - an thou will lack one who help thee - an thou won't escape from I Itority up til I-man downstroy thy name invocation from this world.

6; As thou have firmed up thy collar of reasonin - an as thou have ilivated thy ras self pon I country - pon the time I-man quickly did this thing like unto a eye wink - thou will know I that I-man were thy Irator ~ as thou are before I like unto grass before the wind that fiyah eat - an as thou are like unto the dust that winds spill an scattar from Earth - thou are like unto them alongside I.

7; Fe thou have aroused I anger - an fe thou didn't know thy Irator - an I-man shall neglect all thy kindred - an neither will I-man preserve him who neared pon thy fortress.

8; An now return from all thy sin that thou worked ~ if thou return from thy sin an totally appease ina mournin an sadness before JAH - an if thou beg toward him ina clean reasonin - JAH will forgive thee all thy sin that thou worked before Him" - him told him.

9; At that time Meqabees wore dust an mourned before JAH becau him sin - fe JAH have vexed pon him.

10; Fe Him eyes are revealed - fe Him don't withhold - an fe Him ears are opened - fe Him don't neglect - an fe Him don't mek the word Him spoke false - an fe Him quickly do she at one time - fe JAH knew lest Him preserve the chastisemant Him spoke by the prophet Word.

11; Him cast him clothes an wore sackcloth an sprinkled dust pon him head an cried an wept before him Irator JAH becau him sin that him worked.

Chapter 3.

1; An the prophet came from Riemat an told him - fe Riemat that are Mo`ab part are near fe Sorya.

2; Him dug a pit an entered up til him neck an wept firm tears - an him entered repentance becau him sin that him worked before JAH.

3; An JAH told the prophet thus: - Return from Yihuda country Riemat toward the Mo`ab official Meqabees Him told him. Tell him - "JAH told thee thus" - Tell him - "Him told thee - I-man JAH Who am thy Irator sent thee by I Accord that thou might downstroy I country - lest thou say - 'Mi destroyed the honoured country 'Iyerusaliem by mi Power firmness an mi army abundance' - yet it aren't thou who did this thing.

4; Fe she have saddened I by all she greed an she perfidy an she lustfulness.

5; An I-man neglected an cast she by thy hand - an now JAH forgave thee thy sin becau thy childran whom thou birthed ~ it aren't becau thou who firmed up thy collar of reasonin an say 'Mi incircled the country 'Iyerusaliem by mi authority firmness.'

6; As persons who doubt aren't disciplined fe enter repentance - don't be a doubter - an now enter repentance bein disciplined ina thy complete reasonin."

7; However persons are admired who enter repentance ina them complete reasonins an who don't again return toward thirst an sin by all that entered toward repentance becau them sin.

8; Persons are admired who return toward them Irator JAH bein disciplined ina mournin an sadness - ina bowin an many pleas. Persons are admired who are disciplined an enter repentance - fe Him have told them - Unu are I moneys who entered repentance after unu misled persons who entered repentance.

9; Him told arrogant Meqabees pon the time him returned toward Him ina repentance after him misled - I-man forgive thee thy sin becau thy fright an thy alarm; fe I-man am JAH thy Irator Who bring hardship pon children by a faada sin up til seven generations if the child work the sin that the faada worked - an Who do Charity up til ten thousand generations fe persons who love I an keep I LAW.

10; An now I-man will firm up I Oath with thee becau these thy childran whom thou birthed - an JAH Who rule all an Who honoured 'Isra'iel said - I-man will accept the repentance thou made becau thy sin that thou worked.

11; At that time him proceeded from the pit an bowed fe the prophet ~ him swore sayin - "As mi have saddened JAH - mek mi what thou loved - yet mek JAH do mi thus thus lest mi separate from thee-I ~ as wi have no Law - mi didn't live firmed up ina Him Command like unto mi faadas ~ thou know that wi faadas taught wi an that wi worship idols.

12; Fe mi are a sinner who lived firmed up ina mi sin - who firmed up ina mi collar of reasonin firmness an mi reasonin arrogance whereby mi saddened JAH Command - but up til now mi hadn't heard JAH servants the prophets Word - an mi didn't live firmed up ina Him LAW an Him Command that Him commanded mi."

13; Him told him sayin - "As there are none from your kindred precedin unu who trusted him sin - mi knew that the prophet raceived repentance today."

14; "But now quit thy worshippin idols an return toward knowin JAH that thou might have true repentance" him told him ~ him fell an bowed at the prophet feet - an the prophet lifted up an commanded him all the goodly Work that are due him.

15; An him returned toward him house doin also like unto JAH commanded him.

16; An that Meqabees returned him body toward worshippin JAH - an him downstroyed from him house the idols an also the sorcery - persons who worship idols an pessimists an magicians.

17; An mornin an evenin like unto them faadas do - him would examine the childran him captured an brought from 'Iyerusaliem ina all JAH Commands an Him Order an Him LAW.

18; An from the childran him captured - him appointed knowin ones pon him house.

19; An again from the infants him appointed knowin children who keep levelled children who were small - who enter toward the beddin that them might teach them JAH LAW that 'Isra'iel childran do ~ him would hear from captured 'Isra'iel childran the Order an the LAW an the Nine Laws - that Mo`ab persons order an them mosques that them mek were vain.

20; Him downstroyed them mosques - them idols an them sorcery - an the sacrifice an the grapes sacrificed fe the idols mornin an evenin from the goat kids an fattened sheeps flocks.

21; An him downstroyed him idols whom him worship an beg an believe ina all him Work while him sacrificed sacrifice afternoon an at noon - an fe all priests told him - an him idols fe whom him do them accord.

22; As it would seem fe him that them save him ina all that them told - him wouldn't scorn all the thing them told him.

23; But that Meqabees quit them Work.

24; After him heard the Ra`ay thing - whom them call a prophet - him accomplished him Work ina repentance ~ as 'Isra'iel childran would sadden Him at one time - an pon the time Him chastised them ina the tribulation - as them know an also cry toward JAH - all Him kindreds worked goodly Work more than 'Isra'iel childran ina that season.

25; Pon the time Him heard that them were seized an abused by peoples hand who firm up tribulation pon them an that them cried toward Him - Him thought of them faadas oath an at that time Him would forgive them becau them faadas Yis'haq - 'Abriham - an Ya`iqob.

26; An pon the time Him saved them - them would forget JAH Who saved them from tribulation - an them would return toward worshippin the idols.

27; An at that time Him would arouse pon them peoples who firm up tribulation pon them - an pon the time them firmed up tribulation pon them an saddened them - them would cry toward JAH ~ as Him love them becau them were Him Itority Iration - at that time Him would be nice an forgive them.

28; An pon the time Him kept them - them again returned toward sin that them might sadden Him by them hands Work that were firm an by worshippin idols ina them councils.

29; But Him would arouse pon them Mo`ab an 'Iloflee - Sorya - Midyam an Gibts persons; an pon the time them enemies defeated them - them would cry an weep ~ pon the time them firmed up pon them an taxed them an ruled them - JAH would arouse princes fe them that Him might save them pon the time Him loved.

Chapter 4.

1; An ina 'Iyasu time are a day when Him saved them.

2; An ina Giediewon time are a day when Him saved them.

3; An ina Somson time an ina Deebora an Bariq an Yodeet time are a day when Him saved them - an lodgin whether pon male or pon dawta - Him would arouse princes fe them that them might save them from them enemies hands who firm up tribulation pon them.

4; An like unto JAH loved - Him would save them from persons who firm up tribulation pon them.

5; An them would be totally Irie ina all the Work that Him accomplished fe them ~ them would be Irie ina them land seed an ina multiplyin all them flocks ina wilderness an them livestock.

6; An Him would bless them plants an them livestock fe them - fe Him sight them up ina Eye of Mercy - an fe Him wouldn't diminish them livestock pon them - fe them are kind persons childran an Him would totally love them.

7; But pon the time them were evil ina them Work - Him would cast them ina them enemies hands.

8; An pon the time Him downstroyed them - them would seek Him ina worship - an them would return from sin an march toward JAH ina repentance.

9; An pon the time them returned ina them complete reasonin - Him would atone them sin fe them ~ Him wouldn't think of them former sin pon them - fe Him know them that them were flesh an blood - fe them have this world misleadin thoughts pon them - an fe them have demons ina them.

10; But pon the time that Meqabees heard this Order that JAH worked ina Him worshippin place the Temple - him were slain ina repentance.

11; After him sight up an heard this - him didn't scorn workin goodly Work; him didn't scorn workin all the goodly Work that 'Isra'iel childran work pon the time JAH forgave them - an after them trespassed from Him LAW - them weep an would cry pon the time JAH whipped them - an again Him would forgive them - an them would keep Him LAW.

12; An Meqabees likewise would straighten up him Work - an him would keep Him LAW - an him would live firmed up ina 'Isra'iel Irator JAH Command.

13; At that time after him heard all the Work whereby 'Isra'iel childran boast - Him would boast like unto them ina keepin JAH LAW.

14; Him would urge him kindred an childran that them might live firmed up ina JAH Command an all Him LAW.

15; An him would forbid the order that 'Isra'iel forbid - an him would hear an keep the Law that 'Isra'iel keep - an when him kindred are another Mo`ab man - him would forbid the food that 'Isra'iel forbid.

16; An him would send forth tithes ~ him would give all that were first birthed an that him owned from him cows an him sheeps an him donkeys - an returnin him face toward 'Iyerusaliem him would sacrifice the sacrifice that 'Isra'iel sacrifice.

17; Him would sacrifice sin an vow sacrifices - a sacrifice whereby welfare are done an a accord sacrifice - an the Itinual sacrifice.

18; An him would give him first crops - an him would gush an pour the grapes that 'Isra'iel pour - an him would give this fe him priest whom him I-pointed - an likewise him would do all that 'Isra'iel do - an him would sweeten him ishence.

19; Him built a candlestick an a bowl an a seat an a tent an the four links of rings - an diluted oil fe the Hola of Holas lamps - an the curtain that 'Isra'iel mek ina the Hola of Holas pon the time them served JAH.

20; An like unto them worked goodly Work pon the time them lived firmed up ina Him Order an Him LAW an pon the time JAH didn't neglect an cast them ina them enemies hands - Meqabees also would work goodly Work like unto them.

21; Him would beg toward 'Isra'iel Irator JAH everytime that Him might be him Teacher an lest Him separate him from 'Isra'iel childran whom Him chose an who did Him Accord.

22; An again him would beg Him that Him might give him childran ina Tsiyon an a house ina 'Iyerusaliem - that Him might give them Heavenly Seed of Virtue ina Tsiyon an a Heavenly House of Soul ina 'Iyerusaliem - an that Him might save him from the downstruction spoken by the prophet tongue - that Him might accept him repentance ina all the mournin him wept before JAH bein sad an enterin repentance...

23; an lest Him downstroy childran ina this world pon him - an that Him might keep him ina him proceedin an enterin.

24; Kindreds from Mo`ab peoples beneath Meqabees Itority were Irie that them might believe - fe them chief live firmed up ina straight Work - an them would check up him judgemant an fulfill him accord - an them would scorn them country language an them country justice ~ them would overstand that Meqabees Work surpassed an were straight.

25; An them would come an hear Meqabees charity an Truth judgemants.

26; Him had much money ~ him had dawta slaves an male slaves an camels an donkeys - an him had five hundred horses that wear breastplates ~ him would totally defeat the 'Amalieqans an 'Iloflans an Sorya persons - but formerly when him worshipped idols him lived when them defeated him.

27; Him prevailed - yet but from him worshippin JAH onward - when him went toward battle there are none who defeated him.

28; But them would come ina them idols Power that them might fight him - an them would call them idols names an curse him - however there were none who defeat him - fe him have made him faith pon him Irator JAH.

29; An when him did thus an when him defeated him enemies - him lived when him ruled peoples ina him Itority.

30; Him would revenge an downstroy wronged persons enemy fe them ~ him would judge Truth fe a child whose mother an faada dead pon him.

31; An him would raceive widows ina them trouble time - an him would give from him food an satta them who hungered - an him would clothe the naked from him clothes.

32; An him would be Irie ina him hands Work - an him would give from the money him had without begrudgin - an him would give tithes fe the Temple ~ Meqabees dead havin lived ina Irie Ites when him did this.

Chapter 5.

1; An him dead quittin him childran who were small - an them grew up like unto them faada taught them ~ them kept them house Order - an them would keep all them kindred - an them wouldn't mek poor ones cry - nor widows nor a child whose mother an faada dead pon him.

2; Them would fear JAH - an them would give them money alms fe poor ones - an them would keep all the trust them faada told them - an them would calm the child whose mother an faada dead pon them an widows ina them trouble time - an them would be them mother an faada ~ them would mek them cast from persons hand who wrong them - an calm them from all the downsturbance an sadness that found them.

3; Them lived five years while them did thus.

4; After this the Keledans king Tseerutsaydan came ~ him downstroyed all them country - an him captured Meqabees childran an downstroyed all them villages.

5; An him plundered all them money ~ them lived firmed up ina all evil Work an sin - ina adultery - insult an greed an not thinkin of them Irator - yet persons who don't live firmed up ina JAH LAW an Him Command an who worship idols seized them also an took them toward them country.

6; Them eat what a beast bit an the blood an the carcass - an what a scavenger beat an cast - all that JAH don't love - yet them have no order from all the true Commands written ina 'Oreet.

7; Them don't know JAH them Irator - Who sent them forth from them mothers wombs an fed them by what are due - were them Medicine.

8; Them marry from them aunt an them faada wife - them step mother - an them go toward robbery an evil thing an sin an adultery - yet them have no order ina Judgemant time - an them work all evil Work an them marry them aunts an them sistren an them have no LAW.

9; An all them roads are dark an slippery - an them Work are sin an adultery.

10; But those Meqabees childran would keep ina all them Order ~ them wouldn't eat what a scavenger beat nor what dead an lodged ~ them wouldn't work all the Work that the Keledans childran work - fe them many Works are evil that weren't written ina this book - that sinners work - an doubters an criminals - betrayers totally filled of robbery an sin an pagans childran.

11; All the Work them Irator JAH love aren't there alongside them.

12; An again them would worship a idol called Bi'iel Fiegor ~ them would trust it like unto them Irator JAH when it were deaf an dumb. Fe it are the idol that a person hand worked - fe it are the person hand Work that a smith worked who work silver an gold - that have no breath nor knowledge - an it had nothing that it sight up nor hear.

13; It don't eat nor drink.

14; It don't kill nor save.

15; It don't plant nor uproot.

16; It don't harm it enemy nor benefit it friend.

17; It don't impoverish nor honour.

18; It will be a hindrance fe mislead the Keledans persons who were lazy - yet it don't chastise nor forgive.

Chapter 6.

1; JAH enemy Tseerutsaydan who were arrogant appointed them who veil an falsehood priests fe him idols.

2; Him would sacrifice sacrifice fe them an pour the grapes fe them.

3; An it would seem fe him that them eat an drink.

4; An while it dawned him would give them cows an donkeys an heifers - an him would sacrifice sacrifice mornin an evenin - an him would eat from that defouled sacrifice.

5; An again him would downsturb an obligate other persons that them might sacrifice fe him idols - yet it weren't that only them do it.

6; Pon the time them sight up Meqabees childran that them were handsome an that them worship them Irator JAH - the idols priests loved that them might mislead them fe sacrifice sacrifice an fe eat from that hated sacrifice - but these honoured Meqabees childran refused them.

7; As them keep them faada command - an as them have firmed up ina workin goodly Work - an as them totally fear JAH - it failed them fe agree...

8; pon the time them bound them an insulted them an robbed them.

9; Them told fe the king Tseerutsaydan that them refused sacrifice an bowin fe him idols.

10; An becaudis thing the king vexed ~ him were sad an commanded that them might bring them - an them brought an stood them before him - an the king told them fe him idols - "Sacrifice a sacrifice fe mi idols."

11; An them spoke an told him - "An InI won't answer thee ina this thing - an InI won't sacrifice sacrifice fe thy defouled idols."

12; Him frightened them by Works that abounded - yet him couldn't able fe them - fe them have disciplined them reasonins believin ina JAH.

13; Him flamed a fiyah an cast them ina fiyah - an them gave them bodies fe JAH.

14; After them dead them arose an were sight up fe him at night drawin them swords when him had reclined pon him lordship throne - an him totally feared.

15; "Mi sirs - tell mi alright - what should mi do fe unu? Don't tek mi body ina death - that mi might do all thou commanded mi."

16; Them told him all that are due fe him while them said - "Think that JAH were thy Irator - an JAH are there Who shall dismiss from this thy kingdom where thou are arrogant - an Who shall lower thee toward *Gehannem* of Fiyah with thy faada Deeyablos ~ when InI worshipped InI Irator JAH without a iniquity livin that InI wronged thee - an when InI bowed fe Him ina fearin Him JAH-ness - like unto thou burned InI ina fiyah - thou will finish all thy hardship by that also.

17; Fe Him are Who Irated all - Earth an Heaven an sea an all that are within she.

18; An fe Him are Who Irated moon an Sun an stars - an fe Him Who Irated all the Iration are JAH.

19; Fe there are no other irator withou Him ina Earth nor Heaven - fe Him are Who able fe all - an fe there are nothing that fail Him. As Him are Who kill an Who save - Who whip ina tribulation an Who forgive - when InI bowed fe Him ina fearin JAH - like unto thou burned InI ina fiyah - thou will finish thy hardship by that" them told him.

20; "As Him are Who rule Earth an Heaven - there are none who escape from Him Itority.

21; There are none from the Iration Him Irated who departed from Him Command - apart from thou who are a criminal - an criminals like unto thee whose reasonins thy faada Seythan hid - an thou an those thy priests an thy idols will downscend together toward *Gehannem* where are no exits up til Iternity.

22; Thy teacher are Seythan who taught thee this evil Work that thou might do a evil thing pon InI - yet as it aren't only thou who do this - unu will downscend toward *Gehannem* together.

23; Fe thou mek thy ras self like unto thy Irator JAH - yet thou didn't know JAH Who Irated thee.

24; An thou are arrogant ina thy idols an thy hand Work up til JAH mek thee wretched ~ Him shall canvict thee pon all thy sin an iniquity that thou worked ina this world.

Chapter 7.

1; Woe fe unu who don't know JAH Who Irated unu - fe thy idols who are like unto thee - an fe thee - an fe unu have that unu might regret a regrets that won't profit pon the time unu were sad bein seized ina *See'ol* difficulty - an woe fe thee - fe unu who don't keep Him Word and Him LAW.

2; Unu will have no exit from she up til Iternity - thy priests an thou who sacrifice fe them like unto your Irator JAH - fe thy idols who have no breath nor soul - who won't revenge an downstroy him who did a evil thing pon them - nor do a goodly thing fe him who did a goodly thing fe them.

3; Woe fe unu who sacrifice fe them - fe them are a person hands Work where Seythan live - lodgin there fe mislead lazy ones reasonin like unto thee - that him might lower unu toward *Gehannem* of Fiyah - an the priests who serve demons commanded fe unu an your idols.

4; As unu don't know that there are nothing that will profit unu - unu wrong an err.

5; As fe the animals that JAH Irated fe be food fe unu - an dogs an beasts - them are better than unu - fe besides one death there are no more candemnation pon them.

6; But as unu will dead an raceive hardship ina *Gehannem* Fiyah where are no exits up til Iternity - animals are better."

7; Havin spoken this - them went an were hidden from him.

8; But that Tseerutsaydan lodged when him trembled - seized by a firm fright - an fright didn't quit him up til it dawned.

Chapter 8.

1; An him lived firmed up ina reasonin malice an arrogance.

2; An as iron have been called firm - like unto Dan'iel sight it up pon him kingdom - him turned ina peoples countries ina him area.

3; Him lived firmed up ina evil an all him laziness an ina downsturbin persons.

4; An him totally downstroy what InI spoke formerly - an him eat a person money.

5; Fe him are diligent fe evil like unto him faada Deeyablos who firmed up him collar of reasonin - an him downstroy what remained with him army.

6; Him say - "Mi era became like unto the Sun era" - yet him don't know JAH that Him were him Irator.

7; An ina him reasonin him think that the Sun are found from him.

8; Him arise in Power - him camp ina Tribe of Zablon lot an begin a formation ina

Meqiedonya - an him receive him food from Semarya - an them give him presents from Semarya.

9; Him camp ina nomads region - an him reach up til Seedona - an him cast a tax pon 'Akayya - an him elevate him collar of reasonin up til the flowin sea - an him return an send messengers up til Hindekie sea.

10; An likewise him elevate him collar of reasonin up til Heaven.

11; Him live firmed up ina bein arrogant an ina evil - yet him don't have humblin him ras self.

12; An him path are toward darkness an slipperiness - an toward crime an bein arrogant - an toward sheddin blood an tribulation.

13; An all him Work are what JAH hate ~ him do like unto robbery an evil an sin teacher Deeyablos taught him ~ him mek a child cry whose mother an faada dead pon him - an him aren't nice fe a poor one.

14; An him defeated an downstroyed peoples kings by him authority.

15; An him ruled enemies chiefs - an him ruled many peoples - an him taxed them like unto him loved.

16; Even if him downstroyed - him didn't quit ~ there are no person whom him didn't snatch Iginnin from Tersies sea up til 'Iyareeko sea.

17; Him would bow fe idols ~ him would eat what dead an lodged - the blood - what a sword bloated an cut - an what were sacrificed fe idols ~ all him Work are without justice - yet him have no justice ~ as him have been who alarm peoples beneath him authority - him would tax them tax like unto him loved.

18; As him do all that him loved before him - there are no fearin JAH before him - an him live ina malice before JAH Who Irated him.

19; Him didn't do it like unto him Irator - an like unto him did a evil thing pon him companion pon the time him vexed an seized him - JAH shall also pay him him hardship.

20; As JAH have said - I-man shall revenge an downstroy sinner persons who don't live by I Command - that I-man might downstroy them name invocation from this world - like unto Him downstroyed peoples who were precedin him - Him shall revenge an downstroy him pon the time when Him downstroy.

21; An like unto evil persons did evil things - them shall raceive them hardship.

22; But bein commanded from JAH - goodly Work shall follow persons who work goodly Work.

23; Fe like unto 'Iyasu downstroyed the five Kene'an kings ina cave ina one day - an like unto him made Sun stand ina Geba'on by him priah that him might downstroy them armies - Sun have stood amidst Heaven up til him downstroyed 'Ewiewon an Kenaniewon - Fierziewon an Kiethiewon an 'Iyabusiewon armies - an like unto him killed around twenty thousand persons at one time - an like unto him killed them - an like unto him bound them makin foot from neck - an like unto him killed them ina cave by spear - an like unto him fitted a stone pon them...

24; Tribulation like unto this shall find all persons who sadden JAH ina them evil Work.

Chapter 9.

1; "O thou weak man who aren't JAH - why are thou proud? thou who are sight up today bein a man are Earth ashes tomorrow - an thou will totally be worms ina thy grave.

2; Fe thy teacher are Deeyablos who return all persons sin hardship toward him ras self becau him misled InI faada 'Adam - an *See'ol* will find thee again - an she will find persons who work thy sin.

3; Fe ina firmin up him collar of reasonin an makin him ras self proud - like unto him refused fe bow fe 'Adam whom the Irator Irated...

4; thou also have refused fe bow fe thy Irator JAH like unto thy teacher Deeyablos did.

5; Like unto thy precedin faadas - who don't know them Irator JAH ina worship - will go toward *Gehannem* - thou also will go toward *Gehannem*.

6; Like unto Him revenged an downstroyed them becau them evil Work that them worked ina this world - an like unto them downscended toward *Gehannem*...

7; thou also will downscend toward *Gehannem* like unto them.

8; As thou have aroused Him anger - an as thou have neglected fe worship JAH Who gave thee Itority pon the five kingdoms - do it seem fe thee that thou will escape from JAH Itority?

9; Thou don't do thus that thou do Him Accord - thus Him examined thee - but if thou work goodly Work ina this world - JAH will accomplish all thy Work fe thee-I - an Him will accomplish an bless all the Work thou seized ina thy hand fe thee-I - an Him will subject thy Antiquity of enemies an thy day enemies fe thee-I.

10; Thou will be Irie ina thy enterins an thy proceedins an ina thy child birthed from thy nature - an ina thy flocks an thy fatnesses - an ina all Work where thou placed thy hand - an ina all that thou thought ina thy heart ~ as Itority have been given thee-I from alongside JAH that thou might do thus an might work an plant an demolish - all will be commanded fe thee-I.

11; However if thou won't hear JAH Word nor live firmed up ina Him LAW - like unto criminals who were precedin thee - an who don't worship JAH by what are due - an who didn't believe firmed up ina HIM straight LAW - there are nothing whereby thou will escape from JAH Itority - fe JAH Judgemant are Truth.

12; All are totally revealed before Him - yet there are nothing hidden from before Him.

13; Him are Who seize the kings Itority an Who overturn powerful ones thrones.

14; Him are Who Ilivate them who were downbased an Who lift up them who fell.

15; Him are Who loose them who were bound an Who arouse them who dead ~ as pardon dew are found from alongside Him - pon the time Him loved Him shall arouse persons whose flesh were demolished an rotten an were like unto dust.

16; An havin aroused an judged persons who worked evil Work - Him will tek them toward *Gehannem* - fe them have saddened Him.

17; Fe them are who demolished JAH Order an Him LAW - an Him will downstroy them child from this world.

18; As kind persons Work are more difficult than sinner persons Work - sinner persons don't love that them might live ina kind persons counsel.

19; Like unto Heavens were distanced from Earth - likewise kind persons Work were distanced from evil persons Work.

20; But sinner persons Work are robbery an sin - adultery an iniquity - greed an perfidy Work ~ it are bein drunk ina iniquity an robbin a person money.

21; It are quickly goin toward sheddin a person blood - an it are goin toward downstruction that don't benefit - an it are makin a child weep whose mother an faada dead pon him ~ it are eatin blood an what dead an lodged - an it are eatin camel an boar flesh - an it are goin toward a dawta ina she blood before she are cleansed - an toward a dawta ina childbirth.

22; All this are sinner persons Work ~ she are Seythan trap that were a wide an prepared path - an that tek
toward *Gehannem* that live firmed up foriva - an toward *See'ol*.

23; But righteous ones path that were totally narrow are what tek toward welfare - an innocence an humbleness - an Inity an Love - an priah an fast - an flesh purity - toward keepin from what don't benefit - from eatin what a sword bloated an cut an what dead an lodged - an from goin toward a youtmon wife an from adultery.

24; Them keep from what weren't commanded by LAW - from eatin disgustin food an from all hated Work - an from all the Work that JAH don't love - fe sinner persons do all this.

25; As fe kind persons - them distance from all the Work that JAH don't love.

26; Him love them an shall keep them from all them tribulation like unto Trust money.

27; Fe them keep Him Order an Him LAW an all that Him love - but Seythan rule sinner persons.

Chapter 10.

1; Fear JAH Who Irated unu an kept unu up til today - yet unu the nobles an the kings - don't go pon Seythan path.

2; Live ina the LAW an Command of JAH Who rule all - yet don't go pon Seythan path.

3; As pon the time 'Isra'iel childran came toward 'Amalieq that them might inherit Kiethiewon an Kenaniewon an Fierziewon country - Siefor child Balaq an Bele`am...

4; whom thou cursed are cursed - an him whom thou blessed blessed ~ don't go pon Seythan road - fe him have said - "An mi will give thee much silver an gold that honour thee - that thou might curse fe mi an - an havin cursed - that thou might downstroy fe mi."

5; An fe Bele`am have come makin him sorcery reward a morale - an fe Siefor child Balaq have shown him the place where 'Isra'iel childran camped.

6; Fe him have done him pessimism - an fe him have sacrificed him sacrifice - an fe him have slaughtered from him fattened cows an sheeps - an fe him have loved that him might curse an downstroy 'Isra'iel childran.

7; Him returned a curse toward a bless - yet but as JAH didn't love that him might curse them by Him Word - don't go pon Seythan road.

8; "As thou are the kindred that JAH chose - as thou are JAH Lodgin that shall come from Heaven - mek persons be cursed who curse thee-I - an mek persons who bless thee-I be blessed" him said.

9; Pon the time him blessed them before him - after this Siefor child Balaq were sad - an him totally vexed an commanded that him might curse them.

10; Fe the kindred that JAH blessed have come toward this country - an Bele`am told him - "Mi won't curse 'Isra'iel whom JAH blessed."

11; An Siefor child Balaq told Bele`am - "As fe mi - mi had loved that thou might curse fe mi ~ thou blessed them before mi yet but thou didn't curse them ~ if thou had cursed fe mi an told mi 'Give mi' - as fe mi - mi would have given thee a house full of silver an gold - but thou totally blessed them - an thou didn't do a goodly thing fe mi - an mi won't do a goodly thing fe thee."

12; Bele`am said - "What JAH told mi Speak with mi tongue - mi will speak it - yet as fe mi - mi cyaan dare fe ignore JAH thing.

13; Lest mi curse a blessed kindred - as JAH shall vex pon mi if mi love money - as fe mi - mi don't love money more than mi soul.

14; As JAH have told them faada Ya`iqob - Mek persons who bless thee-I be blessed an mek persons who curse thee-I be cursed - lest mi curse blessed Ya`iqob - as fe mi - mi don't love money more than mi soul" him said - an as JAH have told him - Him who bless thee-I are blessed...

15; an a person who curse thee-I unjustly are cursed - accomplish thy path an thy Work that JAH might love thee.

16; An don't be like unto former persons who saddened JAH ina them sin an whom Him neglected - an there are them whom Him downstroyed ina Downstruction Water.

17; An there are them whom Him downstroyed by them haters hands ~ there are them whom Him downstroyed by them enemies hands - bringin enemies who were evil persons who firmed up tribulation pon them - an them captured them lords with them priests an them prophets.

18; An them delivered them toward the foreign country them don't know ~ them totally captured them - an them plundered them livestocks pon them an downstroyed them country.

19; Fe them have demolished the honoured country 'Iyerusaliem fences an ramparts - an them made 'Iyerusaliem like unto a field.

20; An the priests were capture - an the LAW were demolished - an warriors fought ina war an fell.

21; An widows were capture ~ as them have been capture - them wept fe them ras selves - yet them didn't weep fe them husbands who dead.

22; An the childran wept - an elders shamed - an them weren't nice fe neither a grey haired person nor a elder.

23; Them downstroyed all them found ina the country - yet them weren't nice fe beauties nor fe them ina LAW ~ as JAH have vexed pon Him kindreds pon the time Him loved that Him might beforehand downstroy Him Lodgin the Temple - them captured an took them toward the country them don't know an toward peoples.

24; As them sadden them Irator everytime - becaudis thing pon the time JAH neglected 'Isra'iel children - JAH made 'Iyerusaliem fe be ploughed like unto a field.

25; Fe Him are nice fe them becau them faadas - but Him didn't downstroy them at one time ~ as Him love them faadas Yis'haq an 'Abriham an Ya`iqob who reigned fe true an lived firmed up ina straight LAW before them Irator - it are becau them faadas kindness - yet it aren't becau them ras selves kindness that him forgive them.

26; An Him I-pointed them pon honours that were twofold - an them found two Kingdoms - pon Earth an ina Heaven.

27; An unu the kings an the nobles who live ina this passin world - like unto your faadas who lived firmed up ina Work that are due an who were precedin unu likewise inherited the Kingdom of Heaven - an like unto them names were beautiful fe a child children - think of them.

28; An thou - straighten up thy Work - that Him might straighten up thy Kingdom fe thee - an that thy name might be called ina goodly invocation like unto the kind kings who were precedin thee who served JAH ina them beautiful lifestyle.

Chapter 11.

1; Think of JAH slave Mussie who weren't annoyed when him kept around this kindred ina him humbleness an him priah an whom not even one person downstroyed - an him begged toward JAH ina him innocence fe him sista an bredda who backbit him an loved that JAH might downstroy them while him said - "As them have wronged Thee-I - Lord - pardon an don't neglect thy kindreds" - an him atoned them sin fe them - yet Him thought of JAH servant Mussie who weren't annoyed.

2; "Fe I-man have wronged Thee-I - an forgive I Thy slave who am a sinner - fe Thou are Merciful - an fe Thou are a Pardoner - an forgive them them sin."

3; An Mussie likewise atoned them sin fe him sista an bredda who backbit him.

4; An becaudis thing him were called innocent.

5; An JAH totally loved him more than all the priests children who were him bredren - fe Him I-point the priests - an JAH made him like unto Him Ras Self alongside them.

6; But Him also sank beneath Earth Qorie children who challenged ~ Him lowered them toward *See'ol* with them livestocks an them tents when them said "Wi are there - wi are there ina flesh an soul" ~ as him Irator JAH have loved him - an as him didn't depart from Him Command - all the word him spoke would be done fe him like unto JAH Word.

7; An unless thou demolished JAH Command likewise - JAH will do thy accord fe thee-I an will love thy thing fe thee-I - an Him will keep thy Kingdom fe thee-I.

8; An 'Asaf an Qorie children who departed from Mussie command grumbled pon him becau him told them - "Straighten up your reasonins fe be ruled fe JAH."

9; Them grumbled sayin - "How about aren't wi Liewee children who work priesthood Work ina Tent that were special?"

10; Them went an smoked up ishence seizin them censers that them might smoke up - but

JAH didn't accept them plea - an them were burnt by the fiyah ina them censers - an them melted like unto the wax that fiyah melt - an not even one person remained from them ~ as Him have said - Them censers were honoured by them bodies bein burnt - apart from them censers that entered toward JAH Lodgin fe JAH Command - neither them clothes nor them bones remained.

11; Becaudis thing JAH told 'Aron an Mussie - Gather them censers toward the Tent ~ mek it be a instrumant fe I Lodgin wherefor I-man prepared all I-ginnin from outside up til within.

12; An him prepared the honoured Tent instrumants ~ him prepared the rings an the joiners - *Keerubiel* picture sea.

13; Him worked the cups - the curtains - the Tent area grounds fe the mobilisation - the altar an the jugs whereby them sacrifice ina the Tent that were special.

14; Them sacrificed the sacrifice that them sacrifice by them accord - the sacrifice whereby welfare are made - the sacrifice whereby Him atone sin - an the vow sacrifice an the mornin an the evenin sacrifice.

15; All that Him commanded fe Mussie - him commanded them ina the Tent that were special - that them might work Work ina she.

16; Them didn't scorn bein ruled fe them Irator JAH - that Him Name might be praised by them ina the LAW Lodgin Tent of them Irator JAH Who gave them a promise that Him might give them fe give them them faadas inheritance that produce honey an milk that Him swore fe 'Abriham.

17; Them didn't scorn bein ruled fe them Irator JAH - Who swore fe Yis'haq an firmed up Him Worship fe Ya`iqob...

18; an Who firmed up fe 'Aron an Mussie the Tent where Him Worship are kept...

19; an Who firmed up Him Worship fe both 'Elyas an Samu'iel ina the Temple an Tent that Selomon worked up til it became JAH Lodgin ina 'Iyerusaliem - an up til JAH Name Lodgin became JAH Lodgin that honoured 'Isra'iel.

20; Fe she are a supplication - an fe she are a sin atonemant where it are overturned fe them who live ina innocence an fe the priests.

21; An fe she are a place fe persons who do Him Accord where Him will hear them pleas...

22; an JAH LAW Canstruction that honoured 'Isra'iel.

23; Fe she are where sacrifice are sacrificed an where Ishence are smoked up that JAH Who honoured 'Isra'iel be ina goodly Fragrance.

24; An Him would speak bein pon the joiner where Him forgive ina the Tent that were special ~ JAH Light would be revealed fe Ya`iqob childran whom Him chose an fe friends who live firmed up ina Him LAW an Him Command.

25; But persons who ignored JAH LAW will be like unto Qorie childran whom Earth sank - an likewise sinner persons have that them might enter toward *Gehannem* that have no exits up til Iternity.

Chapter 12.

1; Unu who didn't keep the LAW Him commanded unu ina Tent - woe fe unu

'Isra'iel nobles who also didn't do Him Accord - yet unu did your ras selves accord - an this are bein arrogant an pride - greed an adultery - drink an bein drunk - an swearin ina lie.

2; An becaudis thing I anger - like unto chaff are burnt before a fiyah - an like unto fiyah burn the mountain - an like unto a whirl wind spill the crushed chaff from Earth an scattar it toward Heaven - lest it trace be found ina it place - I anger will downstroy unu like unto that.

3; JAH Who honoured 'Isra'iel said - I-man shall likewise downstroy all persons who work sin - an think of JAH Who rule all an fe Whom nothing fail.

4; Him love persons who love Him - an fe persons who live firmed up ina Him Command - Him will atone them iniquity an them sin fe them ~ don't be dull an stingy of heart by not believin.

5; An mek your reasonins straight fe be ruled fe JAH - an believe ina Him that unu might firm up your bodies - an I-man shall save unu from your enemy hand ina your tribulation day.

6; An ina your plea time I-man tell unu - Check - I-man am there with unu ina Support ~ I-man shall save unu from your enemy hand ~ as unu have believed ina I - an as unu have done I Command - an as unu didn't depart from I LAW - an as unu have loved what I-man love - JAH Who rule all said - I-man won't neglect unu pon your tribulation day.

7; Him love them who love Him - fe Him are a Pardoner - an fe Him are nice - an Him keep persons who keep Him LAW - like unto a trust money.

8; Him return Him anger fe them many times ~ becau Him were who know them that them are flesh an blood - as Him are a Pardoner - Him didn't downstroy all ina Him chastisemant - an pon the time them souls were separated from them flesh - them will return toward them Earthliness.

9; As Him have Irated them bringin from not livin toward livin - them won't know the place where them live up til JAH love that Him might bring them from not livin toward livin ~ again Him separated them souls from them flesh - an Earth nature returned toward it Earthliness.

10; An again Him Accord shall bring them from not livin toward livin."

11; But Tseerutsaydan who denied JAH multiplied bein arrogant before JAH ~ him made him ras self lofty up til the day that him loved pon the time him quit Him.

12; "An mi era became like unto Heaven era - an mi are who send forth Sun - an mi won't dead up til Iternity" him said.

13; An before him finished speakin this thing the Angel of Death whose name are called Thilimyakos alit an struck him heart ~ him dead ina that iwa ~ as him didn't praise him Irator - him were separated from him beautiful lifestyle an him perished arisin from him arrogance abundance an him Work evil.

14; But when the Keledans king army had camped ina the city an the country squares lovin fe fight him - pon the time him dead - them proceeded an downstroyed him country ~ them plundered all him livestock - an them didn't preserve a elder who near an sight up ramparts.

15; Them plundered all him money - an them took him tiny money - an them burned him country ina fiyah an returned toward them country.

Chapter 13.

1; But these five Meqabees childran who believed gave them bodies fe death refusin fe eat the sacrifice sacrificed fe idols.

2; Fe them have known that pretendin with JAH surpass from pretendin with persons - an JAH anger from the king anger.

3; Havin known that this world will totally pass an that the Irie Ites won't live firmed up foriva - them gave them bodies fe fiyah that them might be saved from fiyah ina Heaven.

4; An as them have known that bein made Irie ina Garden one day are better than livin many eras ina this world - an that findin Thy Pardon one iwa Lord - are better than many eras - them gave them bodies fe fiyah.

5; What are InI era? Like unto a shadow - like unto passin wax melt an perish pon a fiyah edge - aren't it like unto that?

6; But Thou Lord live foriva - an Thy Era aren't fulfilled - an Thy Name invocation are fe a child childran.

7; An Meqabees childran thought that it seemed all this ~ refusin fe eat a disgustin sacrifice them chose believin ina JAH.

8; Knowin that them will arise with persons who dead - an meanin becau JAH - knowin that Judgemant shall be judged after Resurrection of Council - becaudis thing them gave them bodies fe martyrdom.

9; Unu persons who don't know nor believe persons who dead risin - knowin that the Life them find later will surpass from this them passin Earthly Life - arisin from these five Meqabees childran who gave them bodies together fe the death and whose appearance were handsome - after this them knew Resurrection.

10; Becau them believed ina Him knowin that all shall pass - an becau them didn't bow fe idols - becau them didn't eat a disgustin sacrifice that don't give Support - them gave them bodies fe death that them might find thanks from JAH.

11; Fe becaudis thing knowin that Him will mek them Irie ina flesh an soul ina later era - them didn't know this world flavour an death tribulation a serious thing fe them who have child an wife - an knowin that Resurrection be made ina flesh an soul pon the Day of Advent - them gave them bodies fe death.

12; An knowin that persons who kept JAH LAW - with the nobles an the kings who believed JAH Word an were nice...

13; shall live reignin fe a child childran many eras ina Kingdom of Heaven where are no sadness an tribulation nor death - an knowin ina them reasonins what will be done later - like unto wax melt amidst a fiyah - becaudis thing them gave them bodies fe death.

14; Believin that them faces will shine seven hands more than the Sun - an that them will be Irie ina Him Love pon the time all arose ina flesh an soul - them gave them bodies fe death.

Chapter 14.

1; But the Samrans an 'Ayhuds thing - the Seduqans who don't believe persons who dead risin - an the Fereesans thing quite totally sadden I - an it help I fe I reasonin ~ "Wi will dead tomorrow" 'Ayhuds say - "Mek wi eat an drink ~ wi will dead tomorrow ~ there are no Irie Ites wi will sight up ina grave."

2; But the Samrans say - "As wi flesh will be dust - it won't arise.

3; Becau she were invisible like unto wind an like unto iyunder voice - check - she are here - an becau she were what them don't call an invisible - as soul won't arise if flesh dead - pon the time Resurrection are done wi will believe wi souls arisin.

4; But as beasts will eat she an as worms will eat she ina the grave - wi flesh are sight up alongside all ~ she will become dust an ashes.

5; An those beasts who ate she will become dust - fe them have been like unto grass - an fe them have become dust like unto them weren't irated - an fe them trace won't be found - but wi flesh won't arise."

6; An the Fereesans say - "Wi believe as fe persons who dead arisin - however Him will bring an Inite souls with another flesh that are ina Heaven - that aren't pon Earth ~ where will demolished an rotten fleshes be found?"

7; But the Seduqans say - "After wi soul proceeded from wi flesh - wi won't arise with persons who dead - an flesh an soul have no arisin after them dead - an after wi dead wi won't arise."

8; An becaudis thing them totally err - an as them speak insult pon JAH Lordship - them thing sadden I.

9; As them didn't believe JAH Who honour them - them have no hope fe be saved - however them have no hope fe dead an arise an be saved.

10; O 'Ayhudan who are blind of reasonin - when thou are whom Him Irated bringin from not livin toward livin - an scorned like unto spit - will thou mek JAH ignorant - Who made thee a person? Will it fail JAH Who Irated thee ina Him Example an Him Appearance fe arouse Initin thy flesh an thy soul?

11; As thou won't escape from JAH Itority - don't think a thing that are thus ~ thou will arise without thou lovin - fe there are the hardship thou will raceive ina *See'ol* where thou were seized pon the time thou dead - an it shall be judged pon thee without thou lovin.

12; Fe the sin found from demons that demons place ina thy reasonin are worked alongside thee after thou were birthed from thy mother womb - an fe she are worked abundantly pon the time thou grew up.

13; Them place she ina thy body pon the time thou dead - an she will bring hardship pon them pon the time them worked she.

14; Like unto there are sin ina them collar of reasonin - as there are persons who work sin bein seized by she - she kindreds will present demons.

15; All sinner persons souls shall come from Heaven edge where them are - an thy sin likewise shall introduce thee
toward *Gehannem* pullin an bringin thy soul from where thou are.

16; An after thy flesh lived separate from thy soul - JAH Charity dew shall arouse thee bein seven fold like unto InI faada 'Adam flesh.

17; Thou who live ina grave - thou also err ina thy error - yet mek it not seem fe thee that thou only mislead the others ~ thou say

- "The arisin that persons who dead shall arise aren't there" - that them might depart from JAH Command an err.

18; Him shall arouse thee that Him might give thee thy hardship like unto thy Work that thou worked - yet who shall quit thee that thou might remain bein dust?

19; But at that time - whether wind ina wind be thy nature - or if Water ina Water be thy nature - or if Earth ina Earth be thy nature - or if fiyah ina fiyah be thy nature - it shall come.

20; An if a soul that lodged ina thee be what lived ina *See'ol* - she shall come.

21; An righteous ones souls that live ina Garden ina Ites shall come.

22; But thou 'Ayhudan - Samran - Fereesan - Seduqan - will live ina *See'ol* up til it are judged pon thee.

23; At that time thou will sight up that JAH shall pay thee the hardship like unto thy sin becau thou misled persons.

24; "Persons who dead won't arise ~ as wi will dead - mek wi eat an drink" - an becau thou sat ina Mussie chair an misled by thy words while thou said - "Persons who dead won't arise" - thou will sight up that Him shall pay thee thy hardship.

25; An without thy knowin *'Oreet* Book - an when thou teach the books word - becaudis thing thou erred ~ it would be better had thou remained without learnin from thy misleadin a person.

26; It would have been better if thou didn't know the books word - when thou promulgate JAH kindreds ina thy evil teachin an thy worthless words.

27; Fe JAH don't favour havin sight up a face - an fe Him shall give the grace an glory Him prepared fe Him friends - persons who teach goodly Work - but thou have that thou might raceive thy reward like unto thy Work an the things that thou spoke.

28; But there are nothing whereby thou will escape from JAH Itority Who shall judge pon thee - an Him have that Him might pay thee like unto thy Work - fe them whom thou taught an thou together will raceive a sentance.

29; Know that persons who dead shall arise - an if them are persons who kept Him LAW them shall arise - an like unto Earth send forth grass pon the time rain rained - as Him Command shall send them forth from a grave - it aren't possible fe it fe remain demolished an rotten.

30; Like unto moist wood drink dew an send forth leaves pon the time Him satta she rain fe Earth - like unto wheat bear forth fruit - an like unto grain produce buds - like unto it aren't possible fe she fe withhold that she might prevent she fruit if JAH loved...

31; an like unto it aren't possible fe a dawta who canceived fe close an prevent she womb pon the time labour seized she - like unto it aren't possible fe she fe escape without birthin...

32; as dew have alit toward she bein commanded from JAH - at that time she shall produce them at one time - yet after she heard JAH Word - a grave also likewise cyaan prevent the persons gathered alongside she from arisin.

33; An fleshes shall be gathered ina the place where them corpses fell - an them places where souls live shall be opened - an souls shall return toward the flesh where them were formerly separated.

34; An pon the time a drum were beaten - persons who dead shall quickly arise like unto a eye wink - an havin arisen them shall stand before JAH - an Him shall give them them reward like unto them hand Work.

35; At that time thou will sight up that thou arise with dead ones - an thou will marvel at all the Work thou worked ina this world - an pon the time thou sight up all thy sins written before thee - at that time thou will regret a useless regret.

36; Thou know that thou will arise with dead ones an that thou will raceive thy hardship like unto the Work that thou worked.

Chapter 15.

1; But persons who found them reward by them goodly Work shall be Irie at that time ~ persons who ignored while them said - "Persons who dead won't arise" shall be sad at that time pon the time them sight up that persons who dead arose with them evil Work that don't benefit.

2; That - them Work that them worked shall canvict them - an them ras selves shall know that it canvict them without one livin who will dispute them.

3; Pon the day when Judgemant an mournin are done - pon the day when JAH shall come - pon the day when Definite Judgemant are judged - persons who forgot JAH LAW shall stand ina the place where them stand.

4; Pon the day when there shall be total darkness - an pon the day when mist are pulled - pon the day when flashes are sight up an when lightnin are heard...

5; an pon the day when quakes an fright an heatwave an sleet frost are made...

6; pon the day when a evil person who worked evil Work raceive hardship - an pon the day when a clean person raceive him reward like unto him worked clean Work - an pon the day when persons who forgot JAH LAW raceive the hardship like unto a sinner person worked sin - them shall stand ina the place where them stand.

7; Fe pon the day when a master aren't more honoured than him slave - an pon the time when a mistress aren't more honoured than she slave...

8; an pon the time when the king aren't more honoured than a poor one - an pon the time when a elder aren't more honoured than a infant - pon the time when a faada aren't more honoured than him child - an pon the time when a mother aren't more honoured than she child...

9; pon the time when a wealthy one aren't more honoured than a poor one - an pon the time when a arrogant one aren't more honoured than a downbased one - an pon the time when the great aren't more honoured than the small - she are the day when Judgemant are judged - fe she are the day when them raceive sentance an hardship - an fe she are the day when all will raceive hardship like unto them worked sin.

10; An fe she are the day when persons who worked goodly Work raceive them reward - an fe she are the day when persons who worked sin raceive hardship.

11; An as she are the day when persons who found them reward are made Irie - persons who forgot JAH LAW shall stand ina the place where them stand. Persons who mek liars - who digest books while them said -

"Persons who dead won't arise" - them shall sight up Resurrection.

12; At that time this world sinners - who didn't work goodly Work ina this world - shall weep pon them sin that them worked - becau sadness found them without calmin.

13; An all likewise - kind persons who worked goodly Work - them Irie Ites won't be fulfilled up til Iternity - fe them have worked goodly Work when them were ina this world.

14; Fe them have known that them will arise after them dead - an them didn't depart from them Irator LAW.

15; Becau them didn't depart from Him LAW - them shall inherit two welfares ~ Him multiplied them seed ina this world - an Him honoured them childran.

16; Him bequeathed them the Kingdom of Heaven where shall be found the welfare him swore fe them faadas pon the time when persons who dead arise - an pon the time when rich ones become poor.

17; Persons shall weep who worked sin - who don't believe persons who dead arisin - who don't keep JAH LAW - an who don't think of Arisin Day.

18; At that time them will sight up the tribulation that shall find them an shall have no endin - an where are no calmin nor welfare - an it have the sadness that have no rest nor calmin ina them reasonin.

19; An a fiyah that don't perish an worms that don't sleep shall find them.

20; An ina the place where are them flesh are fiyah - sulphur - whirl wind - frost - hail - sleet ~ all this shall rain over them.

21; Fe persons who don't believe persons who dead arisin - there are fiyah of *Gehannem* pon them.

Chapter 16.

1; Thou - please think of what are pon thy flesh - an thy feet an thy hands nails - an thy head hair - fe them proceed quickly pon the time thou cut them ~ know Resurrection by this - that thou have a reasonin - an that thou have religion an knowledge.

2; Thy feet an thy hands nails an thy head hair - thou say - "Where do these come from?" ~ aren't it JAH Who prepared it that them might proceed - that thou know arisin that shall be done pon thy flesh that aren't pon another flesh - that thou might know that thou will arise after thou dead?

3; Becau thou misled persons while thou said - "There are no Resurrection of the dead ones" - pon the time when dead ones arise thou will raceive thy hardship like unto thou worked sin an iniquity.

4; An as even what thou planted now won't remain refusin that it might grow - whether it be wheat or barley - thou will sight she up pon the time the day arrived when thou raceive thy hardship.

5; An again - the plant thou planted won't say - "I-man won't grow" - an be it a fig wood or a grape vine - it fruit an it leaf won't be changed.

6; If thou plant grapes - it won't be changed that it might be a fig - an if thou plant figs - it won't be changed that it might be grapes - an if thou sow wheat it won't be changed that it might be barley.

7; All - ina each of the seeds - ina each of it kinds - each of the fruits - each of the woods - each of the leaves - each of the roots - send forth fruit havin raceived Pardon Dew blessin by what are found from JAH - yet if thou sow barley also it won't be changed that it might be wheat.

8; An all likewise - that a grave might produce flesh an soul - she shall produce persons like unto JAH sowed pon she ~ the flesh an soul that JAH sowed shall arise bein Inited - yet persons who worked goodly Work won't be changed ina persons who worked evil Work - an persons who worked evil Work also won't be changed ina persons who worked goodly Work.

9; Pon pon the time the iwa arrived when a drum are beaten - persons who dead shall arise by the Pardon Dew found from JAH ~ persons who worked goodly Work shall arise ina Life Resurrection - an them reward are the Garden where are Irie Ites that JAH prepared fe kind persons - where are no tribulation nor disease - an that are clean ones lodgin where them won't again dead after this.

10; But persons who worked evil Work shall arise a Definite Judgemant arisin - an with Deeyablos who misled them...

11; an with him armies - demons who don't love that even one person might be saved from all 'Adam childran...

12; them shall downscend toward *Gehannem* that were darkness edge - where are tooth grindin an mournin - where are no charity nor pardon - an where are no exits up til Iternity - that are beneath *See'ol* foriva. Fe them didn't work goodly Work ina them Life ina this world when them were ina them flesh.

13; Becaudis thing it shall be judged pon them pon the time when flesh an soul arise bein Inited.

14; Woe fe persons who don't believe the flesh an soul arisin whereby JAH show Him miracles abundance together.

15; An all an each one shall raceive him reward like unto him Work and him hands weariness.

Chapter 17.

1; A wheat kernel won't grow nor bear fruit unless she were demolished. But if a wheat kernel are demolished she will send roots toward Earth ~ she will send forth leaves ~ there will be buds ~ it will bear fruit.

2; Unu know that the one wheat kernel will become many kernels.

3; An all likewise - this kernel grow risin up from Water an wind an Earth dew - fe wheat cyaan bear fruit without Sun - but Sun are becau fiyah stead.

4; An wind are becau a soul stead - an wheat cyaan bear fruit without wind - an the Water give Earth fe drink an satta she.

5; An after Earth that are ashes drank Water - she produce roots - an she tips are lofty upward ~ she bear fruit around what JAH blessed she.

6; But a wheat kernel are 'Adam example - ina whom lodged a resonatin soul that JAH Irated - an likewise a grape wood drink Water an send forth roots - an the thin root kinds drink Water.

7; Fe Pardon Dew found from JAH give fe drink vines tips that were long - an it send the Water upward toward the leaf tips ~ it bud up from the Sun heat - an by JAH Accord it bear fruit.

8; It shall be a goodly fragrance that mek a reasonin Irie - an pon the time them ate it - it shall satta like unto Water that don't mek thirsty an grain that don't mek hungry - an pon the time them immersed it - it will be the cluster blood.

9; An like unto it were told ina Psalm sayin - "Grapes mek a person reasonin Irie" - pon the time them drank it - it mek a person heart Irie - an pon the time a person who came loose opened him mouth an drank it - him are drunk ~ him drink an fill ina him lungs - an the blood flow toward him heart.

10; As grapes drunkenness totally mislead - an as it deprive him him mind - it mek the pit an the cliff like unto a wide meadow - an him don't know obstacles an thorns pon him feet an hands.

11; JAH did thus pon she fruit an grape wood that Him Name might be praised by persons who believe dead persons arisin an who do Him Accord.

12; Ina the Kingdom of Heaven Him shall mek persons Irie who believe persons who dead arisin.

Chapter 18.

1; Unu persons who don't believe persons who dead arisin - around what error unu err! An pon the time them took unu toward the place unu don't know - unu will regret a useless regrets - an becau unu didn't believe the arisin that persons who dead shall arise Inited ina soul an flesh - an pon the time persons cast unu toward *Gehannem*...

2; if unu work whether the good or the evil - unu will raceive your reward like unto your Work - fe unu have misled them companions reasonin while unu said - "Wi know that persons who dead - who were dust an ashes - won't arise."

3; As them death have no exit - an as them have no Power fe them chastisemant that shall come pon them - an as them weren't firm ina them tribulation - becaudis thing them mislead them companions ~ fe them have that them might stand ina JAH Square.

4; Pon the time Him vexed pon them ina Him wrath them will totally fear ~ becau them didn't know that them were Irated bringin from not livin toward livin - as them speak JAH LAW without knowin - it shall be judged pon them all becau them worked evil.

5; Them don't know *Gehannem* where them will go - fe becau them were angry an becau them were crooked ina them Work - them teach fe them companions like unto them reasonin thirst measure - an fe them are evil ones who teach a crooked thing while them said - "There are no Resurrection of dead ones."

6; At that time them shall know that persons who dead shall arise - an them shall know that it shall be judged pon them becau them didn't believe the persons who dead arisin that are fe all 'Adam childran.

7; Fe all InI are 'Adam childran - an fe InI have dead becau 'Adam - an fe death judgemant have found InI all from alongside JAH becau InI faada 'Adam error.

8; InI will again arise there with InI faada 'Adam that InI might raceive InI hardship by InI Work that InI worked - fe the world have been ruled fe death by InI faada 'Adam ignorance.

9; By 'Adam infringin JAH Command - becaudis thing InI raceived hardship ~ InI flesh ina grave melted like unto wax - an InI bodies perished.

10; An Earth drank InI marrow ~ InI perished an InI comeliness perished ina grave - an InI flesh were buried ina grave - an InI beautiful words were buried ina Earth.

11; An worms proceeded from InI shinin eyes - an InI features perished ina grave an became dust.

12; Where are youtmons features comeliness - who were attractive - whose stance were handsome an whose word thing succeeded? How about where are warriors firmness?

13; Where are the kings armies - or how about the nobles lordship? Where are adornin ina horses an adornin ina silver an gold an adornin ina shinin weapons? Didn't it perish?

14; Where are sweet grape drink - an how about food flavour?

Chapter 19.

1; O Earth who gathered the nobles an the kings an rich ones an elders an dawtaz who were attractive an beauties who were attractive - woe arisin from thee-I.

2; O Earth who gathered persons who were warriors - them who have comeliness - an them who were fine of leg - an them who have reasonin an knowledge - an them whose words have words that were beautiful like unto a hummin harp an like unto a lyre an a violin beat...

3; an them who have a tune that mek Irie like unto grape drink mek Irie - an them whose eyes shine like unto a mornin star...

4; an them who sketch what were firm like unto them right hands lift up what are given an withheld an like unto them were - an them whose feet were beautiful fe sight up - an them who run like unto rushin wheels - woe arisin from thee-I.

5; O death who separated attractive persons souls from them flesh - woe arisin from thee-I - fe thou have been sent by JAH Accord.

6; As thou have gathered many persons whom JAH produced from thee-I an returned toward thee-I - thou Earth - woe arisin from thee-I ~ InI were found from thee-I ~ InI returned toward thee-I by Accord of JAH ~ InI were Irie over thee-I by JAH Accord.

7; Thou became a carpet fe InI corpses ~ InI recurred over thee-I - an InI were buried within thee-I ~ InI ate thy fruit - an thou ate InI flesh.

8; An InI drank the Water found from thy springs - an thou drank InI blood springs ~ InI ate the fruit found from thy Earthliness - an thou ate InI body flesh.

9; Like unto JAH commanded thee-I fe be InI food - InI ate grain from thy Earthliness that have beautiful dew - an thou raceived InI fleh comeliness an made it dust fe thy food like unto JAH commanded thee-I.

10; O death who gathered the nobles an the kings who were powerful - woe arisin from thee-I ~ thou didn't fear arisin from them famousness an them frightenin - like unto JAH Who Irated them commanded thee-I ~ o death - woe arisin from thee-I - an thou didn't scorn the sufferah.

11; An thou weren't nice fe persons whose features are beautiful - an thou didn't quit powerful ones an warriors ~ thou didn't quit poor nor rich ones - neither kind nor evil ones - neither childran nor elders - neither dawtaz nor males.

12; Thou didn't quit persons who think a goodly thing an who didn't depart from the

LAW - an thou didn't quit them who were like unto animals ina them Work - who think a evil thing - who were totally beautiful ina them features comeliness - ina them thing flavour an ina them words ~ o death - woe arisin from thee-I.

13; Thou didn't quit persons whose words were angry an whose mouths were full of curses ~ thou gathered persons who live in darkness an ina light an them souls ina thy places ~ o death - woe arisin from thee-I.

14; An Earth gathered the persons flesh who live whether ina cave or ina Earth - up til a drum are beaten an persons who dead arise.

15; As persons who dead shall arise quickly like unto a eye wink by JAH Command an pon a drum bein beaten - persons who worked evil Work shall raceive them hardship ina them sin abundance measure that them worked it - an persons who worked goodly Work shall be Irie.

Chapter 20.

1; An believe I that all InI Work that InI worked ina this world won't remain nor be hidden pon the time InI stood before Him fearin an tremblin.

2; An pon the time InI didn't seize provisions fe InI path - an pon the time InI won't have clothes fe InI bodies...

3; pon the time InI won't have a staff fe InI hands nor shoes fe InI feet...

4; an pon the time InI won't know the paths where demons tek InI - whether it be slippery or smooth - or be it dark - an whether it be thorns or nettles - or whether it be a Water depth or a pit depth - believe I that InI Work that InI worked ina this world won't remain nor be hidden.

5; InI won't know the demons who tek InI - an InI won't hear them thing.

6; As them are black ones - an as them lead InI toward darkness - InI don't sight up them faces.

7; An like unto the prophet spoke sayin - "Pon the time I soul were separated from I flesh - Lord I Lord - Thou know I path - an them hid a trap pon that path where I-man went - an I-man sight up returnin toward the right ~ I-man lacked one who know I - an I-man have nothing there whereby I-man will escape" - as them tek InI toward darkness - InI won't sight up them faces.

8; As him know that demons ridicule pon him - an as them will lead him toward the path him don't know - him speakin this are becaudis - an if him return leftward an rightward - there are no person who know him.

9; Him are alone amidst demons - an yet there are none who know him.

10; Angels of Light who are subtle are who are sent toward kind persons that them might raceive righteous ones souls - an might tek toward a Light place - toward the Garden - where welfare are found.

11; Demons an Angels of darkness are who are sent that them might raceive them an might tek them toward *Gehannem* that were prepared fe them that them might raceive them hardship by them sin that them worked.

12; Woe fe sinner persons souls who tek them toward downstruction - who have no welfare nor rest - nor escapin from the tribulation that found them - nor proceedin from *Gehannem* up til Iternity.

13; As them have lived firmed up ina Qayel Work - an as them have perished by Bele'am iniquity price - an as them have lacked what them will do - woe fe sinner persons - fe them pretext fe raceive interest an presents that ina downgression them might tek a foreigner money that weren't them money.

14; Them shall raceive them hardship ina *Gehannem* by them sin that them worked.

Chapter 21.

1; Where are persons who gather a foreigner money that weren't them hands Work nor them money?

2; Fe them tek a person money for free - an fe them shll be gathered without knowin the day when them dead that shall arrive pon them - however them quit them money for a foreigner.

3; Fe like unto them faadas - them are sinners kindreds who worry an seize sinners like unto them whether it be by theft or by robbery - an them childran won't be Irie by them faadas money.

4; As them have gathered fe them ina downgression - an as it are like unto misty urine an like unto the smoke that wind scattar an like unto wiltin grass - an like unto wax that melt arisin from before a fiyah - as sinners glory shall perish like unto that - there are none whom them faadas money will benefit ~ like unto Daweet spoke sayin - "I-man sight up a sinner man...

5; bein honoured an famed like unto a cordia an like unto a cypress - but pon the time I-man returned I-man lacked him ~ I-man searched an didn't find him place" - there are none whom them faadas money will profit nor benefit.

6; Becau them gathered a person money ina downgression - it seemin fe them that them won't dead - like unto persons who wrong them companions won't boast - sinner persons downstruction are likewise at one time.

7; Unu lazy ones - think that unu will perish an that your money will perish with unu - an if your silver an your gold abound it shall be rusted.

8; An if unu birth many childran them shall be fe many graves - an if unu work many houses them shall be demolished.

9; Fe unu didn't fulfill your Irator JAH Accord - an if unu multiply livestock them shall be for your enemies capture - an all the money unu seized ina your hands won't be found - fe it have been what weren't blessed.

10; Whether it be ina house or ina forest - an be it ina wilderness or a pasture place - an be it ina grape threshinfloor or ina grain threshinfloor - it won't be found.

11; Becau unu didn't keep JAH Command - as JAH won't save unu with all your house hold from the tribulation - there shall be sadness pon unu arisin from all your enemies - yet unu won't be Irie ina your children birthed from your nature.

12; But from Him plenty - Him won't trouble persons who kept Him Order an Him LAW ~ Him give all who begged Him - yet Him bless them childran birthed from them nature an also them land fruit fe them.

13; An Him mek them rulers pon all peoples ina them area that them might rule lest them be who are ruled - an Him give them all Him plenty ina them pasture place.

14; Him bless fe them all them seized ina them hand - all them field fruit - an all them livestocks places - an Him mek them Irie in them childran birthed from them nature.

15; An Him don't diminish them livestocks pon them ~ Him save them from all them tribulation an from weariness an illness an downstruction - an from them enemy them don't know an from him them know.

16; An Him will dispute fe them ina Judgemant time - an Him shall save them from a evil thing an from tribulation an from all who dispute them ~ ina the first era if a priest lived who work the Tent Work - who keep the LAW an keep the Tent Order an live firmed up ina JAH Accord - by the first Order an all the LAW as them would give him the tithe an what were birthed first Iginnin from man up til livestock - Him would save them from all the tribulation.

17; Like unto Mussie commanded Newie child 'Iyasu - there was a country of sanctuary ina all them country ~ by not knowin an by knowin up til them judged judgemant pon whom them canvicted an fe whom them acquitted...

18; if a person lived who killed a soul - him would be measured there that him might be saved.

19; Him told them - "Examine ina your reasonins that him have a quarrel with him formerly - an be it by axe or be it by a stone or be it by wood - as it have fallen from him hand by not knowin - if him say "That person pon whom it fell dead pon mi" - examine an save him ~ if him did it ina not knowin mek him be saved.

20; But if him do it knowin - him will raceive him hardship like unto him sin - an there are none who will pardon him; but if him kill him ina not knowin - as him have done it ina not knowin - examine an save him lest him dead.

21; Him worked fe them that them might distance from all the sin - yet Mussie would work like unto this fe 'Isra'iel children lest them depart from JAH LAW.

22; Him commanded them that 'Adam childran - who live firmed up ina JAH Command from worshippin idols an eatin what dead an lodged an what a sword bloated an cut - an who distance from all evil work like unto him worked fe them - that them might work it an might totally distance from all that aren't due.

23; Him commanded them lest them depart from the Command Him worked fe them ina the Tent example ina Heaven - that them might save them bodies an might find them lodgin with them faadas.

24; As them have been birthed from Siet an 'Adam who did JAH Accord - persons who believed ina JAH Word an lived firmed up ina Him Command will be called kind persons children.

25; As InI are 'Adam children - as Him have Irated InI ina Him Example an Him Appearance that InI might work all goodly Work that mek JAH Irie - Him won't scorn it.

26; As Him totally won't separate Him friends - if InI work goodly Work - InI shall inherit the Kingdom of Heaven where are welfare with persons who work goodly Work.

27; Him totally love persons who beg him cleanly - an Him hear them ina them priah - an Him accept the repentance of persons who are disciplined an enter repentance ~

Him give firmness an Power fe persons who keep Him Order an Him LAW an Him Command.

28; Persons who did Him Accord shall be Irie with Him ina Him Kingdom foriva - an whether them be persons who preceded or who arose later - them will present praise fe Him Iginnin from today up til Iternity.

Mek glory due fe JAH foriva - an the secand Meqabyan arrived an were fulfilled.

Book of Meqabyan III

Chapter 1.

1; Kristos shall rejoice Gibts persons - becau Him shall come toward them ina later era that Him will revenge an downstroy Deeyablos - who wronged them who were kindly an innocent - an who misled persons - an who hate him Irator Work.

2; Him shall revenge an downstroy him ~ Him shall return him lordship toward wretchedness an bein downbased - fe him have been arrogant ina him reasonin.

3; Him shall return him lordship toward bein downbased - fe him have said - "As mi will enter toward the sea midst - an as mi will proceed toward Heaven - an as mi will sight up depths - an as mi will grasp an seize 'Adam childran like unto bird chicks - who are it who are loftier than mi?

4; Becau mi became by them reason that mi might distance them from the straight LAW of JAH - as mi will strengthen pon persons who live ina this world unless them did JAH Accord - there are none who will depose mi from mi authority" him said.

5; "Fe mi will be a reason fe return them toward a path that were smooth fe go toward *Gehannem* with mi.

6; Persons who loved Him an kept Him LAW hate mi becaudis thing - but persons who departed from them Lord LAW an who erred will come toward mi an love mi an keep mi oath ~ as mi will mek them reasonin evil an change them thoughts lest them return toward them Irator JAH - them will do mi command like unto mi commanded them.

7; An pon the time mi showed them this world money - mi will mislead them reasonin from straight LAW - an pon the time mi showed them beautiful an attractive dawtaz - mi will distance them by these from straight LAW.

8; An pon the time mi showed them shinin Hindekie jewels an silver an gold - mi will distance them by this also from straight LAW that them might return toward mi Work.

9; An pon the time mi showed them thin clothes an red silk an white silk - an linens an white silk - mi will distance them by this also from straight LAW - an mi will return them toward mi thoughts ~ pon the time mi multiplied money an livestocks like unto sand an showed them - by this also mi will return them toward mi Work.

10; An pon the time mi showed them jealousy done in arrogance becau dawtaz an becau anger an quarrels - by all this mi will return them toward mi Work.

11; An pon the time mi showed them signs - mi will lodge ina them companions reasonin - an mi will lodge a sign thing that were fe each of the ras selves ina them reasonin - an mi showed them words signs an misled them.

12; An fe persons ina whom mi lodged mi lodgin - mi will show them signs - an be it ina stars gait - or be it ina cloud proceedin or ina fiyah flickerin - or be it ina beasts an birds cries - as them are mi lodgins - mi will lodge signs ina them reasonin pon them by all this.

13; Them will speak an give signs fe them companions - an like unto those them naysayers told them - mi will precede an be a sign fe them.

14; Mi will do them words signs fe them - that persons who examined them might be misled - an that them might give a wage fe magicians - an that them might tell fe them companions sayin - 'There are no savants like unto so-an-so an so-an-so fe whom it are done like unto them spoke - an who know prophecy - an who separate good an evil - an fe whom all are like unto them spoke - an fe whom it are done like unto them word.'

15; Mi will be Irie pon the time them spoke this - that persons who perish an err by mi might totally abound an that 'Adam children might perish - fe JAH have downbased mi from mi rank becau them faada 'Adam - pon mi sayin 'Mi won't bow fe 'Adam who are downbased fe mi.'

16; An mi will tek toward downstruction all him childran who live firmed up ina mi command ~ mi have a Oath from JAH Who Irated mi - that all persons whom mi misled might downscend toward *Gehannem* with mi.

17; An pon the time Him multiplied Him anger pon mi - an pon the time Him commanded that them might bind an cast mi toward *Gehannem* - pon the time mi Irator commanded sayin thus - mi interceded with mi Lord ~ mi interceded before Him while mi said - 'As Thou have vexed pon mi - an as Thou have admonished mi by Thy chastisement - an as Thou have chastised mi by Thy wrath - Lord mi Lord - adjourn mi that mi might speak one thing before Thee-I.'

18; An mi Lord answered fe mi sayin - Speak - I-man will hear thee ~ at that time mi began mi plea toward Him sayin - 'After mi were downbased from mi rank - mek the persons whom mi misled be like unto mi ina *Gehannem* where mi will raceive tribulation.

19; An mek them be fe Thy Lordship who refused mi - who didn't err by mi - who didn't keep mi command - that them might do Thy Command an might fulfill Thy Accord an might keep Thy Word - pon the time them didn't err by mi like unto mi misled them havin refused like unto mi taught them - an pon the time Thou loved mi - mek them tek the crown Thou gave fe mi.

20; Give them the crown of the authorities called Seythans who were sent with mi ~ seat them pon mi throne pon Thy Right that were a wilderness from mi an mi hosts.

21; An mek them praise Thee-I like unto Thou loved - an mek them be like unto mi hosts an like unto mi ~ becau Thou hated mi an loved them who were Irated from ashes an Earth - as mi authority have perished - an as them authority have been lofty - mek them praise Thee-I like unto Thou loved.'

22; Mi Lord answered fe mi sayin - As thou have misled them while them sight up an while them heard - if thou misled them without them lovin I Order - mek them be fe thee like unto thy accord an like unto thy word.

23; If them quit the Books Word an I Command an came toward thee - an if thou misled them while them downstruction also saddened mi - mek them raceive tribulation ina *Gehannem* like unto thee - Him told mi.

24; Unu will raceive tribulation ina *Gehannem* up til the Iternity - yet unu will have no exits from *Gehannem* up til the Iternity - fe them whom thou misled nor fe thee.

Chapter 2.

1; But I-man shall bequeath thy throne ina lordship fe them whom it failed thee fe mislead - like unto I slave 'Iyob ~ JAH Who rule all said - I-man will give the Kingdom of Heaven fe persons whom it failed thee fe mislead.

2; An mi provoke pon 'Adam childran ina all ~ if it were possible fe mi fe mislead them - mi won't quit them that them might firm up ina goodly Work ~ fe mi provoke pon all 'Adam childran - an mi sweeten this world Irie Ites fe them.

3; Be it by lovin drink an food an clothes - or by lovin things - or by withholdin an givin...

4; or be it by lovin fe hear an sight up - or be it by lovin fe caress an go - or be it by multiplyin arrogance an things - or be it by lovin dreams an slumber...

5; or be it by multiplyin drunkenness an drink - or be it by multiplyin insults an anger - be it by speakin games an useless things...

6; or be it by quarrels an by backbitin them companion - or be it by sightin up this world dawtaz who were attractive - be it by smellin perfumes fragrance that mislead them...

7; mi hate them by all this lest them able fe be saved ~ mi distance them from JAH LAW that them might enter with mi toward the downstruction whereby mi were downbased from mi rank."

8; An the prophet told him - "Thou who downstroy persons - perish ~ pon the time thou departed from JAH LAW an committed crime ina thy reasonin firmness an thy arrogance - an by saddenin thy Irator an not worshippin thy Irator ina thy reasonin firmness - will thou thus be arrogant pon JAH Iration?

9; Pon the time thy Irator vexed pon thee - Him downbased thee from thy rank becau thy evil Work ~ why do thou tek 'Adam toward sin - him whom him Irator Irated from Earth - whom Him made like unto Him loved - an whom Him placed fe Him praise?" him told him.

10; "Pon the time thou - who are subtle an were Irated from wind an fiyah - were arrogant ina sayin 'Mi are the Irator'...

11; pon the time thou boasted - as JAH have sight up thy evil Work an thou have denied JAH with thy hosts - Him Irated 'Adam who will praise becau thy stead - that him might praise Him Name without diminishin.

12; As thou have made thy ras self prouder than all Angels hosts who are like unto thee - becau thy arrogance JAH Irated 'Adam with him childran that them might praise JAH Name becau the praise that thou praise with thy hosts whom Him scorned.

13; An becaudis thing JAH downstroyed thee separatin from all Angels chiefs like unto thee - an thy hosts Irated ina one counsel with thee - an thou - unu proceeded an erred from JAH praise becau your useless reasonin arrogance an becau your reasonin firmness - an unu were arrogant pon your Irator - that aren't pon another.

14; Becaudis thing Him Irated 'Adam from Earth that Him might be praised by downbased persons - an Him gave him a Command an Law sayin Don't eat lest him eat from fig fruit.

15; An Him I-pointed him pon all the Iration Him Irated ~ Him notified him sayin - Don't eat from one fig fruit that bring death - lest thou bring death pon thy ras self - yet eat fruit from all the woods amidst the Garden.

16; An pon the time thou heard this Word - thou lodged perfidy ina him arisin from the thing thou spoke ina thy tongue fe Hiewan who were found from 'Adam side bone.

17; Thou misled 'Adam who were clean - ina firm perfidy that thou might mek him a Law demolisher like unto thee.

18; Pon the time thou misled Hiewan - who were Irated bein like unto a innocent dove an who don't know thy malice - thou made she betray by thy thing that succeeded an thy crooked word - an after thou misled that Hiewan who were Irated beforehand - she also went an misled JAH Iration 'Adam who were Irated from Earth beforehand.

19; An thou made him betray a downsturbance that aren't by thy arrogance - an thou made him fe deny that him might deny him Irator Word - an thou downstroyed 'Adam ina thy arrogance.

20; An ina thy malice thou distanced him from him Irator Love - an by thy reason thou sent him way from the Garden where Irie Ites are - an by thy hindrance thou made him quit the Garden food.

21; Fe Iginnin from Antiquity thou have quarreled with the innocent Iration 'Adam that thou might lower him toward *See'ol* where thou will raceive hardship - an that thou might send him way from the Love that brought him an Irated him from not livin toward true livin - an by thy false thing thou made him thirst a drink from the Garden.

22; An when him are Earthly - Him made him a subtle Angel who totally praise him Irator ina him flesh an him soul an him reasonin.

23; An Him Irated many thoughts fe him - like unto harps praise ina each of them styles.

Chapter 3.

1; But Him Irated one thought fe thee - that thou might totally praise while thou were sent toward where thy Irator sent thee.

2; But fe 'Adam were given five thoughts that were evil an five thoughts that were goodly - ten thoughts.

3; An again him have many thoughts like unto sea waves - an like unto a whirl wind that scattar dust liftin up from Earth - an like unto the sea waves that shake - an arisin from him unnumbered thoughts abundance ina him heart like unto unnumbered rain drops - 'Adam thoughts are like unto that.

4; But thy thought are one ~ as thou aren't fleshly - thou have no other thought.

5; But thou lodged ina snake reasonin ~ ina evil perfidy thou downstroyed 'Adam who were one limb - an Hiewan heard the snake thing - an havin heard - she did like unto she commanded she.

6; After she ate a fig fruit - she came an misled JAH first Iration 'Adam - an she brought death pon him an pon she childran becau she infringed she Irator Command.

7; Them proceeded from the Garden fe JAH by Him true Judgemant ~ Him calmed them ina the land where them were sent by them childran birthed from them nature an by them crops found from Earth - yet Him didn't distance them from the Garden quarrelin.

8; An pon the time thou expelled them straight from the Garden - that them might plant plants an childran fe be calmed an fe renew them reasonin ina the Earth fruit that Earth prepared from she Earthliness - an that them might be calmed by Earth fruit an the Garden fruit that JAH gave them...

9; JAH gave them woods more verdant than the Garden woods - an Hiewan an 'Adam - whom thou sent way from the Garden pon them eatin it - were totally calmed from sadness.

10; As JAH know fe calm Him Iration - them reasonins are calmed becau them childran an becau the crops found from Earth.

11; As them have been sent toward this world that grow nettles an thorns - them firm up them reasonins ina Water an grain.

Chapter 4.

1; Jah have that Him might ransom 'Adam - an Him shall shame thee ~ Him will save a sheep from a wolf mouth ('Adam from Deeyablos).

2; However thou will go toward *Gehannem* seizin with thee the persons whom thou ruled.

3; Persons who kept them Irator JAH LAW shall be Irie with them Irator JAH Who hid them from evil Work that Him might mek them Him fortune - an that them might praise Him with honoured Angels who didn't infringe them Irator JAH LAW like unto thee.

4; But JAH - Who chose an gave thee more than all Angels like unto thee that thou might praise Him with Him servant Angels - withheld from thee a lofty throne ina thy arrogance.

5; But thou became famous an were called one who love godhood - an thy hosts were called demons.

6; But persons who loved JAH shall be Him kindreds like unto honoured Angels - an the *Surafiel* an *Keerubiel* who praise Him streach forth them wings an praise without slackness.

7; But ina thy arrogance an thy laziness thou downstroyed thy praise that thou might praise Him everytime with thy host an thy kindreds Irated ina thy features.

8; Lest the praise of JAH - Who Irated thee makin a tenth tribe - be diminished pon the time thou forgot the praise of JAH Who Irated thee - it havin seemed fe thee that it aren't posssible fe Him fe Irate a Iration like unto thee - an lest the praise of JAH - Who Irated thee - be diminished pon the time thou were separated from thy bredren Inity - Him Irated 'Adam becau thy stead.

9; But ina thy reasonin arrogance thou neglected the praise of JAH Who Irated thee - an Him vexed pon thee ~ Him ridiculed thee - an Him bound an banished thee ina *Gehannem* with thy hosts also.

10; Him brought Soil from Earth with Him glorified Hands - an addin fiyah an Water an wind - Him Irated 'Adam ina Him Example an Him Features.

11; Him I-pointed him pon all the Iration Him Irated ina Him Itority - that Him praise might be filled by the praise thou would praise Him ~ 'Adam praise became one with Angels praise - an them praise were level.

12; But ina thy collar of reasonin firmness an thy arrogance thou were downbased from thy rank - an havin departed from JAH Lordship - Who Irated thee - thou downstroyed thy ras self.

13; Know that Him praise weren't diminished - fe JAH have Irated 'Adam who praised Him ina him reasonin counsel lest Him JAH-ness praise be diminished.

14; Fe Him know all before it are done - an Him knew thee before Him Irated thee that thou will demolish Him Command ~ as there are a counsel hidden alongside Him before Him Irated the world - pon the time thou denied Him - Him Irated Him slave 'Adam ina Him Features an Him Example.

15; Like unto Selomon spoke sayin - 'Before hills were Irated an before the world succeeded bein Irated - an before winds that are Earth grounations were Irated...

16; an before Him firmed up hills an mountains grounations - an before this world Work firmed up - an before moon an Sun light shone - before eras an stars caretakin were known...

17; an before daylight an night alternated - an before the sea were delineated by sand - before all the Irated Iration were Irated...

18; an before all sight up today were sight up - before all the names called today were called - Him Irated I Selomon' - Angels like unto unu an thou an Him slave 'Adam were ina JAH Reasonin.

19; Him Irated 'Adam that Him glorified Name might be praised pon the time thou mutinied - an that Him might be praised by Him downbased slave 'Adam who were Irated from Earth pon the time thou were arrogant.

20; Fe bein ina Heaven JAH hear poor ones plea - an Him love downbased persons praise.

21; Him love fe save havin lodged ina persons who fear Him - yet as Him don't love horse Power - an as Him don't step meanin fe the lap of a concubine - JAH shall ignore arrogant ones thing.

22; An them shall weep while them cried becau them sin that them worked.

23; It failed thee fe plead ina repentance.

24; But 'Adam who were Irated from Earth returned ina repentance while him totally wept before JAH becau him sin.

25; But ina thy collar of reasonin firmness an thy heart arrogance thou didn't know Love Work an thou didn't know repentance ~ it failed thee fe plead before thy Irator JAH ina repentance an mournin an sadness.

26; But that 'Adam who are ashes an Earth returned toward repentance ina mournin an sadness - an him returned toward humbleness an Love Work.

27; But thou didn't downbase thy reasonin an thy ras self fe JAH Who Irated thee.

28; As fe 'Adam - him downbased him ras

self an pleaded pon the iniquity him wronged ~ him weren't proud.

29; As thou have totally produced crime - it were found from thee - yet it aren't him who produced that error ~ ina thy arrogance thou took him with thee toward thy downstruction.

30; Before him Irated unu both - as Him have known unu that unu were sinners - an as Him have known your Works - Him know that this that were done were ina thy heart arrogance.

31; But Him returned that 'Adam - who were without arrogance or malice - ina repentance mournin an sadness.

32; Fe a person who wrong an don't plead ina repentance have multiplied him iniquity more than him earlier iniquity - but ina thy heart arrogance it failed thee fe plead ina repentance - but a person who plead an weep enterin repentance before Him Irator JAH...

33; him entered repentance fe true - an him found Work whereby him will be saved that him might fear him Lord Heart - an him pleaded before him Irator - fe him have pleaded before Him ina bowin an much repentance - an arisin from the earlier tribulation Jah shall lighten him sin fe him lest Him vex pon Him slave - an Him will forgive him him former sin.

34; If him didn't return toward him former sin an if him did this - this are perfect repentance ~ 'Adam didn't forget fe think of him Irator nor fe implore him Irator JAH ina repentance.

35; An thou - plea ina repentance toward thy Irator JAH - an don't wrong them becau them were flesh an blood - fe JAH Who Irated them know them weakness - an don't wrong the persons Him Irated by Him Itority.

36; An after them soul were separated from them flesh - them flesh shall be dust up til the day that JAH love.

Chapter 5.

1; Know JAH WHo Irated thee-I ~ as JAH have Irated thee-I ina Him Features an Him Example when thou are Earth - don't forget JAH Who firmed thee-I up an saved thee-I an Whom 'Isra'iel glorified ~ Him placed thee-I ina Garden that thou might be Irie an might dig Earth.

2; Pon the time thou demolished Him Command - Him sent thee way from the Garden toward this world that Him cursed becau thee - that grow nettles an thorns.

3; *Fe thou are Earth - an fe she are Earth - fe thou are dust - an fe she are dust - fe thou are Soil - an fe she are Soil - fe thou are fed the grain found from she - an fe thou will return toward she* - fe thou will be Soil up til Him love that Him might raise thee - an fe Him shall examine thee the sin thou worked an all the iniquity.

4; Know what thou will answer Him at that time ~ think of the good an evil thou worked ina this world ~ examine whether the evil would abound or whether the good would abound ~ try.

5; If thou work a goodly thing - it are a goodly thing fe thee-I that thou might be Irie pon the day when persons who dead will arise.

6; But if thou work evil Work - woe fe thee - fe thou will raceive thy hardship like unto thy hands Work an like unto thy reasonin evil ~ fe if thou work a evil thing pon thy companion an if thou didn't fear JAH - thou will raceive thy hardship.

7; An if thou betray thy companion an if thou call JAH Name an swear ina lie - as thou will raceive thy hardship like unto thy Work - woe fe thee.

8; An thou tell thy false thing fe thy companion simulatin Truth - but thou know that thou spoke a lie.

9; An thou persuade the persons with thee thy false thing simulatin Truth - an thou multiply false things that weren't Truth - an thou will raceive thy hardship like unto thy sin ~ thou deny thy companion while thou tell thy companion 'mi will give thee' what thou won't give him.

10; An pon the time thou said 'Mi will give' ina thy pure reasonin - demons mek application fe thee like unto dogs - an them mek thee forget all - an if thou withhold or if thou love that thou might give - them don't know the person fe whom them gather - yet as Him have said - Them shall fatten - this world money appetise thee that thou might fatten the money that won't benefit thee an that thou won't eat.

11; An again - as Him have said - 'Adam liar childran mek a balance false ~ as fe them - them go from robbery toward robbery - this world money appetise thee.

12; O persons - don't mek hope ina distortin scales an balances - an ina stealin a person money - an ina makin a person money one ina downgression - an ina infringin your companions money - an ina stealin him field - ina all the lies unu do fe your ras selves profit that aren't fe your companions.

13; If unu do this unu will raceive your hardship like unto your Work.

14; O persons - be fed by your hands Work that were straight - yet don't desire robbery ~ don't love that unu might totally rob an eat a person money without justice by what aren't due.

15; An if unu eat it - it won't satta unu ~ pon the time unu dead unu will quit it fe another - yet even if unu fatten - it won't benefit unu.

16; An if your money abound - don't distort your reasonins ~ as sinner persons money are like unto the smoke that proceed from a griddle an the wind tek it - better than sinner persons money are the likkle money them accumulated ina Truth.

Chapter 6.

1; Think of the day when unu will dead ~ pon the time your souls were separated from your flesh - an pon the time unu quit your money fe another - an pon the time unu went pon the path unu don't know - think of the tribulation that shall come pon unu.

2; An the demons that will raceive unu are evil - an them features are ugly - an them are frightenin ina them splendour - an them won't hear your words - an unu won't hear them words.

3; An becau unu didn't do your Irator JAH Accord - them won't hear unu ina your plea pon the time unu begged them ~ becaudis thing them will totally frighten unu.

4; But persons who fulfilled JAH Accord have no fear - fe demons fear them. But demons shall ridicule sinner persons souls pon them.

5; But kind persons souls shall be Irie pon Angels ina Irie Ites - fe them shall totally mek them Irie becau them scorned this world - but angels who are evil shall raceive sinner persons souls.

6; Pardon Angels shall raceive kind persons an righteous ones souls - fe them are sent from JAH that them might calm righteous ones souls ~ as Angels that were evil are sent from Deeyablos that them might ridicule pon sinner persons souls - demons shall raceive sinner persons souls.

7; Sinner persons - woe fe unu ~ weep fe your ras selves before the day when unu dead arrive pon unu ~ pon the time unu reach toward JAH...

8; enter repentance ina your era that are there before your era pass - that unu might live ina Irieness an Ites without tribulation nor disease - yet as after unu dead your era won't return that passed - weep.

9; Lest it be pon unu toward a vain accord that distance from JAH - ina your firm criticism mek lovin fe be lavished an food an Irie Ites not be found ina unu ~ as a body that are sated without measure won't think of JAH Name - Deeyablos wealth shall lodge pon it - yet as the Hola Spirit won't lodge ina it - mek lovin the Irie Ites not be found ina unu.

10; Like unto Mussie spoke - Mussie havin said - "Ya`iqob ate an were sated an fattened an tall an wide - an JAH Who Irated him were separated from him.

11; An him lifestyle distanced from JAH" - as a body that were sated without measure nor moderation won't think of JAH Name - mek lovin Irie Ites not be found alongside unu ~ as belly satiety without measure are bein like unto a boar an like unto a wanderin horse - mek drinkin an eatin without measure an adultery not be found ina unu.

12; But a person who eat ina measure shall live firmed up ina JAH Support - an him shall live firmed up like unto the horizon an like unto a tower that have a stone fence; a person who forgot JAH LAW shall flee without one livin who chase him.

13; A kind person shall live ina bein raspected like unto a lion.

14; But persons who don't love JAH won't keep Him LAW - an them reasonins aren't straight.

15; An JAH shall bring sadness an alarm pon them when them are ina this world - an bein seized ina tremblin an fright - an bein seized ina the tribulations without number by them money bein snatched - bein bound by them hands ina chains from them masters hands...

16; lest them be who rested from the tribulation - an lest them lifestyle be ina Irie Ites - lest them rest when them are ina alarmin tribulations that are pon each of them ras selves - Him shall bring sadness an alarm pon them.

Chapter 7.

1; But like unto Daweet spoke sayin - "I-man believed ina JAH ~ I-man won't fear havin said - 'What would a person mek I?'" - there are no fright an alarm pon persons who believed ina JAH.

2; An again like unto him spoke sayin - "If warriors surround I - I-man believed ina Him ~ I-man begged JAH one thing ~ I-man seek that" - persons who believed ina Him have no fright pon them ~ a person who believed ina Him shall live ina Life foriva - an him won't fear arisin from a evil thing.

3; Who are a person who shamed believin in JAH? how about who ignored Him fe a desire?

4; As Him have said - I-man love him who loved I - an I-man shall honour him who glorified I ~ I-man shall keep him who returned toward I ina repentance - who are a person who shamed believin ina Him?

5; Judge Truth an save the widow body ~ save them that JAH might save unu from all that oppose unu ina evil thing ~ keep them ~ as kind persons childran are honoured - them are given makin a profit - an yet Him shall save your childran after unu - fe them won't be troubled fe grain.

Chapter 8.

1; 'Iyob believed ina JAH ~ as him didn't neglect fe praise him Irator JAH - JAH saved him from all the tribulation that 'Adam childran enemy Deeyablos brought pon him ~ him said - "JAH gave ~ JAH withheld ~ it happened like unto JAH loved pon I - an mek JAH Name be praised by all pon Earth an ina Heaven" - yet as him didn't sadden him reasonin - JAH saved him.

2; An pon the time JAH sight up 'Iyob that him heart were cleansed from sin - Him raceived him ina much honour.

3; An Him gave him money that abounded more than him money that preceded ~ fe him have totally indured him tribulation - an Him cured him from him wounds becau him indurin all the tribulation that arrived pon him.

4; An if unu like unto him indure the tribulation arisin from demons sent toward unu - unu will be admired.

5; Indure the tribulation ~ that JAH might be fe unu a fortress Refuge from persons who hate unu - an that Him might be a fortress Refuge fe your children children an fe your children after unu - don't sadden your reasonins arisin from the tribulation that came pon unu ~ believe ina Him - an Him shall be a fortress Refuge fe unu.

6; Beg Him ~ Him will hear unu ~ mek hope - an Him will forgive unu ~ beg Him - an Him will be a Faada fe unu;

7; Think of Merdokyos an 'Astier - Yodeet an Giediewon an Deebora an Bariq an Yoftahie an Somson...

8; an other persons like unto them who were disciplined fe believe ina JAH an whose enemies didn't defeat them.

9; Fe JAH are True - an fe Him don't favour havin sight up a face - but persons raceived hardship who love that them might work sin pon them ras selves ~ all persons who fear Him an keep Him LAW shall keep bodies - an Him shall give them bein I-loved an honour.

10; Him shall mek them Irie ina them proceedin an them enterin - ina them Life an them death - an ina them arisin an sittin ~ Fe Him save - an Him seclude.

11; Fe Him sadden - an Him pardon.

12; Fe Him mek poor - an Him honour ~ Him mek wretched - an as Him honour - Him mek them Irie.

Chapter 9.

1; An whether it be what are ina Heaven - or whether it be what are pon Earth - an be it either subtle or stout - everything n all Him money live bein firmed up ina Him Order.

2; There are nothing that departed from JAH LAW an Him Order - Who Irated all the world ~ be it a vulture track that fly ina Heaven - Him command toward it destination where Him loved.

3; An Him command a Earth snake path that live ina cave toward where Him loved - an a boat path that go pon sea - apart from only JAH there are none who know it path.

4; An apart from only JAH - there are none who know the path where a soul go pon the time it were separated from it flesh - be it a righteous or a sinner soul.

5; Who know where it will turn - that it would turn ina wilderness or pon a mountain? or that it would fly like unto a bird - that it would be like unto Heaven dew that alight pon a mountain...

6; or that it would be like unto deep wind - or that it would be like unto lightnin that straighten up it path...

7; or that it would be like unto stars that shine amidst the deep - or that it would be like unto sand pon a sea shore that are piled amidst the deep...

8; or that it would be like unto a horizon stone that firmed up pon the sea deep edge - or like unto a wood that give she beautiful fruit that grew by a Water spout...

9; or that it would be that I likened unto the reed that heat of the Sun burnt - an that wind lift an tek toward another place where it didn't grow - an whose trace aren't found...

10; or that it would be like unto misty urine whose trace aren't found - who know JAH Work? who are Him counsellors? how about with whom did Him counsel?

11; As JAH Thoughts are hidden from persons - who will examine an know Him Work?

12; As Him have Irated Earth pon Water - an as Him have firmed she up without stakes - there are none who examine an know JAH Counsel or Him Wisdom - an Him Irated Heaven ina Him perfect Wisdom an firmed it up ina winds - an Him streached forth a lofty cosmos like unto a tent.

13; Him commanded clouds that them might rain rain pon Earth - an Him grow grass - an Him grow fruits without number fe be food fe persons - that InI might believe ina JAH an be Irie ina Inity.

14; JAH are Who give 'Adam childran the Irie Ites an all the fatness an all the satiety ~ JAH are Who give that them might satta an praise JAH Who gave them fruit from Earth...

15; an Who dressed them ina beautiful robes - Who gave them all the I-loved plenty - the Irieness an the Ites that are given fe persons who fulfill JAH Accord.

16; Him give bein I-loved an honour ina the house Him prepared an ina the Kingdom of Heaven fe them faadas who keep JAH LAW.

17; Him give bein I-loved an honour ina the place Him prepared an ina the Kingdom of Heaven fe them faadas who lived firmed up ina Him Worship an Him LAW - an who didn't depart from Him LAW - whom Him famed an raised that them might keep Him Order an Him LAW - an I-man sight up what JAH do fe Him friends ina this world by weakenin them enemies an by keepin them bodies.

18; I-man sight up that Him give them all them begged Him an that Him fulfill them accord fe them ~ don't depart from JAH - an fulfill JAH Accord.

19; Don't depart from Him Command an Him LAW - lest Him vex pon unu an lest Him downstroy unu at one time - an lest Him vex an whip unu ina the tribulation from where unu lived formerly - lest unu depart from your faadas Order where unu were formerly - an lest uour lodgin be ina Gehannem where are no exits up til the Iternity.

20; Keep your Irator JAH LAW when your soul are separated from your flesh that Him might do goodly Work fe unu pon the time unu stood before JAH.

21; Fe Earth an Heaven Kingdoms are fe Him - an fe Kingdom an capability are fe Him - an fe bein nice an pardonin are only fe Him.

22; As Him mek rich an Him mek poor - as Him mek wretched an Him honour - keep JAH LAW.

23; An Daweet spoke becau Him while him said - "Man seem vain - an him era pass like unto a shadow."

24; Him spoke becau Him sayin - "But Lord - Thou live foriva - an Thy Name Invocation are fe a child childran."

25; An again him said - "Thy Kingdom are all the world Kingdom - an Thy Rulership are fe a child childran" ~ Thou returned a kingdom fe Daweet bringin from Sa'ol.

26; But there are none who will I-point Thee-I ~ there are none who can dismiss ~ Thou sight up all - yet there are none who can sight up Thee-I.

27; An Thy kingdom won't perish foriva fe a child childran ~ there are none who will rule Him - but Him rule all ~ Him sight up all - but there are none who sight Him up.

28; As Him have Irated man ina Him Features an ina Him example that them might praise Him an might know Him Worship ina straight reasonin without doubt - Him examine an know what kidneys smoked up an what a reasonin transported.

29; Yet them bow fe stone - fe wood - an fe silver an gold that a person hand worked.

30; An them sacrifice sacrifice fe them up til them sacrifice smoke proceed toward Heaven - that them sin might live firmed up before JAH - but yet them refused fe worship JAH Who Irated them ~ Him shall downcuse them becau all them sin that them worked ina worshippin them idols.

31; Them learned bowin fe idols an all stained Work that aren't due - naysayin by stars - sorcery - worshippin idols - evil accord - an all the Work that JAH don't love - yet them didn't keep JAH Command that them learned.

32; As them didn't love fe worship JAH that them might save them bodies from sin an iniquity by Him servants the Angels an by money that them praise before JAH - them work all this ina lackin goodly Work.

33; An pon the time them all arose together from the graves where them were buried an where them bodies perished - them souls shall stand empty before JAH - an them souls lived ina the Kingdom of Heaven prepared fe kind persons.

34; But sinner persons souls shall live ina *Gehannem* - an pon the time graves were opened - persons who dead shall arise - an souls shall return toward the flesh that them were separated formerly.

35; Like unto them were bithed ina them nakedness from them mother belly - them shall stand ina them nakedness before JAH - an them sins that them worked Iginnin from them infancy up til that time shall be revealed.

36; Them shall raceive them sin hardship pon them bodies - an whether them likkle or much sin - them shall raceive them hardship like unto them sin.

Chapter 10.

1; Fe the blood of soul found from JAH shall lodge ina them like unto it lodged ina them formerly - an if unu didn't believe persons who dead arisin - hear that Irations shall arise ina rainy season without bein birthed from them mother nor faada.

2; An Him command them formerly by Him Word that them dead.

3; An them flesh bein demolished an rotten an again renewed - them shall arise like unto Him loved.

4; An again pon the time rain alit an pon the time it sated Earth - them shall live havin arisin like unto them were Irated formerly.

5; As them who are everlivin ina bloodly soul an who live ina this world an them whom Water produce have been Irated - Him havin said Mek them be Irated - an as JAH Itority lodge pon the Water - she give them a bloodly soul by Him Itority an by Him Word.

6; As them are Irated by Him Itority an by Him Word without a faada nor mother - thou blind of reasonin who say "Persons who dead won't arise" - if thou have knowledge or Wisdom - how will thou say persons who dead won't arise by them Irator JAH Word?

7; As persons who dead - who were ashes an dust ina grave - shall arise by JAH Word - as fe thou - enter repentance an return toward thy religion.

8; Like unto Him Word spoke formerly - them shall arise by the Pardon Dew found from JAH - an that Word shall turn all the world an arouse the persons who dead like unto Him loved.

9; An know that thou will arise an stand before Him - an mek it not seem fe thee ina thy reasonin dullness that thou will remain ina grave.

10; It aren't thus ~ thou will arise an raceive thy hardship like unto the Work measure that thou worked - whether it be goodly or evil - yet mek it not seem fe thee that thou will remain - fe this Day are the day when them will raceive hardship.

11; An ina Resurrection time thou will raceive thy hardship by all thy sin that thou worked ~ thou will finish thy sin hardship that were written Iginnin from thy infancy up til that time - an thou have no reason that thou will pretext pon thy sin like unto this world Work that thou might deny thy sin.

12; Like unto thou mek thy false word truth before thee - an like unto thou mek the lie thing that thou spoke truth - thou have no reason that thou will pretext like unto this world Work.

13; Becau it were that she know pon thee all thy evil Work thou worked - an becau it were that she will reveal pon thee before she Irator JAH - as JAH Word shall lodge pon thee an speak pon thee - thou have no reason pon what thou pretext.

14; Thou will shame there becau thy sin that thou worked ~ it are that thou might be thanked with persons who are thanke pon them beautiful Work - yet lest thou shame before man an Angels pon the day when Judgemant are judged - quickly enter repentance ina this world before thou arrive toward there.

15; Persons who praise JAH with Angels shall raceive them reward from them Irator without shamin - an them shall be Irie ina the Kingdom of Heaven - however unless thou worked goodly Work when thou are ina thy flesh ina Life - thou have no fortune with righteous ones.

16; As thou weren't prepared when thou have knowledge an when thou have this world where thou enter repentance - there shall be a useless regret pon thee - an fe thou didn't give a morsel fe the hungry when thou have money.

17; An fe thou didn't clothe the naked when thou have clothes - an fe thou didn't save the wronged when thou have Itority.

18; Fe thou didn't teach the sinner person when thou have knowledge - that him might return an enter repentance - an that JAH might forgive him him sin that him formerly worked ina ignorance - an fe thou didn't fight with demons who quarrel with thee when thou have Power that thou able fe prevail.

19; An fe thou didn't fast nor pray when thou have firmness that thou might weaken thy infancy Power that are pon flesh - an that thou might subject thy ras self fe Rightness that aren't favorin pon flesh...

20; that aren't favorin Irie Ites when it are ina this world ina beautiful drink an sweet food - an that aren't adornin ina thin clothes an silver an gold...

21; an as thou didn't fast nor pray when thou have firmness that thou might subject thy ras self fe Rightness that aren't adornin ina honoured Hindekie jewels called emerald an phazyon - there shall be a useless regret pon thee ~ this aren't a person ornamant that are due.

22; As fe a person ornamant - it are purity - Wisdom - knowledge - lovin one another by what are due without envyin nor jealousy nor doubtin nor quarrels ~ while thou loved thy companion like unto thy ras self...

23; an without thy doin a evil thing pon a person who did a evil thing pon thee-I - it are lovin one another by what are due - that thou might enter toward the Kingdom of Heaven that are given fe person who indured the tribulation - that Him might give thee the honoured Kingdom of Heaven an thy reward pon makin hope ina the Kingdom of Heaven ina Resurrection time with honoured persons ina knowledge an Wisdom.

24; An don't say "After wi dead wi won't arise" - fe Deeyablos cut off hope of persons who speak an think this lest them be saved in Resurrection time ~ them will know that them have hardship pon them pon the time Advent arrived pon them ~ ina Resurrection time persons will be totally sad who worked sin ina not knowin that Him might think of them sin pon them - fe them didn't believe ina Him that them will arise pon that Day.

25; Becaudis thing them shall be reproached like unto them Work evil measure that them worked ina this world - an them shall sight up the Resurrection that them denied whereby them will arise together ina flesh.

26; Them shall weep at that time becau them didn't work goodly Work ~ it would have been better fe them if them wept ina this world if it are possible fe them lest them be who weep ina *Gehannem*.

27; If InI didn't weep ina this world by InI accord - demons will mek InI weep without InI accord ina *Gehannem* ~ if InI didn't enter repentance ina this world - InI prepare worthless an useless cries an mournin ina *Gehannem*.

28; Prepare goodly Work - that unu might cross from death toward Life - an that unu might go from this passin world toward the Kingdom of Heaven - an that unu might sight up the Kingdom of Heaven Light that surpass light ina this world.

29; Refuse Irie Ites that are ina this world - that thou might be Irie without measure ina the Kingdom of Heaven ina Irie Ites that aren't fulfilled Iginnin from today up til the Iternity with persons who believe persons who dead arisin.

Mek Glory an praise due JAH foriva - an the third book that speak the Meqabyans thing were fulfilled.

SELAH

Additions to Jeremiah The Prophet

~1.1
It came to pass, when the children of Israel were taken captive by
the king of the Chaldeans, that God spoke to Jeremiah saying:
Jeremiah, my chosen one, arise and depart from this city, you and
Baruch, since I am going to destroy it because of the multitude of
the sins of those who dwell in it.
~1.2
For your prayers are like a solid pillar in its midst, and like an
indestructible wall surrounding it.
~1.3
Now, then, arise and depart before the host of the Chaldeans
surrounds it.
~1.4
And Jeremiah answered, saying:
I beseech you, Lord, permit me, your servant, to speak in your presence.
~1.5
And Jah said to him:
Speak, my chosen one Jeremiah.
~1.6
And Jeremiah spoke, saying:
Lord Almighty, would you deliver the chosen city into the hands of the Chaldeans, so that the king with
the multitude of his people might boast and say: "I have prevailed
over the holy city of God"?
~1.7
No, my Lord, but if it is your will, let it be destroyed by your
hands.
~1.8

And Jah said to Jeremiah:
Since you are my chosen one, arise and
depart form this city, you and Baruch, for I
am going to destroy it
because of the multitude of the sins of those
who dwell in it.
~1.9
For neither the king nor his host will be able
to enter it unless I
first open its gates.
~1.10
Arise, then, and go to Baruch, and tell him
these words.
~1.11
And when you have arisen at the sixth hour
of the night, go out on
the city walls and I will show you that
unless I first destroy the
city, they cannot enter it.
~1.12
When Jah had said this, he departed from
Jeremiah.
~2.1
And Jeremiah ran and told these things to
Baruch; and as they went
into the temple of God, Jeremiah tore his
garments and put dust on
his head and entered the holy place of God.
~2.2
And when Baruch saw him with dust
sprinkled on his head and his
garments torn, he cried out in a loud voice,
saying:
Father Jeremiah, what are you doing?
What sin has the people committed?
~2.3
(For whenever the people sinned, Jeremiah
would sprinkle dust on his
head and would pray for the people until
their sin was forgiven.)
~2.4
So Baruch asked him, saying:
Father, what is this?

~2.5
And Jeremiah said to him:
Refrain from rending your garments --
rather, let us rend our hearts! And let us not
draw water for the
trough, but let us weep and fill them with
tears! For Jah will
not have mercy on this people.
~2.6
And Baruch said:
Father Jeremiah, what has happened?
~2.7
And Jeremiah said:
God is delivering the city into the hands of
the
king of the Chaldeans, to take the people
captive into Babylon.
~2.8
And when Baruch heard these things, he
also tore his garments and
said:
Father Jeremiah, who has made this known
to you?
~2.9
And Jeremiah said to him:
Stay with me awhile, until the sixth hour
of the night, so that you may know that this
word is true.
~2.10
Therefore they both remained in the altar-
area weeping, and their
garments were torn.
~3.1
And when the hour of the night arrived, as
Jah had told Jeremiah
they came up together on the walls of the
city, Jeremiah and Baruch.
~3.2
And behold, there came a sound of trumpets;
and angels emerged from
heaven holding torches in their hands, and
they set them on the walls
of the city.

~3.3
And when Jeremiah and Baruch saw them, they wept, saying:
 Now we know that the word is true!
~3.4
And Jeremiah besought the angels, saying:
 I beseech you, do not
 destroy the city yet, until I say something to Jah.
~3.5
And Jah spoke to the angels, saying:
 Do not destroy the city
 until I speak to my chosen one, Jeremiah.
~3.6
Then Jeremiah spoke, saying:
 I beg you, Lord, bid me to speak in your presence.
~3.7
And Jah said:
 Speak, my chosen one Jeremiah.
~3.8
And Jeremiah said:
 Behold, Lord, now we know that you are delivering
 the city into the hands of its enemies, and they will take the people
 away to Babylon. What do you want me to do with the holy vessels of
 the temple service?
~3.10
And Jah said to him:
 Take them and consign them to the earth, saying:
  Hear, Earth, the voice of your creator
  who formed you in the abundance of waters,
  who sealed you with seven seals for seven epochs,
  and after this you will receive your ornaments (?) --
~3.11
 Guard the vessels of the temple service until the gathering of the beloved.
~3.12
And Jeremiah spoke, saying:
 I beseech you, Lord, show me what I should do for Abimelech the Ethiopian, for he has done many
 kindnesses to your servant Jeremiah.
~3.13
 For he pulled me out of the miry pit; and I do not wish that he
 should see the destruction and desolation of this city, but that you
 should be merciful to him and that he should not be grieved.
~3.14
And Jah said to Jeremiah:
 Send him to the vineyard of Agrippa, and I will hide him in the shadow of the mountain until I cause the
 people to return to the city.
~3.15
 And you, Jeremiah, go with your people into Babylon and stay with
 them, preaching to them, until I cause them to return to the city.
~3.16
 But leave Baruch here until I speak with him.
~3.17
When he had said these things, Jah ascended from Jeremiah into heaven.
~3.18
 But Jeremiah and Baruch entered the holy place, and taking the
 vessels of the temple service, they consigned them to the earth as
 Jah had told them.
~3.19
And immediately the earth swallowed them.
~3.20
And they both sat down and wept.
~3.21

And when morning came, Jeremiah sent Abimelech, saying:
Take a basket
and go to the estate of Agrippa by the mountain road, and bring back
some figs to give to the sick among the people; for the favor of the
Lord is on you and his glory is on your head.

~3.22
And when he had said this, Jeremiah sent him away; and Abimelech went
as he told him.

~4.1
And when morning came, behold the host of the Chaldeans surrounded
the city.

~4.2
And the great angel trumpeted, saying:
Enter the city, host of the Chaldeans;
for behold, the gate is opened for you.

~4.3
Therefore let the king enter, with his multitudes, and let him take
all the people captive.

~4.4
But taking the keys of the temple, Jeremiah went outside the city and
threw them away in the presence of the sun, saying:
I say to you, Sun,
take the keys of the temple of God and guard them until the day
in which Jah asks you for them.

~4.5
For we have not been found worthy to keep them, for we have become
unfaithful guardians.

~4.6
While Jeremiah was still weeping for the people, they brought him out
with the people and dragged them into Babylon.

~4.7
But Baruch put dust on his head and sat and wailed this lamentation,
saying:
Why has Jerusalem been devastated? Because of the sins of the
beloved people she was delivered into the hands of enemies -- because of
our sins and those of the people.

~4.8
But let not the lawless ones boast and say:
"We were strong enough to
take the city of God by our might;"
but it was delivered to you because of our sins.

~4.9
And God will pity us and cause us to return to our city, but you will
not survive!

~4.10
Blessed are our fathers, Abraham, Isaac and Jacob, for they departed
from this world and did not see the destruction of this city.

~4.11
When he had said this, Baruch departed from the city, weeping and
saying:
Grieving because of you, Jerusalem, I went out from you.

~4.12
And he remained sitting in a tomb, while the angels came to him and
explained to him everything that Jah revealed to him through
them.

~5.1
But Abimelech took the figs in the burning heat; and coming upon a
tree, he sat under its shade to rest a bit.

~5.2
And leaning his head on the basket of figs, he fell asleep and slept

for 66 years; and he was not awakened from his slumber.

~5.3
And afterward, when he awoke from his sleep, he said:
I slept sweetly for a little while,
but my head is heavy because I did not get enough sleep.

~5.4
Then he uncovered the basket of figs and found them dripping milk.

~5.5
And he said:
I would like to sleep a little longer, because my head
is heavy. But I am afraid that I might fall asleep and be late in
awakening and my father Jeremiah would think badly of me; for if he
were not in a hurry, he would not have sent me today at daybreak.

~5.6
So I will get up, and proceed in the burning heat; for isn't there
heat, isn't there toil every day?

~5.7
So he got up and took the basket of figs and placed it on his
shoulders, and he entered into Jerusalem and did not recognize
it -- neither his own house, nor the place -- nor did he find his own
family or any of his acquaintances.

~5.8
And he said:
Jah be blessed, for a great trance has come over me today!

~5.9
This is not the city Jerusalem -- and I have lost my way because I came
by the mountain road when I arose from my sleep; and since my head
was heavy because I did not get enough sleep, I lost my way.

~5.10
It will seem incredible to Jeremiah that I lost my way!

~5.11
And he departed from the city; and as he searched he saw the
landmarks of the city, and he said:
Indeed, this is the city; I lost my way.

~5.12
And again he returned to the city and searched, and found no one of
his own people; and he said:
Jah be blessed, for a great trance has come over me!

~5.13
And again he departed from the city, and he stayed there grieving,
not knowing where he should go.

~5.14
And he put down the basket, saying:
I will sit here until Jah takes this trance from me.

~5.15
And as he sat, he saw an old man coming from the field; and Abimelech said to him:
I say to you, old man, what city is this?

~5.16
And he said to him:
It is Jerusalem.

~5.17
And Abimelech said to him:
Where is Jeremiah the priest, and Baruch the secretary,
and all the people of this city, for I could not find them?

~5.18
And the old man said to him:
Are you not from this city, seeing that you remember Jeremiah today, because you are asking about him after such a long time?

~5.19
For Jeremiah is in Babylon with the people; for they were taken
captive by king Nebuchadnezzar, and Jeremiah is with them to preach
the good news to them and to teach them the word.
~5.20
As soon as Abimelech heard this from the old man, he said:
If you were not an old man,
and if it were not for the fact that it is not lawful for a man to upbraid one older than himself, I would laugh at
you and say that you are out of your mind -- since you say that the
people have been taken captive into Babylon.
~5.21
Even if the heavenly torrents had descended on them, there has not
yet been time for them to go into Babylon!
~5.22
For how much time has passed since my father Jeremiah sent me to the
estate of Agrippa to bring a few figs, so that I might give them to
the sick among the people?
~5.23
And I went and got them, and when I came to a certain tree in the
burning heat, I sat to rest a little; and I leaned my head on the
basket and fell asleep.
~5.24
And when I awoke I uncovered the basket of figs, supposing that I was
late; and I found the figs dripping milk, just as I had collected
them.
~5.25
But you claim that the people have been taken captive into Babylon.

~5.26
But that you might know, take the figs and see!
~5.27
And he uncovered the basket of figs for the old man, and he saw them
dripping milk.
~5.28
And when the old man saw them, he said:
O my son, you are a righteous man,
and God did not want you to see the desolation of the city, so
he brought this trance upon you.
~5.29
For behold it is 66 years today since the people were taken captive
into Babylon.
~5.30
But that you might learn, my son, that what I tell you is true --
look into the field and see that the ripening of the crops has not
appeared.
~5.31
And notice that the figs are not in season, and be enlightened.
~5.32
Then Abimelech cried out in a loud voice, saying:
I bless you, God of heaven and earth,
the Rest of the souls of the righteous in every place!
~5.33
Then he said to the old man:
What month is this?
~5.34
And he said:
Nisan (which is Abib).
~5.35
And taking some of figs, he gave them to the old man and said to him:
May God illumine your way to the city above, Jerusalem.

6

~6.1
After this, Abimelech went out of the city and prayed to Jah.

~6.2
And behold, an angel of Jah came and took him by the right hand
and brought him back to where Baruch was sitting, and he found him in
a tomb.

~6.3
And when they saw each other, they both wept and kissed each other.

~6.4
But when Baruch looked up he saw with his own eyes the figs that were
covered in Abimelech's basket.

~6.5
And lifting his eyes to heaven, he prayed, saying:

~6.6
You are the God who gives a reward to those who love you. Prepare
yourself, my heart, and rejoice and be glad while you are in your
tabernacle, saying to your fleshly house, "your grief has been
changed to joy;" for the Sufficient One is coming and will deliver
you in your tabernacle -- for there is no sin in you.

~6.7
Revive in your tabernacle, in your virginal faith, and believe that
you will live!

~6.8
Look at this basket of figs -- for behold, they are 66 years old and
have not become shrivelled or rotten, but they are dripping milk.

~6.9
So it will be with you, my flesh, if you do what is commanded you by
the angel of righteousness.

~6.10
He who preserved the basket of figs, the same will again preserve you
by his power.

~6.11
When Baruch had said this, he said to Abimelech:
Stand up and let us pray
that Jah may make known to us how we shall be able to send
to Jeremiah in Babylon the report about the shelter provided for you
on the way.

~6.12
And Baruch prayed, saying:
Lord God, our strength is the elect light which comes forth from your mouth.

~6.13
We beseech and beg of your goodness -- you whose great name no one is
able to know -- hear the voice of your servants and let knowledge come
into our hearts.

~6.14
What shall we do, and how shall we send this report to Jeremiah in
Babylon?

~6.15
And while Baruch was still praying, behold an angel of Jah came
and said all these words to Baruch:
Agent of the light, do not be
anxious about how you will send to Jeremiah; for an eagle is coming
to you at the hour of light tomorrow, and you will direct him to
Jeremiah.

~6.16
Therefore, write in a letter:
Say to the children of Israel: Let the stranger who comes among you be set
apart and let 15 days go by;

and after this I will lead you into your city, says Jah.

~6.17
He who is not separated from Babylon will not enter into the city;
and I will punish them by keeping them from being received back by
the Babylonians, says Jah.

~6.18
And when the angel had said this, he departed from Baruch.

~6.19
And Baruch sent to the market of the gentiles and got papyrus and ink
and wrote a letter as follows:
Baruch, the servant of God, writes to Jeremiah in the captivity of Babylon:

~6.20
Greetings! Rejoice, for God has not allowed us to depart from this
body grieving for the city which was laid waste and outraged.

~6.21
Wherefore Jah has had compassion on our tears, and has
remembered the covenant which he established with our fathers
Abraham, Isaac and Jacob.

~6.22
And he sent his angel to me, and he told me these words which I send
to you.

~6.13
These, then, are the words which Jah, the God of Israel, spoke,
who led us out of Egypt, out of the great furnace:
Because you did
not keep my ordinances, but your heart was lifted up, and you were
haughty before me, in anger and wrath I delivered you to the furnace
in Babylon.

~6.24
If, therefore, says Jah, you listen to my voice, from the mouth
of Jeremiah my servant, I will bring the one who listens up from
Babylon; but the one who does not listen will become a stranger to
Jerusalem and to Babylon.

~6.25
And you will test them by means of the water of the Jordan; whoever
does not listen will be exposed -- this is the sign of the great seal.

~7.1
And Baruch got up and departed from the tomb and found the eagle
sitting outside the tomb.

~7.2
And the eagle said to him in a human voice:
Hail, Baruch, steward of the faith.

~7.3
And Baruch said to him:
You who speak are chosen from among all the
birds of heaven, for this is clear from the gleam of your eyes; tell
me, then, what are you doing here?

~7.4
And the eagle said to him:
I was sent here so that you might through me send whatever message you want.

~7.5
And Baruch said to him:
Can you carry this message to Jeremiah in Babylon?

~7.6
And the eagle said to him:
Indeed, it was for this reason I was sent.

~7.7
And Baruch took the letter, and 15 figs from Abimelech's basket, and
tied them to the eagle's neck and said to him:
I say to you, king of

the birds, go in peace with good health and carry the message for me.
~7.8
Do not be like the raven which Noah sent out and which never came
back to him in the ark; but be like the dove which, the third time,
brought a report to the righteous one.
~7.9
So you also, take this good message to Jeremiah and to those in
bondage with him, that it may be well with you-take this papyrus to
the people and to the chosen one of God.
~7.10
Even if all the birds of heaven surround you and want to fight with
you, struggle -- Jah will give you strength.
~7.11
And do not turn aside to the right or to the left, but straight as a
speeding arrow, go in the power of God, and the glory of Jah
will be with you the entire way.
~7.12
Then the eagle took flight and went away to Babylon, having the
letter tied to his neck; and when he arrived he rested on a post
outside the city in a desert place.
~7.13
And he kept silent until Jeremiah came along, for he and some of the
people were coming out to bury a corpse outside the city.
~7.14
(For Jeremiah had petitioned king Nebuchadnezzar, saying: "Give me a place where I may bury those of my people who have died;" and the king gave it to him.)
~7.15
And as they were coming out with the body, and weeping, they came to where the eagle was.
~7.16
And the eagle cried out in a loud voice, saying:
I say to you,
Jeremiah the chosen one of God, go and gather together the people and
come here so that they may hear a letter which I have brought to you
from Baruch and Abimelech.
~7.17
And when Jeremiah heard this, he glorified God; and he went and
gathered together the people along with their wives and children, and
he came to where the eagle was.
~7.18
And the eagle came down on the corpse, and it revived.
~7.19
(Now this took place so that they might believe.)
~7.20
And all the people were astounded at what had happened, and said:
This is the God who appeared to our fathers in the wilderness through
Moses, and now he has appeared to us through the eagle.
~7.21
And the eagle said:
I say to you, Jeremiah, come, untie this letter
and read it to the people --
So he untied the letter and read it to the people.
~7.22
And when the people heard it, they wept and put dust on their heads,
and they said to Jeremiah:
Deliver us and tell us what to do that we may once again enter our city.

~7.23
And Jeremiah answered and said to them:
Do whatever you heard from
the letter, and Jah will lead us into our city.
~7.24
And Jeremiah wrote a letter to Baruch, saying thus:
My beloved son,
do not be negligent in your prayers, beseeching God on our behalf,
that he might direct our way until we come out of the jurisdiction of
this lawless king.
~7.25
For you have been found righteous before God, and he did not let you
come here, lest you see the affliction which has come upon the people
at the hands of the Babylonians.
~7.26
For it is like a father with an only son, who is given over for
punishment; and those who see his father and console him cover his
face, lest he see how his son is being punished, and be even more
ravaged by grief.
~7.27
For thus God took pity on you and did not let you enter Babylon lest
you see the affliction of the people.
~7.28
For since we came here, grief has not left us, for 66 years today.
~7.29
For many times when I went out I found some of the people hung up by
king Nebuchadnezzar, crying and saying: "Have mercy on us, God-ZAR!"
~7.30
When I heard this, I grieved and cried with two-fold mourning, not
only because they were hung up, but because they were calling on a
foreign God, saying "Have mercy on us."
~7.31
But I remembered days of festivity which we celebrated in Jerusalem
before our captivity; and when I remembered, I groaned, and returned
to my house wailing and weeping.
~7.32
Now, then, pray in the place where you are -- you and Abimelech -- for
this people, that they may listen to my voice and to the decrees of
my mouth, so that we may depart from here.
~7.33
For I tell you that the entire time that we have spent here they have
kept us in subjection, saying:
Recite for us a song from the songs of Zion [see Ps 136.3c/4] -- the song of your God.
~7.34
And we reply to them:
How shall we sing for you since we are in a foreign land? [Ps 136.4]
~7.35
And after this, Jeremiah tied the letter to the eagle's neck, saying:
Go in peace, and may Jah watch over both of us.
~7.36
And the eagle took flight and came to Jerusalem and gave the letter
to Baruch; and when he had untied it he read it and kissed it and
wept when he heard about the distresses and afflictions of the people.
~7.37
But Jeremiah took the figs and distributed them to the sick among the
people, and he kept teaching them to abstain from the pollutions of

the gentiles of Babylon.
6
~8.1
  And the day came in which Jah brought the people out of Babylon.
~8.2
And Jah said to Jeremiah:
  Rise up -- you and the people -- and come to the Jordan and say to the people:
  Let anyone who desires Jah
  forsake the works of Babylon.
~8.3
  As for the men who took wives from them and the women who took
  husbands from them -- those who listen to you shall cross over, and you
  take them into Jerusalem; but those who do not listen to you, do not
  lead them there.
~8.4
  And Jeremiah spoke these words to the people, and they arose and came
to the Jordan to cross over.
~8.5
  As he told them the words that Jah had spoken to him, half of
those who had taken spouses from them did not wish to listen to
Jeremiah, but said to him:
  We will never forsake our wives,
  but we will bring them back with us into our city.
~8.6
So they crossed the Jordan and came to Jerusalem.
~8.7
And Jeremiah and Baruch and Abimelech stood up and said:
  No man joined with Babylonians shall enter this city!
~8.8
And they said to one another:
  Let us arise and return to Babylon to our place --
And they departed.
~8.9
But while they were coming to Babylon, the Babylonians came out to
meet them, saying:
  You shall not enter our city, for you hated us and
  you left us secretly; therefore you cannot come in with us.
~8.10
  For we have taken a solemn oath together in the name of our god to
  receive neither you nor your children, since you left us secretly.
~8.11
And when they heard this, they returned and came to a desert place
some distance from Jerusalem and built a city for themselves and
named it 'SAMARIA.'
~8.12
And Jeremiah sent to them, saying:
  Repent, for the angel of
  righteousness is coming and will lead you to your exalted place.
6
~9.1
  Now those who were with Jeremiah were rejoicing and offering
sacrifices on behalf of the people for nine days.
~9.2
But on the tenth, Jeremiah alone offered sacrifice.
~9.3
And he prayed a prayer, saying:
  Holy, holy, holy, fragrant aroma of the living trees,
  true light that enlightens me until I ascend to you;
~9.4
  For your mercy, I beg you --

for the sweet voice of the two seraphim, I beg --
  for another fragrant aroma.
~9.5
And may Michael, archangel of righteousness, who opens the gates to
  the righteous, be my guardian (?) until he causes the righteous to
  enter.
~9.6
I beg you, almighty Lord of all creation, unbegotten and
  incomprehensible, in whom all judgment was hidden before these things
  came into existence.
~9.7
When Jeremiah had said this, and while he was standing in the
  altar-area with Baruch and Abimelech, he became as one whose soul had
  departed.
~9.8
And Baruch and Abimelech were weeping and crying out in a loud voice:
  Woe to us! For our father Jeremiah has left us -- the priest of God has
  departed!
~9.9
  And all the people heard their weeping and they all ran to them and
  saw Jeremiah lying on the ground as if dead.
~9.10
And they tore their garments and put dust on their heads and wept
  bitterly.
~9.11
And after this they prepared to bury him.
~9.12
And behold, there came a voice saying:
  Do not bury the one who yet lives,
  for his soul is returning to his body!
~9.13
And when they heard the voice they did not bury him, but stayed
  around his tabernacle for three days saying, "when will he arise?"
~9.14
  And after three days his soul came back into his body and he raised
  his voice in the midst of them all and said:
  Glorify God with one voice!
  All of you glorify God and the son of God who awakens us --
  messiah Jesus -- the light of all the ages, the inextinguishable
  lamp, the life of faith.
~9.15
But after these times there shall be 477 years more and he comes to
  earth.
~9.16
And the tree of life planted in the midst of paradise
  will cause all the unfruitful trees to bear fruit,
  and will grow and sprout forth.
~9.17
And the trees that had sprouted and became haughty and said:
  "We have supplied our power (?) to the air,"
  he will cause them to wither, with the grandeur of their branches,
  and he will cause them to be judged -- that firmly rooted tree!
~9.18
And what is crimson will become white as wool --
  the snow will be blackened --
  the sweet waters will become salty, and the salty sweet,
  in the intense light of the joy of God.
~9.19
And he will bless the isles
  so that they become fruitful by the word of the mouth of his messiah.

~9.20
For he shall come,
  and he will go out and choose for himself twelve apostles
    to proclaim the news among the nations--
    he whom I have seen adorned by his father
    and coming into the world on the Mount of Olives --
  and he shall fill the hungry souls.
~9.21
  When Jeremiah was saying this concerning the son of God -- that he is
coming into the world -- the people became very angry and said:
This is a repetition of the words spoken by Isaiah son of Amos,
  when he said:
I saw God and the son of God.
~9.22
Come, then, and let us not kill him by the same sort of death with
  which we killed Isaiah, but let us stone him with stones.
~9.23
  And Baruch and Abimelech were greatly grieved because they wanted to
hear in full the mysteries that he had seen.
~9.24
But Jeremiah said to them:
Be silent and weep not, for they cannot kill me
  until I describe for you everything I saw.
~9.25
And he said to them:
Bring a stone here to me.
~9.26
And he set it up and said:
Light of the ages,
  make this stone to become like me in appearance,
    until I have described to Baruch and Abimelech everything I saw.
~9.27
Then the stone, by God's command, took on the appearance of Jeremiah.
~9.28
And they were stoning the stone, supposing that it was Jeremiah!
~9.29
  But Jeremiah delivered to Baruch and to Abimelech all the mysteries
he had seen, and forthwith he stood in the midst of the people
desiring to complete his ministry.
~9.30
Then the stone cried out, saying:
O foolish children of Israel,
  why do you stone me, supposing that I am Jeremiah?
  Behold, Jeremiah is standing in your midst!
~9.31
And when they saw him, immediately they rushed upon him with many
stones, and his ministry was fulfilled.
~9.32
  And when Baruch and Abimelech came, they buried him, and taking the
stone they placed it on his tomb and inscribed it thus:
  This is the stone that was the ally of Jeremiah.

THAT WHICH JAH SPOKE TO JEREMIAH BEFORE THE CAPTURE OF JERUSALEM AND HOW THE CAPTURE HAPPENED

~1.1
  In those days Jah spoke to Jeremiah, saying: Arise,
depart from this city with Baruch, since I am going to destroy
it because of the multitude of the sins of those who dwell in it.
~1.2
For your prayers are like solid pillars in its

midst, and like an indestructible wall surrounding it.
~1.3
Now, then, depart from it before the host of the Chaldeans
surrounds it.
~1.4
And Jeremiah spoke, saying: I beseech you, Lord, permit me,
your servant, to speak in your presence.
~1.5
And Jah said: Speak.
~1.6
And Jeremiah said: Lord, would you deliver this city into
the hands of the Chaldeans, so that they might boast that they
had prevailed against it?
~1.7
My Lord, if it is your will, rather let it be destroyed by
your hands and not by the Chaldeans.
~1.8
And God said: You, arise, depart.
~1.9
But they will not boast. Unless I open (the gates), they are
not able to enter.
~1.10
Therefore go to Baruch and tell him.
~1.11
And at the sixth hour of the night go up on the city walls
and see that unless I open (the gates), they are not able to
enter.
~1.12
And when he had said these things he departed from him.
~2.1
And Jeremiah departed and told Baruch; and as they went into
the temple they tore their garments and mourned much.
~3.1
And at the sixth hour when they had gone up on the city
walls, they heard the sound of trumpets.
~3.2
And the angels came from heaven, holding torches in their
hands, and they set them on the walls of the city.
~3.3
And when they saw them they wept and said: Now we know that
the word that God spoke is true.
~3.4
And they besought the angels, saying: We beseech (you) not
to destroy the city until we speak to God.
~3.6
Then Jeremiah spoke, saying: I beg you, Lord, bid me to
speak in your presence.
~3.7
And Jah said: Speak.
~3.8
And Jeremiah said: Behold, Lord, we know that you are
delivering the city into the hands of its enemies, and your
people depart for Babylon.
~3.9
What then will we do with your holy vessels?
~3.10
And God said: Consign them to the earth, saying: Hear,
earth, the voice of your creator, who founded you upon the
waters, who sealed you with seven seals for seven epochs, and
after this you will receive your ornaments.
~3.11
Guard the vessels of the temple service until

the gathering
of the beloved.
~3.12
And Jeremiah spoke again, saying: I beseech you, Lord, what
should I do for Abimelech the Ethiopian, for he has done many
kindnesses to your servant?
~3.13
For he drew me up out of the miry pit where they threw me,
and I do not wish that he should see the destruction and
spoiling of the city because he is little-souled.
~3.14
And Jah said to Jeremiah: Send him to the vineyard of
Agrippa, and I will hide him in the shadow of the mountain until
the people are about to return from the captivity.
~3.15
And you, Jeremiah, go with your people into Babylon and
stay with them, preaching to them, until I cause them to return.
~3.16
But leave Baruch here.
~3.18
Then they went into the temple, and taking the vessels of
the temple service, they consigned them to the earth as Jah
had told them.
~3.21
And at morning, Jeremiah said to Abimelech: Take a basket,
child, and go to the estate of Agrippa by the mountain road, and
bring back figs to the sick of the people; for their favor is on
you, and glory is on your head.
~3.22
And immediately he went to the field.
~4.1
And when he had departed and the sun had appeared at dawn,
behold, the host of the Chaldeans, having arrived, had
surrounded the city of Jerusalem.
~4.2
And the great angel trumpeted, saying: Enter the city, the
entire host of the Chaldeans; for behold, the gates are opened
for you.
~4.4
Then Jeremiah, taking the keys of the temple, went outside
the city and throwing them away in the presence of the sun,
said: Take them and guard (them) until the day in which Jah
asks you for them.
~4.5
For we have not been found worthy to keep them.
~4.6
And Jeremiah went with the people into captivity in Babylon.
~4.11"-12"
But Baruch departed from the city and remained sitting
in a tomb.
~5.1
And Abimelech, taking the figs in the burning heat and
coming upon a tree, sat under its shade to rest a bit.
~5.2
And leaning his head on the basket, he fell asleep for
seventy times. And this happened according to the commandment of
God because of the word which he spoke to

Jeremiah: I will hide
him.
~5.3
And after awakening he said: I slept sweetly for a little
while, and because of this my head is heavy because I did not
get enough sleep.
~5.4
And uncovering the figs, he found them dripping milk, as if
he had gathered them shortly before.
~5.5
And he said: I would like to sleep a little longer, but
since Jeremiah sent me in much haste, if I do this I will be
late and he will be distressed.
~5.6
For isn't there toil and heat every day? Rather, I should
leave quickly, and I will heal him and then I can sleep.
~5.7
And taking the figs, he went into Jerusalem and he did not
recognize either his house or that of his relatives or of his
friends.
~5.8
And he said: Jah be blessed, a trance came over me
today!
~5.9
This is not the city. Lacking sleep, I have gone astray.
~5."11"z"1"
And he departed from (the city) and searching for the
landmarks he said: Indeed, this is the city; I went astray.
~5.12
And entering again and searching, he found no one of his
relatives or of his friends; and he said: Jah be blessed, a
great trance has come over me!
~5.13
And going out, he stayed there grieving, not knowing what
he should do.
~5.14
And putting down the basket, he said: I must sit here until
Jah takes the trance from me.
~5.15
And as he was sitting, behold, an old man was coming from
the field, and he said to him: I say to you, old man, what city
is this?
~5.16
And he said: It is Jerusalem, child.
~5.17
And Abimelech said: And where is Jeremiah the priest of
God, and Baruch the secretary, and all the people of the city,
for I could not find them?
~5.18
And the old man said to him: Are you not from this city?
Today you remembered Jeremiah and asked about him.
~5.19
Jeremiah has been in Babylon with the people since they
were made captives by Nebuchadnezzar the king seventy times ago;
and how is it that you, being a young man and never having been
(old), then, are asking about the things which I have never
seen?.
~5.20
And when he had heard these things,

Abimelech said to him:
If you were not an old man, and if it were not for the fact that
it is not lawful for a man of God to upbraid one older than
himself, I would laugh at you and say that you are out of your
mind for saying that the people went captive into Babylon.
~5.21
Even if the heavenly torrents had opened, and the angels of
God came to take them with power and authority, not yet would
they have (time) to go into Babylon!
~5.22
For how much time has passed since my father Jeremiah sent
me to the estate of Agrippa because of a few (figs), so that I
might give them to the sick of the people?
~5.23
And coming to a tree from out of the heat, I fell asleep
for a little bit.
~5.24
Supposing that I was late, I uncovered the figs and found
them dripping milk just as I had collected (them).
~5.25
And you say that the people were taken captive into
Babylon.
~5.26
But that you might know, and not account me a liar, take
the figs and see.
~5.28
And when the old man saw these things he said: O child, you
are the son of a righteous man, and God did not want to show you
the desolation of this city and he brought this trance upon you.
~5.29
Behold, it is seventy times (since) the people were taken
captive into Babylon with Jeremiah from this day.
~5.30
But so that you may learn, my child, that what I tell you
is true, look into the field and see that the ripening of the
crops has not yet appeared.
~5.31
And notice that the figs are not in season, and be
enlightened and be persuaded that I am telling the truth.
~5.32
Then Abimelech, just as from great sobriety and observing
the land accurately, and the trees in it, said: Blessed be the
God of heaven and earth, the Rest of the souls of the righteous.
~5.33
And he said to the old man: What month is this?
~5.34
And the old man said: The twelfth.
~5.35
And giving some figs to the old man, he departed when he
had blessed him.
~6.1
   And rising up, Abimelech prayed that it might be revealed to
him what he should do.
~6.2
And behold, an angel of Jah came and took him by the
right hand and brought him safely to the tomb in which Baruch

was sitting.
~6.3
And seeing one another, they wept much, and then they prayed
to God and rejoiced, glorifying and praising him.
~6.4
And Baruch, seeing the figs which were picked seventy times
before still dripping milk, was astonished, and said:
~6.11
Let us pray to God that Jah may make known to us how,
then, we will give knowledge to Jeremiah concerning the shelter
made for you, and now (your) incredible awakening.
~6.15
And while they were doing this, they heard an angel which
was sent to them:
~6.16
Write a letter to Jeremiah (saying) what he must do unto
the people as I say to you. And he told them everything that
they should write, and he also delivered over this: Behold, in a
few days God will lead you out of Babylon into Jerusalem. And
early tomorrow when an eagle comes, bind the letter and a few
figs on its neck so that it may carry these things to Jeremiah
in Babylon.
~6.18
And when he had said these things he departed from them.
~6.19
 And immediately taking papyrus Baruch sat down and wrote
the things which he heard from the angel.

~7.1
And coming early, the eagle cried out. And going out, they
praised God.
~7.7
And when they had prayed they bound the letter and ten figs
on its neck.
~7.8
And when they had prayed for it they sent it away, having
commanded it to return to them again.
~7.12
And it went away to Babylon (and having arrived) it sat on
a pillar outside the city.
~7.13
And according to the stewardship of God, Jeremiah was going
out of the city with all the people to bury a corpse.
~7.14"-15"
And they were mourning and were about to bury it in the
place which Jeremiah received from Nebuchadnezzar which he
yielded for the burying of dead Jews.
~7.16
And the eagle cried out with the voice of a man and said: I
say to you Jeremiah, take the letter which I have brought to you
from Baruch and Abimelech and let all the people of Jerusalem
hear it.
~7.17
And when Jeremiah heard, he glorified God.
~7.18
And the eagle sat on the corpse and immediately it arose.
~7.20
Everyone seeing this knew that the letter was sent from

God. And when all had glorified God at what had happened,
~7.21
Jeremiah untied the letter and read it before all.
~7.22
And when they heard it they shouted out and rejoiced
greatly.
~7.24
And Jeremiah also wrote on papyrus of all the tribulations
and misfortunes that had happened to them.
~7.35
And he tied it to the neck of the eagle and blessing it, he
sent it off.
~7.36
And again it took this letter to Baruch and Abimelech, and
when they had read it they wept and with thanks they glorified
God because they had not been tested with such tribulations.
~7.37
But Jeremiah gave the figs to the sick of the people, and
they were all healed, as many as ate of them.
~8.1
 And when the appointed day had been attained,
~8.2
God said to Jeremiah: Take the entire night and go out of
Babylon and come to the Jordan.
~8.3
And there you will separate the rulers of the Babylonians
who took wives from your nation and the women of the Babylonians
who joined together with your people. And those who do not hear
you the Jordan will separate. They will not cross with you.
~8.4
And Jeremiah did as God commanded him.
~8.5
And in separating them at the Jordan, most of those who had
joined (with the Babylonians) did not wish to listen to
Jeremiah, but said: It is better for us to return to Babylon
than to forsake our wives.
~8.8
And they departed for Babylon.
~8.9
But they were not welcomed by the Babylonians who said:
Because you left us and departed secretly,
~8.10
We have sworn an oath among ourselves not to receive you or
your children.
~8.11
But these who were not received, either by Jeremiah or by
the Babylonians departed into a desert place some distance from
Jerusalem and built for themselves a city which is called
Samaria, which is what they named it.
~9.1
 And Jeremiah with the people went into Jerusalem and they
rejoiced, bringing up their sacrifices for nine days.
~9.2
And on the tenth day Jeremiah offered his sacrifice to God.
~9.3
And he prayed
~9.7
until his soul went up and his body fell down dead in the
altar-area.

~9.8
Then Baruch and Abimelech came to mourn Jeremiah.
~9.9
And when all the people heard they ran to them and saw
Jeremiah lying on the ground dead.
~9.10
And they tore their garments and put dust on their heads
and they all wept bitterly.
~9.11
And after this they prepared to bury him.
~9.12
And behold, there was a voice from heaven saying: Do not
bury the one who yet lives.
~9.13
And when they heard the voice they stayed beside him,
praying for three days.
~9.14
And after three days his soul came back into his body and
he raised his voice in the midst of them all, saying: With one
voice all of you glorify God and his son who awakens us, messiah
Jesus, the light of all the ages, the inextinguishable lamp, the
life of our nature.
~9.15
For after these times there shall be 377 years more.
~9.21
And as he preached the good news of the messiah to them as
he saw and heard enigmatically when his soul went up, all the
people shouted: These are the words which Isaiah of old spoke to
our fathers: I saw God and his son.
~9.22
And they killed him with a wooden saw, sawing him asunder.
Come then, let us stone him.
~9.23
And when they heard these things, Baruch and Abimelech were
greatly grieved because of the death of Jeremiah and had not
heard in full the mysteries which the prophet who had gone up
had seen and heard.
~9.24
And he, knowing their thoughts, said: Be silent; they will
not kill me until everything which I saw and heard I describe
for you.
~9.25
And he said to them: Bring a great stone to me. And they
brought it to him.
~9.26
And the prophet said: Lord, make this stone like me in
appearance so that the people will stone it until I tell my
brothers the things which I saw and heard.
~9.27
Then, by the commandment of God, the stone took on the
appearance of the prophet,
~9.28
And they stoned it instead of him.
~9.29
And he told them everything that he saw and heard. Desiring
to complete his ministry, he went into the midst of the people.
~9.30
And by the command of God the stone went up and cried out
in the voice of a man, saying: O foolish children of Israel, why

do you stone me, supposing that I am Jeremiah, who is standing
in your midst?
~9.31
Then, out of great sobriety, they saw the holy one, and
taking up stones they killed him. And he was stoned by his
fellow captives of Jerusalem who owed him much good, and he did
not speak against them neither was he angry, but thus he
received the overpowering of the stones, as through them he went
up into heaven.
~9.32
And when Baruch and Abimelech came, they buried him, and
taking the stone they placed it on his tomb, inscribing on it:
This is the stone that was the ally of Jeremiah.
~9.33
And the sacred vessels Jeremiah laid away according to the
command of God, sealed in this stone by his finger in the name
of God. Through the writing of iron, the imprint has become on
the stone a shadowy cloud, because it is indistinguishable. And
the stone is in the desert where formerly the ark was prepared
with the others. And this Jeremiah spoke: Jah went up to
heaven from Zion, but he will come again to visit Zion, and the
coming of the messiah will be the sign whenever every nation
worships the cross, glorifying and praising God, to whom becomes
all glory forever and ever, Amen.